PAUL'S LETTER TO THE ROMANS

Paul's Letter to the Romans

A Socio-Rhetorical Commentary

Ben Witherington III

with Darlene Hyatt

WILLIAM B. EERDMANS PUBLISHING COMPANY
GRAND RAPIDS, MICHIGAN / CAMBRIDGE, U.K.

Wm. B. Eerdmans Publishing Co.
2140 Oak Industrial Drive N.E., Grand Rapids, Michigan 49505 /
P.O. Box 163, Cambridge CB3 9PU U.K.

Printed in the United States of America

11 10 09 08 07 06   7 6 5 4 3 2

Library of Congress Cataloging-in-Publication Data

Witherington, Ben, 1951-
    Paul's Letter to the Romans: a socio-rhetorical commentary /
Ben Witherington III, with Darlene Hyatt.
        p.   cm.
    Includes bibliographical references and index.
    ISBN-10: 0-8028-4504-5
    ISBN-13: 978-0-8028-4504-7 (pbk.: alk. paper)
    1. Bible. N.T. Romans — Commentaries. 2. Bible. N.T. Romans —
Socio-rhetorical criticism.   I. Hyatt, Darlene.   II. Title.
BS2665.53W58   2004
227′.1077 — dc22

                                                2003064340

www.eerdmans.com

This commentary is dedicated to my Durham colleagues who have taught NT there during the last thirty years and to the new bishop of Durham, my old friend Tom Wright. It is also dedicated to my pastor, Dr. A. W. Gwinn, a very present help in difficult times, and a very able expositor of the Good News which Paul brokered for Gentiles like us. A special thanks to Darlene Hyatt for helping by providing some of the application materials in this commentary. I could not have done this without all of your help in so many different ways.

Contents

Preface

As I write this preface, the Society of Biblical Literature is offering a remarkable seminar entitled "Romans through History and Cultures" in which papers are presented analyzing Romans through the eyes of the Church Fathers and Mothers on the one hand and through various cultural lenses as well (e.g., in the 2001 meeting we heard a paper analyzing Romans 8 from the perspective of classical Confucianism). If anyone was prone to wonder if anything new could ever be said about the most studied and commented on document from the biblical period, this seminar shows that new light can still be shed on this enduring classic. In that spirit, it is my hope that, since a full-scale socio-rhetorical commentary has not yet been attempted, there will be new light shed by what one finds in the following pages, which take that line of approach.

I do not pretend that this is the definitive work on Romans (considering the volume of literature on this book, no study could be either exhaustive or all-encompassing), but I hope it moves the conversation along in some fruitful and even in some fresh directions. One of the more surprising things I have discovered along the way is that there really has never been, since the English Reformation, a major exegetical study of Romans which intentionally takes into account Arminian and Wesleyan readings as opposed to more Augustinian/Lutheran/Calvinist readings of Romans. Discussion of Romans in the nineteenth and twentieth centuries was overwhelmingly shaped by the Reformed tradition, to the point that even some Lutheran scholars, such as Krister Stendahl, wondered if another line of approach might be helpful in shedding fresh light on Paul's text.

A measure of the impact of the Reformed reading of Romans is also shown by the fact that even in many Catholic circles since Vatican II the Lu-

theran and Calvinist reading of Romans has been assumed to be fully representative of what Protestants have to say about this book.[1] This is hardly surprising
since Karl Barth's *Römerbrief* so shaped twentieth-century Protestant discussion, including to significant degree even the commentary by the Methodist NT
scholar C. K. Barrett.[2]

If, as one scholar has put it, Christian theology since the Reformation has
sometimes become footnotes to Paul, it is fair to say that the study of Pauline
theology is sometimes in danger of becoming footnotes to Romans.[3] I do not
intend to write this commentary through the lens of Wesleyan theology. Exegesis should precede, not follow, theological commitments and readings. Nevertheless, it appears to me that there are significant deficiencies to various of the
Reformed readings of Romans, as a careful survey of work on Romans by both
ancient Church Fathers and modern exegetical scholars will show in detail.

Perhaps an example (as a foretaste and in order to stir up the pot a bit) of
the different sort of reading I will be pursuing is in order. I will argue that
Romans 7 is not a statement of Pauline autobiography. To read it as such is to
ignore the use of the rhetorical technique of "impersonation" (as well as the use
of diatribal style). Nor in Romans 8–11 does Paul inform his audience that certain individuals have been selected from a mass of unredeemed humanity and
predestined from before the foundation of the earth to be saved or lost. Such a
reading of Romans 8–11 overlooks the early Jewish discussions affirming both
divine sovereignty and human freedom, in particular the fact that those discussions were about a collective and corporate entity known as Israel, as the people
of God. It is striking how even in the Mishnah when an author wishes to affirm
"all Israel will be saved" he quickly adds a list of exclusions. God will save his
people, but that provides no pre-ordained guarantees for those individual Jews
or Christians who repeatedly violate his commandments. Paul follows the line
of these sorts of Jewish discussions, not the later line of Augustine.

Though this commentary will focus on the contributions social and rhetorical analysis can make to the interpretation of Romans, theological and ethical issues can hardly be overlooked or avoided. I have dealt with the exegetical
issues in more detail in this commentary than in some of my previous socio-
rhetorical commentaries because of the enormous weight this letter carries in
exegetical and theological discussions today. It is hoped that the reader will
make a good faith attempt to hear Paul on his own terms, and not just through

---

1. E.g., J. Fitzmyer's *Romans* (New York: Doubleday, 1992).

2. Note the foreword to Barrett's volume in the Black's New Testament Commentary
series (Peabody: Hendrickson, 1991), pp. vii-viii, where he credits Barth along with Luther
and Calvin.

3. W. Meeks, ed., *The Writings of St. Paul* (New York: Norton, 1972), p. 435, referring to
Sydney Ahlstrom.

the various voices of his later interpreters. Such an attempt will prove well worth the effort.

Readers will no doubt detect the debt I owe to those who taught me Romans at the University of Durham — C. K. Barrett and C. E. B. Cranfield — who both also wrote important commentaries on the book, and also to the Durhamite who came after them, J. D. G. Dunn, who has also written a major and very helpful commentary on Romans. Perhaps it is the daily witnessing of the magnificent Norman cathedral constructed over a period of forty years that inspires attempts to construct a commentary on the most formidable and towering of Paul's letters.

Easter 2003

Abbreviations

AusBR	*Australian Biblical Review*
BAGD	W. Bauer, W. F. Arndt, F. W. Gingrich, and F. W. Danker, *Greek-English Lexicon of the New Testament and Other Early Christian Literature.* 2nd edition; Chicago: University of Chicago, 1979
BEvT	Beiträge zur evangelischen Theologie
Bib	*Biblica*
BJRL	*Bulletin of the John Rylands Library*
BZ	*Biblische Zeitschrift*
CBQ	*Catholic Biblical Quarterly*
CIL	*Corpus inscriptionum latinarum*
CTM	*Currents in Theology and Mission*
ET	*Expository Times*
ETSMS	Evangelical Theological Society Monograph Series
FS	Festschrift
HTR	*Harvard Theological Review*
ICC	International Critical Commentary
Instit. Or.	Quintilian, *Institutio Oratio*
Int	*Interpretation*
JBL	*Journal of Biblical Literature*
JETS	*Journal of the Evangelical Theological Society*
JQR	*Jewish Quarterly Review*
JSNT	*Journal for the Study of the New Testament*
JSNTS	*Journal for the Study of the New Testament* Supplements
JTSA	*Journal of Theology for Southern Africa*
LW	*Luther's Works*
LXX	Septuagint

MT	Masoretic Text
NEB	New English Bible
Neot	*Neotestamentica*
NewDocs	*New Documents Illustrating Early Christianity* (North Ryde: Macquarie University/Grand Rapids: Eerdmans, 1976-97)
NICNT	New International Commentary on the New Testament
NovT	*Novum Testamentum*
NTS	*New Testament Studies*
OGIS	*Orientis graeci inscriptiones selectae,* ed. W. Dittenberger. 2 vols., 1903-05.
RB	*Revue Biblique*
RelStud	*Religious Studies*
SBL	Society of Biblical Literature
SBLDS	Society of Biblical Literature Dissertation Series
SBLSP	*Society of Biblical Literature Seminar Papers*
ST	*Studia Theologica*
TGl	*Theologie und Glaube*
ThH	Théologie historique
TQ	*Theologische Quartalschrift*
TynBul	*Tyndale Bulletin*
WW	*Word and World*
WUNT	Wissenschaftliche Untersuchungen zum Neuen Testament
ZNW	*Zeitschrift für die Neutestamentliche Wissenschaft*
ZTK	*Zeitschrift für Theologie und Kirche*

Bibliography

This bibliography is not intended to be exhaustive, only representative of some of the best resources available for the understanding of Romans, concentrating particularly on socio-rhetorical resources that shed light on this text.

Introductory Guides

There are several useful guides to Romans which can be commended. In view of the fact that Romans is so formidable and so much has been written about it, one or more of these guides is a good place to start in order to avoid getting lost in the sea of literature on the book. There have been two efforts of late to read through Romans and chart its narrative and ideational progress, both of which have their merits and can be commended. K. Grieb's *The Story of Romans: A Narrative Defense of God's Righteousness* (Louisville: Westminster/ J. Knox, 2002) is conversant with recent discussions of Romans and seeks to read the letter in light of the biblical stories which undergird and sometimes surface in the text. L. T. Johnson's *Reading Romans: A Literary and Theological Commentary* (Macon: Smyth and Helwys, 2001) is very readable and gives a bit more detailed attention to some exegetical issues than does Grieb. A more issues- and prolegomena-oriented approach is found in R. Morgan's *Romans,* in the NT Guides series (Sheffield: Sheffield Academic, 1995). D. Moo's *Encountering the Book of Romans* (Grand Rapids: Baker, 2002) is more geared to a lay or perhaps college audience and has various charts and pictures.

Perhaps pride of place of all these sorts of volumes should go to C. Bryan's *A Preface to Romans: Notes on the Epistle and Its Literary and Cultural*

Setting (Oxford: Oxford University Press, 2000), which is the best companion to this present commentary because it deals with the relevant ancient literature and Greco-Roman rhetoric. For an introduction to the scholarly debate about Romans no volume is more helpful than the volume edited by K. P. Donfried, *The Romans Debate* (second ed., Peabody: Hendrickson, 1991). For an introduction to some recent trends in Pauline studies and the search for the historical Paul see my *The Paul Quest: The Search for the Jew of Tarsus* (Downers Grove: InterVarsity, 1998). For very helpful information taken from the study of extrabiblical inscriptions and applied to the NT, in this case to Romans, see the now eight-volume series, *New Documents Illustrating Early Christianity,* earlier volumes edited by G. H. R. Horsley, later volumes by S. Llewelyn (emanating from Macquarie University in Sydney, Australia, 1981-97). Thankfully the series has now been taken up by Eerdmans.

Commentaries

This list could go on for miles, and what is often overlooked is that some of the older commentaries are as valuable as some from our own era. For example, it is very fruitful indeed to read Origen, John Chrysostom, Philipp Melanchthon, John Calvin, Martin Luther, and other of the earlier divines on Romans, not least because many of them have a more thorough grasp of the Greek text than do some modern commentators, and in the case of Chrysostom we have the added bonus of a person for whom koine Greek was still a living language and Greco-Roman rhetoric was still an art well understood and practiced. The following commentaries from the modern era can be commended.

Of the large full-scale commentaries dealing with all the exegetical particulars three stand out. The most helpful and the one most conversant with the general state of scholarly discussion of Pauline studies, the new perspective on Paul, Paul in the setting of early Judaism, and other relevant considerations is J. D. G. Dunn's two-volume work in the Word Biblical Commentary Series (Dallas: Word, 1988). Secondly there is C. E. B. Cranfield's ICC commentary, also in two volumes (Edinburgh: Clark, 1975 and 1979). The great merit of Cranfield is his close attention to grammatical details and to history of interpretation. Unlike Dunn, however, Cranfield has insufficient interaction with Pauline scholarship of the modern era. Cranfield's volumes were the replacement for the older ICC volume of W. Sanday and A. C. Headlam (fifth ed., Edinburgh: Clark, 1902). Thirdly and more recently there is D. Moo's thousand-page volume in the New International Commentary series (Grand Rapids: Eerdmans, 1996). Moo's volume does a good job of covering the waterfront in terms of the literature on Romans but in the end turns out very much like previous commentaries from a conservative Reformed perspective (that is, the actual exposition often sounds like Calvin, some of the Puritan divines, and C. Hodge). It is none the worse for this, but it has a very old-fashioned ring while still being conversant with much recent discussion. Missing is any real detailed engagement with social science or rhetorical treatments of Romans or Paul. J. A. Fitzmyer's *Romans* (New York: Doubleday, 1992) deserves to be mentioned with these volumes, especially because of his awareness and use of the history of Catholic exegesis of Romans, which many commentators either ignore or are ignorant of.

Because of the importance of Romans, it is fortunate for the English-speaking world that some of the really seminal or important foreign-language commentaries on Romans, particularly German ones, have been translated into English. Of course the most influential Romans commentary of the twentieth century was K. Barth's *Der Römerbrief,* which first appeared in 1929 and was translated into English in 1933 (Oxford University Press). When Barth produced his *Kurze Erklärung des Römerbriefes* in 1956, it was in turn translated into English in 1959 (Richmond: John Knox Press). Barth's original work was a landmark work which was to affect most subsequent commentators in the twentieth century, perhaps most notably C. K. Barrett.

What finally eclipsed the influence of Barth's *Romans* was E. Käsemann's *An die Römer,* which, when it reached its fourth edition (Tübingen: Mohr, 1980), having been hailed as a classic exposition, was translated into English as *Commentary on Romans* (Grand Rapids: Eerdmans, 1980). Because of the prolix nature of both Barth's and Käsemann's German prose, these two vigorous and stimulating commentaries did not have their full impact on the English-speaking world until they were translated. A much smaller commentary which has been translated from the German and can be commended is P. Stuhlmacher's *Der Brief an der Römer,* which came out in 1989 in Germany and was translated in 1994 (Louisville: Westminster/J. Knox). There are several other important German commentaries on Romans of recent vintage which have not been translated into English yet, most notably those of O. Michel (1978), R. Pesch (1983), and H. Schlier (1977). Since M. J. Lagrange's important work on Romans, which appeared in 1950, there have not been any very influential commentaries on Romans written in French, except one can mention that of A. Viard (1975).

Good small or mid-sized commentaries on Romans written at less than the most highly technical level are hard to come by. This is because Romans requires vigorous interaction. The most helpful recent mid-sized commentary on Romans is that of N. T. Wright, who provides 375 pages of very lucid prose conversant with recent scholarship and dealing with the more profound theological and ethical issues arising out of the letter. It can be found in *The New Interpreter's Bible* vol. X, ed. L. E. Keck (Nashville: Abingdon, 2002). Another

excellent, though now somewhat dated, exposition is the second edition of
C. K. Barrett's volume in the Black's New Testament Commentary series (Peabody: Hendrickson, 1991). Another mid-sized volume, in the Sacra Pagina series, is that of B. Byrne (Collegeville: Liturgical, 1996). Byrne does a good job of
referring to and brokering recent foreign-language (particularly German) discussion of Romans in a way that these other mid-sized commentaries do not.
C. Talbert's recent commentary (Macon: Smyth and Helwys, 2002) has numerous user-friendly features such as charts, detailed sidebar discussions of more
technical topics, and a good use of the Graeco-Roman resources. We can also
mention J. Zeisler's *Paul's Letter to the Romans* (London: SCM, 1989).

One mid-sized classic German commentary which has been recently
translated is that of A. Schlatter, originally published as *Gottes Gerechtigkeit. Ein
Kommentar zum Römerbrief* in 1935, and then translated six decades later as
Romans: The Righteousness of God (Peabody: Hendrickson, 1995). This work
heavily influenced Käsemann and others and has the great merit that it does
not constrict the Pauline discussion of righteousness to the matter of right
standing before God. "Righteousness" is seen rather in the first instance as
theocentric and then, in a derived sense, as anthropocentric, having to do not
merely with the position but also ultimately the condition of the believer. All of
Romans then is seen as a revelation of God's righteousness, which in turn has to
do with human righteousness in response.

The English translation of F. J. Leenhardt's commentary, entitled *The
Epistle to the Romans* (New York: World, 1961), is still helpful, especially in re-
gard to the structure of Romans. Also helpful and very interesting is *Erasmus'
Annotations on the New Testament: Acts — Romans — I and II Corinthians,* ed.
A. Reeve and M. A. Screech (Leiden: Brill, 1990), annotations on the Latin text,
but based on Erasmus's reflections on his Greek text.

Of the more popular level commentaries on Romans, P. Achtemeier's
Romans (Atlanta: John Knox, 1985) can be commended, as can D. Moo's *Encountering the Book of Romans* (Grand Rapids: Baker, 2002).

Rhetorical Resources[1]

For bibliographic help on matters social, rhetorical, and historical in general
see my *Conflict and Community in Corinth* (Grand Rapids: Eerdmans, 1995),
48-67. Most of the following works deal specifically with Romans.

1. Special thanks to Duane Watson for providing me with the initial list of these resources.

Aletti, J.-N., "L'argumentation paulinienne en Rm 9," *Bib* 68 (1987), 41-56.

―――, *Comment Dieu est-il juste? Clefs pour interpréter l'épître aux Romains* (Paris: Éditions du Seuil, 1990).

―――, "La présence d'un modèle rhétorique en Romains. Son rôle et son importance," *Bib* 71 (1990), 1-24.

―――, "The Rhetoric of Romans 5–8," in *The Rhetorical Analysis of Scripture: Essays from the 1995 London Conference,* ed. S. E. Porter and T. H. Olbricht (JSNTS 146; Sheffield: Sheffield Academic, 1997), 294-308.

―――, "Rm 1,18–3,20. Incohérence ou cohérence de l'argumentation paulinienne?" *Bib* 69 (1988), 47-62.

―――, "Romains 2. Sa cohérence et sa fonction," *Bib* 77 (1996), 155-77.

―――, "Romains 5,12-21. Logique, sens et fonction," *Bib* 78 (1997), 3-32.

―――, "Rom. 7.7-25 encore une fois. Enjeux et propositions," *NTS* 48 (2002), 358-76.

Aune, D. E., "Romans as a *Logos Protreptikos* in the Context of Ancient Religious and Philosophical Propaganda," in *Paulus und das antike Judentum,* ed. M. Hengel and U. Heckel (WUNT 58; Tübingen: Mohr, 1991), 91-121; abbreviated version in *The Romans Debate,* ed. K. P. Donfried (second ed.; Peabody: Hendrickson, 1991), 278-96.

Black, D. A., "The Pauline Love Command: Structure, Style, and Ethics in Romans 12:9-21," *FilolNT* 2 (1989), 3-22.

Boers, H., *The Justification of the Gentiles: Paul's Letters to the Galatians and Romans* (Peabody: Hendrickson, 1994).

Botha, J., "Creation of New Meaning: Rhetorical Situations and the Reception of Romans 13:1-17," *JTSA* 79 (1992), 24-37.

―――, "Social Values in the Rhetoric of Pauline Paraenetic Literature," *Neot* 28 (1994), 109-26. On 13:1-7.

―――, *Subject to Whose Authority? Multiple Readings of Romans 13* (Emory Studies in Early Christianity; Atlanta: Scholars, 1994).

Bouwman, G., *Paulus aan de Romeinen. Een retorische analyse van Rom 1–8* (CahLV 32; Averbode: Werkgroep voor levensverdieping, 1980).

Burton, K. A., "The Argumentative Coherence of Romans 7.1-6," in *SBL Seminar Papers 2000,* 452-64.

Byrskog, S., "Epistolography, Rhetoric and Letter Prescript: Romans 1.1-7 as a Test Case," *JSNT* 65 (1997), 27-46.

Campbell, D. A., "Determining the Gospel through Rhetorical Analysis in Paul's Letter to the Roman Christians," in *Gospel in Paul: Studies in Corinthians, Galatians and Romans for Richard N. Longenecker,* ed. L. A. Jervis and P. Richardson (JSNTS 108; Sheffield: Sheffield Academic, 1994), 315-36.

―――, *The Rhetoric of Righteousness in Romans 3.21-26* (JSNTS 65; Sheffield: Sheffield Academic, 1992).

————, *The Rhetoric of Righteousness in Romans 3:21-26* (JSNTS 65; Sheffield: Sheffield Academic, 1992).

————, "A Rhetorical Suggestion Concerning Romans 2," *SBLSP 1995*, ed. E. H. Lovering, Jr. (Atlanta: Scholars, 1995), 140-67.

————, "Towards a New, Rhetorically Assisted Reading of Romans 3.27–4.25," in S. E. Porter and D. L. Stamps, eds., *Rhetorical Criticism and the Bible*, 355-402.

Classen, C. J., "St. Paul's Epistles and Greco-Roman Rhetoric," in S. E. Porter and T. H. Olbricht, eds., *Rhetoric and the New Testament*, 265-91.

Cosby, M. R., "Paul's Persuasive Language in Romans 5," in *Persuasive Artistry: Studies in New Testament Rhetoric in Honor of George A. Kennedy*, ed. D. F. Watson (JSNTS 50; Sheffield: Sheffield Academic, 1991), 209-26.

Cosgrove, C. H., "Rhetorical Suspense in Romans 9–11: A Study in Polyvalence and Hermeneutical Election," *JBL* 115 (1996), 271-87.

Crafton, J. A., "The Dancing of an Attitude: Burkean Rhetorical Criticism and the Biblical Interpreter," in S. E. Porter and T. H. Olbricht, eds., *Rhetoric and the New Testament*, 429-42.

————, "Paul's Rhetorical Vision and the Purpose of Romans: Toward a New Understanding," *NovT* 32 (1990), 317-39.

Dewey, A. J., "Acoustics in the Spirit: A Hearing of Romans 10," *PEGLMBS* 9 (1989), 212-30.

————, "A Re-Hearing of Romans 10:1-15," *SBLSP 1990*, ed. D. L. Lull (Atlanta: Scholars, 1990), 273-82.

Donfried, K. P., "False Propositions in the Study of Romans," *CBQ* 36 (1974), 332-55, reprinted in *The Romans Debate*, ed. K. P. Donfried (second ed., Peabody: Hendrickson, 1991), 102-25.

Du Toit, A. B., "Persuasion in Romans 1:1-17," *BZ* 33 (1989), 192-209.

Elliott, N., *The Rhetoric of Romans: Argumentative Constraint and Strategy and Paul's Dialogue with Judaism* (JSNTS 45; Sheffield: Sheffield Academic, 1990).

Feuillet, A., "Les attaches bibliques des antithèses pauliniennes dans la première partie de l'épître aux Romains (1–8)," in *Mélanges bibliques en hommage au R. P. Béda Rigaux*, ed. A. Deschamps and R. P. André de Halleux (Gembloux: J. Duculot, 1970), 323-49.

Fiore, B., "Invective in Romans and Philippians," *PEGLMBS* 10 (1990), 181-89.

————, "Romans 9–11 and Classical Forensic Rhetoric," *PEGLMBS* 8 (1988), 117-26.

Forbes, J., *Analytical Commentary on the Epistle to the Romans Tracing the Train of Thought by the Aid of Parallelism* (Edinburgh: Clark, 1868).

Fraikin, D., "The Rhetorical Function of the Jews in Romans," in *Anti-Judaism in Early Christianity*, Vol. 1: *Paul and the Gospels*, ed. P. Richardson (Studies in

Christianity and Judaism 2; Waterloo: Wilfrid Laurier University, 1986), 91-105.

Gienuisz, A., "Rom 7,1-6: Lack of Imagination? Function of the Passage in the Argumentation of Rom 6,1–7,6," *Bib* 74 (1993), 389-400.

Girardin, B., *Rhétorique et théologique. Calvin. Le commentaire de l'épître aux Romains* (ThH 54; Paris: Beauchesne, 1979).

Grobel, K., "A Chiastic Retribution-Formula in Romans 2," in *Zeit und Geschichte. Dankesgabe an Rudolf Bultmann zum 80. Geburtstag*, ed. E. Dinkler (Tübingen: Mohr, 1964), 255-61.

Hellholm, D., "Amplificatio in the Macro-Structure of Romans," in S. E. Porter and T. H. Olbricht, eds., *Rhetoric and the New Testament*, 123-51.

———, "Die argumentative Funktion von Römer 7.1-6," *NTS* 43 (1997), 385-411.

———, "Enthymemic Argumentation in Paul: The Case of Romans 6," in *Paul in His Hellenistic Context*, ed. T. Engberg-Pedersen (Minneapolis: Augsburg Fortress, 1995), 119-79.

Jaquette, J. L., "Life and Death, *Adiaphora*, and Paul's Rhetorical Strategies," *NovT* 38 (1996), 30-54.

Jennrich, W. A., "Rhetoric in the New Testament: The Diction in Romans and Hebrews," *CTM* 20 (1949), 518-31.

———, "Rhetorical Style in the New Testament: Romans and Hebrews" (Ph.D. dissertation, Washington University, 1947).

Jewett, R., "Ecumenical Theology for the Sake of Mission: Romans 1:1-17 + 15:14–16:24," *SBLSP 1992*, ed. E. Lovering, Jr. (Atlanta: Scholars, 1992), 598-612.

———, "Following the Argument of Romans," *WW* 6 (1986), 382-89; expanded version in *The Romans Debate*, ed. K. P. Donfried (second ed.; Peabody: Hendrickson, 1991), 265-77.

———, "The Rhetorical Function of Numerical Sequences in Romans," in *Persuasive Artistry: Studies in New Testament Rhetoric in Honor of George A. Kennedy*, ed. D. F. Watson (JSNTS 50; Sheffield: Sheffield Academic, 1991), 227-45.

———, "Romans as an Ambassadorial Letter," *Int* 36 (1982), 5-20.

Jolivet, I. J., "An Argument from the Letter and Intent of the Law as the Primary Argumentative Strategy in Romans," in S. E. Porter and T. H. Olbricht, eds., *The Rhetorical Analysis of Scripture*, 309-35.

Jüngel, E., "Ein paulinischer Chiasmus. Zum Verständnis der Vorstellung vom Gericht nach den Werken in Röm 2,2-11," in *Unterwegs zur Sache*, ed. E. Jüngel (BEvT 61; Munich: Kaiser, 1972), 173-78 = "Das Gesetz zwischen Adam und Christus: Eine theologische Studie zu Röm 5,12-21," *ZTK* 60 (1963), 70-74.

Kinneavy, J. L., *Greek Rhetorical Origins of Christian Faith* (New York: Oxford University Press, 1987).

Kirby, J. T., "The Syntax of Romans 5.12: A Rhetorical Approach," *NTS* 33 (1987), 283-86.

Lagrange, M.-J., "Langue, style, argumentation dans l'épître aux Romains," *RB* 12 (1915), 216-35.

McDonald, P. M., "Romans 5.1-11 as a Rhetorical Bridge," *JSNT* 40 (1990), 81-96.

Melanchthon, P., *Commentarii in epistolam ad Romanos hoc anno M.D.XL. recogniti et locupletati* (Argentorati: C. Mylium, 1540).

Mesner, D. E., "The Rhetoric of Citations: Paul's Use of Scripture in Romans 9" (Ph.D. diss., Northwestern University, 1991).

Moxnes, H., "The Quest for Honor and the Unity of the Community in Romans 12 and in the Orations of Dio Chrysostom," in *Paul in His Hellenistic Context,* ed. T. Engberg-Pedersen (Minneapolis: Augsburg Fortress, 1995), 203-30.

Myers, C. D., "Chiastic Inversion in the Argument of Romans 3–8," *NovT* 35 (1993), 30-47.

North, J. L., "'Good Wordes and Faire Speeches' (Rom 16.18 AV): More Materials and a Pauline Pun," *NTS* 42 (1996), 600-14.

Porter, C. L., "Romans 1.18-32: Its Role in the Developing Argument," *NTS* 40 (1994), 210-28.

Porter, S. E., "The Argument of Romans 5: Can a Rhetorical Question Make a Difference?" *JBL* 110 (1991), 655-77.

———, "The Rhetorical Scribe: Textual Variants in Romans and Their Possible Rhetorical Purpose," in S. E. Porter and D. L. Stamps, eds., *Rhetorical Criticism and the Bible,* 403-19.

———, "Romans 13:1-7 as Pauline Political Rhetoric," *FilolNT* 3 (1990), 115-39.

Porter, S. E., and T. H. Olbricht, eds., *Rhetoric and the New Testament: Essays from the Heidelberg 1992 Conference* (Sheffield: Sheffield Academic, 1993).

———, *The Rhetorical Analysis of Scripture* (Sheffield: Sheffield Academic, 1997).

Porter, S. E., and D. L. Stamps, eds., *Rhetorical Criticism and the Bible* (Sheffield: Sheffield Academic, 2002). There are several essays in this volume of relevance for the study of the rhetoric of Romans, though most of them (with the exception of the one by D. A. Campbell) are critical of such an approach to Paul's letters.

Reed, J. T., "Indicative and Imperative in Rom 6,21-22: The Rhetoric of Punctuation," *Bib* 74 (1993), 244-57.

Reid, M. L., *Augustinian and Pauline Rhetoric in Romans Five: A Study of Early Christian Rhetoric* (Mellen Biblical Press Series 30; Lewiston, NY: Mellen Biblical Press, 1996).

———, "A Consideration of the Function of Rom 1:8-15 in Light of Greco-Roman Rhetoric," *JETS* 38 (1995), 181-91.

———, "Paul's Rhetoric of Mutuality: A Rhetorical Reading of Romans," *SBLSP 1995,* ed. E. H. Lovering, Jr. (Atlanta: Scholars, 1995), 117-39.

————, "A Rhetorical Analysis of Romans 1:1–5:21 with Attention Given to the Rhetorical Function of 5:1-21," *PRS* 19 (1992), 255-72.

Rolland, P., "L'antithèse de Rm 5–8," *Bib* 69 (1988), 396-400.

Sampley, J. P., "The Weak and the Strong: Paul's Careful and Crafty Rhetorical Strategy in Romans 14:1–15:13," in *The Social World of the First Christians: Essays in Honor of Wayne A. Meeks,* ed. L. M. White and O. L. Yarbrough (Minneapolis: Fortress, 1995), 40-52.

Schoeni, M., "The Hyperbolic Sublime as a Master Trope in Romans," in S. E. Porter and T. H. Olbricht, eds., *Rhetoric and the New Testament,* 171-92.

Scroggs, R., "Paul as Rhetorician: Two Homilies in Romans 1–11," in *Jews, Greeks and Christians: Religious Cultures in Late Antiquity* (FS W. D. Davies), ed. R. Hamerton-Kelly and R. Scroggs (Leiden: Brill, 1976), 271-98.

Siegert, F., *Argumentation bei Paulus gezeigt an Röm 9 bis 11* (WUNT 34; Tubingen: Mohr, 1985).

Snyman, A. H., "Stilistiese tegnieke in Romeine 7:7-13," *NduitseGT* 27 (1986), 23-28.

————, "Style and Meaning in Romans 8:31-9," *Neot* 18 (1984), 94-103.

————, "Style and the Rhetorical Situation of Romans 8.31-39," *NTS* 34 (1988), 218-31.

Spencer, A. B., *Paul's Literary Style: A Stylistic and Historical Comparison of II Corinthians 11:16–12:13, Romans 8:9-39, and Philippians 3:2–4:13* (ETSMS; Jackson: Evangelical Theological Society, 1984).

Stowers, S. K., *The Diatribe and Paul's Letter to the Romans* (SBLDS 57; Chico: Scholars, 1981).

————, "Paul's Dialogue with a Fellow Jew in Romans 3:1-9," *CBQ* 46 (1984), 707-22.

————, *A Rereading of Romans: Justice, Jews, and Gentiles* (New Haven: Yale University Press, 1994).

————, "Romans 7.7-25 as a Speech-in-Character (προσωποποιία)," in *Paul in His Hellenistic Context,* ed. T. Engberg-Pedersen (Minneapolis: Augsburg Fortress, 1995), 180-202.

Strauss, D. J., "'N Voorstel vir Gekontroleerde Perikoop — En Kolongroep-verdeling in Romaine 5," in *Oor styl en retoriek by Paulus,* ed. A. H. Snyman (Acta academica 6; Bloemfontein: Universiteit van die Oranje-Vrystaat, 1986), 52-78.

Theobald, M., "Glaube und Vernunft. Zur Argumentation des Paulus im Römerbrief," *TQ* 169 (1989), 287-301.

Thurin, L. "Romans 7 Dehistoricized," in S. E. Porter and D. L. Stamps, eds., *Rhetorical Criticism and the Bible,* 420-40.

Tobin, T. H., "Controversy and Continuity in Romans 1:18–3:20," *CBQ* 55 (1993), 298-318.

Von Dobschütz, E., "Zum Wortschatz und Stil des Römerbriefs," *ZNW* 33 (1934), 51-66.

Vorster, J. N., "The Context of the Letter to the Romans: A Critique on the Present State of Research," *NeoT* 28 (1994), 127-45.

————, "The Rhetorical Situation of the Letter to the Romans — An Interactional Approach" (D. D. thesis, University of Pretoria, 1991).

————, "Strategies of Persuasion in Romans 1.16-17," in S. E. Porter and T. H. Olbricht, eds., *Rhetoric and the New Testament*, 152-70.

Vos, J. S., "Die hermeneutische Antinomie bei Paulus (Galater 3.11-12; Römer 10.5-10)," *NTS* 38 (1992), 254-70.

Vouga, F., "Romains 1,18–3,20 comme *narratio*," in *La narration. Quand le récit devient communication*, ed. P. Bühler and J.-F. Habermacher (Lieux Théologiques 12; Geneva: Labor et Fides, 1988), 145-61.

————, "Römer 1,18–3,20 als *narratio*," *TGl* 77 (1987), 225-36.

Wire, A. C., "'Since God Is One': Rhetoric as Theology and History in Paul's Romans," in *The New Literary Criticism and the New Testament*, ed. E. S. Malbon and E. V. McKnight (JSNTS 109; Sheffield: Sheffield Academic; Valley Forge: Trinity, 1994), 210-27.

Wonneberger, R., "Textgliederung bei Paulus. Eine Problemskizze am Beispiel von Römer 3,21, 1.Korinther 13 und Römer 5," in *Sprachtheorie und Pragmatik. Akten des 10. Linguistischen Kolloquiums, Tübingen 1975*, vol. 1, ed. H. Weber and H. Weydt (Linguistische Arbeiten 31; Tübingen: Niemeyer, 1976), 305-14.

Wuellner, W., "Paul's Rhetoric of Argumentation in Romans: An Alternative to the Donfried-Karris Debate over Romans," *CBQ* 38 (1976), 330-51, reprinted in K. P. Donfried, *The Romans Debate, 128-46*.

Articles from the SBL "Romans through History and Culture" Seminar

These articles are listed separately not only because they are of such recent vintage but also because they represent first attempts to read Paul in conjunction with various modern cultural contexts, some historical settings that post-date the NT period, and various philosophical and ideological perspectives. In other words, these are exercises to one degree or another in what I would call hermeneutics. They are valuable because they produce new readings of Paul, but most scholars such as myself who have been traditionally trained in the classics, ancient history, biblical studies, and the like, and not in modern cultures or other historical settings, are not really competent to critically evaluate such efforts.

Early papers (from before 2000) by various contributors to this seminar can be found in C. Grenholm and D. Patte, eds., *Reading Israel in Romans: Legitimacy and Plausibility of Divergent Interpretations* (Harrisburg: Trinity, 2000).

Anderson, V. N., "Can Kierkegaard Help Us Understand the Role of the Law in Romans 7.7-12? Tools for a Kierkegaardian Reading of Paul," *SBLSP 2002*, 111-35.
Bingham, D. J., "Irenaeus's Reading of Romans 8," *SBLSP 2001*, 131-50.
Clements, R., "(Re)constructing Paul: Origen's Readings of Romans in *Peri Archōn*," *SBLSP 2001*, 151-74.
Draper, J. A., "Bishop John William Colenso's Interpretation to the Zulu People of the *Sola Fide* in Paul's Letter to the Romans," *SBLSP 2000*, 465-93.
Ehrensperger, K., ". . . Let everyone be convinced in his/her own mind": Derrida and the Deconstruction of Paulinism," *SBLSP 2002*, 53-73.
Eisenbaum, P., "'A Remedy for Having Been Born of Woman': Jesus, Gender, and Genealogy in Romans," *SBLSP 2000*, 494-519.
Gignac, A., "Taubes, Badiou, Agamben: Reception of Paul by Non-Christian Philosophers Today," *SBLSP 2002*, 74-110.
Hornsby, T. J., "The Gendered Sinner in Romans 1–7," *SBLSP 2000*, 520-58.
Lung-Kwong, L., "Identity Crisis Reflected in Romans 14.1–15.13 and the Implications for the Chinese Christians' Controversy on Ancestral Worship," *SBLSP 2002*, 1-32.
Rakotoharintsifa, A., "Peace in the Epistle to the Romans and the Malagasy Culture," *SBLSP 2002*, 33-52.
Tan, Y.-H., "Judging and Community in Romans: An Action within the Boundaries," *SBLSP 2000*, 559-82.
Yeo, K.-K., "Messianic Predestination in Romans 8 and Classical Confucianism," *SBLSP 2001*, 81-107.

Other Works

On Paul and the Law see the discussion and bibliography in my *Grace in Galatia* (Grand Rapids: Eerdmans, 1998), 141-56.

Aageson, J. W., "Scripture and Structure in the Development of the Argument in Romans 9–11," *CBQ* 48 (1986), 265-89.
Achtemeier, P., "Unsearchable Judgments and Inscrutable Ways: Reflections on the Discussion of Romans," *SBLSP 1995*, 521-34.
Adcock, F. E., "Women in Roman Life and Letters," *Greece and Rome* 14 (1945), 1-22.

Aletti, J. N., "Romains 2: Sa Coherence et sa Fonction," *Bib* 77 (1996), 170-74.

Allison, D. C., "The Pauline Epistles and the Synoptic Gospels: The Pattern of the Parallels," *NTS* 28 (1982), 1-32.

Aus, R. D., "Paul's Travel Plans to Spain, and the 'Full Number of the Gentiles' of Romans 11.25," *NovT* 21 (1979), 232-62.

Babcock, W. S., ed., *Paul and the Legacies of Paul* (Dallas: SMU Press, 1990). This volume has a variety of interesting articles, largely ignored by Pauline scholars, about the reception and use of Paul by figures as diverse as the Apostolic Fathers, Origen, Chrysostom, and Augustine.

Badenas, R., *Christ the End of the Law: Romans 10.4 in Pauline Perspective* (Sheffield: JSOT, 1985).

Balsdon, J. P. V. D., *Roman Women: Their History and Habits* (London: Bodley Head, 1962).

Barrett, C. K., *From First Adam to Last* (London: Black, 1962). This is a slender but quite important study which helps us understand difficult things like Pauline typology, incorporative personality, and related notions.

Bassler, J., "Divine Impartiality in Paul's Letter to the Romans," *NovT* 26 (1984), 43-58.

―――, *Divine Providence: Paul and a Theological Axiom* (Chico: Scholars, 1982).

Bauckham, R., *Gospel Women: Studies in the Named Women in the Gospels* (Grand Rapids: Eerdmans, 2002). This study is important for studies of Romans as it gives us one of the most recent and detailed treatments of Junia and whether or not she might have been not only an apostle, but also the same person as Joanna the wife of Chuza, mentioned in Luke 8.1-3.

Baxter, A. G., and J. Zeisler, "Paul and Arboriculture: Romans 11.17-24," *JSNT* 24 (1985), 25-32.

Beckheuer, B., *Paulus und Jerusalem. Kolleckte und Mission im theologischen Denken des Heidenapostels* (Frankfurt: Lang, 1997).

Beker, J. C., "The Relationship between Sin and Death in Romans," in R. T. Fortna and B. R. Gaventa, eds., *The Conversation Continues: Studies in Paul and John in Honor of J. Louis Martyn* (Nashville: Abingdon, 1990), 55-61.

Bell, R. H., "Romans 5.18-19 and Universal Salvation," *NTS* 48 (2002), 417-32.

Benko, S., "The Kiss" in Benko, *Pagan Rome and the Early Christians* (Bloomington: Indiana University Press, 1984), 79-102.

Betz, H. D., *Paulinischen Studien* (Tübingen: Mohr, 1994). Betz has in many ways been a trailblazer in the study of Paul and rhetoric and in trying to understand how Christianity emerged from the shadow of Judaism. In his view, Paul was the one who began to set the pattern of Christianity as a separate religion.

Borg, M., "A New Context for Romans XIII," *NTS* 19 (1972-73), 205-18.

Brooten, B., *Women Leaders in the Ancient Synagogues* (Chico: Scholars, 1982).

Brown, M. J., "Paul's Use of *Doulos Christou Iēsou* in Romans 1.1," *JBL* 120 (2001), 723-37.

Brown, R. E., "Further Reflections on the Origins of the Church of Rome," in R. T. Fortna and B. R. Gaventa, eds., *The Conversation Continues*, 98-115.

Brown, R. E., and J. P. Meir, *Antioch and Rome: New Testament Cradles of Christianity* (New York: Paulist, 1983). This book helped set in motion the reevaluation of the social setting of the church in Rome.

Bruce, F. F., "Paul and the Powers That Be," *BJRL* 66 (1983-84), 78-96.

Bultmann, R., *Der Stil der paulinschen Predigt und die kynisch-stoische Diatribe* (reprint, Göttingen: Vandenhoeck und Ruprecht, 1984).

Burer, M. H., and D. B. Wallace, "Was Junia Really an Apostle? A Re-examination of Rom. 16.7," *NTS* 47 (2001), 76-91.

Byrne, B., "Living Out the Righteousness of God: The Contribution of Rom. 6.1–8.13 to an Understanding of Paul's Ethical Presuppositions," *CBQ* 43 (1981), 557-81.

————, "Rather Boldly (Rom. 15.15): Paul's Prophetic Bid to Win the Allegiance of the Christians in Rome," *Biblica* 74 (1993), 83-96.

Caird, G. B., "Expository Problems: Predestination — Romans ix–xi," *ET* 68 (1956-57), 324-27.

Campbell, W. S., "The Rule of Faith in Romans 12.1–15.13," in D. M. Hay and E. E. Johnson, eds., *Pauline Theology*, vol. III, 259-86.

Carson, D. A., P. O'Brien, and M. A. Seifrid, eds., *Justification and Variegated Nomism*, vol. 1 (Grand Rapids: Baker, 2001). This is perhaps the first full-scale response to E. P. Sanders's reading of early Judaism with regard to issues such as covenantal nomism and works of the Law. It is a helpful reevaluation of the evidence, with a promise of a second volume that evaluates Paul in the light of these data.

Cervin, R. S., "A Note Regarding the Name Junia(s) in Romans 16.7," *NTS* 40 (1994), 464-70.

Clarke, A. D., "The Good and the Just in Romans 5.7," *TynBul* 41 (1990), 128-42.

————, "Jew and Greek, Slave and Free, Male and Female: Paul's Theology of Ethnic, Social, and Gender Inclusiveness in Romans 16," in P. Oakes, ed., *Rome in the Bible and the Early Church*, 103-25.

Cranford, M., "Abraham in Romans 4: The Father of All Who Believe," *NTS* 41 (1995), 71-88.

Cullmann, O., *The State in the New Testament* (London: SCM, 1957).

Dahl, N. A., "Two Notes on Romans 5," *ST* 5 (1952), 37-38.

Das, A. A., *Paul, the Law, and the Covenant* (Peabody: Hendrickson, 2001). A helpful corrective to some aspects of the new perspective on Paul vis-à-vis covenantal nomism. Paul *was* in the end concerned about self-righteousness, and his critique of the Law was not limited to the boundary-marker or ethnic aspects of the Law. In Paul's view the Mosaic Law could not give life or empower one to obey.

Davies, G. N., *Faith and Obedience in Romans: A Study in Romans 1-4* (Sheffield: Sheffield Academic, 1990).

Davies, W. D., *Paul and Rabbinic Judaism* (New York: Harper, 1948).

Deidun, T. J., "Romans," in *A Dictionary of Biblical Interpretation*, ed. R. J. Collins and J. L. Houlden (Philadelphia: Trinity, 1990), 601-4.

Donaldson, T. L., *Paul and the Gentiles: Remapping the Apostle's Convictional World* (Minneapolis: Fortress, 1997). This is a very helpful attempt to locate Paul in the context of Second Temple Judaism. It proposes that Paul believed in not only the salvation of Gentiles but also the restoration of Israel.

Donfried, K. P., "A Short Note on Romans 16," in K. P. Donfried, ed., *The Romans Debate* (second ed., Peabody: Hendrickson, 1991), 44-52.

Donfried, K. P., and P. Richardson, eds., *Judaism and Christianity in First-Century Rome* (Grand Rapids: Eerdmans, 1998).

Dunn, J. D. G., *Baptism in the Holy Spirit* (London: SCM, 1970).

———, "In Quest of Paul's Theology: Retrospect and Prospect," *SBLSP 1995*, 704-21. Already here we see Dunn arguing for Romans as the center and the place to start when it comes to deciphering Paul's theology.

———, "The Law of Faith, the Law of the Spirit, and the Law of Christ," in *Theology and Ethics in Paul and His Interpreters*, ed. E. H. Lovering and J. L. Sumney (Nashville: Abingdon, 1996), 62-82.

———, "'Righteousness from Law' and 'Righteousness from Faith': Paul's Interpretation of Scripture in Romans 10.1-10," in G. F. Hawthorne and O. Betz, eds., *Tradition and Interpretation*, 216-28.

———, "Romans 13:1-7 — A Charter for Imperial Quietism?" *Ex Auditu* 2 (1986), 55-68.

———, "Spirit Speech: Reflections on Romans 8.12-27," in S. K. Soderlund and N. T. Wright, ed., *Romans and the People of God*, 82-91.

———, *The Theology of Paul the Apostle* (Grand Rapids: Eerdmans, 1998). This is an excellent survey of Paul's thought which is old-fashioned in some respects and new-fangled in others. It shows what happens when a scholar takes Romans as his point of departure or touchstone. Compare and contrast this volume with my *Paul's Narrative Thought World*.

Dunn, J. D. G., ed., *Paul and the Mosaic Law* (Tübingen: Mohr, 1996).

Dupont, J., "Le Seigneur de tous (Ac 10:36; Rm. 10.12). Arrière-fond scripturaire d'une formule christologique," in G. F. Hawthorne and O. Betz, eds., *Tradition and Interpretation*, 229-36.

Du Toit, A. B., "*Dikaiosune* in Rom. 6. Beobachtungen zur ethischen Dimension der paulinischen Gerechtigkeitsauffassung," *ZTK* 76 (1979), 261-91.

Eastman, S., "Whose Apocalypse? The Identity of the Sons of God in Romans 8.19," *JBL* 121 (2002), 263-77.

Elliott, J. K., "The Language and Style of the Concluding Doxology to the Epistle to the Romans," *ZNW* 72 (1981), 124-30.

Elliott, N., "Romans 13.1-7 in the Context of Imperial Propaganda," in R. A. Horsley, ed., *Paul and Empire*, 184-204,

Epp, E. E., "Text-Critical, Exegetical, and Socio-Cultural Factors Affecting the Junia/Junias Variation in Rom. 16.7," in *New Testament Textual Criticism and Exegesis: Festschrift J. Delobel,* ed. A Denaux (Leuven: Leuven University Press, 2002), 227-91.

Esler, P. F., *Conflict and Identity in Romans* (Minneapolis: Fortress, 2002). This important work is not so much a commentary on Romans as a social-scientific reading of the entire text which helpfully focuses on the crisis of identity in Rome and shows how social-scientific resources on individual and group identity illuminate the text.

Evans, C. A., "Paul and the Prophets: Prophetic Criticism in the Epistle to the Romans (with Special Reference to Romans 9–11)," in S. K. Soderlund and N. T. Wright, eds., *Romans and the People of God,* 115-28.

Fee, G. D., *God's Empowering Presence: The Holy Spirit in the Letters of Paul* (Peabody: Hendrickson, 1994). Easily the most thorough treatment of the Holy Spirit in Paul's letters. A landmark study.

Fitzmyer, J., "The Consequent Meaning of *Eph' Hō* in Romans 5.12," *NTS* 39 (1993), 413-17.

———, "Paul's Jewish Background and the Deeds of the Law," in his *According to Paul: Studies in the Theology of the Apostle* (New York: Paulist, 1993), 18-35.

Fortna, R. T., and B. R. Gaventa, eds., *The Conversation Continues: Studies in Paul and John* (Nashville: Abingdon, 1990).

Furnish, V. P., *The Love Command in the New Testament* (Nashville: Abingdon, 1973). A formative study which set in motion a closer examination of the connections between the ethics of Jesus and Paul in regard to love and other matters.

———, *The Moral Teaching of Paul* (Nashville: Abingdon, 1979).

———, *Theology and Ethics in Paul* (Nashville: Abingdon, 1968). Important for its stress on the relationship between the indicative and imperative in Paul's writings.

Gager, J. G., *The Origins of Anti-Semitism* (New York: Oxford, 1983).

Gagnon, R. A. J., "The Meaning of *humōn to agathon* in Romans 14.16," *JBL* 117 (1998), 675-89.

Garlington, D. G., *The Obedience of Faith: A Pauline Phrase in Historical Context* (Tübingen: Mohr, 1991).

Gaston, L., *Paul and the Torah* (Vancouver: University of British Columbia, 1987).

Gathercole, S. J., "A Law unto Themselves: The Gentiles in Rom. 2.14-15 Revisited," *JSNT* 85 (2002), 27-49.

Georgi, D., "God Turned Upside-Down. Romans: Missionary Theology and Roman Political Theology," in R. A. Horsley, ed., *Paul and Empire*, 148-57.

Gillmann, F. M., "Another Look at Romans 8.3: 'In the Likeness of Sinful Flesh,'" *CBQ* 49 (1987), 597-604.

Godsey, J., "The Interpretation of Romans in the History of the Christian Faith," *Interpretation* 34 (1980), 3-16.

Gorday, P., "Paulus Origenianus: The Economic Interpretation of Paul," in W. S. Babcock, ed., *Paul and the Legacies of Paul*, 141-63.

Grieb, K., "Affiliation with Jesus Christ in His Sacrifice: Some Uses of Scripture to Define the Identity of Jesus Christ in Romans" (Ph.D. diss., Yale University, 1997).

Griffin, M. T., *Nero: The End of a Dynasty* (New Haven: Yale University Press, 1985).

Guerra, A. J., *Romans and the Apologetic Tradition: The Purpose, Genre, and Audience of Paul's Letters* (Cambridge: Cambridge University Press, 1995).

Hammerton-Kelly, R., "Sacred Violence and Sinful Desire: Paul's Interpretation of Adam's Sin in the Letter to the Romans," in R. T. Fortna and B. R. Gaventa, eds., *The Conversation Continues*, 35-54.

Havemann, J. C. T., "Cultivated Olive — Wild Olive: The Olive Tree Metaphor in Romans 11.16-24," *Neot* 31 (1997), 87-106.

Hawthorne, G. F., and O. Betz, eds., *Tradition and Interpretation in the New Testament* (Grand Rapids: Eerdmans, 1987).

Hay, D. M., *Glory at the Right Hand: Psalm 110 in Early Christianity* (Nashville: Abingdon, 1973).

Hay, D. M., and E. E. Johnson, eds., *Pauline Theology*, vol. III: *Romans* (Minneapolis: Fortress, 1995). Vigorous discussion of Paul's theology in Romans, but often with too much isolation from the other letters. This is forgetting that while Paul had a theology, expressed variously depending on the situation, letters do not have theologies. This volume should be compared to some of the essays in the Festschrift for V. P. Furnish edited by Lovering and Sumney.

Hays, R. B., "Adam, Israel, Christ — The Question of Covenant in the Theology of Romans: A Response to Leander E. Keck and N. T. Wright," in D. M. Hay and E. E. Johnson, eds., *Pauline Theology*, vol. III, 68-86.

————, *Echoes of Scripture in the Letters of Paul* (New Haven: Yale University Press, 1989). A helpful and influential study which helped advance intertextual study of Paul's letters.

————, "Have We Found Abraham to Be Our Forefather according to the Flesh: A Reconsideration of Rom. 4.1," *NovT* 27 (1985), 76-98.

————, "The Righteous One as Eschatological Deliverer: A Case Study in Paul's Apocalyptic Hermeneutics," in *Apocalyptic and the New Testament: Essays in Honor of J. Louis Martyn,* ed. M. Soards and J. Marcus (Sheffield: Sheffield Academic, 1988), 191-225.

Heckel, T. K., *Der Innere Mensch. Die paulinischen Verarbeitung eines platonischen Motivs* (Tübingen: Mohr, 1993).

Hooker, M. D., "Adam in Romans 1," *NTS* 6 (1959-60), 297-306.

————, "A Further Note on Romans 1," *NTS* 13 (1966-67), 181-83.

Horsley, R. A., ed., *Paul and Empire* (Harrisburg: Trinity, 1997).

————, ed., *Paul and Politics* (Harrisburg: Trinity, 2002). These two volumes present something of a mixed bag of sociological studies of Roman culture and essays on elements in Paul's thought. They are always challenging and interesting, but often seem to overplay both the impact of the imperial cult on Paul's thinking and also the radical nature of Paul's own politics.

Humphrey, E. M., "Why Bring the Word Down? The Rhetoric of Demonstration and Disclosure in Romans 9.30–10.21," in S. K. Soderlund and N. T. Wright, ed., *Romans and the People of God,* 129-48.

Jeffers, J., *Conflict at Rome: Social Order and Hierarchy in Early Christianity* (Minneapolis: Fortress, 1991).

Jervis, A. *The Purpose of Romans: A Comparative Letter Structure Investigation* (Sheffield: Sheffield Academic, 1991).

Jewett, R., "Paul, Phoebe, and the Spanish Mission," in *The Social World of Formative Christianity and Judaism,* ed. J. Neusner et al. (Philadelphia: Fortress, 1988), 142-61.

————, "Response: Exegetical Support from Romans and Other Letters," in R. A. Horsley, ed., *Paul and Politics,* 58-71.

Johnson, D. G., "The Structure and Meaning of Romans 11," *CBQ* 46 (1984), 91-103.

Johnson, E. E., *The Function of Apocalyptic and Wisdom Traditions in Romans 9–11* (Atlanta: Scholars, 1989).

————, "Romans 9–11: The Faithfulness and Impartiality of God," in D. M. Hay and E. E. Johnson, eds., *Pauline Theology,* vol. III, 211-39.

Joubert, S., *Paul as Benefactor: Reciprocity, Strategy, and Theological Reflection in Paul's Collection* (Tübingen: Mohr, 2000).

Karris, R. J., "Romans 14.1–15.13 and the Occasion of Romans," in K. P. Donfried, *The Romans Debate,* 65-84.

Kearsley, R. A., "Women in Public Life in the Roman East: Iunia Theodora, Claudia Metrodora, and Phoebe Benefactress of Paul," *TynBul* 50 (1999), 189-211.

————, "Women in the World of the New Testament," *Ancient Society* 15 (1985), 124-77.

Keck, L. E., "Christology, Soteriology, and the Praise of God (Romans 15.7-13)," in R. T. Fortna and B. R. Gaventa, eds., *The Conversation Continues,* 85-97.

————, "The Function of Romans 3.10-18 — Observations and Suggestions," in

God's Christ and His People: Studies in Honor of Nils Alstrup Dahl (Oslo: Universitetsforlaget, 1977), 141-57.

————, "What Makes Romans Tick?" in D. M. Hay and E. E. Johnson, eds., *Pauline Theology*, vol. III, 3-29.

Kim, S., "God Reconciled His Enemy to Himself: The Origin of Paul's Concept of Reconciliation," in *The Road to Damascus: The Impact of Paul's Conversion on His Life, Thought, and Ministry*, ed. R. N. Longenecker (Grand Rapids: Eerdmans, 1997), 102-24.

————, *Paul and the New Perspective: Second Thoughts on the Origin of Paul's Gospel* (Grand Rapids: Eerdmans, 2002). A critique of Dunn's critique of Kim's earlier work, not really a survey or detailed critique of the "new perspective on Paul." The focus is not on Romans.

Klassen, W., "Coals of Fire: Signs of Repentance or Revenge?" *NTS* 9 (1962-63), 337-50.

Kümmel, W. G., *Römer 7 und Die Bekehrung des Paulus* (Munich: Kaiser, 1974). This was such an important monograph, challenging the older Lutheran view that the "I" in Romans 7 was autobiographical, that it was reprinted forty-five years after it first came out in 1929. Still an important volume.

Lambrecht, J., "Paul's Logic in Romans 3.29-30," *JBL* 119 (2000), 526-28.

————, *The Wretched "I" and Its Liberation* (Louvain: Peeters, 1992).

Lampe, P., *Die städtromischen Christen in den erst beiden Jahrhunderten* (Tübingen: Mohr, 1987). This very important monograph is now fortunately going into a second edition, to be published in English. It has done as much as any volume to push forward the sociological study of Romans.

Levine, A. J., "Nanos, *The Mystery of Romans*," *JQR* 89 (1998), 222-24.

Lincoln, A. T., "From Wrath to Justification: Tradition, Gospel, and Audience in the Theology of Romans 1.18–4.25," in D. M. Hay and E. E. Johnson, eds., *Pauline Theology*, vol. III, 130-59.

Lindemann, A., "Paul in the Writings of the Apostolic Fathers," in W. S. Babcock, ed., *Paul and the Legacies of Paul*, 25-45.

Little, J. A., "Paul's Use of Analogy: A Structural Analysis of Romans 7.1-6," *CBQ* 46 (1984), 82-90.

Loane, H. J., *Industry and Commerce of the City of Rome (50 BC–AD 200)* (Baltimore: Johns Hopkins, 1938).

Longenecker, B. W., *Eschatology and the Covenant: A Comparison of 4 Ezra and Romans 1–11* (Sheffield: JSOT, 1991).

Longenecker, R. N., "The Focus of Romans: The Central Role of 5.1–8.39 in the Argument of the Letter," in S. K. Soderlund and N. T. Wright, eds., *Romans and the People of God*, 49-69.

Lovering, E. H., and J. L. Sumney, eds., *Theology and Ethics in Paul and His Interpreters* (Nashville: Abingdon, 1996).

Lyonnet, S., "L'histoire du salut selon le ch. 7 de l'épître aux Romains," *Bib* 43 (1962), 117-51.

MacDonald, M. Y., *The Pauline Churches* (Cambridge: Cambridge University Press, 1988).

Malherbe, A., "'Mē genoito' in the Diatribe and in Paul," *HTR* 73 (1980), 231-40.

Marcus, J., "The Circumcision and the Uncircumcision in Rome," *NTS* 35 (1989), 67-81.

Marshall, I. H., "Romans 16.25-27 — An Apt Conclusion," in S. K. Soderlund and N. T. Wright, eds., *Romans and the People of God*, 170-84.

Martin, R. P., "Reconciliation: Romans 5.1-11," in S. K. Soderlund and N. T. Wright, eds., *Romans and the People of God*, 36-48.

Martyn, J. L., "Romans as One of the Earliest Interpretations of Galatians," in his *Theological Issues in the Letters of Paul* (Nashville: Abingdon, 1997), 37-45. This is a revised form of a 1988 article.

Meeks, W. A., *The First Urban Christians: The Social World of the Apostle Paul* (New Haven: Yale University Press, 1983). A seminal study which was a catalyst for more sociological studies of Paul. He draws on G. Theissen's seminal work and pushes the discussion a stage further.

————, "Judgment and the Brother: Romans 14.1–15.13," in G. F. Hawthorne and O. Betz, eds., *Tradition and Interpretation*, 290-300.

Meyer, P. W., "The Worm at the Core of the Apple: Exegetical Reflections on Romans 7," in R. T. Fortna and B. R. Gaventa, eds., *The Conversation Continues*, 62-84.

Meyers, C. D., "The Place of Romans 5.1-11 within the Argument of the Epistle" (Ph.D. dissertation, Princeton Theological Seminary, 1985).

Michaels, J. R., "The Redemption of Our Body: The Riddle of Romans 8.19-22," in S. K. Soderlund and N. T. Wright, eds., *Romans and the People of God*, 92-114.

Minear, P. S., *The Obedience of Faith: The Purposes of Paul in the Epistle to the Romans* (London: SCM, 1971). This volume helped emphasize the importance of the ethical material in chs. 12–15 for understanding Romans.

Moo, D., "The Theology of Romans 9–11," in D. M. Hay and E. E. Johnson, eds., *Pauline Theology*, vol. III, 240-58.

Morris, L., "The Meaning of *hilastērion* in Rom. 3.25," *NTS* 2 (1955/56), 33-34.

Nanos, M., *The Mystery of Romans* (Minneapolis: Fortress, 1996). This is a very interesting volume which, despite some of its flawed theses, nonetheless does a fine job of making clear that Paul is not combating any Jewish or Jewish Christian opponents in Romans. It is rather the "Hellenizing" agenda Paul may be combating, particularly in chs. 14–15, when he deals with his dominantly Gentile audience.

Oakes, P., ed., *Rome in the Bible and the Early Church* (Grand Rapids: Baker, 2002). Interesting articles, two of which are on Romans.

Obeng, E. A., "Abba Father: The Prayer of the Sons of God," *ET* 99 (1987-88), 363-66.

Osiek, C., "The Oral World of the First-Century Christians," a paper delivered at the SBL North American meeting in 1993.

Osten-Sacken, P. Von der, *Römer 8 als Beispiel paulinischen Soteriologie* (Göttingen: Vandenhoeck und Ruprecht, 1975).

Packer, J. I., "The 'Wretched Man' Revisited: Another Look at Romans 7.14-25," in S. K. Soderlund and N. T. Wright, ed., *Romans and the People of God,* 70-81.

Penna, R., "Les Juifs à Rome au temps de l'Apôtre Paul," *NTS* 28 (1982), 321-47.

Peterman, G. W., "Romans 15.26: Make a Contribution or Establish Fellowship?" *NTS* 40 (1994), 457-63.

Piper, J. A., *The Justification of God: An Exegetical and Theological Study of Rom. 9.1-23* (Grand Rapids: Baker, 1983).

Porter, C. L., "Romans 1.18-32: Its Role in the Developing Argument," *NTS* 40 (1994), 210-28.

Räisänen, H., *Paul and the Law* (Tübingen: Mohr, 1983).

———, "Paul, God and Israel: Romans 9–11 in Recent Research," in *The Social World of Formative Christianity and Judaism: Essays in Tribute to Howard Clark Kee,* ed. J. Neusner et al. (Philadelphia: Fortress, 1988), 178-206.

Reasoner, M., "The Theology of Romans 12.1–15.13," in D. M. Hay and E. E. Johnson, eds., *Pauline Theology,* vol. III, 287-99.

Refoulé, F., "*. . . Et ainsi tout Israel sera sauvé": Romains 11,25-32* (Paris: Cerf, 1984).

Richards, R. E., *The Secretary in the Letters of Paul* (Tübingen: Mohr, 1991).

Robinson, O. F., *The Criminal Law of Ancient Rome* (Baltimore: Johns Hopkins, 1995).

Romaniuk, K., "Was Phoebe in Romans 16,1 a Deaconess?" *ZNW* 81 (1990), 132-34.

Sanders, E. P., *Paul and Palestinian Judaism* (Philadelphia: Fortress, 1977). Perhaps the most influential monograph on Paul and his Jewish context in the last three decades. It championed the view that Paul reasoned from solution to plight when it came to issues such as the Law, salvation, and the future of Israel.

———, *Paul, the Law and the Jewish People* (Minneapolis: Fortress, 1983). Not as influential as *Paul and Palestinian Judaism,* this book still helped push forward "the new perspective" on Paul.

Schlier, H., "Die 'Liturgie' der apostolischen Evangeliums (Römer 15,14-21)," in *Das Ende der Zeit: Exegetische Aufsätze und Vorträge* (Freiburg: Herder, 1971), 171-76.

Schnabel, E. J., *Law and Wisdom from Ben Sira to Paul* (Tübingen: Mohr, 1985).

Seifrid, M., "Natural Revelation and the Purpose of the Law in Romans," *TynBul* 49 (1998), 115-29.

Sherwin-White, A. N., *Roman Society and Roman Law in the New Testament* (Oxford: Clarendon, 1963).

Snodgrass, K. "Justification by Grace to the Doers: An Analysis of the Place of Romans 2 in the Theology of Paul," *NTS* 32 (1986), 72-93.

Soderlund, S. K., and N. T. Wright, eds., *Romans and the People of God* (Grand Rapids: Eerdmans, 1999).

Song, C., "Reading Romans through the Macro-Structure of the Diatribe," *SBLSP 2001*, 260-77.

Stanley, C. D., *Paul and the Language of Scripture: Citation Techniques in the Pauline Epistles and Contemporary Literature* (Cambridge: Cambridge University Press, 1992).

Stendahl, K., *Paul among Jews and Gentiles* (Philadelphia: Fortress, 1977). The seminal essay about Paul's introspective consciousness (or, better said, lack thereof), reprinted here, was originally written in 1963 and led, along with the important monograph of Kümmel, to a reevaluation of what Romans 7.7-25 was actually discussing.

Stowers, S. K., *The Diatribe and Paul's Letter to the Romans* (Chico: Scholars, 1981).

—————, *A Rereading of Romans: Justice, Jews and Gentiles* (New Haven: Yale University Press, 1994). Both of these volumes by Stowers are important for pushing for a rereading of Paul's Romans in light of the diatribe style. Much more than just a recognition of a literary motif in Romans (à la R. Bultmann), Stowers's insights give a new perspective on texts like Romans 2–3, especially in this more recent volume.

Swetnam, J., *Jesus and Isaac* (Rome: Biblical Institute Press, 1981).

Theissen, G., *Psychological Aspects of Pauline Theology* (Philadelphia: Fortress, 1987). This is a fascinating volume with detailed exposition, but it also shows how modern readings of texts like Romans 7 over-psychologize Paul and fall into the trap Stendahl warned about.

—————, *The Social Setting of Pauline Christianity* (Philadelphia: Fortress, 1982). In North America even more than in Europe this was a very influential study which spawned a plethora of sociological studies of Paul's works, including Romans.

Thielman, F., "The Story of Israel and the Theology of Romans 5–8," in D. M. Hay and E. E. Johnson, eds., *Pauline Theology*, vol. III, 169-95.

Thompson, R. W., "The Inclusion of Gentiles in Rom. 3.27-30," *Bib* 69 (1988), 343-46.

Thorley, J., "Junia a Woman Apostle," *NovT* 38 (1996), 18-29.

Towner, P., "Romans 13.1-7 and Paul's Missiological Perspective," in S. K. Soderlund and N. T. Wright, eds., *Romans and the People of God*, 149-69.

Van den Beld, A., "Romans 7.14-25 and the Problem of Akrasia," *RelStud* 21 (1985), 495-515.

Van der Horst, P. W., "Only Then Will All Israel Be Saved: A Short Note on the Meaning of *kai houtōs* in Romans 11.26," *JBL* 119 (2000), 521-25.

Volf, J. M. G., *Paul and Perseverance: Staying In and Falling Away* (Louisville: Westminster/John Knox, 1990). A helpful study, even though it does not grasp the nettle when it comes to Paul's actual belief that the apostasy of a saved person was possible, however seldom.

Wagner, G., *Pauline Baptism and the Pagan Mysteries: The Problem of the Pauline Doctrine of Baptism in Romans 6.1-11 in the Light of Its Religio-Historical Parallels* (Edinburgh: Oliver and Boyd, 1967).

Wagner, J. R., "The Christ, Servant of the Jew and Gentile: A Fresh Approach to Romans 15.8-9," *JBL* 116 (1997), 473-85.

Watson, F., *Paul, Judaism, and the Gentiles* (Cambridge: Cambridge University Press, 1986). This volume offers something of a sociological approach to Paul, mainly to Romans. Watson suggests that there were at least two congregations in Rome, the Pauline Gentile Christians and the Jewish Christians. The problem is that the Gentiles in Rome are not Paul's converts, and the persons he knows in Rome seem to be almost entirely, if not entirely, Jewish Christians.

————, "The Two Roman Congregations: Romans 14.1–15.13," in K. P. Donfried, ed., *The Romans Debate*, 203-15.

Watts, R., "'For I Am Not Ashamed of the Gospel': Romans 1.16-17 and Habakkuk 2.4," in S. K. Soderlund and N. T. Wright, eds., *Romans and the People of God*, 3-15.

Weaver, P. C., *Familia Caesaris* (Cambridge: Cambridge University Press, 1972). It is possible that some of those greeted in Romans 16 were slaves of Caesar, in which case we see Paul building social networks even in high places. Weaver helps us understand what this sort of contact might mean.

Wedderburn, A. J. M., "Adam in Paul's Letter to the Romans," in *Papers on Paul and Other New Testament Writers*, ed. E. A. Livingstone, JSNTS 3 (Sheffield: Sheffield Academic, 1980), 413-30.

————, "Paul's Collection: Chronology and History," *NTS* 48 (2002), 95-110.

————, *The Reason for Romans* (Edinburgh: Clark, 1988). This book makes it clear that Paul had a variety of interlocking purposes for writing Romans. Wedderburn rightly stresses that particular issues Paul knew of in Rome played a part, though he is wrong that one of them was an antagonism between Judaizing Christians and Law-free Christians. There is no evidence of Judaizing Christians in Rome, but plenty for "Hellenizing" Christians.

————, "The Soteriology of the Mysteries and Pauline Baptismal Theology," *NovT* 29 (1987), 53-72.

Westerholm, S., *Israel's Law and the Church's Faith: Paul and His Recent Interpreters* (Grand Rapids: Eerdmans, 1988). Another helpful critique of the Sanders-Dunn-Wright new perspective on Paul.

Wilken, R., "Free Choice and the Divine Will in Greek Christian Commentaries on Paul," in W. S. Babcock, ed., *Paul and the Legacies of Paul*, 123-40.

Williams, S. K., *Jesus' Death as Saving Event: The Background and Origin of a Concept* (Missoula: Scholars, 1975).

Wink, W., *Naming the Powers: The Language of Power in the New Testament* (Philadelphia: Fortress, 1984).

Winter, B. W., "Roman Law and Society in Romans 12–15," in P. Oakes, ed., *Rome in the Bible and the Early Church*, 67-102.

————, *Seek the Welfare of the City: Early Christians as Benefactors and Citizens* (Grand Rapids: Eerdmans, 1994). This volume shows what a detailed knowledge of the Greco-Roman world can do to illuminate the text of the NT, including Paul's Romans. Paul's social strategy turns out to be more radical in some ways and more conservative in others than is often thought.

Witherington, B., "The Influence of Galatians on Hebrews," *NTS* 37 (1991), 146-52.

————, "Not So Idle Thoughts about *Eidōlothuton*," *TynBul* 44 (1993), 237-54.

————, *Paul's Narrative Thought World: The Tapestry of Tragedy and Triumph* (Louisville: Westminster/John Knox, 1994). What I have attempted in this study is a somewhat detailed analysis of Paul's thought based on the key narratives or stories which underlie and undergird all his arguments.

————, *Women in the Earliest Churches* (Cambridge: Cambridge University Press, 1988).

Wright, N. T., *The Climax of the Covenant: Christ and the Law in Pauline Theology* (Edinburgh: Clark, 1991). In some ways this is Wright's most satisfying and tightly argued monograph. It helps set up his later discussions of "righteousness" and covenantal faithfulness, and Jesus and Israel.

————, "The Law in Romans 2," in *Paul and the Mosaic Law*, ed. J. D. G. Dunn (Tübingen: Mohr, 1996), 131-50.

————, "New Exodus, New Inheritance: The Narrative Substructure of Romans 3–8," in S. K. Soderlund and N. T. Wright, eds., *Romans and the People of God*, 26-35.

————, "Romans and the Theology of Paul," in D. M. Hay and E. E. Johnson, eds., *Pauline Theology*, vol. III, 30-67.

Yinger, K., "Rom. 12.14-21 and Nonretaliation in Second Temple Judaism: Addressing Persecution within the Community," *CBQ* 60 (1998), 74-96.

Zeisler, J. A., "The Just Requirement of the Law (Romans 8.4)," *AusBR* 35 (1987), 77-82.

————, *The Meaning of Righteousness in Paul* (Cambridge: Cambridge University Press, 1972).

Introduction

Embarking on a study of Romans is rather like beginning a long journey — it requires a certain amount of preparation, patience, and faith, as the goal of understanding this formidable discourse is not reached for a considerable period of time. This is all the more the case because people have put up more signposts along this path than any other biblical path, many of which have frankly led readers off the main highway onto various dead-end streets. In particular, attempts to de-particularize this letter and treat it as some sort of introduction to Pauline thought or generalized treatise or essay, and even attempts to treat it as just another letter like Paul's earlier letters,[1] in the end prove to lead the student of this important discourse in wrong and unfruitful directions.[2]

For example, this letter clearly states that it was written in part to prepare the audience for Paul's long anticipated journey to Rome (1.11-13). It is written to an audience that includes few if any of Paul's own converts, and those mentioned in ch. 16 are mostly coworkers rather than converts. Though Paul is indeed the apostle to the Gentiles, rhetorically speaking, he cannot approach his

---

1. Which is not to say that I am endorsing treating Romans in a vacuum as an independent entity. This was one of the less helpful tendencies of the SBL Pauline Theology Seminar in the 1990s. Isolating Romans, as if it were a self-contained literary entity, is an unhelpful approach, not least because Romans contains so many echoes of Paul's earlier letters, particularly Galatians and the Corinthian correspondence, though Paul has nuanced and rephrased things to suit his Roman audience's perceived needs and situation. It is also unhelpful to study the text of Romans in isolation because Paul perceives his letters as only part of a total communication effort, which would also include oral instructions carried by the bearer of the letter, in this case probably Phoebe.

2. See the overview by P. Achtemeier, "Unsearchable Judgments and Inscrutable Ways: Reflections on the Discussion of Romans," *SBL Seminar Papers 1995*, pp. 521-34.

communication act in this letter in the same way as if he were addressing his Galatian or Corinthian or Philippian converts. Notice the readjustment evident in verses like 1.11-12, where Paul begins to speak about imparting a gift and then realizes that he needs to speak of mutual sharing.

The art of persuasion had to be pursued differently in a letter written to those who were not Paul's converts and thus not inherently under his authority, compared to letters written to those who were Paul's converts and who recognized that they were. The nature of Romans is bound up with the nature of its audience and the rhetorical role Paul is able to play in relationship to them, which in turn partially determines the overall intended purpose and effect of Romans. It will not do to judge Romans and its rhetoric in the same sort of way one would judge Galatians or 1 Corinthians. While this letter is partially an attempt to establish rapport with and authority over the Roman Gentile Christians, it is not an example of exercise of the authority we would see where Paul already had a power relationship.

It is also a great temptation to try to understand the Roman road by examining one or another portion of the road without taking into account where the whole road is leading. It is all too easy to get caught up in the voluminous literature on a particularly controversial passage, such as ch. 7, and make the mistake of thinking that understanding that particular passage is the key to understanding the whole document. The problem with this approach is that one loses the sense of the flow of the overall argument or arguments and so loses perspective. One is also in danger of treating asides or supplementary arguments as if they are the major points in Paul's overall act of persuasion. But there is also the danger of treating one large portion of Romans, such as Romans 1–8, as the essence of the document, which leads to treating what follows ch. 8 as if an afterthought or appendix or of less importance to understanding what Paul is trying to accomplish. From a rhetorical point of view this is an enormous blunder.

Like any major sporting event, Romans is not over till it's over, and you cannot tell what is really exercising the speaker and where his rhetoric is leading unless you follow the discourse to the end in Romans 16. For one thing, without attention to the clues in *both* the *propositio*s and the *peroratio*s one cannot know where Paul himself is placing the emphasis in this discourse. This is as important as determining whether Romans is in the main a deliberative, forensic, or epideictic piece of oratory.

In other words, understanding the rhetorical structure and nature of this *whole* letter is perhaps more important than in any of Paul's other letters. Paul is not writing to correct problems or misunderstandings his own ministry with the audience has created (unlike the Corinthian letters), nor is this a progress-oriented letter to those long since converted by Paul (unlike Philippians). Paul must pick and choose his words here in Romans very carefully, knowing that first impressions are important. This document is more like an ambassadorial sort of document than a letter-essay to friends or understudies. It also should not be seen as an introduction to Pauline thought, since it leaves out many of Paul's most important ideas about resurrection, the return of Christ, the Lord's Supper, and many other subjects as well.

Even when one stands on what seems to be the familiar ground of major theological themes like the subject of *dikaiosynē* ("righteousness"), it turns out that even what this term means to Paul has often been misconstrued. Consider for example what A. K. Grieb says at the beginning of her recent study on the narrative substructure of Romans: "Romans is a sustained argument for the righteousness of God that is identified with and demonstrated by the faithfulness of Jesus Christ understood primarily as his willing obedience to suffer death on the cross."[3] This is correct as far as it goes, but it fails to adequately deal with what is going on in chs. 12–15 and misses the fact that Romans is also about human righteousness that derives from God's saving activity on behalf of his people and indeed on behalf of the world. Romans is not just about theology proper. It is also about ethics and praxis.[4] Romans is intended to be a rhetorical word on target for the Roman congregation which helps establish a viable relationship between Paul and these mostly Gentile Christians, whom he feels he has some apostolic responsibility toward.

There is no evidence that Paul is polemicizing against Judaism or Jewish Christian opponents in this letter, as M. Nanos has rightly stressed.[5] For one thing the rhetoric of this letter is not by and large forensic in character. For another, if Paul is doing any apologetics at all in this document, it is in chs. 9–11, and there he is defending his Jewish heritage, Jewish Christians, and also non-Christian Jews.[6] Romans should never have been seen as a justification for anti-

---

3. A. K. Grieb, *The Story of Romans* (Louisville: Westminster/John Knox, 2002), p. ix. C. Talbert, *Romans* (Macon: Smyth and Helwys, 2002), p. 14, says almost exactly the same thing: "Romans is about the gospel of the righteousness of God revealed in the faithfulness of Jesus that issues in salvation for all who believe." Talbert rightly adds the dimension of the intended effect of the gospel on its recipients. Romans is not just about God or God in Christ. It also has a thoroughgoing anthropological dimension.

4. I would also differ with Grieb in that she sees Romans as a defense of God's righteousness, while I would see it as an explanation and exhortation based on God's righteousness. I do, however, quite agree with her that chs. 9–11 are central to Paul's argument.

5. M. D. Nanos, *The Mystery of Romans* (Minneapolis: Fortress, 1996).

6. A. J. Guerra helpfully analyzes all of Romans as an example of a protreptic letter, following D. Aune and others. This categorization comports nicely with the conclusion that in Romans we have an example of deliberative rhetoric. Cf. A. J. Guerra, *Romans and the Apologetic Tradition* (Cambridge: Cambridge University Press, 1995) to D. E. Aune, "Romans as a *Logos Protreptikos*," in *The Romans Debate*, ed. K. P. Donfried (2nd ed.; Peabody: Hendrickson, 1991), pp. 278-96.

Semitism or an argument that God had now rejected his first chosen people.
More will be said on these subjects in due course.

Authorship and the Text-Critical Issues in Chapter 16

About the authorship of this document there is little or no debate. Paul wrote it.
But there is considerable debate about the integrity of this letter insofar as its
ending is concerned. Basically the debate centers on whether ch. 16 was in
whole or in part originally written to the Christians at Rome. How one evaluates a variety of questions including the nature, purpose, and audience of
Romans is affected by how one views this issue. The doxology we presently find
at 16.25-27 in some manuscripts is also found at the end of ch. 14 in other
manuscripts and in both places in still other manuscripts, and it is omitted in
still other manuscripts. Furthermore, these verses are found at the end of ch. 15
in our earliest fragment of Romans — ℘46.

Needless to say, this has led to endless speculation in regard to whether
the letter originally ended after ch. 14, ch. 15, or all or part of ch. 16. Some have
even suggested that ch. 16 was originally a separate letter attached later, and it
has been conjectured that it was originally written to a different audience, perhaps to some Pauline converts in Ephesus. This last conjecture is in part fueled
by the quandary over how Paul could know so many Roman Christians when
he had never visited or written to them before. But let us consider for a moment
the textual evidence more closely.

First of all it is important to consider the source of one or another of the
shorter versions of Romans. It is Marcion who ends Romans at 14.23, placing
the doxology at this juncture. Marcion's agenda against the OT and the Jewish
origins of Christianity is well known, and the OT is frequently cited in ch. 15.
Origen in fact tells us that Marcion did expunge the last two chapters of
Romans. Furthermore, various of our earliest and best witnesses provide a
strong case for the document not ending at ch. 14. There are thus good textual
and theological reasons not to think this document originally ended at ch. 14.

Several basic rules of text criticism come into play in consideration of ch.
16 (in whole or in part): (1) the more difficult reading should be preferred;
(2) the reading which best explains the others is likely to be original; (3) duplication suggests uncertainty about proper placement of a text. It may suggest
that a scribe who found the doxology in more than one place in his sources and
did not wish to leave anything out conflated the readings in his copy. This
seems clearly to be what happened with the manuscripts that have the doxology
in both ch. 14 and ch. 16. Putting the doxology at the end of ch. 14 destroys the
continuity between chs. 14 and 15. One plausible hypothesis based on this third

principle suggests that the original document was 1.1–16.23. Marcion truncated this down to 1.1–14.23, and he or someone who used his copy added the doxology found at 16.25-27. This may mean that 16.25-27 is not from Paul's hand, or it may mean that it is a Pauline fragment from somewhere else later tacked on to Romans, or it is still possible that it is the original ending of Romans. Whichever is the case, H. Gamble's detailed study shows that from a text-critical point of view there is little merit to the argument that ch. 16, or all of it except the final doxology, does not belong with this letter.[7] This conclusion is of no small importance because it means that Paul had many contacts in Rome, and the theory that he was writing some generalized treatise to Roman Christians because he was oblivious to their particular situation simply will not work. His rhetorical finesse and cautiousness in dealing with particular issues in Rome in this letter must not be missed, lest we think him ignorant or oblivious to the actual situation in Rome in A.D. 56-57.

Integrity

The discussion above does not, however, answer the question raised by T. W. Manson and others about the originality of 16.1-23 — whether it might originally have been part of another letter.[8] Against the theory that this portion of Romans was originally directed to Ephesus one must note that Paul in general refrains from sending many greetings to churches he already knows (there are none in 1 and 2 Corinthians, Galatians, Philippians, and 1 and 2 Thessalonians). This suggests that Paul has a specific rhetorical strategy for including these names in a letter to a congregation he does not have an apostolic relationship with — namely he wishes to establish credibility and rapport and make the audience more receptive to his coming and sharing with them. The names and the various greetings improve his honor rating with at least a part of the audience. The rhetorical effect at the end of the letter is to cement the fact that he already has some relationship with some Christians in Rome, so that his words need to be taken seriously and respected. He is drawing on his existing social networks to establish a basis for Rome being his own future launching pad for missions in the west. The greetings also provide avenues for those who have questions to ask those who know Paul, perhaps in particular Phoebe, for whom the beginning of ch. 16 serves as something of a note of introduction to the Roman Christians.

---

7. H. Gamble, *The Textual History of the Letter to the Romans* (Grand Rapids: Eerdmans, 1977).

8. See the argument of Manson, "St. Paul's Letter to the Romans — and Others," now reprinted in *The Romans Debate*, pp. 3-15.

The expulsion of Jews, and probably Jewish Christians, from Rome took place in A.D. 49, but such edicts normally fell into abeyance when an Emperor died. Claudius passed away in October A.D. 54. Most scholars think Romans was written no earlier than 55-56. In my judgment it was written in late 56 or early 57 prior to Paul's last trip to Jerusalem (see below).[9] In any case, Paul is apparently dealing with a overwhelmingly Gentile group of Christians in Rome who are more well established than the Jewish Christians there (another reason to mention some Jewish Christians by name in ch. 16 and give them a higher honor rating), since at least the leaders among the Jewish Christians are probably only recently back in Rome and getting reestablished.

While one of Paul's purposes in writing this letter is to begin to garner support for his future mission work in the west, another is that he clearly wants the Roman Christians to recognize, endorse, and embody the vision of Jew and Gentile united in Christ which is manifested by the collection and the response Paul is hoping it will receive in Jerusalem. If the Roman Christians are to embody such a vision, Paul must help them to overcome their divisions about food, and taxes, and other matters.

As Cranfield says, it is understandable that some copies of Romans later sent to other Christian communities might have excluded ch. 16 as being of no relevance to them.[10] But it is also understandable how ch. 16 in some form might have been a separate letter of introduction for Phoebe who was to be Paul's agent in Rome, or at least a note of reminder to Phoebe as to whom she should make contact with and greet on Paul's behalf in Rome (see 16.1). If ch. 16 was a separate document, it is understandable why our earliest manuscript, 𝔓 46, has the doxology after 15.33. On the other hand, P. Lampe probably provides us with a stronger argument to the contrary when he says: "Paul would never have ended a letter with Romans 15.33. Formulations like 'the God of peace [with you]' never conclude a letter but precede requests to greet — greetings like the ones in Romans 16. The *de* in Romans 16.1, on the other hand, presupposes a *previous* text. That means that Romans 15 and 16 mutually presuppose each other. Why separate them?"[11] This makes good sense, and it means we do need to see ch. 16, even if one of its functions is to introduce Phoebe to the Roman Christians, as an integral part of this letter.

---

9. See my *New Testament History* (Grand Rapids: Baker, 2001), p. 198.

10. C. E. B. Cranfield, *A Critical and Exegetical Commentary on the Epistle to the Romans* (ICC; Edinburgh: Clark, 1975-79), 1:5-11.

11. P. Lampe, "The Roman Christians of Romans 16," in *The Romans Debate*, p. 217.

Date

There are a few chronological clues which help us to date Romans. Firstly, we know that Paul wrote this letter shortly before he took the collection to Jerusalem (15.23-28). This in turn must mean that he wrote it after the Corinthian correspondence. Furthermore, 16.1 probably indicates that Romans was written from Corinth: Phoebe from Corinth's port of Cenchreae is carrying the letter with her as she sails to Rome. Notice also the greeting at 16.23 from Gaius, presumably the one also mentioned in 1 Cor. 1.14. If we consider the relevant data from Acts 15.25 and 20.2ff., this suggests that the letter was written while Paul had some leisure to reflect on his gospel and some of the previous things he had written (noting the echoes of Galatians and Corinthians in Romans). Another chronological clue is that Paul seems to assume that his ministry in the eastern portion of the Empire is done. No time better suits the composition of this letter than the three-month winter stay in Corinth Paul had prior to his trip to Jerusalem in spring 57.

Audience

It is clear enough that Paul writes to those in Rome who believe in Jesus. Clearly enough it was not written to non-Christian Jews in Rome. But there is considerable debate about the makeup of that Roman Christian audience. Was it mostly Gentile Christian, mostly Jewish Christian, or a balance of the two? Should we think of any sort of overarching church structure in Rome, or only individual house church meetings that had occasional contact with other such meetings? Is it significant that Paul does not speak of the *ekklēsia* in Rome, or would we be reading too much into that silence to conclude it reflects an un-unified group of Christians in Rome? Who founded the Christian community in Rome?

Peter is not mentioned in the letter, nor does Paul connect Peter with Rome in his other letters.[12] Paul specifically refers to the Roman believers as "among the other Gentile peoples" (1.13; cf. 15.15ff.). "To you Gentiles" in 11:13 comports with the tenor of 9.3ff.; 10.1-2; 11.23-31, where Paul addresses Gentiles about the status of Jews, including non-Christian Jews. In 3.1 and perhaps 7.1ff. Paul is rhetorically debating an imaginary Jew, using the diatribe style.[13] This should not be taken as an indication that Paul had Jewish or Jewish Christian opponents in Rome. Nevertheless, a text like 15.7ff. does suggest there are some

---

12. The church Father Ambrosiaster says that the Romans accepted Christianity without any notable miracles and without apostles proclaiming the faith to them.

13. See S. Stowers, *A Rereading of Romans* (New Haven: Yale University Press, 1994).

Jewish Christians in the audience, as does 16.7-11. And the knowledge of the LXX required to make sense of some of Paul's arguments, for example in chs. 1–4 and 9–11, suggests that there were in the audience some Jewish Christians and some Gentile Christians who had been among the God-fearers, that is, Gentiles who had attended synagogue services but had not fully converted to Judaism.

In sum, Paul as the apostle to the Gentiles is primarily addressing Gentile Christians in Rome, although he is happy for Jewish Christians to overhear this conversation. It is Gentile Christians in Rome that he feels mainly need exhorting, and it is Gentile Christians in Rome he feels he has some claim on, since he is the apostle to the Gentiles. The defense of Jews and Jewish Christians in chs. 9–11 to Gentile Christians needs to be given the weight it deserves. Paul wishes to make clear that Jews and Gentiles alike have the same responsibilities before God (cf. 1.16; 2.9ff., 25ff.; 3.29; 10.12) and that God is impartial when it comes to matters of both justice and mercy. God is the God of both Jews and Gentiles. Thus, just to reiterate, Paul is focusing on Gentile Christians in Rome, though his audience probably contains some Jewish Christians, as well as former God-fearers (in all likelihood). But saying that the vast majority of the audience are Gentiles tells us very little about the social level or character of Roman Christians or the social structure of Roman Christianity.[14]

The Social Level and Structure of Roman Christianity

It will be well to begin with the more detailed data first. As P. Lampe has suggested, ch. 16 seems to suggest that Paul knows of at least five house churches in Rome — one sponsored by Priscilla and Aquila (16.5), one that includes Asyncritus, Phlegon, Hermes, Patrobas, and Hermas (16.14), one that includes Philologus, Julia, Olympas, and Nereus and his sister (16.15), the Christians in the house of Aristobolus (16.10), and the Christians in Narcissus's household (16.11).[15] This means that there had to have been some early Christians in Rome

---

14. R. E. Brown ("Further Reflections on the Origins of the Church of Rome," in *The Conversation Continues: Studies in John and Paul,* ed. R. T. Fortna and B. R. Gaventa [Nashville: Abingdon, 1990], pp. 98-115) speaks of four different groups of Christians, each of which included Jewish and Gentile Christians and had varying positions on the Law, ranging from a demand that all submit to it to denial of any lasting significance in the Jewish rituals for Jews or Gentiles. This neglects the fact that the church in Rome in Paul's day was a largely Gentile enterprise, with Gentiles setting the dominant cultural agenda and Jewish Christians marginalized, neglected, or not welcomed into the fellowship of the majority.

15. But note that the "you" (plural) who are exhorted to greet these various individuals and groups are apparently not included in any of these groups. In short, it appears likely that the Gentile majority is not included in any of these five or so house churches. See pp. 375-400 below on ch. 16.

of significant enough social status to have more than just a room in an *insula* (in modern terms, an apartment house). A patron was a wealthy person who acted as a benefactor and protector of another person. There have to have been some patron-like Christians who hosted church meetings in their homes. But this very factor, the existence of various house churches with no centralized authority structure, "reinforced a tendency to fragmentation and dissension."[16] It is no accident that in the same chapter which mentions various different house churches we also find an exhortation against divisions and dissensions (16.17-19).

Perhaps one reason there was no central organization to the church in Rome is that it had no apostolic foundation, nor was it simply an offshoot of the synagogue communities in Rome. It seems likely that the first Christians in Rome were ordinary Jews and God-fearers who had heard the gospel in Jerusalem, and brought the message home with them (see Acts 2.10-11). But it is perhaps possible that someone like Andronicus or Junia, who were "apostles in Christ" before Paul was (16:7), which is to say within only a matter of a couple of years after the death of Jesus, had brought Christianity from Jerusalem to Rome.[17] Cranfield makes a plausible case for the Aristobolus mentioned in 16.10 being the grandson of Herod the Great and the brother of Herod Agrippa I. From Josephus we learn that this Aristobolus lived in Rome and was a friend of the Emperor Claudius (*Wars* 2.221-22; *Antiquities* 18.273-76; 20.13). Aristobolus may have died in the late 40s, but his household would have continued to exist, and would have included a number of Jews. Paul does not greet Aristobolus, but his greeting to those of his household is probably a greeting mainly to Jewish Christians.[18] Further support for this suggestion may come from the fact that the next person greeted is someone named Herodion, a name which also suggests a connection with the family of Herod, but certainly a Jewish Christian since Paul calls him "my kinsman." Paul is telling the Gentile Christians he addresses to pass these greetings on to Jewish Christians. This is just another part of his strategy to unite the Jewish and Gentile believers in Rome, for if a Gentile Christian goes and conveys greetings to a Jewish Christian in another household, then the hospitality conventions would come into play, creating *koinōnia*. This is all the more the case if we take seriously the meaning of the key hospitality verb here (*aspazomai*, to wrap one's arms around) and the exhortation about the holy kiss.[19]

We need to remember that the juridical status of individuals — whether

---

16. W. L. Lane, "Roman Christianity during the Formative Years from Nero to Nerva," in *Judaism and Christianity in First-Century Rome,* ed. K. P. Donfried and P. Richardson (Grand Rapids: Eerdmans, 1998), p. 214.

17. On 16.7 see pp. 387-90 below. They are said to have been in prison with Paul, but where? It would have to have been in the eastern part of the empire.

18. See Cranfield, *Romans,* 2:791-92.

19. On this see pp. 395-96.

they were free-born, slave, or freed — does not necessarily tell us much about their socio-economic status. Many freedmen and freedwomen were wealthy, and there were even wealthy slaves. To judge from the names in ch. 16, it would appear that many of these people, perhaps as many as two-thirds of them, had slave origins, even if now many of them were freedmen and freedwomen. (Many of these names are nicknames rather than proper names, and often slaves would have nicknames.) The general social level of Christians in Rome at this juncture seems to have been about the same as Jews in Rome, which is to say the majority of them were of the lower echelon of society.[20]

Apparently Priscilla and Aquila were free-born, and it may not be an accident that only they and Urbanus are called Paul's coworkers in Rome (notice however that Rufus's mother seems to have been a patroness — 16.13). The upshot of this is that Paul is very cognizant of the social structure in Rome and realizes the advantages to having higher-status persons as his co-workers. They would be more likely to be able to establish their own house church situations and would be naturally looked up to by others. It is also no accident that Paul stresses that Andronicus, Junia, and Herodion are his fellow Jewish Christians. In trying to help rehabilitate the honor of such folk in Rome, Paul stresses their status as apostles or the like, as a supplement to the kind of rhetoric we find in chs. 9–11. As Lampe says, "Paul has a special interest in emphasizing the Jewish origin of Christians (16.7, 11, 21). . . . The kins(wo)men in Romans 16 are living proofs of the same grace toward Israel. They and Paul himself are the 'remnant at the present time, chosen by grace' (11.5)."[21]

It is Lampe's conclusion that some fourteen of the twenty-six persons mentioned in ch. 16 were not born in Rome, which may explain in part why Paul knows them. Early Christians, for a variety of reasons, were often mobile. This would also help explain the lack of unity and structure in the Roman church. Only a minority of the converts had lived in Rome all their lives or for a very long time.

Paul is trying to construct a church structure (1) that is rather egalitarian in character, recognizing both male and female apostles, patrons, and co-workers, (2) that involves both Jewish and Gentile Christians together in worship and fellowship, with respect for differences, (3) that at the same time pays no attention to whether one is of slave or free or freed origins, and (4) that takes advantage of those of higher social status, making them hosts and patrons of the community. The socio-economic status hierarchy is left somewhat intact, but any sort of ethnic hierarchy or gender hierarchy is not. It is interesting that in the

---

20. J. C. Walters, "Romans, Jews and Christians," in *Judaism and Christianity in First-Century Rome,* ed. K. P. Donfried and P. Richardson (Grand Rapids: Eerdmans, 1998), pp. 175-95, here 176-80.

21. Lampe, "The Roman Christians of Romans 16," p. 226.

case of Aristobolus and Narcissus there seem to be meetings in their houses,[22] but they are not Christians, apparently, for Paul does not directly greet them. In short, Paul seems to be keen on constructing a high group, but not necessarily high grid identity in this congregation in Rome, and he sees the Gentile majority as a major key to this.[23] At present they exist in a low group-identity condition, but with some stratification based on whether one was a Gentile or not. They must revise their views on Jews and Jewish Christians, and accept the leadership of some of Paul's fellow Jewish Christians.[24]

Rome and Its Christians in the Middle of the First Century A.D.

Rome in the mid-fifties A.D. had a new and ambitious emperor — Nero. Later historians were to argue that Nero's first five years as emperor went rather well. There was no reason to expect that Nero might become some persecuting monster whom Christians of a later era, including John of Patmos, would see as an antichrist figure. In fact, Nero during this period ended the private treason trials of prominent people. Under the tutelage of the philosopher Seneca and with the guidance of others such as Burrus he seemed to be a clement dictator, until at least 59, when he killed his own mother in order to take matters more entirely into his own hands. Apparently, Agrippina had intended to rule with her son, and Nero baulked at that prospect (*Sibylline Oracles* 4.119-21). Nero was the last of the Julio-Claudian emperors, but not the last to pursue dreams of grandeur at the expense of others, including Christians in Rome.[25]

Rome was the hub of the ever-expanding empire. Anyone like Paul with an urban ministry strategy and a desire to reach the West could not possibly ignore this city of vital importance. It was the empire's largest city and had a large proportion of slaves in its population.

22. Or are we to think there are some Christian slaves in these houses, but meetings are held elsewhere?

23. See now the article by A. D. Clarke, "Jew and Greek, Slave and Free, Male and Female," in *Rome in the Bible and the Early Church,* ed. P. Oakes (Grand Rapids: Baker, 2002), pp. 103-25. I have used language here from the group-grid sociology model. "High group"= high group cohesiveness. "High grid"= highly articulated and stratified leadership structure.

24. Notice that Paul does not directly greet his friends, but rather has the Roman Christians pass on such greetings. This is part of his strategy to build community between Jewish and Gentile believers in Rome. Another interesting bit is that Paul introduces his coworker Timothy to the church in Rome (16.21). The eastern churches all knew Timothy, but presumably he was not known in Rome. Could this mention be some sort of preparation to send Timothy to Rome in advance of Paul's coming, but separately from Phoebe? Paul seems to be establishing his social networks in Rome by several means.

25. See my *New Testament History,* pp. 278ff.

The city also had a large Jewish population. By the time of Claudius, Nero's predecessor, some 40,000 to 50,000 out of a population of at least 400,000 were Jews, not all of whom were expelled when the edict of expulsion was announced in 49. The Jewish population was originally composed largely of Jews brought in as slaves beginning in 63 B.C. The evidence suggests that while some Roman Jews were at the upper end of the socio-economic spectrum in the middle of the first century, most were not. Most seem to have lived in the Transtibertinum, the region just across the Tiber from the central part of Rome, apparently a low-rent district noted for its insulae, not its palatial mansions, where many Christians also lived.[26]

It was probably the leadership of the Jewish community that was expelled by Claudius's edict, and Acts 18.2 suggests this included Jewish Christian leaders such as Priscilla and Aquila. There is then good reason for one to think that Paul is writing at a time when Jewish Christians, and in particular their leadership, are just beginning to reestablish themselves in Rome. They have been marginalized by the expulsion, and Paul is addressing a largely Gentile Christian audience in Rome which has drawn some erroneous conclusions about Jews and Jewish Christians. M. Nanos has challenged the common understanding of the historical situation in Rome vis-à-vis the edict.[27] As I have shown elsewhere, there is nothing very surprising about an emperor expelling Jews from Rome.[28] This happened already in A.D. 19 during the reign of Tiberius (Dio Cassius 57.18.5), and the focus of the concern then was on Jewish leaders. Tiberius sent many Jews to Sardinia and had some of the leaders executed there. But even during the reign of Claudius, we are told of his having to deal with difficulties involving Jews in Alexandria, and on balance Dio's statements about the curtailment of Jewish practices in Rome in A.D. 41 (60.6.6) seems likely to reflect a historical occurrence.

Julio-Claudian emperors were known to be anti-Semitic, like many other patrician Romans.[30] Claudius was particularly concerned in the Alexan-

---

26. On the Jewish catacombs and synagogues see I. Levinskaya, *The Book of Acts in Its First Century Setting*, vol. 5: *Diaspora Setting* (Grand Rapids: Eerdmans, 1996), pp. 182-93. The earliest evidence is from the second century A.D. See A. D. Clarke, "Rome and Italy," in *The Book of Acts in Its First Century Setting*, vol. 2: *Graeco-Roman Setting* (Grand Rapids: Eerdmans, 1994), pp. 455-78.

27. Nanos, *The Mystery of Romans*, pp. 372-87.

28. Jews were expelled from Rome for specifically religious reasons several times beginning in 139 B.C., when the praetor Hispalus expelled Jews, Chaldeans, and Asian astrologers for bringing eastern religions into Rome. There was always a concern that eastern religions were causing the neglect of Rome's traditional gods. See Valerius Maximus, *Factorum et dictorum memorabilium* 1.3.3. See my *The Acts of the Apostles: A Socio-Rhetorical Commentary* (Grand Rapids: Eerdmans, 1998), pp. 539-44.

30. This attitude is clearly reflected in the popular literature of the day. Jews are de-

drian difficulties that Jews not try to be Hellenes. Mixing of the cultures, with the suspicion of the pollution of Hellenistic or Greco-Roman culture by things Jewish, was the issue, and he would be alarmed if many Gentiles, perhaps even notable Gentiles, became adherents of Judaism or even Jewish Christianity. So the edict is believable not only on the grounds of Claudius's previous conduct in relationship to Jews in Alexandria and Rome, but also on the grounds of how Claudius felt about the pollution of Hellenistic culture by Jewish customs and the like. If, with Nanos himself, one takes Luke seriously as a historian, then the burden of proof must be on those who suggest that the conjunction of Acts 18.2 with Suetonius (*Life of Claudius* 25) and with Orosius, who dates the expulsion to A.D. 49, should not lead to the conclusion that there was an expulsion of a considerable number of Jews and Jewish Christians from Rome at that time.

Nanos believes that, not only during the reign of Claudius but even when Paul wrote Romans, Christians were operating under the umbrella of the Jewish synagogue. But the following evidence argues otherwise: (1) Acts 28 purports to deal with a later period in Nero's reign, namely A.D. 60-62. It does not support the idea that Christians were meeting under the authorization of the synagogue at this point, or even that they had earlier in the 50s. To the contrary, the synagogue leaders seem remarkably poorly informed about this "sect" and their knowledge seems decidedly secondhand. They must ask Paul why this "sect" is so widely spoken against. This suggests little direct contact of any duration between the Christians and the Jewish leaders in Rome.

(2) Nanos is probably right that Acts 18 speaks hyperbolically of the expulsion of *all* Jews from Rome. Presumably Luke means the Jewish leadership or those who were instigating disturbances, both Jews and Jewish Christians. But Nanos's attempt to deny that Priscilla and Aquila were already Christians is weak. We are not told that Paul proselytizes them when he comes to Corinth, and we know it was his regular practice to stay with Christians, not non-Christian Jews, wherever he went.

(3) That Josephus does not mention the expulsion of Jews from Rome in A.D. 49 is in no way surprising. The expulsion would have been an embarrassment to an apologist for the Jews such as Josephus, especially since he was the apologist for Jews in Rome.

(4) It is not convincing to argue that the reference to "Chrestus," which is quite regularly an alternate Latin spelling for "Christus," probably has nothing to do with Jewish messianic squabbles in Rome about Jesus. It is asking too much to expect that there were two Jewish messianic figures called Chrestus/Christus about which there might be debate in Rome. Indeed, Acts 28 suggests

picted in Juvenal, *Satires* 2.11 and 14.105 as lazy and beggars and in 6.541-44 as fortune-tellers. In Persius, *Satire* 5.184 they are viewed as "superstitious."

that the name of Jesus and his sect had a high degree of odium and notoriety associated with it throughout the Diaspora Jewish communities in the empire.

(5) It will also not do to underplay Roman anti-Semitism, nor will it do to suggest that Roman authorities were unable to distinguish Christians from Jews during this period. The obvious answer to this is that clearly Nero was able to make such distinctions, and if he was, Claudius might well have been able to do so as well, being a far more astute student of history and of the peoples of the empire than was Nero.[31] Judaism, like Christianity, was viewed as a "superstition" by most Romans. Since Judaism was an ancient religion, Claudius allowed Jews to continue their religious customs so long as they did not pollute Hellenistic culture in general. Any religious disturbance that caused trouble in Rome would have raised the anti-Semitic fears of Roman authorities, and it is believable that they dealt with the matter as Acts 18 describes.

Nanos says rightly that reading Romans while bearing in mind the edict of Claudius and what Luke, Suetonius, and Orosius say leads to the implication that there were already two communities, Jewish and Christian, who had had difficulties even when they tried to interact in A.D. 49. But he is keen to discredit some of this evidence. The balance of the historical evidence, including Romans itself, suggests that Christians had not been under the Jewish umbrella or closely associated with the Jewish synagogue for a long time before Paul ever arrived in Rome. Indeed, it may be that A.D. 49 and the edict marked and made the final split between these two communities in Rome, making it a permanent reality at least in that locale.[32]

In a remarkable and programmatic essay Hans Dieter Betz argues at length that one of the things Paul is in fact trying to do in Romans is provide a foundation for the Christian faith as a distinct "religion" — distinct from non-Christian Judaism and from paganism of various sorts. In this view Paul attempts to "define his version of the gospel message as religion."[33] As 12.1-2 suggests, Paul is proposing to his largely Gentile audience a "reasonable religion" or a reasonable and logical form of worship distinct from Judaism and pagan worship, not least in that it involves no priests, temples, or animal sacrifices. To

31. See rightly, Walters, "Romans, Jews and Christians," pp. 179-80: ". . . the ancient materials are silent regarding how Christians were identified and prosecuted in 64 C.E.; nonetheless they were identified and prosecuted, and the implication of that datum for the existence of features which distinguished Christians from non-Christian Jews, and the Christian communities from Jewish communities should not be underplayed."

32. Walters, "Romans, Jews and Christians," pp. 178-79, rightly follows Lampe in seeing the split as already in place by the time Paul wrote Romans, a split to a large degree caused by the edict. Walters is probably correct in saying that non-Christian Jews after the expulsion realized the wisdom of dissociating themselves from adherents of Jesus.

33. H. D. Betz, "Christianity as Religion: Paul's Attempt at Definition in Romans," in *Paulinischen Studien* (Tübingen: Mohr, 1994), pp. 206-39.

the contrary, it involves presenting oneself as a living sacrifice. Christ has provided the one necessary and sufficient atoning sacrifice, so that forms of religion that involve priests, temples, and sacrifices are obsolete.

Betz, in my judgment, is correct that we already find in Galatians the seeds of what Paul assumes to be the case in Romans: (1) Judaism is an extant form of religion that Paul left behind when he had his Damascus road experience. (2) Christ came to redeem those under the Law, out from under that Law, as well as to provide redemption for Gentiles. (3) The Law was an interim arrangement as part of the Mosaic covenant, but now there is a new covenant which is linked with the Abrahamic covenant. (4) The people of God are defined as Jew and Gentile united in Christ. Paul does not uphold a two-track model of fulfillment of prophecy, salvation, or ecclesiology (using the term loosely). (5) Abraham is called "our Father" not because Gentiles were being integrated into Judaism through Jesus but because Abraham is the father of both Jews and the nations and so the forefather of a universal religion, and the nations are being integrated into the people of God via Jesus. The root that Paul refers to in Romans 9–11 is the forefathers plus Jewish Christians like Paul, Peter, and James, not non-Christian Judaism. In other words, Paul both early and later, both in Galatians and Romans, takes a sectarian approach to these matters. (6) In antiquity, foundational sacrifices were often thought to give rise to new religions, and Paul presents Christ's death as such a sacrifice.[34]

Paul's audience, while perhaps able to conceive of a philosophy of life not requiring visits to temples and animal sacrifices, could not conceive of a logical or reasonable religion not requiring such. Once Paul defines the faith he talks about as a reasonable religion, he must speak of the foundational sacrifice. This is part of the deliberative rhetoric Paul uses to help convince his audience that they were adherents of something far greater and more reasonable than a primitive superstition.[35] They were adherents of the Good News of salvation for all people and all types of people, and of their integration into one body or assembly of God.[36]

Some consideration should be given to Paul's own Sitz im Leben, his own social situation in Corinth and how it may have affected what he says in this letter.[37] Paul writes from Corinth and is staying with Gaius, whom, we are told in

34. See Betz, "Christianity as Religion," p. 228.
35. It is surely not incidental or accidental that Judaism did not provide early Christianity with its core symbols as it emerged into the light of day as a distinctive religion. The cross, the chi ro, the ichthus, and other such symbols were generated out of the distinctive experience of Jesus or early Christian thinking about the Christ event. See K. P. Donfried, "In the First Century: The Nature and Scope of the Question," in *Judaism and Christianity in First-Century Rome*, p. 4.
36. Betz, "Christianity as Religion," pp. 232-34.
37. I thank my teaching assistant Abson Joseph for prompting me to think along these lines.

1 Cor. 1.14, he has baptized. On the whole, he has has been treated well by the Romans in Corinth, including Gallio (see Acts 18), and he has even converted one of them, Erastus, the city's aedile or director of public works, who, among other duties, collected taxes. We should not be surprised to find Paul endorse the strategy he does in Romans 13 when it comes to respecting Roman authorities and paying one's taxes. In A.D. 56-57, Paul had no reason to suspect that Christians, particularly the Gentile Christians he was mainly writing to, were likely to be abused by Nero or other officials. After all, it was Nero who allowed Jews and Jewish Christians to come back to Rome when he took the throne. We need to hear both sides of the conversation between Paul and the Roman Christians, for a text without a context (historical, social, literary, and rhetorical) is just a pretext for whatever the individual reader wants it to mean.

Structure and Rhetoric

There have been many attempts to discern the structure of Romans ranging from the sublime to the ridiculous. One popular older view was that in chs. 1–8 we have the exposition of Paul's Gospel, in chs. 9–11 a diversion, and in chs. 12–15 loosely connected exhortations. The merit of this overly simplistic analysis is that it recognizes that chs. 12–15 mainly deal with ethical matters, while chs. 1–8 mainly deal with theological matters. It does no justice to chs. 9–11.

Much more helpful is the outline of Cranfield, which suggests that the quotation of Hab. 2.4 (LXX) in Rom. 1:17 sets up what immediately follows as a sort of exegesis of this text. 1.17–5.11 explains how sinners are justified by grace through faith, and 5.12–8.39 deals with the phrase "shall live," that is, the consequences of being set in right relationship with God.[38]

Cranfield puts his finger on a crucial point. But it is not just the quotation from Habakkuk but the entire *propositio* in 1.16-17 that sets up what follows. There is to be an abiding emphasis on the gospel being for the Jew first and also for the Gentile. Paul must stress this precisely because of the situation in Rome — Jewish Christians are struggling to reestablish themselves in Rome, and all the while they are being written off by Gentile Christians. Paul will argue to the contrary that Jewish Christians are the root and Gentiles the branches and that God has not given up on non-Christian Jews either. In other words this is an ambassadorial letter of sorts, intended not only to help mend fences in Rome but to promote the larger agenda of the gospel which is represented by the collection — namely Jew and Gentile united in Christ. As such it is largely an example of deliberative rhetoric, the rhetoric of advice and consent. So Paul offers

38. Cranfield, *Romans*, 1:28-29.

theological and ethical arguments intended to produce unity and concord, so that there can indeed be one true *ekklēsia* in Rome and indeed throughout the empire, made up of Jews and Gentiles united in Christ. What connects the advice to the Roman Christians, the collection, and Paul's journey to Jerusalem and planned journey to Spain is his belief in a universal unifying gospel meant for all humankind, which unites them all with the true God, and also with each other.

One of the more complete attempts to discern the rhetorical structure of the letter is that of Jewett, who suggests the following outline:

> *exordium* 1.1-12
> *narratio* 1.13-15
> *propositio* 1.16-17
> *probatio* 1.18–15.13
> *peroratio* 15.14–16.27[39]

The difficulties with this outline are several. In the first place, the different tenor and approach to argumentation in chs. 9–11 need to be noted. These chapters are a *refutatio* of Gentile misunderstandings about Jews and Jewish Christians and God's salvation plan as it involves them. Furthermore, it is clear how very exercised Paul is in that section of the document to make his point. There are amplification and hyperbole to a degree not found in chs. 1–8. Why is this? Because Paul has finally arrived at what has concerned him the most about the theological misunderstanding in Rome. In chs. 1–8 he treads carefully through what could be called common ground, but in chs. 9–11 he comes to grips with a major issue, following which in chs. 12–15 he must deal with the ethical fallout in Rome of the bad theology he has confronted.

Paul understands that he does not have the same clout in Rome that he has in his own churches. He must therefore follow the method known as *insinuatio,* not dealing at first with what most disturbs him but building rapport with his audience. Nevertheless, he already hints at the gauntlet he intends to throw down in chs. 9–11 when he says in the *propositio* that the Gospel is *for the Jew first.* God has not changed his mind about his chosen people.

The other difficulty with Jewett's outline is that 15.14–16.27 is much too extensive to be a *peroratio.*[40] It is important to recognize the epistolary framework of this discourse and not mistake some of that for rhetorical structure. But at the same time it is a mistake to overemphasize the epistolary framework

---

39. R. Jewett, "Following the Argument of Romans," in *The Romans Debate,* p. 268.

40. Talbert, *Romans,* p. 14, simply quotes Jewett in this analysis without critique or comment other than to caution against trying to force Romans into some rhetorical procrustean bed. This is inadequate.

of what is basically a series of rhetorical arguments.[41] Nearer the mark is the suggestion of N. Elliott that we may find the *peroratio* in 15.14-32,[42] though this as well is too expansive and includes the epistolary element of the travel plans and prayer mentioned in vv. 23-32. Therefore, 15.14-22 can serve as the *peroratio* with a final exhortation against divisions thrown in for good measure at 16.17-19, which supplements the *peroratio* and in fact serves as a sort of second *peroratio* for Jewish Christians.[43] Paul intersperses rhetorical and epistolary elements at the end of the document, as he does at the beginning where there is overlap between the *exordium* and the initial thanksgiving prayer or health wish often found in ancient letters.

A further attempt to delineate the rhetorical structure of Romans has been made by M. Reid. He sees the *exordium* in 1.8-15, he calls 1.16-17 the *transitus*, 1.18–3.20 is said to be the *narratio*, 3.21-31 the *propositio*, and the *probatio* consists in 4.1–11.36. 12.1–15.13 is labeled parenesis, and the *peroratio* is found in 15.14-33. Ch. 16 is not seen as part of the rhetorical stucture.[44] There are pluses and minuses to this analysis. On the one hand Reid has properly recognized that 3.21-31 and 15.14-33 do play the role of *propositio* and *peroratio,* and he is also right in his designation of the parenesis section. On the other hand the failure to see arguments in 1.18–3.20 is significant. That segment certainly does not appear to be a *narratio,* and 1.16-17 is surely more than just a transition. Finally, Reid also fails to note that the difference in tone and substance in

41. It is also a mistake to overemphasize the epistolary character of Romans, which is in the main confined to the outer edges of the discourse. Epistolary elements intermingle at the beginning and end of Romans with the dominant rhetorical structure. Notice the cautions of "Demetrius" in *On Style* 228-34 against seeing essays with only brief epistolary openings and closings as "letters." He says: "If one writes logical subtleties . . . in a letter, one is writing, certainly, but one is not writing a letter. The aim of a letter is to be affectionate in brief, and to lay out a simple subject in simple terms. . . . The one who utters sententious maxims and exhortations seems to be no longer talking familiarly in a letter but speaking with contrivance." There can be little doubt that "Demetrius" would not have seen Romans as a proper letter. My point is that one needs to emphasize what makes up the bulk of the material in Romans, and that is the rhetorical arguments, not the epistolary framework.

42. N. Elliott, *The Rhetoric of Romans* (Sheffield: JSOT, 1990), p. 86.

43. In a rhetorical discourse the final argument is emphatic by placement, as it intends to be the last and lasting thing left in the mind of the audience. Recognizing the rhetorical nature of Romans, even though it has an epistolary shell or framework, means that we cannot allow Paul's parting shots to be seen as afterthoughts or as incidental. Rather, 16.17-19 is a clear indicator that there were divisions among Christians in Rome, and Paul's discourse has offered help in healing those divisions and in unifying Jew and Gentile there. C. Bryan in *A Preface to Romans* (Oxford: Oxford University Press, 2000), p. 14, suggests that Rom. 16.17-20 is where Paul takes up the stylus and adds his own final exhortation. This may be correct.

44. M. Reid, "Paul's Rhetoric of Mutuality: A Rhetorical Reading of Romans," *SBL Seminar Papers 1995,* pp. 117-39.

chs. 9–11 means that that section cannot simply be included as one more part of the *probatio* (see below). Reid fails also to note that a *narratio* is not, and parenesis is not normally, a feature of epideictic rhetoric.

The problems with seeing Romans as epideictic rhetoric are several:[45] Epideictic rhetoric is the rhetoric of praise or blame, and it is hard to see Romans as focusing on that. As C. Bryan points out, Romans is profoundly an attempt at persuasion and dissuasion about various things, not just an affirmation or praise of shared values, and persuasion and dissuasion is properly speaking deliberative rhetoric (*Ad Herennium* 1.2.2; 3.2.2). As Bryan goes on to add, 14.1–15.13 is clearly in the form of deliberative rhetoric, trying to persuade the Romans to do something about their behavior.[46] Furthermore, Paul's rhetoric follows the Greek pattern of oratory. We have no evidence that he knew, for example, Cicero. His training was in what Aristotle or Theophrastus or Isocrates or others in the Greek tradition said about the proper rhetorical forms. Note carefully what Quintilian says about epideictic rhetoric in the Greek tradition: "This class [of rhetoric] appears to have been entirely divorced by Aristotle, and following him by Theophrastus, from the practical side of oratory (which they call *pragmatica*) and to have been reserved solely for the delectation of audiences, which indeed is shown to be its peculiar function by its name, which implies display" (*Instit. Or.* 3.7.1). He goes on to say that epideictic rhetoric is meant to serve the purpose of offering praise or blame to gods or human beings, which is certainly not the major focus of Romans. Furthermore, Romans is certainly not an example of the rhetoric of display. Chs. 12–15 are far too "pragmatic" to have been included in either an epideictic or forensic piece of rhetoric.

Furthermore, the focus of epideictic rhetoric is on the present, rather than the past or the future, and yet in Romans we not only have parenesis which attempts to persuade the audience to change their conduct in the near future, but also material such as chs. 8 and 9–11 in which Paul reflects on the future and on what God in Christ intends to do — redeem the creation as well as the creature, Israel as well as the Gentile world. Paul also speaks of his future journey to Jerusalem, and then Rome, and then Spain, intending thereby to get the Romans to think ahead, prepare to receive Paul and his gospel, and be ready to help support the missionary thrust further west. Deliberative rhetoric is the suitable sort to support such an agenda in this letter, not epideictic rhetoric.

---

45. Perhaps the first formidable attempt to argue that Romans is an example of epideictic rhetoric was that of W. Wuellner, "Paul's Rhetoric of Argumentation in Romans," in *The Romans Debate*, pp. 128-46. He is followed to some extent by R. Jewett. One of the problems with Wuellner's approach is that he depends too much on modern rhetorical handbooks and their analysis (e.g., on Lausberg, Perelmann, and others), rather than spending enough time in the primary sources on rhetoric from the Greco-Roman world. This same problem is encountered in the work of J. N. Vorster (see his works listed in the bibliography, p. xxv above).

46. Bryan, *A Preface to Romans*, pp. 21-22.

There is also the matter of style. The rhetoric of Romans is not like the Asiatic and more flamboyant style we find for instance in Ephesians, or in the epideictic showpiece in 1 Corinthians 13. Listening to Romans is in part like hearing a debate, and in part like hearing an exhortation. Both such exercises are intended to bring about change in the audience in regard to how they believe and behave. Finally, a *narratio* is out of place in a piece of epideictic rhetoric, but is quite appropriate in a deliberative piece, especially when it includes travel plans meant to suggest that Paul is coming for a visit to reinforce the rhetoric in this letter.

Paul does not assume that he can appeal to a broad-based set of values with his audience, when it comes to practical matters especially. He has to argue his case, so the divisions in Rome can be overcome, hopefully before his arrival. D. Aune has suggested that we see Romans as a protreptic letter using deliberative rhetoric, attempting to convert his largely Gentile audience to his viewpoint.[47] I would suggest Romans is a deliberative discourse which uses an epistolary framework, and in some ways comports with a protreptic letter.

One of the more interesting and peculiar features of Romans is the alternation between sections with many allusions, quotes, and echoes of the OT and sections with virtually none. For instance, 1–4.25 and chs. 9–11 have a plethora of such allusions, but 5.1–8.39 has virtually none, and there is little in the parenesis in chs. 12–15. R. Longenecker has suggested that in 5.1–8.39 Paul simply offers a sampling of his distinctive message to Gentiles.[48] I think there is something to this. One could argue that up to ch. 5 Paul is presenting the gospel to the Jew first,[49] as he would render it in the synagogue, and in chs. 5–8 we have the gospel as he would present it to Gentiles. Then Paul turns to the issue that might disconfirm the thesis that the gospel is for the Jew first, namely the rejection of the message by most Jews (chs. 9–11), after which he offers corrective parenesis for his largely Gentile audience based on that correction of their theological assumptions (chs. 12–15). The Jesus tradition more than the OT undergirds this parenesis offered to the mostly Gentile audience. There are a logic and a flow to the discourse which are often overlooked.

In other words, we have a back-and-forth rhetorical approach. The goal of the discourse up to the end of ch. 15 is not only to make clear that God is impartial, caring about justice and redemption for all (the gospel is for the Jew first and also for the Gentile), but also that God is faithful to his promises as well, and expects of all the obedience of faith. God wants Jews and Gentiles united in Christ, and division is the antithesis to the realization of such a vision. This is

---

47. D. Aune, "Romans as Logos Protreptikos," in *The Romans Debate,* pp. 278-96.

48. R. Longenecker, "The Focus of Romans," in *Romans and the People of God,* ed. S. K. Soderlund and N. T. Wright (Grand Rapids: Eerdmans, 1999), pp. 61, 67.

49. Which would explain why we have the diatribal dialogue with imaginary Jews in this section of Romans.

why in the end, Paul's parting exhortation in ch. 16 is an attack on those who use sophistic rhetoric to create divisions among the Christians in Rome (16.17-19).

This analysis of the rhetoric of Romans comports nicely with the conclusions most scholars are drawing about Romans on other grounds. For instance, as C. Talbert suggests, "A consensus seems to be building . . . that the main need in the Roman church addressed by Paul was that of resolving the disunity between Jew and Gentiles. If so then the spiritual gift Paul wanted to impart was his Gospel, which was to be the basis of unity for the Roman congregations."[50]

In my view the rhetorical structure of Romans is as follows:

Expanded epistolary opening: addresser and addressee   1.1-7a

Epistolary greeting   1.7b

Exordium/epistolary wish-prayer   1.8-10

Narratio   1.11-15

Propositio   1.16-17

Probatio

    Argument I: The bankruptcy of pagan religious experience
       and God's judgment on it

       Part a: The unbearable likeness   1.18-32

       Part b: A critique of a judgmental Gentile hypocrite   2.1-16

    Argument II: Censoring a censorious Jewish teacher   2.17–3.20

Recapitulation and expansion of *propositio*/main thesis   3.21-31[51]

    Argument III: Abraham as the forefather of a universal religion,
       of those who obtain righteousness by grace through faith   4.1-25

---

50. Talbert, *Romans*, p. 12.

51. In his perceptive reading of the rhetoric of Romans, Melanchthon quite properly identifies the *exordium* and preliminary matters in ch. 1, says that the first main rhetorical argument begins at 1.18, finds in 3.21-31 the main exposition of the proposition that is only foreshadowed and prepared for earlier on, takes ch. 4 and the example of Abraham as the first "proof" of the proposition, followed by several others, takes 5.1ff. as the confirmation or amplification of the main proposition, sees in chs. 9–11 an entirely new discussion, and at 12.1 another and more ethical division in the argument. He seems to see in 15.14-24 the *peroratio* as well. See P. Melanchthon, *Commentary on Romans*, trans. F. Kramer (St. Louis: Concordia, 1992). One must look at the key junctures in the text to see Melanchthon's view of the rhetorical structure, as he does not neatly sum it up in any one place. For a very helpful review of Melanchthon's rhetorical analysis and commentary on Romans see C. J. Classen, "St. Paul's Epistles and Ancient Greek and Roman Rhetoric," in *Rhetoric and the New Testament*, ed. S. E. Porter and T. H. Olbricht (Sheffield: Sheffield Academic Press, 1993), pp. 265-91, here pp. 271-78.

Language, Style, and Intertextuality

On first blush it might seem odd that Paul would address a largely Gentile audience of Romans in Greek rather than Latin. After all, Paul knew very well that Latin was the language of Rome, as it was also the official and legal language of the Roman colony from which place he wrote Romans. Yet in fact Greek had long before become the predominant language of Rome, not least because it was one of the most cosmopolitan cities in the Empire. Cicero explains that while knowledge and use of Latin was not uncommon in the Empire, its sphere of use and influence was much narrower than that of Greek and so "if anyone thinks that the glory won by writing Greek is somehow less than that given to the one who writes in Latin, he is entirely wrong for Greek letters are read in almost every nation there is, whereas Latin letters are confined to their own quite narrow boundaries" (*Pro Achaia* 23). It is certainly the case that the majority of Jews in Rome were Greek-speaking in the first century A.D. as the funeral inscriptions in the Jewish catacombs make evident.

But what of Paul's use of Greek? Certainly it is common or koine Greek that he uses, but this does not mean that it is rudimentary or lacking in eloquent passages. Unlike the Gospels and Acts, and even though Paul frequently quotes and alludes to the OT in this letter, he largely avoids Aramaisms and Semitisms. The anacolutha (interruptions of syntax) in Romans, as in his other letters, may be put down to the fact that he uses a scribe (see 16.22), who presumably at times had trouble keeping up. As has often been noted, Paul's style is that of an orator, a rhetor rather than a writer, a fact which should have long ago sent exegetes scrambling to study how oratory in the Greco-Roman world was undertaken. Part and parcel of this "oral" approach is Paul's choice to use the diatribe format in Romans 2 and elsewhere, as well as personification (see ch. 7) and other standard rhetorical devices. It must be kept steadily in view that Paul's letter was meant to be read aloud, indeed meant to be orally delivered by a Pauline co-worker, not merely handed over to a congregation. In this case it may be that it was Phoebe who would be the proclaimer of this formidable discourse (see 16.1).

But when one is dealing with an audience which one wishes to exercise some sort of authority over, and yet one does not already have a relationship with most of the audience, one must attend to the rhetorical techniques that help establish ethos and authority, one of which is the use of authoritative sources which the audience will recognize as carrying weight. In this case these include: (1) Christian traditions such as we find in 1.3-4, (2) portions of the LXX, (3) the teaching of Jesus, and even (4) allusions to Paul's earlier rhetorical discourses. Elsewhere, in Galatians, Paul has called some combination of this sort of material that has authority for Christians, "the Law of Christ." It will be well if we deal with the issue of intertextuality (or in some cases, since it is oral tradition which is being used, inter-traditionality) at this juncture. Let us consider first Paul's allusions to his own earlier discourses.

Paul is not given to simply quoting his own previous letters, but he does recycle ideas and phrases more in Romans than in any of his other documents. J. Fitzmyer speaks of Romans as an irenic discussion of many of the topics which have come up in various of Paul's earlier letters.[52] It is in part this fact which has led to the suggestion that Romans should be seen as an introduction to Pauline thought, or in even more grandiose terms as P. Melanchthon once called it "a summary of all Christian doctrine." But too much is missing from Romans for either of these labels to be appropriate, and in any case the rhetorical function of such allusions is ignored in such pronouncements. There are at least some in Rome who are familiar with the gospel Paul has previously preached, in particular his coworkers such as Priscilla and Aquila.

It is important in building a case for exhortation to establish that one has been consistent in one's teaching and preaching. It must be the same gospel Paul has offered in the east that he is now offering to Rome. Otherwise he will be seen to be simply currying favor in the fashion of sophistic rhetoric, attempting to please an audience by telling them what they wish to hear. He believes that it is the one gospel that he preaches which brings Good News to both Jew and Gentile alike. Accordingly, he echoes ideas and phrases from his earlier letters, mostly Galatians, 1 Thessalonians, and 1 and 2 Corinthians, that represent important elements of the gospel and of his experience and ministry (the few correspondences with Philippians may well indicate influence in the other direction, with Philippians echoing Romans). Fitzmyer gives a full list of such parallels;[53] the following is representative:

1.16-17	salvation by faith and the revelation of God's righteousness	Gal. 2.15-21; 2 Cor. 5.21; Phil. 3.9
4.1-23	Abraham the model of justifying faith	Gal. 3.6-9, 14-19; 4.21-31
4.24-25	Christ crucified for trespasses and raised for justification	2 Cor. 5.15; Gal. 2.19-21
7.4	death to the Law through Christ and resurrection	Gal. 2.19-20; 2 Cor. 5.15
7.25; 8.1-2	freedom from death, sin, and Law through Christ	1 Cor. 15.57
8.14-15	adoption, Abba	Gal. 4.5-6
9.3-4; 11:1	Paul's ancestry and kinsmen	2 Cor. 11.22; Phil. 3:5

---

52. J. A. Fitzmyer, *Romans* (New York: Doubleday, 1992), p. 73.
53. Fitzmyer, *Romans*, pp. 71-73.

10.12	no distinction between Jew and Gentile	Gal. 3.28
12.9-13	love	1 Corinthians 13
14.1–15.13	the strong guided by love for the weak	1 Corinthians 8–10
14.17	what the kingdom of God is not	1 Cor. 4.20

Most of the parallels occur outside chs. 1–4 and 9–11, that is, where the fewest allusions or quotations from the OT are found (e.g., the lists of Scripture quotations in 3.10-18 and 9.25-29). Paul most often draws on his own previous diction and ideas in chs. 12–15, where he also alludes to the Jesus tradition.

Romans is thus a tradition-laden epistle. Paul relies on earlier teaching, ideas, and phrases as part of his attempt to undergird the authority of the discourse and its exhortations. He takes no chance that this message may be dismissed, rejected, or ignored, not least because he is counting on not merely conveying but also receiving some "gift" from the Romans when he arrives in Rome. Romans, like an ambassadorial letter, is eliciting support and rapport and is building a social network in preparation for the visit of the apostle to the Gentiles.[54]

54. For a helpful study of Paul's citation of Scripture in comparison with that of some of his contemporaries see C. D. Stanley, *Paul and the Language of Scripture: Citation Techniques in the Pauline Epistles and Contemporary Literature* (Cambridge: Cambridge University Press, 1992).

THE COMMENTARY

Epistolary Prescript and Greeting — 1.1-7

The prescript to Romans is more expansive than those of some of Paul's other letters, which may reflect the fact that here he is not writing to his own converts, and presumably the issue of ethos and authority is more of a concern with this audience than with some others. It is also surely no accident that already in this prescript Paul will stress the indebtedness of Christians to their Jewish heritage both in the Scriptures and in the person of the Jew Jesus. Traditional material is probably drawn on in this prescript, so that from the first Paul positions himself with those who affirm and indeed stress the Jewish heritage of Jesus and his followers. One should note how this material prepares for what is to come in ch. 9, but notice that there are also echoes of this material in the final doxology in 16.25-27.

Paul, slave of Jesus Christ, called apostle, set apart for the gospel of God which was promised beforehand through his prophets in the Holy Writings, concerning his Son who came to be born from the seed of David according to the flesh, who was marked out/appointed Son of God in power according to the Spirit of holiness from the resurrection of the dead, Jesus Christ our Lord, through whom we received grace and apostleship unto the obedience of faith in all the non-Jewish peoples for his name's sake, in whom you also are called of Jesus Christ. To all those in Rome[1] — beloved of God, called saints. Grace and peace to you from God our Father and the Lord Jesus Christ.[2]

1. A few manuscripts omit "in Rome," including Origen's text of Romans. This is perhaps a deliberate and later excision meant to make this document into a more general or universal treatise. See B. M. Metzger, *A Textual Commentary on the Greek New Testament* (3rd ed.; London: United Bible Societies, 1971), p. 505.

2. It is my practice here, as in my other socio-rhetorical commentaries, to offer a fresh

29

This rich introduction to the discourse begins already the attempt to establish both rapport with the audience and Paul's authority in relationship to them. Though they are not his converts he received an apostleship that included the task of accomplishing "the obedience of faith" in all the nations, or put another way, among all the non-Jewish peoples. This would include the vast majority of his audience.

It is important to bear in mind from the outset that Paul is drawing on and alluding to a storied world. He begins this work with a reference to his own story (called and set apart for a specific role by God) and the story of Jesus (born in the Davidic line requisite of a messianic figure and marked out as Son of God in power after his resurrection). Paul assumes he shares or can share in common with his audience the generative narratives underlying and undergirding his discourse from the outset. Neglect of the storied world out of which he does his theological and ethical reflection has led to misreadings of texts as varied as chs. 2 and 7. To treat Romans as some sort of theological treatise involving merely abstract and logical constructs will not do. Paul certainly knows how to use logic and rhetoric to argue his case well, but he does not do so like a late western philosopher or logician but rather as an early Jewish Christian evangelist well trained in the art of persuasion.[3]

At the very outset Paul calls himself a slave or servant of Christ. It is possible that he wishes thus to set himself within the prophetic tradition (see Ps. 105.26, 42; Amos 3.7; Zech. 1.6), but he uses the same sort of introduction in Phil. 1.1 and Gal. 1.10. Furthermore, other important OT figures besides the prophets are regularly identified in this way, which suggests that "servant" is an honorific title (2 Kgs. 18.12, of Moses; Judg. 2.8, of Joshua; 2 Sam. 7.5, of David).[4] It is an honor to be a servant of the great King.[5] C. K. Barrett suggests that Paul

---

and also rough translation throughout the commentary, because I have found that often translators, in smoothing out the rough edges of Paul's rhetoric, in fact interject something into the text that Paul was not intending. Thus, this translation, while hopefully not woodenly literal, tends more toward the literal than to a more free-flowing dynamic equivalency model.

3. On what undergirds Paul's theology and rhetoric see my *Paul's Narrative Thought World: The Tapestry of Tragedy and Triumph* (Louisville: Westminster/John Knox, 1994), pp. 1ff., and see K. Grieb, *The Story of Romans: A Narrative Defense of God's Righteousness* (Louisville: Westminster/John Knox, 2002), pp. 1-18, which gives further proof of the fruit of paying attention to Paul's narrative subtext.

4. See C. Talbert, *Romans* (Macon: Smyth and Helwys, 2002), p. 27.

5. It has even been suggested that Paul is using the phrase "servant of Jesus Christ" as a sort of technical term alluding to the household of Caesar. This in part depends on the assumption that slaves from Caesar's household were part, perhaps a significant part, of Paul's audience in Rome. Even if there were a few such persons in Paul's audience, it is a mistake to take the list in ch. 16 as representing the majority of those whom Paul is addressing. In fact, ch. 16 mainly lists the Jewish Christian minority in Rome, whom Paul knows. But see M. J. Brown, "Paul's Use of *Doulos Christou Iēsou* in Rom. 1.1," *JBL* 120 (2001): 723-37.

may be drawing on language that refers to servants of a king. While Greeks did not see themselves as a king's slaves, Jews who were ministers of a king often did (1 Sam. 8.17; 2 Sam. 14.22).[6] In any case, Paul is making it clear that he is a man who belongs to and is under the authority of Jesus. His will is not his own, and his mission, his apostleship, is a task to which he has been called and assigned. Paul does not see himself as one who is free to do as he pleases.[7] He is called to be a missionary among the Gentiles.

The term *apostolos* means a "called out and set apart person" and probably has a background in the Jewish concept of the *shaliah*, the person who was a legal agent of the one who sent him to undertake some task, imbued with the power and authority of the sender. A *shaliah* was sent on a mission with a quite specific commission, and here Paul makes clear what his own commission is.[8] He is not defensive about his apostleship but is, rather, comfortable with mentioning that he is a slave of Jesus at the outset. This document is not an exercise in the rhetoric of defense or attack, and it should not be read as a broadside against Paul's opponents, who are nowhere in evidence in this document. The diatribal style of discourse in ch. 2 and elsewhere should not be misconstrued in that way. As E. Käsemann stresses, the tasks of the apostle are always associated with God's work of eschatological salvation.[9]

Somewhat surprisingly Paul refers here to "the gospel of God" rather than the gospel of Jesus Christ. A deliberate theocentric note is sounded here and elsewhere in Romans, though for Paul christocentrism is a form of theocentrism. But is this an objective or subjective genitive? Is this the Good News *about* God or Good News which *comes from* God? Since Paul is setting forth his credentials to an audience which by and large does not know him personally, it is probable that he refers in this way to a gospel which comes from God. His use of *euangelion* refers, clearly enough, to the oral proclamation of a positive message. In the light of the use of this term of emperors at their births[10] or when they accomplished something dramatic, it is also clear that

---

6. See C. K. Barrett, *A Commentary on the Epistle to the Romans* (Peabody: Hendrickson, 1991), p. 18.

7. As C. Bryan, *A Preface to Romans: Notes on the Epistle and Its Literary and Cultural Setting* (Oxford: Oxford University Press, 2000), p. 58, puts it, everyone in Paul's world belonged to someone or something. No one simply belonged to themselves. Even the Julio-Claudian emperors saw themselves as the sons of the divine Julius Caesar. A person's identity was established in relationship to other persons or groups of persons. Slaves of a very important person could be very important and powerful persons themselves by means of derived authority. Such was the case with Paul.

8. Bryan, *A Preface to Romans*, p. 58.

9. E. Käsemann, *Commentary on Romans* (Grand Rapids: Eerdmans, 1980), pp. 5-6.

10. E.g., Augustus, about whom there was an inscription in Asia Minor saying that his birthday was for the entire world the beginning of the *euangelion* or good news concerning

Paul intends an implicit anti-imperial sort of rhetoric. The one who really offers salvation and true Good News for human beings is the God who has sent Jesus and raised him from the dead.

This message of salvation was, in Paul's view, promised beforehand through the prophets whose oracles were inscribed in the Holy Scriptures. The content of this Good News is made clear in vv. 3-4. Paul does not speak of prediction in advance by these prophets, but rather of promise in advance. This is interesting in view of the covenantal significance of promises to Abraham and others. This message is about God's Son who was born from David's seed. Cranfield points out that *genomenou* (from *ginesthai*) is not the word ordinarily used for birth. Paul uses it here and in Gal. 4.4 and Phil. 2.7. It is not impossible that this reflects his belief that Jesus' birth took place without human fatherhood, though we cannot be sure.[11]

In order to understand vv. 3-4, one must pay close attention to the two parallel clauses — *kata sarka* and *kata pneuma*. Many of the Church Fathers thought they found here a testimony about the two natures of Christ, human and divine. But, against this, v. 3 does not focus on Jesus' human nature per se, but rather on his human lineage through David, and v. 4 is not about what Christ is according to his divine nature but rather about what happened to Jesus at the resurrection, when God's Spirit raised him from the dead and designated or marked him out as Son of God in power.[12] In other words, these are comments about two phases in the trajectory of Jesus' career. It is not at Jesus' birth or baptism but at his resurrection that Paul wants to speak of Jesus as *kata pneuma*. But resurrection has to do with Jesus' body, with his being raised out of the realm of the dead. One cannot then see a contrast here between what Jesus was physically and what he became spiritually. This is not about apotheosis or divination of the soul in the spiritual realm or heaven. In short, when Jesus became what he was after the resurrection, he did not cease to be the bodily person he was before. Perhaps *kata* (literally "according to") should be translated "in the sphere of" here.[13] The unusual phrase "Spirit of Holiness" is surely not a reference to Jesus' human spirit. Rather it refers to the effect of the Holy

---

him. See Talbert, *Romans*, p. 30. The term is also used of good news about Greek states being guaranteed freedom or autonomy (*OGIS* 6.10-34). It does not, however, appear to me that the term is a technical one in either of these cases.

11. C. E. B. Cranfield, *A Critical and Exegetical Commentary on the Epistle to the Romans* (ICC; Edinburgh: Clark, 1975-79), 1:59.

12. The verb *horizein* has the sense of designate, appoint, or even install in Acts 10.42; 11.29; 17.26; 17.31; Heb. 4.7. This does not make its usage here adoptionist as the phrase "in power" modifies "Son of God." Jesus was the Son of God in weakness or vulnerable humanness prior to the resurrection. See B. Byrne, *Romans*, Sacra Pagina (Collegeville: Liturgical, 1996), p. 44.

13. See rightly Barrett, *Romans*, p. 20.

Spirit on Jesus — Jesus enters an entirely sanctified or glorified condition when he is raised from the dead by the Spirit.

Does "in power" modify the noun phrase "Son of God," the verb "marked out/appointed," or less likely "the Spirit"? Käsemann rightly notes the parallels in the hymn fragments in 1 Tim. 3.16 and Heb. 1.13. This favors the conclusion that Paul means here that at the resurrection Jesus enters a phase of his career where he becomes Son of God *in power*. Previously, he was Son of God in weakness. He did not assume the role of glorified and exalted and all-powerful Lord until after the resurrection (so also Philippians 2), when he was appointed to such a role.[14]

It is interesting that Paul uses the phrase "from the resurrection of the dead."[15] Paul here and elsewhere (see 1 Corinthians 15) affirms the concept of a resurrection of one (and later of some — namely those who are in Christ) out from among the dead.[16] In other words, Paul does not operate with a concept of the general resurrection of all the dead at one juncture in time. Like some other early Jews he works only with a concept of the resurrection of the righteous or saints. The resurrection of Jesus was the firstfruits of the resurrection of the righteous, and as such inaugurated the eschaton.

V. 5 affirms that Paul has received both "grace and apostleship," or if we have here a verbal hendiadys (two terms representing one thing) the grace of apostleship. Grace is, of course, God's undeserved benefit and love, and it is interesting that Paul wishes to affirm it in close connection with apostleship. He believes that being chosen an apostle was an undeserved benefit or blessing (cf. 1 Cor. 15.9). But here he is probably also affirming that the task/role/office cannot be undertaken without God's empowerment/blessing/enabling. Grace and commissioning as apostle are required if Paul is to do what God expects of him. Here as elsewhere, when Paul speaks of doing something by grace, he is referring to some extra strength or power and authority bestowed by God that one would not otherwise have.

14. Sometimes this has been seen as a pre-Pauline adoptionist formula, but Paul is certainly not suggesting that Jesus was not Son of God before the resurrection (see, e.g., Gal. 4.4, where it is stressed that Jesus was sent by God and was his Son even before he was born of woman). Rather, the phrase is referring to a new role Jesus assumed, the role and status of Son of God in power (= Lord) at and after the resurrection. See J. A. Fitzmyer, *Romans* (New York: Doubleday, 1992), p. 235; D. Moo, *The Epistle to the Romans* (NICNT; Grand Rapids: Eerdmans, 1996), p. 48.

15. The parallel construction here needs to be taken seriously. Both the clause about Jesus' human descent and the clause about the role he took on begin with the preposition *ek*. If we arranged the Greek in perfect parallelism the text would read: "who was born *from/out of* the seed of David in the sphere of the flesh, who was appointed *from/out of* the resurrection of the dead in the sphere of the Spirit of holiness."

16. See J. D. G. Dunn, *Romans 1–8,* Word Biblical Commentary (Dallas: Word, 1988), pp. 15-16.

Here we must say a bit more about the deliberative rhetoric Paul is offering and why he seems to adopt a somewhat humble and irenic tone in this discourse as compared to his letters to his own converts. Before he can advise or instruct, his authority must be declared and made plain to an audience which likely does not recognize that he has any authority over them. And since the authority of the speaker is the most crucial issue when one offers up declarative rhetoric, he must establish his credentials up front.[17]

Furthermore, as Quintilian stresses, "It also makes a great deal of difference who it is that is offering the advice: for if his past has been illustrious, or if his distinguished birth or age or fortune excites high expectations, care must be taken that his words are not unworthy of him. If on the other hand he has none of these advantages he will have to adopt a humbler tone" (*Instit. Or.* 3.8.48). Paul is addressing an audience of largely Gentile Christians over which, as it would appear to them, he has no authority. Since it is quite clear from chs. 9–11 that this audience has an issue with Jews and Jewishness and what God thinks about these matters, Paul cannot appeal to his own illustrious past as a Jew, as he does in 2 Corinthians, Philippians, and elsewhere. He has no fortune to tout, nor does it appear that he can appeal to a distinguished birth.[18] He does not possess, as far as the Gentile Christians in Rome would be concerned, the signs of honor that normally produced instant respect in Rome. Accordingly, it must suffice that he take a different rhetorical tact — he will stress that he is an apostle, indeed the apostle of the Gentiles, up front, and at the same time will take a hubris-free or humble approach to his discourse. Indeed, he will even go so far as to introduce himself first as a slave of Christ before calling himself apostle to the Gentiles. He is simply following the sort of advice he knew applied in his situation if Romans was to be a rhetorically effective piece of discourse.

Certainly one of the most debated of phrases in a document full of debatable points is "obedience of faith." Cranfield lists the following possible meanings: obedience to a body of doctrines known as "the faith," obedience to the authority of faith, obedience to God's faithfulness attested in the gospel, the obedience that *faith* works, the obedience required by faith, believing obedience, and faith that is a form of or consists in obedience.[19] Cranfield, Käsemann, and Talbert favor some version of the last option. So Paul might mean that believing in Christ is a form of submission to Christ and so is obedi-

---

17. See pp. 1-20 above.

18. Paul was quite reluctant to use his Roman citizenship to give himself clout when first entering into a new situation. The evidence from Acts shows that he used it in the main as a sort of trump card, in extremis. See my *The Paul Quest: The Search for the Jew of Tarsus* (Downers Grove: InterVarsity, 1998), pp. 69-73. He wanted the gospel to be presented without using human status or extant social hierarchies as a tool to coerce adherence.

19. Cranfield, *Romans,* 1:66ff.

ence to Christ's demand that we believe in him. One may compare Gal. 3.2 and Rom. 10.16 and 15.18. But does God, in Paul's view, demand faith or rather call us to faith? Are we not called to both trust and then also to obey? Paul's specific concern here is with the obedience of faith among Gentiles, and it is quite apparent from chs. 12–15 that Paul wants not just trust or faith from Gentile converts but also obedience to God's demands. I would suggest that in fact Paul refers here to the obedience that flows forth from saving faith.[20]

In v. 5 he puts special stress on his apostleship being to *all* the peoples, including, of course, the Romans. He believes that he has a task of winning the "obedience of faith" even from the Romans, even though they are not his converts. He has a divine commission to accomplish this task even in Rome, and when he does so it will be not for his own personal glory but for the sake of God's name. It was critical that from the very outset Paul establish his ethos, his authority in relationship to his audience, before he addressed them properly. It was not enough to ingratiate himself with the audience and establish rapport, as he does in the verses that follow; he also had to make clear his divine commission and task in relationship to the Roman Christians themselves. He wants to bestow on them a spiritual gift. Well and good. By what authority does he assume any claim on those who are not his converts? By God's commission that he be apostle to *all* the non-Jewish peoples.[21]

To further punctuate his authority over the audience, Paul adds in v. 6 "among which non-Jewish peoples you are included." He thus stresses the overwhelmingly non-Jewish character of his audience. He is not unaware of the Jewish Christians in Rome or intending that they not hear this discourse. But his focus will be on those that he has specific apostolic authority and commission to deal with — Gentiles. Especially with a new audience of already converted Christians, Paul must be careful not to step beyond his divine commission.[22]

He reminds his readers that they are among "the called of Jesus Christ." The Roman Christians, just like Paul, have a divine call on their lives. They have been called to the obedience of faith by no less a person than Jesus himself. The divine call to which they have responded requires of them that they live in a certain way, which includes harmony with one another. The uses of "you"

---

20. See Barrett, *Romans,* pp. 22-23; Barrett rightly objects to treating faith and obedience here as synonymous.

21. It is better to use the term "peoples," rather than "nations," because the modern concept of nation-state did not even exist in Paul's day. He is not writing to Italians but to Romans. Paul is speaking of non-Jewish ethnic or people groups. Sometimes, since for the most part he is evangelizing only Greek-speaking persons, he calls them Greeks (as opposed to "barbarians," which simply meant non-Greek-speaking peoples).

22. On the evidence for some Jewish Christians being in the Roman church, and Paul being aware of their presence, see pp. 1-20 above, and also pp. 350-405 below on chs. 15 and 16.

(hymeis) in v. 6 are emphatic. The form of "to be" here already contains the subject "you" (plural), so we could in fact translate the clause as "among which peoples you are, even you called of Jesus Christ."

With "to *all* those in Rome . . ." (v. 7) Paul probably now includes in the address Jewish Christians as well, even though vv. 5-6 have made very evident that his focus is on the non-Jewish Christians in Rome.[23] "All" is emphatic and is repeated in v. 8.

Paul gives the entire Christian audience in Rome two epithets: "beloved of God" and "called saints/holy ones."[24] God's love is indeed a major theme of this epistle. Paul usually uses *agapētos* ("beloved") of the love of Christians for their fellow believers (as in 12.19; 16.5-12), though in 11.28 he uses it of God's love for un-

---

23. Grieb, *The Story of Romans*, p. 9, is typical of many who think Paul says here "to all of God's beloved in Rome, who are called to be saints" when in fact what the Greek says is "to all who are in Rome, beloved of God, called saints." Nothing suggests that we should insert the words "who are" after "God," nor that we should insert the verb "to be" between "called" and "saints," making the clause about saints a subordinate one. If anything, the simple word "and" after the word "God" would be in order. Furthermore, if one translates the clause "called to be saints" it suggests that they are not yet in this condition, when in fact Paul is talking about those who are called "saints" already.

24. There is an interesting emphasis here on being "called," which is closely related to but not identical with being chosen. Notice for instance the assemblage of verbs in 8.29-30 — foreknew, predestined, called, justified, glorified. To be called can be distinguished from being known in advance or destined in advance or justified or glorified. That particular chain of verbs is in fact preceded by the phrase "those who love him, who are called according to purpose/choice" (v. 28), using a form of the same two verbs as are found here. It is appropriate to ask, Who have demonstrated that they are the "called"? Answer: "those who love God" and are loved by God. Who are those whom God foreknew? Those already mentioned in v. 28 — namely Christians, namely those who love God. God foreknew quite well who would respond to his call and who would not. He knew them through and through. The destining, the justifying, the glorifying are all predicated on what God knew in advance about those who would love God. See pp. 226-32 below.

A valid distinction can be made between being called and being chosen. If you are called, and you respond — respond by grace and in faith and love to God — then you are among the chosen, the beloved of God. To use a mundane analogy, when someone calls your name to be on a sport team, you then have a choice as to how you will respond. If you respond positively, then you have been "picked." If you do not, then you have not been chosen.

The great mystery of divine sovereignty and human response enabled by grace should be resolved neither by denying the sovereignty and saving power and initiative of a loving God nor by simply affirming human free will. Paul knows nothing of modern notions of pure libertarian voluntarism any more than he affirms pure fatalism. What Paul does know is that love must be freely given and freely responded to, if it is to be a truly loving response. It can be enabled by grace, but love cannot be coerced. Even when we rightly think of the notion of radical rescue of the lost or misdirected, such as was the case of Paul himself, it was still necessary for Paul to choose to respond properly once he was "saved," and this God graciously enabled him to do.

believing Israel (cf. 9.25). God's love preceded his calling of persons, and indeed was the basis of the call. In a memorable discussion of God's love, V. P. Furnish has said that God's love is not like a heat-seeking missile directed by something inherently attractive in the target audience.[25] It is, rather, that which makes a person lovely and loveable. Such a person is transformed by God's love. It is the greatest blessing and honor of humankind to be beloved and called by God.

Paul's vision of the people of God is clear from the first. He uses terms formerly used of Israel, namely "beloved" and "called," even of his largely Gentile audience, because he believes that Jew and Gentile united in Christ and in his gospel are the eschatological people of God and stand in continuity with Abraham and OT Israel.[26] With "called holy ones" he does not mean that they are "saints" in the modern sense of the term. What follows in this letter makes it clear they were far from perfect people. Perhaps, as J. Fitzmyer suggests, Paul is uses *hagios* ("holy, saint") in its OT sense of "dedicated" or "consecrated," that is, voluntarily separated from profane and immoral aspects of life. Fitzmyer suggests the translation "called to be his consecrated/dedicated people."[27] This comports nicely with 12.1: A sacrifice is something dedicated or consecrated to God, and the Roman Christians are called to give themselves to God as an act of worship.[28] They, too, are beloved of God and his called holy ones.[29]

---

25. See V. P. Furnish, *The Love Command in the New Testament* (Nashville: Abingdon, 1973), pp. 23ff.

26. See Moo, *The Epistle to the Romans*, p. 54. It is very possible that Paul, having referred to all believers in Rome, has then divided them into two different categories — the beloved of God would refer to the Gentiles, and those "called saints" would be the Jewish Christian minority in Rome. The term "saints" is repeatedly used of Israel, indicating that they are God's set apart people (cf. Deut. 7.6; 33.3; Ps. 50.5; Isa. 4.3; Dan. 7.18-22). If this is correct then Paul acknowledges the division in Rome from the outset of the document. See pp. 375-80 below. F. Watson, *Paul, Judaism, and the Gentiles* (Cambridge: Cambridge University Press, 1986), pp. 96-98, has put his finger on something when he notes that there seem to be basically two major groups of Christians in Rome, who are not for the most part meeting together, as is witnessed to in chs. 14–16. If this is correct then 12.13 becomes especially pointed because it urges that the Gentiles share with Jewish Christians in need. The only more generic use of "saint" in Romans that may include Gentiles seems to be 8.27.

27. Fitzmyer, *Romans*, p. 237.

28. See pp. 280-89 below.

29. Though modern notions of sanctification should not be read into these terms, Paul is interested not just in Christians' position before God but also in their moral condition. They are to be set apart not just by an act of God but also in their own active belief and behavior. It is not impossible that in fact Paul is differentiating two groups in Rome — the Gentiles whom he calls beloved of God, and the Jewish Christians whom he calls saints. This would seem to comport with the usage of "saints" in 15.25, 31 and 16.15 (cf. also the usage in Ephesians). See R. Jewett, "Ecumenical Theology for the Sake of Mission," in *Pauline Theology*, ed. D. M. Hay and E. E. Johnson, vol. 3: *Romans* (Minneapolis: Fortress, 1995), p. 95.

This theology does not make Paul a supersessionist, not least because he will argue vigorously in chs. 9–11 that non-Christian Jews still have a future as God's people, when Jesus returns and they recognize their Messiah. God has not reneged on his promises to Israel. No, Paul is a completionist and takes the already extant union of Jews like himself and Aquila and Priscilla with Gentiles in Christ as a foretaste and a foreshadowing of that great universal family re-union of all of Abraham's descendents, both Jewish and Gentile, when the Mes-siah of Israel, who is also the Saviour of non-Jews, returns. Paul sees it as his particular mission as apostle to the Gentiles to aid this process of union and re-union by activities such as writing this letter, visiting Jerusalem and conveying the collection, visiting Rome, and pressing on to the non-Jewish peoples in the western end of the empire.

He has thus prepared his audience in this preface for one of the most magisterial exercises in the rhetoric of concord and reconciliation ever penned. He will call his audience to the obedience of faith, an obedience which entails believing, loving, serving, uniting with other believers, however different their lifestyles may be (see chs. 12–15), and avoiding and healing divisions (16.17-19).[30] It will entail open-hearted acceptance of Jewish Christians by the Gentile majority in Rome and a willingness to see that God has not given up on his first chosen people, even if many of them have already rejected the gospel. In other words, Romans is an exercise in anti-supersessionist rhetoric, since all, both Jews and Gentiles, are included in God's plan of salvation through his Son.

V. 7b concludes this section of the document with Paul's standard greet-ing of "grace and peace." He does not merely greet his audience on his own, but passes along greetings from God the Father and the Lord Jesus Christ. The stan-dard Greek greeting was *chaire,* a word that meant "joy" before it came to mean simply "greetings," in much the same way as "good day" or "goodbye" (a con-traction of "God be with ye") have become perfunctory. Paul uses, instead, *charis,* "grace." There is nothing perfunctory about grace for Paul. He combines this modified Greek greeting with the traditional Jewish greeting *shalom* or "peace/be well." He thus wishes the audience both God's unmerited favor and blessing and God's peace or rest.

Paul refers to God as "our Father," that is, the Father of both Jewish Chris-tians like Paul and also of the predominantly non-Jewish Christians in his audi-ence. Paul strives for union and communion with his audience and within his audience from the first, beckoning God to grace and give peace to them. Be-cause God is one and is their common Father, Paul's vision and hope is that the

---

30. Dunn, *Romans 1–8,* pp. 17-18, rightly points out that the term "obedience" or "obey" comes up at various places in this letter (cf. 1.5; 5.19; 6.16; 15.18; 16.19, 26; on "obey" see 6.12, 15-17; 10.16). Here it is germane to stress that this is not the sort of rhetoric one finds in a forensic discourse, which does not involve parenesis.

Christians in Rome might be one with each other and with him, the one who proclaims a universal gospel for the Jew first but also for non-Jewish peoples.

Bridging the Horizons

It seems at first strange to establish one's credentials at the beginning of a letter. Right at the beginning of this letter Paul calls himself a slave. Slavery was not, generally speaking, anyone's desire or career goal in the first century. Indeed, it was seen by most as a humiliating condition. It is doubtful that most of the Gentiles in Paul's largely Gentile audience would have been familiar enough with the OT to remember the concept of the prophets as God's servants or slaves, so Paul is taking something of a risk. But there is a profound truth underlying Paul's introduction of himself as a slave. He believes that human beings are created to serve their Creator, not to be gods in their own little worlds. Indeed, Paul believes that we are all created for relationship, not to be lords of the universe.

At the same time, it was a position of power and authority to be the imperial slave of a great ruler, whether of Nero or of Christ. So perhaps Paul wants his audience to draw an analogy between himself and an imperial slave, a conjecture made all the more likely by his mention of some of these slaves in ch. 16.[31]

In keeping with this is the fact that Paul turns around immediately and calls himself an apostle of Jesus Christ. This is certainly a more honorific title, but an apostle is a sent one, one who is under authority and has a specific task or function to undertake. An apostle may be at the top of the leadership structure of the early church, so far as human roles are concerned, but he is still someone who is under the authority and guidance of Christ. His is a derived authority. There are no independent human authorities in the church, nor is there anyone who has inherent authority. This is why we speak of someone being "called" (by another), "commissioned" (by another), or "ordained" (by another). This relational language indicates the real nature of such roles. They are given, not earned. They are assigned, not achieved.

31. See pp. 379-90 below.

Exordium and *Narratio* — 1.8-15

In an epistolary piece of rhetoric there is an overlap between the wish-prayer and the *exordium,* though the rhetorical function of the two is the same. A regular feature of such prayers/*exordia* is that they give a preview of what is to come later on in Paul's discourse. The *exordium* also normally contains praise to God for something that in fact has been causing difficulties — in this case, apparently, the nature of the Roman Gentile Christians' faith. Their faith is reported all over the world, but Paul does not say what is reported about it. Is it strong or weak? Is it inclusive or ethnocentric? Are they acting in proportion to their faith, or are their actions going beyond or even against their faith? These are the sort of questions which will need to be raised. The *exordium* flows quite naturally into the brief *narratio* at v. 11, which then continues through v. 15.

Quintilian says that an *exordium* is not required in deliberative oratory but may be included. But "even if we introduce an *exordium* we must content ourselves with a brief prelude, which may amount to no more than a heading" (*Instit. Or.* 3.8.10). Certainly Rom. 1.8-10 meets this requirement. Quintilian says of *narratios* in deliberative rhetoric that "Statements as to external matters which are relevant to the discussion may . . . frequently be introduced" (3.8.11). Paul must recount why he has not managed to get to Rome, even though he has been visiting Gentile regions for years. He must make clear at the same time that he is still eager to come to Rome.

Aristotle stresses that both private exhortation and legislative proposals to the assembly (*ekklēsia*) and arguments to support them are the subject of deliberative rhetoric (*Rhetoric* 1358b).[1] In chs. 12–15 Paul will give ethical exhorta-

---

1. See N. Elliott, *The Rhetoric of Romans: Argumentative Constraint and Strategy and Paul's Dialogue with Judaism* (JSNTS 45; Sheffield: Sheffield Academic, 1990), p. 99.

tion, and in chs. 1–11 he will try to persuade the Romans about his gospel so that they will change in their relationship to Jewish Christians and Jews. He will undertake both under the banner or theme of "righteousness," both God's and that of believers, with ch. 16 an appropriate final deliberative attempt to effect unity and reconciliation between the largely Gentile Christian audience and the Jewish Christian minority. Paul is already setting up what he intends to do both in this letter and when he comes to Rome by saying what he does in 1.12-13 about fruit in Rome and mutual sharing.

Quintilian stresses that "appeals to emotions . . . are especially necessary in deliberative oratory" (*Instit. Or.* 3.8.12) and goes on to list strong emotions such as anger, hatred, ambition, reconciliation, and pity. Paul readily displays emotion from the beginning of this document, stressing how he longs to see the Roman Christians, will later express great anxiety and pathos over his fellow Jews (chs. 9–11), and then will exhort the Roman Christians to love. He is following the rules of deliberative oratory. Emotion is especially to be displayed at the beginning and at the end of major portions of a deliberative discourse. We see this clearly at the end of the theological segment of the discourse in chs. 9–11, and then again at the end of the pragmatic portion of the discourse in ch. 15.

Paul is, however, in something of a bind. He wishes to give instruction and advice to the Roman Christians, but they are not his converts. How then to exercise authority over them? This is no small question for one embarking on a deliberative discourse because "what really carries greatest weight in deliberative speeches is the authority of the speaker. For he who would have all men trust his judgment as to what is expedient and honorable should possess and be regarded as possessing genuine wisdom and excellence of character" (*Instit. Or.* 3.8.13). He must then step carefully, emphasize his apostolic status in relationship to Gentiles, and use the technique of *insinuatio* if he is to get his message across.

First of all then I give thanks to my God through Jesus Christ concerning all of you, because your faith is proclaimed in the whole of the world. For my witness is God, whom I worship/serve in my spirit in the gospel of his Son, how ceaselessly I have made remembrance of you always in my prayers, begging if somehow sometime at last I will be led along a good route according to the will of God to come to you.

For I long to see you so that I might share some grace gift with you unto your strengthening. That is, I mean to be encouraged at the same time in you through the [sharing] in one another's faith — yours and mine. But I do not wish you to be ignorant, brothers, how often I proposed to come to you, and was often prevented up until now, in order that I might acquire some fruit among you just as also [I have] among the rest of the non-Jewish peoples. Greeks and non-Greek-speaking peoples, wise and unlearned I am indebted to. Hence, with respect to me there is eagerness to preach the Gospel even/also to you, those who are in Rome.[2]

It is clear in this *exordium* either that Paul has little he wishes to thank God for about the Roman Christians or that he is simply eager to get on with the discourse. One should compare the more ample wish-prayers/*exordia* in 1 Corinthians or 1 Thessalonians. Faith, however, is certainly one of the major themes of this discourse, and the fact that Paul can praise the faith of the Romans in this way is significant. Since Rome was the center of the social networks of the empire and since communication went out from Rome throughout the empire, it is not surprising that Paul writes that the Romans' faith has been "proclaimed" in the whole empire. Doubtless this is rhetorical hyperbole to some degree, but Paul is stressing that their faith is well known.[3] And with such notability comes some responsibility. How the Roman Christians respond to the divisions among them, to the Collection, and to Paul's mission to the West will be noticed. Paul is deliberately putting them on notice that they and their behavior are being observed. They seem to have a generally good reputation and honor rating as faithful Christians, such that their faith is trumpeted throughout the Mediterranean crescent. The *exordium* thus sets the stage for the discussion of faith, in particular the faith of those in Rome, especially the Gentile Christians Paul is mainly addressing. Paul is here following the rhetorical strategy advised for establishing rapport in one's introductory remarks, for by "speaking [positively] of the person of our hearers goodwill is secured. . . . if we show in what esteem they are held" (*Ad Herennium* 1.5.7).

In comparison to what we find in the LXX and other Jewish texts in Greek, Paul places an extraordinary emphasis on *pistis,* trust/faith. The breadth and extent of Paul's usage of these terms is not fully explained by what we find in the LXX (though cf. Hab. 2.4; Gen. 15.6; Exod. 14.31). J. L. Kinneavy has pointed out that it is in rhetoric that we most often find *pistis* and its cognates in Greek literature, and particularly in political or deliberative rhetoric, where issues of persuasion and dissuasion, of faith and trust, are at stake. So Paul's emphasis on *pistis* may in part be attributed to Paul's predominant use of deliberative rhetoric in his letters as he writes to an audience that existed in a rhetoric-saturated context.[4]

---

2. A precious few manuscripts omit the reference to "those in Rome" including Origen and G. On this see above, p. 29 and notes. The inclusion of these words is well supported textually, and the omission likely reflects the later generalizing tendency.

3. See rightly, C. Bryan, *A Preface to Romans* (Oxford: Oxford University Press, 2000), p. 62.

4. See J. L. Kinneavy, *Greek Rhetorical Origins of Christian Faith* (New York: Oxford University Press, 1987).

Paul calls in God as a witness that he has been exceedingly eager to come and be with the Roman Christians. That Paul has made remembrance of them in his prayers probably means something more than just calling them to mind and mentioning their existence. The rhetorical force of words like "ceaselessly," to which is redundantly added the word "always," "begging," and "at last" conveys how very deeply concerned Paul is about the Roman Christians and how very badly he wants to visit them. This is, of course, a way of building rapport with the audience and making them feel important and cared for. But Paul adds "according to the will of God." If it were up to him he would have already come to Rome. Thus, in just a few lines, he has appealed to the Romans' sense of pride (in their reputation as persons of faith) and has sought to make them feel that they are very important to him.

In v. 9, "in the gospel of his Son" probably pushes the translation of *latreuō* ("worships/serves") in the direction of "serve" since Paul serves his God by proclaiming that gospel. But one could also say that he worships his God in his spirit when he proclaims that Good News.[5] Nevertheless, in the Bible this verb always refers to some sort of religious service, which could be worship or witness.[6] If it is worship, it is viewed here as an interior act.

Worship and prayer are closely linked here. We gain the impression that Paul prays a great deal and that he always remembers to pray for the Romans when he prays. "Begging" makes clear that Paul has no problems with petitionary prayer, with actually beseeching God for some particular outcome. But we know that while Paul wrote this letter in A.D. 56-57, he was not to get to Rome until about A.D. 60.

The transition to the *narratio* in v. 11 is smooth as Paul continues to express his feelings for the Romans in various ways. He longs to see them because he wishes to impart a grace gift to them in order that he might strengthen them. The use of *charisma* here should be compared to the usage in 5.15-16; 6.23; and 11.29. Here Paul lays a few of his cards on the table. The real truth of the matter, from his viewpoint, is that the faith of the Roman Gentile Christians needs some strengthening and indeed even some redirecting. Some commentators have thought that Paul was referring to this letter itself or its contents as the gift he longed to convey to them. But if that were the case, then why link this with a statement about longing to see them? He could convey the gift of the content of this letter without a personal visit. Is he just using a round-about way of saying he would rather say all this in person? That is possible, but there is something else against this conclusion.

5. See N. T. Wright, "Romans," in *The New Interpreter's Bible*, vol. 10 (Nashville: Abingdon, 2002), p. 422.

6. See G. D. Fee, *God's Empowering Presence: The Holy Spirit in the Letters of Paul* (Peabody: Hendrickson, 1994), p. 485.

Paul turns around in v. 12 and says that there actually needed to be some mutual sharing between the apostle and these Christians. They need, says Paul, to share with each other out of each's wellspring of faith. Notice again the reference to the Romans' faith. Paul seems to have added v. 12 for two good reasons: (1) He is not writing to his own converts and so must nuance things a bit so that his message and authority will not be rejected. He says that it is a matter of giving and receiving so that the Roman audience will not feel that he is coming to take over. (2) Paul does not want to give the impression at the outset that the Romans are in need of some major attitude adjustments or that their faith is somehow seriously defective. They do need some adjustments and their faith does need some corrective and strengthening, but it is not apropos to bring this up in the *exordium*, where the aim is to establish a good feeling in the audience about the writer so that they will be receptive to what follows. Paul proceeds much more irenically here with an audience not already indebted to him and under his authority, compared, for instance, to his approach in Galatians 1.

But he must also be to some degree candid about why he wants to come to Rome, and so he adds in v. 13 that he hopes to acquire some fruit among the Roman Christians when he comes. The *narratio* then recounts that at various times he has attempted to come to the hub of the empire but has been prevented. This simply makes clear that he regards the Roman congregations as important and that he wishes he could have visited them before the writing of this letter. It also conveys that when Paul comes he does not intend to simply be passing through or making a courtesy call to an already extant church. He wants to "acquire some fruit" while there. He has acquired such fruit among other non-Jewish groups and as apostle to non-Jews feels it is his responsibility to do so in Rome with the Romans as well.

Paul in fact terms it in v. 14 a matter of being indebted to all non-Jewish peoples, whether they speak Greek or not or are learned or not, regardless, that is, of their cultural or educational or social status. This combines Jewish and Gentile ways of speaking, dividing up the world into Jews and all the other non-Jewish peoples, then into Greeks and "barbarians."[7] By "Greeks" was meant Greek-speaking persons, which would include most Romans. "Barbarians" were simply non-Greek-speaking persons. He characterizes Rome as among the "non-Jewish" peoples. The modern concept of nation or nation-state does not really apply here.[8] "That Paul should be thus prepared to designate the Gentile

7. See K. Grieb, *The Story of Romans: A Narrative Defense of God's Righteousness* (Louisville: Westminster/John Knox, 2002), p. 6.
8. Greco-Roman persons might well have assumed that the two different ways of characterizing people that Paul uses here were identical. In other words, there were the educated Greek-speaking persons, and then there were the rustic, somewhat foolish and primitive non-Greek-speaking persons. Paul had certainly evangelized both Greeks and non-Greek-

world in categories of culture and rationality (rather than of races or geographical areas) is striking; it indicates his confidence in the power of his message even in the face of hellenistic sophistication."[9] He also distinguishes between those who are wise and those who are unlearned. He is neither a snob nor an elitist, and his message is not just for the well-educated or socially higher status persons. It is for all persons, and Paul hopes to come to Rome to share with all different kinds of persons.

Paul's desire is not merely to write about the gospel, as he does in this letter, but actually to proclaim the message in Rome orally and personally. "If it is indeed the case that Paul knows the Roman church to be divided and weakened by factional infighting, by claims to superiority of one group over another, then he has already undermined all such claims. The gospel by which they stand is God's and those who are Christ's *belong* to Christ. There is implied therefore already the question that Paul will later pose explicitly to those who would create or nourish disputes: 'Who are you to pass judgment on someone else's household slave? . . .' (14.4)."[10]

Some have seen a contradiction between what is said here and 15.20-24. Probably P. Stuhlmacher is correct in suggesting that what Paul means (as he will say in the *peroratio*) is that he wishes not to evangelize the already Christian Romans but rather to clarify for them the essence of the Good News as he understands it and also its practical implications vis-à-vis Jewish and Gentile Christian relationships.[11]

Bridging the Horizons

There is a certain degree or tone of frustration to this segment of Romans. Paul has longed to come to Rome and visit with the Christians there but he has been prevented from doing so. Now he is hoping it will finally happen even if by a

---

speaking persons, as Acts 13–14 bears witness (cf. especially the episode in Lystra). Romans often prided themselves on the way they had adopted and adapted Greek and Greek culture. They assumed they had even improved on it some. Claudius, for example, was a thoroughgoing "Hellene," as was Nero, who even competed in the poetry contests of the Olympic games in Greece. Of course he won! See B. Byrne, *Romans,* Sacra Pagina (Collegeville: Liturgical, 1996), p. 56.

9. J. D. G. Dunn, *Romans 1–8,* Word Biblical Commentary (Dallas: Word, 1988), p. 33.

10. C. Bryan, *A Preface to Romans: Notes on the Epistle and Its Literary and Cultural Setting* (Oxford: Oxford University Press, 2000), p. 63.

11. P. Stuhlmacher, *Paul's Letter to the Romans* (Louisville: Westminster/John Knox, 1994), p. 27.

circuitous route. Here we see Paul coping with a certain degree of frustration, even frustration with God perhaps.

To some degree this frustration is a reflection of Paul's eagerness to proclaim the gospel in a portion of the Gentile world he has not previously visited. We get a strong sense of Paul the missionary here. Notice also the level of confidence Paul has in the gifts and graces God has given him. He truly believes he has something worth sharing with the Romans, and he believes it will bear fruit if he can once get to Rome. Of course circumstances would conspire such that Paul would get there later than he hoped, and not as a free man either. But notice too that he recognizes that his audience also has things to share with him that could benefit his Christian life. He does not conceive of his visit to Rome as purely a matter of his helping them. Indeed, he will go on to speak in ch. 15 about the possibility of their supporting him on his way to Spain.

Propositio — 1.16-17

It would be hard to overestimate the importance of a *propositio* in a rhetorical discourse. It sets forth the basic theme or proposition which the author will then advance by a series of arguments. It has been characteristic of some treatments of these verses to see the quotation of Habakkuk as the key foreshadowing what follows in chs. 1–8, but in fact the entire *propositio* needs to be given its due weight. The stress, for example, on the gospel being the power of God for salvation of the Jew first as well as the Gentile foreshadows the discussion in chs. 9–11. Furthermore, the reference to faithful living or living by faith in v. 17 is precisely what chs. 12–15 will focus on. Of course the reference to the righteousness of God is crucial and indicates one of the major themes to be dealt with throughout chs. 1–11. But no one should miss that the one word, with its cognates, which gets repeated four times in this *propositio* is faith/faithfulness/believing. This whole discourse will be an attempt to instruct about the nature of faith and faithfulness. God's own faithfulness in Christ to Jews and his impartiality when it comes to Jews and Gentiles will be under discussion, as will human faith and faithfulness.

Quintilian tells us that it is important, if there are multiple propositions (which is perfectly appropriate: *Instit. Or.* 4.4.2-5), or a cluster of related propositions to be dealt with in the arguments, that they should be enumerated up front, and so there must be a sort of partition *(partitio)* of these propositions, instead of just a presentation of one proposition. In my judgment this is precisely what we find in Rom. 1.16-17:

1. First Paul signals the deliberative nature of the discourse by indicating it will be about honor and what is honorable: "I am not ashamed of the gospel . . ." (cf. Aristotle, *Rhetoric* 1369b on honor and 1383b-85a on

47

shame).[1] The implication is that Paul's *largely* Gentile audience should also not be ashamed of a gospel that is for the *Jew first* as well as for them.

2. The discourse will be about the gospel as the power of God for salvation of the Jew first, as well as the Gentile. This will be reflected in the alternation between Gentiles and Jews in chs. 1–11 and will finally culminate in the discussion of God's plan for Jews in chs. 9–11, a plan not merely to save but to unite all in Christ. The discussion about the relationship of Jew and Gentile will continue in chs. 12–15 when the subjects of divisions and of the weak and strong come to the fore.

3. The crucial subject of the righteousness and justice of God will be broached at various points throughout the entire discourse, but in the *refutatio* in chs. 9–11 Paul must address what is not the case in regard to God's justice so far as the Jew's future is concerned. He must undercut certain inappropriate theological notions held by some Gentiles in the audience.

4. This righteousness of God is revealed in the gospel most clearly, though it is also revealed in creation and in the human realm.

5. The phrase *ek pisteōs eis pistin* is of course a crux interpretum, but it seems likely that it is not just an emphatic way of saying "through faith alone." Rather one must give full weight to the prepositions: "from faith unto faith" or, more likely, "from the Faithful One unto faith." Faith and faithfulness are the heart of the matter in this discourse.

6. The quotation of Habakkuk in v. 17b probably should not be read in a messianic way (taking "the righteous one" as Jesus). The focus in this discourse is both on God's faithfulness and on humans who have faith and live out the obedience of faith. Thus, while the Habakkuk quotation can be taken as referring to Romans 1–4 (the righteous through faith) and Romans 5–8 (shall live),[2] I am more persuaded that Paul is probably in the main preparing for the exhortation in Romans 12–15. Thus, Romans 1–11 is in the main about the grace and righteousness and faithfulness of God the faithful one, while Romans 12–15 is about how those who are righteous through faith shall live out the obedience of faith.

In other words, this *propositio* involves a *partitio* and comprehensively introduces the major topics and proofs found in 1.18–ch. 15. It is a major mistake to treat chs. 1–8 as what this discourse is mainly about and chs. 9–11 as a theological afterthought, followed by a potpourri of unrelated ethical exhortations.

---

1. On honor and shame as important topics in deliberative rhetoric see N. Elliott, *The Rhetoric of Romans: Argumentative Constraint and Strategy and Paul's Dialogue with Judaism* (JSNTS 45; Sheffield: Sheffield Academic Press, 1990), p. 117.

2. See pp. 16-18 above on Cranfield's outline.

"Partition may be defined as the enumeration in order of our own propositions. . . . this is indispensable on the ground that it makes the case clearer and the judge [audience] more attentive and ready to be instructed, if he knows what we are speaking about and what we are going subsequently to speak about" (*Instit. Or.* 4.4.1).

For I am not ashamed of the gospel, for it is the power of God unto salvation of everyone who believes, the Jew first and also the Greek. For the righteousness of God has been revealed from the Faithful One unto [those who have] faith, just as it is written: "The righteous from faith shall live."

Since the subject of God's righteousness comes up in the *propositio,* it is important to say something about the deliberative nature of this discourse at this juncture. This discourse is deliberative in both its so-called theological and in its parenetic sections. Quintilian makes clear that the appeal to what is honorable is considered a higher form of deliberative oratory than the appeal to expediency or personal benefit. The topics or themes usually addressed when the matter is one of character and honor are "right, justice, piety, equity, and mercy" (*Instit. Or.* 3.8.25-29). Religion is an appropriate topic for deliberative oratory (3.8.29). Romans 1–11 is indeed about whether God is impartial, faithful, and just in regard to his promises, whether he is merciful and concerned with equity between Jews and Gentiles. Then, of course, Paul will turn around in chs. 12–15 and suggest that his audience must be like God in being just, merciful, equitable, pious, and in the right, in particular in right standing with God. In other words, Paul has chosen the highest road of the various forms of deliberative oratory. He has chosen to address topics which Rome's own Quintilian says ought to be addressed in a deliberative speech about what is honorable. Paul aims his rhetoric right at the heart of empire and suggests that it is his God who does and God's people who should fulfill the virtues most admired by Romans and called honorable by them.

Quintilian says also that "it is an easy task to recommend an honorable course to honorable men" (3.8.38), and Paul treats his audience as honorable persons, though they have their weaknesses. In his summation or *peroratio* in ch. 15 he will say that he is convinced that his audience is full of goodness, complete in knowledge, and competent to instruct each other (15.14). His irenic tone throughout this letter reflects his rhetorical decision to appeal to the best in his audience rather than focusing too negatively on the worst. It is the rhetorical situation, not his lack of knowledge about what is happening in Rome, that dictates how Paul approaches things.

Among the appropriate topics for a deliberative rhetorical piece when it reaches its pragmatic portion are advice about peace, public works or services, and revenue (including taxes: cf. *Instit. Or.* 3.8.14). It will be seen that Paul begins Romans 12 with a statement about appropriate service, even the service of love to one another, continues in ch. 13 with a discussion of authorities and taxes, carries on in ch. 14 with a discussion about how the weak and strong can make peace and produce harmony and concord, and then in ch. 15 urges that they accept one another and appeals to a spirit of unity.

But if the audience is to heed such exhortations the theological underpinnings must first be shown. What the reader/hearers ought to believe about God's plan of salvation and reconciliation for the Jew first and also for the Gentile must first be addressed at length before they can be exhorted to obey and so live out the union of all peoples in Christ. Put another way, chs. 1–11 tell what humans have done in their fallenness and how God has responded in Christ, and chs. 12–15 tell what Christians in Rome ought to do, on the basis of what God has done, as the proclamation of the gospel makes clear. God's character, the character of Paul, and the character of the audience are all at stake in what the Romans believe and how they behave on the basis of their beliefs.

Paul begins his discussion in v. 16 with the issue of shame. It could be that we have the rhetorical device *litotes,* saying in a more reserved and negative way what is meant as a positive, namely, "I am proud of the gospel."[3] The gospel is not mere words, it is power. It is "not one miracle among others. It is the epiphany of God's eschatological power pure and simple."[4] Of course Paul is not suggesting that there is some magic in the words themselves. He is talking about the powerful effect they may have when the Spirit applies them. There is perhaps a deliberate echo of Mark 8.38/Luke 9.26 in the beginning of this verse.[5] If so, then Paul is alluding to the fact that he stands in line with the Jesus tradition and Jesus' affirmation about witnessing about the Good News. The "post-Easter interpretation of the Christ event [is] being consciously formulated in continuity with the proclamation of Jesus."[6] Paul then improves his ethos with his audience by suggesting he is following the agenda of Jesus.

The term *sōtēria* occurs here for the first time in Romans and, as Cranfield points out, is used of the human relationship with God.[7] Paul uses another term *(ruesthai)* when he wants to refer to rescue from ordinary temporal dangers. He uses "salvation" of what occurs in past, present, and future. When it speaks of the future, it usually has in view deliverance from or beyond

3. See K. Grieb, *The Story of Romans: A Narrative Defense of God's Righteousness* (Louisville: Westminster/John Knox, 2002), p. 10.

4. E. Käsemann, *Commentary on Romans* (Grand Rapids: Eerdmans, 1980), p. 22; cf. N. T. Wright, "Romans," in *The New Interpreter's Bible,* vol. 10 (Nashville: Abingdon, 2002), p. 423.

5. See the discussion in J. D. G. Dunn, *Romans 1–8,* Word Biblical Commentary (Dallas: Word, 1988), pp. 38-39.

6. Dunn, *Romans 1–8,* p. 38.

7. C. E. B. Cranfield, *A Critical and Exegetical Commentary on the Epistle to the Romans* (ICC; Edinburgh: Clark, 1975-79), 1:87-91.

final judgment (Rom. 5.9; 13.11; 1 Cor. 3.15; 5.5; Phil. 1.19). 2 Cor. 6.2 and Rom. 8.24 and our present text show that it also involves a present experience, a result of what God has already done in Christ on the cross. What seems usually to be meant is the restoration of the image of God, the new creation, referring to the transformation that has already happened to the believer as a result of the finished work of Christ on the cross and in the resurrection (cf. 1 Cor. 1.18; 2 Cor. 2.15 for present tense references to salvation, and see Rom. 8.24, 30 for past tense references). Thus one can say "I have been saved, I am being saved, and I will be saved," but not "I am saved," if by that one means that the process of salvation is already complete. There is always the working out of salvation with fear and trembling to be done while one lives in the flesh (Phil. 2.12), and there is also the matter of deliverance from final judgment or through Christ's judgment in the future. One is not eternally secure until one is securely in eternity, not until one has passed through all three stages of salvation.

Notice the emphasis on salvation being for *all* who believe. This emphasis will be continued in 3.22; 4.11; and 10.4, 11. Paul preaches an inclusive rather than exclusive gospel, and here perhaps the real thrust is against notions that God has given up on his first chosen people or other sorts of inappropriate election mentality. Many Romans believed that the gods had favored them over other peoples, including Jews, as was shown by their success in wars and in building the empire. This sort of "election" mentality could well have aided in creating a belief in the divine superiority of Gentiles, and in particular of Romans over Jews. Anti-Semitism did not arise out of nothing in Rome but in part out of the belief in the superiority of one's own race or ethnic group. But the emphasis on "all" is reinforced and balanced by the reference to "to the Jew *first.* . . ."

Thus it is stressed that this salvation is for Jews first and also for Gentiles. In light of chs. 9–11 the meaning of this cannot be limited to the notion that Jews were first offered salvation and then Gentiles were. Paul still sees that God has a plan for the salvation of non-Christian Jews in the future.[8] But even the Jews' place is qualified by "to all who have faith," and Paul clearly means not just any sort of faith but rather faith or nodal trust in God through Christ.

In v. 17 we hear for the first time of the *dikaiosynē* of God. Some contextual matters should be considered at this juncture. First, there is a parallel between vv. 17 and 18 in that both speak of a revelation, but in v. 17 the revelation happens in "it," that is, in the gospel, while in v. 18 it is revealed from heaven. Second, Paul has been talking about the power of God unto salvation (v. 16) and it is natural to see *dikaiosynē* as having something to do with that. In fact, Paul is about to go on and discuss at least two of the attributes of God (1.18ff.), and there is no reason why he could not be referring to the righteous character of God in 1.17.

8. See pp. 236-50 below.

A Closer Look: Righteousness in the LXX, Early Judaism, and Paul

Dikaiosynē occurs over 300 times in the LXX, where it is used of both God and human beings. There can be little doubt that as applied to human beings, the term usually has an ethical rather than forensic flavor, indicating conduct that is pleasing to God, in accord with the Law, and morally correct (see Isa. 5.7). It is often used of a godly and moral person (Proverbs 10-13).

The noun phrase *dikaiosynē tou theou* ("righteousness of God") does not occur in the LXX, but there are two references to "the Lord's righteousness" (1 Sam. 12.7; Mic. 6.5), and some 48 times, most often in Isaiah or the Psalms, *dikaiosynē* is juxtaposed with a personal pronoun referring to God. Perhaps the most relevant of these references are those that juxtapose God's salvation and his righteousness, such as Ps. 51.14 or Isa. 46.13. But against the argument of D. Moo it is not correct to say that God's righteousness *is* God's saving intent.[9] Rather it is God's righteousness, which is to say his fairness and faithfulness to his promises, which prompts his saving activity. He will not allow something unjust ultimately to overwhelm his righteous ones.

Do we find the notion of righteousness as gift in the LXX? Moo points to Pss. 35.27-28 ("Let those who desire my righteousness shout and be glad. . . . And my tongue will declare your righteousness") and 51.14. But is this correct? Psalm 51 connects being rescued/saved with God's righteousness, but does not equate them. God's righteousness is the basis of his vindicating or saving the psalmist. It is the psalmist who is saved, but it is God's righteousness which is praised, as also in Psalm 35. However, Ps. 37.5-7 does refer to the believer's righteousness and the justice of his cause being made evident by God. It is not said that this righteousness comes as a gift from God. The attempt to connect God's righteousness and eschatological deliverance or salvation in Mic. 7.9 needs nuancing. There is nothing in this text about the believing speaker being righteous or reckoned as righteous. Indeed, what is said is that the speaker has sinned against God and will bear God's wrath until God pleads his case and establishes his right (7.8). Then it will be God's righteousness which he and his enemy will both see. Again, a transfer of righteousness or a conveying of righteous status is also not in view in Isa. 46.13. In the previous verse one hears "Listen . . . you who are far from righteousness. I am bringing my righteousness near . . . and my salvation will not be delayed." God's righteousness and salvation are mentioned together and the unrighteousness of the audience is mentioned in the same breath. I see no evidence that God's righteousness is simply equated with his saving activity, though they are often closely associated. There are, however, plenty of instances where God's righteousness is seen as the basis or motivation of his saving activity (cf. Ps. 31.1; Exod. 15.13; Ps. 71.2; Isa. 38.19; 63.7).[10]

But there are also plenty of references where God's righteousness expresses it-

9. D. Moo, *The Epistle to the Romans* (NICNT; Grand Rapids: Eerdmans, 1996), p. 81.

10. Moo, *Romans*, p. 82, recognizes that these references are a matter of association not identification.

self in judgment on either Israel's enemies or unfaithful Israelites. Here "justice" would be an apt translation, rather than "vindication" (Pss. 50.4-6; 97.2; Isa. 59.17; cf. Psalm 119 on the judgments of God's righteousness). In both vindication and judgment, God is the one who does what is right according to the situation and according to what he has said he would do.

Finally, texts like Ps. 71.1-2 in the LXX and *Epistle of Aristeas* 280 both quite clearly speak of human beings being made righteous or given righteousness so that they are enabled to act in a righteous or just manner. It would be wrong to say this concept is not to be found in early Jewish sources or in the Greek OT. I would submit that texts like Rom. 5.9 and probably Phil. 3.9 stand in this tradition.[11]

There are some striking parallels in the Qumran material to what is said in Rom. 1:17-18. In CD 20.20 we hear that believers should hold on "until salvation and righteousness are revealed for those who fear God." There as here salvation and righteousness are what must be revealed. They are still in some sense in the future, and the context in CD suggests that righteousness there refers to God's righteous action of judgment on sin, which will also entail deliverance for God's people.

Some have understandably stressed the forensic character of *dikaiosynē*, and so the term has often been translated as though it referred to a legal verdict, meaning pardon, acquittal, and thus a re-establishing of right standing with God. This is a frequent Protestant interpretation. In the Jewish discussion acquittal is something that transpires at the last day of judgment, not now.

Phil. 3.9 refers to believers not having a *dikaiosynē* based on works of the Law, but rather one that comes through the faithfulness of Christ and from God.[12] There at least it appears that Paul is talking not about an attribute of God but rather a gift from God to believers. This in turn leads to the traditional question of whether Protestant or Catholic exegetes are right about the nature of the gift. Traditional Catholic exegesis has talked about *dikaiosynē* as an ethical quality infused or transferred into the believer; it does not have to do just with some legal standing or status one has before God. It has both an objective and subjective dimension.

In Phil. 3.9 the discussion is about something that is true of believers. But when we consider some of the other Qumran parallels it seems unlikely Paul is referring even in Philippians to an infused righteousness. For example, 1QH 4.37: "You forgive the unjust and purify one from guilt by *your righteousness.*" Or again, 1QH 7.19: "in your righteousness you have raised me up," and 11.30: "purify me through your righteousness." In each case the righteousness belongs to God, not to the believer, but nonetheless is said to have an effect, even probably a subjective effect (purifying) on the believer.

But Paul's use of *dikaiosynē* is not monolithic. For instance, in 1 Cor. 1.30 and 2 Cor. 5.21, where Christ himself is called God's *dikaiosynē* (as are believers), what would it mean to say that Christ is God's right-standing, if we translated it that way? And further, what would it mean to say that we *are* God's right standing, rather than

11. See C. Talbert, *Romans* (Macon: Smyth and Helwys, 2002), p. 40.
12. See my discussion of this verse in *Friendship and Finances in Philippi* (Harrisburg: Trinity Press, 1994), p. 93.

saying we have right standing with God? It appears then that Paul can use the term in a range of ways.

The following conclusions about *dikaiosynē* seem warranted: (1) The term does not ever seem to refer in Paul's letters to any "innate" quality in a believer, not least because Paul believes all have sinned and fallen short of God's glory. (2) *Dikaiosynē* can in some instances, it appears, refer to the righteousness/justice of God himself, as in Rom. 1.16-17. But (3) Paul's main concern is not with abstract qualities in God, but rather with God's saving purposes, and so with the effect of the righteousness of God on human beings, as Phil. 3.9 makes clear. This last usage is similar to what we find at Qumran. It is God's righteousness which has an effect on believers. (4) This effect comes about through the believer's faith. (5) Paul uses *dikaiosynē* in conjunction with his soteriological language about the saving work of Christ. He does not use it in conjunction with the exercise of God's wrath (unlike *orgē* in Rom. 1.18), which distinguishes the Pauline usage from what we find sometimes in the LXX. But on the other hand, it would appear that Paul sees God's righteous wrath as the negative expression of the same aspect of God's character — his justice, holiness, and righteousness. (6) The forensic notion of legal standing cannot be read into all the uses of the term by Paul.

We will have to evaluate the Pauline usage of *dikaiosynē* and its cognates on a case-by-case basis as we work through Romans. For now, it is sufficient to say that Paul believes that God saves the ungodly and that that salvation is a gift. It involves a declaration of no condemnation, as Rom. 8.1 makes evident. There is then probably some forensic overtone to some of Paul's discussion, but not as much as is often thought,[13] and the notion of salvation as a gift is important to Paul. There is also some truth to the claim that *dikaiosynē* is a relational term, by which is meant God or a person is "righteous" or "just" in relationship to someone else.[14] How *dikaiosynē* fits into the Pauline eschatological scheme of things we shall see.[15]

---

13. See Talbert's remark in *Romans*, p. 39, about the assumption of a courtroom sense in the early Jewish use of the term: "The declarative, courtroom component, while present ([e.g. in] LXX Isa. 50.8), is minimal."

14. See C. Bryan in *A Preface to Romans* (Oxford: Oxford University Press, 2000), pp. 76-77.

15. It is interesting that most of the Church Fathers were quite clear in their belief that the phrase "the righteousness of God" referred in the first instance to an attribute of God and secondly to a derived attribute of believers obtained through faith, and not to something like the concept of God's covenant faithfulness. Cf. the difference of emphasis with the discussion in Wright, "Romans," pp. 396-404, or Grieb, *The Story of Romans*, pp. 12-13. In other words, it is not simply a cipher for the notion that God will be true to his promises to his people and so keep his Word, though that notion is not excluded. Sometimes the Fathers saw this righteousness as the basis of a believer's right-standing and so "justification" as well (e.g., Ambrosiaster, who speaks of God justifying the ungodly and also sees the citation of Habakkuk in Romans 1 as indicating that it is the "just" person who will live by faith). See the discussions of the Fathers on this righteousness in G. Bray, ed., *Romans* (Ancient Christian Commentary on Scripture; Downers Grove: InterVarsity, 1998), pp. 30-33.

Having partially worked our way through one difficult issue, we now are confronted with another in the phrase *ek pisteōs eis pistin* in v. 17. The notion that this is simply an intensified way of saying "by faith" or "by faith alone" is well known. But this translation entirely ignores the usual force of the preposition *ek*. One could also argue that *ek pisteōs* modifies the noun phrase "the righteousness of God," not the verb "revealed." Cranfield argues for this view and takes it to mean "right-standing from God by faith."[16] The word order certainly does not favor such a view, and one suspects that Cranfield reads back his understanding of the Habakkuk quotation (taking it to mean "the righteous by faith shall live") into this part of the verse.

But there is a further problem with the Habakkuk quotation. Hab. 2.4 could be read to mean either "the righteous will live by their faith" or perhaps "the righteous will live by their faithfulness." Habakkuk's concern is with life on earth and how it should be carried out, not with the gift of eternal life. Paul's quotation of this text is nearer to the LXX than the Hebrew, but is not verbatim even from the LXX. It is more of a paraphrase of sorts. The Hebrew reads "the righteous shall live by his faith/faithfulness."[17] It is clear enough that the text of Habakkuk has as its context a revelation which should be written down and which speaks of the end, including judgment on the wicked. Cranfield takes Paul's quotation of Habakkuk, as we have seen, such that *ek pisteōs* modifies the subject rather than the verb, but both the Hebrew text itself and probably both recensions of the LXX (see below) seem to suggest otherwise. As Talbert puts it, "If Paul had intended to associate 'out of faith' with 'the righteous one,' he would have written *ho de ek pisteōs dikaios*."[18]

Here we must compare Gal. 3.11, where the same portion of Habakkuk is quoted. It seems clear in this instance that Paul is not referring to Christ.[19] His concern is with what is or should be the case with the Galatians. I see no compelling reason to introduce Christ in Rom. 1.17 either. There are in fact two versions of the LXX text. LXXa understands the Hebrew to mean "my righteous one shall live by his faithfulness" while LXXb understands it to mean "the righteous shall live on the basis of my (that is, God's) faithfulness." Since in neither Galatians nor Romans does Paul bring in the pronoun "my," it seems clear that he is focusing on what is true of the believer, not what is true of God or Christ.[20] What is notably in common in the case of both the Hebrew text and

16. Cranfield, *Romans*, 1:100-102.

17. This is the reading found at Qumran as well; see 1QpHab 8.1-3.

18. Talbert, *Romans*, p. 42.

19. On all of this see R. Watts, "'For I Am Not Ashamed of the Gospel': Romans 1.16-17 and Habakkuk 2.4," in *Romans and the People of God*, ed. S. K. Soderlund and N. T. Wright (Grand Rapids: Eerdmans, 1999), pp. 3-15.

20. See my discussion in *Grace in Galatia* (Grand Rapids: Eerdmans, 1998), p. 234, as opposed to R. B. Hays, "The Righteous One as Eschatological Deliverer: A Case Study in

the two versions of the LXX is that "faith/faithfulness" modifies "shall live" not "the/my righteous one." There is no good reason to think that Paul is viewing the text any differently. Therefore the quotation is about the righteous one living by faith or faithfulness. In short, it is about the sort of thing Paul will discuss in Romans 12–15.

This brings us back to the phrase "from faith unto faith." I would suggest it means "From the faithful one unto those who have faith."[21] "The faithful one" may be God, or it may be Christ, since he is seen as the means through or from which the revelation of God's righteousness comes. Proof we are on the right track in reading the phrase in this way is found in the very similar phrase in 3.22, which not coincidently is part of an amplified or expanded version of the *propositio.* "Paul's summary of 'the gospel' in 1.3-4 and his summary of 'God's righteousness' in 1.16-17 will do further business with each other as the work progresses, and their contrapuntal interweaving will support other tunes, other harmonic progressions."[22]

Bridging the Horizons

Salvation is of course a familiar term in Christian circles, and much of the church is used to thinking of it in almost exclusively spiritual terms. It is interesting that *sōtēria* in Greek literature outside the NT normally refers to being rescued, healed, or helped in some temporal or temporary way during this lifetime. Paul's concept of salvation does include such ideas, but clearly his focus is elsewhere. When he says that the person who is righteous by faith will live, he is not referring to longevity on this earth. He is referring to that other way of speaking of salvation — eternal life.

He speaks of the gospel as "power." He does not merely mean that the words that one proclaims may be powerful. He means that the gospel is a vehicle that a powerful God uses to change lives and so save people. I once heard Fred Craddock tell the story of a young female student at Emory who came into his office mystified. She explained that she was not a Christian and had not attended church. There came a time when she had reached a low ebb in her life and in fact had intended to commit suicide. She had gone to a high bridge and was going to jump into the river below. What stopped her was that suddenly as

Paul's Apocalyptic Hermeneutics," in *Apocalyptic and the New Testament: Essays in Honor of J. Louis Martyn,* ed. M. Soards and J. Marcus (Sheffield: Sheffield Academic Press, 1988), pp. 191-225.

21. See Dunn, *Romans 1–8,* pp. 43-44.
22. Wright, "Romans," p. 427.

she was about to jump a verse of Scripture popped into her mind: "My life is not my own. I have been bought with a price."

The young woman came and asked Dr. Craddock, the great NT scholar and homiletician, to explain what had happened to her. He began to ask her questions. "Are you sure you have never read the Bible?" "Yes," she said, "quite sure." "Are you sure you have never attended church?" "Yes," she said, and then she hesitated, "Oh, when I was a little girl my grandmother took me to vacation Bible school." "Do you remember anything about that?" Craddock asked. "Only that we were asked to write out some sentences on little slips of paper and memorize them. I guess they were Bible verses." Craddock smiled and said, "You see, God stored that gospel word up in your heart, so that one day it would save you." And so indeed it had.

Argument One, Part One — 1.18-32: The Unbearable Likeness

It will be well to summarize in advance the flow of Paul's theological arguments in 1.18–11.36 in order to map out his rhetorical strategy. This way, we will have a framework in which we may evaluate his individual arguments along the way. Otherwise, it is all too easy to get bogged down in the dense texture of the individual arguments. The intended effect of the theological arguments is cumulative, climaxing in chs. 9–11. If one misses this fact, one can set the emphasis in the wrong place, as so often has happened when bits and pieces of Romans have been used to build theological systems which Paul, as an early Jewish Christian, would hardly have recognized as his own.

Paul's audience is mainly Gentile Christians, and it is their beliefs and their behavior he is mainly concerned about altering. The problem is that he is dealing with entrenched habits of the heart and, furthermore, does not have the same clout he would have if his audience were mostly his own converts. What sort of rhetorical strategy then will work in such a situation?

Paul chooses to use foundational arguments that have a leveling effect, putting Gentile and Jewish Christians on the same footing. This, in effect, raises the status or standing of the Jewish Christians, who are currently at a disadvantage in Rome. Paul on the one hand will argue that all have sinned and fallen short of the glory of God, so any attempts by Gentiles to portray themselves as inherently better than Jews or Jewish Christians or more favored by God will not work. On the other hand, Paul will make clear that God's plan of salvation by grace through faith, while in essence impartial, does not mean that God will renege on promises to those he already had a relationship with before Christ — namely Jews. Supersessionist rhetoric in Rome is undercut.

It is especially important that this sort of rhetorical strategy come from someone like Paul who, while a Jew, is nonetheless widely recognized to be the

apostle to the Gentiles. The assumption in the Gentile church would presumably be that if anyone knows what the case is with the relationship between
Gentiles and God, it is Paul. Paul's first leveling argument in 1.18-32 will deal
with all persons outside Christ, but in particular Gentiles and their fallen condition and sin. He will then in a diatribal format deal with Jews outside Christ,
which, while also a leveling argument, also preserves the priority and privileges
bestowed on Jews by God. These arguments, very much like the first arguments
we find in Galatians, are based on human experience. Paul then in 3.21-31 will
revisit, revise, and expand the *propositio* in preparation for a second line of argumentation, this time not from experience but rather from ancient written
authorities, namely the Scriptures.[1] This sort of argument from Scripture, with
some pauses to draw conclusions based on scriptural stories, will continue right
through chs. 9–11.

In ch. 4, as in Galatians 3, Paul will appeal to the example of Abraham in
Scripture. Paul has not changed his views about the role of the Law and the Mosaic covenant, but, because he is dealing with a different situation than in
Galatia, where opponents were attempting to persuade the Galatians to Judaize,
how he presents the Law differs somewhat in Romans. There is no need to
polemicize against the Law, for the Roman Gentile Christians show no signs of
being about to get themselves circumcised and submit to the Mosaic covenant.
To the contrary, they are more likely to devalue the Law and the Jewish heritage
in general.

Nonetheless, Paul will still make clear in Romans that the Christian,
whether Jewish or Gentile, is not to submit to the Mosaic covenant. Christ is the
end of the Law or Torah so far as it being either a means of salvation or an obligatory way of responding to God's gift of salvation (ch. 10). In other words, it is
not just works-righteousness that Paul does not affirm for anyone, it is also
covenantal nomism, if the covenant in question is the Mosaic one.[2] Christians
are under a new covenant, which has a new Law, even though that new covenant
involves the reaffirmation of portions of the Mosaic covenant. Paul then will discourse on this new way for all to respond to God's grace in chs. 12–15. Among
other things it involves a new sort of graciousness and tolerance for differing
practices in regard to worship and eating and other matters. Things which were
previously seen as obligatory in Mosaic Law are now seen as blessed options.

1. Melanchthon calls the Abraham argument the first "proof" of the main proposition,
and he is quite right about this conclusion. This means the arguments that precede the amplified version of the proposition in Romans 3 are ground-clearing as well as leveling arguments ("all have sinned . . ."). They help remove the obstacles in the way of Paul making the
case for his gospel and for how it can be lived out in a practical way in Rome.

2. See now the discussion in A. A. Das, *Paul, the Law, and the Covenant* (Peabody:
Hendrickson, 2001).

Argument four, found in 5.1-11, is in fact a continuation of argument three about Abraham, and in this argument Paul will explain what follows from or is implied by (note the "therefore" in 5.1) the Abraham argument. Unlike in Galatians, where Paul takes an example from everyday life (Gal. 3.15ff.) before returning to another argument based on a very creative handling of Scripture (Sarah and Hagar, Gal. 4.21–5.1), in Romans Paul will proceed directly in argument five (Rom. 5.12ff.) to another act of persuasion based in Scripture, this time grounded in the story of Adam. It is unfortunately seldom noted that the story of Adam is either the text or the subtext for not only argument five, but all the way through Romans 7. This story, which tells what is true of all humanity (for all have died in Adam), underlies and undergirds everything that is said from 5.12 to 7.25. Of course Paul will intersperse comparison and contrast between those who are in Adam and those who are in Christ along the way, but it was the fundamental failure of Luther and before him of Augustine not to see that ch. 7 is not an attempt to describe the condition of the Christian. Adam's experience is described in 7.7-13 (where the "I" stresses that we were all "in Adam"), and then Paul will describe in 7.14-25 what is presently true for those who are still "in Adam" and outside Christ. The rhetorical technique of intercalation allows Paul in 7.25a to introduce the argument which will begin in 8.1 about the condition of those who are in Christ, and then conclude the previous argument in 7.25b.

The argument in ch. 8, much like what we find in 5.1-11, is in fact a drawing out of the implications and conclusions for Christians of what has been said in 5.12–7:25. Notice the "therefore" followed by "now" which begins ch. 8. Paul will describe here what is "now" positively the case for those who are in Christ. He has foreshadowed and prepared for this discussion in 7.4-6. While it is understandable, in view of the powerful rhetorical conclusion to this argument at the end of ch. 8, that many see an end to the main theological discussion here, this is a fundamental mistake. The *probatio* does indeed end with a flourish at the end of ch. 8, but as in Galatians, where Paul concludes the theological arguments with the allegory of Hagar and Sarah, which is a *refutatio,* here too in Romans a *refutatio* thoroughly grounded in Scripture is presented in chs. 9–11 which are the climax of the theological arguments. This is of no small importance because, according to the rules of rhetoric, the last major argument is the one that the rhetor wants his audience to feel the impact of the most. By the principle of end stress, it is this argument which is most likely to be the most revealing about the actual situation in Rome's Christian community and is most likely to present Paul placing his cards most clearly on the table as he prepares to come and visit the Roman Christians. It is no accident that Paul concludes this argument, and not the one in ch. 8, with the doxology in 11.33-36. At the end of ch. 11 Paul has reached the climax of his theological and philosophical arguments and must turn to their pragmatic, political, and ethical implications, which he does in the arguments in chs. 12–15.

So Paul has pursued on a grander scale a rhetorical strategy and technique similar to what we find in Galatians: first arguments grounded in experience, then arguments grounded in Scripture, and then practical arguments based on what has preceded in the discourse.[3] There is nothing haphazard or careless about Paul's approach. The imperative will indeed be well grounded in and prepared for in the indicative. The intended rhetorical effect of all of this is a leveling effect coupled with a unifying effect. Leveling was needed if unifying was to happen. In Paul's view Jew and Gentile united in Christ needed to be modeled in Rome as well as elsewhere in the empire, and before he could really elicit the support of Roman Christians further west, there needed to be this sort of effort at overcoming separation and divisions in Rome. Both the theological and the practical arguments are intended to further that larger aim.

The largely Gentile audience needed, in addition, to embrace Paul's vision that God has given up on no one, not even on Jews who have hitherto rejected Christ. Paul's theology of election in Christ and of Christ as the Elect One does not entail the notion of God's permanent rejection of any living being, and certainly not from "before the foundation of the world." Whoever will respond in faith to God's grace may come, for God in Paul's view is an equal-opportunity Savior of both Jew and Gentile, both male and female, both slave and free, regardless of previous sin and rejection of God. The continuing mission to the West could not be grounded in the false idea of rejection following election when it comes to Jews, or even of a selection within election which amounts to eternal soteriological rejection. In short, the continuing mission could not be grounded in the view that God had replaced his first chosen people with another one, for that would mean that God was unfaithful.

Indeed, as Paul embarks on the journey to Jerusalem to present the collection, he seems to see it as a symbol of the desire of the largely Gentile church to be united with the largely Jewish mother church in Jerusalem, and so for the prophecies to be fulfilled of the in-gathering of the Gentiles into the people of God, as recognized in Zion, so that salvation for all, for the Jew first and also for the Gentile, could be celebrated in Jerusalem. Paul hopes that the Roman Christians will catch the vision and will support what he goes to do in Jerusalem, in preparation for his own visit in Rome. If they do that, they will have to own and embrace the rhetorical force of the discourse we call Romans.

---

3. Some time ago, J. L. Martyn, "Romans as One of the Earliest Interpretations of Galatians," in his *Theological Issues in the Letters of Paul* (Nashville: Abingdon, 1997), pp. 37-45, posited that Romans was a reworking of some elements in Galatians. There is some truth to this, not only at the level of ideas, but also as we have seen in regard to the rhetorical structure of both documents.

For the wrath of God from heaven is being revealed against every form of ungodliness and human injustice obstructing the truth in unrighteousness, for what may be known of God is evident among them, for God has made himself evident to them. For since the creation of the universe his invisible nature, I mean his eternal power and deity, being understood, are perceived, so that they are without excuse. For, knowing God, they did not glorify or give thanks to him as God, but rather were made empty-headed in their speculations and were darkened in their hearts without understanding. Asserting themselves to be wise, they were made foolish and exchanged the glory of the incorruptible God for the likeness of images of corruptible humans, birds, four-legged creatures, and reptiles.

For this reason, God handed them over to the desires of their hearts unto the impurity of the degrading of their bodies with one another. They exchanged the truth of God for a lie and worshipped and served the creature rather than the Creator, who is blessed forever, amen. Because of this God handed them over unto the dishonorable lusts, for females exchange the natural function for that which is against nature, and similarly males, leaving the natural function with women, burned in their desire for one another, man in man, perpetrating the indecency and receiving the inevitable corresponding penalty of the perversion of themselves in one another. And just as they did not put to the test the knowledge of God they had, God gave them up unto a discredited mind, to do that which was not fitting — the full range of all sorts of unrighteousness (evil, greed, malice, full of envy, murder, rivalry, deceit, malignity; whisperers, slanderers, God-haters, insolent, arrogant, boastful, inventive scoundrels, rebellious sons, without discernment, treacherous, devoid of natural affection, merciless),[4] who, knowing perfectly well the just pronouncements of God, that those doing such things are worthy of death, not only continue to do such things, but even approve of those practicing such things.

How will Paul begin his arguments, hoping to persuade his audience to change? Horace in *Ars Poetica* 191-92 says that as a rule one must not introduce a god into the plot of one's story unless things have gone so far wrong that only a deity could untangle the mess.[5] When Paul paints his picture of a world gone wrong in the arguments leading up to the restatement of the *propositio* in

---

4. Remarkably, there are no major textual issues in this argument except that there is some variation in the vice list in v. 29 in different manuscripts. The Textus Receptus, following a few other manuscripts, inserts *porneia*, sexual immorality, at the head of the list. It is possible that it was added because of the similarity it has to the word "evil" in Greek (*ponēria*). One could envision a manuscript in which the letters of *ponēria* were transposed, and thereafter, for fear of leaving something out, both terms were included in this manuscript tradition. However, the fact that א, A, B, and various other good manuscripts do not include the term probably means it is not original. See B. M. Metzger, *A Textual Commentary on the Greek New Testament* (3rd ed.; London: United Bible Societies, 1971), p. 447.

5. See C. Talbert, *Romans* (Macon: Smyth and Helwys, 2002), p. 55 on this.

3.20ff., Christ is nowhere mentioned except in passing at 2.16. The argument moves from plight to solution, even if Paul has thought through the plight in light of the solution.[6] Basically he will be dealing with God's righteousness in two veins — the righteousness of God as expressed through the gospel and responded to as such is connected with salvation, but if one experiences God's righteousness outside that gospel context, it leads to condemnation and judgment, as 1.18ff. will make evident.

Underlying the discourse in 1.18–3.20 is not merely Jewish polemics against Gentile vice, but quite specifically the sort of discussion one finds in Jewish sapiential literature. In particular, Paul draws repeatedly on the Wisdom of Solomon in Romans 1 (and again in ch. 9) to help make his case. This was already noticed by W. Sanday and A. C. Headlam, who offered the following list of parallels:

Romans	Wisdom of Solomon
1.20	13.1, 5, 8 (cf. 2.23; 18.9): since God is knowable, humans are not excusable.
1.21	13.1
1.22	12.24: idolatry is the source of all sorts of evil.
1.23	12.1; 14.8, 12; 13.10-14
1.24	14.12
1.25	13.17; 14.11, 21
1.26	14.12, 16, 22-24: idolatry results in immorality, including sexual immorality.
1.27	14.31; 16.24: immorality is self-destructive and self-punishing.
1.28, 32	14.22b: idolatry leads to mental corruption.
1.29	14.25-27[7]

These parallels are both too numerous and too closely spaced together in both Romans and Wisdom to be coincidental. It is for a typically Jewish critique of pagan idolatry and immorality that Paul draws on Wisdom, but his purpose in thus showing that such pagans deserve God's wrath is to demonstrate their need for the gospel. He endorses the idea, found in Wis. 11.16, that "One is punished by the very thing in which one sins."

This critique undercuts any pride in Roman ethnic identity outside Christ. No reveling in the beautiful pagan temples, the Roman triumphs, or the

---

6. On which see E. P. Sanders, *Paul and Palestinian Judaism* (Philadelphia: Fortress, 1977), especially the final chapters on Paul.

7. W. Sanday and A. C. Headlam, *Romans* (fifth ed., ICC; Edinburgh: Clark, 1902), pp. 51-52. I have supplemented their list with the help of Talbert, *Romans*, p. 63.

Roman social life will do. All pagan aspects of Roman culture fall under the searching criticism that it is all a matter of idolatry which in turn leads to immorality. False religion leads to sinful behavior. "The concept of making idols was the beginning of fornication, and the invention of them was the corruption of life" (Wis. 14.12). Since we know from 1 Corinthians 8–10 that Paul tried to implement his understanding of the Acts 15 decree by urging his Gentile converts in Corinth to stay away from temples where this sort of idolatry and immorality was believed to transpire,[8] it comes as no surprise that he is stringently against such conduct in Rome.[9] The net effect of this critique is that it deflates Gentile notions of cultural superiority and so places Roman Jew and Gentile in Christ on more equal footing.

In v. 18 Paul likely introduces a contrast with what has gone before by means of the *gar*. He has been talking about the righteousness of God as it is seen and expressed through the gospel and related to through faith. Now he will go on to explain what God's righteousness amounts to for those who have exchanged the truth about God for a lie, namely, God's wrath. God gives up such persons to their idolatry and moral iniquity.[10] Paul refers to those who are already experiencing the wrath of God, just as he has spoken and will speak of those who are currently experiencing God's salvation. God's wrath is already being revealed (present passive).[11] As with God's *dikaiosynē*, this is something already being made known and playing a role on the stage of human history.

There are always those who have difficulty coping with the notion that a loving God might also be a wrathful God. Cranfield responds to this concern or complaint helpfully:

> That Paul would attribute to God a capricious, irrational rage is more than improbable. But a consideration of what Dodd calls "the highest human ideals of personality" might well lead us to question whether God could be the good and loving God, if he did not react to our evil with wrath. For indignation against wickedness is surely an essential element of human goodness in a world in which moral evil is always present. A man who knows, for

8. See my *Conflict and Community in Corinth* (Grand Rapids: Eerdmans, 1995), pp. 186-230.

9. That Paul is here specifically envisioning what goes on in pagan temples, as well as in other pagan cultural venues, is probably indicated by the reference to the exchanging of God's glory for the sort of images and statues one finds in pagan temples.

10. E. Käsemann, *Commentary on Romans* (Grand Rapids: Eerdmans, 1980), pp. 37-38.

11. Clearly for Paul there is an already-and-not-yet dimension to God's wrath (cf. 12.19), just as there is an already-and-not-yet dimension to God's salvation. Paul is, however, not the only early Jew who spoke about God's wrath in the present tense (see, e.g., 1 Macc. 3.8; *Testament of Reuben* 4.4), nor is he the only early Jew who believed the eschatological age was dawning (cf. John the Baptist or some of the Qumran community).

example, about the injustice and cruelty of apartheid, and is not angry at such wickedness cannot be a thoroughly good man; for his lack of wrath means a failure to care for his fellow man, a failure to love.[12]

In other words, when we think of God's wrath we should not think of some irrational passion on the part of God, but rather of his righteous and wholly justified indignation against sinful belief and sinful behavior.

But how is God's wrath *now* being revealed against all forms of ungodliness? Doubtless it is right to point out that Paul believes he already lives in the eschatological age, in which God's salvation and judgment are and will be manifest. Probably, Paul is thinking along the lines of OT prophets like Joel who saw in mundane things like locust plagues, floods, and the like preliminary manifestations or foreshadowings of the day of judgment. So here vv. 24 and 26 hold the key to understanding this segment of the text. Because of pagan idolatry, God has given up Gentiles to the ethical consequences of their actions — to unclean and degrading behavior. Bad theology or worship, in a morally structured universe, leads to bad ethics. God's wrath is seen not so much in what he does, but in what he allows to happen. "He gave them up," says Paul repeatedly, probably echoing Ps. 106.41. Degrading worship leads to debauchery of the individual and to his or her ethical demise, and so there are both vertical and horizontal dimensions to sin.

Paul believes that all religious actions have ethical implications and personal consequences, as did other early Jews. For instance, *Jubilees* 21.22 urges that one must be cautious not to commit some major willful sin lest God deliver the sinner into the power of his own sin. More pointed however is *Testament of Gad* 5.10: "By whatever human capacity anyone transgresses, by that he is also chastised." "God's wrath, then, takes the form of God's giving humans up to the chaos for which we have voted."[13] What differentiates Paul's discourse from the usual Jewish polemics against paganism is that Paul believes that since the Christ-event has transpired the eschatological action of God for both salvation and judgment is already in play.

In v. 18 we hear of the pagans holding down or obstructing the truth in unrighteousness. Paul does not believe in either the noble savage or the totally ignorant pagan. Rather, he believes that sinful humanity, in this case pagans, universally repress the knowledge of God available to them and so are held accountable. As his argument will go on to suggest, he believes persons are judged according to the light they have received and what they do with that light. No one is condemned for not knowing God or Christ, but rather for suppressing and ignoring the knowledge of God they do have available to them.

12. C. E. B. Cranfield, *A Critical and Exegetical Commentary on the Epistle to the Romans* (ICC; Edinburgh: Clark, 1975-79), 1:109.
13. Talbert, *Romans,* p. 58.

Does *gnōston* in v. 19 refer to what is actually known about God, or to what is knowable about God? Against Cranfield, vv. 21, 28, and 32 suggest that Paul is not just talking about God making himself objectively known, so that it was possible for a pagan to know God to some degree. Rather, Paul is saying that in some sense they actually do subjectively know God.[14] Otherwise, they could not have exchanged this truth for a lie or suppressed this knowledge. Paul deliberately uses a different verb, *phaneroun* "make evident," to speak of what is apparent from examining creation, as opposed to "reveal," which Paul uses of the source of knowledge of God's salvation plan and Son. "Paul admits that God's uprightness is *revealed* in the gospel, but he also maintains that people can perceive or come to a certain awareness of God's 'eternal power and divinity' from reflection on what he has *made evident* in material creation."[15] Pagans are not judged for choosing not to avail themselves of knowledge of God but for rejecting the knowledge of God they actually have — knowledge that God exists and is powerful. *Gnōston* is an aorist participle and is much more easily understood to mean "having known." The complaint in v. 21 must be taken seriously.

Thus Paul is indeed talking about what has come to be called natural revelation in creation and natural knowledge of God based on this natural revelation. Unfortunately, that natural knowledge can be twisted, suppressed, misinterpreted, and totally perverted so that one ends up worshiping the creature rather than the Creator. And this is what Paul believes has happened. Thus again, the root problem is not ignorance but rather suppression of knowledge.

This comports with what we know of Greco-Roman reflection on such matters. For example, Cicero argues that when one examines the heavens and earth one cannot but believe that some god or higher power is responsible for such a magnificent, intricately designed, and enormous structure (*Tusculan Disputations* 1.29.70). In fact, in the Greek philosophical tradition, natural theology goes back at least to Plato (*Timaeus* 28A-30C, 32A-35A) and was continued by his successors (e.g., Aristotle, *De Mund.* 6.397b-399b). This tradition of natural theology is found in early Jewish thinkers influenced by both their own tradition and the Greco-Roman tradition (e.g., Philo, *Rewards and Punishments* 43-46; *Abraham* 33.185; Josephus, *Antiquities* 1.154-56). So Paul stands in a long and time-honored line of those who have reflected about natural theology. But behind natural theology is, in the case of these Jewish writers, a theology of natural revelation. Paul believes, as Rom. 1.19 states, that there is only knowledge of God available through nature, because God has chosen to reveal himself in that fashion. He does not speak of humans ascending to or pursuing knowledge of God on their own.[16]

14. See Cranfield, *Romans*, 1:106-22.
15. J. A. Fitzmyer, *Romans* (New York: Doubleday, 1992), p. 273.
16. See on all this Talbert's helpful discussion in *Romans*, pp. 60-62.

But why should people suppress what they know of God through God's self-revelation? Paul will not come to grips with that sort of question until he discusses Adam in ch. 5. It is well to keep in mind that "Paul's purpose here is less to show a universal condition of humanity than to describe for the people of his own world how the rejection of God leads to destruction and despair."[17]

Paul does not seem here to have in mind a knowledge of God that humans have because they are created in God's image or have a conscience and so a capacity for religious and moral judgment. In view of the mention of the beginning of creation in v. 20, it seems more likely that he has in mind the sort of creation theology one finds in Psalm 8.[18] A person knows God by examining God's creation. This is of course not to say that Paul believes there is a saving knowledge of God outside Christ and special revelation. He has already told us in v. 16 that the place where saving knowledge of the righteousness of God can be found is in the gospel.

V. 20 speaks of the invisible attributes of God, which is explicated to mean his "eternal power and deity." These things are revealed in creation, but in view of the fallen condition of human beings they do not help us much, for without new creation fallen persons only repress such knowledge. It is important to recognize that Paul is discussing fallen humanity in general here, and pagan humanity in particular. He is of course well aware that at various junctures in the Hebrew Scriptures Israel is depicted as also committing these same sorts of sins of idolatry (e.g., worshiping a golden calf) and immorality. But he will turn more specifically to those under the Law a little later in his discourse. He may speak mainly of Gentiles at first in this discourse because, though he believes salvation is indeed for the Jew first, he is mainly addressing Gentiles and wishes to confront them from the very outset.

A Closer Look: Two Ways to Misread 1.18-32

One of the perennial debates concerning Rom. 1.18-32 is over whether Paul affirms some sort of natural theology or a possibility of some sort of true knowledge of God apart from the gospel or special revelation. This debate is by and large a post-

17. L. T. Johnson, *Reading Romans: A Literary and Theological Commentary* (Macon: Smyth and Helwys, 2001), p. 32.

18. As G. Bray, ed., *Romans* (Ancient Christian Commentary on Scripture; Downers Grove: InterVarsity, 1998), p. 34, points out: "The Fathers generally believed in the possibility of coming to a true, albeit limited, knowledge of God by using the resources of the human mind to contemplate the mysteries of the universe. To their way of thinking, this did not open the door to a form of salvation by works. Rather it merely increased the horror of condemnation that humanity incurred for having turned away from God."

Reformation and even post-Enlightenment debate which the early Church Fathers were innocent of. Hard-line fideism does not seem to comport with what Paul is actually saying here. He does not deny that some things can be actually known about God from examination of creation. He also does not affirm that such knowledge amounts to saving knowledge of God. But what is evident in creation is not the same as what is revealed through special revelation and in particular through the Gospel. Käsemann, Nygren, Moo, and others have overreacted against the notion of a natural revelation of God's existence in creation. But the issue in Rom. 1.18-32 is not so much what is known through examination of the creation as what fallen persons do with that knowledge.

A second track that is not helpful in interpreting this material is to read the story of Adam into Rom. 1.18-32. Hooker,[19] Wedderburn,[20] and Dunn all have attempted to argue that Genesis 2–3 underlies this text, but, as Fitzmyer says, if any portion of Genesis is alluded to here it is Genesis 1.[21] But in truth, as we have pointed out, the real echoes are of Wisdom of Solomon 10–14, not Genesis 2–3.

Neither of these lines of argument helps us to hear Paul's words in light of either the early Jewish sapiential discussion which he is drawing on, or the rhetorical context of a largely Gentile audience to whom he is offering his act of persuasion.

Paul says of those he castigates in 1.18-32 that they are without excuse and are ungrateful, not even giving thanks to God for their existence. Instead, they have engaged in vain reasonings and useless speculations. In v. 21 we hear about how the heart is darkened by such speculations. Here as elsewhere Paul means by "heart" the control center of the personality, which entails thought, feeling, and will. It is Paul's view that human beings, created in God's image, will always worship something, and the only alternative to true worship in a universe where there is only one true God is worship of creation or one or another of God's creatures. Possibly Paul is thinking of the images of the emperor in Rome and elsewhere that were testimonies to idolatry (cf. Acts 17; Wis. 14.17: "When people could not honor monarchs in their presence, since they lived at a distance, they imagined their appearance far away and made a visible image of the king whom they honored, so that by their zeal they might flatter the absent one as though present").[22] According to v. 24 degraded minds lead to degraded bodies. Notice the repeated theme that "God gave them up" in vv. 24, 26, 28 to

19. See, e.g., M. Hooker, "Adam in Romans 1," NTS 6 (1959-60): 297-306, and "A Further Note on Romans 1," NTS 13 (1966-67): 181-83.

20. See A. J. M. Wedderburn, "Adam in Paul's Letter to the Romans," in Papers on Paul and Other New Testament Writers, ed. E. A. Livingstone, JSNTS 3 (Sheffield: Sheffield Academic Press, 1980), pp. 413-30; cf. J. D. G. Dunn, Romans 1–8, Word Biblical Commentary (Dallas: Word, 1988), pp. 53-62.

21. See Fitzmyer, Romans, p. 274.

22. See K. Grieb, The Story of Romans (Louisville: Westminster/John Knox, 2002), p. 28.

both a debased mind and debased behavior. "They were given over, not so they could do what they did not want to do, but so that they could carry out exactly what they desired. . . . To hand over means to permit, not to encourage or force. . . ."[23]

Vv. 26-27 are about as clear a condemnation of homosexual and lesbian behavior as exists in the NT. Paul speaks of actions, not inclinations, attitudes, or genetics.[24] He says quite literally that those who practice such behavior have exchanged the natural function of intercourse for that which is against nature. In both Jewish and Greco-Roman tradition there was a long history of seeing such behavior as "unnatural" or counter to the way God originally created and intended things to be (Plato, *Laws* 1.2; Ovid, *Metamorphoses* 9.758; Lev. 18.22; 20.13; Philo, *Abraham* 26.135; *Special Laws* 2.14.50; Josephus, *Apion* 2.25, 199; *2 Enoch* 10.4).[25] Paul certainly believes there is a natural order of things that God put into creation which ought to be followed. In v. 27 he speaks of a corresponding penalty for such "unnatural" behavior. "The punishment not only fits the crime, but directly results from it as well."[26] Such behavior is a constant means of putting God to the test. The just decree of God concerning all the listed vices is that those who do them deserve death — and yet God has sent his Son to call both Gentile and Jew to a better way, a way out of human darkness and fallenness. In Paul's view homosexual behavior flows naturally from idolatry in that it is a rejection of the creation order that the Creator God set up in the first place.[27] "For him it is a way in which human beings refuse to acknowledge the manifestation of God's activity in creation."[28]

Vice lists such as we find in vss. 29-31 were common in antiquity and are regularly found in Paul's letters (Rom. 13.13; Gal. 5.19-21; 1 Cor. 5.10-11; 6.9-10; 2 Cor. 12.20-21; Col. 3.5, 8; and undoubtedly there are echoes here of Wis. 14.23-26).[29] It is interesting that Paul tends to focus on the corruption of the heart or

---

23. Ambrosiaster, *Commentary on Paul's Epistles* 81.47; see Bray, *Romans,* p. 44. Cf. the comment of Chrysostom: "What could God have done about this? Could he have forced them to do what is right? Yes, but that would not have made them virtuous" (*Homilies on Romans* 3). In Chrysostom's view, neither human love nor human virtue is possible if all things are predetermined or compelled by God.

24. See the treatments of this difficult subject by R. B. Hays, *The Moral Vision of the New Testament* (San Francisco: Harper, 1996), pp. 379-406, and R. A. J. Gagnon, *The Bible and Homosexual Practice* (Nashville: Abingdon, 2001), pp. 229-303.

25. See Dunn, *Romans 1–8,* pp. 65-66.

26. N. T. Wright, "Romans" in *The New Interpreters Bible,* vol. 10 (Nashville: Abingdon, 2002), p. 433.

27. See the helpful discussion in C. Bryan, *A Preface to Romans* (Oxford: Oxford University Press, 2000), pp. 84-89.

28. Fitzmyer, *Romans,* p. 276.

29. One of the reasons Paul's rhetorical skill is often overlooked is because of what gets

mind here and so deals with the attitudes of mind from which individual sinful acts spring. This is probably no accident. In some respects this is much like what we find in 1QS 4.9-11, but for Paul's largely Gentile audience he may intend a deliberate resemblance to the vice lists found in the Greek philosophical tradition (see Plato, *Gorgias* 525; *Republic* 4.441c), particularly Stoicism. No less famous a Stoic than Seneca was an advisor and mentor to Nero at the very time Paul wrote Romans, and Seneca's influence and the popularity of Stoicism was surely not minimal in Rome. Thus it may indeed have been part of Paul's rhetorical strategy to offer up critiques of pagan culture that had some contact with the popular philosophy extant in Rome in that day. Such a critique might be more readily received by Gentiles than one which only echoed Jewish sources. As Epictetus said, "There are certain punishments assigned as it were by law for those who are disobedient to the divine dispensation" (*Discourses* 3.11.1). In v. 32 Paul implies that some knowledge of God still remains even when it has been repressed. One is still held responsible for what they have done with what they knew about God.[30] "This is written with the flourish of ancient rhetoric, in the style of the preacher of all ages, and would be recognized for what it is — a dramatic expression of a widespread malaise, of a human condition whose character as a whole is demonstrated by its failure to control or to find an answer to its most depressing features and worst excesses."[31]

Bridging the Horizons

Karl Barth tells a gripping story about a man out walking one winter night in his own region of Switzerland who is confronted suddenly with a blinding snowstorm. In the storm he loses his way and wanders in uncharted directions. When the storm subsides, he looks behind him and discovers to his shock and horror that he has walked across an only partially frozen lake with thin ice. From his place of safety on the shore, he gives thanks to God for his mercy on his foolish behavior. He should not have willfully wandered around in the blizzard, but simply stopped where he was when it began.[32] For a fallen person, given up to one's own desires and refusing to acknowledge God and his claim on one's life,

lost in translation. As Wright, "Romans," p. 434 points out, the last four vices listed have a rhyming and alliterative form — *asnetous, asynthetous, astorgous, aneleēmonas;* only the NIV has really effectively given a bit of the sense of this: "senseless, faithless, heartless, ruthless." Cf. the NJB: "without brains, honor, love, or pity."

30. See Talbert, *Romans*, p. 70

31. Dunn, *Romans 1–8*, p. 70.

32. K. Barth, "Saved by Grace," in *Deliverance to the Captives*, trans. M. Weiser (New York: Harper, 1978), pp. 35-42.

life is much like what happened to the man in Barth's story. One wanders around without being able to see the potential consequences of one's actions, never realizing one is teetering on the brink of disaster by such wandering. Paul's description of fallen existence, here especially of the fallen existence of Gentiles, comports well with Barth's story. It speaks well to the fact that, for fallen creatures, the image of God in which they have been created can be an unbearable likeness which they repeatedly try to efface by trying to erase the memory of God and to distort God's likeness in them by means of sinful beliefs and behaviors.

This passage implies quite a great deal about the nexus of belief and behavior. It assumes that bad theology, or at least deliberately ignoring good theology by ignoring God, leads to misbehavior. It also assumes something about the will of God. It assumes that there is both an active and a passive dimension to God's will. God does not actively will sin but does allow it to happen by giving people up to the lusts of their hearts. There is a problem if one ignores either of these truths. While it is of course true that human beings are not perfectly consistent (e.g., sometimes true believers misbehave, and sometimes those with a bad theology or almost no theology can act in ethically responsible ways), as a general rule it is true that what one believes affects how one behaves. At a minimum, if one believes that there is no God or will be no ultimate or final consequences to misbehavior, one is more likely to misbehave. Paul here is talking about something even more dramatic than that. He is referring to persons in rebellion against God who deliberately reject what they know about God and turn instead to sinful ways.

If, at the other extreme, one has a theology of election that does not allow for viable secondary causes, then ultimately one makes God the author of sin. Sometimes a work like Luther's *The Bondage of the Will* seems to leave no room for human beings to make viable moral choices and so rightly be held responsible for their misbehavior. Or again, Jonathan Edwards's *Freedom of the Will* can give the impression that all that freedom means is that human beings do not *feel* compelled by God to do what they do, when actually they could not have done otherwise. There is no genuine power of contrary choice. It is hard to see how this sort of theology escapes the criticism that it ultimately makes God the author of sin and is a form of determinism or even fatalism.

Paul does not say that God wills everything that happens. To the contrary, he says here that God gave up the people he describes to their own devices and will and choice of behavior. God allowed them to follow the path of sin because they had determined for themselves to go in that direction.

Another problem with determinism is that no good action should be seen as virtuous if a person could not have done otherwise, or at least there should be no talk of rewards and the like if a person did something good quite apart from their own intention and will. Both Jesus and Paul do speak of rewards for virtuous behavior.

This is not to deny that all good deeds done by fallen persons are done with the aid of grace, but grace is not normally seen as some inexorable force that predetermines how one will use the grace given. Grace is a power given that enables a person to choose the good. It does not usually force a person to do something. In other words, grace is usually something that can be resisted or positively drawn upon. There are moments in life, no doubt, when one is overwhelmed by grace, but this is by no means always the case. Sometimes we reject the leading and guiding of God's love and grace in our lives, and it is part of the divine mystery that God allows such things to happen, as Romans 1 says.

Argument One, Part Two — 2.1-16: Critique of a Judgmental Gentile Hypocrite

Rom. 2.1-16 is in fact a continuation of, or based on, the argument in 1.18-32.[1] 2.1 begins with the inferential conjunction *dio,* connecting it to what comes before. What differentiates 2.1-16 from what precedes is that here for the first time in Romans Paul uses the rhetorical technique known as *prosopopoeia,* impersonation, or better said, speech in character. We have a shift to direct address and the second person singular.[2] It has been recognized at least since the time of Origen and Chrysostom that Paul uses a variety of rhetorical figures and techniques in this discourse, including dialogue with an imaginary interlocutor (in diatribal format),[3] as well as impersonation. We actually find both of these techniques in Romans 2, as has been amply demonstrated by S. Stowers.[4]

There are two types of speech in character technique.[5] In the first type,

---

1. This is rightly stressed by C. L. Porter, "Romans 1.18-32: Its Role in the Developing Argument," *NTS* 40 (1994): 210-28.

2. See the discussion by Porter, "Romans 1.18-32," p. 223, although his thesis that Paul in the rest of his discourse sets out to refute the argument found in Rom. 1.18-32 will not fly. What is opposed in 2.1-16 is not the judgments found in 1.18-32, which reflect a revelation from God, but a posture of judgmentalism by one sinner against another.

3. Most recent commentators recognize the diatribal style being adopted and adapted here. See, e.g., J. D. G. Dunn, *Romans 1–8,* Word Biblical Commentary (Dallas: Word, 1988), pp. 78-79.

4. See especially S. Stowers, *A Rereading of Romans: Justice, Jews, and Gentiles* (New Haven: Yale University Press, 1994), pp. 16ff.

5. C. Bryan, *A Preface to Romans* (Oxford: Oxford University Press, 2000), p. 92 n. 68, is right that "In terms of rhetorical technique, in this section of his argument (2.1–3.20) Paul alternates between passages of *synkrisis* ('comparison') (2.12-16; 2.25-29), and passages of dialogue with the imaginary objector (2.1-11; 2.17-24; 3.1-9), concluding with a lengthy series of

the character of a known person is impersonated. In the second, a particular type of person (a husband, a general, a farmer, or the like) as well as his ethos or character is impersonated. In other words, both the person and his character are fictive in the second form of this technique. Various writers on rhetoric, including Cicero, Quintilian, Theon, Hermogenes, and Aphthonius discuss this rhetorical technique at some length, but, as is usually the case, Quintilian is the best summarizer of the collective wisdom on the matter:

> I regard impersonation as the most difficult of tasks, imposed as it is in addition to the other work involved by a *deliberative* theme. For the same speaker has on one occasion to impersonate Caesar, on another Cicero, or Cato. But it is a most useful exercise because it demands a double effort. . . . For orators of course it is absolutely necessary. [Types of persons as well as real persons are impersonated such as] sons, parents, rich men, old men . . . misers, superstitious persons, cowards, and mockers. . . . All these roles may be regarded as part of impersonation, which I have included under deliberative themes, from which it differs merely in that it involves the assumption of a role. (*Instit. Or.* 3.8.49-52)[6]

> This technique adds wonderful variety and animation to oratory. With this figure we present the inner thoughts of our adversaries as though they were talking with themselves. . . . Or without diminishing credibility we may introduce conversations between ourselves and others, or of others among themselves, and give words of advice, reproof, complaint, praise, or pity to appropriate persons . . . peoples may find a voice . . . or [we may] pretend that we have before our eyes things, persons, or utterances. (9.2.30-33)

Diatribe, that is, dialogue with an imaginary interlocutor, is a tool of deliberative rhetoric, not surprisingly since the original setting for deliberative rhetoric was the assembly where one would have dialogue or debate over the course of action to pursue or policy to enact. The *Rhetorica ad Herennium* 4.65 sees the diatribe as a deliberative figure in the form of amplification. The primary setting of diatribe was the school where the teacher employed the Socratic method.[7]

---

authoritative citations (3.10-18)." He demurs, however, from saying which bits are likely the voice of the objector and which are Paul.

6. Notice the stress on the association of this technique with deliberative rhetoric. The presence of this device at various places in Romans provides another strong piece of evidence for seeing Romans as deliberative in character.

7. See S. Stowers, *The Diatribe and Paul's Letter to the Romans* (Chico: Scholars Press, 1981), pp. 57ff. Also R. Bultmann, *Der Stil der paulinischen Predigt und die kynisch-stoische Diatribe* (repr.; Göttingen: Vandenhoeck and Ruprecht, 1984).

A Closer Look: The Making of a Diatribe

What exactly was a diatribe?[8] It was a dialogical form of argumentation developed by ancient teachers such as Teles, Dio of Prusa, and Maximus of Tyre in the Cynic and Stoic schools of philosophy. It may also have some origins even further back in the Socratic dialogues as presented in the works of Plato. The format was one of vigorous debate on some important topic "peppered with apostrophes, proverbs and maxims, rhetorical questions, paradoxes, short statements, parodies, fictitious speeches, antitheses, and parallel phrases."[9]

Paul uses diatribal form especially in Rom. 2.1-6, 17-24; 3.1-9, 3:27–4.25; 9.19-21; 10.14-21; 11.17-24; 14.4, 10-11.[10] Among characteristic elements of diatribe we see in Romans are dramatic exclamations such as *mē genoito* (3.4, 6, 31; 6.2, 15; 7.7, 13; 9.14; 11.1, 11)[11] and the language of drawing inferences — for example, *ti oun,* "what then?" (3.1, 9; 4.1; 6.1, 15; 7.7; 8.31; 9.14, 30; 11.7). Paul's form of diatribe is most like that of Epictetus, which makes us aware that he is using the diatribe in a pedagogical manner, not for polemics or to attack opponents.[12]

The diatribal style, with one exception (14.4, 10-11), is confined to the theological portion of the discourse. This may suggest that Paul felt that there would be more debate about the theological underpinnings of his parenetic advice than about the ethical advice itself. More importantly, the diatribe was one form of speaking which rhetoricians embraced and took up into their arsenals as part of the art of persuasion. Paul's prevalent use of this form in this particular letter tells us something important about what Paul is about in this document. He believes that he must pull out all the rhetorical stops not only to make an impression on his Roman audience but to change their settled habits of thinking about the relationships of Jews and Gentiles in and out of the church, among other subjects. The careful and competent use of rhetoric and the diatribal style is part of his means to establish his authority and ethos in relationship to an audience that lives in a rhetoric-saturated environment and so persuade them on a whole variety of things ranging from his gospel to his mission to the collection, and also in regard to their own beliefs and behavior. Paul thus believes that to be an effective communicator and apostle in relationship to Romans, one must do

8. See now C. Song, "Reading Romans through the Macro-Structure of the Diatribe," *SBL Seminar Papers 2001*, pp. 260-77.

9. J. A. Fitzmyer, *Romans* (New York: Doubleday, 1992), p. 91.

10. See Song, "Reading Romans," pp. 260-61, who lists as standard features: (1) vivid dialogue mode; (2) imaginary interlocutor addressed in the second person singular; (3) characteristic rejection phrases like *mē genoito*; (4) vocatives such as *anthrōpe.* Song's evaluation is based on a comparion of Romans to Epictetus's *Discourses* in particular.

11. See the discussion by A. Malherbe, "'Mē genoito' in the Diatribe and in Paul," *HTR* 73 (1980): 231-40.

12. See, rightly, Song, "Reading Romans," p. 269. I do not, however, agree that Romans 1–14 was a diatribe originally performed by Paul before his students! (See p. 272.)

as the Romans do. Furthermore, by the use of this distancing technique, Paul could more successfully critique his audience and their flaws in reason and praxis. Thus Paul can set about the business of "discriminating undesirable attitudes or sentiments through a fictive device, without directly confronting (and possibly alienating) the real audience."[13] Failure to recognize that Paul is using such rhetorical techniques in Romans has led to all sorts of false conclusions, for example, that he is combating actual Jewish or Judaizing opponents in his audience[14] or that he is describing himself and his struggles as a Christian in ch. 7.

It is clear that Paul is critiquing a type of person in 2.1-16 — the supposedly morally superior judgmental person, as v. 1 makes evident. In particular Paul is focusing on those persons who would condemn others in the terms found in 1.18-32 but exempt themselves from judgment, as if they were morally superior. But, in light of 2.17, is Paul already critiquing the Jewish morally superior type of person at 2.1, or someone else?

That Paul is dialoguing with an imaginary morally superior Gentile[15] makes good sense on several levels.[16] We know from ch. 1 and elsewhere that the majority of the audience is Gentile and that Paul is especially addressing Gentiles in Rome since he is the apostle to the Gentiles and so has some right to address them. Furthermore, there are signals within the discourse: (1) Paul is critiquing those who at some juncture had done or were still doing some of the things listed in 1.18-32 (see 2.3), (2) he refers to "those who sin apart from the Law" first in 2.12, and this is surely a reference to Gentiles, and (3) the aside in 2.14-15 is a specific comment about Gentiles.

As N. Elliott rightly stresses, Paul's rhetorical approach is that of *insinuatio.* "Paul does not address them directly: he will not apply any of his arguments to their own lives until ch. 12. They are nonetheless addressed implicitly."[17] Thus in the imaginary dialogue, though Paul is addressing a "type" of person who is not a Christian, nevertheless there is an implicit message for his

13. N. Elliott, *The Rhetoric of Romans* (Sheffield: Sheffield Academic Press, 1990), p. 186.

14. For an excellent critique of the assumption that Paul is engaging in a debate with a Jew already here in 2.1-16 see Elliott, *Rhetoric of Romans,* pp. 168-223. Elliott is right, however, unlike Stowers, that later in this chapter Paul will critique some early Jewish views of things through the diatribe beginning at 2.17.

15. Stowers, *Rereading,* p. 37.

16. Stowers is by no means the first to suggest that the interlocutor here is not a Jew. Chrysostom, for example, thought it was a pagan authority figure (an *archōn* — *Homily on Romans* 5.1). Even nearer the mark is T. Zahn, who suggests it is a pagan philosopher or moralist.

17. Elliott, *The Rhetoric of Romans,* p. 126.

Gentile Christians in the audience — namely go and do otherwise. Elliott rightly puts it this way: "no one in the audience should expect to be exempt from God's righteous requirement by virtue of an appeal to divine mercy that is not accompanied by true repentance (2.5) and good works (2.6-11). Paul wants the Christians in Rome to take that message seriously. There is no good reason, *on rhetorical grounds*, to insulate the letter's intended audience from the persuasive force of the apostrophe or its implicit call to repentance."[18] Paul's assumption in Romans is not different from his assumption in 1 and 2 Corinthians, namely that there are some partially socialized Gentile Christians in the audience who have brought some of their pagan assumptions and values into their church life, and they need to be sensitized to this fact.

Who then is Paul "impersonating" when he critiques the type of the morally superior Gentile and then the Jew? Here the focus is on "you" from the very outset in ch. 2.1 and 2.17. But in ch. 7, the focus of the impersonation is on "I." But I would suggest there is something quite subtle going on in ch. 2. Paul is in a sense impersonating himself as if he were already in Rome, addressing a mixed audience of Gentiles but also some Jews, and as if he were able to speak to them prophetically and with the voice of God. He imagines himself in that setting and is impersonating a person who already has considerable moral authority in relationship to the entire audience he is addressing. Perhaps he also imagines the rhetor, perhaps Phoebe in this case (see 16.1), who will orally deliver this letter, facing the audience, and turning first to the Gentile majority and then to the Jewish Christian minority as she attempts to persuade the audience, speaking for Paul. It is of course difficult to deliver an oration in advance. It is like practicing a sermon when alone at home. It requires imagination and putting oneself into one's own public character and into the location and occasion when the discourse will actually be delivered. Paul has done that effectively in ch. 2.

Finally, we should note that D. A. Campbell has helpfully suggested that we should see the arguments in chs. 2–3 as a sort of rhetorical *reductio ad absurdum*.[19] Paul will argue that all have sinned and fallen short of God's glory, so that no one has a right to a morally superior attitude or position. Since no one wants to be judged on the basis of their deserts, which would lead to one degree or another of condemnation for all, not to salvation for some good Jews and Gentiles, and condemnation for others. Therefore, judging one another is summarily ruled out.

18. Elliott, *The Rhetoric of Romans,* p. 126.

19. See D. A. Campbell, "A Rhetorical Suggestion Concerning Romans 2," *SBL Seminar Papers 1995,* pp. 140-67. Campbell's full spelling out of the argumentative logic of these chapters on pp. 165-67 is very helpful.

Therefore, you (singular) are without excuse, oh human being, whoever you are who judge, for in the matter for which you judge the other person, you condemn your own self, for you are doing the same things, you judger. But we know that the judgment of God is according to truth upon those doing such things. But you (singular) think about this, oh human who judges others for doing such things, and yet you do the same thing, because you yourself, will you escape the judgment of God? Or do you make light of the wealth of the kindness and the tolerance and his patience, being unaware that the kind act of God is meant to lead you to repentance/ change of mind? But according to your hardness and unrepentant heart, you are storing up wrath against yourself on the day of wrath and the revelation of the just judgment of God, who will give each his due according to his works. To those on the one hand according to the steadfastness of good works who seek glory and honor and incorruptibility [he will give] eternal life. But on the other hand to those out of self-seeking ambition and disobedience to the truth, letting themselves be persuaded by wrong, wrath, and rage — distress and anguish upon every human life doing evil, to the Jew first, also the Greek. But glory and honor and peace to all those doing the good, the Jew first, also the Greek. For there is no partiality with God. For whosoever sins outside the Law, even outside the Law will perish. And whosoever sins in the Law, through the Law will be judged. For not the hearers of the Law are righteous before God but the doers of the Law will be shown to be in the right. For when a pagan not having the Law does by nature the things of the Law, this one not having the Law is a law unto himself; whoever shows the works of the Law written in his heart, bears witness also of his conscience and with one another the inner debate, now accusing, now defending, in the day when God judges the secrets of human beings according to my gospel through Jesus Christ.[20]

Paul may seem on the surface to be speaking here about human beings in general, but in fact he is focusing on Gentiles. He provides a strong critique of those in his audience who might have the tendency to see themselves as morally superior to their fellow Gentiles, and indeed to their fellow Christians as well. One might well ask what sort of Roman Gentile might reflect such attitudes as we find critiqued here. There are at least two: God-fearers who had already imbibed the usual Jewish critique of pagan idolatry and immorality before becoming Christians, and Romans who had absorbed the philosophy of self-mastery reflected in the letters of Seneca and the writings of Epictetus.[21]

There were in fact many Romans who were not at all happy with the prof-

---

20. There are no significant textual problems in this section of Romans.

21. I disagree with N. T. Wright's suggestion that Paul is addressing an imaginary Jewish interlocutor in 2.1-16, as if that Jew was a pagan moralist. See his "Romans" in *The New Interpreter's Bible*, vol. 10 (Nashville: Abingdon, 2002), p. 438. 2.1-16 must not be lumped together with 2.17ff.

ligate lifestyle of many of their contemporaries and were on a quest to find a more peaceful and less emotionally and morally chaotic life. When such persons became Christians they already had an orientation that lent itself to the adoption of the sort of critique of the Gentile world found in Rom. 1.18-32. Paul then is cautioning such Christians: "God justly condemns the idolatry and vice of the Gentile world. *Therefore* you, a Gentile who has just emerged from that world, have no right to judge others as if you had attained some special status apart from your actual works (2.6-11). In fact, when you judge others you are manifesting a hubris, arrogance, and pretentiousness . . . that characterizes Gentile sin; you are doing the 'same kind of things'."[22] Unlike Stowers, however, I do not think Paul is accusing the "you" addressed here of committing all the same sort of moral sins listed in 1.18-32, or of idolatry. Paul is accusing such a person of judgmentalism and some hypocrisy, and thus of carrying forward a pagan life into Christian existence to some degree. S. K. Williams rightly points out that 2.1-16 shares with 3.25-26 the same language of restraint and the holding back of judgment for a time for amendment of life, which is language Paul uses to remind Gentiles of how God has been patient with them.[23] This language Paul has drawn from his Jewish milieu: "For with the other nations, the Lord patiently holds back from punishing them until they have attained the full measure of their sins . . ." (2 Macc. 6.14), though Paul uses the language to a different end.

There was a special timeliness to Paul's remarks here to his largely Gentile audience as has been made abundantly clear by Stowers:

> Paul wrote Romans early in Nero's reign, when golden age ideology and hopes may have reached their highest peak since Augustus. About the same time that Paul wrote Romans, Nero's tutor and advisor, Seneca, addressed *On Clemency* to the emperor. Seneca here presents Nero as the one who has the potential to save the empire from sin and usher in the golden age. The great multitude of the people are "unruly, seditious, without self-mastery, ready for mutual destruction if it throws off the yoke of rule." "We have all sinned: some in serious ways, some in less serious ways; some by deliberate intent, some impulsively or led astray by the wickedness of others." (1.6.3-4; cf. 1.22.2)[24]

Paul, like Seneca, recognizes that self-mastery is a good thing, but also, nonetheless, that all are still sinners and so cannot put themselves in a position of moral superiority.

22. Stowers, *A Rereading of Romans*, p. 103.
23. S. K. Williams, *Jesus' Death as Saving Event: The Background and Origin of a Concept* (Missoula: Scholars Press, 1975).
24. Stowers, *A Rereading of Romans*, p. 124.

From the first, in vv. 1 and 2, Paul contrasts human and divine ability to judge others. Humans lack not only the omniscience but also the purity of heart and character required to judge others properly. They are all too often guilty of the same sort of sins they criticize. Indeed, they may be more apt to critique the very sins they are most prone to. God however, unlike human beings, judges strictly according to the truth about a person and his or her words and deeds. Paul appropriately asks then how a person will escape the judgment of God after judging others for the same sins he or she is guilty of. It seems likely that Paul is in part offering some reflections here based on what he knows of the Jesus tradition, particularly on a saying like what we find in Matt. 7.1-2/ Luke 6.37-38.

As Fitzmyer points out, "human being" in vv. 1 and 3 should be compared to the use of the plural in 1.18. In neither case is Paul simply referring to all human beings. It is "you who judge" and perhaps by implication particularly those in Paul's audience who judge while still doing the sorts of things that are being addressed here. In other words, as interesting and generally valid as K. Barth's critique of human religiosity may be,[25] it is not the target of Paul's critique here. Paul's target is the morally judgmental person who is hypocritical. "It is not the presumption on one's moral merit, but the presumption on God's grace [and patience — see v. 4] — precisely in its undeservedness! — that Paul attacks here."[26]

Scholars have often puzzled over this entire passage because it seems to conflict with Paul's theology of justification by grace through faith. It seems on the surface to suggest that people will be judged on the basis of their works or deeds.[27] There are two viable explanations for this seeming contradiction: (1) Paul could indeed be focusing here on Gentiles outside of Christ (even though the critique of judgmentalism could also apply to those in Christ), and he does indeed believe that they will be judged on the basis of their works, just as he believes Jews outside of Christ will be judged on the basis of what they do in relationship to the Law's requirements. But of course Paul also believes, as 1.18-32 shows, that people will be judged, or, better said, are being judged, on the basis of what they have done with what they know of God as well. (2) While Paul believes that initial justification or conversion is by grace through faith, he also affirms that Christians' works, what they do after conversion, will be judged by God. This is clear from 1 Cor. 3.12-15, but 2 Cor. 5.10 is even more transparent: "we must all appear before the judgment seat of Christ so that ev-

---

25. See K. Barth, *The Epistle to the Romans* (New York: Oxford University Press, 1933).

26. Elliott, *The Rhetoric of Romans*, p. 185.

27. Notice how already in 1.18-32 persons experience the wrath of God on the basis of both what they do with their knowledge of God and how they behave as a result of that rejection of knowledge.

eryone may receive what is due them for the things done while in the body, whether good or bad." That is, while Paul certainly affirms salvation by grace through faith, he also affirms a judgment on the works of every human being, whether Christian or not. What is not made clear is the relationship between salvation by grace through faith and a judgment on all persons' works. Perhaps, 1 Corinthians 3 gives a clue: while a minister's works may prove to be worthless when tested on judgment day, he nonetheless will escape judgment of himself as a person, but only just — as through fire.

V. 4 suggests that the person Paul is critiquing shows contempt for God by not emulating God's behavior. If even God is patient, tolerant, and kind in order to lead fallen persons to repentance, how can the interlocutor not also be that way? *Metanoia,* "repentance," was a word familiar to Gentiles. It usually conveyed the sense of a change of mind in Stoic thought, or sometimes even remorse for something done in the past. The Hebrew equivalent is *shub,* which means to turn back or return. In Christian contexts the term is virtually equivalent to "convert." Paul does not use the word often (but see 2 Cor.7.9-10; 12.21). In fact all of these ideas — returning to God, changing one's mind, remorse for sin, and the understanding that such things are necessary dimensions of converting are within the semantic field of this term. If we ask how Paul's largely Gentile audience would have heard the term, they may have focused on the concept of "change of mind" and so of lifestyle.[28]

V. 5 seems to reaffirm the conclusion that Paul in the main is addressing non-Christian Gentiles here (but with an implicit warning to Christian Gentiles who act in the same way), for here he describes a person stubborn and unrepentant in heart who is storing up his quotient of wrath for the judgment day. V. 6 quotes Prov. 24.12 (cf. Ps. 62.12 for the reward side of judgment). Just as there is a tension or balance in Paul's theology between divine sovereignty and viable human choice, so there is also a tension between salvation by grace through faith and judgment of works. It is a mistake to affirm one side of the conundrum at the expense of the other, since Paul affirms both. Perhaps the real problem is that we cannot always see or understand, especially this far removed from the context of Paul's thinking, how such apparent antinomies go together.

The positive values listed in v. 7 — glory, honor, and immortality — are indeed things that Romans valued highly. Paul seems to be contrasting two groups of people here — the godly and the wicked. The one group seeks honor and immortality, the other their own selfish gain, which involves injustice. V. 10 has a triad similar to the one in v. 7, but here peace is substituted for immortality. But on closer inspection, Paul is not talking about those who are self-seeking, for clearly enough such persons are contrasted to "those who do good" in v. 8. No, Paul is arguing that those who persist in doing good have the pros-

28. See Dunn, *Romans 1–8,* p. 82.

pect of receiving from God glory, honor, peace, immortality, and everlasting life. In other words, Paul is talking about eschatological reward or blessing for the godly, not about the goals good persons should seek to establish for themselves in this life. His point in this paragraph is that God does not show favoritism to Jew or Gentile when it comes to rewarding the doing of good and punishing the doing of evil. J. Bassler has placed enormous stress on divine impartiality as a major theme for Paul in this letter.[29] While I agree that one should not overlook the stress on this idea in this passage,[30] as Elliott says "in Rom. 2.11-16 . . . the argumentative flow is not from other premises toward 'impartiality' but *from* God's impartiality as an axiom . . . *toward* the main thesis, 'there is no excuse before God's judgment' (cf. 1.20; 2.1) since God judges 'what is hidden in human hearts' (2.16)."[31]

The Law is brought into the discussion in vv. 12-16. There seems little reason to dispute that Paul has in mind the Mosaic Law. But precisely because Paul speaks of those outside the Law, he makes clear that they are not judged on the same basis as those under the Law. He says that such Gentiles who unknowingly but naturally conform to the Law are in a sense a law unto themselves.[32] Paul quite naturally, as a Jew, tends to view God's judgment of pagans as well as immoral Jews from the perspective he already had as a Pharisee. Judged by the standards of the Law, only those who do what the Law required would be declared legally righteous. Paul will however go on to insist later in his discourse that all have sinned and fallen short of God's glory.

V. 15 is important for our discussion. Here Paul is clearly talking about Gentiles, and he says of them that they have in a sense the Law written on their hearts, or, putting it another way, they have a conscience bearing witness to them, and there is an inner debate with the conscience accusing or defending a person's decisions and actions.[33] Paul does not view the conscience as moderns

---

29. See J. Bassler, *Divine Impartiality: Paul and a Theological Axiom* (Chico: Scholars Press, 1982).

30. See especially Bassler's "Divine Impartiality in Paul's Letter to the Romans," *NovT* 26 (1984): 43-58.

31. Elliott, *The Rhetoric of Romans*, p. 122.

32. Paul is surely not talking about Gentile Christians here. Those referred to here act "by nature" rather than by the Spirit; but see N. T. Wright, "The Law in Romans 2," in *Paul and the Mosaic Law*, ed. J. D. G. Dunn (Tübingen: Mohr, 1996), pp. 131-50; and also S. J. Gathercole, "A Law unto Themselves: The Gentiles in Rom. 2.14-15 Revisited," *JSNT* 85 (2002): 27-49. Note that D. Moo, *The Epistle to the Romans* (NICNT; Grand Rapids: Eerdmans, 1996), pp. 149-50; Dunn, *Romans 1–8*, p. 98; and Fitzmyer, *Romans*, p. 310, all stress that the phrase "by nature" is surely adverbial and modifies the verb "do." See A. A. Das, *Paul, the Law, and the Covenant* (Peabody: Hendrickson, 2001), pp. 178-82.

33. See the discussion by K. Snodgrass, "Justification by Grace to the Doers: An Analysis of the Place of Romans 2 in the Theology of Paul," *NTS* 32 (1986): 72-93.

often do, as primarily a negative inner voice. In his view conscience can either approve or disapprove, commend or condemn, render an account of what has been thought, said, or done.[34] This verse however provides us something of a foreshadowing of 7.14-25, where we hear of precisely the sort of inner moral struggle mentioned in passing here, and Paul is definitely not referring to a Christian here in 2.15. He has in view the Gentile pagan.

The reference to the Law written on the heart does not signal that Paul is referring to a Jew, and it need not do so in ch. 7 either, though we will discuss that matter at the appropriate point. Nor is Paul speaking purely hypothetically here. As Barrett says, Paul does not say "if Gentiles were to do the Law . . ." but rather "when they do the Law." Furthermore, Barrett is also right that Paul does not speak here of the Law written on pagans' hearts, but rather of the effect of the Law written on their hearts, so Jer. 31.33 is not in view here, any more than Gentile Christians are.[35] So Paul assumes that sometimes some Gentiles fulfill some of the requirements of the Law, just as Jews do. This does not mean they always do so, or do so perfectly, for Paul will go on to call all sinners. It does mean that there is some obedience to the will or Law of God among those who are not Christians, with Gentiles in focus here.

V. 16 concludes this first argument about and with Gentiles and their behavior. It includes the only reference to Christ in 1.18–2.16. Since Paul affirms that God will judge people "through Jesus Christ" (cf. 2 Thess. 2.8), it is clear that he does not believe in just an impersonal process of "wrath" which affects persons in the present in a moral universe (see 1.18-32), but also in a future eschatological Day of Judgment. There was already a tradition in early Judaism which could associate a messianic figure with future judgment (*Psalms of Solomon* 17–18; cf. Isa. 11.1-10).[36] Indeed, Paul says that such a notion is part of "my gospel," which must mean that he preached such an idea. 1 Thess. 1.9-10 seems to be a summary of what he preached on this subject. There Jesus is described as the One who will return from heaven and who rescues believers from the wrath to come. Here in Romans Paul also affirms that God will judge everyone's secrets. This presumably would involve not only deeds but also what is in human hearts as well.

34. The last participle, *apologoumenōn,* is a legal term and refers to rendering an account in the papyri (P. Wis. 55.1). See *NewDocs* 2:92.

35. See C. K. Barrett, *A Commentary on the Epistle to the Romans* (Peabody: Hendrickson, 1991), pp. 49-50.

36. See Wright, "Romans," p. 438.

Bridging the Horizons

It is often difficult to talk about human fallenness in a voluntaristic culture where life seems to be all about the plethora of choices one can viably make. Yet it is important, in light of what Paul says especially in Romans 2–3 and 5–7, to do so. Is it really the case that human beings have theologically and ethically fallen in such fashion that they cannot get up without divine intervention? Paul's answer to that query seems to be yes. But let us be clear about what Paul is not claiming. In the first place, he is not claiming that anyone is unredeemable. He is not suggesting that God has written off anyone from the outset or that anyone is so bad or the image of God in them so effaced that they could not be saved, redeemed, restored, righted. Nor, when Paul speaks of human fallenness, is he suggesting that our fallen natures are utterly corrupt. Sin is extensive, in that it affects every aspect of a human's being — body, mind, heart, will, emotions, and so relationships and behavior. But sin is not so intensive that it is impossible for a given person to do anything good or helpful or to ever be loving or kind or the like.

Though Paul does not speak about "prevenient" grace, he does say in Romans 2 that some persons outside of Christ not only have the effects of the Law written on their hearts but also have a conscience and sometimes do things that conscience can approve. People are not as bad as they might be, nor as good as they ought to be. "Total depravity" is an unhelpful phrase if it is taken to mean more than that sin has affected and corrupted every aspect of human nature. But at the same time the judgment that all have sinned (save Christ) and have fallen short of God's highest and best for them is rightly seen as a universal judgment. There are no exceptions. Thus it seems that Paul would be uncomfortable with the notion of a truly unfettered or free human will, though he would probably be willing to talk about a grace-enabled ability that allows the power of choice and indeed of contrary choice. Whatever is the case about this, Paul does indeed believe humans are responsible for their actions, and more particularly he believes that at the final judgment Christians especially will be held accountable by Christ for their actions. These things must be taken into account as one reads through Romans.

Argument Two — 2.17–3.20:
Censoring a Censorious Jewish Teacher

Having critiqued Gentiles outside Christ, Paul now turns to Jews outside Christ, continuing to use the diatribal format. It is no accident that Paul will appeal here to specific scriptural texts and ideas, as if he were indeed dialoguing with a Jew (e.g., 2.24; 3.4, 10-18). Indeed, a full third of this segment of argumentation involves quotations, largely from Isaiah and the Psalms. This favors the suggestion that there were at least a few Jewish Christians in Paul's audience, as well as former "God-fearer" Gentiles, to appreciate the rhetorical force and direction of such citations.

Paul thus employs a twofold rhetorical strategy in this section — both the diatribe and a catena of Scriptures — to reinforce the message he wishes to convey here, particularly that all stand guilty before God without a basis for boasting since all have fallen short of perfect obedience to the will of God. The message is, then, not only about the impartiality of God,[1] though that is emphasized, but also about the fact that all humans are equally in need of mercy in view of their sin, including particularly those Jews who should have been teachers to the blind but in fact proved to be less than good exemplars of what the Law required. Having the Law is no guarantee of doing the Law, and merely having it is no protection against God's judgment on disobedience, for all human behavior will be judged by God. Even being a Jewish teacher does not exempt one from God's righteous judgment on sin and so from the need to hear and heed the gospel proclamation.[2]

---

1. On which one must cf. Deut. 10.17; 2 Chron. 19.7; *Jubilees* 5.16; 21.4; 30.16; 33.18; *Pss. Sol.* 2.18; Sir. 35.12.

2. See A. T. Lincoln, "From Wrath to Justification," in *Pauline Theology*, ed. D. M. Hay and E. E. Johnson, vol. 3: *Romans* (Minneapolis: Fortress, 1995), pp. 143-44.

But if you call yourself a Jew, rely upon the Law, boast in God, know the Will [of God], and approve after testing the things which are best, being instructed from the Law, being persuaded that you yourself are a guide of the blind, a light of those in darkness, an instructor of the foolish, a teacher of infants, having the formulations of knowledge and of the truth in the Law — so then teacher of others, are you not teaching yourself? Preacher [preaching] not to steal, are you stealing? Saying not to commit adultery, are you committing adultery? Detesting idols, are you robbing temples? You who boast in the Law, are you dishonoring God through the transgression of the Law? For "the name of God through you is blasphemed among the Gentiles," just as it is written. For on the one hand circumcision is of use if you would do the Law. But if on the other hand you are a breaker of the Law, your circumcision has become uncircumcision. If then the uncircumcised keeps the just ordinances, is not his uncircumcision reckoned as circumcision? And he judges you, the one who by nature is uncircumcised [but] carrying out the Law, you who, though you have the written code and circumcision, break the Law. For [it is] not the one who is outwardly a Jew, nor the one who is outwardly in the flesh the circumcision, but the one who is inwardly a Jew, and has the circumcision of the heart in the spirit and not the letter, who [seeks] the praise not from humans but from God.

What then is the extra advantage of being a Jew or what benefit is there to circumcision? Much in every way. For first they were entrusted with the words of God. For what if some have been unfaithful? Will not their unfaithfulness nullify the faithfulness of God? Let it not happen! But God must be true, but all humans false, just as it is written: "so that you may be vindicated in your word, and victorious when you are tried." But if the unrighteousness of us serves to show God's righteousness, what shall we say? Is God not unrighteous to loose his wrath? (I speak according to human logic.) Let it not happen! Otherwise how could God judge the world? But if the truth of God abounds unto his glory in my refusal of the truth, why then am I judged as a sinner? And is it not just as we are blasphemed and just as some affirm that we say "Do evil so good may come"? The judgment of them is deserved.

What then? Are we superior? Not at all.[3] For we have already accused Jews and Gentiles to be under sin, just as it is written, "None are righteous, not even one. None are understanding, none are seeking out God. All have turned away,

---

3. There is a difficulty here in regard to what to make of *ou pantōs*. Does it mean "not at all" or "not altogether"? There is also the question of which verb and which form of the verb are original. The reading "are we superior" is surely to be preferred, and since Paul is trying to level the playing field between Jew and Gentile here, it seems more likely that the phrase in question would mean "not at all." For the issue here is not whether Jews have some advantages over Gentiles, which is admitted, but whether that makes them superior to Gentiles, and Paul's view is that it does not.

they have together become useless. None are about the doing of goodness, not even one. Open graves are their throats, their tongues deceive. The poison of snakes is upon their lips. Their mouths are full of curses and bitterness. Their feet are quick to shed blood. Ruin and misery [are] in their ways, and the way of peace they do not know. There is no fear of God before their eyes."

But we know that whatever the Law says it speaks to those under the Law, in order that all mouths might be stopped and all the world be held guilty before God. Therefore, no one, from works of the Law, will be declared righteous, from among all humans before him, for through the Law we become conscious of sin.[4]

In his tour de force argument to provide us with a real rereading of Romans, S. Stowers is able to point out how harmful the misreading of Rom. 2.17–3.20 has been for the history of Christendom since the Reformation. He points out that the attempt to see in this passage a characterization of all Jews or the typical Jew or Judaism in general has caused an enormous amount of harm, not least to efforts at Jewish-Christian dialogue. It is thus important to rightly understand what is going on in this passage and to be especially clear as to who the imaginary interlocutor is that Paul is dialoguing with in diatribe format here.[5] Just as Paul's dialogue with the judgmental and hypocritical Gentile in 2.1-16 was not intended to be a broadside against any and all Gentiles, so too it is a serious mistake to see 2.17–3.20 as a broadside against all Jews, not least because Paul provides us with more than enough clues to make evident this is not the case.[6]

In the first place, Paul tells us in vv. 19-20 that he is dealing with someone who fancies himself a teacher, and not just any sort of teacher, but a teacher for both those who are in the dark and are spiritually blind and those who are foolish and mere infants. The ABCs that this teacher is teaching and preaching in fact seems to boil down to the Decalogue and involves a critique of idolatry and immorality based on the Decalogue.[7] The echo in v. 19 of Isa. 42.6-7 (where Is-

---

4. There are no significant textual issues in this section of Romans.

5. See here S. Stowers, *A Rereading of Romans: Justice, Jews, and Gentiles* (New Haven: Yale University Press, 1994), pp. 143-58.

6. C. K. Barrett, *A Commentary on the Epistle to the Romans* (Peabody: Hendrickson, 1991), p. 52, makes the following helpful comment: "These critics preach virtue, some from the philosopher's platform, some from the pulpit of the synagogue. . . . We should probably not be wrong in the guess that the most notorious example of the class was the unconverted Paul."

7. Against N. T. Wright, "Romans," in *The New Interpreter's Bible*, vol. 10 (Nashville: Abingdon, 2002), p. 445, who says Paul is speaking of the entire Jewish people, at least in principle. When he clarifies this he says that Paul is suggesting that immorality or bad behavior by some Jews falsifies the ethnic boast of Israel as a people. He also urges that, though Israel is supposed to be a light to the world, the bearers of the solution have become part of the

rael is called on to be a light to blind Gentiles) is a key clue that Paul is referring to a teacher of Gentiles (like himself). V. 24 gives a further clue that the audience of this Jewish teaching is Gentile.

1 Cor. 5.9–6.20 shows that Paul thought that the commandments here mentioned as violated were known to be violated by Gentiles elsewhere. As was true of the characterization of the pretentious, censorious, and hypocritical Gentile, here Paul is especially concerned with the issue of hypocrisy of his dialogue partner, in this case a teacher who does the very sort of things he criticized. Perhaps here again Paul is reflecting on the Wisdom of Solomon, since the underlying attitude of the Jewish teacher seems to be that expressed in Wis. 15.2: "Even if we sin, we are yours [God's], knowing your power, but we will not sin because we are accounted as yours." It would have been especially unhelpful to Paul's case that he will make in chs. 9–11 and later in Romans on behalf of Jews and Jewish Christians if here he were to simply castigate and denigrate all Jews or all things Jewish, or to caricature all Jews as hypocrites and immoral. As Barrett suggests, Paul has in mind a hypocritical Jewish teacher or missionary here.[8]

It will be useful at this juncture to say something about Paul's view of "sin," or more properly his use of the term *hamartia*. Paul distinguishes between "sin" and "transgression" (a different Greek word), the latter being a violation of a known law. *Hamartia* is a broad umbrella term including things such as sins committed in ignorance (cf. Lev. 5.5 LXX), missing the mark, and sins of omission as well as of commission. Paul almost always uses *hamartia* in the singular (but see 1 Cor. 15.3). It is clear that he sees it as a power over fallen persons' lives, and he uses the term as a collective noun encompassing all kinds of sin and all sins. In fact, as we shall see in Romans 7, he can even personify sin. Over half of Paul's total use of *hamartia* and cognate words occurs in Romans 5–7, because throughout that portion of his discourse, from 5.12 on, he focuses on Adam and those who are in Adam. And the chief thing he wants to say there is that Adam sinned and fallen human beings have been sinning ever since the beginning. If humans are to be rescued or saved, the sin problem must be dealt with decisively.

---

problem. Underlying his analysis is the conclusion that in fact ethnic Israel has been replaced or superseded first by Christ, who becomes Israel in a sense, and then by the church of Jew and Gentile united in Christ, as is shown by his exegesis of 11.25-26. Wright does not address Stowers's argument about the sort of person Paul is speaking about here. Diatribes generally describe a particular kind of person or vice that is being critiqued. See N. Elliott, *The Rhetoric of Romans* (Sheffield: Sheffield Academic Press, 1990), pp. 128-30, who makes clear that Paul is not setting up Jews in general as the archetypal braggart.

8. Barrett, *Romans*, p. 53. See also M. Seifrid, "Natural Revelation and the Purpose of the Law in Romans," *TynBul* 49 (1998): 115-29, who rightly stresses that Paul is speaking to individuals or types of individuals, not to ethnic groups here. We should not read ch. 3 back into chs. 1–2.

In contrast to what the OT says about deliberate sin, Paul believes that even sin with a high hand, even deliberate sin against humans or God has been atoned for in the death of Christ. There was no such provision for deliberate sin in the OT (see Num. 15.31). Crimes against the neighbor could not be atoned for. There was only punishment. And rebellion against God was considered an even more heinous offense without the possibility of atonement.[9]

Paul will go on and argue that the Law is inadequate to deal with sin, and that salvation by grace through the work of Christ is essential for all human beings. But he does not argue that case by caricaturing all Jews as if all were hypocrites and grossly immoral people. He does indeed believe that all people have sinned and need Christ for salvation, both Jew and Gentile. But it is no part of his agenda to paint Judaism as without merit or strengths, nor does he have any intention to portray the Law as anything other than holy and good or to argue that God's first chosen people have been abandoned by God.

Thus it is important that Paul's carefully nuanced and balanced critique of his own Jewish heritage be understood properly. This material gives no license to anti-Semitism. What Paul is urging is simply: "In view of God's impartiality, the need of all peoples for God's grace, and the Jewish teacher's refusal to acknowledge God's way of dealing with Gentiles, Paul thinks that the interlocutor's condescending and arrogant attitude of superiority over gentiles is grossly misplaced."[10] In other words, Paul is trying in his first two major arguments to put his audience on one level. There will be no room for Gentile or Jewish boasting about ethnic or moral superiority when Paul gets through. All are equally in need of and indebted to God's grace, and all should be as compassionate as God is toward the lost and spiritually blind. The groundwork will have been laid for a clear presentation of the case for salvation by grace through faith in Christ being what all need.

This argument begins at 2.17 with an address to a Jew in the second person singular. This in itself is probably significant. Paul, for example, does not stereotype by saying "you (plural) Jews." The Jew in question is not a nominal Jew or a secular Jew. He boasts in God, has been instructed in the Law, and relies on the Law. He is clearly a very religious Jew. In addition he knows God's will and has critical judgment. The sort of conditional sentences Paul is offering here are "real" conditions. He knows of such conduct and situations. V. 19 indicates that this individual is persuaded or convinced that he is and ought to be a teacher of Gentiles. It is not hard to imagine that Paul is remembering some of the folks he had to deal with in Galatia (the so-called Judaizers), or perhaps, writing from Corinth, he is thinking about the "super-apostles" or

---

9. See rightly C. Bryan, *A Preface to Romans* (Oxford: Oxford University Press, 2000), pp. 100-102.

10. Stowers, *A Rereading of Romans*, p. 152.

"false apostles" there. But perhaps he is remembering himself before his Damascus road experience, or someone he knew during his pre-Christian days in Jerusalem who was an instructor or proselytizer of Gentiles. In any case, Paul does not object to this person teaching such subjects. He does not object at all to seeing the Law as the repository of knowledge and truth. He objects to the inconsistency of not practicing what one preaches regarding idolatry or immorality.

With the close connection in v. 22 between adultery and idolatry it is quite possible to believe that Paul is referring to the sort of thing he believes goes on in pagan temples, particularly at dinner parties in the sacred precincts.[11] But what does he mean by "robbing temples"? Is he referring to taking away something from a visit to a pagan temple?[12] This is entirely possible. There were small votive "dolls" of sorts, small statues of a god or a goddess that a visitor to a temple might well buy and take home. These were not mere souvenirs but were often thought to bring the favor of the deity with them wherever they went, not unlike what we see in the OT story about the *teraphim* (Gen. 31.19). Acts 19.23-27 is also instructive at this point.[13] But would a religious Jew actually visit a pagan temple? The truth of the matter is that Jews carried on such syncretistic practices in several major cities of the empire. An especially high-status cultured Jew might well have socialized with pagans, perhaps even in temples on occasion. Grave inscriptions reflect these syncretistic tendencies on the part of both Jews and Christians.[14]

Paul then in vv. 25-28 critiques a person who bears the outward sign of Jewish faith in the form of circumcision but fails to keep the covenant that circumcision signifies.[15] Inconsistency and hypocrisy are again Paul's target, especially since this person portrays himself as a teacher of Gentiles. Paul is quick to

11. On which see my discussion in *Conflict and Community in Corinth* (Grand Rapids: Eerdmans, 1995), pp. 191-95, 243-47.

12. Barrett, *Romans*, p. 54, suggests the pilfering of offerings from pagan temples, but if anything of this sort were in view it would probably refer to eating the things offered to pagan deities in the temple, and then perhaps taking home some of the meat from the sacrifices there. It is interesting that Philo, *On the Confusion of Languages* 163, also links together theft, adultery, and sacrilege, but he also adds murder. In both cases however the Decalogue stands behind their discussions, and in Paul's case the apostolic decree probably also lies in the background; Paul takes this decree to be a summary order to Gentile Christians to stay away from pagan temples and the things that go on there, as a way of honoring the Decalogue and not alienating oneself from all Jews and Jewish Christians. See my discussion in "Not So Idle Thoughts about *Eidōlothyton*," *TynBul* 44 (1993): 237-54.

13. See my discussion in *The Acts of the Apostles: A Socio-Rhetorical Commentary* (Grand Rapids: Eerdmans, 1998), pp. 589-92.

14. On which see, e.g., *New Docs* 1.

15. See J. Marcus, "The Circumcision and the Uncircumcision in Rome," *NTS* 35 (1989): 67-81.

add that he does not mean that circumcision is of no value. But what is of infi-
nitely more value is keeping God's commandments whether or not one is circumcised. Paul will stress that circumcision of the heart is also of far more value
than outward circumcision.[16] A real Jew is one who has had his heart transformed or circumcised by the Spirit, which can operate inwardly in a way that
the written code cannot.[17] Here Paul draws on Deut. 10.16 and Jer. 4.4, which
speak of the circumcision of the heart. The latter text indicates that the phrase
refers to repentance, but the former text seems closer to Paul's thrust, which suggests that the phrase refers to a humble response to God's grace and love.

The radical nature of Paul's reevaluation of the faith of his fathers, and in
particular of the Law, is sometimes underplayed or underappreciated. On the
other hand, some scholars have gone so far as to portray Paul as if he were indeed an anti-Semite. It is hard indeed to get the balance right. We will have
something to say in due course about covenantal nomism and the critique of
E. P. Sanders and others which led to the "new" perspective on Paul.[18] Here it is
appropriate to note Barrett's helpful summary of the material in these verses
and their import for such a discussion:

> Paul makes clear beyond all doubt what he means by keeping, and by trans-
> gressing, the Law. It is possible to neglect so weighty a command as circum-
> cision — and fulfil the Law; it is possible to observe the letter of the Law, in-
> cluding circumcision — and transgress the Law. This is not rabbinic
> Judaism or any other kind of orthodox Judaism. Paul's new Christian con-
> viction, that Jesus, whom the Law had cast out, crucified, and cursed, was
> the risen Lord in heaven, led him to a revaluation of religion and in partic-
> ular of the Law, the basis of his own national religion, far more radical than
> is often perceived. He not merely had a new faith, and a new theology; in
> the light of these he came to the conclusion that the old faith — the Old
> Testament and Judaism — meant something different from what he had
> thought. It was not a closed system, complete in itself, requiring only strict
> and unimaginative obedience; for those who had eyes to see it pointed for-
> ward to Christ, and the Gospel. . . . That Paul believed that non-Christian
> Jews were in some important matter wrong is evident; it is equally evident
> that he continued to think of them as his kinsmen and to long for their sal-

---

16. On the spiritualizing of circumcision by Philo and other Jewish writers to make it
meaningful to a Greco-Roman audience see A. J. Guerra, *Romans and the Apologetic Tradition*
(Cambridge: Cambridge University Press, 1995), pp. 62-63.

17. In early Judaism there was some emphasis on circumcision of the heart as opposed
to the body, or at least as more important than the outward ritual. See *Jubilees* 1.23; 1QpHab.
11.13; Philo, *De Migratione Abrahami* 92. See C. Talbert, *Romans* (Macon: Smyth and Helwys,
2002), pp. 87-89.

18. See below pp. 102-7.

vation (9.1-3; 10.1). He was less patient with those who tried to make the best of both worlds and enjoy both faiths; he was the true radical.[19]

V. 29 also suggests that a true Jew will not be doing things for public acclaim, or looking for human praise for his accomplishments. A true Jew's praise or due comes from God. Paul nowhere here suggests that there is no such person as a true Jew, and in fact he will now go on to make clear that he is not even saying that outward circumcision has no value. What he is saying is that there is no room for arrogance, boasting, judging, or hypocrisy by Gentile or by Jew, for all must stand before God in humility and admit they have sinned and fallen short of God's glory.

A Closer Look: When Wright Is Wrong; Getting the Story Straight

N. T. Wright attempts to argue that the subtext in Romans 3–8 is the story of Israel,[20] and in particular the story of the exodus and the redemption of God's people from bondage. There are several problems with this view: (1) It arises out of the assumption that Paul is engaging in a theology wherein the story of Israel is taken over by the church as Christ's story or its own story or both. In fact, Paul will go on and insist in chs. 9–11 that non-Christian Israel still has its own story and that God intends to complete that story. It would totally undercut Paul's attempt to put the largely Gentile audience in Rome in its place if he were to argue that after all they were right that the Jewish people of God had basically been superseded. Wright would not disagree with the proper conclusion that Gentiles are seen as being grafted into the Jewish people of God via Christ, but how one interprets this fact is all-important. Paul believes Jews who are temporarily broken off will one day be grafted back into God's people. See pp. 271-76 below.

(2) It is not the Moses part of Israel's story that underlies Romans 4 and 5 but the stories of Abraham and Adam. Again in ch. 7 the focus is on the story of Adam and those who are in Adam, which is a more universal story, much more applicable to the largely Gentile audience than the story of Moses and the exodus. (3) Gentile Roman Christians did not view themselves as slaves in need of being liberated from the great Pharaoh. Quite the opposite, they were more in danger of being too enamored with their own pharaoh, Nero, who when this letter was written seemed a fine emperor to most. It would hardly be an effective rhetorical technique to suggest that they needed to identify with the story of the exodus. (4) It is telling that when Paul chooses to tell the story of Christ's atoning sacrifice in 3.21-31, with further development in ch.

19. Barrett, *Romans*, pp. 56-57.
20. When it comes to the subtext of this material, it is of course important to get the story straight. Wright, "New Exodus, New Inheritance: The Narrative Substructure of Romans 3–8," in *Romans and the People of God*, ed. S. K. Soderlund and N. T. Wright (Grand Rapids: Eerdmans, 1999), pp. 26-35.

5, there are no OT quotations or really any convincing allusions to Exodus discussions of sacrifice and liberation. Only Deut. 6.4 is echoed (in 3.30), and that has to do with God's oneness, with the heart of the Shema, not the story of the exodus. As for Romans 5–8, as is well known,[21] there are hardly any echoes there of any part of the OT other than the story of Adam, much less any specific allusions to the exodus. It is important to understand not only Paul's logic of argumentation which lies on the surface of Romans 3–8, but also the nature of the narrative subtext.

Many, perhaps most, commentators recognize the dialogical and diatribal form of the material in 3.1-9, but the difficulty is that some readings of the dialogue are less helpful than others. In particular, if one attributes the wrong bits to Paul, one can get the wrong impression of Paul's views on Jews and the Law, among other vital subjects. Stowers assigns vv. 1, 4, 6, and 9a to the interlocutor and the balance to Paul.[22] On this reading, the questions in vv. 3, 5, 7, and 8 are not objections from the interlocutor but Paul's own probing questions meant to make the dialogue partner rethink things. In the diatribe it is traditionally the teacher who asks the probing or daring questions, as in Socratic dialogue.

It is a crucial point of this segment that Paul in v. 3 stresses that some Jews have indeed been unfaithful. Whom does Paul have in mind? Perhaps 15.31 provides a clue: Paul speaks there of "the disobedient ones in Judea." He would seem to mean in the main those Jews who have rejected Christ and opposed his Gentile mission. He will go on to say in chs. 9–11 that such Jews have been temporarily broken off from God's people, but could be grafted back in. In any case, Paul does indeed want to affirm that even if all Jews were unfaithful, God would still remain faithful.[23]

But if individual Jews may prove unfaithful and be broken off, at least temporarily, from God's people, then what advantage can there be to being a Jew? If election does not guarantee final salvation for each individual Jew, what advantage can there be to being among God's chosen people? Paul says that there is much advantage because Jews have been entrusted with the very words or oracles of God. Seifrid is absolutely right at this juncture to stress that what sets Jews apart from Gentiles is not the sort of general knowledge of the existence or will of God available to all, but rather the possession of the oracles which reveal both the divine judgment and the divine salvation of God.[24]

21. See pp. 23-25 above.

22. Stowers, *A Rereading of Romans*, p. 165.

23. This matter is complex because Paul knows that God has made both conditional and unconditional promises. He is apparently alluding to the unconditional ones here.

24. M. Seifrid, "Natural Revelation and the Purpose of the Law in Romans," *TynBul* 49 (1998): 125-26.

There are other advantages, but this one is seen as paramount here (cf. 9.4). It is to be noticed that Paul also has already mentioned that the word of God in the form of the gospel is also entrusted to and for the Jew first, though it is also for the Gentile. This in itself should have been sufficient proof that God had not unfaithfully abandoned his first chosen people for another. Romans 3.3 is also of importance because it demonstrates that Paul can use the phrase *tēn pistin tou theou* to refer to the faithfulness of God rather than faith in God.[25] The Scripture quotation in v. 4 is placed on the lips of the interlocutor. "Everyone a liar" is from Ps. 116.11 and then "so that you may be proved right/justified when you speak . . ."[26] is word-for-word from the LXX of Ps. 51.4. In general, Paul does use the LXX, not surprisingly since if his largely Gentile audience knows any version of the OT it is the LXX, few if any of them knowing Hebrew or Aramaic.

That the second question in v. 5 expects an answer of No is indicated by the use of *mē* at the beginning: "Is it not unrighteous/unjust for God to unleash his wrath [if my unrighteousness highlights God's righteousness]?" Interestingly, vv. 6-8 become somewhat personal for Paul because he alludes to the fact that he has been charged with antinomianism, with actually advocating immoral behavior so that God's righteousness could be better or once again demonstrated. This is no small aside here since it demonstrates once again that Paul was a radical and that his views on salvation by grace through faith were liable to be misunderstood by Jews and by others as some sort of immoral or at least amoral message.

V. 9 not only introduces the lengthy series of quotations that follows but also demonstrates something fundamental about what Paul believes about human beings and sin, and in this case about Jews. He does believe that there are advantages to being a Jew, such as having been entrusted with God's Word. But Jews do not have the advantage of a morally superior position, not least because "to whom more is given more is required," and, as Paul reminds his audience, he has already established that both Jews and Gentiles are all "under sin," a phrase probably meant to convey the idea of bondage.

Vv. 10-18 provide us with a lengthy pastiche or collection of Scriptures meant to establish the point just made — that all have sinned and fallen short of God's glory.[27] Paul refers to the source of these quotations as "the Law," but

---

25. See rightly Barrett, *Romans*, p. 60.

26. Here we have the word *dikaiōthēs*, which would surely seem to mean more than just "counted righteous" here, since it is referring to God.

27. It seems likely that Justin Martyr either knows Romans or knows this catena of Scripture that Paul uses, for Justin uses an abbreviated form of it in *Dialogue with Trypho* 27.9-12. See L. E. Keck, "The Function of Romans 3.10-18 — Observations and Suggestions," in *God's Christ and His People: Studies in Honor of Nils Alstrup Dahl* (Oslo: Universitetsforlaget, 1977), pp. 141-57.

of course they come primarily from the Psalms[28] and Isaiah.[29] Here as in 1 Cor. 14.21 Paul uses the term more broadly to refer to the whole Hebrew Scriptures. From a rhetorical point of view, the appeal to ancient authorities is not only valid but especially necessary if one's own authority is not securely established with an audience, as with Paul in Rome. The first quotation is especially interesting, whether it comes from Ps. 14.1 or Ps. 53.3, because Paul has introduced into the text the word "righteous," which is found in neither the Greek nor the Hebrew texts of these passages. They instead have "good." V. 13 juxtaposes quotations from Pss. 5.9 and 140.3, which have similar subject matter. V. 14 quotes Ps. 10.7, vv. 15-17 quote Isa. 59.7-8, and v. 18 provides a rendering of Ps. 36.1.

Most of the audience are Gentiles, and for them the rhetorical effect of all this quoting comes from what the words actually say and how they sound. The net effect is to make very clear how very lost and wicked humankind can be.[30] But that this whole segment of quotations is directed mainly to the imaginary Jew is made apparent in vv. 19-20, where Paul says that the "Law" (here meaning the whole of Scripture) speaks to those who are under the Law. Paul has already established the accountability of Gentiles to God and silenced their pretensions to moral superiority in his first argument, but here he silences Jews, showing that they are condemned out of the very source they claim gives them an advantage over Gentiles. Thus is the whole world held guilty[31] before God.[32]

---

28. Chrysostom, *Homilies on Romans* 7: "Note that Paul was in the habit of referring to the whole Old Testament as the Law . . . for here he calls a Psalm, 'the Law.'" See G. Bray, ed., *Romans* (Ancient Christian Commentary on Scripture; Downers Grove: InterVarsity, 1998), p. 94.

29. It is interesting that there was a division of opinion among the Church Fathers as to what "Law" was referring to here. Chrysostom and Ambrosiaster argued it was the Mosaic Law, but Origen and others thought it was the natural law written even on Gentile hearts. The quotations from the OT itself of course make it likely that Chrysostom and Ambrosiaster were more nearly on the right track. See Bray, *Romans,* p. 88.

30. This catena of quotations may well be pre-Pauline, but even if so, we have no right to overlook it, because it constitutes something Paul wanted his audience to hear, something he believed to be worth saying, and something that served his larger rhetorical purposes.

31. As Seifrid, "Natural Law," p. 126, points out, the natural rendering of the word *hypodikos* is "guilt." This is the normal meaning in secular Greek, and also in Josephus (*Vita* 74) and Philo (*De Specialibus Legibus* 2.249). As Seifrid says, this also comports better with the previous chain of OT references, which were about guilt, not accountability. Paul had already argued that Gentiles were accountable to God without the Law (2.12-16). Why would he reverse his field and now argue that the Law is necessary for such accountability? Finally, Seifrid is also right to hear an echo of the OT in the phrase "that every mouth may be closed," and when one examines the relevant texts (Pss. 63.11; 107.42; Job 5.16) one finds that they deal with the silencing of the guilty.

32. Some have protested the view that Paul could be talking about the universal sinfulness of every last human being (see, e.g., Stowers, *A Rereading of Romans,* passim) and have

So this leads to the conclusion of this entire argument — therefore no one[33] will be declared righteous in God's sight by observing the Law, for what in fact happens is that the Law even more clearly reveals human sin, so that humankind becomes more aware of sin. Paul is thinking about the eschatological verdict when we appear before Christ at the end of history. The final declaration of righteousness or acquittal is yet in the future.[34]

Here for the first time in Romans we have the key phrase "works of the Law." Does it refer merely to ethnic identity markers such as circumcision, food laws, and sabbath laws, or to the entire Law? It would seem to be the latter, as I have argued elsewhere.[35] Paul does not qualify the phrase in any way that might suggest that he had only a part of the Law in mind, and surely he would have needed to do so writing to an audience that was by far mostly made up of Gentiles.[36] "Works of the Law" is not found in the text echoed (Psalm 143): Paul adds the phrase. In regard to Dunn's suggestion that Paul refers here only to boundary-defining rituals, Fitzmyer replies that "this restricted sense of the phrase is hardly correct for it contradicts the generic sense of 'law' about which Paul has been speaking since 2.12 and to which he refers in 3.20b."[37]

Seneca (*Moral Letters* 28) says that "knowledge of sin is the beginning of salvation." But in fact, to judge from Romans 7, what knowledge of sin leads to is despair over the human ability to save oneself or to achieve or earn salvation.

---

tried to argue that this was not a Jewish view of things. In fact, however, there were other early Jews who affirmed that none were righteous. Rabbi Eliezer, who lived at the end of the first century A.D., also affirmed the universal sinfulness of humanity, including all Jews (see Babylonian Talmud *Sanhedrin* 101a). This also seems to be clearly affirmed at Qumran (cf. 1QH 4.29f.; 7.17; 9.14f. — "None is righteous according to thy sentence, nor guiltless in thy judgment"). Thus universal sinfulness is not a uniquely Christian idea, though perhaps it was not the dominant view in early Judaism.

33. The term *sarx* here, "flesh," refers to humans in their mortality and frailty. It is probably not used in the more loaded sense we sometimes find in Paul.

34. See R. B. Hays, *Echoes of Scripture in the Letters of Paul* (New Haven: Yale University Press, 1989), p. 50: "Thus, the underlying purpose of Rom. 3.9-20 is to establish beyond all possible doubt the affirmation that God is just in his judgment of the world. The passage rebuts the rhetorical suggestion of Rom. 3.5-7 that God might be considered unfair *(adikos).*"

35. See my *Grace in Galatia* (Grand Rapids: Eerdmans, 1998), pp. 341-56. See also Talbert, *Romans*, pp. 90-95.

36. See B. Byrne, *Romans*, Sacra Pagina (Collegeville: Liturgical, 1996), p. 121; J. Fitzmyer, *Romans* (New York: Doubleday, 1992), pp. 337-39.

37. Fitzmyer, *Romans*, p. 338. Fitzmyer also demonstrates that the Qumran material so often cited by Dunn, Wright, and others does not by any means support their case, including especially 4QMMT. Paul is indeed objecting to at least one existing trend in early Judaism that can be called a form of "works righteousness." See Fitzmyer, "Paul's Jewish Background and the Deeds of the Law," in his *According to Paul: Studies in Theology of the Apostle* (New York: Paulist Press, 1993), pp. 18-35. Cf. also Lincoln, "From Wrath to Justification," p. 146.

When awareness of sin comes from knowing and trying to obey the Law, then it becomes apparent that only in Christ can there be right standing with and approbation from God.[38] This leads directly into the repetition and expansion of the *propositio* in 3.21-31.

Bridging the Horizons

"Not many of you should become teachers," say the Scriptures, and portions of this passage simply reinforce that truth. In particular we can see how knowledge can lead to arrogance, judgmentalism, airs of superiority, and indeed to the misuse of power. Unfortunately we see this outcome of erudition all too often in the academy whether in publications or in the regular meetings of the SBL and SNTS. The irony of this is of course that such posturing really masks insecurities and lack of ego strength and provides classic examples of rhetorical over-compensation for such insecurities and feelings of low self-worth. And part of the game is to pour cold water on other persons' accomplishments, lifting oneself up by putting others down. Sometimes this takes the form of proving one's scholarly acumen by "justification by doubt." If one can deconstruct another person's work, one has proved one's critical pedigree and acumen. There is nothing wrong with a healthy critique of another person's views or with dialogue and debate in diatribe form, but this should not entail ad hominem attacks. Paul's concern for behavior that agrees with one's teaching is paramount here. At the end of the day, the amount known of the oracles of God is less important than the practice of what one knows.

The flip-side to this discussion, however, is the danger of using texts like this one to justify anti-intellectualism. It is amazing how often Paul, surely one of the great probing minds of his age, one who encourages people to study and learn, has been used to castigate the pursuit of knowledge or education. If arrogance and judgmentalism by teachers are ruled out by this text, so is the dismissive attitude of those who feel threatened by vigorous debate about matters of the faith or assume that, if one has the Holy Spirit, the hard work of study and learning is not really required. I once had a student who was really quite miffed that he had to do a great deal of study to get through divinity school. One day in nearly total frustration he came up to me and said, "I don't know why I have to do all this studying when I can just get up into the pulpit and the Spirit will give me utterance." My overly quick response was, "It's too bad you don't give the Spirit more to work with." I have thought about this response over the years and realized that while this student did need his consciousness

---

38. E. Käsemann, *Commentary on Romans* (Grand Rapids: Eerdmans, 1980), pp. 89-90.

raised about the importance of studying the Scriptures, the way to encourage this was not a quick quip, but rather a more gentle and less condescending retort. In short, I too have been convicted by what Paul says in Rom. 2.17–3.20.

There is a trap in focusing on Paul's insistence on a Law-free Gospel, the trap of cheap grace. Paul is not encouraging lawlessness by making clear that Christians are not under the Mosaic Law and covenant. Indeed he will argue that Christians are under the Law of Christ. The issue here, however, is not only how one obtains right standing with God (by grace through faith), but also one's attitude and approach to the Word of God when it has been entrusted to believers as a gift. Paul's theology is that a gift never becomes a possession in the sense of something one can do with as one pleases. The Word of God, including the Law, was entrusted to Israel as a gift, and therefore there could be no ground for boasting. A gift is not an accomplishment or achievement. If a friend gives me a copy of her latest book, though in one sense it is mine, in another sense it is not. I am not free to claim that I wrote it or that I have the right to the definitive interpretation of it. Possession of a gift must not lead to an attitude of possessiveness, much less to a sense of entitlement and arrogance. In other words, the Word must not be used as a tool for having and exercising power over others for the sake of gratifying one's own pride or desire for control.

Recapitulation and Expansion of *Propositio* — 3.21-31: The Manifestation of the Righteousness of God Apart from the Law

One of the things which has characterized the discussion from the *propositio* in 1.16-17 up to the recapitulation and amplification in 3.21-31 is that Paul basically does not discuss Jesus or any specifically Christian subject.[1] This is because he is dialoguing with Gentiles and then with Jews outside Christ, and he speaks rather as a missionary might (cf. Acts 17.16-34). But now he must turn and repeat and expand upon the thesis statement, adding more explicitly christological content, as he prepares to show his audience how they in fact fit into the story of God's plan for the salvation of all who are in Adam by being linked to the story of Abraham through the salvific and faithful work of Christ.

This recapitulation can be divided into two parts: the proclamation (vv. 21-26) and the diatribe (vv. 27-31).[2] The diatribe is only one of Paul's rhetorical tools in Romans, and he feels free to oscillate back and forth between differing styles of discourse, even within one rhetorical unit, such as this one. Vv. 21-26 contain the expanded recapitulation of 1.16-17, vv. 27-31 set out in brief fashion the consequences of the thesis statement. W. S. Campbell has urged that this section is a key to the structure and thought of the whole document, and he is surely correct.[3] Once one recognizes this sec-

---

1. On the rhetorical device of amplification here and elsewhere in Romans see D. Helmholm, "Amplification in the Macro-Structure of Romans," in *Rhetoric and the New Testament: Essays from the 1992 Heidelberg Conference*, ed. S. E. Porter and T. H. Olbricht (JSNTS 90; Sheffield: Sheffield Academic Press, 1993), pp. 123-51.

2. See J. A. Fitzmyer, *Romans* (New York: Doubleday, 1992), p. 342.

3. W. S. Campbell, "Romans iii as a Key to the Structure and Thought of the Letter," *NovT* 23 (1981): 22-40. For a fresh rereading of some of this material see D. A. Campbell, "Toward a New Rhetorically Assisted Reading of Romans 3.27–4.25," in *Rhetorical Criticism and the Bible*, ed. S. E. Porter and D. L. Stamps (Sheffield: Sheffield Academic, 2002), pp. 355-402.

tion as the amplified version of the *propositio*, this conclusion becomes all the more evident.

But now, apart from the Law, the righteousness of God has been made clear, as is attested to by the Law and the Prophets, but the righteousness of God through the faithfulness of Jesus Christ, unto all who believe, for there is no differentiation. For all have sinned and lack of the glory of God, being righteous freely of his grace through the ransom which is in Christ Jesus, whom God set forth/predestined as a means of propitiation through the faith[4] in his blood as a proof of his righteousness, through the overlooking of previously committed sins, in the tolerance of God, for the proof of his righteousness in the present time, unto his being righteous and setting right those from faith in Jesus.

Where then is boasting? It is precluded. Through doing the Law, of works? No, but through the law of faith. For we reckon to be righteous believing human beings without works of the Law. Is God the God of Jews alone? Not also of Gentiles? Yes also of Gentiles. If indeed there is one God, who sets right the circumcised by faith and the uncircumcised through the [same] faith. Law, do we then nullify it through the faith? Let it not happen! On the contrary we confirm law.

It would be hard to overestimate the importance of this segment of Paul's discourse, for here we have the first full and clear statement of Paul's view of how God can be both righteous and the righter and redeemer of sinful human beings. I have intentionally in this section avoided the traditional terms "justify" and "justification" because they obscure the relationship between what is said about God's character and action as righteous and about those he sets right and calls to be righteous.

Here we find that Paul can use *nomos*, "law," in several ways, not always of the Mosaic Law. For example, in v. 21 it is perfectly clear that the subject is the Mosaic Law, since there is a definite article and the noun is coupled with a reference to the Prophets. But in v. 27 we have a contrast between the doing of works of Law (probably the Mosaic Law) and "the law/rule/principle of faith." It is then possible that in v. 27 Paul is saying that the rule of law is not nullified through faith. Rather faith establishes law — not the Mosaic Law, but rather the law of faith, otherwise known as the obedience of faith. There is no definite article in v. 27, making it uncertain what law Paul has in mind.[5]

---

4. There is a textual issue in v. 25 as to whether we should follow the manuscripts that have the definite article before "faith" or those that omit the definite article. The evidence is rather evenly divided, but probably the article was originally in the text. See B. M. Metzger, *A Textual Commentary on the Greek New Testament* (3rd ed.; London: United Bible Societies, 1971), p. 449.

5. This becomes all the more an issue since Paul keeps using the phrase "the faith" with the definite article, but in v. 31 he refers to law without an article.

In this expansion of the thesis statement, Paul speaks of what is *now* true apart from the Law. The Law paradoxically enough brought awareness of sin, and thus the righteousness of God, as a saving force, must be revealed apart from the Law. Of course it is ironic that the Law testifies to that from which it cannot deliver. This section is the very heart of Paul's arguments in all of 1.16b–15.13,[6] or, better said, it is the thesis that all these arguments support and are built upon.

"But now" surely refers to the era of salvation, namely what is true since Christ died and rose again. The righteousness of God has been made clear.[7] But clear to whom? To those who have saving faith. Käsemann says that "witnessed" or "attested" refers here to a witness that has a legally binding force, appealing as Paul does to "the Law and the Prophets,"[8] a phrase that Paul uses only here.

V. 22 tells us that this righteousness is revealed either through faith in Christ or through the faith/faithfulness of Christ. The latter would presumably be a shorthand way of referring to Christ's death: his faithfulness and obedience even to death on the cross revealed the righteousness of God. This interpretation is favored by several things: (1) It relieves us of the redundancy of Paul referring to Christian faith twice in this sentence. Instead, both objective and subjective means are referred to: the righteousness of God is revealed through the faithfulness of Christ (i.e., through the Christ-event), and it is revealed to all who believe. This, then, would be an expanded form of *ek pisteōs eis pistin* in the brief introductory *peroratio* in 1.16-17. (2) This reading also gives proper force to the two prepositions "through" and "unto," one referring to the means and the other the ultimate object or recipient of the revelation. (3) This comports well with the parallel *dia* clause in v. 24, which tells us that the gift of righteousness or being righted comes through the liberation or ransom provided in the Christ-event.[9]

Since this truth about God's saving righteousness has been revealed to all who have faith, there is no differentiation between one sort of sinner and another.[10] All have sinned and fall short of God's glory. Notice that the verb here is in the aorist — "have sinned." This could be a futuristic aorist, with Paul

6. C. E. B. Cranfield, *A Critical and Exegetical Commentary on the Epistle to the Romans* (ICC; Edinburgh: Clark, 1975-79), 1:199.

7. Notice the perfect tense of the verb here. Cf. Rom. 1.16-17. The revelation took place in the Christ-event in the past but has an enduring impact into the present.

8. E. Käsemann, *Commentary on Romans* (Grand Rapids: Eerdmans, 1980), pp. 93-94.

9. See the discussion by K. Grieb, *The Story of Romans: A Narrative Defense of God's Righteousness* (Louisville: Westminster/John Knox, 2002), pp. 37-38.

10. The LXX does indicate that God makes a distinction between Jew and Gentile (Exod. 8.23), but that is within the Pentateuch or Law. As Barrett says in his *Commentary on the Epistle to the Romans* (Peabody: Hendrickson, 1991), p. 70, in a situation defined outside of or apart from the Law such a distinction ceases to exist.

looking back from the perspective of final judgment.[11] Dunn is right to stress the shocking character of the assertion that there is no difference between Jews and Gentiles.[12] Part of the very essence of early Judaism was the attempt to remain separate or distinct in certain ways. The Mosaic Law was full of regulations which had the explicit purpose of distinguishing Israelites from the nations around them in the way they looked, dressed, ate, believed, and behaved.

The verb *hysterountai* in v. 23 means "lack, fail to obtain, be wanting, or fall short." Probably here Paul means that because all have sinned they lack the glory of God. This translation is supported by 1.23, which speaks of people exchanging such glory for something else when they choose to sin. Later rabbinic discussion talked about how Adam had such glory but lost it,[13] but we find the notion already in 3 *Baruch* 4.16: "Adam was divested of the glory of God," and *Apocalypse of Moses* 21.6: "O wicked woman, what have I done to you that you have deprived me of the glory of God?" So the reference to lost glory may prepare for the discussion of Adam and those who are in Adam which will follow in Romans 5–7.[14] To speak of a "lack" suggests a loss of glory, so we must speak of a once and future glory.[15] Fitzmyer's objection that Paul has not introduced Adam yet and so cannot be talking about lost glory fails to come to grips with the fact that the thesis statement here deliberately foreshadows in miniature the ideas which are to be discussed thereafter.[16]

In 2 Cor. 3.18 Paul speaks of the believer being changed from glory into glory, but Paul can of course speak of future glory as well — "Christ in you the hope of glory." If one stresses the word "all" here in Rom. 3.23, then Paul would necessarily be talking about a future glory all humans still lack. The normal meaning of the term *doxa* is "radiance," the brilliance shed by the bright presence of something or in this case someone — God or Christ (cf. 5.2; 8.18, 21, 30).

A Closer Look: "Justified" Concepts and Covenantal Nomism

It is hardly an exaggeration to say that the work of E. P. Sanders, beginning with his landmark study *Paul and Palestinian Judaism* in the late 1970s and continuing on to the present, has led to various new avenues for discussing and evaluating Paul's writings and early Judaism and the relationship between the two. Enough time has passed

---

11. See Cranfield, *Romans*, 1:204-5.
12. See J. D. G. Dunn, *Romans 1–8*, Word Biblical Commentary (Dallas: Word, 1988), p. 167.
13. See Cranfield, *Romans*, 1:204.
14. See rightly, Dunn, *Romans 1–8*, p. 168.
15. See Barrett, *Romans*, p. 71.
16. Fitzmyer, *Romans*, p. 347.

now that a proper assessment is in order, especially here since it affects how we understand what Paul says about Judaism, works of the Law, and what is commonly called "justification by faith." Here we want to deal with two major subjects: "covenantal nomism" as a description of the nature of early Jewish religion and Paul's use of righteousness language in his discussion of salvation.

Most scholars now recognize the excesses and problems with the older Protestant ways of evaluating early Judaism, particularly the caricature that was reinforced by influential compendiums like Strack-Billerbeck's volumes comparing the NT to Jewish writings, which suggested that Judaism was nothing more than a religion of works righteousness. Sometimes such comparisons even went so far as to make it sound as if there were no religion of grace and faith and being set right with God in the OT, something the Paul who wrote Romans 4 would vigorously dispute. More nuanced views which suggested that the OT is one thing, but early Judaism, simply a religion of works righteousness, is another, also have their problems, as Sanders has extensively demonstrated in his treatment of the primary sources.[17] Sometimes scholars such as H. Räisänen have been bold enough to say that Paul himself simply caricatures early Judaism and its view of the Law.[18] This is in fact too bold, because there were a variety of views in early Judaism about the Law and works of the Law.

There was, in fact, a considerable body of opinion in early Judaism to which Paul might be reacting when he uses phrases like "works of the Law" to describe a works righteousness approach to the issue of salvation, both in obtaining salvation and in sustaining it. This becomes especially clear in 2 Enoch but also in 4 Ezra, but such ideas are already latent in texts like *Jubilees* 15.3-4; Sirach 44.19-21; or CD 3.2.[19] The point is not that these documents deny that God initiated a relationship with his people out of his own grace or that part of the covenantal nomism equation is fulfilled. It is, rather, that their authors believed that final or eschatological salvation for anyone is a reward for strenuous obedience to the Law. For example, 2 Baruch 51.3 speaks of those who at the last judgment are justified by obedience to the Law. In fact, as D. A. Carson stresses, "the emphasis is overwhelmingly on meriting salvation by works of obedience to the Law, with the result that human achievement takes center-stage and God's grace, while presupposed, is effectively marginalized."[20] A document like 2 Baruch is nuanced, but still when "God bestows mercy on the righteous," it is *"because of their good works."*[21] The importance of this material is simply that Paul has

17. See not only E. P. Sanders, *Paul and Palestinian Judaism* (London: SCM, 1977), but also his *Paul, the Law, and the Jewish People* (Philadelphia: Fortress, 1983).

18. H. Räisänen, *Paul and the Law* (Tübingen: Mohr, 1983).

19. See the discussion in C. Talbert, *Romans* (Macon: Smyth and Helwys, 2002), pp. 95-98.

20. D. A. Carson, "Summaries and Conclusions," in *Justification and Variegated Nomism,* ed. D. A. Carson et al. (Grand Rapids: Baker, 2001), pp. 518-19. This entire volume should be consulted, and a second volume, *The Paradoxes of Paul,* is promised.

21. R. Bauckham, "Apocalypses," in *Justification and Variegated Nomism,* ed. Carson et al., p. 182.

not set up a straw man argument in regard to works righteousness and some early Jewish beliefs and writings.

Sanders paid little attention to the works of Josephus when he evaluated early Jewish views on various subjects in *Paul and Palestinian Judaism*.[22] But there are some interesting parallels between Josephus's view of the Law and Paul's. For example, as P. Spilsbury points out, Josephus says in *Apion* 2.174 something very similar to what we find in Rom. 3.1-2, namely that "the only advantage the Jews have is their association with Moses, who in his extreme sagacity discovered the truth about God and formulated laws in keeping with God's will. Those who experience God's blessing, therefore, will be those who accept the Law as their 'standard and rule' and who live under it 'as under a father and master.'"[23]

Sanders's discussion of the Qumran material and its soteriology must be given its due, but, as M. Bockmuehl demonstrates, a good deal more needs to be said. Bockmuehl pays especial attention to 1QS, some of the new fragments from Cave 4, as well as CD, 1QH, and of course 4QMMT.[24] He points out that this material often presents a complex tension between voluntarism and predestination when it comes to individuals. In 1QS and 1QH personal commitment to the faith is necessary for salvation, and one can also later become apostate. But there are also texts which speak of the destiny of both the just and the wicked being foreordained by God. Sometimes the words for righteousness can be used forensically (see 1QS 10–11); nonetheless it is through God's righteous character and acts that sins can be forgiven, and this forgiveness is not available for those outside the community. "Thus atonement for sins is an act of God *for believers;* God does not atone for the sins of Belial's lot (2.8)."[25] Bockmuehl stresses the unsystematized and non-monolithic or inconsistent nature of this material. Still, we "might have in Qumran a developing example of the sort of exclusivistic preoccupation with 'works of the Law' [see 4QMMT] against which Paul of Tarsus subsequently reacts in his letters to Gentile Christians."[26]

In his discussion of *Jubilees*, P. Enns notes that "covenantal nomism" hardly describes what we find there.[27] As Carson helpfully summarizes the matter: "In Jubilees,

22. This deficiency he partially makes up in his considerably later work *Judaism: Practice and Belief, 63 B.C.E.–66 C.E.* (Philadelphia: Trinity, 1992), but he does not really relate the findings there to the study of Paul.

23. P. Spilsbury, "Josephus," in *Justification and Variegated Nomism,* ed. Carson et al., p. 258.

24. On this latter source and its relevance for the discussion of Paul's use of the phrase "works of the Law" see my excursus on Paul and the Law in *Grace in Galatia* (Grand Rapids: Eerdmans, 1998), pp. 341-56.

25. M. Bockmuehl, "1QS and Salvation at Qumran," in *Justification and Variegated Nomism,* ed. Carson et al., here p. 400. It is somewhat ironic that sometimes Calvin and Luther sound more like this Qumran material than like Paul on these matters.

26. Bockmuehl, "1QS and Salvation at Qumran," pp. 413-14.

27. P. Enns, "Expansions of Scripture," in *Justification and Variegated Nomism,* ed. Carson et al., pp. 73-98, here pp. 92-97.

election is certainly by grace. But that is mere initiation; final salvation finally depends on obedience. More importantly, for the Jews for whom Jubilees is written, the 'getting in' is by birth; it is something inherited. All the focus of their own experience is on staying in. It appears that Enns is right: in the configuration of Jubilees the 'getting in' is not really into salvation, but into a kind of preliminary election, with the salvation being accomplished by the 'staying in.'"[28] This is hardly what Sanders has in mind by the phrase "covenantal nomism." It is far more like self-salvation or works righteousness.

The net effect of these various discussions is that it becomes clear that Sanders's umbrella concept of covenantal nomism has some holes in it, if it is meant to rule out the fact that various early Jews did indeed take a line which Paul could have critiqued under the banner of "works of the Law" = works righteousness, especially in regard to the matter of final salvation.

What may we say about Paul's righteousness language in light of this discussion? In the first place it needs to be borne in mind how very sectarian and radical Paul is. His discussion of the inward or secret Jew and of circumcision of the heart in Romans 2–3 is already pushing him in new directions, even beyond ordinary remnant theology.[29] He is a creative thinker, and his theology and ethics are not simply products of his early Jewish or early Christian background.

In the second place, the evidence as a whole suggests that we should not immediately read a phrase like "the righteousness of God" in early Jewish or Jewish Christian sources through the lens of forensic categories. Occasionally the phrase does have a forensic sense, but this must be determined from the context. More often it refers to the character of God, which he actively expresses in his salvific work or sometimes in judgment. It is for this reason that I have avoided the traditional language of "justification" and "justify" and have preferred instead some form of usage that includes "right" or "righteous" in it. Romans 4 will discuss the matter of being reckoned as righteous, but *dikaiosynē* means more than just this to Paul. It is not just about a declaration or forensic pronouncement, and the phrase "legal fiction" hardly does justice to this profound idea. God does not simply consider the sinner righteous as a result of the finished work of Christ. Through that salvific work of Christ a person has been *set right* — which means not only set back into a right relationship with God, or reckoned as righteous, but also set in the right moral direction as well.

Paul frequently associates *dikaiosynē* with God's divine saving activity, and it involves far more than just a declaration by God of no condemnation. I do not wish to neglect the "reckoned as righteous" concept, but it limits Paul's understanding of *dikaiosynē* too much. Paul believes that a person in Christ is already a new creature, has a circumcised heart, and is indwelt by the Holy Spirit, who bears witness with and to that person's spirit that he or she is a child of God. Of course all of this should not be loaded into the term *dikaiosynē*, but the term should be evaluated by the terminological company it keeps. Paul has a vision of believers becoming righteous by grace

28. Carson, "Summaries and Conclusions," p. 546.
29. See Barrett's remark, p. 83 above.

through faith in Christ. This of course begins by regaining right-standing with God, being set right, being set on the right moral course. But since Paul also affirms what can be called final *dikaiosynē* it is important not to radically separate the term from notions of sanctification, for final "justification" depends in one sense on that sanctification. As 1 Cor. 1.30 makes evident, *dikaiosynē* should be associated with notions of holiness and redemption in Christ.

I would further maintain that Paul himself is far closer to the notion of covenantal nomism in his own theology than Sanders realizes. Paul of course believes in God's initiative of grace, in this case in Christ, but he also believes that adherence to "the Law of Christ" (as he calls it in Galatians) or to "the obedience of faith" is not optional for Christians who wish to stand before the final judgment of Jesus and hear the declaration "well done, good and faithful servant; inherit the rewards of the kingdom."

Paul also affirms the concept of apostasy, as do various of these other early Jewish documents, which also have a strong stress on God's sovereignty. Paul of course believes that a Christian must rely on God's grace daily in order to obey, avoid sin, and avoid apostasy, but the point is that he does not believe that how one lives one's life as a Christian has no effect on whether one will obtain final salvation and the resurrection. Paul is sectarian in his approach to these matters in much the same way that some of the Qumranite writers were, which is to say he takes a minority line, but in doing so he neither caricatures the faith of all early Judaism nor sounds so very different from some other early Jewish sectarian writers, except in regard to how he sees Christ fitting into the equation of salvation.

In his study of the use of righteousness language in relationship to God in the Hebrew Scriptures and their milieu, M. Sefrid establishes that while the phrase "the righteousness of God" is often associated with salvation, nonetheless there are a significant number of texts where it refers to punishment as an expression of that righteousness (e.g., Psalm 98).[30] Furthermore, Sefrid shows that the phrase is not simply used in a forensic rather than an ethical sense in the Hebrew Scriptures or in early Jewish literature. He is also able to demonstrate that "God's righteousness" is not simply equated with God's covenant faithfulness. "All 'covenant-keeping' is righteous behavior, but not all righteous behavior is 'covenant-keeping.' It is misleading, therefore, to speak of 'God's righteousness' as his 'covenant-faithfulness.'"[31]

Sefrid is right then that when Paul speaks in Rom. 1.17 of the revelation of God's righteousness and then goes on in 1.18-32 to speak of the revelation of God's wrath he is not dealing with two entirely different concepts or matters, the former having to do with salvation, the later with judgment. God's righteous character and will are expressed both through the gospel and outside the gospel, both in creation and in God's Law. Creation, Law, and gospel all include judgment. The gospel involves judgment

30. See the entire discussion by M. Sefrid, "Righteousness Language in the Hebrew Scriptures and Early Judaism," in *Justification and Variegated Nomism,* ed. Carson et al., pp. 415-42.

31. Sefrid, "Righteousness Language in the Hebrew Scriptures and Early Judaism," p. 424.

on Jesus in lieu of judgment on believers, and purgative rather than punitive sanctifying work in the believer is also an expression of God's righteousness or holiness. That judgment can be involved in the expression of God's righteousness outside the gospel in the form of righteous wrath is shown in Rom. 1.18-32 and elsewhere in Paul, and in texts like Psalm 98.

It is right to point out, however, that in the Hebrew Scriptures the association of righteousness with salvation is four times more common than the association of God's righteousness with judgment, which tells us something about the emphasis in the Hebrew Scriptures on God's mercy and forgiveness even when God continues to be righteous and just. Hopefully it does not need to be said that we do not have mainly a wrathful and graceless deity in the OT, and a wrath-free graceful deity in the NT, despite Marcion's and others' misreadings. And Paul follows this lead by most often associating "the righteousness of God" with the gospel and salvation of human beings. It is time for us to once again appreciate the early Jewish matrix out of which Paul's language about righteousness comes and to be thankful for the discussions of Sanders and his respondents, which have helped us get beyond the older and less helpful Protestant thinking both about early Judaism and about what Paul means by *diakaiosynē*, even though Sanders was overreacting to the older Protestant complaint about legalism and works righteousnesss in early Judaism.

V. 24 is particularly difficult to translate. It means something like "being set right freely by his grace through the liberation/ransom which is in Christ." Barrett strikes the right note: "It is far better, and more in harmony with Paul's teaching as a whole to suppose that . . . *dikaioun* does mean 'to make righteous,' but at the same time to recognize that 'righteous' does not mean 'virtuous,' but 'right,' 'clear,' 'acquitted,' in God's court. Justification then means no legal fiction but an act of forgiveness on God's part. . . . Far from being a legal fiction, this is a creative act changing the relation between God and man."[32] The key term *apolytrōseōs* is a compound of *lytron*. It is hardly accidental that in the next verse Paul speaks of a *hilastērion*. Here the discussion by Cranfield should be consulted in full.[33]

A *lytron* is most definitely a ransom to emancipate slaves. While "liberation" may be an adequate translation here, it is likely that to the Gentile ear, especially in Rome where a huge percentage of the population was enslaved, including a good part of Paul's Christian audience in all probability, Paul's words refer to a "ransom," for this is the nuance present in profane Greek.[34] It is also the meaning found in such Jewish texts as *Epistle of Aristeas* 12, 33 and Josephus,

32. Barrett, *Romans*, p. 72.
33. Cranfield, *Romans*, 1:206-12.
34. Barrett, *Romans*, p. 73.

Antiquities 12.27. In view of 1 Cor. 6.20 and 7.23, Paul obviously does use the idea of being bought with a price. It is also certainly true that this sentence conveys the sense of a decisive act of deliverance by God which has brought about the believer's righteous status.[35]

V. 25 is a statement about Christ and may be a quote from a Christ hymn, in view of the fact that the sentence starts awkwardly with *hon.*[36] The verb *proetheto* means "display" or "show forth publicly." The crucifixion of Jesus publicly displays God's eternal purpose for humanity. Implicit in this way of putting things is that God purposed for Jesus to die on the cross as an atonement. His crucifixion did not happen purely on the basis of human machinations.[37] Dunn argues: "Assuredly the logic of Paul's exposition is that the wrath of God . . . is somehow averted by Jesus' death (cf. 2 Macc. 7.38) but the passage also portrays God as offerer of the sacrifice rather than its object."[38] Actually, however, God is not only the offerer but also the recipient of the sacrifice, for it is his own wrath which is averted!

There has been unending debate on the term *hilastērion,* which can mean anything from mercy seat to expiation to propitiatory sacrifice.[39] In other contexts it is clear that it refers to a propitiatory sacrifice, not merely to expiation. It is, in addition, not true that *hilaskesthai* in the LXX is not associated with God's wrath (cf. Exod. 32.12-14; Dan. 9.16-19).[40] Propitiation of wrath is the normal meaning in Greek literature. In view of Paul's Roman audience it may be helpful to compare a Greek inscription found at Cos which reads: "The people, for the Emperor Caesar, son of God, Augustus, for salvation to the gods [offer this] propitiatory sacrifice *(hilastērion)*."[41] The word refers, then, not merely to the cleansing of the effects of sin (i.e., guilt) but the propitiation of the wrath of a deity. We have already heard in chs. 1–2 about this wrath as a present reality and about averting the future wrath of God. So Paul probably refers here to a propitiatory sacrifice, though it is a mistake to take him as meaning that God propitiates human beings. Rather, "This amounts to the paradoxical claim that God propitiates God. . . . The paradox is rooted in the nature of God. It is the nature

35. See the dissertation by K. Grieb, "Affiliation with Jesus Christ in His Sacrifice: Some Uses of Scripture to Define the Identity of Jesus Christ in Romans" (Ph.D. diss., Yale University, 1997).

36. See my discussion of the hymns in *Jesus the Sage: The Pilgrimage of Wisdom* (Minneapolis: Fortress, 2000), chapter 6.

37. See Dunn, *Romans 1–8,* p. 170.

38. Dunn, *Romans 1–8,* p. 171.

39. L. Morris, "The Meaning of *hilastērion* in Rom. 3.25," *NTS* 2 (1955/56): 33-34.

40. See the helpful discussion in C. Bryan, *A Preface to Romans: Notes on the Epistle and Its Literary and Cultural Setting* (Oxford: Oxford University Press, 2000), p. 111.

41. See W. R. Paton and E. L. Hicks, *The Inscriptions of Cos* (Oxford: Clarendon, 1891), no. 81, cf. no. 347.

of God to be irreconcilably opposed to sin; it is the nature of God to love sinners and to seek reconciliation with them. No one but God could resolve the problem; and God himself could be faithful to both aspects of his being only at the cost of the Cross."[42] Probably we should translate the word here as "means of propitiation" since it refers to Christ and his blood. It is said that this *hilastērion* benefits those who have faith in Christ's blood. This is very strange language indeed unless Paul believed Christ was some sort of atoning and appeasing sacrifice.[43]

It must be noted that we are talking about God's plan here. He is the subject of the verb *proetheto.* The word may mean "predestine" here, in which case Paul is arguing that Christ is the elect, chosen, predestined one through whom salvation is effected.[44] Most commentators, however, take the verb as meaning "set forth publicly," "display," or even "purpose" or "intend" here.

V. 25a must not be divorced from v. 25b, which says that Christ was set forth as a "proof" (or a "demonstration" — see 2 Cor. 8.24). But how could Christ's death be a demonstration or proof of God's righteousness? The phrase which follows, "through the overlooking of previous sins," may give a clue.[45] There came a point at which God had to vindicate his own righteousness, because previously he had overlooked human sin because of his mercy (see 2.4). Christ's death is then seen as a judgment and at the same time a payment of the price for those sins. Better said, his death was a propitiatory sacrifice for those who committed those sins — namely, all humanity, as specifically referred to in v. 23 where "all" is in the emphatic position at the beginning of the sentence. Here it is important to stress that Paul believes Christ died for the sins of all, not just for some subset of humanity called the elect. Christ's death is a sufficient atonement for the sins of all human beings, but it is effective only for those who appropriate its benefits through faith, as v. 22 makes evident. God's saving righteousness, which is also his mercy through the death of Christ, does not automatically benefit a person. A person must believe to receive this bene-

42. Barrett, *Romans,* p. 74.

43. See rightly, N. T. Wright, "Romans," in *The New Interpreter's Bible,* vol. 10 (Nashville: Abingdon, 2002), p. 476; D. Moo, *The Epistle to the Romans* (NICNT; Grand Rapids: Eerdmans, 1996), pp. 231-36. The sense "mercy seat" for *hilastērion* is of course technically possible (see Lev. 16.2), but Paul is not just conjuring up OT imagery; he is discussing the atoning sacrifice of Jesus here and explaining what it accomplishes.

44. See, for example, Ambrosiaster, *Commentary on Paul's Epistles* 81: "in Christ, God put forward i.e. appointed himself as a future expiation for the human race if they believed" (G. Bray, ed., *Romans* [Ancient Christian Commentary on Scripture; Downers Grove: InterVarsity, 1998], p. 102). Ambrosiaster sees the sense as "put forward in advance" = "predestine."

45. This translation of *dia tēn paresin* is to be preferred to the translation that suggests that the phrase means forgiveness. Rather, overlooking something is in view. See Luke 11.42; Heb. 12.12; Sir. 23.2. See Bryan, *A Preface to Romans,* pp. 112-13.

fit. Christ's death both vindicates and displays God's righteous judgment on sin and demonstrates God's desire to set right sinful humankind.

V. 26 is awkward as well, but what it affirms is that God previously showed tolerance (cf. 2.4) by not exacting the due penalty on sin, but now God has demonstrated his righteousness by exacting the punishment on Christ "in the now time."[46] *Kairos* can refer to the right or critical or precisely correct time. In Paul's letters it is used of the time determined by God. The phrase "the now time" *(ho nyn kairos)* then connotes the time of salvation since and including the Christ-event. Paul clearly believes that the eschatological age has broken into human history through Christ. God is able to be and remain righteous and holy even when he sets right believing human beings by grace because of what Christ did on the cross. Otherwise, either God's holiness/righteousness or his mercy/love would have been compromised by a forgiveness that overlooks and either does not punish wickedness or does not solve the way a righteous God can rightly relate to a sinful human being, to the sanctifying benefit of that human being. How otherwise will one lacking glory obtain it? How otherwise can a holy God dwell within human beings? Pardon without atonement would not have been just or right for a God in whom there is no darkness or shadow of turning.[47] "Rom. 3.21-26 makes the essentially simple point that Christ, and above all his death, is the definitive eschatological revelation of the saving righteousness of God. This point responds to Paul's previous argument that all humanity, including Israel, stands in need of salvation. Therefore, where law, circumcision and good works have failed, the vehicle of salvation for both Jew and Greek is Christ and the Cross."[48]

Since all this is true, boasting by anyone, even a pious Jew or Gentile, is ruled out (v. 27). 2.17 should be compared. Paul here returns to the diatribe format, as if he has given a brief sermon in vv. 21-26 and now allows time for questions and answers. Here the diatribe uses a less confrontational "we," as opposed to "you."[49] The "rhetorical questions" of diatribe "are gifts to us later readers. . . . They help us to track the important turning points in Paul's argument, like markers left on a wilderness trail."[50]

---

46. It is very profitable to compare the *propositio* in Gal. 2.15-21 to this passage, which is the full form of the *propositio* for Romans. In both cases the discussion is so densely packed with ideas and key phrases that the grammar becomes awkward at more than one juncture. Paul is struggling to summarize the key assumptions that undergird his entire set of arguments in each of these crucial letters.

47. On Paul's theology of sacrifice and atonement see A. A. Das, *Paul, the Law, and the Covenant* (Peabody: Hendrickson, 2001), pp. 113-44.

48. D. A. Campbell, *The Rhetoric of Righteousness in Romans 3.21-26* (Sheffield: Sheffield Academic Press, 1992), pp. 202-3. This is the most comprehensive, helpful treatment of this portion of the *peroratio*.

49. See Dunn, *Romans 1-8*, p. 184.

50. Grieb, *The Story of Romans*, p. 46.

There is a radical element to what Paul is saying here. The psalmist repeatedly speaks of God vindicating or saving the righteous. But here Paul is
talking about the setting right and rescuing of the sinner or ungodly person.
Strictly speaking, the sinner has no right to be vindicated or "justified" in the
ordinary sense of those terms, which is one reason I find this sort of language
not entirely helpful in translating the *dikaioō/dikaios/dikaiosynē* word group.
Furthermore, Paul is talking about something more than just reckoning a person as righteous or pardoning him or her, though that is included. He has more
than a forensic declaration in mind. He is also talking about the actual righting/
setting right/converting/changing of a person. Käsemann has a way of stating
Paul's point in its starkest form: "Grace is simultaneously judgment because it
fundamentally sets even a religious person in the place of the godless."[51]

There is necessarily some debate about the term *nomos* in v. 27b. Does it
refer to the Mosaic Law or to the "law/principle of faith"? I would suggest that
Paul is saying here that boasting is excluded through the principle of faith,[52]
and I suspect that the phrase "law of faith" should be compared to "obedience
of faith," which certainly does not have the Mosaic Law in mind. Of course Paul
does also use *nomos* in v. 28 of the works of the Mosaic Law. But Paul is engaging in the appropriate rhetorical technique of wordplay in order to get the attention of the audience and make them rethink some things, giving them a new
perspective.[53] He is contrasting the Law of works with the law of faith.[54]

V. 28 can be seen as a brief summary of Paul's views about "getting in,"
namely that it is by faith and not by works of the Law that a person is set right.

51. Käsemann, *Romans*, p. 102.
52. See Fitzmyer, *Romans*, p. 363.
53. Dunn, *Romans 1–8*, pp. 185-86, misses the rhetorical play here and so wants to suggest that Paul means "What kind of understanding of the law is this?" But the issue here is not
the understanding of the Mosaic Law or any law, but rather the kind of ruling principle or
law that excludes boasting. Paul is not talking about the Mosaic Law as understood through
the eyes of faith. Paul's argument about the Law is salvation-historical, not epistemological
or hermeneutical. In his view the Mosaic Law is obsolete or obsolescent, because the new
covenant dawned when Christ came and died and rose again. See my discussion in *Grace in
Galatia*, pp. 341-56. To argue as Dunn does (*Romans 1–8*, p. 191) that Paul intends to undermine only the Law's function in marking out Jewish privilege and prerogative is not to take
the measure of the radical nature of Paul's eschatological approach to the Law and the Mosaic covenant in general.
54. Barrett, *Romans*, p. 79, who recognizes that in the second case he cannot simply
mean the Jewish Law. See Moo, *Romans*, pp. 247-49: "the question in v. 31: 'Do we then nullify
the law through faith?' . . . does not make sense unless Paul has, in this context, fully separated
'faith' from the Law of Moses. And this same careful distinction between believing and 'doing' (the law, works of the law) is maintained throughout Romans (cf. 2.25-29; 3.20; 4.2-8;
9.31–10.8)." Moo then rightly concludes that *nomos* must mean "principle" here, at least when
it is linked with faith. Cf. however Das, *Paul, the Law, and the Covenant*, pp. 194-98.

It was Origen, not Luther, who first added the word "only" to this verse ("we reckon that it is by faith alone . . ."), though Luther certainly did the most to popularize the notion. It is important to bear in mind that there is no manuscript support for such an addition here, though it certainly is implied in what Paul says. But after "getting in" the obedience of faith is also expected.

In vv. 29 and 30 the argument takes what is perhaps a surprising turn. Here Paul in diatribal format turns another common idea on its head — namely that the one God has one special people. Paul asks whether, if there is only one God, he is really the God of the Jews only. Is he not the God of all the other human beings he also created? If he is the God of the Jews only, this would seem to deny that he is the sole God. The implication is that there is one God, who has one people, but they are drawn from the whole of humanity. The biblical God's claim and salvation extend to all the race of humans.[55] He sets right the circumcised by faith, and the uncircumcised through faith as well.[56] Paul does not have just any sort of faith in mind, but, as the rest of this section shows, faith in Christ.[57] Thus both Jew and Gentile are set right by grace through faith.[58]

Does this then mean that the Law has been nullified? "Certainly not" is the answer. Rather law, as the just and righteous claim of God on his people, is affirmed. If Paul is referring more specifically to the Mosaic Law here, he may mean that it is confirmed as the witness to God's righteousness it was said to be in v. 21. But it is equally possible here that Paul continues to oscillate back and forth between two senses of *nomos* and here at the end of this section is merely saying that God's imperatives and his demands on the lives of his people for obedient faith continues. But possibly 3.31 should be seen as transitioning to 4.1 and the beginning of the next argument, where Paul will demonstrate how the Law is established by his argument, namely by being the witness to the concept of being set right by grace through faith. To use Genesis as a witness is to establish the Torah, at least in one sense.

55. Cf. J. Lambrecht, "Paul's Logic in Romans 3.29-30," *JBL* 119 (2000): 526-28, to R. W. Thompson, "The Inclusion of Gentiles in Rom. 3.27-30," *Bib* 69 (1988): 343-46.

56. It is probably best to consider the use of *ek* and *dia* just stylistic variation in this case.

57. Despite the best efforts of J. Gager, L. Gaston, K. Stendahl, S. Stowers, and others, it will not do to suggest that Paul has a two-track model of salvation and a two-track model of the people of God. Faith here refers to faith in Christ, and it alone is seen as saving faith by Paul. That is the measure of his radicality. Contrast J. Gager, *The Origins of Anti-Semitism: Attitudes toward Judaism in Pagan and Christian Antiquity* (New York: Oxford University Press, 1983), p. 262, to Sanders, *Paul, the Law, and the Jewish People*, p. 196.

58. See N. Elliott, *The Rhetoric of Romans: Argumentative Constraint and Strategy and Paul's Dialogue with Judaism* (JSNTS 45; Sheffield: Sheffield Academic Press, 1990), p. 157.

Bridging the Horizons

As K. Grieb says, Paul uses three major metaphors in this section to describe salvation: it involves being set right (a legal metaphor), redemption (a metaphor from slavery), and atonement (a sacrificial metaphor).[59] But though Paul is using language metaphorically (for example, Christ's death did not literally conform to the rules of a blood sacrifice), it is a mistake to assume that he does not mean what he says. In Paul's view he is describing real spiritual transactions that resulted from the historical death of Christ. God's wrath against sin was assuaged, humans were cleansed from their sin (both propitiation and expiation being involved), they were set free from the bondage of sin (redemption), and they were set back in right relationship with God and with each other (atonement), if only they will appropriate these benefits through faith. The death of Jesus is an act in which he modeled the obedience of faith, and so it is called his "faithfulness." Thus, as it turns out, the "righteousness of God" turns out to be about both judgment and redemption, judgment on sin in the person of the sin-bearer Jesus and consequent redemption and liberation of the sinner. This affects both the sinner's position in relationship to God and the sinner's condition. Reconciliation and cleansing are both effected by Christ's atoning sacrifice.

Of course many moderns have difficulties with the view of God implied here. Along with the concept of a God who has wrath or righteous anger, they have even more difficulty with a God who requires that his Son give up his life in such a horrible fashion, as an atoning sacrifice. But unless Christ's death on the cross is both the one necessary and also the sufficient sacrifice for the sins of the world, then God is in no sense a loving God. What parent would require such a thing of his or her only child? Thus some modern discussions have even talked about the cross and the crucifixion as an example of child abuse! This would be correct, if there were some other way God could be both just and the justifier or righter of fallen human beings. But Paul seems to think this was indeed the only way for God to remain both holy and loving and be reconciled to his estranged children. If this perspective is right, then Christ's death, instead of a hideous tragedy or mistake, is the greatest display of God's love that ever happened in human history. In the cross one sees the gamut of God's character and the extent of divine love all at once.

It is characteristic of God that he is faithful even when humans are faithless, and so it is no surprise that Paul would speak of the faithfulness, even unto death, of Christ. But it may be asked: to what or whom is Jesus faithful? To God, to the divine plan for his life, to what he has promised his followers? Phil. 2.5-11 speaks of Christ's obedience even unto death, which implies that God required

---

59. Grieb, *The Story of Romans*, p. 35.

this action of him. In the main it seems that when Paul speaks of the faithfulness of Christ he means Christ's faithfulness to God's salvation plan.

There is, however, another dimension to this which reflects a certain tension: how can God be at one and the same time both impartial, no respecter of persons, and at the same time faithful to his promises to his people? The answer seems to be that God found a way both to manifest his righteousness and to achieve his desire for setting right a world gone wrong, a way that was outside the Law and through and in Jesus Christ. God will honor his promises made in a previous covenant, but he will inaugurate a whole new covenant that is more inclusive of all persons and is based on a more universal condition of grace and faith. Indeed, his promises to Israel are to be gathered up and fulfilled in Jesus in the context of the new covenant, not the continuation of the old one. So both Israel and Gentiles find themselves on a new footing with God as a result of the Christ-event. God is not keeping two contracts and two sets of laws with humankind at the same time.

Argument Three — 4.1-25: Abraham as Forefather of All the "Righteous" by Faith

In 3.21 Paul has argued that his thesis was in fact announced in the Law and Prophets. There is a sense in which 4.1-12 provides the validation for that particular claim.[1] The link between Paul's thesis and this argument is made apparent by the particle *oun* — "then" or "therefore." Abraham becomes a linchpin in Paul's argument concerning how righteousness and a right relationship with God have come to human beings quite apart from the Law. This is very different from the sort of argument one finds in 2 *Baruch* 57.2, where Abraham is said to be able to be righteous and keep the Law because God has already written the Law on his heart. Put another way, the deliberative nature of Paul's argument here is clear because, as Guerra says, "Romans 4 is an outstanding instance of the creative reinterpretation of Scripture, for the purpose of promoting a new community and its value system, evidencing its protreptic orientation."[2] Abraham turns out to be not only the example to follow but also the forefather of both Jews and Gentiles and so the proof that Jews and Gentiles were meant to be united in Christ as Abraham's heirs.[3]

It is useful to compare how Paul uses the example of Abraham here and in his argument in Gal. 3.6-14. The appeal to the example of Abraham is briefer in Galatians and cites Scripture less extensively. Romans associates Abraham

---

1. See J. A. Fitzmyer, *Romans* (New York: Doubleday, 1992), p. 369.

2. A. J. Guerra, *Romans and the Apologetic Tradition: The Purpose, Genre, and Audience of Paul's Letters* (Cambridge: Cambridge University Press, 1995), p. 125.

3. Furthermore, the argument here prepares for Paul's climactic argument in chs. 9–11. N. Elliott, *The Rhetoric of Romans: Argumentative Constraint and Strategy and Paul's Dialogue with Judaism* (JSNTS 45; Sheffield: Sheffield Academic Press, 1990), p. 221, rightly notes: "Romans 4 lays the groundwork for the discussion in Romans 9–11 by characterizing Abraham's faith as trust in God's ability to 'do what has been promised.'"

and Sarah with an argument about life from the dead by means of divine miracle, as further illustrated by the resurrection of Jesus, while Galatians has an argument about the cross connected with the blessing of Abraham being extended to Gentiles in and through Jesus. In both arguments, the issue of priority — which came first, the promise to one who believed or action on the basis of a work of the Law, namely circumcision — is important. The issue of boasting in works and of payment due for works accomplished comes up only in Romans. In Galatians Paul argues against a serious temptation by the audience to get themselves circumcised and keep the Law. In Romans Paul is trying to get the audience to place more value on their Jewish inheritance and on the fact that Abraham is the father of all who believe, and he is trying to undercut the boasting and ethnic and cultural arrogance of Roman Gentiles. The great leveler is of course that all have sinned and are equally saved by grace through faith. And now we discover that all, both Jews and Gentiles, are in the debt of Abraham the Jew, the paradigmatic man of faith.

This appeal to a historical example from a sacred text which is a shared authority for both author and audience comes after the expanded version of the *propositio,* but also after arguments based on human experience, both Gentile and Jewish. This order of argumentation, experience and then Scripture, is also followed in Galatians, though in Galatians all the arguments follow the one and only statement of the *propositio* in Gal. 2.15-21. Quintilian stresses that the strongest kind of proof from analogy is the proof from historical example (*Instit. Or.* 5.11.6-8). The appeal to examples is a staple item in deliberative rhetoric, for, as Aristotle says, "examples are most suitable for deliberative speakers, for it is by examination of the past that we divine and judge the future" (*Rhetoric* 1.9.40). The use of such examples is in fact an inductive method of persuasion. Quintilian associates its usage with the use of the diatribe (*Instit. Or* 5.11.2-3). Paul then is going right by the rhetorical book here when he presents his historical example in the context of a dialogue in diatribe form.[4]

This form moves the argument forward typically by beginning with rhetorical questions the audience will know and assent to the probity of, and then more difficult questions follow which only the logic of the argument is likely to persuade them to accept. In this case, all the questions come in the first paragraph. What did Abraham obtain? What does the Scripture say? Is the blessing on both the circumcised and uncircumcised? How then is it reckoned? Before or after Abraham was circumcised? The drift of the argument is meant to lead to the conclusion that faith is reckoned as righteousness and that Abraham's example of strong trust in God's promise should be followed. This is of no small

---

4. Melanchthon, who was probably the most rhetorically adept of those who lived around the time of the Reformation, argued that we have here a "proof" of the proposition, which is certainly correct. On his rhetorical analysis see p. 21 n. 51 above.

importance for Paul's later arguments in chs. 9–11. There Paul will insist that God does not renege on his promises to Israel, any more than he did on his promises to Abraham. The Gentiles in Paul's audience then, if they assent to the Abraham argument and the logic of what it says about God's and our righteousness and God's promises to his people, must then also come to recognize that supersessionist notions of Gentiles replacing Jews permanently in God's people are completely erroneous because God keeps his promises to all. Gentiles, who in a sense got into the people of God because of a promise made to a Jew named Abraham, are hardly in a position to deny God's other promises to Jews, as we shall see.

What then shall we say Abraham, our forefather[5] according to the flesh, obtained? For if Abraham was set right by works, he has a boast, though not before God. For what does the Scripture say: "Abraham believed God and it was reckoned to him for righteousness." To the one who works, wages are not reckoned according to grace but according to due. But to the one not working, but believing in the righteousness of the ungodly, faith is reckoned to him for righteousness. Just as even David speaking a blessing over the human being to whom God reckons righteousness without works: "Blessed are those whose transgressions are forgiven, and whose sins are covered. Blessed is the man to whom the Lord will surely not reckon sin." The blessing then, Is it thus upon the circumcised or also upon the uncircumcised? For we say: To Abraham faith was reckoned for righteousness. How then is it reckoned? When he was circumcised or when he was uncircumcised? Not when he was circumcised but when he was uncircumcised. And the sign of circumcision he received, a seal of the righteousness of faith of those who are uncircumcised, unto his being the father of all the believers among the uncircumcised, unto whom also had been reckoned righteousness, and the father of the circumcised, those not from circumcision alone but also those following in the footsteps[6] of faith our father Abraham walked when uncircumcised.

For the promise to Abraham or his seed [came] not through the Law, his heirs to be of the world, but through the righteousness of faith, for if those were heirs from the Law, the faith is invalidated and the promise nullified. For the Law causes wrath. But where there is no Law, nor is there transgression. For this reason, from faith, in order that according to grace, unto the promise being reliable/firm to all the seed, not only to those from the Law but also to those from the faith of Abra-

---

5. The term "forefather" occurs nowhere else in the NT, and some later manuscripts replace it with the Greek word for "father." See B. M. Metzger, *A Textual Commentary on the Greek New Testament* (3rd ed.; London: United Bible Societies, 1971), p. 450.

6. On the metaphorical phrase "walking in the tracks of the faith of Abraham" see *NewDocs* 3:68. On this same page an interesting inscription is cited, which refers to the footprints of a god made when the god appeared in that place.

ham (who is the father of all of us, just as it is written that "the father of many nations I have appointed you"), before whom he put his faith in the God who gives life to the dead and calls the things that are not into existence, who beyond hope yet in hope believed so as to become the father of many nations according to what had been said: "Thus shall your seed be." And not weakened in faith,[7] he considered his own body as good as dead/impotent, being about 100 years old, and the deadness of the womb of Sarah, but in the promise of God not hesitating in unbelief but having been strengthened in faith, gave glory to God, and being fully convinced that what he promised he has power even to do it. Therefore, "it was reckoned to him as/for righteousness." But it was not written for him alone that "it was reckoned to him," but also for us it is to be counted, to those believing in the resurrection of Jesus our Lord from the dead, who was handed over for our transgressions and raised for our being set right.[8]

The Jewish discussion out of which the material in 4.1-12 was germinated needs to be kept in view,[9] and there is reason to see this as perhaps a continuation of the dialogue with the Jewish teacher which began in ch. 3. Abraham was seen in some early Jewish literature as the paradigm of the one who was "faithful" and to whom it was reckoned as righteousness. For example, among the reflections on the "deeds of the fathers" in 1 Macc. 2.51-52: "Was not Abraham found faithful in temptation, and it was reckoned to him as righteousness?" Paul takes a very different approach. His argument will be based on the order of the narratives about Abraham in Genesis. There is, then, a quite specific narrative logic to his case. God credited Abraham's faith as righteousness (Gen. 15.6) before Abraham was ever circumcised (Gen. 17.10; cf. Gal. 3.17-18) and before Abraham had been tested as well (Genesis 22). Paul does not simply amalgamate the Abraham story and draw conclusions. There is a before and after dimension to the story, and Paul's logic follows the narrative flow. This brings up an

---

7. Various Western manuscripts have "He was so strong in faith. . . ." But on balance the translation in the text seems more likely. Metzger, *A Textual Commentary on the Greek New Testament,* p. 451, says: "here Paul does not wish to imply that faith means closing one's eyes to reality, but that Abraham was so strong in faith as to be undaunted by every consideration."

8. The noun *dikaiōsis* is rare in the NT; indeed, it occurs only here and in Rom. 5.18. Unless it is just a matter of stylistic variation (as it may be in 5.18), the term should not be translated "righteousness," but rather "being set right" or possibly, if the forensic idea is dominant, "acquittal." The translation "vindication" should be resisted, since Paul, technically speaking, does not believe that sinners are vindicated by God, but rather forgiven, pardoned, set right. Only the righteous may rightly call for God to vindicate them.

9. As P. Achtemeier, *Romans* (Atlanta: John Knox, 1985), p. 78, points out, the odd use of the verb "find" here in 4.1 reflects the earlier Jewish discussion of Abraham; see Sir. 44.19; 1 Macc. 2.52.

important point for understanding Paul: he does not think through issues as a systematic theologian might, lining up a series of topics or ideas and then assessing them. There is a narrative logic to his thought patterns. He does theology out of his storied world and into the world of his audience. So what we have in Romans is not so much "an introduction to Pauline theology" as an excellent and fulsome example of his theologizing out of his own storied world and into a rhetorical and social situation. Paul would disagree with those Jewish predecessors who contended that Abraham was reckoned righteous on the basis of his deeds or faithful obedience rather than his trust in God. He does not use Abraham as the poster child for obedience to the Law, as we find in Mishnah *Kiddushin* 4.14: "We find that Abraham our father had performed the whole Law before it was given. . . ." To the contrary, Paul uses Abraham as the paradigmatic example of faith reckoned as righteousness.

One argument in favor of seeing Rom. 4.1-12 as a continuation of the discussion with the imaginary Jewish teacher that seemed to have concluded at 3.20 is that 4.1 seems to be a continuation, with Paul picking up where he left off. This would mean that in the phrase "our forefather according to the flesh" Paul or his imaginary dialogue partner is recognizing that they have a common physical descent from Abraham.[10] "What then shall we say?" is a form of rhetorical question Paul regularly uses, including in Romans (see 3.5; 4.1; 7.7; 8.31; 9.14, 30). So the diatribe format continues into ch. 4:

> Interlocutor (Jewish teacher): "Okay, if what you have just argued is true, what then shall we say Abraham our forefather according to the flesh found?"[11]
> Paul: "Well, if Abraham was set right from works, he has (grounds for) a boast, but not before God, for what does the Scripture say. . . ?"
> Interlocutor: "Is the blessing then valid for the circumcised only, or also for the uncircumcised?
> Paul: "For the latter also, for we can say. . . ."
> Interlocutor: "In what state was he then when it was counted? In a state of circumcision or uncircumcision?
> Paul: "Not in a state of circumcision. . . ."[12]

10. See C. Bryan, *A Preface to Romans: Notes on the Epistle and Its Literary and Cultural Setting* (Oxford: Oxford University Press, 2000), pp. 118-19.

11. A few manuscripts (K, L, P) connect the phrase *kata sarka* with the verb "found" — i.e., "What did Abraham find according to the flesh?" But this reading, in addition to being not all that well supported, really makes less sense of the text. How would Abraham's finding something out about righteousness be "according to the flesh"?

12. Compare S. K. Stowers, *A Rereading of Romans: Justice, Jews, and Gentiles* (New Haven: Yale University Press, 1994), pp. 232-50, and especially his critique of R. B. Hays, "Have We Found Abraham to Be Our Forefather according to the Flesh? A Reconsideration of Rom.

If this is a proper way to read the resumption of the diatribe, then it is a mistake to engage in a long discussion of how Paul could address his largely Gentile audience and speak of Abraham as their forefather *kata sarka*. Paul is making no such blunder, and paying attention to the rhetorical structure is crucial. He will clearly enough go on to say in vv. 11-12 that Abraham is the father of all who have faith (both the uncircumcised and the circumcised). Clearly enough the climax of the diatribal argument comes in those verses, and then Paul draws important conclusions in vv. 13-25 about faith and law and righteousness based on the previous dialogue.

Paul thus adopts the format of dialogue followed by summary conclusions based on the dialogue. The major questions in this segment of the diatribe are raised by Paul's dialogue partner. He presupposes the sort of view of Abraham found in the early Jewish discussion cited above. Paul counters with his own line of argumentation which is more driven by the narrative logic of Genesis as the various events are told in sequence. This is in part because Paul thinks salvation-historically, or perhaps better said eschatological-historically. History as well as the future is re-envisioned in light of the eschatological Christ-event.

V. 3 is a crucial quotation of Gen. 15.6 LXX (which has the passive "was counted," unlike the Hebrew, which has the active "he counted").[13] It needs to be stressed that Paul is not speaking here of Christ's righteousness counting in place of Abraham's righteousness or, for that matter, in place of later Christian believers' righteousness. The text is quite explicit — the exchange is between Abraham's faith and Abraham's righteousness. The former is credited or reck-

---

4.1," *NovT* 27 (1985): 79. Hays thinks that there is only one voice, Paul's, in this section, but Stowers is able to show how this interpretation overlooks the way in which a diatribe can be set forth in the very same fashion we find here in Romans. Hays' argument requires that we take Abraham as the object of the verb "found," which is taken to be a first person plural ("what we found Abraham . . ."). This also means that we must take "What then shall we say?" as a separate sentence. But the verb "find" here is in infinitival form, not in the first person plural; in addition, it is grammatically awkward to take the infinitive as the beginning of a new sentence. See D. Moo, *The Epistle to the Romans* (NICNT; Grand Rapids: Eerdmans, 1996), p. 259; B. Byrne, *Romans*, Sacra Pagina (Collegeville: Liturgical, 1996), p. 148. It is more likely that *heurēkenai* is dependent on the verb *eroumen* and introduces a noun clause: "what then shall we say Abraham to have found (or to be found by Abraham). . . ?" See the further discussion in K. Grieb, *The Story of Romans: A Narrative Defense of God's Righteousness* (Louisville: Westminster/John Knox, 2002), pp. 46-47. Also M. Cranford, "Abraham in Romans 4: The Father of All Who Believe," *NTS* 41 (1995): 71-88.

13. Dr. A. J. Levine in oral conversation kindly pointed out to me that on the basis of the Hebrew text of this verse, some medieval Jewish exegetes interpreted the "he" to be Abraham and so took the verse to mean that Abraham trustingly reckoned/counted God as righteous. The Hebrew text is ambiguous enough to allow for such an interpretation, unlike the LXX.

oned in lieu of or as the latter. Where then does the idea of imputed righteousness come from? It comes ultimately from Erasmus, and the Lutheran adoption
of his reading of this material, as we shall now see.

A Closer Look: Imputed Righteousness Versus Reckoned Righteous

If Romans 4 is *not* in fact talking about Christ's righteousness being imputed to Abraham or to believers, where does that notion come from? Fitzmyer has helpfully unrav-
eled the mystery of the history of Protestant interpretation of this matter.[14] First we
need to note that Erasmus chose to depart from the Vulgate rendering, which has
"Abraham believed God, and it was reputed *(reputatum)* to him unto justice
(iustitiam)." Instead Erasmus, drawing on the language common among lawyers of
his day, renders the text as follows: "Abraham believed God and it was imputed
(imputatum) unto him for justice." This rendering is found in Erasmus's *Novum
Instrumentum* of 1516. Now this might not have been very important except that
Melanchthon used Erasmus's NT, and as Fitzmyer says, later Lutheran orthodoxy followed Erasmus's rendering and understanding of the matter. Hence was borne a
rather strictly forensic understanding of *diakaiosynē*, to the point where imputed
righteousness or imputed justification became a received idea.

Luther himself does not always go quite this far. He is prepared to say that only
by the accrediting of a merciful God and by faith in his word do we become just.[15] He
also is prepared to say that all of our good is in fact outside ourselves and located in
Christ.[16] But, as scholars have pointed out, Luther does not usually use the language
of imputation.[17]

The "crediting" language ("it was reckoned") is not forensic language but commercial or bookkeeping language. There is precedent for use of such language of human conduct in Ps. 106.31 and 1 Macc. 2.52 (cf. Phlm. 18). In early Judaism there was
the belief in the good and evil deeds of a person being recorded in ledgers (Esth. 6.1;
Dan. 7.10; *Testament of Benjamin* 11.4; *Jubilees* 30.17).[18] While there are probably some

14. See Fitzmyer, *Romans*, p. 374, to whom I am indebted here.
15. M. Luther, *LW* 25.24-75.
16. M. Luther, *LW* 25.267.
17. See the discussion of A. E. McGrath, "The Righteousness of God from Augustine to
Luther," *ST* 36 (1982): 403-18.
18. At this juncture, a brief note about Jas. 2.20-24 is in order. James is arguing that
faith without deeds is dead. (See my discussion of this material in H. Shanks and
B. Witherington, *The Brother of Jesus* [San Francisco: Harper, 2003], pp. 156-62.) So James
starts with the story of Abraham offering his son Isaac as a sacrifice, seeing this as a reason
why Abraham was considered a righteous person. His faith was made complete by what he
did. Then in v. 23 James quotes the same Scripture Paul uses, Gen. 15.6, but as a fulfillment of
the notion that it was not by faith alone but by faith plus deeds that Abraham was reckoned

legal overtones when Paul couples the Genesis 15 passage with a passage about sins being covered and forgiven and not credited (see below),[19] it is a mistake to simply read Paul's righteousness language through a forensic filter, not least because Paul believes that God requires of his people that, once saved, they actually lead righteous lives. Paul would likely be appalled by the notion that he is talking about some sort of legal fiction, including the idea that Christ is righteous in the believer's place in such a way that believers are not required to be righteous. Even worse would be the notion that when God looks at believers, he simply sees Christ's righteousness and reckons it to their accounts, instead of believers having to live holy lives. This would seem to mean that God is deceived about the actual sinful condition of believers or is willing to look the other way and will no longer hold them accountable for such condition or behavior. It is my guess that Paul would have concluded that either of these notions would amount to God being less than totally righteous. It would certainly involve God re-

---

as righteous. This sounds closer to the early Jewish views, which start with Abraham's obedience and work their way back to the faith passage, than to Paul. V. 24 provides the conclusion that people are set right or are righteous with God, not by faith alone, but also because of what they do.

Is this a flat contradiction of Paul's Abraham argument in Galatians or Romans? No, not exactly. It appears possible that James is arguing against "garbled" Paul, a misrepresentation of the Paul he knew, because in fact Paul is no antinomian, as will become clear in Romans 12–15. Nor would Paul have objected to the idea of working out one's salvation in deeds, which is to say that he believed one must practice what one believes. Whether he would have spoken quite as James does about faith being completed by deeds is uncertain, though the phrase "the obedience of faith" may point in this direction. For Paul, it is so important to make clear that salvation or right standing with God is not obtained by doing deeds of the Law that he would likely have avoided such language, unless it was offered in a context where it was evident that he was not talking about how one enters the community of faith.

19. Notice, however, that the text is speaking about human sin not being credited. There is nothing here about Christ's righteousness being credited to the believer. The idea about crediting Christ's righteousness seems to have been primarily derived from 1 Cor. 1.30. This text reads literally: "who [i.e., Jesus] was made our wisdom by God, righteousness, and sanctification, and redemption." So is Paul saying that Jesus is all these things for or on behalf of the believer? Probably not, for the actual full sentence in the Greek reads as follows: "But you are (from God in Christ, who was made our wisdom by God), righteousness, and sanctification, and redemption." Christ is certainly identified with Wisdom here, but *sophia* is separated from the other predicate nouns here precisely because it is applied to one subject, Jesus, while the other three nouns are applied to another subject, believers. As I have said at more length in *Conflict and Community in Corinth* (Grand Rapids: Eerdmans, 1995), p. 117: "Salvation (as expressed in these three metaphors) comes to believers through a crucified Christ, and thus there is a sense in which believers *are* these things, just as they are frequently called *hagioi*." If one compares 2 Cor. 5.21, we find that believers are said to be the righteousness of God through Christ, and in 1 Cor. 6.11b we hear about believers being washed, consecrated, and set right. So Paul in 1 Cor. 1.30 is speaking not only of what Christ is (our wisdom), but also of what believers are through Christ.

quiring more of his people under the Law than he does under the new covenant, and this hardly comports with the intensification of demands we find in both Pauline parenesis and the Jesus tradition, including portions of the Sermon of the Mount, that Paul draws on in Romans and elsewhere.[20]

Abraham had faith/trust (in God) and that faith was counted to him as righteousness. Paul is speaking of basic trust in God here, not of "the faith" in the sense of a specific set of things believed. He is not suggesting that Abraham was a Christian before the time of Christ. Fitzmyer puts it this way: "Abraham believed in Yahweh's promise of numerous progeny, and this faith was 'booked to his credit' as uprightness. . . . By 'faith' is meant Abraham's acceptance of Yahweh at his word and his willingness to trust and abide by it even when he had no perceptible evidence. It involved his personal confidence and included hope in a promise that no mere human could guarantee (4.18)."[21] The issue here is fundamental trust in God. Paul did not understand the narrative logic of Genesis as suggesting that, once Abraham's faith was counted as righteousness, this took the place of his needing to go on and be obedient to God or personally righteous. Abraham's initial act of faith or trust is credited as righteousness, but then later in Genesis, Abraham is called to various forms of obedience.

Paul wants to use this text to make clear once more that boasting is excluded, even in the case of the father of true religion. The theme of boasting was already found in 2.17 in the earlier portion of the dialogue with the Jewish teacher, and this is one of the links that suggests that the dialogue with the Jewish teacher is continuing here. If Abraham was righteous on the basis of works, then it was a matter of God giving him his just due (again, commercial language), not evaluating him on the basis of grace. But since it was his faith that was credited as righteousness, it was a matter of grace. It may properly be asked — why? If it is Abraham's faith which is being exercised, why is it not seen as his contribution towards the exchange? Abraham offers his faith and God takes it as righteousness. But while Abraham certainly must exercise his faith, Paul believes that faith is also a gift from God. There is no simple quid pro quo involved. God has graciously enabled Abraham to trust, he does so, and it is graciously credited as righteousness. If faith is counted as righteousness, then these two things can be distinguished.[22] In vv. 4-5 Paul poses faith and works as opposites, echoing the contrast between the principle of faith and works of the Law found in 3.27-30. He is showing in the life of Abraham another reason that

20. See pp. 280-90 below.
21. Fitzmyer, *Romans*, p. 373.
22. C. K. Barrett, *Commentary on the Epistle to the Romans* (Peabody: Hendrickson, 1991), p. 83.

the Mosaic Law and its works are inadequate to produce or maintain right standing with God.[23]

This argument stands at the opposite end of the spectrum to what we find in *Jubilees* 11–16, where Abraham is the exemplar of one who kept the Mosaic Law, even before it was written (see *Jubilees* 23.10; 24.11; cf. also Sirach 44.20-21).[24] This tradition of interpretation was continued right through and beyond the NT era (cf. CD 3.2-3; Mishnah *Kiddushin* 4.14: "Abraham our father had performed the whole Law before it was given."). In short, while other Jews saw Abraham as an example of faithfulness, faithful obedience to God's precepts in the Mosaic Law, Paul by contrast saw him as the exemplar of basic trust in God, which is the meaning of *pistis* here.

"Works" in this discussion do not have to do with boundary markers, but any sort of activity by which one could put God in one's debt. As Westerholm puts it: "Since the issue (works of the law vs. faith in Jesus Christ) permits re-statement in terms of a general distinction between 'works' and 'faith,' the point of attack cannot be limited to statutes in the Law which serve as Jewish 'identity markers.' "[25] So when Paul says in 3.20 that by works of the Law no one shall be set right, for the Law merely provides knowledge of sin, he is not suggesting that it is merely circumcision and other boundary-defining laws that provide such knowledge.[26] In fact, Paul now will go on to cite a Scripture that implies that Abraham (see the application to Abraham in v. 9), like, or even as one of, the ungodly, was "justified" quite apart from works or faithful obedience to the Law. He was "set right" much as the largely Gentile audience of Paul's was — by grace through faith. In other words, even Abraham, and even David who was cited earlier, fell short of perfect obedience to the Law. Even for them it was not a sufficient means for "getting in" or "staying in."

In short, there are major flaws in the new perspective on Paul engendered by Sanders and followed by Dunn and to some degree Wright and others, which suggests that Paul is mainly attacking Jewish particularistic nationalism or ethnocentrism.[27] On the contrary, we have seen in the arguments in Romans 2–3 that Paul is attacking arrogance, boasting, self-righteousness based on

23. A. A. Das, *Paul, the Law, and the Covenant* (Peabody: Hendrickson, 2001), p. 205.

24. It is in part the reading of the Abraham story in the sapiential tradition of early Judaism that Paul is critiquing.

25. S. Westerholm, *Israel's Law and the Church's Faith* (Grand Rapids: Eerdmans, 1988), p. 119.

26. See G. N. Davies, *Faith and Obedience in Romans: A Study in Romans 1–4* (Sheffield: Sheffield Academic Press, 1990), p. 118.

27. See the thorough treatment of these difficulties for the new perspective on Paul by Das, *Paul, the Law, and the Covenant*, pp. 192-214. See also B. Longenecker, *Eschatology and the Covenant: A Comparison of 4 Ezra and Romans 1–11* (Sheffield: Sheffield Academic Press, 1991).

works and accomplishments, judgmentalism, and the like. In his Abraham argument he continues along this line to level the playing field: "all have sinned and now lack the glory they should have," and even "faithful" Abraham is not set right by his faithfulness, but rather by God's grace and the response of trust.

In v. 5 Paul speaks of the God who sets right the ungodly. This is very striking to anyone (such as Paul's imaginary interlocutor) who knows the OT, which says in a variety of places that God will not justify the wicked (Exod. 23.7) and that God despises those who do so (Prov. 17.15; Isa. 5.23). To the contrary, God vindicates the just or righteous or innocent or those wrongly accused. There are also plenty of texts in the OT where God is said to have mercy and forgive sin. But the point is that Paul believes that he lives in a different time, an eschatological time after the Christ-event. It is only because of the death of Christ that God can set right the ungodly and not be unjust in doing so. The OT texts in question know nothing of a situation where God could be both righteous and the one who sets right the ungodly.

One of the Jewish techniques of exegesis that Paul continues to use, most appropriately if he is to impress an imaginary Jewish teacher, is called *gezerah shewah*. This technique involves setting two passages beside each other which have a common key term and allowing one to aid interpretation of the other.[28] Here Gen. 15.6 is exegeted in the light of Ps. 32.1-2. The latter text, found in vv. 6-8, is taken verbatim from the LXX, and introduces into the conversation the issue of forgiveness and sins being covered, which is not present in the Genesis text in question. By means of this exegetical exercise Paul is able to imply that the counting of righteousness entails the negative corollary of not counting sin. He does not make a great deal out of this here, but it lays the groundwork for later argumentation. The quotation of the Psalm propels Paul's argument back to the Genesis text in that, when the interlocutor asks about the Psalm text who receives this blessing of forgiveness, the circumcised or the uncircumcised, Paul is able to respond "the uncircumcised" on the basis of the condition of Abraham in Gen. 15.6.

Vv. 11-12 bring the argument to a close with the conclusion that Abraham then is in fact the father of both the circumcised and the uncircumcised who have faith. He is the father of all true believers. There is an important proviso. The Jew, Paul says, must not rely on circumcision "only" *(monon)* but must also follow in the footsteps of Abraham and go on the journey of faith. This conclusion has some extraordinary features. The order in which it is stated suggests that Abraham is in the first place the father of believing Gentiles, since he believed and had the credit of righteousness before he was circumcised and then became the father of believing Jews as well once he was circumcised. Paul is not an advocate of the notion that Abraham can become the father of Gentiles only

28. See Byrne, *Romans,* p. 146.

if they become proselytes, follow the Law, and presumably are also circumcised. Further, Paul has already said in ch. 3 and will reiterate in 9.6-13 that the true Jew, the one who is really the descendent of Abraham, is one who has faith and in that way follows Abraham.

The question then becomes: What was the point of Abraham being circumcised? Circumcision becomes a "seal," after the fact of the righteousness that comes through faith. Circumcision is called a "sign" in Gen. 17.11, and we are told in *Jubilees* 15.26 that the Gentile lacks the sign on his body that he belongs to the Lord. It would appear that Paul deliberately calls circumcision a "seal" here to say something further or a bit different than just that it is a "sign." Paul elsewhere uses "seal" *(sphragis)* of a "confirmation" (cf. 1 Cor. 9.2). He takes Abraham's circumcision to refer back to his faith and his righteousness through faith, not forward to his obligation to keep the Law in order to be righteous. Circumcision, then, instead of inaugurating something, is seen as confirming a preexisting condition. This can only be called a tour de force argument.

Why is Paul seemingly belaboring the circumcision issue as it is connected to the Abraham story when it does not appear that the issues are the same in Rome as they were in Galatia, where there were Judaizers? The answers probably have to do with the fact that early Jews associated the origins of the practice of circumcision on the eighth day with the Abraham story (see Gen. 17.1-27, especially v. 12). Circumcision was believed in some circles to give access to heaven or the messianic kingdom (cf. CD 16.4-6; *Jubilees* 15.31-33). It was no mere ritual, and in any case it came to be seen as the sign of both the Abrahamic and the Mosaic covenants. This being the case, it appears that in early Judaism a good deal of the thinking about the Mosaic covenant was amalgamated with or read back into the story of Abraham. Paul, however, is attempting to distinguish these covenants and to suggest a significance to circumcision that confirms, rather than takes precedent over, Abraham being counted as righteous through faith.

Paul realizes that his reading of the Abraham story in Genesis 15 is bound to raise questions about why the Law was added and what its purpose might be. He tries to begin to deal with this question in vv. 13-25, and along the way he introduces a second portion of the Abraham story to bolster his case. In v. 13 Paul contends that it was not because of the Law that the promise came to Abraham or his seed — the promise that the world would be his inheritance.[29] Here he is thinking of Gen. 22.17-18: all the nations of the world will be blessed through Abraham's seed. Some voices in Jewish tradition had broadened the promise of "land" to include the whole "world" or, eschatologically speaking, all the bless-

---

29. The original promise to Abraham involved "the land" rather than "the world," but already in early Jewish literature, in Sir. 44.19-21, the promise involves the world. Once again we see that Paul is following a sapiential reading of the OT tradition.

ings of the age to come. Paul follows this tradition in v. 13. So to determine who is an heir of Abraham and why is to say who has a place in the world to come, and how it is that they do.[30]

In Galatians Paul argues that Christ is *the* seed of Abraham, and so the blessing comes to the Gentiles as well as Jews through Christ. The promise of blessing through the seed comes after Abraham's circumcision and after he offers up Isaac. Yet even so, says Paul here in Romans, this promise is not based on Abraham's works or merits. In Paul's way of thinking, a promise "falls within the sphere of gift, that is of grace."[31] If the promise had been given on the basis of Law or as a quid pro quo for works of the Law such as circumcision, then it would be a contractual arrangement, and grace and faith would not enter into it. Thus, Paul reasons, if the heirs were heirs on the basis of the Law and works of the Law, then faith and the promise would be in effect nullified (v. 14). Faith, grace, and promise stand on one side of the ledger, and works, Law, and sin stand on the other. This explanation is not sufficient by itself, so Paul adds the further explication that the Law causes wrath and that where there is no Law, there is no transgression (v. 15).

V. 15 is important for understanding the logic of Paul's argument and of his view of the Law. Paul basically believes that the existence of the Law turns sin into transgression, a willful violation of a known Law. One is thus all the more accountable, and the wrath of God results. This is not to say that God does not express his wrath against sin that is not transgression, as 1.18-32 has made evident. The point is that with the Law there are even more accountability and a risk of even greater wrath.

Vv. 16-18 are grammatically difficult, though the gist of what Paul says is reasonably clear. He links together grace, faith, and the promise and explains that God did things as he did so that the promise might be "secure" or "reliable" both for those who are linked to Abraham by faith alone (Gentiles) and for those linked to him by circumcision and "works of the Law" as well as by faith. Had the promise been based on the Law, then only those who did works of the Law could inherit it. Since it is based on grace and appropriated through faith, everyone can inherit. Paul relies on Gen. 17.5 and 15.5 (both in their LXX form) to support his case that from the outset Abraham was meant to be the forefather not only of Jews but also of Gentiles. "God's gracious out-

---

30. Byrne, *Romans*, p. 143. It is also the case, however, that Paul is making clear that Gentiles are saved in the same way as Abraham, which is to say that it has a Jewish precedent. He will go on to argue that Gentiles have been grafted into a Jewish tree known as the people of God. The idea is to take the air out of the Gentile balloon, and not just the Jewish balloon, when it comes to ethnocentric preening and assumptions of superiority or precedence as God's favorites.

31. Barrett, *Romans*, p. 89.

reach to man is of such a character that it can only be received in unconditional openness."[32]

In vv. 18-25 Paul will discourse on another Abraham story, the miraculous
pregnancy of Sarah and the birth of Isaac which resulted. According to Genesis
17 Abraham was already 100 years of age, and even more critically Sarah had
been unable to conceive (and was now 90 years old), when the miracle pregnancy happened. Thus, Paul is able to say that the conception of Isaac was an
example of God quickening the dead, that is, both Abraham's body, which was
"as good as dead," and Sarah's barren womb, and in fact calling into being
things which do not exist. Paul sees this miracle as an example of creatio ex
nihilo, and to him it is closely analogous to the raising of Jesus from the dead.

There is an apropos turn of rhetorical phrase in v. 18 describing Abraham's faith that God could act in spite of the circumstances — par' elpida ep'
elpida. A literal rendering would be something like "beyond hope in hope." Paul
describes Abraham's faith in another way in v. 19: Abraham was not "weakening
in his faith" in the promise, despite his bodily condition. This description is
probably important in light of the later discussion of the "weak" among the Roman Christians, who were mainly Jewish Christians.[33] Abraham, as it turns out,
is the example of faith for both Gentile and Jewish Christians in Rome. But
what would it mean to be beyond hope and yet hopeful? Barrett suggests "it is
when human hope is exhausted that God-given hope . . . comes into effect; in
the midst of human death and non-existence it looks to God who quickens and
creates."[34] In Paul's view, the remarkable resurrection power of God to bring
life out of death and something out of nothing was in evidence long before Jesus' resurrection. It was already in evidence in Abraham's time and life.

But there is further rhetorical force to Paul's continuing reiteration that
Abraham is the father of many (non-Jewish) nations. As we shall see in chs. 9–
11, there seems to have been a real problem with Gentile Christians in Rome ap-
preciating their Jewish heritage. Paul has to emphasize to them who are the root
and vine and who are wild olive branches grafted in later. Here Paul will prepare for that discussion by making clear that Abraham is the Gentiles' father too,
not just the father of Jews. Abraham is their father not just as the paradigm of
the sort of faith Gentile Christians have and ought to have, but also because
they share in salvation through the promise made to Abraham. Furthermore, it
was God who appointed Abraham to be the father of many nations. This was
God's plan from the first. God did not supersede an original plan for Jews with
one for Gentiles. Rather Jews and Gentiles were in the plan from the time of the
human progenitor of God's people — Abraham.

---

32. J. D. G. Dunn, Romans 1–8, Word Biblical Commentary (Dallas: Word, 1988), p. 215.
33. See pp. 325-40 below.
34. Barrett, Romans, p. 91.

V. 20 stresses that Abraham did not give way to unbelief but rather was strengthened in faith during the time of testing, and gave glory to God. Faith "is strong precisely because it looks solely to God and does not depend on human possibilities. . . . It is not that faith ignores or denies historical realities . . . rather, says Paul, Abraham took them fully into account . . . that is why his faith can be called strong. . . . By implication faith is weak when it allows itself to be determined by or depend upon what lies within human power. . . . Paul takes for granted that faith is not a fixed packet but can grow strong and grow weak. . . ."[35] Abraham was convinced that the promise itself was powerful and that what God had said would be accomplished. It is this remarkable faith, and not just any sort of faith, that was reckoned as righteousness — a faith that hoped against hope, a faith that in the time of testing did not give way to unbelief, a faith that gave glory to God then,[36] a faith that was convinced and convicted that God could bring life out of death and accomplish what was humanly impossible, a faith which is described in Heb. 11.1 as "the assurance of things hoped for and the conviction about things not seen." Notice the participle "being fully convinced" (plērophorētheis), which Paul correlates with strong faith here.

Paul returns to the theme of faith reckoned as righteousness at the end of this argument, quoting again from Gen. 15.6, and then in vv. 24-25 he draws the analogy to Christians who place such faith in the One who raised Jesus "our Lord" from the dead. V. 25 may indeed involve a quotation from an early Christian creedal formula, but, if so, it is one that Paul endorses. It may also allude to Isa. 53.12. "Handed over" refers in all probability to God's action, just as raising from the dead was what God did for Jesus.[37] The emphasis is both on Christ being given up for *our transgressions* and being raised for *our being set right/acquittal.* The passage thus ends stressing the Christian believers' being set right. Nothing is said about Christ's righteousness being imputed to the believer.[38] In fact, the second *dia* clause seems likely to be prospective, in which case the reference is to believers' final acquittal or being set right when they appear before the *bēma* seat of Christ.

Jesus who is handed over and raised is called "our Lord." The fact of Jesus' humanness and indeed even his horrific death did not in any way in Paul's mind make him less than the divine Lord. Thus while some might regard speaking of a Lord who was raised from the dead as oxymoronic, in Paul's view

---

35. Dunn, *Romans 1–8*, pp. 220-21.

36. As Barrett, *Romans*, p. 92, points out, Abraham does the very thing that those mentioned in 1.21 did not do — honor and glorify the Creator God in the proper way.

37. See Dunn, *Romans 1–8*, p. 224.

38. I agree with those scholars who think that the story of the binding of Isaac, particularly in its later rabbinic form, plays little or no role in shaping Paul's presentation here.

this aptly describes two important things that are both true of Jesus. In Phil. 2.5-11 Paul will say that it was precisely at the resurrection that Jesus was given the divine name Lord. This verse is a perfect segue into the argument which begins in Rom. 5.1.

Bridging the Horizons

There are certainly times when faith is stretched to the limits, times when it is indeed a matter of hoping against all the visible evidence and natural conditions, hoping against hope. Jim Wallis of the magazine *Sojourners* once defined hope as "trusting God in spite of all the evidence, then watching the evidence change."[39] Abraham certainly falls into the category of one who trusted God at various junctures without having the "ocular proof," as Shakespeare's Othello called it. Paul juxtaposes two stories about Abraham here as examples of true faith in action, and one may choose one or the other to focus on. What is equally interesting is that Paul does not go on to elaborate about the ultimate test of Abraham's faith when he had to offer up Isaac to God. Rather he focuses on Abraham's initial trust in God and then on his trust regarding the miraculous conception of Isaac. I suspect the reason for this is that the Isaac story could be read as an example of Abraham's faithfulness or obedience to God, and Paul instead wishes to focus on faith rather than faithfulness here where the issue is how one comes to be reckoned righteous.

It is important in teaching and preaching this material that one focus on what the text does say and not on what it does not say. Romans 4 is about Abraham's nodal trust in God, which God reckoned as righteousness. It is not about Christ's righteousness being imputed to Abraham or to those who follow his example. The discussion is about faith vs. works, not Christology vs. anthropology. Furthermore, the dominant metaphor is not forensic but commercial — the reckoning of a credit because of faith and the non-reckoning of a debit, namely sin. These factors should guide the way one teaches and preaches this material.

---

39. Cited by Grieb, *The Story of Romans*, p. 53.

Argument Four — 5.1-11:
The Results of Rectification

The story of Abraham leads to certain conclusions, which Paul has amply pointed out in ch. 4. But there are also certain further implications to that story, especially as it is compared to the story of Christians, that Paul wants to highlight. He uses no OT quotations (there is one allusion) and argues in terms that a Gentile could readily understand and identify with. The language of peace, reconciliation, and the pacification of enemies would be familiar to those in Rome used to hearing the honorific propaganda about the emperor and his accomplishments, vis à vis the Pax Romana.[1] But here the Lord through whom this was accomplished was Jesus, and the means he used was dying rather than killing. There is a close thematic relationship between 5.1-11 and 8.1-39, for in both segments we find the themes of rectification, hope, eschatological glory, patience in suffering, the love of God, the Spirit of God, and the death of Christ.[2] Here finally in this text, as in ch. 8, Paul is clearly and openly describing Christian experience.

Lest we think that Paul emphasizes only the positive side of things, we should note that Romans 5-8 contains 45% of the references to death and 32% of the references to life in all the undisputed Paulines.[3] In short, one may say that Paul is dealing with (spiritual) life and death issues in Rom. 5–8.

---

1. See the important essay by N. Elliott, "Paul and the Politics of Empire," in *Paul and Politics,* ed. R. A. Horsley (Harrisburg: Trinity, 2002), pp. 17-39, and also N. T. Wright, "Paul's Gospel and Caesar's Empire," pp. 160-83 in the same volume.

2. See N. A. Dahl, "Two Notes on Romans 5," *ST* 5 (1952): 37-38.

3. For details see F. Thielman, "The Story of Israel and the Theology of Romans 5–8," in *Pauline Theology,* vol. 3: *Romans,* ed. D. M. Hay and E. E. Johnson (Minneapolis: Fortress, 1995), pp. 169-95, here p. 178 n. 31.

While 5.1-11 is a transitional passage, a good case can be made that it is the conclusion of the arguments in 1.18 through ch. 4, drawing out the implications for Christians of what has been argued. Then Paul will begin again in 5.12 with the story of the world gone wrong, as in 1.18ff., and work his way to the climax in ch. 8, which speaks of the destiny of those in Christ.[4] This is not to suggest that the progression and nature of the arguments in 1.18–5.11 are identical to what one finds in 5.12–8.39 by any means, but the two are complementary in the way they move from disgrace to grace.

R. N. Longenecker has suggested that in 1.16–4.25 Paul has set out what he believed he had in common with his audience's worldview, whereas in 5.1–8.39 he speaks of matters of his own distinctive preaching.[5] The problem with this conclusion is that it does not recognize the relationship of 5.1-11 with the material in ch. 4, which it builds on and draws implications from. And in fact, since Paul is actually critiquing Gentile hubris in ch. 2, it is doubtful that he really thinks that his audience already agrees with what he says there. There may well however be something to the suggestion that the material in 5.12–8.39 does reflect and is distilled from Paul's distinctive preaching to Gentiles.[6] Certainly we do find important Pauline themes in this section of the letter.

What can be said is that when Paul takes up the mantle again at 5.12 the argument becomes more personal in the sense that Paul will deal with Adam in particular, then those who are in Adam, whereas 1.18-32 began more generally with fallen humanity, and in particular pagans. The end of the first cycle through the story of fall and redemption became personal with the example of Abraham, and then the implications for Christians are made plain in Rom. 5.1-11, whereas the second cycle through the story begins with the stories of Adam and of Christ, and then one oscillates between what is the case for Adam (7.6-

4. This is the suggestion of F. J. Leenhardt, *The Epistle to the Romans* (New York: World, 1961), pp. 24-25. He is followed in this by C. Talbert, *Romans* (Macon: Smyth and Helwys, 2002), pp. 129-31. See also C. D. Myers, "The Place of Romans 5.1-11 within the Argument of the Epistle" (unpublished Ph.D. diss., Princeton Theological Seminary, 1985).

5. R. N. Longenecker, "The Focus of Romans: The Central Role of 5.1–8.39 in the Argument of the Letter," in *Romans and the People of God,* ed. S. K. Soderlund and N. T. Wright (Grand Rapids: Eerdmans, 1999), pp. 49-69. Using the same sort of divisions of the letter, R. Scroggs ("Paul as Rhetorician: Two Homilies in Romans 1–11," in *Jews, Greeks and Christians: Religious Cultures in Late Antiquity* [FS W. D. Davies], ed. R. Hamerton-Kelly and R. Scroggs [Leiden: Brill, 1976], pp. 271-98) has actually suggested that chs. 1–4 and 9–11 contain a Jewish homily from Paul, and chs. 5–8 contain one directed to Gentiles. As we have seen, this will not work, not least because 1.18-32 is directed toward Gentiles, as are chs. 9–11.

6. See also S. Kim, "God Reconciled His Enemy to Himself: The Origin of Paul's Concept of Reconciliation," in *The Road to Damascus: The Impact of Paul's Conversion on His Life, Thought, and Ministry,* ed. R. N. Longenecker (Grand Rapids: Eerdmans, 1997), pp. 102-24.

13), for those in Adam (especially 7.14-25), and for those in Christ (8.1-39). The role of the Mosaic Law comes up in both sets of discussions.

Having been set right then by faith, we have⁷ peace with God through our Lord Je-sus Christ, through whom also we have gained the access into this grace in which we stand, and we boast in the hope of the glory of God. Not only so, but also we boast in the suffering, knowing that suffering produces patience, but patience pro-duces tested character, and tested character produces hope. But hope does not dis-appoint because the love of God is poured out in our hearts through the Holy Spirit who was given to us. If indeed Christ, being weak for us, at the appointed time died for the ungodly. . . . For scarcely for a righteous person will anyone die. Well, per-haps for a good person someone might dare to die. But God introduced his own love for us because while we were sinners Christ died for us. How much more then, having been set right then by his blood, shall we be saved through him from the wrath [of God]. For if, being enemies, we were reconciled to God through the death of his Son, how much more having been reconciled shall we be saved by his life. But not only that, but boasting in God through our Lord Jesus through whom now we receive the reconciliation.

There is significant debate in regard to whether Paul is saying in 5.1 that believers have peace with God as a consequence of being set right with God, or whether it happens concurrently with being set right. It is doubtful that we should agree with Cranfield that what Paul is referring to here is having a righ-teous *status* before God, if by this some idea of imputed righteousness is im-plied.⁸ What Paul is talking about is neither an inherent nor a given attribute of believers but rather an action of God which set them right, so that they have a new or renewed relationship with God as a result of the work of Christ. If God were simply to impute to believers his righteousness, then there would be no basis to require righteousness of them after their conversion.

The peace Paul is talking about here is not inner tranquility, but rather the cessation of hostilities, and so, like the term *dikaiōthentes*, it has to do with a restored or fixed relationship that exists between two parties. The language of

7. The subjunctive reading "we might have" has superior external support, but since Paul is stating facts rather than exhorting here, the indicative seems to be the preferable read-ing, and it also has good manuscript support. The hortatory section of this discourse does not begin until 12.1. See B. M. Metzger, *A Textual Commentary on the Greek New Testament* (3rd ed.; London: United Bible Societies, 1971), pp. 452, on the manuscript evidence. There was no pronunciation difference between the indicative and subjunctive versions of "we have" in Paul's day, and so the scribe may have heard it one way while Paul meant it the other way.

8. C. E. B. Cranfield, *A Critical and Exegetical Commentary on the Epistle to the Romans* (ICC; Edinburgh: Clark, 1975-79), 1:256-59.

obtaining peace on the basis of justice/righteous action was familiar and regularly used of the pacification efforts of the Roman emperor, who, it was
claimed, was being just as he established the Pax Romana.[9] "Romans was written at the beginning of Nero's rule, when propaganda based on such prophetic
and theological speculations, with intense eschatological expectations, enjoyed
great popularity. For Paul, Jesus is what the *princeps* claimed to be: representative of humanity, reconciler and ruler of the world. Jesus is all this because he
demonstrates the association and identification of God with those in rebellion
against God. He represents the weakness of God and thus the dominion of
grace, the sole form of dominion befitting both humanity and God."[10] There is
then a revolutionary dimension to what Paul is saying here, especially when the
ears who are hearing it are largely Roman Gentiles who know the rhetoric of
empire by heart. Paul will take a further step in the direction of co-opting the
empire's rhetoric and claims in ch. 13, where he will argue that Nero and his
subordinate authority figures are servants of the God of the Bible.[11]

Paul probably also has in mind the Jewish concept of shalom, which comprehensively represents the blessings of salvation, which brings wholeness as well
as holiness (see Isa. 48.18; cf. 2 Thess. 3.16). One may say that being set back in
right relationship with God necessarily entails being at peace with God and being
reconciled with God. Another part of the package is that through Christ the believer also has access to an ongoing source of grace, which Paul can describe as the
grace in which "we stand," the perfect tense of the verb indicating something with
ongoing effects. Paul says the believer has gained unfettered or free access to this
grace. But this language may suggest even more, because grace here seems to be
seen as a sort of sphere which the believer enters and stands within.[12]

The image may be of a weak person who is able to stand up and with-
stand whatever life brings through the divine power and love of God. Cranfield
notes that it implies the privilege of being introduced into the presence of
someone of higher station than oneself.[13] It is grace that enables a believer to
stand and also grace which enables one to boast in the glory of God. Here in
this context, boasting is not a negative thing, since it is boasting in God. The
verb could be translated "exult" to convey this positive sense.[14] More particu-

9. See D. Georgi, "God Turned Upside Down — Romans: Missionary Theology and
Roman Political Theology," in *Paul and Empire*, ed. R. A. Horsley (Harrisburg: Trinity, 1997),
pp. 148-57.

10. Georgi, "God Turned Upside Down," p. 154.

11. See pp. 305-8 below.

12. See J. D. G. Dunn, *Romans 1–8*, Word Biblical Commentary (Dallas: Word, 1988),
p. 248.

13. Cranfield, *Romans*, 1:259.

14. See C. K. Barrett, *Commentary on the Epistle to the Romans* (Peabody: Hendrickson,
1991), p. 96.

larly, Paul boasts in two different things — in the eschatological hope and in the present sufferings which produce good character.

A person's existence is defined by the master he or she serves.[15] What a person boasts in or about reveals who that master is. Probably Jer. 9.23ff. lies in the background here. It speaks of the perfectly legitimate boasting in the Lord. Since God by definition already has glory, it is not likely that Paul means the hope of giving God glory. Paul could be referring here to seeing the glory of God when Christ comes, but more likely he refers to the hope of being conformed to Christ's glorious image at the resurrection (see Romans 8). Paul never defines life in heaven as glory. Indeed, in 2 Corinthians 4–5 he makes evident that life in heaven involves being absent from the body, which he can also call a state of nakedness before God. This is seen not as glorious but embarrassing. Rom. 3.23 perhaps refers to the glory humans lost in the fall which must be regained in the eschaton.[16]

In v. 3 we have a "not only . . . but also" construction. Paul mentions here another reason for boasting, namely suffering, presumably the woes and trials of faith, including persecution, as in 2 Cor. 6.4 and 12.10. It is then not just any sort of suffering Paul is boasting about, for he is no masochist, but specifically suffering for the sake of the faith. Apparently Paul believes that believers fill up the allotment of messianic suffering (see Rom. 8.17). Dunn puts the matter as follows: "the sufferings believers endure in the period of overlap between the old age (of Adam) and the new age (of Christ) are bearable because they are a sharing in Christ's sufferings and death."[17] But there are further reasons to boast in one's afflictions in that they prevent a person from placing confidence in himself and not in God alone (see 2 Cor. 11.30). And Paul also exults in suffering because it is a clear sign that the eschatological age has dawned and such sufferings "mark out the path to glory (cf. Col. 1.24)."[18]

One boasts in suffering not just because it produces long-term glory, down the road, but also because it produces Christian character here and now — including, according to vv. 3-4, patience, which in turn produces tested character,[19] which in turn produces a hope which does not disappoint. We have here an elliptical chain where one has to assume that the same verb ("produce") functions in each case. Notice the "we know" which introduces the chain. This is the voice of shared Christian experience. Unlike some kinds of hope, Paul is

15. E. Käsemann, *Commentary on Romans* (Grand Rapids: Eerdmans, 1980), pp. 133-36.

16. See p. 102 above.

17. Dunn, *Romans 1–8*, p. 250.

18. Barrett, *Romans*, p. 97.

19. *Dokimē* is a rare word. It means "tested and approved." In view of its lack of attestation prior to the time of Paul (and nowhere else in the Greek Bible), Dunn, *Romans 1–8*, p. 251, suggests that Paul may have coined the term.

not advocating mere wishful thinking, for it is a hope which has already been partially realized in the Spirit's presence and in God's love in the life of the believer. Such a hope only whets the appetite, for it serves as a preview of coming attractions.

In an honor and shame culture such as Paul lived in, to have believed in a false god, to have placed one's hope in a hoax, and for this to become public knowledge was one of the ultimate forms of humiliation (see Ps. 22.5; 25.3, 20). It is likely that Paul's audience would hear what he says here about shame in light of what Stoics like Seneca said about suffering being part of a divine education program meant to produce virtue in a person. "Toward good persons God has the mind of a father . . . and he says, 'Let them be harassed by toil, by suffering, by losses, in order that they may gather true strength. Who has struggled constantly with his ills becomes hardened through suffering, and yields to no misfortune. . . . Are you surprised if that God, who greatly loves the good, who wishes them to become supremely good and virtuous, allots to them a fortune that makes them struggle?" (*On Providence* 2.5-6). The same idea can be found in the Jewish tradition in *4 Maccabees* 10.10-27; 17.12-18. "Suffering in this view is not so much correction of misdirection as conditioning that builds one up for greater virtue."[20]

Here also Paul speaks of God pouring his love into the inner being of the believer (here called the heart). The verb "poured out" is in the perfect, indicating the enduring effect on the believer of the pouring out of love. He is not talking about the pouring out of the Spirit here. Rather, the Spirit is the agent through whom the love of God comes into the being of the believer. The Spirit is also seen as a gift, bringing with him all the other benefits and blessings of God. Probably the presence of the Spirit is seen as a sort of pledge, the source of the assurance that the believer's hope is not in vain. Salvation here, as in 13.11, is envisioned as having a yet unrealized future dimension. The phrase "love of God" is found only here and in 8.39 and 2 Cor. 13.13, and in each case it refers to God's love for us rather than our love for God (despite Augustine's interpretation of Rom. 5.5).

This is indeed the first reference to God's love in Romans, and it is significant that Paul talks about it in such experiential terms. Paul refers not merely to believing in or knowing about this love but also to experiencing it in the inner person in an abundant way, through the metaphor of a rainstorm.

"In our hearts," "underscores the same point since it is precisely the fact that God has effected his work at the level of their motive and emotive center . . . , through the Spirit and in fulfillment of the promise of Jer 31:31-34 (cf. 2 Cor 3:3), which in Paul's view most clearly distinguished the first Christians. . . ."[21]

---

20. Talbert, *Romans*, p. 135, whose lead I am following here. He is also right that Paul has followed here the rhetorical rules for using a train of logic to build to an appropriate climax.

21. Dunn, *Romans 1–8*, p. 253.

In v. 6 Paul states the basis of all this — at the appointed time, when humankind was weak, Christ died for the ungodly, indeed even died for his enemies. A crescendo of terms is used for those Christ died for: weak, ungodly, sinners, enemies.[22] Christ acted as part of God's appointed plan, which had as its object the whole human race, since all have sinned and fallen short of God's glory. The sense of v. 7 is brought out by Cranfield as "it is a rare thing for someone to lay down his life for a just person, much less for one who is his benefactor" (see Ps. 73.1 for this sense of "the [do]-gooder").[23] How much more surprising then is Christ's death for the ungodly. It does not follow normal human behavior patterns or human logic. How very different is the logic here compared to Sirach 12.1-7, which advises to recognize whom you are doing good to and "give to the godly person but do not help the sinner." Seneca advised giving help to those who deserved it (*De Beneficiis* 4.27.5), and Aristotle (*Ethics* 9.8.1169a) speaks of doing good for one's friends. Paul's logic runs counter to the normal conventions of the day.[24] He stresses that God's action in Christ is without human analogy.[25] But God "introduced his love" (or "demonstrated" it — *sunistēmi* can mean either) for believers in the fact that Christ died for them while they were still sinners (v. 8). This fact gives believers further hope that they shall be saved from the wrath to come.

It appears we have here an instance of a *kal wayomer* type of argument (from the lesser to the greater, "if . . . then how much more . . ."), as also in vv. 9, 10, 11, 15, and 17. Many of the rhetorical techniques and forms of argumentation known in early Judaism were in fact derived ultimately from Greco-Roman rhetoric, and their use by Jews is another example of the effect Greek culture had on Jews from the time of Alexander on.[26] Quintilian explains that one form of amplification which involves comparison "seeks to rise from the lesser to the greater, since by raising what is below it must necessarily exult that which is above" (*Instit. Or.* 8.4.9-10). One form this type of amplification takes is an "if x . . . then how much greater . . ." form. Quintilian goes on to say that in *argumentation* where the greater is inferred from the lesser, though this resembles amplification as a figure of speech, it is in fact aiming at proof rather than just embellishment (*Instit. Or.* 8.4.12). Here Paul is in the midst of argumentation, and

22. Dunn, *Romans 1–8*, p. 254.

23. The definite article before the word "good" suggests a particular class or type of person, such as generous benefactors. See Cranfield, *Romans*, 1:264-65; A. D. Clarke, "The Good and the Just in Romans 5.7," *TynBul* 41 (1990): 128-42.

24. See Talbert, *Romans*, p. 137, on these texts.

25. Dunn, *Romans 1–8*, p. 256.

26. The Hellenizing effect is of course more in evidence in some Jewish writers than others; for example, Philo definitely reflects the effect of Greek philosophy and of rhetoric on someone who remained thoroughly Jewish. On his rhetorical adeptness see B. Winter, *Are Paul and Philo among the Sophists?* (Cambridge: Cambridge University Press, 1997).

so we must not think of embellishment here but the enhancement of his proof and persuasion.

The reference to Christ's blood in v. 9 builds on what Paul has said in 3.25. He does not refer to the blood of Christ all that frequently (cf. 1 Cor. 10.16; 11.25-27; Eph. 1.7; 2.13; Col. 1.20). Here rescue from wrath is said to come by Christ's blood, which surely favors the view that Christ's death is what assuaged and propiated that wrath.[27]

Salvation is viewed here as future. It involves being rescued from the coming wrath of God. In fact, more often than not, Paul speaks of salvation in the future tense (see Rom. 5.10; 9.27; 10.9, 13; 11.26; cf. 1 Cor. 3.15; 7.16; 9.22).[28] Being set right and reconciled are present realities, while salvation is seen as essentially in the future. Barrett sets out vv. 9-10 in parallel to show that the form of argumentation is the same — having been set right (v. 9)/reconciled (v. 10), through the death of Jesus (both verses), we shall be saved (both verses).[29] It follows from this that "reconciled" is another way to speak of being set right. It refers to the restoration of a relationship, the setting of a relationship back on the right track so that there is no more alienation, estrangement, or hostility. "And since the process of salvation is yet incomplete, it also means that the believer is not yet delivered from the outworking of wrath in the present (cf. 1:18-32) or from the necessity of being judged in the last day (cf. 14:10; 1 Cor 3:14-15; 2 Cor 5:10)."[30] Both the tense of "will be saved" and the eschatological context here make evident Paul is not talking about some spiritual experience in the present, but rather deliverance and perhaps resurrection at the end of human history.

So v. 10 merely restates the argument in different terms. Human beings have been called weak, sinners, and ungodly, and now enemies of God. "Enemy" suggests open rebellion or warfare against God, a condition aptly described in 1.18-32.[31] Reconciliation took place through the death of God's Son[32]

---

27. See N. T. Wright, "Romans," in *The New Interpreter's Bible,* vol. 10 (Nashville: Abingdon, 2002), p. 519, and the discussion pp. 108-10 above.

28. On the verb *sōzō* being used of the present experience of the believer, see 1 Cor. 1.18; 15.2; 2 Cor. 2.15.

29. Barrett, *Romans,* p. 100.

30. Dunn, *Romans 1–8,* p. 258.

31. See pp. 62-72 above.

32. Jesus is referred to here as God's Son for the first time since 1.3-4. The importance of this is of course that it rules out the notion that Paul thought Jesus became the Son of God at the resurrection. On the contrary, Paul believed that Jesus was the Son of God during his life and when he died on the cross as well, however paradoxical it might be thought to speak of God sacrificing his own Son in order to be reconciled to his own enemies. Chrysostom puts it this way: "The fact that we who were such terrible sinners were saved is a very great sign, indicating how much we were loved by him who saved us. For it was not by angels or

while those being reconciled were still openly hostile to God.[33] Achtemeier puts the matter this way: "If Christ's death means God made peace with us even though we were enemies, surely Christ's resurrection means God will save us now that we are his friends."[34] It may well be that Paul is thinking of himself being at odds with God and persecuting God's people before his Damascus road experience.

V. 11 simply gathers up and reiterates what has been said previously, as is appropriate in a rhetorical argument.

Bridging the Horizons

Reconciliation, says Cicero, is a sign of greatness. In our passage it is seen as a miracle of God. Just how much it is a miracle and an act of grace can be attested to by anyone who has gone through the trauma of becoming alienated from another that one loves. It is even worse for one who has largely been the cause of alienation through a sin or error. Human beings do not forgive as readily as God. Nor, if they do forgive, do they necessarily go the extra mile by actually reaching out in reconciliation to the one who has sinned. I have had occasion to experience what it is like to feel unforgiven for a very long period of time because reconciliation was not forthcoming. It reminded me that the biblical notion of forgiveness, as God practices it, entails reconciliation. God does not merely forgive or cease hostilities. He reaches out in love and offers reconciliation. He not only offers reconciliation, he pours love into the heart of the sinner by means of the Holy Spirit, so that the sinner can respond in love to God. Certainly one of the most powerful expositions of this truth is seen in Rembrandt's famous painting of the Prodigal Son housed in the Hermitage in St. Petersburg, Russia. The Father goes forth and embraces his son, placing his hands lovingly and gently on the kneeling and repentant child while others watch in amazement at the father's behavior.

Reconciliation is indeed a sign of greatness, a sign of a great miracle. If it was practiced anywhere near as much as it is preached, both the church and the world would be far more liveable and gracious places. There is a certain pro-

---

archangels but by his only begotten Son that God saved us" (*Homily* 9 on Romans). See G. Bray, ed., *Romans* (Ancient Christian Commentary on Scripture; Downers Grove: InterVarsity, 1998), p. 134.

33. On the theme of reconciliation here and elsewhere in the Pauline corpus see R. P. Martin, "Reconciliation: Romans 5.1-11," in *Romans and the People of God*, ed. Soderlund and Wright, pp. 36-48. Reconciliation of course implies estrangement in the first place.

34. P. Achtemeier, *Romans* (Atlanta: John Knox, 1985), p. 91.

gression to Paul's statement here — having been set right leads to peace with God, a current standing in grace, and a hope for the future. There are past, present, and future dimensions to salvation and its benefits. It is not just about pardon and release, not just about peace with God, not just about having grace sufficient to stand and to resist sin day by day, not simply about having a legitimate hope. It is about all these things, and all of these benefits accrue in the present. Paul does not even speak about glorification here or the final future. Yet he does speak of one future dimension to salvation: if one has been set right in the present, one will be saved from the wrath to come. The salvation process is not complete in the present. It is completed only in the future, with the final deliverance from wrath and the assumption of the resurrection body. Paul's entire discussion of salvation is eschatologically driven, and includes very few otherworldly dimensions.

Argument Five — 5.12-21:
From First Adam to Last (a Comparison)

By now in his discourse, Paul has established a definite pattern. After the initial thesis statement in 1.16-17, an argument with a judgmental Gentile is presented, followed by an argument with a judgmental Jewish teacher. This in turn leads to the amplified version of the thesis statement in 3.21-31. The discourse with the Jew continues in ch. 4, where Paul presents Abraham as exhibit A of righteousness through faith and as the spiritual forefather of Gentiles as well as Jews. This in turn is followed by another summary statement in 5.1-11 of Christian theological implications for the life of the Christian based on the previous argument.

We will then not be surprised to find Paul present a further historical example in his next argument, in this case Adam, as a basis for drawing yet further conclusions about the Christian life in ch. 6. This argument involves a *synkrisis* or comparison between Adam and Christ, just as the argument in ch. 4 involved an implied comparison between Abraham and Christian believers.[1] What is not generally recognized is that the story of Adam not only undergirds but underlies the entire discussion from 5.12 to the end of ch. 7, and it is only at that juncture that Paul feels free to give a full discussion of the implications of what he has been saying for Christian life, which he does in ch. 8, which concludes the *probatio* portion of Paul's arguments.

The rhetoric of comparisons needs to be explored briefly here, and in particular the rhetoric of a specific kind of comparison, since Paul is not simply comparing Adam to Christ, but rather the effects of Adam's actions on the human race with the effects of Christ's action. Quintilian tells us that as a rule all deliberative speeches are based on comparisons (*Instit. Or.* 3.8.23-24), and so it

---

1. See C. Talbert, *Romans* (Macon: Smyth and Helwys, 2002), pp. 150-51.

is not a surprise that Paul resorts to this technique here and to a lesser degree elsewhere in Romans.[2] Hermogenes says regarding comparisons done in a narrative mode that examples are most vivid when the differences are highlighted as clearly as the similarities (*Progymnasta* 2).[3] Paul in fact stresses the differences, for clearly enough the point is that the gift is not just like the trespass, but exceeds it in effect. Thus, this is not intended to be a comparison of exact equals but is a way of highlighting both misdeeds and good deeds and their effects. The "how much more" form of argument is turned to in the midst of this comparison as well (see above on vv. 9 and 10).[4]

The effect of the comparison here, set in a deliberative piece of rhetoric, is rather like a Rembrandt painting — the dark backdrop of Adam's sin serves to highlight the brightness and clarity of God's grace gift. The comparison by contrast also brings to the fore another key point — namely, that those who are in Christ and feeling the effects of the reign of his grace in their lives are no longer in Adam and do not labor under the reign of sin, which Paul has described as the condition from Adam to Moses (and beyond until Christ). Thus by this comparison, Paul has prepared the way for the contrast between the "I" in ch. 7 and the person in Christ, described in ch. 8. The former is laboring under the bondage of sin, and the latter has been set free by the Spirit from that bondage, as we shall see. Quintilian says that comparisons of this sort are to be done on the basis of the character of the two parties (*Instit. Or.* 4.2.99). In this case it is not just the characters of Adam and Christ which are contrasted, but also of all those in Adam and all those in Christ.

Quintilian is very clear in including "the lesser to the greater" form of argument as a regular part of a proper comparison (*Instit. Or.* 5.10.88; 8.4.13). Paul's argument here would likely have been recognized as a sophisticated form of rhetorical comparison that moves from the dark to the light, the lesser to the greater. The psychological dynamics of the technique are that if the listener grants the premise in regard to the example of Adam (namely that his sin affected all humanity), there is a strong pull to grant the conclusion that that is how Christ has affected humanity. It was important that one conclude the argument on the positive, or "greater" side, which is of course what Paul does with a flourish in v. 21, where the duel between sin and grace, death and eternal life, is won with grace and life reigning longer and more profoundly in the life of the believer.

---

2. There is some comparison going on in chs. 2–3, and also in the exposition on Abraham in ch. 4, but here we have the clearest instance of *synkrisis* in Romans.

3. I owe this reference to my Australian friend and colleague Christopher Forbes, who has studied rhetorical comparisons at length, as well as their relevance for studying Paul's letters.

4. On which see pp. 137-38 above.

So it is that through one human being sin entered the world, and through sin, death, and thus death spread to all human beings, because all sinned. For until the Law, sin was in the world, but sin was not reckoned, not being against the Law. But death reigned from Adam to Moses, even upon those who did not sin in the same likeness of the trespass of Adam, who is a type of the Coming One.

But not like the trespass is thus also the grace gift. For if through the trespass of the one the many died, how much more the grace of God and the gift in grace of the one human being Jesus Christ abounded to the many. And the gift is not like the sin by the one. For on the one hand the judgment from the one unto condemnation, but on the other hand, the grace gift after many trespasses unto acquitting judgment. For if death reigned because of the trespass of the one through that one, how much more those receiving the abundance of the grace and the gift[5] of righteousness will reign in life through the one Jesus Christ. So then, as through one trespass unto all humans unto condemnation, thus also through one human being's act of justice/righteous deed unto all humans for the putting right of life. For as through the disobedience of the one human, many were made sinners, thus also through the obedience of the one many were constituted righteous. But the Law intruded in order to increase the trespass. But where the sin increased, the grace superabounded, in order that just as the sin reigned in death, so also the grace reigned through righteousness unto everlasting life through Jesus Christ our Lord.

The logic of argumentation in 5.12-21 will seem strange to many moderns because it deals with the concept of one affecting many for ill or good, and not only affecting them but determining their destiny to a real extent. Paul can also say in the midst of this argument that death spread to all humans because they all sinned, but then turn around and say that death reigned over even those who did not trespass in the same fashion Adam did. Some have drawn an analogy with the notion of federal headship over a group of people (e.g., when the President declares war on another nation, whether the citizens will it or not, they are affected by this decision and are in effect also at war with the nation in question). This analogy does get at some of the dimensions of Paul's argument. But there is a dimension of corporate personality or, better said, incorporative personality to Paul's argument as well. Paul says that death reigned because of Adam's trespass through Adam to all of his progeny, just as through Christ those receiving grace will reign in life. All in Adam feel the effect of that incorporation, while all those in Christ experience the very resurrection life of Christ through him. This notion goes well beyond the modern concept of federal

---

5. It is interesting that a variety of manuscripts and Church Fathers, including Chrysostom, have an additional "and" after the word "gift," thus distinguishing the gift from the righteousness. The text without the additional *kai* is, however, very well supported and is probably original.

headship, and it is not a surprise that this passage became a mainstay in later arguments about original sin and its taint and effect.

Adam is viewed as not merely sinning, but disobeying a direct commandment of God. Therefore his sin can be called a trespass or transgression — a willful violation of a known law. This will become important when we consider 7.7-13. Incidentally, Paul nowhere blames Eve for original sin here.

Paul is using a form of reasoning involving typology which he has used previously (e.g., 1 Corinthians 10). Adam is said to be a type of Christ, in that his action affects all those who are "in" him. This is not the same sort of trope as an allegory, such as we find in Galatians 4. Typology is reasoning by analogy using historical examples and based on Paul's reading of salvation history and its most seminal figures. So Paul does not attempt to suggest that some aspects of the Adam story are symbolic. Paul's Roman audience was likely familiar with notions of the emperor as head of the body, which is the empire, such that what affects the emperor affects the empire and what the emperor decides also affects the empire, like it or not. In other words, Roman political realities provided something of an analogy to the concept of incorporative personality used here.

Nowhere in Romans does Paul spend much time on the story of Moses. This is largely true of his other letters as well (except in 2 Cor. 3.7-18). Paul believes that the story of Moses and those involved in the Mosaic covenant is not the generative narrative for Christians, whether Jew or Gentile. The Adam story, the Abraham story, and the Christ story are generative narratives for Christians, stories with lasting impact on their lives. Paul sees the story of Moses, like the Mosaic covenant and the Mosaic Law, as *pro tempore*. It was meant to guide God's people between the time of Moses and Christ. But once the eschatological age dawned through the Christ-event, the Moses story could no longer be the controlling narrative of God's people, precisely because now is the era of the new covenant. The Mosaic story thus becomes a story about a glorious anachronism, or, as Paul puts it in 2 Corinthians 3, a fading glory. That story is to be respected and honored as a temporary part of God's plan for his people, but it is not a story that one is *required by Law* to obey any more, for Christ came to redeem even those under the Law out from under the Law.[6] Such is the nature of the radical eschatological theology of Paul. This will become clearer when we consider further what Paul will say about the Law in ch. 6.[7]

As Cranfield says, vv. 12-21 do not stand in isolation but indicate some

---

6. See my discussion in *Grace in Galatia* (Grand Rapids: Eerdmans, 1998), pp. 287-90.

7. It is interesting that Paul concentrates by and large on how believers are a part of the story of one or another incorporative personality, Gentiles even becoming heirs of Abraham, but he spends little time on the notion that Christians are incorporated into Israel (however, see below, pp. 250-75).

further conclusions to be drawn from the previous argument in 5.1-11.[8] The *dia touto* of v. 12 refers back to the material in the preceding eleven verses and should be translated "because of this."[9]

Here we are dealing with some of the most difficult material in all of Romans in terms of grammar and interpretation. It is possible, for instance, to take v. 12a to be an anacoluthon, involving the protasis of a sentence which has no apodosis or at least not until after the protasis is restated and the sentence is finally concluded in v. 18. But Barrett, among others, sees an apodosis right in v. 12, which gives a vastly different sense to the first verse: "Therefore, as through one man sin entered the world [and through sin came that man's death], so also death came to all humans because they sinned." This is very different from what we find in Käsemann or Cranfield: "Therefore, as through one man sin entered the world, and through sin death, and so death came to all men in turn, because all sinned. . . ."[10] Barrett's rendering requires the insertion of the idea of "that man's death" and that an analogy be drawn between Adam's situation and everyone else's: both Adam and all others sinned and both received the death penalty. But against this interpretation of v. 12 is the fact that the whole section is comparing Adam and his progeny with Christ and those in him, not Adam with all other humans. There are also grammatical problems. "Through him" is in the emphatic position in the protasis, which suggests that Paul is going to tell us in the apodosis what is true "through" another person. It is not unusual for Paul to start a sentence and then digress or qualify the sentence, as he does here.[11] The essentially oral nature of Paul's discourse needs to be remembered. Not only is Paul dictating to a scribe rather than writing, reflecting, and revising, he also expects his discourse to be delivered orally. Paul's letters, much like reading the text of a sermon which is a transcript of an oral message, involves encountering certain grammatical infelicities caused by starting and stopping and occasionally digressing.

Paul's argument here is thus more difficult than the notion that all people are their own Adams, that as a result of their individual sins, like Adam's, their deaths result.[12] At issue is whether or not Paul subscribed to

---

8. C. E. B. Cranfield, *A Critical and Exegetical Commentary on the Epistle to the Romans* (ICC; Edinburgh: Clark, 1975-79), 1:271.

9. This in turn means that we should see the argument in 5.1-11 as both retrospective and prospective.

10. On the theological implications of what Paul says here, see J. C. Beker, "The Relationship between Sin and Death in Romans," in *The Conversation Continues: Studies in John and Paul,* ed. R. T. Fortna and B. R. Gaventa (Nashville: Abingdon, 1990), pp. 55-61.

11. See Cranfield, *Romans,* 1:272.

12. For the argument that each person is their own Adam, cf. *2 Baruch* 54.15: "Adam is therefore not the cause, save only of his own soul, but each of us has been the Adam of his own soul."

some sort of notion of original sin passed down to and/or through the race of humanity.[13]

The final clause of v. 12 is heavily debated, especially in regard to how to translate *eph' hō*. There are at least six possibilities, but we may boil them down as follows: One basic question is whether we should take these words as a conjunction, "because," or take the *hō* as a masculine relative pronoun referring either to death or to "one man."[14] *Hamartia* is ruled out as an antecedent by its feminine gender ending. In 2 Cor. 5.4 and Phil. 3.12 and 4.10 *eph' hō* is used causally — "because of,"[15] not "in which" or "to which."[16] Thus the phrase means "because all sinned," and here concrete acts of sin are in view. There is, however, one further viable possibility. *Eph' hō* could certainly have a consequential force meaning "with the result that." Fitzmyer cites numerous examples of such consequential use of *eph' hō*, including Plutarch, *Cimon* 8.6.4 and *Aratus* 44.4.1.[17] But the Pauline parallels support the translation "because."

Some have argued that what is meant is not our individual sinning, but rather our participation in Adam's sin. On this view not merely do humans imitate Adam's sin, they do so in consequence of Adam's original sin.

Paul is not suggesting that Adam and Christ are alike in all respects, not even in the way they affect the race that flows forth from them. The point of comparison is simply that in both cases the act of one man had far-reaching consequences for all those who came after him and had integral connection

13. See the discussion in R. H. Bell, "Romans 5.18-19 and Universal Salvation," *NTS* 48 (2002): 417-32. He (mistakenly) concludes that Paul is also affirming universal salvation here.

14. Erasmus's opinion on this matter proved controversial in view of the enormous influence of Augustine and also Ambrosiaster, who argued that all persons sinned in Adam because they were seminally present in him. (See G. Bray, ed., *Romans* [Ancient Christian Commentary on Scripture; Downers Grove: InterVarsity, 1998], pp. 136-37.) In his annotations on the Latin text of the NT, his long marginal note about Rom. 5.12 urged that the *in quo* of the Latin, when traced back to the Greek original *eph' hō*, meant "because" or "for that" rather than "in whom" (i.e., in Adam). This seems to call into question the doctrine of original sin. See *Erasmus' Annotations on the New Testament. Acts–Romans–I and II Corinthians,* ed. A. Reeve and M. A. Screech (Leiden: Brill, 1990), p. xiii and pp. 366-77, for the actual Erasmean notes on the text.

15. See Talbert, *Romans,* p. 148. However, he prefers the Orthodox rendering: "wherefore, from which it follows"; in other words, a logical inference is indicated by this phrase — since death passed to all, therefore it follows that all sinned. But this is not how Paul uses the phrase elsewhere.

16. The rather novel suggestion that the phrase means "with the result that" of Fitzmyer in "The Consequent Meaning of *eph' hō* in Romans 5.12," *NTS* 39 (1993): 413-17, is helpfully critiqued by N. T. Wright, "Romans," in *The New Interpreter's Bible,* vol. 10 (Nashville: Abingdon, 2002), p. 527.

17. See the endorsement of this view by C. Bryan, *A Preface to Romans: Notes on the Epistle and Its Literary and Cultural Setting* (Oxford: Oxford University Press, 2000), pp. 128-29.

with him. In all other respects, and at some length in vv. 13-17, Paul wishes to distinguish Adam and Christ. Thus, it is not necessary to argue that Christ's salvation must pass to or affect everyone in the exact same manner as Adam's sin, for, as Paul says, the gift of salvation is in many ways not like the trespass. Paul's "universalism is of the sort that holds to Christ as the way for all."[18]

Paul begins by stating that because of the action of one man, the destiny of the whole race was affected. *Kosmos* probably means humanity here, though it could mean world. Notice that Paul is clear that death enters the world because of sin. It is not viewed as a natural occurrence, at least insofar as humanity is concerned. As 1 Corinthians 15 makes clear, Paul sees death as an enemy, not a friend. He is quite clear that death spread to all because of Adam's sin, but it was not as though this negative result was not deserved because all did in fact sin. Thus, while it is true that humans die because of the sin of Adam, it is also true that death is a just outcome in view of the fact that all have sinned. Humans do not die simply because of Adam's sin, but because of Adam's sin and their own sin. There can be no question that Paul believed in a historical Adam who affected the whole historical process.[19] It is also possible that like his contemporary, the author of 4 Ezra, he believed in a seminal transmission of a fallen identity passed from Adam to his offspring (see 4 Ezra 3.7-22). *Jubilees* 3.17-32 blames Adam, Eve, and the serpent equally for sin and death entering the world. By contrast, Paul says nothing here about Eve. Sirach 25.24 is even a greater contrast with Romans 5: Eve was the cause of sin and death entering the world, an opinion also found in *Life of Adam and Eve* 3. Wis. 2.24 blames the devil for death's entry into the world. *2 Baruch* 54.19 says that "Adam was responsible for himself only; each one of us is his own Adam." By contrast, 4 Ezra 7.48 complains: "O Adam, what have you done? For though it was you who sinned, the fall was not yours alone, but ours also who are your descendants."[20]

V. 13 somewhat abruptly introduces the Law. Paul says until the Law (surely the Mosaic Law), sin was in the world. Sin is almost personified here, as death was in v. 12.[21] Sin was in the world, but it was not reckoned or counted, there being no Law. Paul cannot mean that God simply ignored sin since he surely knows the story of Noah. Thus what Paul seems to mean is that sin was not reckoned[22] as transgression, for the latter involves a willful violation of a known law. Transgres-

18. Wright, "Romans," p. 529.

19. See rightly C. K. Barrett, *Commentary on the Epistle to the Romans* (Peabody: Hendrickson, 1991), p. 104.

20. For discussion and further illumination on these texts see Talbert, *Romans*, pp. 147-48.

21. This is an important point, because in 7.7-13 Paul will also personify sin when he deals with the story of the fall. See pp. 179-90 below.

22. Again we have the use of commercial rather than forensic language. The term means "put in a ledger." See Barrett, *Romans*, p. 104.

sion, then, in the case of all of humanity (except Adam) does not come on the scene until the time of Moses. This explains why death still reigned between Adam and Moses, even over those who had not sinned in the form of transgression, as Adam did. Death as a consequence for sin still held sway even before the Law of Moses, but a different sort of punishment entered the picture with Moses, just as a different view of sin entered the picture with the Mosaic Law.

In v. 14 we hear that Adam is the type of the Coming One.[23] *Homoiōmati*, used here of sins that are unlike Adam's transgression, refers to a likeness, a mark made by striking or an impression, form, or pattern made by a mold. *Typos*, on the other hand, refers to something or someone that prefigures something or someone else, in this case someone or something that belongs to the eschatological age. "Adam in his universal effectiveness for ruin is the type which . . . prefigures Christ in his universal effectiveness for salvation."[24] It is Adam's transgression, his one deed that affects all just as the Christ-event affects all, which makes him the type of Christ. "Paul sees history gathering at nodal points and crystalizing upon outstanding figures . . . who are notable in themselves as individual persons, but even more notable as representative figures. These . . . incorporate the human race, or sections of it, within themselves, and the dealings they have with God they have representatively on behalf of their [people]."[25]

Having initiated the analogy, Paul in v. 15 proceeds to clarify by saying that the trespass is in fact not exactly like the gift of grace. Again we have a "how much more" argument. If the trespass affected many and many died, the grace

---

23. It is worth noting that Paul does not suggest that Christ is the antitype of Moses. When discussions about Jesus' faithfulness, even unto death, get started, it is important to remember the point of comparison that Paul makes here. Christ's faithfulness is not covenant faithfulness to the Mosaic Law. It is simply faithfulness to enact the divine will, the plan of salvation that God intended. Christ is the last Adam, not the last Moses nor Israel reduced to one person. In other words, Paul insists that Christ stands in a more universal relationship to all of humanity, including Gentiles, than Moses or Israel did. It is not an accident that Paul chooses Abraham and Adam as his points of comparison in these chapters. Christ is, as we shall see in the discussion of ch. 10 (see pp. 260-65 below), the end of the Mosaic Law.

Furthermore, Christ is not in covenant relationship with God, as Israel was. He is not obliged to keep the Adamic, Abrahamic, Mosaic, or Davidic covenants. To the contrary, in Pauline theology he brings in or enacts through his death and resurrection the new covenant, which at one and the same time fulfills the Abrahamic one and ends the Mosaic one. All these covenants, including the new one, are between God and his people, not between God and Christ. But see N. T. Wright, "Romans and the Theology of Paul," in *Pauline Theology*, vol. 3: *Romans*, ed. D. M. Hay and E. E. Johnson (Minneapolis: Fortress, 1995), pp. 30-67, and the response by R. B. Hays, "Adam, Israel, Christ — The Question of Covenant in the Theology of Romans: A Response to Leander E. Keck and N. T. Wright," in the same volume, pp. 68-86.

24. Cranfield, *Romans*, 1:283.

25. C. K. Barrett, *From First Adam to Last: A Study in Pauline Theology* (New York: Charles Scribner's Sons, 1962), p. 5.

of God and the gift that comes through the one man Christ will abound to many all that much more. While *polloi* can be used to mean "all," it may be significant that Paul switches here to using *polloi,* whereas before he has used *pantes.* He does not wish to convey the notion of universal salvation.[26]

In v. 16 the same principle is restated but with an added factor. Here we learn that judgment followed only one misdeed and resulted in the condemnation of all, whereas the grace gift followed many misdeeds and resulted in a judgment of acquittal and, in fact, in salvation. In the former case an act followed as punishment for a deed, in the latter case an act followed God's long patience with many more sins, and it was not an act of condemnation. Thus, as Paul was trying to say, there is almost no comparison between the trespass and the grace gift. The one trespass led to death reigning through the one misdeed, but how much more did the grace and the gift of being set right by God and acquitted accomplish, for it will result in believers reigning in life through Christ. Paul may be drawing on the old apocalyptic notion of the reign of the saints, possibly in connection with millennial ideas (cf. 1 Corinthians 15). The important thing to note is that this reign is envisioned as happening sometime in the future, not in the present. The life Paul is referring to is also something received in the future, and so not at conversion. It is part of the hope previously mentioned.

V. 18 expands the notion a bit further by speaking of the *dikaiōsis* of life. Some have translated this as if the two words referred to the same thing: "right standing, that is, life." But more likely Paul is referring to a *dikaiōsis* which results in life; or perhaps, if we translate the phrase as "the setting right of life," we can get at the gist of the matter. Adam's act led to the condemnation of all, but Christ's righteous act led to the setting right of life for all. There is a problem with translating *dikaiōsis* as "right standing" here because in fact Paul did not believe that Christ's death automatically gave all humans right standing with God apart from a faith response.

So what Paul has in mind is that Christ's "act of justice" wiped the slate clean, and thus life was set right. Humans were then in a position to have once again a right relationship with God, whereas that potential was not present before Christ died. In this entire context Paul has been discussing the vast superiority of Christ and his effect on humankind to that of Adam and his effect.[27] The condemnation of Adam is reversed in Christ. In Christ, human destiny

26. Ambrosiaster, *Pauline Commentary* 15.84, says that the acquittal will not be universal like the condemnation, for the very good reason that not all believe. See Bray, *Romans,* p. 147.

27. Why is Christ's action seen as superior? P. Achtemeier, *Romans* (Atlanta: John Knox, 1985), p. 98, helpfully answers: "The implied reason is that it takes much more power to overcome (by obedience) the effects of sin once that power has been let loose than it took originally (by disobedience) to allow sin to enter."

changed. At the very least, the emphasis on the effect for and upon all of both Adam and Christ implies that Paul does not believe it was God's intent to send Christ to die for the select few. Christ's act of justice was for the whole human race. This argument does not state the conditions under which all might receive the benefit of Christ's act.[28] Paul speaks of this blessing as a "gift," and a gift is that which must be received and unpacked, not something that has an automatic effect, and of course it can be rejected.[29]

In v. 19 we hear of the obedience of the one man Christ, and here Paul surely has in mind Christ's obedience unto death on the cross which made possible the righting of things, as he earlier stated. It was Christ's obedience, called his "faithfulness" in ch. 3,[30] which "constituted" or "made" many to be set right in regard to their relationship with God. The verb here does not mean "reckon" but rather "make." This is to be contrasted with the disobedience of Adam which "made" many sinners. As Fitzmyer rightly says, Adam's act not merely made humans liable to punishment, it constituted them as sinners.[31] The effect of Adam's sin is both relational and personal. The action of that one person has drastic effects on many. As Achtemeier puts it, those who belong to the race of Adam are under the power and reign of sin. The only way to escape this is to join another race of humanity — those who are in Christ.[32] Barrett argues that "the words 'sinners' and 'righteous' are words of relationship, not character."[33] But this distinction cannot be made between the relational position and the condition of a person when Paul uses "made" rather than "reckoned." Paul believes that Christ's death affects not only the believer's position in relationship to God but also the believer's condition, as v. 1 has made clear.

In v. 20 we learn that the Law intruded into the historical process. The verb translated "intrude" is an interesting choice. Just as Paul has personified sin and death in this discussion, so here he personifies the Law, treating it as an actor on the historical stage who could intrude into some process.[34] The *hina*

---

28. Note Barrett's comment (*Romans*, p. 107): "but it would be as wrong to deduce from these passages a rigid universalism as to suppose that they meant 'many' and therefore not 'all.'"

29. One of the "earmarks" of good rhetoric is the use of poetic devices such as assonance, alliteration, rhythm, and rhyme. G. D. Fee, *God's Empowering Presence: The Holy Spirit in the Letters of Paul* (Peabody: Hendrickson, 1994), p. 498, notes the way *paraptōma* and *charisma* have the same ending and suggests that Paul uses the latter term here for rhetorical effect. One may translate these terms similarly as well — act of sin, and act of grace — for each refers to some specific event or action.

30. See pp. 99-110 above.

31. J. A. Fitzmyer, *Romans* (New York: Doubleday, 1992), p. 421.

32. Achtemeier, *Romans*, p. 96.

33. Barrett, *Romans*, p. 109.

34. See rightly Fitzmyer, *Romans*, p. 422.

clause here could indicate either purpose or result — the Law intruded for the purpose of increasing sin or, more likely, with the result that sin increased (cf. Gal. 3.19). How so? There are at least three points to be made: the Law revealed sin and made it evident; sin increased in the sense that it became more sinful as sin was turned into trespass — willful violation of a known Law; and sin increased in the sense that the Law gave sinful humanity a target, ideas of more things to rebel against or further acts of rebellion against God. Perhaps then Paul sees the Law as deliberately sent by God to reveal human sin to humanity.[35] The Law could count sin, but it could not counter it.[36] But however much sin increased as a result of the Mosaic Law coming into the historical process, grace abounded even more with the inbreaking of the Christ-event into the historical process. So just as sin reigned in death, so grace reigned through righteousness unto eternal life through Jesus Christ.

In v. 21's parallel construction, the question is whether "righteousness" refers to divine righteousness or human right standing. But if this is a true parallel construction (which the *hōsper* at the beginning of the clause suggests) then "righteousness" may be an elliptical reference to Christ's death. Just as sin reigned through the death that Adam brought into the world, so also grace reigned through the death/act of justice/expression of righteousness of Jesus with the result of eternal life.[37] Paul then would be concluding his rhetorical comparison by comparing the effect of the death Adam brought into the process and the effect of the death Jesus brought into the historical process. The aorist tense of the verb makes very good sense if the reference in "righteousness" is to Christ's act of justice — his death. It makes far less sense if we take Paul to be referring to human right standing with God, which of course has been established only for some by the time Paul wrote.

What does it mean to say "sin reigned in death"? Perhaps Paul refers thus to the notion that since we are all going to die, there comes a certain fatalism into human thinking. Sin becomes the attempt to have as much pleasure as one can while alive — to eat, drink, and be merry knowing that death is coming. The hovering cloud of death leads those under it to look for diversions and ways to distract themselves from the inevitable and also ways to spit into the prevailing wind. As Ecclesiastes suggests, what is the point of being good if it all

---

35. See pp. 179-90 below on ch. 7.

36. See K. Grieb, *The Story of Romans: A Narrative Defense of God's Righteousness* (Louisville: Westminster/John Knox, 2002), p. 66: "Later (in 7.7-25) Paul will argue that the law cannot control sin; all it can do is count it."

37. Grace here is also personified. Paul is using rhetorical techniques here which he will pick up again in ch. 7, when he retells the story of Adam using the dramatic device of the first person. We will discuss the rhetorical use of personification on pp. 179-85 below when we reach ch. 7. Personification falls under the heading of figures of thought. See Quintilian, *Instit. Or.* 9.2.30.

ends in death? Thus the reality and finality of death cause sin to reign in human life. Therefore, to deal with the human sin problem Christ also had to deal with the death problem. Eternal life had to be on offer if the reign of sin was to be ended. Once again we see what a very negative and highly theological view of death Paul has.

This section and the next three major sections in Romans all end with a reference to the lordship of Christ. Perhaps, as Fitzmyer avers, Paul is stressing that Christ has established his lordship over the human process, eclipsing the lordship of sin, death, and the Law.[38] The Law, as we shall see, while being holy, just, and good, unfortunately can be death-dealing rather than life-giving when its recipients are fallen human beings.

Bridging the Horizons

There is certainly a lot of talk about brokenness in Christian circles today. This is hardly surprising when just as many Christian marriages as non-Christian marriages end in divorce. We have broken hearts, broken homes, broken promises, and broken marriages, and the question is: Can they really be fixed? All this brokenness is but a manifestation of the general human brokenness which has as its root the ultimate human dilemma of the breakdown of our relationship with God, and the sad effects of that broken relationship. It might seem to follow that if one fixes one's relationship with God, then these other forms of human brokenness could be worked out. There is some real truth to that assumption and hope. But there is also a place for a reality statement, and it is this — even when brokenness sometimes gets fixed, the signs and some of the lasting effects of that brokenness still exist.

Consider for a minute a beautiful porcelain vase sitting on a mantlepiece. The cat jumps up and knocks the vase to the marble hearthstone below and breaks it. Can the pieces be glued back together? Yes, they can. Will the vase ever look or be the same again? No it will not. It will bear the signs of its brokenness always, and it will probably need to be handled more carefully hereafter. It is the same with human lives and relationships, even Christian ones.

Furthermore, when Jesus calls us to take up our crosses and follow him, he is calling believers to a form of brokenness. The old self needs to die. The self-centered orientation needs to be shattered. And the healing that comes beyond this brokenness does not involve simply picking up the pieces and gluing them back together so that we can go on being our old selfish selves. Rather, they are reconfigured into a new whole, a new self. Just as the risen Christ still

38. Fitzmyer, *Romans*, p. 422.

bore the stigmata, we too will bear the marks of our former brokenness as new persons in Christ. The old is both transfigured and transformed, but it is not entirely transcended in this lifetime, if by that one means it is totally left in the past. We are called to remember where we have come from, what kind of persons we once were, to own up to our past and claim that God's power is made perfect in our very weaknesses. A cross-shaped life does not ever reach the place in this lifetime where it no longer needs to bear the cross or to stand in its shadow. The reason for this is sin, which, while it does not reign in the Christian's life, nonetheless remains as a living force and a danger. C. K. Barrett in reflecting on the human condition outside of Christ says this:

> The ruin of the old creation, as of the old man, Adam, was sin. Sin could never be a private matter, but corrupted the whole race, which consisted of men born out of true relation with God and condemned constantly to worsen their relationship, whether they carelessly ignored it or self-righteously essayed to mend it. Like planets robbed of the centre of their orbit they could not possibly keep a proper course. The more they sought life for themselves, the more they forsook God and plunged into death. Their lot could be changed only by a new creation, from a new beginning.[39]

It is this larger context of fallenness in which one must interpret individual instances and types of brokenness. It follows from this that those who do not believe in human fallenness will have a very difficult time explaining why it is that humans are the only creatures that foul their own nests.

There is a balance to be struck between the admonitions to individual responsibility for sin and what may be called corporate responsibility. Paul certainly believes both that human beings have been affected by the sin of our ancestors, particularly Adam, and that we are responsible for our own sin. Both things are true. It is true both that we are conditioned to sin because we have inherited a fallen human nature and that when we willingly sin we are held responsible for such actions. Paul does not believe in "free will" in the modern sense of the term, but he does appear to believe in grace-enabled will, the ability of all persons by God's common grace to choose to avoid particular acts of sin. Yet, at the same time this is not always the case. Romans 7 makes it clear that Paul also sees the impotence of the human will at some junctures in the face of powerful temptation and sin, if one is outside of Christ. Paul is prepared to speak about the addictive power of sin or the dichotomy in the life of a fallen person between knowing what is the good and doing it. He is also a realist about the Christian life, holding the view that while temptation and sin remain for the Christian, they do not reign in the Christian life.

---

39. Barrett, *Romans*, p. 111.

Argument Six: Shall Sin, Death, and the Law Continue Now That Christ Has Come?

Part One — 6.1-14: Shall We Go On Sinning So That Grace May Increase?

A series of closely related concepts (sin, death, the Law vs. grace, life, etc.) was introduced once Paul began to tell the story of Adam in 5.12-21. In chs. 6–7 Paul will address a series of questions that arise out of his telling of the Adam story in comparison to the Christ story in ch. 5. The stories of Adam and those in him and of Christ and those in him continue to undergird and underlie the discussion leading up to ch. 8. "Paul's thought is still determined by the Adam/Christ contrast of 5:12-21. The death here spoken of is the death of Adam, and those in Adam and of the Adamic epoch."[1]

In one large argument in four parts encompassing all of chs. 6–7, Paul will discourse on human fallenness in the light of the Christ-event. His thought does indeed move, as Sanders has suggested, from solution to plight.[2] Thus some of what Paul will say about life outside of Christ he says from the perspective of Christ rather than through the lens of the Law. And certainly some of the things Paul is prepared to say in this letter about sin, death, and the Law he would have put differently when he was a Pharisee. His conversion changed his perspective on these matters in various respects. To some extent Paul must forestall some possible false conclusions that one might draw from the argument in 5.12-21. This he begins to do in 6.1-14.

Clearly enough, the *ti oun* of v. 1 looks back to what has preceded. On the basis of what he has said in ch. 5, Paul will set in motion a discussion punctuated by a series of rhetorical questions (6.1-3, 15, 16, 21; 7.1, 13, 24) that will not be

---

1. J. D. G. Dunn, *Romans 1–8*, Word Biblical Commentary (Dallas: Word, 1988), pp. 307-8.

2. E. P. Sanders, *Paul and Palestinian Judaism* (London: SCM, 1977). The entire Pauline section of the book, roughly the last third of the book, should be consulted.

over until the end of ch. 7. "The sustained deliberative tone and syllogistic progression evident here were characteristics attributed by the rhetorical handbooks to the figure of conversational reasoning, *ratiocinatio,* which by simulating dialectical reasoning lends to the speaker's handling of a controversial subject the appearance of the self-evident."[3] Quintilian reminds us that deliberative rhetoric is always involved with questions where some doubt exists (*Instit. Or.* 3.8.25). Paul's argument in ch. 5 has probably raised as many questions as it has answered, and, as a good rhetorician, Paul needs to forestall objections by answering in advance some of the possible questions that could arise in Rome from hearing the previous argument.

The first of these questions is, Shall we continue sinning so grace may increase? The definitive answer to this question will not come until 8.12-13. This reminds us that the attempt to treat chs. 6–8 in terms of theological topics instead of in terms of the flow of the argument and the underlying flow of narrative substructure will lead to misunderstanding. Paul will resolve these logical dilemmas in specifically Christian terms. He is not arguing with Jewish opponents; he is trying to teach a largely Gentile Christian audience.

What then shall we say? Shall we continue to sin in order that the grace may increase? Let it never happen! For we have died to sin, how then shall we still live in it? Or do you not know that whoever was baptized into Christ Jesus was baptized into his death? We were buried then with him through baptism into death, in order that just as Christ was raised from the dead through the glory of the Father, thus also we should walk in newness of life. For if we have grown together in the likeness of his death, also we shall . . . of his resurrection. Recognizing this, that our old self was crucified with him, in order that the body of death be destroyed, that we no longer be a slave to sin. For the one having died is freed from sin. But if we have died with Christ, we believe that also we will live with him. Knowing that Christ has been raised from the dead, he no longer can die, death no longer rules him. For the death that he died, he died to sin once for all, but the life he lives, he lives to God. Thus also you reckon yourselves dead to sin, but alive to God in Jesus Christ. Therefore, do not let sin reign in your mortal body, unto the obedience of its desires. Do not any longer lend your members to sin as weapons/instruments of unrighteousness, but lend yourself to God, as from death to life also your members as instruments/weapons of righteousness to God. For sin will not rule you, for you are not under Law, but under grace.[4]

3. N. Elliott, *The Rhetoric of Romans: Argumentative Constraint and Strategy and Paul's Dialogue with Judaism* (JSNTS 45; Sheffield: Sheffield Academic Press, 1990), p. 236. See Cicero, *De Inventione* 1.57; *Rhetorica ad Herennium* 4.23-24.

4. There are no significant textual difficulties in this section of Paul's discourse.

The danger of any gospel of grace is that it will be understood in an antinomian way. But Paul goes even beyond that to deal with an even more extreme idea: if sin is what prompts God's outpouring of grace, then does it not follow that the more we keep sinning the more grace will abound? Paul says in v. 2 that continuing to sin is not an option for Christians, because they have died to sin and must not attempt to continue living in it. In what sense have believers already died to sin? Paul surely does not mean that they are immune to temptation, but he does want to insist that sin no longer reigns in the Christian's body and life.[5] Another way of putting this is that the old self of the believer was crucified with Christ so that the Christian is no longer a slave to sin. There is still the matter of reckoning oneself dead to sin as well, as the passage will go on to say, but this exhortation is based on the indicative statement that the old self has in fact died. Paul further exhorts his audience not to allow sin to reign in their mortal bodies, by which he means being a slave to its desires.

There is an interesting dialectic here between the condition of the redeemed person being set free from the reign of sin and death through Christ and at the same time still standing in danger of re-enslavement, of allowing sin to once again reign in his or her body. Such re-enslavement amounts to moral apostasy. "Sin's rule was up to and in death; but death has already occurred, and where death has already occurred sin's *rule* is past."[6] Small points of grammar

---

5. C. E. B. Cranfield, *A Critical and Exegetical Commentary on the Epistle to the Romans* (ICC; Edinburgh: Clark, 1975-79), 1:299-300, lists four possible meanings of the idea that believers have already died to sin, and he seems to favor the notion that it simply refers to how God regards believers — they have died to sin in God's sight, or perhaps believers through baptism have accepted that God sees them this way. Underlying this is the old theology of imputed righteousness, but in fact Paul is talking about believers having died in some sense, not about how they perceive themselves or how God perceives them. Cranfield mentions a moral sense that for him amounts to the believer trying harder and harder to approximate dying to sin daily. This last suggestion involves a flagrant disregard for the aorist tense of the verb — Paul says "we have died" not "we are dying" or "we die daily." Paul is talking about the spiritual transformation that happens within the believer at conversion and that is depicted in baptism. As we have said, he is affirming that sin no longer reigns in or over the believer's life, even including over his body. Rhetorically, it is quite wrong to read back a certain sort of interpretation of ch. 7 into ch. 6. Paul's audience could not know what Paul was going to say in ch. 7 when they heard ch. 6. This argument's first part must be allowed to stand on its own and be grounded in what comes before, not what comes afterwards.

6. Dunn, *Romans 1–8*, p. 307. This amounts to neither an ethic of sinlessness nor a naive view of human nature. Paul is simply saying that Christians are no longer under the reign of sin; and as 1 Cor. 10 makes evident, they can resist or escape temptation without being forced to sin. The point is simply this: once one is a new creature in Christ, one is no longer in bondage to sin. Sin no longer makes Christians an offer they can't refuse. Neither their nature nor temptation compels them to sin. The horror of sin in the Christian life is that it is freely chosen or submitted to.

and word usage often make a difference. In v. 2 Paul does not use the ordinary relative pronoun *hoi* but *hoitines* instead. This means not merely "we" but "we in our essential nature."[7] Paul is referring to something within the very nature of the believer that died at conversion.

He offers some interesting though brief comments on baptism in v. 3. Believers were baptized into Christ, which entailed being baptized into Christ's death and being buried with him.[8] Paul is not interested in pursuing an argument about baptism and its nature. He simply refers to the ritual all Christians participate in and asks his audience whether they realize the theological and spiritual implications of this ritual. What is said here should be compared to 1 Cor. 12.13, but one must also take into account what Paul says about water baptism in 1 Corinthians 1, where Paul says that he is glad he did not baptize more Corinthians because baptism was a cause of division and dissension there. Paul's emphasis in his letters is on salvation by grace through faith, not on what is accomplished by the baptismal ritual. He warns the Corinthians in 1 Cor. 10.1-5 about reliance on a sacrament. What then shall we make of what Paul says in Romans 6 about baptism?

First of all, we note that Paul here talks about baptism into Christ, whereas in 1 Cor. 12.13 he refers to baptism into Christ's body. Secondly we notice that in neither Rom. 6.3 nor 1 Cor. 12.13 does Paul speak of human administrants of baptism; indeed in 1 Cor. 12.13 baptism seems to be "by" the Holy Spirit. Is then the baptismal ritual an outward and visible sign of a spiritual transaction which may or may not transpire during the baptismal ritual? This would seem to be Paul's view, for otherwise it is very difficult to explain how he could be thankful he did not baptize more people than he did.[9] The emphasis in both Rom. 6.3 and 1 Cor. 12.13 is on the spiritual reality which water baptism depicts. When one is joined to Christ, one is buried with him or, one

---

7. See C. K. Barrett, *Commentary on the Epistle to the Romans* (Peabody: Hendrickson, 1991), p. 113.

8. On the issue of whether Paul is drawing on language from the mystery religions, particularly the religion of Isis and Osiris, see the judicious discussion by Dunn, *Romans 1–8*, pp. 308-11. It is possible that Paul chose his language about being baptized into Jesus' death deliberately to echo the mystery rite's talk about death of the old self and being born again (see Apuleius, *Metamorphoses* 11.16-23). Paul's largely Gentile audience then would have understood Paul to be referring to a real, and not merely a notional, change in the devotee. As Dunn says (p. 311) there would have been an understanding that Paul is talking about a phenomenon similar to that which was believed to transpire in the mystery rite, but "without thereby identifying the two, or calling into question the distinctive claims of each."

9. See rightly D. Moo, *The Epistle to the Romans* (NICNT; Grand Rapids: Eerdmans, 1996), p. 366: "we must assume from the fact that faith is emblazoned in every chapter of Romans while baptism is mentioned in only two verses that genuine faith, even if it has not been 'sealed' in baptism, is sufficient for salvation."

might say, plunged into his death.[10] A spiritual transaction happens in the life of the person who is uniting himself with Christ such that he is freed from the reign of sin, in particular the tyranny of passions and desires. It seems clear as an inference from this that Paul believes that those outside Christ are bound to and in sin. They are not and cannot be free from sin.

In v. 4 Paul indicates that through baptism the believer is buried with Christ "into death." Death is not seen here as an event, as we might speak of the time of death, but rather as a state which one enters.[11] Baptism throughout this segment is correlated with burial and death, not with resurrection and new life. Resurrection, including the resurrection of Jesus, is paired with the believer walking in newness of life. The reason for this is not hard to find. Paul believes that the Christian has yet to experience the resurrection, at which juncture there will be full conformity to the image of God's Son. Having gone through the transformation which is symbolized by baptism, believers should walk in newness of life. So Paul believes that Christians are capable of "walking" in a very different fashion than they have previously, "in newness of life," not merely that they ought to do so. The phrase "through the glory of the Father" may refer to the fact that there was a manifestation of divine glory in the risen Jesus, but it could mean through the powerful outreaching presence of the Father.[12]

V. 5 uses even more dramatic imagery and ideas. The text reads literally, "for if we have grown together in the image of his death. . . ." This conditional statement is in the form of a "real" or "genuine" condition, not something merely hypothetical. Paul believes this condition already exists. But what does he mean? Barrett takes him to be referring to being joined to Jesus' death by means of the image of Jesus' death, that is, through baptism.[13] But this is not what the text actually says. The perfect tense of the verb in v. 5a suggests an ongoing state or condition, and there is no precedent for using "likeness" to refer to baptism.[14] Paul is probably referring to believers being fused together in the likeness of Christ's

---

10. In Apuleius, *Metamorphoses* 11, Lucius explains his initiation into the cult of Isis and says that it entailed a voluntary death that led to a new birth and to the freedom to serve Isis. Paul then is using language that would not likely be totally foreign to his Gentile audience in Rome. On the parallels between the discussion here and the mystery religions see G. Wagner, *Pauline Baptism and the Pagan Mysteries* (Edinburgh: Oliver and Boyd, 1967). Cf. A. J. M. Wedderburn, "The Soteriology of the Mysteries and Pauline Baptismal Theology," *NovT* 29 (1987): 53-72.

11. See Dunn, *Romans 1–8*, p. 314.

12. Tertullian (*On the Flesh of Christ* 15), combating Gnosticism, among other things, makes the helpful comment: "We insist . . . that what has been abolished in Christ is not 'sinful flesh' but rather 'sin in the flesh' — not the material stuff but its condition; not the substance but the flaw."

13. Barrett, *Romans*, p. 116.

14. See Dunn, *Romans 1–8*, p. 317.

death, by which he is indeed referring to how the death of the old self, the so-called sin nature, knits believers together, eliminating our isolation and alienation from one another.[15] V. 6 then reiterates the idea in a slightly different way, but here the stress is on how believers have been unified through the death of Jesus, which in turn leads to the image of his death in us as the old person dies. Thus believers bear the likeness of his death in themselves, and believers are promised that they will bear the likeness of his resurrection when Christ returns.[16]

V. 6 also explains a bit more clearly that the old person, the person the believer used to be, was crucified with Christ. Paul is not merely referring to Christ in some sense bearing death for the believer, for he goes on to say that the body of sin in human beings has been done away with. Three things then are done away with: the old self, the body of death, and slavery to sin. The verb *katargeō* means at the very least "render ineffective" (see 3.3, 31; 4.14; 1 Cor. 1.28; Gal. 3.17), but Paul also uses it in the stronger sense of "abolish" (1 Cor. 6.13; 15.24, 26; 2 Thess. 2.8).[17]

This verse will be exceedingly important for the understanding of 7.14-25. Precisely what Paul says here is no longer the case for the believer is described in 7.14-25 as still being the case for the "I" there. Here Paul says the believer's old self, body of death, and enslavement to sin have been abolished or crucified. The language could hardly be more direct and emphatic.[18] The body of sin, described here, is no different from the body of death that the "I" cries out for deliverance from in 7.24. Furthermore, Paul is speaking of a process here. The old self has been crucified (cf. Col. 3.9-10; Eph. 4.22-24) in order that the body of death might be rendered powerless, ineffective, paralyzed, or even abolished, which is to say the same thing as that one is no longer a slave to sin.[19]

15. See C. Bryan, *A Preface to Romans: Notes on the Epistle and Its Literary and Cultural Setting* (Oxford: Oxford University Press, 2000), p. 137, notes that Cyril of Jerusalem stressed that the word "likeness" indicates that while Christ actually died, we experience only the likeness of his death in some spiritual way. This is likely correct.

16. See B. Byrne, *Romans,* Sacra Pagina (Collegeville: Liturgical, 1996), p. 191: "believers obviously do not share in Christ's historical, physical death upon the cross. What they 'conform to' is the ethical pattern expressed in Christ's death to sin (cf. vs. 6), his self-giving love (Rom. 15.3), and obedience (5.19; cf. Phil. 2.8)."

17. See Moo, *Romans,* p. 358. N. T. Wright, "Romans," in *The New Interpreter's Bible,* vol. 10 (Nashville: Abingdon, 2002), p. 539, says "the NIV's 'rendered powerless' is a possible meaning of the Greek, but Paul's intention seems to be to insist that 'this body of sin' should be destroyed, not simply left to one side without power."

18. See Wright, "Romans," p. 541: "If Paul had wanted to say . . . that Christians have not completely 'died to sin,' that the old Adam still lingers on in some way, he has chosen an extremely misleading way of saying it."

19. Thus a subtle psychodynamic is going on here. The old self-centered, selfish person has been crucified, has experienced death. Because that self no longer exists, the bondage to the fallenness in and of the flesh, the bondage to sinful desires of various sorts, no longer has

"Body of death" or "body of sin," as the earlier reference to the desires of the flesh makes evident, is a reference to the body insofar as it is affected by sin and its punishment — death. Here as in his discussion of Gentile sin in chs. 1–2 Paul is drawing on some of the early Jewish sapiential treatments of the subject (on the body in debt to sin see Wis. 1.4; cf. Sir. 18.22). Paul is in essence saying that the believer is freed from domination by the fallenness of the flesh, the desire to sin, the desire to rebel or sin in the face of death.[20] One must still live in one's body, but its fallenness no longer controls the believer. When there is an ethical tension in the Christian life, Paul speaks of it as flesh vs. Holy Spirit (see Galatians 5) or an outer and inner contrast of deterioration and renewal (2 Corinthians 4), but not as an old person–new person tension, as if the two could coexist in some schizophrenic manner in the same person at the same time.[21] "The implication is that prior to our dying with Christ to sin we had no freedom to choose whom we would serve. The only freedom we had was a freedom to sin. After dying with Christ to sin, our freedom from sin is not automatic but must be chosen. With the power of sin broken, we have the freedom to make a choice for righteousness. 'Your members' refers not just to one's body parts, but to the various facets of one's personality or self. . . . Romans 6:1-14 says that grace does not have libertine consequences because those who have been baptized into Christ cannot act as if they were still in Adam."[22]

V. 7 explains one of the benefits of being a new person in Christ: one is

---

control. The new self is not controlled or dominated by the old passions. The body insofar as it is prone to sin and tending toward death has been set free from sin's control, though not from vulnerability to sin. The freedom to choose comes because there is a new control center of the personality — the new self or new creature.

20. See P. Achtemeier, *Romans* (Atlanta: John Knox, 1985), p. 105: "If we do not yet share the glory of Christ's resurrection, however, the share in his death is enough for now: It has broken the enslaving power of sin over us. Because of Christ, we have, for the first time, a real choice: For the first time, we can choose not to sin! For the first time, it is possible that exhortations to good can be followed. That is why, of course, we now, for the very first time, find moral exhortations in Paul's letter to Rome!"

21. It is interesting that Barrett, *Romans*, p. 117, recognizes that the position most advocated here commends itself for its simplicity, but then rejects it, in part because of the common Protestant interpretation of ch. 7. Against his reading of other Pauline texts, Col. 3.9-10 speaks of the believer having "put off" the old person and having put on the new self — both actions taken in the past. Eph. 4.21-24 speaks of what believers were taught in the past about putting off the old self and putting on the new. The problem dealt with there is the temptation to go back to old patterns of sinful behavior, acting as if one was still the old self. Paul certainly believes moral and spiritual apostasy by a Christian is possible, and he warns against it. Neither the text in Colossians nor the one in Ephesians supports the "schizophrenic" or "multiple personality disorder" interpretation of Christian life in which one is both the old and new person simultaneously.

22. C. Talbert, *Romans* (Macon: Smyth and Helwys, 2002), p. 166.

freed from the slavery to sin one has previously experienced. The verb *dedikaiōtai* here has sometimes been translated "has been justified/acquitted" (perfect passive), but it can just as well mean "has been freed" (cf. Sir. 26.29; Acts 13.38-39; and especially 1 Cor. 6.11), and this is certainly how a largely Gentile audience was likely to take the term (see *Corpus Hermeticum* 13.9). The following prepositional phrase, which must mean "from sin" points us in the direction of "freed" as the proper translation as well. Again Paul is not just talking about a change in the way God views a person, and while it is possible to talk about being "acquitted of sin," being "acquitted *from* sin," makes less sense. The rest of the context here is basically not forensic in character, involving as it does a discussion of baptism and the real transformation wrought by conversion. Babylonian Talmud *Shabbat* 151a may be of some help here: "When one dies, one is freed from the obligation of the Law and its precepts." But it is equally true that when one dies, one is freed from sin.[23]

In v. 8 as in v. 5 ("we shall be") Paul is talking about what believers will be or become at the eschaton. But Paul begins to focus more on Christ here and in the next verse. Christ, having already been raised from the dead, can die no more. This statement makes it as clear as can be that when Paul speaks of the resurrection of Jesus he is not merely talking about the resuscitation of a dead person, as was the case with the raising miracles in the Gospels. He is referring to an eschatological event which had never happened before it happened to Jesus. This is very clear in 1 Corinthians 15, where Jesus is said to be the firstfruits of the eschatological resurrection. So Christ can never die again. The corollary to this is that the risen Christ is also immune to sin. So too with believers: until they die they will not be immune to sin, and until they rise again they will not be immune to death.

That Christ died to sin once and for all (v. 10) of course has meaning for Christ, in that once he died, he became immune to sin. But there is more to it than that, for Christ died for all and for the sins of all, and the death of Christ made the final payment for all sin. He died but once, but the benefit is perpetual. "Once for all" highlights the linear and historical view of things that Paul has, in contrast to the more cyclical view of things associated with various pagan cults,[24] and even in the OT sacrificial system sacrifices needed to be offered repeatedly because their efficacy was only partial and limited to particular sins committed in the past.[25] Barrett suggests that Paul also means that Christ died

---

23. See the discussion by J. A. Fitzmyer, *Romans* (New York: Doubleday, 1992), pp. 436-37.

24. See Dunn, *Romans 1-8*, p. 323.

25. The book of Hebrews admirably expounds on this notion of Christ's death being the one necessary and sufficient sacrifice for all time, thus ending any need for further sacrifices. Hebrews is likely indebted to several Pauline letters, including Romans; see my article, "The Influence of Galatians on Hebrews," *NTS* 37 (1991): 146-52.

sinless, which does seem to be Paul's view of Christ's nature and earthly life.[26] Paul then adds that Christ "lives to God." The theocentric nature is clear enough, and "God" throughout this discourse refers to God the Father, with the exception of one reference in 9.5.[27] There is a sense in which Christ was oriented to us and died for us, fulfilling his obligations and ministry to the human race, but ever since the resurrection Jesus has lived for and to God. His orientation has been toward God since his death.

Christ then provides the pattern for the Christian life, and Paul quickly moves from christology to anthropology and a moment of exhortation (v. 11). Paul is dealing here with how the believer thinks about and orientates his or her life. It is no accident that Paul has first stressed the real change in the believer, who has left the old self behind, before he talks about "reckoning" or considering oneself dead to sin. Why should the believer need to reckon himself or herself dead to sin, if in fact the old person has already been crucified, is dead and buried? The answer is of course that the believer still lives in a mortal body which is not immune to sin and temptation. Even if the control center of the personality has been changed and is being renewed, the external part of who one is has not yet been renovated, a change which will not happen until the resurrection of believers. The inner-outer tension still exists. Furthermore, people may become so habituated to sin that they find it hard to believe that they are actually free now. Therefore, there must be a conscious effort to continually reckon oneself dead to sin, no longer subject to its enticement. This in no way denies the inward change Paul has already spoken of. Indeed, it is precisely because of the inward change that the believer is able, with the help of the indwelling Holy Spirit and God's grace, to reckon self dead to sin, despite still living in a vulnerable body. The physical body is indeed the weak chink in the Christian's armor, which is why it is that Paul spends so much time exhorting his converts about the sins of the flesh.

The phrase "in Christ Jesus" occurs for the first time here in Romans. It is important because it makes clear that believers are alive, not in themselves, but in Christ, if we are talking about the new life that comes from Christ and through the Spirit. Salvation does not make the believer a self-contained individual who has no needs. On the contrary, it joins the believer in a spiritual union to Christ, through whom life comes to the believer, and at the same time it joins the believer to the body of believers. Being-in-relationship, not being an independent entity, is the goal and is to be seen as normal, unlike what much self-actualization literature tries to suggest.

Having begun the brief exhortation in v. 11, Paul continues in v. 12 to draw

26. Barrett, *Romans*, p. 118; this is presumably why Paul will later say in this letter that Christ died in the "likeness" of sinful flesh.

27. On which see below, pp. 251-52.

out the practical ethical implications of what he has just argued. Reckoning one-self dead to sin means not letting sin reign or have dominion in one's mortal body, which is to say not letting the passions of the flesh take over and rule one's thinking and living. Paul interestingly calls this a form of false obedience. The image is of the passions being the master and the person being the slave who feels the obligation to obey. As v. 13 adds, the believer has a choice whether to al-low the body to become an instrument or weapon of unrighteousness or an in-strument in service to God. *Hopla,* the word from which "hoplite" comes, can re-fer to a weapon, or, as in 13.12, to armor (cf. 2 Cor. 6.7; 10.4). The hoplites were the spear carriers in the Greek army. With images of slavery it is not surprising that Paul will also add an image of warfare here. Chrysostom says "The body, like a military weapon, is not in itself inclined to either vice or virtue. It can go either way, depending on the user. . . . The flesh becomes either good or evil ac-cording to the mind's decision, not because of its own nature" (*Hom. Rom.* 11).[28]

We sometimes talk of using sex as a weapon, and Paul is likely talking about using the body as a weapon for unrighteousness, a weapon which wounds and destroys other lives when they are treated as sex objects rather than sexual persons to be treated with respect. The reference to the sinful desires has pushed Paul's discourse in this direction. Paul uses "lend" here in the present imperative and then the aorist imperative. Thus Paul is saying "do not any longer lend" (on-going or repeated action) your members to sin but "lend" (one-time decision about orientation) yourself to God and your members as instruments of righ-teousness. What is most noteworthy about this is that Christians have a con-scious decision to make. They will not automatically do the right and righteous thing. They must choose the right path and work out their own salvation as God works within the body of Christ to will and to do. Paul uses "members" *(melē)* rather than "limbs" here, referring thus not just to the bodily limbs but our hu-man faculties in general.[29] Nothing that we are is to be used in service of sin. In the contrast between unrighteousness *(adikia)* and righteousness the focus is clearly on behavior. Whatever unrighteousness means here, righteousness must be the commensurate opposite, which is to say that *dikaiosynē* here is not about being reckoned righteous but about righteous deeds.[30] This is what using one's faculties as instruments of righteousness to God is all about.[31] Both unrigh-teousness and righteousness are personified as leaders that one serves.

28. See G. Bray, ed., *Romans* (Ancient Christian Commentary on Scripture; Downers Grove: InterVarsity, 1998), p. 165.

29. Barrett, *Romans,* p. 119.

30. See B. Byrne, "Living Out the Righteousness of God: The Contribution of Rom. 6.1–8.13 to an Understanding of Paul's Ethical Presuppositions," *CBQ* 43 (1981): 557-81.

31. Again, this is not to deny that sometimes there is a forensic flavor to some of Paul's use of the "right"/righteous/righteousness word group, but it seems to be so in a distinct mi-

V. 14 draws this argument to a conclusion. Paul says that sin will not rule the believer, because "you are not under Law, but under grace." This is a fundamental principle for Paul, and it applies to all believers, both Gentile and Jewish. They are not, or in the case of Jewish Christians, no longer, obligated to keep the Mosaic Law, which, as 5.14, 20 suggests, is the Law Paul has in mind here. Paul seems to have been accused of being antinomian precisely because some of his critics rightly perceived him to be taking a radical stance in relationship to the Mosaic Law. What they did not understand is that he believed another Law, the Law of the new covenant, the "Law of Christ," was to be obeyed by Christians. Paul is not antinomian, but he is opposed to submission to a Law that is part of a covenant that, in view of the eschatological situation, is obsolete or becoming obsolete. As Galatians 3–4 makes evident, he sees submission to the Mosaic Law as a retrograde action for Christian believers.[32] It is like the Israelites wishing to go back to Egypt and bondage after wandering in the wilderness.

Paul has said that the effect of the Law coming on the scene was that it turned sin into trespass, and thereby sin actually increased. In 1 Cor. 15.56 he says that the power of sin is the Law. Rom. 5.20 says literally that the Law slipped into the historical process in order to increase the trespass. Sin is far more likely to dominate and rule a person under the Law, because it provides more ways to become a lawbreaker than Adam had. Sin gains power in the fallen world when the Law enters the picture because the Law makes sin twice as deadly, for it becomes clear that sin is a willful violation of God's will, God's revealed design for human life.[33]

But sin will not rule the believer because, instead of being under the Mosaic Law,[34] they are under grace, which empowers them to shake off the bond-

---

nority of cases, and it is certainly not Paul's focus when he is addressing those who are already Christians. Even Moo, *Romans,* p. 386, recognizes that *dikaiosynē* here must have a moral rather than forensic sense. My point is that this is also the case in various other places in Romans and elsewhere in the Pauline corpus (cf. Phil. 1.11; Eph. 4.24; 5.9).

32. See my extended treatment of this subject in *Grace in Galatia* (Grand Rapids: Eerdmans, 1998), pp. 252-67.

33. Barrett, *Romans,* p. 120, argues that "Law opens the way to the upward striving of human religion and morality, and therefore colors all human activity with sin, for it represents man's attempt to scale God's throne. Those who live under the reign of grace, however, have given full scope to God's freedom, since instead of pressing upwards towards God they humbly wait for his descent in love." Legalism, and the attempt to achieve standing with God by keeping rules, is of course a human problem, but it is not at the root of Paul's critique of the Mosaic Law. The root of the problem seems to be that the Law does not have the power to change fallen human beings. It can inform them but not transform them. The Law was something good that God gave to his people as a temporary guardian and protector and reminder. On "works righteousness," see pp. 85-110 above.

34. Moo, *Romans,* p. 390, makes a valiant effort to distinguish between the Mosaic Law

age to sin and even overcome the temptation to sin. In this verse Paul provides the necessary transition to the next argument, which the rhetorical question in 6.15 shows is prompted by the conclusion of this first part of the major argument in 6.1–7.25. By the time this argument is over, Paul will have made clear how life in Adam, which involves sin and death and a wrestling with the Law and its strictures, is not the life Christians are called to live.

Bridging the Horizons

In America we spend a lot of our rhetorical energy talking about freedom. Most of the time what we are talking about is freedom to live as we like, and to some degree freedom from meddlesome interference in our private lives by government or laws and the like. The premise behind such comments is that if outside forces would just leave us alone, we would indeed be free. This is most definitely not Paul's view of the human condition or for that matter of freedom. Consider for a moment the matter of sin. As I have said elsewhere, sin is, in fact, not as advertised. Sinning does not prove one's freedom, much less make one free. "Ironically, sin, once committed, does not aid one to become one's own master, but rather proceeds to become one's master; sin reigns as a lord in the fallen creature (cf. Rom. 6.6; 6.12; 6.17; 6.19-20)."[35]

Consider the parable of the ravenous eagle. In an ever-narrowing circle he floats above the Niagara River. He spots a deer carcass on an ice floe heading toward Niagara Falls. He believes he has time to eat and fly away before the ice reaches the falls. He says in his mind "I am free and strong, I can fly away at the last moment." And so the eagle circles down to the carcass, sinks his talons into

---

as a system and particular Mosaic commandments. He argues that some individuals under the Law, such as David, were able to escape its condemning power, and he also argues that Christian believers could still be obligated to individual Mosaic laws but not to the Law as a system. Unfortunately, this is not Paul's view, as Romans and Galatians make very clear. Paul believes that the Law has condemning power for all persons under it since all sin and fall short of God's glory, and furthermore, he believes that the Mosaic Law is a package deal — to submit to one commandment, such as the commandment to be circumcised, then implicitly involves one in submitting to them all. Part of the problem here comes from the assumption of Moo, and other scholars such as Cranfield, that Paul somehow operates with a one-covenant model, such that the new covenant is a renewal or continuation of the Mosaic covenant. The allegory in Galatians 4 makes it evident that Paul can talk about plural covenants and that he distinguishes between the Mosaic covenant and the new covenant, which is linked back to the Abrahamic covenant.

35. Witherington, *Paul's Narrative Thought World* (Louisville: Westminster/John Knox, 1994), p. 290.

the carcass, and begins to eat and eat, feeding his deep hunger. All the time, he can hear the increasingly loud noise of the rushing waters, but his mind tells him, "It will be okay. I can fly away at the last moment." What the eagle does not realize is that his talons have frozen to the carcass of the deer, and when the moment comes for flight, the eagle is unable to escape and goes over the falls with the ice floe. This accurately describes the addictive power of sin.

This is why salvation has to be seen as a radical rescue mission, not a human self-help program. Humankind has fallen and cannot get up apart from the grace of God transforming human nature. After dying with Christ, however, and after the breaking of the bondage to sin, while sin remains a potential and a possibility for Christians it no longer reigns in their lives. Another lordship now rules in their lives, the lordship of Christ. Instead of being servants to sin, they have become servants to Christ. This is the perspective Paul has on sin, conversion, and the new life in Christ. "Since they are no longer 'in Sin,' they should no longer let Sin into them!"[36]

36. K. Grieb, *The Story of Romans: A Narrative Defense of God's Righteousness* (Louisville: Westminster/John Knox, 2002), p. 67.

Part Two — 6.15–7.6:
Slaves to Righteousness

Paul also begins the second part of the argument with a rhetorical question. He is again forestalling objections to his views about sin, death, and the Law, now to what he said in 6.14 about being under grace rather than under Law. The ethical tone of this discussion is clear. Paul is talking about the conduct of Christians, which is to reflect righteousness. Justification/acquittal/being reckoned as righteous is not in view here. The issue is conduct, as the references to obedience make evident. We have not only a series of rhetorical questions here but also an antithetical construction, presenting a series of contrasts. In fact the series of contrasts began just before the end of the first part of the argument in v. 13:

v. 13	weapons of unrighteousness to sin	weapons of righteousness to God
vv. 14-15	not under Law	but under grace
v. 16	sin unto death	obedience unto righteousness
v. 18	free from sin	enslaved to God
v. 19	slave to uncleanness unto lawlessness	slave to righteousness unto sanctification
v. 20	slaves of sin	free for righteousness
vv. 21-22	end is death	end is eternal life
v. 22	free from sin	slaves to God
v. 23	wages of sin is death	grace gift of God is eternal life[1]

We thus hear about sin, death, and Law, over and over, and also about righteousness, grace, sanctification (or cleanness), and eternal life. These contrasts

---

1. J. D. G. Dunn, *Romans 1–8*, Word Biblical Commentary (Dallas: Word, 1988), p. 335.

are between what the audience was and what the audience is now in Christ: "but now. . . ." Of course Paul believes that new persons in Christ can make the mistake of acting like old persons outside Christ, hence the warnings here. Nonetheless, the antitheses between what they were and what they are should not be underplayed. Paul is not speaking hypothetically.

Quintilian commends the sort of rhetorical style and finesse that Paul is displaying here:

> Sometimes the repetition of words will produce an impression of force, at other times of grace. Again slight changes and alterations may be made in words, the same word may be repeated sometimes at the beginning of a sentence and sometimes at the end, or the sentence may open and close with the same phrase. One verb may be made to serve the purpose of a number of clauses, our words may be worked up to a climax, the same word may be repeated with a different meaning or reiterated at the opening of one sentence from the close of the proceeding, while we may introduce words with similar terminations or in the same cases or balancing or resembling each other. Other effects may be obtained by the graduation or contrast of clauses, by the elegant inversion of words, by arguments drawn from opposites, asyndeton, paralepsis, correction, exclamation, meiosis, the employment of a word in different cases, moods and tenses. (*Instit. Or.* 9.1.33-34)

The first two parts of this argument in Romans 6 display almost every one of these markers of good oral style and a learned use of figures of speech, especially the argument from contrasts or opposites (Aristotle, *Rhetoric* 1397a).[2] The adeptness of Paul's rhetoric would simply add additional authority and persuasiveness to his case with the Roman audience.

What then? Are we to commit sin because we are not under Law but under grace? Let it not happen! Do you not know that whomever you lend yourselves to as slaves for obedience, you are slaves to whomever you obey, whether of sin unto death[3] or obedience unto righteousness? But grace/thanks to God that you who were slaves of

---

2. To say that Paul simply uses a few rhetorical devices here and there, or once in a while, is totally to misrepresent the degree of knowledge of rhetoric Paul demonstrates, even in so short a span of argument as we find in Romans 6. Paul knows very well what amounts to an apt use of the art of persuasion with a largely Gentile, rhetoric-hungry and rhetorically adept Roman audience, and he is not afraid to use almost every rhetorical device in the book. Perhaps the most important thing to note about this is that Quintilian is talking about what he calls "embellishments," which require the sort of rhetorical skill that only those who are thoroughly grounded in rhetoric would attempt. Paul's rhetoric is not rudimentary, it is masterful.

3. D and several other manuscripts omit the phrase "unto death," but this seems to be a result of a scribal oversight. See B. M. Metzger, *A Textual Commentary on the Greek New Testament* (3rd ed.; London: United Bible Societies, 1971), p. 454.

sin have become obedient from the heart unto the type of teaching to which you were committed/handed over. Being freed from sin, you were enslaved to righteousness. (I speak in human terms because of the weakness of your flesh.) For just as you lent your members as slaves of uncleanness and of lawlessness unto lawless acts, so now you lend your members as slaves to righteousness unto sanctification. For when you were slaves to sin, you were free of righteousness. What fruit then do you now have from that [freedom]? — things of which you are now ashamed, for the end of that is death. But now, being freed from sin but enslaved to God, you have your fruit unto sanctification, the end of which is eternal life. For the wages of sin is death, but the grace gift of God is eternal life in Christ Jesus our Lord.

Do you not know, brothers, for I speak to those who understand what law is about, that the law governs a person just so long as he is alive? For the woman subject to a husband is bound by the law to the living husband, but if the husband dies, she is set free from the law of the husband. So then she will be an adulteress if while her husband is living she becomes [wife] of another man. But if the husband is dead, she is free from the law, so that she is not an adulteress if she becomes [the wife] of another man. So then, my brothers, you also were put to death to law through the body of Christ, in order that you might belong to another, to the one raised from the dead, in order that we might bear fruit to God. For when we were in the flesh, the passions of sin, these things through the law used to be at work in our members unto the bearing of fruit unto death, but now we are set free from the law, having died to that by which we were subjugated, so as to serve in newness of Spirit and not in oldness of letter.

The conclusion that Paul is largely, if not almost exclusively, addressing Gentiles in this letter is simply reconfirmed in ch. 6, where we find the critique of enslavement to sin, lending one's members to lawlessness and impurity and things of which one should be ashamed. Paul has used these sorts of complaints to critique the Gentile world in ch. 1 (e.g., 1.24) and the first Gentile interlocutor in ch. 2.[4] The critique could apply to anyone who does such things, including Jews, but Paul's focus is largely on Gentiles. That they are not under Law but under grace is a remark made to Christians, explaining what is not now to be the case with them.[5] "Chapters 6-8 present the benefits of Christ as a way to the goal of gentile obedience but without a law-centered regimen of practices aimed at subduing the passions."[6]

4. See the discussion by Dunn, *Romans 1–8*, pp. 346-47: "This evocation of the Jewish critique of Gentile morality and the implicit antithesis between Jewish ideals of priestly consecration and gentile lawlessness is therefore undoubtedly deliberate. It strengthens the implication that Paul was writing the letter with Gentiles largely or principally in view."

5. See the discussion by S. K. Stowers, *A Rereading of Romans: Justice, Jews, and Gentiles* (New Haven: Yale University Press, 1994), pp. 255-58.

6. Stowers, *Rereading of Romans*, p. 257.

V. 15 begins once again with the dialogue or diatribal format. But in ch. 6, unlike the predominant form of discourse in chs. 1–5, Paul is speaking here in the first and second persons plural. He presents negative and positive incentives not to sin. For one thing, the Christian is not under the Law. For another thing the Christian is under grace. Paul will deal with the latter point here, and then turn to the former in ch. 7.[7]

Underlying the discussion here is Paul's attempt to undercut false views of Christian freedom under grace. Freedom is not just freedom from sin, but also freedom for specific lifestyles and tasks that God has called a person to. In particular, it is freedom to serve God. Christian freedom does not entail freedom from any and all sorts of obligations or obedience, freedom to be merely self-indulgent and then presume on the mercies of God. To the contrary, says Paul in v. 16, when the audience became Christians they offered themselves as slaves to God, and this necessarily entails obedience.[8] Formerly they were "obedient" to their sinful inclinations, and Paul says the end of that road is death. In his use of slavery language here he is drawing on the fact that people in the Roman Empire did indeed often volunteer to become slaves because in many cases it gave themselves and their families a more secure living than they would have otherwise.[9] There may indeed have been those in Paul's audience in Rome who had actually done this, for Rome was the slave capital of the empire, a place where more domestic slave labor was used than probably anywhere else in the Mediterranean crescent.[10] Freedom in Christ does not mean being free from all masters and lords. It does not mean radical independence. It means being free to serve the

7. C. K. Barrett, *Commentary on the Epistle to the Romans* (Peabody: Hendrickson, 1991), p. 123.

8. The rhetorical question that begins v. 16 suggests that Paul is speaking about a well-known fact, or something the informed audience will or should know about (cf. 1 Cor. 3.16; 5.6; 6.2-3). It is not simply a question of Paul preferring a lively diatribal style (see Dunn, *Romans 1–8*, p. 341). Rather, Paul is establishing that there are some things his audience should, but may not, know about, which Paul needs to instruct them on. In other words, this is a way of establishing authority with the audience, so that they will be open to what the apostle will say.

9. See the discussion by S. Bartchy, *First-Century Slavery and the Interpretation of 1 Corinthians 7.21* (Missoula: Scholars, 1973).

10. This is of course because the largest conglomeration of patricians with villas was concentrated in Rome, and for many of them manual labor was beneath their dignity. Thus many artisans, educators, and others went to Rome to find employment as slaves in the house of some patrician, as a member of the extended household. In Caesar's household alone hundreds of slaves were employed, often in the very affairs of state. On this see P. C. Weaver, *Familia Caesaris* (Cambridge: Cambridge University Press, 1972). It is possible that some of those greeted in Romans 16 were slaves in the household of Caesar whom Paul knew (cf. Phil. 4.21-22). If this is the case, Paul's connections with them would also improve his honor rating with various parts of his audience in Rome and make them more receptive to his message.

one true Lord and to be under the Law of Christ (see 1 Cor. 9.21; Gal. 6.2).[11] Paul's view of human nature is that we have been made to serve some higher power, and the alternative to serving the one true God is to serve false gods, including the self and one's own selfish desires.[12] For Paul, it is also axiomatic that there is a place for obedience under grace. Indeed, he might well have asked his audience, Why should we assume God would expect less of believers when they have more grace than when they were under Law (or outside the Law)?

Paul speaks about the conversion of his audience in v. 17 and says that while they were once slaves to sin, that is no longer the case since the time they became obedient to the goal of final righteousness,[13] or, to put it another way, since they became obedient from the heart to the Christian teaching to which they were handed over. We might have expected him to say that the "pattern" or type *(typos)* of teaching was handed over to them (using the Jewish language of the handing over of sacred tradition; see 1 Cor. 11.23; 15.3), which is true, but Paul says the reverse. Since he has been emphasizing obedience it is probable that he is thinking of the idea of one submitting to a teaching, like one submitted to the yoke of the Law. These new converts were handed over to a pattern or type of teaching which they were to both believe and obey in the "obedience of faith." This pattern probably involved the imitation of the faithful and obedient Christ, though Paul does not say so here. Nonetheless, *typos* in Paul's letters almost always has a personal reference to a particular individual who provides a pattern of conduct (cf. Rom. 5.14; Phil. 3.17; 1 Thess. 1.7; 2 Thess. 3.9; and especially Col. 2.6 for the idea).[14] The end of such obedience is righteousness, including final righteousness, which is the goal of the Christian life and is counterposed with death in v. 16. *Dikaiosynē* here surely does not refer to God's gracious power or being under the sway of his righteousness, since the discussion here is about the present and future state and condition of the believer, although of course God is the sanctifier of the believer and the one who produces in the believer the state of righteousness.[15]

---

11. See Dunn, *Romans 1–8*, p. 345: "The only real freedom for man is as a slave to God, a life lived in recognition of his creaturely dependence."

12. See C. E. B. Cranfield, *A Critical and Exegetical Commentary on the Epistle to the Romans* (ICC; Edinburgh: Clark, 1975-79), 1:323: "The man who imagines he is free, because he acknowledges no god but his own ego, is deluded; for the service of one's own ego is the very essence of slavery to sin."

13. This is rightly sensed by Dunn, *Romans 1–8*, p. 343: "Paul here has no misgivings about representing 'righteousness' as an 'end product,' a condition or state or relationship yet to be realized (as elsewhere most clearly in Gal. 5.5 . . .). Nor does he seem to have any misgivings about representing righteousness as in some sense the product or result of obedience, even if qualified as obedience enabled by God."

14. Dunn, *Romans 1–8*, p. 343.

15. Pace Dunn, *Romans 1–8*, pp. 344, 347.

Paul says in v. 19 that he is using a merely human illustration when he talks about slavery to sin or to righteousness. He says he must do this because of their human weakness (something Paul can identify with: cf. Gal. 4.13). It is possible that he is indirectly making clear that he is not in fact an advocate of slavery or enslaving oneself to some other human being in the literal sense. He is simply speaking metaphorically about slavery to sin or righteousness. But there is something else going on here. Paul said in ch. 1 that he looks forward to coming to Rome and sharing with the Romans, surely by way of teaching them. His assumption seems to be that they are still neophytes in the faith, and here he reminds them of the original "catechetical" pattern of teaching to which they submitted or were handed over. It was not a pattern that encouraged continuing to sin since one is now under grace.

But there is a rhetorical dimension to what Paul says in this verse. In the first place, arguing from human customs or analogy (here using the example of slavery, in 7.1-6 using an analogy with marriage law of the day) is a form of argument Paul has used before in Gal. 3.15-18.[16] In rhetorical terms the introductory phrase (whether *kata anthrōpon* or, as here, *anthrōpinon legō*) signals an artificial proof, as opposed to an inartificial proof like the earlier appeals to experience or Scriptures. It is a weaker form of argument than the inartificial proof, in part because it is an argument from human analogy or human example (see Quintilian, *Instit. Or.* 5.11.1ff.).

It is not surprising that here in Romans, as in Galatians, Paul has led first with arguments from experience, then from Scripture, and finally from analogy, a form of artificial proof. He believes he has arranged his arguments according to their relative strengths as the audience will evaluate them. To finish with a strong argument he will return to an argument from experience in chs. 7–8, first non-Christian experience "in Adam" and then Christian experience in Christ and in the Spirit in ch. 8. Failure to recognize the progression and nature of Paul's rhetorical arguments has caused no end of misinterpretation of chs. 7–8 and to a lesser degree of what the arguments in ch. 6 are preparing for, as Paul brings the *probatio* or his theological case to a climax in ch. 8.

Paul is not so much shaming his audience, as he has been doing, especially in the first two arguments, as deflating them. He wants all arrogance to be set aside before he gets to the *refutatio* in chs. 9–11, where he will take on a very real problem of ethnic prejudice and supersessionist theological thinking. He has been following the rhetorical technique known as *insinuatio*, which is the indirect approach, where one only alludes to the major bone of contention along the way, or to a need for further instruction, and then reserves that most contentious topic for the end of the discourse or major portion of the discourse, where it is presented with much pathos and directness

16. See my *Grace in Galatia* (Grand Rapids: Eerdmans, 1998), pp. 240-42.

(see Aristotle, *Rhetoric* 1419b).[17] That contentious topic will be dealt with in chs. 9–11. What comes before in chs. 1–8 has been laying the foundation and preparing the way for that discussion. Here Paul helps prepare the way by reminding his audience that they have some weaknesses and are still at an elementary level in their understanding of the faith. He was of course not their original instructor in the faith, but it is noteworthy that he feels he can build on that pattern by simply reminding the Roman Christians about it. He nowhere debates or disputes the original teaching they received. This letter is not about refuting opponents but about directing and to some degree correcting his audience. In part this entails forestalling possible objections to his arguments, as is the case here.

Paul urges that the Romans submit their members, their very faculties, to righteousness, which leads to sanctification. This way of putting things, coupled with the contrast with moral impurity and iniquity, makes it as clear as can be that Paul is referring to an ethical quality of the Christian life, namely righteousness, and that pursuing such a pattern of living leads to cleansing or sanctification. The issue here is not the believer's standing with God or God's own righteousness, but the believer's behavior and quality of life before God, and Paul believes that when one behaves as God desires this in itself has a cleansing or purifying effect. That *hagiasmos* has an ethical or moral or spiritual rather than a ritual sense here is supported by the parallel usage in 1 Thess. 4.3-7, where the issue is clearly sexual purity of some kind.[18]

"One of the dangers for Christians in this new situation is that, thinking themselves free of all lordships, they may fall back unwittingly under the lordship of sin. . . . There is another danger. Facing the new situation, with its new requirements of obedience, Christians may so romanticize the old situation that they think back on it with longing. Maybe it was not so bad after all. Paul is aware of that danger as well. Only think back on what that life led to. . . . All that obedience to sin could accomplish was death."[19] "To think freedom is attained by jettisoning obedience to God is to opt for sin as one's lord."[20] Paul is thus seeking to do some ethical steering even in the midst of a largely theological ar-

17. It is no accident that the greatest display of pathos comes in the final theological argument in chs. 9–11. This is not just because the issue there is near and dear to Paul's heart, though that is true. It is because he has deliberately and in rhetorically adept fashion reserved his discussion of that thorniest of issues until last.

18. Thus Paul, while he is talking about submission to God's righteous will and imperatives for the believer here (see Barrett, *Romans*, p. 124), is actually focusing not on the righteousness God has or bestows but on how believers manifest or reflect God's righteousness in their own lives, by offering all their faculties to a good end. This verse prepares in a sense for what Paul will say in 12.1.

19. P. Achtemeier, *Romans* (Atlanta: John Knox, 1985), p. 110.

20. C. Talbert, *Romans* (Macon: Smyth and Helwys, 2002), p. 168.

gument, in preparation for the parenetic or practical portion of this deliberative discourse, which begins at 12.1.

A further rhetorical question is asked in v. 21. What good fruit did freedom from righteousness bring you? Of course the implied answer is "none." Paul answers for the audience by saying it only brought shame and ultimately spiritual and then physical death. This is to be contrasted with what is now the case with the audience. V. 22 states that the audience have become slaves to God and so their lives do not produce bad fruit, but rather sanctification, the end of which is eternal life. Paul assumes that there is no such thing as freedom from all sorts of mastery or lordship. The only question is whether one will be a slave to God or a slave to sin.[21]

Sanctification is seen here as the intermediate condition between what was true of believers before they were converted and what will be true of believers at the resurrection, where they will inherit eternal life. Sanctification is then something that is supposed to lead to eternal life, not merely happen when one obtains eternal life, just as iniquity in this life leads to death. Holiness of heart and life is what God expects, indeed requires of his people. When one becomes a slave of God, a slave who obeys God's call and will, the process of sanctification, of cleansing, has begun in that human life. It is something that must continue, as the believer continually must submit his faculties to be used in a right and righteous manner.[22] One must present oneself to God as a living sacrifice daily. The promise given here is that believers have been freed from the bondage to sin, but freed for service and obedience to God.

In v. 23 Paul will contrast wages with a free gracious gift. The cost of going on sinning is ultimately death, including spiritual and physical death. "Paul . . . points to death as the 'wages' . . . paid by slave master 'Sin.'"[23] Eternal life, on the other hand, is not something earned by the believer, even if he or she behaves in a holy manner, for holiness is obligatory, not optional, for the Christian. Eternal life is a grace gift. Even if Christian persons managed to live an entirely sanctified life, this would not oblige God to reward them with eternal life, for they will have done no more than what was required of them. Thus Paul does not see eternal life as some sort of quid pro quo for holy living in this lifetime. Salvation is indeed a matter of grace, received through faith, from start to finish.

In the second phase to this part of the argument, in 7.1-6, Paul will draw a further analogy, appealing to what is the case with marriage law.[24] "Rom. 7.1-6

---

21. See Talbert, *Romans*, p. 170.

22. See A. B. Du Toit, "*Dikaiosynē* in Rom. 6. Beobachtungen zur ethischen Dimension der paulinischen Gerechtigkeitsauffassung," *ZTK* 76 (1979): 261-91.

23. B. Byrne, *Romans*, Sacra Pagina (Collegeville: Liturgical, 1996), p. 204.

24. On the argumentative coherence of this segment see K. A. Burton, "The Argumentative Coherence of Romans 7.1-6," in *SBL Seminar Papers 2000*, pp. 452-64. Burton is correct

supports the dissociative argument in 6.15-23 by way of analogy."[25] There may
be some interplay here between use of *nomos* of a ruling principle or law (other
than the Mosaic Law) and of the Mosaic Law as well. The appeal to knowledge
may mean no more than "surely you ought to know," or again Paul may be rhetorically demonstrating the audience's ignorance and need for further instruction.[26] In Roman law of Paul's day a wife was not irrevocably bound to her husband for a lifetime.[27] It appears that Paul is drawing on a Mosaic principle here
that was accepted as valid in the Christian community, and Paul presumes it is
valid in the Roman Christian community.[28]

The second half of v. 1 states the principle which is then discoursed on in
vv. 2-3 and applied in vv. 4-6.[29] The principle is quite clear: the law has validity
over someone as long as one is alive, and it has validity over a relationship so
long as both partners are still alive. But once a person, or one of the marital
partners, dies, the law no longer applies to either the dead or the surviving partner. Paul states in v. 2 that a woman under the authority of a husband is bound
by the law to her *living* husband. The term *hypandros* is found nowhere else in
the NT and probably means "under the authority of the husband," describing
the woman's legal position. He appears to be drawing on Num. 5.20-29 (LXX),
where we find not only the same word but also the matter of the wife's faithfulness or adultery.

Because of what Paul says in v. 2, he can draw the conclusion we find in

---

that we are dealing with an analogy following the rhetorical rules for such devices, and a degree of artificiality or lack of complete conformity to real life is usual (in this regard it is like
some of Jesus' parables). In fact, the analogy falls under the heading of artificial proofs; see
Quintilian, *Instit. Or.* 5.9.1. Aristotle informs us that the analogy is a form of inductive argument (*Ars Rhetorica* 1.2.9). Burton sees the structure here as: (1) principle stated, v. 1; (2) illustration of principle, vv. 2-3; (3) application of principle, vv. 4-6. The emphasis is on the application.

25. N. Elliott, *The Rhetoric of Romans: Argumentative Constraint and Strategy and
Paul's Dialogue with Judaism* (JSNTS 45; Sheffield: Sheffield Academic Press, 1990), p. 242.

26. I do not think there is warrant for seeing a change in audience here. Paul is still addressing a largely Gentile audience. But he is saying here that these Gentiles ought to know
their Jewish heritage, including the Law. He will continue this theme in chs. 9–11. In other
words, we have here a rhetorical use of "those who know" = "those who ought to know." See
D. Moo, *The Epistle to the Romans* (NICNT; Grand Rapids: Eerdmans, 1996), pp. 410-11. This
conclusion is supported by the initial salvo in this verse: "Or are you ignorant. . . ." The answer is that they may well be, but they ought to know their Jewish roots better.

27. See O. F. Robinson, *The Criminal Law of Ancient Rome* (Baltimore: Johns Hopkins
University Press, 1995), pp. 54-71.

28. See my discussion in *Women in the Earliest Churches* (Cambridge: Cambridge University Press, 1988), pp. 62-63.

29. J. A. Little, "Paul's Use of Analogy: A Structural Analysis of Romans 7.1-6," *CBQ* 46
(1984): 82-90.

v. 3: if while the husband is still alive the woman consorts with or attempts to marry another, she is to be called an adulteress. But if the husband is dead, she is not an adulteress, but is free to remarry. Though it is not Paul's purpose to discourse on marriage here, nonetheless it is apparent that he believes marriage, even Christian marriage, to be an earthly relationship dissolved at death. V. 2 focuses on the husband's rights while alive, and v. 3 on the wife's. This is certainly a more egalitarian discussion of marriage and its rights and duties than was often found in the Greco-Roman world.[30]

In v. 4 Paul begins to show what the analogy's significance is for Christian life. Christians have been set free from the Law. Sometimes this argument is seen as hopelessly confused, but in fact Paul's purposes are limited here. He is not drawing elaborate conclusions on the basis of the analogy, only suggesting that freedom from the Law has been gained through a death, and certainly the analogy establishes this point. "Paul's question . . . is: 'How can the death of *another* person affect *my* relationship to the law?'"[31] The analogy answers that question. But Paul is also asking: In what sense has the believer died to the Law in the body of Christ? This could mean that through the physical death of Jesus the Law ceased to have sway over those who would come to believe in Jesus.[32] In any case, the death Paul refers to as a past event has released the believer from being under the power, control, or jurisdiction of the Mosaic Law.[33] The believer is like the woman in the analogy, no longer subject to the old authority of the Law and now free to belong to another, in this case Christ. Paul speaks elsewhere of Christians being under another Law, the Law of Christ, which in this letter he speaks of as the obedience that flows from faith. Here it is enough to establish that Christians are not under the Mosaic Law, just as Paul said of himself in Gal. 2.19.[34]

Vv. 5-6 prepare for the arguments which are yet to come in chs. 7–8, and several points here are crucial.[35] V. 5 says clearly that the believer used to be in the flesh, and the sinful passions used to be at work. The imperfect tense of "be at work" here is often overlooked.[36] The Law, unfortunately, as part of its effect on a fallen person, increased or aroused sin (cf. 5.20). But the believer is no longer "in the flesh" or under the Law because he or she has died to the Law and

30. See my *Women in the Earliest Churches*, pp. 26-64.

31. Achtemeier, *Romans*, p. 114.

32. This seems the most probable interpretation. See Barrett, *Romans*, p. 128.

33. See G. D. Fee, *God's Empowering Presence: The Holy Spirit in the Letters of Paul* (Peabody: Hendrickson, 1994), p. 504.

34. See N. T. Wright, "Romans," in *The New Interpreter's Bible,* vol. 10 (Nashville: Abingdon, 2002), p. 559.

35. See Barrett, *Romans*, p. 128: "The subject matter of this verse reappears, at much greater length, in vv. 7-25." That is correct, and this means that just as Paul is talking about a pre-Christian condition here in this verse, so he is in vv. 7-25 as well.

36. Barrett, *Romans*, p. 128.

the passions of the flesh. As 8.5-8 will make abundantly clear, Paul is describing in 7.5 life before one has the Spirit, which is to say, pre-Christian life. Gal. 5.13-24 shows that we are on the right track here, for there too Paul says believers are not "in the flesh," by which he means that sinful way of life which is in opposition to God and in which one is enslaved to one's own passions.

Thus v. 6 concludes that the believer is no longer bound by or to the Law and so serves in newness of spirit rather than oldness of letter. The spirit in question here is probably the Holy Spirit, just as the letter in question is the old Law, which, Paul says, believers are now not under the authority of.[37] There have been many misinterpretations of Paul's meaning here and in Rom. 2.29 and 2 Cor. 3.6. In all three places, "the contrast between 'Spirit' and 'letter' has nothing to do with several popularizations of this language, e.g., between the 'spirit and the letter' of the law, or between 'literal and spiritual'! This is eschatological and covenantal language. 'Letter' has to do with the old covenant, that came to an end through Christ and the Spirit.[38] As 2 Cor. 3.6 makes clear, the new covenant is a covenant characterized by the effective presence of the Spirit."[39] The issue here then is not hermeneutics but salvation history. The era of the Torah covenant is over.[40] The era of the new covenant, characterized by the full endowment of the Spirit, has dawned. The contrast between old and new could hardly be more clearly drawn, and this prepares for what follows in chs. 7–8.

Bridging the Horizons

On first glance Paul's language about slavery may seem harsh. Though we may be tempted to distance ourselves from the discussion since none of us are liter-

---

37. See Talbert, *Romans*, p. 174: "The language of Romans 7.6, the 'old written code' and 'in the new life of the Spirit' is similar to that in 2 Corinthians 3.6. The context of the Corinthians passage treats the new covenant as a replacement of the old. Likewise here in Romans 7.6 it is the new covenant's contrast with the old Mosaic one that is in view. For Paul the coming of the Spirit meant the end of the time of the Law."

38. See Ambrosiaster (*Comm. on Paul* 81.219-21): "Although Paul regards the [Mosaic] Law as inferior to the law of faith, he does not condemn it. . . . The Law of Moses is not called 'old' because it is evil but because it is out of date and has ceased to function." See G. Bray, ed., *Romans* (Ancient Christian Commentary on Scripture; Downers Grove: InterVarsity, 1998), p. 179.

39. Fee, *God's Empowering Presence*, p. 507.

40. See Chrysostom (*Hom. Rom.* 12): "He does not say that the Law was discharged or that sin was discharged but that we were discharged. How did this happen? It happened because the old self, who had been held down by sin, died and was buried." See Bray, ed., *Romans*, p. 179.

ally slaves, as some of Paul's audience were, this would be a large mistake. Paul wants to stress the bondage to sin of those outside Christ. Though we have not experienced literal slavery, perhaps we can after all relate to this discussion because what Paul is really talking about is slavery to sin and slavery to a law.

The easiest point of analogy of course would be to various sorts of compulsive and addictive behaviors — compulsive eating, or binging and purging, addiction to any number of drugs from nicotine to caffeine to heroin to cocaine. But there are also the addictions of the eyes, addiction to pornography, so-called adult entertainment, and the like. There can also be the addiction to spending money (shopping), or alternatively to hoarding money, or greed. All these sorts of behaviors attest to the fact that humans do not just choose to sin but are also unable to do otherwise without outside intervention, without the grace of God acting in some way. This passage presses the question: What sort of unhealthy and unhelpful desires, behaviors, and habits are running your life, even though you may think you are controlling them?

It is part of the American pledge that we affirm "one nation, under God, with liberty and justice for all." There is in this pledge some sense or awareness that freedom and justice in a dark world are ultimately provisions of God. They are perhaps the two things besides love that the human heart most cries out for in the modern era. However, the freedom (and justice or righteousness) Paul is referring to is not merely freedom from things like slavery or addictive behavior, but freedom for doing righteousness. While there is always a legitimate cry for justice in a world full of injustice, Paul is more concerned to focus on our contribution to setting the world right, our attempt to manifest the righteousness of God in our character and behavior. He places the onus on believers to do so. Paul never gives way to the spirit of victimization and retaliation that so often permeates our world.

Part Three — 7.7-13: Retelling Adam's Tale

Impersonation, or *prosopopoeia,* is a rhetorical technique which falls under the heading of figures of speech and is often used to illustrate or make vivid a piece of deliberative rhetoric (*Instit. Or.* 3.8.49; cf. Theon, *Progymnasta* 8). This rhetorical technique involves the assumption of a role, and sometimes the role is marked off from the surrounding discourse by a change in tone, inflection, or accent, by form of delivery, or by an introductory formula signaling a change in voice. Sometimes the speech would simply be inserted "without mentioning the speaker at all" (9.2.37). Unfortunately, we cannot hear Paul's discourse delivered in its original oral setting, as was Paul's intent. It is not surprising then that many have not picked up the signals that he is using impersonation in Rom. 7.7-13 and also for that matter in 7.14-25.[1]

Quintilian says impersonation "is sometimes introduced even with controversial themes, which are drawn from history and involve the appearance of definite historical characters as pleaders" (*Instit. Or.* 3.8.52). Adam is the historical figure impersonated in Rom. 7.7-13, and the theme is most certainly controversial and drawn from history. The most important requirement for a speech in character in the form of impersonation is that the speech be fitting, suiting the situation and character of the one speaking. "For a speech that is out of keeping with the man who delivers it is just as faulty as a speech which fails to suit the subject to which it should conform" (3.8.51). Quintilian considers the

---

1. C. Talbert, *Romans* (Macon: Smyth and Helwys, 2002), p. 186, rightly notes that "impersonation" was also a rhetorical device used to train those learning to write letters (see Theon 2.1125.22). I am indebted to Dr. Carroll Osburn of Abilene Christian University for inviting me to give the Carmichael-Walling lectureship on this passage. The material appears here in a somewhat different form.

ability to pull off a convincing impersonation as reflecting the highest skill in rhetoric, for it is often the most difficult thing to do (3.8.49). That Paul attempts it, tells us something about Paul as a rhetorician. This rhetorical technique also involves personification, sometimes of abstract qualities like fame or virtue (9.2.36) or in Paul's case sin or grace. Quintilian also informs us that impersonation may take the form of a dialogue or speech, but it can also take the form of a first person narrative (9.2.37).

Since the important work of W. G. Kümmel on Romans 7, it has become a common, perhaps even majority, opinion in some NT circles that the "I" of Romans 7 is not autobiographical.[2] This, however, still does not tell us what sort of literary or rhetorical use of "I" we find there. As Stowers points out, it is also no new opinion that the rhetorical technique known as "impersonation" is what is going on in Romans 7.[3] In fact, this is how some of the earliest Greek commentators on Romans, such as Origen, took this portion of the letter, and later commentators such as Jerome and Rufinus take note of this approach of Origen's.[4] Not only so, Didymus of Alexandria and Nilus of Ancyra also saw Paul using speech in character or impersonation here.[5] The point to be noted here is that we are talking about Church Fathers who not only knew Greek well but who also understood the use of rhetoric.[6] Even more importantly, John Chrysostom (Homily 13 on Romans), who was very much in touch with the rhetorical nature and the theological substance of Paul's letters, did not think Romans 7 was about Christians, much less about Paul himself as a Christian. He took it to be talking about those who lived before the Law and then those who lived outside or under the Law. In other words, it is about Gentiles and Jews outside Christ.

Since the vast majority of Paul's audience is Gentile, and Paul has as part of his rhetorical aims effecting some reconciliation between Jewish and Gentile Christians in Rome,[7] it would be singularly inept for Paul here to retell the story of Israel in a negative way and then turn around in chs. 9–11 to urge Gentiles to appreciate their Jewish heritage in Christ and be understanding of Jews and

2. See W. G. Kümmel, *Römer 7 und das Bild des Menschen im Neuen Testament* (Munich: Kaiser, 1974).

3. S. K. Stowers, *A Rereading of Romans: Justice, Jews, and Gentiles* (New Haven: Yale University Press, 1994), pp. 264-69.

4. Unfortunately we have only fragments of Origen's commentary on Romans. See the careful discussion by Stowers, *A Rereading of Romans*, pp. 266-67. Origen rightly notes that: (1) Jews such as Paul do not speak of a time when they lived before or without the Law; and (2) what Paul says elsewhere about himself (cf. 1 Cor. 6.19; Gal. 3.13; and 2.20) does not fit this description of life outside Christ in Romans 7.

5. See Stowers, *A Rereading of Romans*, pp. 268-69.

6. It appears that the better commentators knew both Greek and rhetoric, the more likely they were to read ch. 7 as an example of impersonation.

7. See pp. 6-15 above.

their fellow Jewish Christians. No, Paul tells a more universal tale here of the progenitor of all humankind and then the story of all those "in Adam," not focusing specifically on those "in Israel" that are within the Adamic category.[8] Even in 7.14-25, Paul is mainly echoing his discussion in 2.15 of Gentiles who have the "Law" within and struggle over its demands.[9]

A Closer Look: The History of the Interpretation of Romans, or Footnotes to Augustine[10]

If the measure of the importance of a text is who it has impacted in a major way, then in many regards Romans is, perhaps after one or the other of the Gospels, the most important NT book. From Augustine to Aquinas to Erasmus to Melanchthon to Luther to Calvin to Wesley and in the modern era to K. Barth, R. Bultmann, and many others its influence has been decisive. But the nature of the impact is in part determined by the way in which and the tradition from which each of these persons has read Romans.

There is a direct line of influence from Augustine to all these other interpreters. But there were interpreters of Romans, and especially of ch. 7, prior to Augustine, and many of them, including luminaries among the Greek Fathers like Origen and Chrysostom in the East and Pelagius and Ambrosiaster in the West, and they did not take Augustine's line of approach to Romans and, in particular, to ch. 7. To a real degree, Augustine skewed the interpretation of this crucial Pauline text, and we are still dealing with the theological fallout, lo these many years later. Philipp Melanchthon was to complain wryly: "This part of the Pauline epistle must be pondered in a particularly careful manner, because the ancients also sweated greatly in explaining these things, and few of them treated them skillfully and correctly."[11] The problem is that

---

8. See Quintilian, *Instit. Or.* 9.2.30-31: "By this means we display the inner thoughts of our adversaries as though they were talking with themselves . . . or without sacrifice of credibility we may offer conversations between ourselves and others, or of others among themselves, and put words of advice, reproach, complaint, praise or pity into the mouths of appropriate persons."

9. The sensitive analysis by J. N. Aletti, "The Rhetoric of Romans 5–8," in *The Rhetorical Analysis of Scripture: Essays from the 1995 London Conference,* ed. S. E. Porter and T. H. Olbricht (Sheffield: Sheffield Academic Press, 1997), pp. 294-308, here p. 300, deserves to be consulted. He makes clear that Paul is not talking about Christians here.

10. In what follows I am indebted to T. J. Deidun for pointing me in the right direction. See especially his helpful summary of the data, "Romans," in *A Dictionary of Biblical Interpretation,* ed. R. J. Collins and J. L. Houlden (Philadelphia: Trinity Press, 1990), pp. 601-4. Also helpful is J. Godsey, "The Interpretation of Romans in the History of the Christian Faith," *Interpretation* 34 (1980): 3-16.

11. P. Melanchthon, *Commentary on Romans,* trans. F. Kramer (St. Louis: Concordia, 1992), p. 156.

Melanchthon thought that Augustine had it right and that the great majority of the Fathers were wrong.

The need to use Romans to dispute the Marcionites and the Gnostics preoccupied patristic interpreters before Augustine and emphasized very un-Augustinian themes such as the created goodness of human flesh and at least some human desire and the integrity of human nature (Chrysostom), free will (Pelagius), and the harmony of gospel and Law (several of the Fathers). In Pelagius's view, sin comes from human beings' free imitation of Adam and can be overcome by imitating Christ. He also suggests that justification, at least final justification, comes through determined moral action. Augustine was to counter Pelagius by insisting on the necessity of grace for justification (see his *On the Spirit and the Letter,* written in A.D. 412).

Augustine's mature interpretation of Romans immediately had enormous weight in the West and was to be, in effect, canonized for the Roman Catholic tradition at the church councils of Carthage in A.D. 418 and of Orange in 529. It was to be canonized, so to speak, for the Protestant line of interpretation by Luther and Calvin. And it was, especially in ch. 7, in various ways an overreaction to Pelagius.[12]

Deidun summarizes Augustine's interpretation thus:

> (1) The "works of the law" which Paul says can never justify, mean moral actions in general without the grace of Christ, not Jewish practices as Pelagius and others maintained.[13] (2) The "righteousness of God" . . . is not an attribute of God but the gift he confers in making people righteous; (3) Rom. 5.12 now became the key text for Augustine's doctrine of original sin: all individuals (infants included) were co-involved in Adam's sin. As is well known, Augustine's exegesis of this verse largely depended on the Latin translation *in quo* ("in whom") of the Greek *eph' hō* ("in that," because) and on the omission in his manuscripts of the second mention of "death," with the result that "sin" became the subject of "spread": sin spread to all (by "generation", not by "imitation").[14] (4) Rom. 7.14-25, which before the controversy Augustine had understood to be referring to humanity without Christ, he now applied to the Christian to deprive Pelagius of the opportunity of applying the positive elements in the passage (esp. vs. 22) to unredeemed humanity. To do this, Augustine was obliged to water down Paul's negative statements: the apostle is describing not the bondage of sin but the bother of concupiscence; and he laments not that he cannot do good *(facere)* but that he cannot do it perfectly *(perficere)*. (5) During this period Augustine came to express more boldly his teaching on predestination. It does not depend on God's advance knowledge of people's merit as Pelagius and others maintained in their interpretation of Rom. 9.10ff. nor even on his advance knowledge of "the merit of faith" as Augustine had supposed in 394 in

---

12. The discussion of Augustine, Luther, and Melanchthon by P. W. Meyer, "The Worm at the Core of the Apple," in *The Conversation Continues: Studies in John and Paul,* ed. R. T. Fortna and B. R. Gaventa (Nashville: Abingdon, 1990), pp. 66-69, is helpful.

13. It is interesting how close Dunn's view on "works of the Law" is to that of Pelagius.

14. On Erasmus's rejection of the Augustinian view, see pp. 116-24 above.

his remarks on the same passage: it depends rather on God's "most hidden judgment" whereby he graciously chooses whom he will deliver from the mass of fallen humanity. Everything is pure gift (1 Cor. 4.7).[15]

Of course all of these points of Augustine are today under dispute among interpreters of Romans, and some are clearly wrong, such as the conclusions based on the Latin text of 5.12. For our purposes it is interesting to note that Augustine, having changed his mind about 7.14-25 in overreaction to Pelagius, had to water down the stress on the bondage of the will expressed in this text in order to apply it to Christians. Luther takes a harder and more consistent line, even though in the end he refers the text to the wrong subject — namely everyone, including Christians. It is also noteworthy that Pelagius does not dispute God's predestining of persons, specifying only that God predestines on the basis of his foreknowledge of the response of believers. It is also important that Augustine talks about God's gift of making people righteous. The later forensic emphasis comes as a result of the translation work of Erasmus, as we have pointed out earlier.[16]

The discussion of merit which Pelagius introduced into the conversation about Romans resurfaces among medieval exegetes after Augustine. Paul's doctrine of "justification" is filtered through Aristotelean thinking, so that grace becomes a *donum superadditum,* something added on top of God's gift of human faculties (see Aquinas). "Divine *charis* became 'infused grace.'"[17] The nominalist school of William of Occam focused on merit, even in a Pelagian way, and it was to this repristinization of Pelagius's case that Luther, an Augustinian monk, was to react in his various lectures and then in his commentary on Romans. But it was not just Pelagius he reacted to. In due course Luther came to see self-righteousness (not concupiscence) as the most fundamental of human sins, and his polemics were directed against both Judaism and Catholicism, which he saw as religions that embodied this besetting sin and were preoccupied with "merit." Luther thinks that Rom. 7.14-25 is about that sin of self-righteousness.

Deidun notes rightly that Luther's exploration of what Augustine says about the righteousness of God led him to criticize Augustine for not clearly explaining the imputation of righteousness. But in fact, as Deidun says, Augustine's "understanding of justification is thoroughly incompatible with the notion of imputation."[18] Luther got the idea from Erasmus, but he is not afraid to critique Erasmus at other points. For instance, drawing on his understanding of Rom. 7.14-25 as validating the notion of the Christian as being "simul justus et peccator," he argued against Erasmus and other humanists in regard to human freedom of the will. And Luther's influential two-kingdom theory (spiritual and temporal) is derived from his exegesis of Romans 13. Christians are subject to earthly powers out of respect and love, but in the spiritual

---

15. Deidun, "Romans," p. 601.
16. See pp. 121-23 above.
17. Deidun, "Romans," p. 601.
18. Deidun, "Romans," p. 602.

sphere subject only to God, not to human authorities such as the pope. Calvin was to follow Luther's line on justification and predestination, except that he at least more explicitly highlighted the notion of double predestination, based on his reading of Rom. 8.29 (see the 1539 edition of his *Institutes*).

The English Reformation or Revival of the eighteenth century did not produce any great commentaries on Romans, not by Wesley, Coke, or Fletcher or later in the Wesleyan tradition by Clarke, Watson (though he offers much exposition on Romans in his Institutes, a rebuttal to Calvin), or Asbury. This helps explain why the Protestant tradition of interpretation of the nineteenth and twentieth centuries continued to be dominated by Lutheran and Calvinist interpreters, including Bultmann, Barth, Käsemann, Cranfield, and others of note. Even the foremost Methodist NT scholar of the last half of the twentieth century, C. K. Barrett, reflects primarily the influence of the Reformed tradition of interpretation in both editions of his Romans commentary, including an acknowledged indebtedness to Barth (and Bultmann).

Winds of change however have blown through NT studies since the late 1970s, and the changed views of early Judaism and, as a result, of Paul and the Law, as well as a reassessment of the social setting and rhetorical character of Romans, have led to various fresh lines of interpretation that seem to be better grounded in the historical setting and matrix of Paul, rather than in the longer history of Protestant interpretation of Romans. It needs to be said that especially since Vatican II, there have also been notable contributions to the discussion of Romans by Catholic scholars such as Cerfaux, Lyonnet, Kuss, Fitzmyer, and Byrne. But these expositors, especially Fitzmyer, seem more indebted to Augustine and Luther than to the scholastic and medieval Catholic traditions.

One can measure the importance of a document by whether it has continued to exercise the best minds in the field with fresh attempts to understand it. This Romans continues to do, for it is not only an enduring classic and the most commented on work in human history, it is also a constant challenge to rethink the Christian faith.

But who is the "I" then who is speaking here? In my view the "I" is Adam in vv. 7-13 and all those who are currently "in Adam" in vv. 14-25.[19] Adam, it will be remembered, is the last historical figure Paul introduced into his discourse, at 5.12, and we have contended that the story of Adam undergirds a good deal of the discussion from 5.12 through ch. 7.[20] More will be said on this below, but suffice it to say here that the old traditional interpretations of 7.7-25 that Paul describes there his own pre-Christian experience or the experience of Chris-

19. See the lengthy discussion by G. Theissen, *Psychological Aspects of Pauline Theology* (Philadelphia: Fortress, 1987), pp. 177-269.

20. On Adam in Romans, see R. Hamerton-Kelly, "Sacred Violence and Sinful Desire: Paul's Interpretation of Adam's Sin in the Letter to the Romans," in *The Conversation Continues*, ed. Fortna and Gaventa, pp. 35-54.

tians fail to grasp the rhetorical finesse and character of the material and must be deemed very unlikely, not only for that reason but also for other reasons we will discuss in due course.[21]

What then shall we say? Is the Law sin? Let it not happen! But I did not know sin except through the Law, for I should not have known desire except the Law said: "You shall not desire/covet." But sin, taking opportunity through the commandment, produced in me all sorts of desires, for without the Law sin is dead. But I was living without the Law once. But with the coming of the commandment, sin was awakened/lived anew. But I myself died, and the commandment which was unto life turned out for me unto death. For sin, taking opportunity through the commandment, deceived me and killed me through it. So the Law is holy, and the commandment holy and just and good. Did then the good become to me death? Let it not happen! But sin, in order to reveal itself as sin, through that which was good produced in me death, in order that sin might become exceedingly sinful through the commandment.[22]

I have commented on this text to some degree elsewhere,[23] but here it is important to give full attention to the narrative. Three things are crucial. First, Paul believes that Moses wrote the Pentateuch, including Genesis. Second, the "law" in Moses' books includes more than the Law given to Moses with the Mosaic covenant. It includes the first commandment given to Adam and Eve.[24] And, third, it appears that Paul saw the "original sin" of coveting the fruit of the prohibited tree as a form of violation of the tenth commandment (cf. *Apocalypse of Moses* 19.3).

An expansive rendering of vv. 8-11 can bring out the Adamic story which is being retold:

21. It is telling that some of the most thorough recent treatments of ch. 7, even from the Reformed tradition, have concluded that Paul cannot be describing the Christian experience here; cf. D. Moo, *The Epistle to the Romans* (NICNT; Grand Rapids: Eerdmans, 1996), pp. 443-50; N. T. Wright, "Romans," in *The New Interpreter's Bible*, vol. 10 (Nashville: Abingdon, 2002), pp. 551-55 (who changed his mind from his earlier view that Christians were in view in 7.14-25); B. Byrne, *Romans*, Sacra Pagina (Collegeville: Liturgical, 1996), pp. 216-26; J. A. Fitzmyer, *Romans* (New York: Doubleday, 1992), pp. 465-73; Talbert, *Romans*, pp. 185-209. See also Meyer, "The Worm at the Core of the Apple," pp. 62-84; J. Lambrecht, *The Wretched 'I' and Its Liberation* (Louvain: Peeters, 1992).

22. There are no real textual problems in this section of Romans.

23. See my *Paul's Narrative Thought World: The Tapestry of Tragedy and Triumph* (Louisville: Westminster/John Knox, 1994), pp. 14-15.

24. It is not surprising that some early Jews saw the commandment given to Adam and Eve as a form of one of the Ten Commandments, specifically the one having to do with coveting. See my *Paul's Narrative Thought World*, p. 14.

> But the serpent [Sin], seizing an opportunity in the commandment, pro-
> duced in me all sorts of covetousness. . . . But I [Adam] was once alive apart
> from the Law, but when the commandment came, Sin sprang to life and I
> died, and the very commandment that promised life, proved deadly to me.
> For Sin [the serpent] seizing an opportunity through the commandment,
> deceived me and through it killed me.

Here indeed we have the familiar primeval tale of human life which began before the existence of the Law and apart from sin. But then the commandment
entered, followed by deception, disobedience, and eventually death.

Those who claim that there is no signal in the text that we are going into
impersonation at v. 7 are simply wrong.[25] "The section begins in v. 7 with an
abrupt change in voice following a rhetorical question, that serves as a transition from Paul's authorial voice, which has previously addressed the readers explicitly . . . in 6.1–7.6. This constitutes what the grammarians and rhetoricians
described as change of voice (enallagē or metabolē). These ancient readers
would next look for diaphonia, a difference in characterization from the
authorial voice. The speaker in 7.7-25 speaks with great personal pathos of coming under the Law at some point, learning about desire and sin, and being unable to do what he wants to do because of enslavement to sin or flesh."[26] We
have here not just a continuation of Paul's discussion of the Law, but a vivid retelling of the Fall that shows that there was a problem with commandments and
the Law from the very beginning of the human story. Paul has moved from talking about what Christians once were (in vv. 5-6[27]) to talking about why they
were that way and why the Law had that effect on them before they became
Christians, namely because of Adam's sin. This is the outworking of the contrast of Adam and Christ in 5.12-21.

Furthermore, there is a good reason not simply to lump vv. 7-13 together
with vv. 14-25, as some commentators still do. In vv. 7-13 we have only past
tenses of the verbs, while in vv. 14-25 we have present tenses. Paul is changing ei-

---

25. See now the very helpful treatment of Paul's rhetorical use of "I" here by J. N.
Aletti, "Rom. 7.7-25 encore une fois: enjeux et propositions," NTS 48 (2002): 358-76. He is also
right that Paul reflects some understanding of both Jewish and Greco-Roman anthropology
in this passage.

26. Stowers, A Rereading of Romans, pp. 269-70.

27. As even C. E. B. Cranfield, A Critical and Exegetical Commentary on the Epistle to the
Romans (ICC; Edinburgh: Clark, 1975-79), 1:337, has to admit, Paul in 7.5 and in 8.8-9 uses the
phrase "in the flesh" to denote a condition that for the Christian now belongs to the past. It is
thus hopelessly contradictory to say "We no longer have the basic direction of our lives controlled and determined by the flesh" (p. 337), and then turn around and maintain that 7.14-25
describes the normal or even best Christian life, even though 7.14 says "we are fleshly, sold under sin," which comports only with the description of pre-Christian life in 7.5 and 8.8-9. This
contradicts the notion that the believer has been released from "the flesh" in a moral sense.

ther the subject, or the time-frame in which he is viewing the one subject. Here it will be worthwhile to consider the issue of the "I" as it has been viewed by various commentators who do not really take into account Paul's use of rhetoric and rhetorical devices, nor note the Adamic narrative subtext to Paul's discourse here.

A Closer Look: The Pauline "I" Chart

Vv. 7-13
    the "I" is strictly autobiographical
    the "I" represents Paul's view of a typical Jewish individual
    the "I" represents the experience of Jews as a whole
    the "I" represents humanity as a whole
    the "I" is a way of speaking in general, without having a particular group of persons in mind

Vv. 14-25
    the "I" is autobiographical and refers to Paul's current Christian experience
    the "I" is autobiographical and refers to Paul's pre-Christian experience as he views it now
    the "I" represents the experience of the non-Christian Jew as seen by himself
    the "I" presents how Christians view Jews
    the "I" is autobiographical and refers to Paul's pre-Christian experience as he viewed it then
    the "I" reflects the so-called "carnal" Christian
    the "I" reflects the experience of Christians in general
    the "I" reflects a person under conviction of sin and at the point of conversion (7.14–ch. 8 provide a narrative of a conversion)

So there is no consensus among scholars who do not take into account the rhetorical signals in the text and do not recognize the echoes and allusions to the story of Adam in vv. 7-13.[28] Sometimes too, as for instance in the case of Käsemann, we have combinations of some of these views. He argues that 7.14-20 reflects the pious Jew, while 7.21-25 reflects all fallen humanity.[29] That there are so many varied conjectures about these texts counts against any of the conjectures being very likely.

    Many commentators through the years have thought Paul was describing

---

28. See the discussion in L. T. Johnson, *Reading Romans: A Literary and Theological Commentary* (Macon: Smyth and Helwys, 2001), pp. 112-16.

29. E. Käsemann, *Commentary on Romans* (Grand Rapids: Eerdmans, 1980), pp. 192-212.

Christian experience, including his own. This we owe in large measure to the influence of Augustine, especially on Luther and those who have followed in Luther's exegetical footsteps. "This entire section of Rom. 7:14-25 is absolutely omnipresent in Augustine's work, and is linked with every other passage in the epistle where the concern is to reinforce the complex interplay of grace and law that Augustine saw in Romans."[30] Furthering the impact of his view is that Augustine shared his opinions on this text in his most influential work, his *Confessions*, as well as in later works relating the text to his own experience.[31] Various important later expositors, such as Luther, resonated with this approach. But this does not constitute any sort of proof that this was what Paul had in mind when he wrote Romans 7. It probably says more about Augustine and Luther, than it does about a rhetorically adept first-century Jewish Christian like Paul, who, K. Stendahl was later to say, does not much seem to reflect the introspective consciousness of the later West.[32] Paul hardly ever talks about his own personal guilt feelings or repentance, and when he does so, he speaks of having persecuted Christians before he was a Christian, not about any internal moral conflict he struggled with as a Christian.[33]

What are the markers or indicators in the text of 7.7-13 that the most probable way to read this text, the way Paul desired for it to be heard, is in the light of the story of Adam, with Adam speaking of his own experience?[34] First, from the beginning of the passage in v. 7 there is reference to one specific commandment: "thou shalt not covet/desire." This is the tenth commandment in an abbreviated form (cf. Exod. 20.17; Deut. 5.21). Some early Jewish exegesis of

30. P. Gorday, *Principles of Patristic Exegesis* (New York: Mellen, 1983), p. 164.

31. Notice that it was a Latin, rather than a Greek, Church Father who made this identification, and only after the strong influence of Manicheanism on him. It does not appear to me that Augustine was all that aware of rhetorical devices and techniques in the Greek tradition.

32. See the famous essay by K. Stendahl with this title in *Paul among Jews and Gentiles* (Philadelphia: Fortress, 1977).

33. Note that Paul's frequent expressions of pathos in his letters, including in Romans, have regularly to do with his concern for his converts, or his fellow Jews, and not with his own personal moral struggles as a Christian. The absence of expressions of guilt about his current conduct, unless ch. 7 is an exception, is noteworthy. Furthermore, Phil. 3.6 strongly indicates that Paul did not have a guilt-laden conscience when he was a non-Christian Jew either.

34. Some commentators, such as C. K. Barrett, *A Commentary on the Epistle to the Romans* (Peabody: Hendrickson, 1991), pp. 134-35, attempt a combination interpretation. Barrett avers that the text is about Adam and also autobiographically about Paul. The rhetorical conventions suggest otherwise, but of course Paul is retelling the story of Adam because of its relevance for his audience's understanding of themselves. They are not to go back down the Adamic road.

Genesis 3 suggested that Adam's sin violated the tenth commandment.[35] He coveted the fruit of the tree of the knowledge of good and evil.

Second, Rom. 7.8 refers to a "commandment" (singular). This can hardly be a reference to the Mosaic Law in general, which Paul regularly speaks of as a collective entity. Only Adam, in all biblical history, was under only one commandment, and it was one about coveting.[36]

Third, v. 9 says "I was living once without/apart from the Law." The only person said in the Bible to be living before or without any law was Adam. The attempt to refer this to persons before their bar-mitzvoth, when they take on the yoke of the Law at 12-13 years of age, while not impossible, seems unlikely. Even a Jewish child who had not yet personally embraced the call to be a "son of the commandments" was still expected to obey the Mosaic Law, including honoring parents and God (cf. Luke 2.41-52).[37]

Fourth, as numerous commentators have regularly noticed, Sin is personified in this text, especially in v. 11, as if it were like the snake in the garden. "Sin took opportunity through the commandment to deceive me." This matches up well with the story about the snake using the commandment to deceive Eve and Adam in the garden. The same verb is used to speak of this deception in 2 Cor. 11.3 and 1 Tim. 2.14.

Fifth, that the "I" "did not know sin except through the commandment" (v. 7) would properly be the case only with Adam, especially if "know" here refers to personal experience of sin (cf. v. 5).[38] The parallel between knowing sin and knowing desire suggests that Paul has in view such experience of sin. As we know from various earlier texts in Romans, Paul believes that all people after Adam have sinned and fallen short of God's glory, and 5.12-21 seems to be presupposed here. But it is possible to take *egnōn* to mean "recognize": I did not recognize sin for what it was except through the existence of the commandment. If this is the point, then it comports with what Paul has already said about the Law turning sin into trespass and sin being revealed as a violation of God's will for humankind. But on the whole it seems more likely that Paul is describing Adam's awakening consciousness of the possibility of sin when the first commandment was given. All in all, the most satisfactory explanation of

35. See 4 Ezra 7.11; Babylonian Talmud *Sanhedrin* 56b. On the identification of Torah with the preexistent Wisdom of God see Sir. 24.23; Bar. 3.36–4.1.

36. See J. D. G. Dunn, *Romans 1–8*, Word Biblical Commentary (Dallas: Word, 1988), p. 381. See Käsemann, *Commentary on Romans*, p. 196: "Methodologically the starting point should be that a story is told in vv. 9-11 and that the event depicted can refer strictly only to Adam. . . . There is nothing in the passage which does not fit Adam, and everything fits Adam alone."

37. But see Barrett, *Romans*, p. 134.

38. Barrett, *Romans*, p. 132, points out the difference between here and 3.20, where Paul uses *epignōsis* to refer to the recognition of sin. Here he simply says "know."

these verses is Paul the Christian rereading the story of Adam in the light of his Christian views about law and the Law.[39]

Certainly one of the functions of this subsection of Romans is to provide an apologia for the Law. Paul is asking: Is then the Law something evil because it not only reveals sin, but has the unintended effect of suggesting sins to commit? Is the Law's association with sin and death then a sign that the Law itself is a sinful or wicked thing? Paul's response is of course "absolutely not!" Sin takes the Law as the starting point or opportunity to produce in the knower all sorts of evil desires (v. 8).[40]

Stowers reads this part of the discussion in light of Greco-Roman discussions of desire and mastery of desire, which may have been one of the things this discourse brought to mind for the largely Gentile audience.[41] But the story of Adam seems to be to the fore here.[42] The basic argument here is how sin used a good thing, the Law, to create evil desires in Adam. In chs. 5–6 Paul has already established that all humans are "in Adam" and have sinned like Adam. Furthermore, Paul has spoken of the desires that plagued his largely Gentile audience prior to their conversions. The discussion here then just further links even the Gentile portion of the audience to Adam and his experience. They are to recognize themselves in this story as children of Adam who have also had desires, sinned, and died. Paul will illuminate the parallels in vv. 14-25, which I take to be a description of all those in Adam and outside Christ.[43]

Paul, then, is retelling the story of Adam from the past in vv. 7-13 and telling the story of all those in Adam in the present in vv. 14-25. This is all in a sense

---

39. See the earlier discussion of this view at some length by S. Lyonnet, "L'histoire du salut selon le ch. 7 de l'épître aux Romains," *Bib* 43 (1962): 117-51, and the helpful discussion of N. Elliott, *The Rhetoric of Romans: Argumentative Constraint and Strategy and Paul's Dialogue with Judaism* (JSNTS 45; Sheffield: Sheffield Academic Press, 1990), pp. 246-50, who comes to the same Adamic conclusion on the basis of rhetorical considerations.

40. Barrett, *Romans*, p. 132, puts it vividly: "The law is not simply a reagent by which the presence of sin is detected: it is a catalyst which aids or even initiates the action of sin upon man."

41. See Stowers, *A Rereading of Romans*, pp. 271-72. He suggests that the tragic figure of Medea might be conjured up by what Paul says, but surely Adam is a more likely candidate to have come to Paul's mind, and that of his audience as well.

42. See P. Achtemeier, *Romans* (Atlanta: John Knox, 1985), p. 122; Dunn, *Romans 1–8*, p. 378.

43. It simply complicates and confuses the matter to suggest that Paul is talking about Israel as well as Adam here. Paul is addressing a largely Gentile audience who did not identify with Israel, but who could understand and identify with the progenitor of the whole human race. That Israel might be included in the discussion of those who are "in Adam" in 7.14-25 is certainly possible, but even there Paul has already described earlier in ch. 2 the dilemma of a Gentile caught between the law and a hard place. My point would be that even in vv. 14-25 he is not specifically focusing on Jewish experience or the experience of Israel.

an expansion on what Paul has already argued in 5.12-21. There is a continuity in the "I" in ch. 7 by virtue of the close link between Adam and all those in Adam. The story of Adam is also the prototype of the story of Christ, and it is only when one is delivered from the body of death and thus transfers from the story of Adam into the story of Christ that one can leave Adam and his story behind, no longer in bondage to sin and now empowered to resist temptation and walk in newness of life, as will be described in ch. 8. Christ starts the race of humanity over again, setting it right and in a new direction, delivering it from the bondage of sin, death, and the Law. It is no surprise that Christ enters the picture only at the very end of the argument in ch. 7, in preparation for ch. 8, using the rhetorical technique of overlapping the end of one argument with the beginning of another.[44]

Some have seen v. 9b as a problem for the Adam view of vv. 7-13 because the verb must be translated "renewed" or "live anew." But notice the contrast between "I was living" in v. 9a with "but Sin coming to life" in v. 9b. Cranfield then is right to urge that the meaning of the verb in question in v. 9b must be "sprang to life."[45] The snake/sin was lifeless until it had an opportunity to victimize some innocent victim, and had the means to do so, namely the commandment. Sin deceived and spiritually killed the first founder of the human race. This is nearly a quotation from Gen. 3.13. One of the important corollaries of recognizing that Rom. 7.7-13 is about Adam (and that vv. 14-25 is about those in Adam and outside Christ) is that it becomes clear that Paul is not specifically critiquing Judaism or Jews here, any more than he is in 7.14-25.[46]

V. 12 begins with *hōste*, "so then," introducing the conclusion about the Law that Paul has been driving toward. The commandment and for that matter the whole Law is holy, just, and good. It did not in itself produce sin or death in

---

44. On which see pp. 204-5 below. This has confused those who are unaware of this rhetorical convention, and have taken the outburst "Thanks be to God in Jesus Christ" to be a cry only a Christian would make, assuming that therefore Rom. 7.14-25 must be about Christian experience. However, if 7.14-25 is meant to be a narrative of a person in Adam who is led to the end of himself and to the point of conviction and conversion, then this outburst should be taken as Paul's interjected reply or response with the gospel to the heartfelt cry of the lost person, a response that prepares for and signals the coming of the following argument in ch. 8 about life in Christ.

45. Cranfield, *Romans*, 1:351-52.

46. As we shall see, there is also nothing in 7.14-25 to suggest that his complaint is specifically with Jews. It is sin and death, and their effects on humankind, and also the Law's effect, whether on Gentiles or Jews, that are critiqued. Furthermore, Paul, despite Luther's insistence, is not critiquing here the self-righteousness of Jews or others caught between a rock and a hard place, when they know what they ought to do but are unable to do it. Sometimes, in order to hear the text without the baggage of later interpretations, one has to deconstruct the later interpretations first.

the founder of the human race. Rather sin/the serpent/Satan used the commandment to that end. Good things, things from God, can be used for evil purposes by those with evil intent. The exceeding sinfulness of sin is revealed in that it will even use a good thing to produce an evil end — death.[47] This was not the intended end or purpose of the Law. Adam was not killed with kindness or by something good. V. 13 is emphatic. The Law, a good thing, did not kill Adam. But sin was indeed revealed to be sin by the Law, and it produced death. This argument prepares the way for the discussion of the legacy of Adam for those who are outside Christ. The present tense verbs in vv. 14-25 reflect the ongoing legacy for those who are still in Adam and not in Christ. Vv. 14-25 should be seen not as a further argument but as the last stage of a four-part argument which began in ch. 6, being grounded in 5:12-21, and will climax Paul's discussion of sin, death, and the Law and their various effects on humankind.

Bridging the Horizons

In using the material in ch. 7, extreme caution is in order, as should be clear from the complex nature and variety of views found in the scholarly literature on this text. Serious missteps can result from unreflectively applying this material to Christians or Jews. Paul is after all not engaging in the all too modern practice of psychologizing one's personal life, and explaining one's current problems on the basis of one's family history. He would be shocked at some of the uses this text has been put to in the modern era.

But he is discussing in vv. 7-13 something important about human sin, namely its relationship to the Law. Adam shows what it is to give in to a serious temptation, and what the effects are of doing so. The Law, which should have been a guard against sin for fallen persons, becomes, in Paul's view, a goad to sin. "Because the commandment of God identifies sin but cannot prevent it, the effect is that sin is potentiated. Another analogy: suppose I experience a mild but nonspecific tickling between my shoulder blades. My teacher warns me, 'Don't scratch in class, young man!' The commandment not only does nothing to take away the itch, it actually makes it worse, by isolating and diagnosing what until then had only been a latent symptom."[48]

---

47. Barrett, *Romans*, p. 136: "Sin in its deceitful use of the law and commandment is revealed not merely in its true colors but in the worst possible light."

48. Johnson, *Reading Romans*, p. 118.

Part Four — 7.14-25: Adam's Lost Race

As important as 7.7-13 is to the understanding of Paul's view of life outside as well as inside Christ, 7.14-25 is even more crucial. We have already reviewed some of the history of interpretation of this material as well as the various conjectures about the "I."[1] Rhetorically, two things must be kept in balance. In the first place, it would be rhetorically inept for Paul to use a fictive "I" in vv. 7-13 and then with no signal change to a non-fictive use of "I." Unless there is compelling evidence to the contrary, the "I" in vv. 14-25 must also be seen as fictive because Paul is continuing another part of the same argument found in vv. 7-13. There must be some sort of continuity. In the second place, the clear marker in the text of the change in verb tenses must be given due respect. This signals that Paul is talking about something that is now true of someone or some group of persons, but nonetheless a group of persons that has some integral relationship with Adam. Käsemann puts the matter well: "*Egō* means mankind under the shadow of Adam: hence it does not embrace Christian existence in its ongoing temptation. . . . What is being said here is already over for the Christian according to ch. 6 and ch. 8. The apostle is not even describing the content of his own experience of conversion."[2] If we prefer the ancient exegetes, G. Bray reminds

---

1. See pp. 187-88 above. There is now a study disputing that Paul is using the technique of "impersonation" here. See L. Thurin, "Romans 7 Dehistoricized," in *Rhetorical Criticism and the Bible,* ed. S. E. Porter and D. L. Stamps (Sheffield: Sheffield Academic, 2002), pp. 420-40. Unfortunately, the author deals almost exclusively with Kümmel and some of the early Church Fathers rather than with the primary source Greco-Roman rhetorical materials. This quite naturally leads to inadequate analysis.

2. E. Käsemann, *Commentary on Romans* (Grand Rapids: Eerdmans, 1980), p. 200. It is interesting that when one compares what look like confessions in the inscriptions, which seem to be parallels to ch. 7, one discovers that they also do not reflect an "introspective conscious-

us "Most of the Fathers believed that here Paul was adopting the persona of an unregenerate man, not describing his own struggles as a Christian. As far as they were concerned, becoming a Christian would deliver a person from the kind of dilemma the apostle is outlining here." He goes on to point out that the Fathers resolved the reference to the person knowing the Law by saying that any rational person would automatically take delight in the Law or natural law.[3]

Sometimes it has been argued that Paul must be specifically referring to Jews in Rom. 7.14-25 because he is talking about someone who is struggling with the Law.[4] But Adam also struggled with the Law, and Paul has said earlier, in ch. 2, that Gentiles have in some fashion the Law of God written on their hearts. And the struggle depicted in 7.14-25 is internal. Paul does not depict a person wrestling with an OT text which he quotes and then debates. This is very different from what we found in the diatribe with the Jewish teacher in chs. 2–3. I take it then that Paul is speaking as broadly as possible about humankind in Adam and not singling out Jews for particular attention here, though his com-

---

ness." Consider, for example, the confession cited in *NewDocs* 8:173, about a woman who entered the Temple of Apollo in a dirty garment and "being punished I confessed and dedicated [this] eulogy because I became whole." The devotee does not come to the temple to confess her sin; indeed, there are no evidences of internal moral struggle at all. She has come in a ritually unacceptable or dirty garment. She confesses that this is so, dedicates a eulogy to Apollo, and so is viewed as being back in a ritually acceptable condition — whole, rather than morally pure. There may be thought to be a miraculous element in this — the god accepts the woman as whole or ritually in a state where her presence in the temple is not defiling, but there is no hint here of the later angst and internal struggles we find in Augustine's confessions. S. Llewelyn's conclusion (p. 175) deserves to be quoted at length:

> In convergence with Stendahl's thesis it is of interest to note that the "sin" acknowledged in confessional inscriptions does not imply an introspective conscience. Many "sins" are committed in ignorance, e.g. the taking of wood from a sacred grove. As in the example cited above, other 'sins' involve the infringement of a purity requirement. Such "sins" do not imply a stricken conscience. Nor indeed does the fact that the confession is made subsequent to the divine punishment. In other words, it is not events in the inner world of the conscience which prompt the confession, but an external misfortune or illness. It would follow then that if Augustine was influenced by confessional inscriptions, he also transformed their significance.

3. G. Bray, ed., *Romans* (Downers Grove: InterVarsity, 1998), pp. 189-90.

4. Despite the influence of later Augustinianism on Luther, it is fascinating to see how Augustine himself interprets this crucial passage. In his commentary on Romans (44), he says "but we must be careful not to think that these words deny our free will, which is not true. The man being described here is under the law, before the coming of grace. Sin overpowers him when he attempts to live righteously in his own strength, without the help of God's liberating grace. For by his free will a man is able to believe in the Deliverer and to receive grace. Thus with the deliverance and help of him who gives it, he will not sin and will cease to be under the law."

ments can be taken as a Christian critique of the Jewish dilemma with sin, death, and the Law as well.[5]

Throughout this chapter a Christian interpretation of a pre-Christian set of conditions is in view.[6] And Paul has couched the discussion in a way that his largely Gentile audience could identify with. Consider Ovid, *Metamorphoses* 7.19-20: "Desire persuades me one way, reason another. I see the better and approve it, but I follow the worse."[7] Or even closer are the words of Epictetus, who says that the sinner does not wish to sin and that the thief does not do what he wishes and does what he does not wish (2.26.1-4). "What I wish, I do not do, and what I do not wish, I do" (2.26.4). Paul is dealing with the effect of law or the Law (as a Jew would see it) on any fallen human being, whether it is the law written on the heart or the Law written on tablets.

There is much pathos here as Paul draws his lengthy sixth argument to a close in an effective and moving fashion. But he is not trying to do psychology here, though what he says has implication for psychological studies of humankind. Rather he is vividly depicting the person outside Christ, coming to conviction about sin and about his incapacity to escape its clutches without outside help. Stendahl's thesis that the "introspective consciousness of the West" is not reflected in first-century literature, including in Paul's letters, but began with Augustine's *Confessions* is, of course, important here.[8]

By an especially adept rhetorical move, before concluding the argument

5. The dangers of reading Paul as describing Jewish experience here, as if he were suggesting that the promises to "Israel according to the flesh" are transferred to "Israel according to the Spirit" (i.e., the church), are well pointed out in R. Clements's helpful discussion of Origen's anti-Semitic hermeneutic in "(Re)Constructing Paul: Origen's Reading of Romans in *Peri Archōn*," in *SBL Seminar Papers 2001*, pp. 151-74.

6. See G. Theissen, *Psychological Aspects of Pauline Theology* (Philadelphia: Fortress, 1987), p. 235: "Rom. 7.13-24, in my opinion, is all too clearly concerned with unredeemed humanity." A. A. Das, *Paul, the Law, and the Covenant* (Peabody: Hendrickson, 2001), p. 227, is quite correct in saying: "absolutely nothing in Rom. 7 suggests that Paul's problem with the law is that it leads to national righteousness and ethnic pride." To the contrary, as Das goes on to say, chs. 6–7 are about all persons outside of Christ. All such fallen persons, whether Gentiles or Jews, have a problem with God's demand on them in the form of Law. "The plight under the law in Rom. 6 and 7 appears to involve both Jews and Gentiles. Paul prepares for this conclusion in Rom. 2.14-16." Das goes on to add: "Dunn's suggestion that the problem with the law is that it leads to a mistaken *understanding* of the law as a source of Jewish national righteousness can hardly account for the language of oppression and existential struggle that characterizes this chapter" (p. 228).

7. See S. K. Stowers, *A Rereading of Romans: Justice, Jews, and Gentiles* (New Haven: Yale University Press, 1994), pp. 280-81.

8. K. Stendahl, "The Apostle Paul and the Introspective Conscience of the West" (1961), reprinted in *Paul among Jews and Gentiles* (Philadelphia: Fortress, 1976), pp. 78-96. See note 2 above for S. Llewelyn's comments in this regard.

of chs. 6–7, Paul will introduce an interjection from himself answering the cry of the lost "I" and praising Christ as the deliverer from the bondage to sin. V. 25a introduces the argument to follow in ch. 8 about life in Christ, in which Paul will speak in the authorial voice, and then the previous argument is concluded in v. 25b.[9] In *Instit. Or.* 9.4.129-30 Quintilian explains the use of this overlap technique when moving from one argument or "proof" to the next. He says that this sort of ABAB structure is effective when one must speak with force, energy, and pugnacity (that is, with pathos). When one is recounting history or narrative this "does not so much demand full rounded rhythms as a certain continuity of motion and connexion of style. . . . We may compare its motion to that of men, who link hands to steady their steps, and lend each other their mutual support" (9.4.129). So then, there is the passing of the baton. Failure to recognize this rhetorical way of introducing the next argument before concluding the previous one has helped lead to the incorrect conclusion that Paul is speaking about Christians in 7.14-25, a mistake various early Greek Fathers who knew rhetoric did not make.[10]

For we know[11] that the Law is spiritual. But I am fleshly, sold under sin. For I do not understand what I do. For I do not practice what I want, but I do what I hate. But if I do not do what I want, I agree that the Law is good. But now it is no longer I myself who does it, but the sin which dwells within me. For I know that nothing good dwells in me, that is, in my flesh. For to will is present to me, but to do the good is not. For the willing to do good is not there, but the evil I do not will, this I practice/commit. But if I do not wish to do this, and nevertheless I do it, then it is sin dwelling in me. For I find then it to be the rule/law with my willing to do the good, that the evil is ready to hand for me. For I rejoice in the Law of God in my in-

---

9. The diatribe format used earlier in Romans has prepared for this with the "I" who is not Paul raising the question, and Paul providing the Christian answer. See pp. 73-95 above. See rightly C. Bryan, *A Preface to Romans: Notes on the Epistle and Its Literary and Cultural Setting* (Oxford: Oxford University Press, 2000), p. 145.

10. Käsemann, *Romans*, pp. 211-12. It will be remembered that Käsemann so struggled with this half-verse that he said it must be a gloss, or if not, he would have to rethink his whole reading of Romans 7. This angst could have been avoided if he had examined the issue from a rhetorical perspective.

11. It is quite possible that the original reading here was *oida men* rather than *oidamen*, which would mean it reads "I know" rather than "we know." This is simply a matter of how one divides the Greek letters; some Church Fathers thought two words were meant here, since we find this in the midst of an "I" passage. B. M. Metzger and the committee, *A Textual Commentary on the Greek New Testament* (3rd ed.; London: United Bible Societies, 1971), p. 454, think "we know" is the far better supported reading. In favor of the first-person singular here is the fact not only that this is an "I" passage but that Paul regularly uses the *men . . . de* construction to set up a contrast.

ner self. But I see another law in my members at war with the law of my mind and making me captive in the rule of sin which is in my members. I am a miserable human being. Who will deliver me from the body of this death? Grace/thanks to God through our Lord Jesus Christ. So then I myself while on the one hand with mind I am a slave to the Law of God, but on the other hand the flesh [is a slave] to the rule/law of sin.

There is an ever-growing body of opinion, led by the reassessment of early Judaism offered by E. P. Sanders and his disciples, that Paul could not possibly be describing here the experience of a Jew as a Jew himself would have described it. If we take, for example, Psalm 119 as a sort of transcript of Jewish experience of the Law, Jews delighted in the Law and saw wrestling with the Law and striving to keep its commandments as a joy, even if such practice was always a work in progress. Nor will it do to suggest that Rom. 7:14-25 is how at least a very rigorous Pharisaic Jew, like Paul, would have described his experience under the Law, for in fact Paul tells us in Phil. 3.6 that in regard to righteousness in the Law he was blameless. As Stendahl says, the evidence is that Paul had a quite robust conscience as a Pharisaic Jew. It is true that Phil. 3.6 does not say that Paul was sinless or perfect, only that, according to the standard of righteous behavior the Law required, no one could fault him for being a law-breaker.[12] Blameless before the Law and sinless are most certainly two different things. Gal. 1.14 only further supports this reading, for in that text Paul says he was making good progress in his faith and was very zealous and excited about keeping the traditions of his ancestors. Furthermore, as we have said, as a Christian Paul also manifests a robust conscience, not a sin-laden one, if the subject is what he has done since he became a Christian. His anxieties are about and for his fellow Christians, not about his own spiritual state. This becomes especially clear in Romans 9 when Paul will say that he could wish himself cut off from Christ if it would produce a turning to Christ by many of his fellow Jews. In fact, one would be hard-pressed to find any mea culpas of any kind in any of Paul's letters when he is describing his experience as a Christian, much less evidence that he saw himself as burdened by the body of death and the bondage to sin. Nor, if Paul when a Jew did not feel like the person described in Rom. 7.14-25, is there any good reason to suppose that other devout Jews felt this way. It is time to stop reading Rom. 7.14-25 through the lens of Augustine and Luther, not least because it keeps fueling skewed views of both early and modern Judaism, which in turn fuel anti-Semitism.

12. Notice how clear it is in Phil. 3.6 that Paul is talking about righteous behavior, not just right standing before God. Righteous behavior by Paul must be what *dikaiosynē* refers to there. This is made especially apparent because in the same verse he has just mentioned his zealous behavior — persecuting Christians.

No, we have here a Christian analysis of the general malaise of fallen humanity when it comes to sin, death, and Law, and the truth is that only by coming to the point of being convicted, convinced, and converted is it likely for fallen persons to see themselves as described here. In other words, we need to take seriously that Paul is describing a crisis experience that leads to a crying out for help here. He is not speaking of the day-to-day mindset of the fallen person, whether devout or not, whether Gentile or Jew. What we have then in 7.14-25 and continuing into the next argument in ch. 8 is a narrative of a conversion and its theological and spiritual implications seen after the fact and from a Christian perspective.

Paul begins v. 14 with his familiar "for we know" formula, a rhetorical technique in which he tries to include the audience as being "in the know," even if they have not yet quite seen it that way. It may mean "for as we all ought to know."[13] The clause does signal what is or ought to be common knowledge among Christians (see Rom. 8.22; 2 Cor. 5.1). We have here a straightforward contrast: the Law is spiritual, but this person is in some respect "fleshly, sold under sin." It is difficult *not* to relate this to vv. 5-6, where it was said that there is a group of persons who *were* in the flesh, but are no longer. Even more directly, in 8.9 Paul will say to Christians "you are not in the flesh." This builds on 8.2, where Paul says that the law of the Spirit of life (clearly not the Mosaic Law) has "freed you from the law of sin and death." "Freed" is in the aorist, speaking of a particular event in the past of the Christian. That is the very event Paul is describing in 7.14-25 — the event of conversion, when freedom from bondage to sin comes. The person in question in 7.14-25 is not as bad as he might be.

Paul has picked up the narrative of a surprising conversion after the person in question both knows that the Law is good and in his mind wants to be obedient to it. This is rather different from the general description of Gentile life in 1.18-32. There knowledge of God and his will is rejected or ignored. Here it is acknowledged, but the striving to conform is failing because of the other "law" in one's members, the ruling passions of the flesh. The person in 7.14-25 is in a moral dilemma because he recognizes the goodness of the Law and wants to obey it, but his fallen nature leads him to do what his mind condemns. He is then a person with a guilty conscience.[14] It is Paul's view, as ch. 8 will show, that

13. See pp. 172-75 above.

14. The view that Paul is describing the so-called carnal Christian here, who is on the road to apostasy, will not work, not only because Paul does not believe the Christian is under the Mosaic Law, but also because in ch. 8 he will address his whole audience as those who have been set free from the "rule" of sin and death. It is, of course, possible for a Christian to commit apostasy, and even to act like the description of the Romans 7 person, but Paul would stress that such behavior is: (a) not acceptable; (b) not inevitable; and (c) not a legitimate option for the believer. There is no legitimate excuse for sin in the believer's life. The bottom line of Cranfield's view of Paul's view of sanctification is that sanctification means not em-

the Christian is in some ways like pre-fallen Adam, not immune to sin and perhaps inclined to sin on various occasions, but it is not inevitable that he do so. Like Adam before the fall, the Christian believer is "posse peccare" and "posse non peccare" by the grace of God, as, for instance, the discussion of temptation in 1 Cor. 10.11-13 shows. But the fallen person is "non posse non peccare" — not able not to sin, as described here in Rom. 7.14-25. The theology of "simul justus et peccator" promulgated by Luther amounts to a very inadequate view of Paul's understanding of grace in the believer's life and of the power that the believer has by that grace to resist temptation, having been set free from the rule or bondage of sin and death. In other words, "simul justus et peccator" ignores Paul's understanding of sanctification, which, while not a counsel of sinless perfection, is nonetheless an assertion about the ability to resist temptation and have victory over sin. While the danger of sin remains for the believer, it no longer reigns. There is no longer the bondage of the will described in 7.14-25.

As v. 16 makes clear, the person in question agrees that the Law is good, but just does not do what he wills to do. There seems to be a power outage. Philosophers may want to debate what it means to say that a person wills one thing but does another. Surely the willing is the starting point or agency through which doing happens. But if one is a deeply conflicted person or in the thrall of strong passions to do something else, then that is another matter. Here Stowers helps us see how a largely Gentile audience would hear this passage:

> [T]his language comes from the tradition of the fragmented personality. Paul unsurprisingly uses Greek tradition to convince Greeks. The *akrasia* depicted here can be partially explained as a conflict between incidental, fragmentary, fluctuating transitory desires and long-term desires.[15] The latter are relatively constant, long-term projects and commitments around which people organize their lives and their identities. Part of what the imaginary Gentile voice is saying is this: "I want to live an overall plan of life like the Jewish law teaches, but my habitually overpowering but transitory desires consistently frustrate that larger goal." The Greek tradition about *akrasia* dramatically represents

---

powerment of the will to resist sin and have victory over it, but apparently only renewal of the mind, for Cranfield says we become increasingly aware of sin as sanctification proceeds. This is, of course, true, but Paul is talking about the liberation of the human will from bondage, not merely release from condemnation for one's sins, or increasing awareness of one's spiritual condition. Paul's point is that the believer can, by drawing on the grace of God, overcome the temptation to sin, and indeed can obey and be faithful to God. As Charles Wesley's hymn says, conversion "loosed the power of canceled sin/he set the prisoner free." But see C. E. B. Cranfield, *A Critical and Exegetical Commentary on the Epistle to the Romans* (ICC; Edinburgh: Clark, 1975-79), 1:341-47.

15. See A. Van den Beld, "Romans 7.14-25 and the Problem of Akrasia," *RelStud* 21 (1985): 495-515.

such moral schizophrenia by speaking as if there were distinct agents in the soul. One agent could even deceive the other (Plautus, *Trinum.* 658 cf. 7.11). Desire resembles giving birth to flames of fire in one's breast: It is a strange power that holds down the will (Ovid, *Met.* 7.17-19).[16]

The person in Rom. 7:14-25 with his mind wants to do one thing, but there is another force at work in his personality which actually controls his willing and doing. Paul is not talking about the Christian who tries hard but whose deeds do not match up with his intentions. The point here is not the falling short or imperfection even of Christian good deeds, but the exceeding sinfulness of sinful deeds. V. 17 makes evident Paul is talking about the person who has indwelling sin, almost as a *habitus,* such that the person is a slave to sin or his passions. With "no good dwells in my flesh" (v. 18) we must compare the closely similar phrase in 7.5. This person intends to do good, but is simply unable to carry out such an intention. Is v. 20 an attempt to exculpate the individual in question, since he cannot help himself, being in the bondage to sin? Probably not, as Paul's point is the bondage of the will, not the excuse-making or excusability of the sinner's behavior. Barrett puts it this way: "Evil behavior is caused by sin, a personal power residing in and dominating the flesh."[17] The language here is strong, bordering on a concept of being possessed. But Paul says nothing of demons here, only of sin and its power over fallen human beings.

Llewelyn thinks that slavery is the controlling metaphor here. The slave's mind may be free to think one way, but his body is enslaved to obey his master.[18] Seneca, a contemporary of Paul and Stoic philosopher, put the matter this way:

> It is an error to think that slavery penetrates to the whole person. The better part is excluded: the body is subject to and at the disposition of its master; the mind, however, is its own master and is so free and able to move that it cannot even be restrained by this prison, in which it is confined, from following its own impulse, setting in motion great ideas and passing over into infinity as a comrade to the gods. And so it is the body that fate surrenders to the master; he buys this, he sells this; the inner part cannot be given by purchase. Whatever issues from this is free. (*De beneficiis* 3.20)

The contrast here between what one thinks and what one does is similar. The person that Paul describes is as surely enslaved to sin as the person Seneca describes is enslaved to a human master.[19]

---

16. Stowers, *A Rereading of Romans,* p. 280.
17. C. K. Barrett, *A Commentary on the Epistle to the Romans* (Peabody: Hendrickson, 1991), p. 139.
18. See *NewDocs* 6:52-53. I owe the finding of the Seneca reference to Llewelyn.
19. For a modern reassertion of the older Augustinian and Lutheran view of 7.14-25 see

Käsemann's theory that the pious Jew is spoken of in vv. 14-19 is based on an understanding of *nomos* as a reference exclusively to the Mosaic Law.[20] But if *nomos* could refer to a commandment given before Moses in vv. 6-13, it can have a wider reference here as well, or perhaps better said, Paul believes that all persons (whether through the law written on the heart or the law written on the tablets) are under the Law of God. There need be no specific reference to Jews here, and indeed, as Stowers shows, Paul seems to have Gentiles in view, in the main.[21] The original prohibition to Adam incorporates all humanity under its condemnation since all humans, in Paul's view, are "in Adam."

In v. 21 Paul seems to use *nomos* in a different sense, which is perfectly possible, as he is rhetorically adept enough to play on words and use them in slightly different senses in the same context (e.g., his use of the name Onesimus and its cognates in Philemon). Thus, it is perfectly possible that here and in 8.2 Paul is indeed speaking of "another law" (as he says here). The appropriate translation might be "rule" or less preferably "principle": "I find it to be a rule/ principle . . . ," and in 8.2: "the rule/principle of the Spirit of life has set me free from the rule/principle of sin and death."[22] If this is correct, Paul is not speaking about the Mosaic Law in these verses.

V. 22 gives us some clues as to Paul's anthropology, though the verse

---

J. I. Packer, "The 'Wretched Man' Revisited: Another Look at Romans 7.14-25," in *Romans and the People of God*, ed. S. K. Soderlund and N. T. Wright (Grand Rapids: Eerdmans, 1999), pp. 70-81.

20. That Jews could occasionally, though exceptionally, describe their condition in a fashion similar to what we find in ch. 7 is clear from 1QS 11.9-10: "As for me, I belong to the wicked humankind, to the company of ungodly flesh. My iniquities, rebellions, and sins, together with the perversity of my heart, belong to the company of worms and to those who walk in darkness." But far from this justifying reading 7.14-25 as referring to the Christian, it rather argues for the opposite, for the person who wrote 1QS 11.9-10 was certainly not a follower of Jesus. J. D. G. Dunn, *Romans 1–8*, Word Biblical Commentary (Dallas: Word, 1988), p. 394, points out: "The illogicality of arguing that the passage here expresses with Christian hindsight the existential anguish of the pious Jew — which as a pious Jew he did not actually experience and as a Christian he still does not experience! — is not usually appreciated." Dunn has a point. However, Paul is not describing day-to-day pre-Christian experience; he is offering a Christian description of a crisis experience in the life of a non-Christian. In this regard it could well be the experience of a pious Jew, such as that from Qumran described above, or a pious Gentile at the point of conversion. There is nothing illogical about such a view. What is illogical is claiming after what Paul clearly says in 7.5-6, and will go on to say in ch. 8, that 7.14-25 is a description of Christian life.

21. Certainly proselytes and God-fearers who were now Christians could be in view, but Paul's view of the Law of God is such that he can even be referring to Gentiles who, while outside the Law, still had the law written on their hearts.

22. There is certainly precedent in Greek usage for the sense rule or principle, even if it is not generally used this way elsewhere in the NT. See H. Räisänen, *Paul and the Law* (Tübingen: Mohr, 1983), p. 50 n. 34.

should not be over-psychologized. The "I" says he rejoices in the Law of God (the Mosaic Law or the Adamic commandment is likely in view) in his inner being. What is the "inner person"? Cranfield wishes to equate it with "my mind," mentioned in vv. 23 and 25 and in 12.2[23] and with the person as renewed by the Holy Spirit (2 Cor. 4.16). If that were the case, Paul would necessarily be talking about Christians here. But if one looks carefully at 2 Cor. 4.16 it becomes clear that the "inner person" is not equivalent to the renewed person in Christ. The inner person is being renewed while the outer person (i.e., the body) is wasting away. The inner person must first exist before it can be renewed, and there is nothing to suggest that Paul is talking about something that exists only in Christians.[24] Paul is clear enough that the mind exists before conversion; thus if there is a parallel between mind and inner self, or an overlap between the two, it does not necessarily imply a mind renewed by the Spirit. Philo, for example, equates the mind with the inner person without adding that he has in view the enlightened person (see de Plantatione 42; de Congressu 97).

Paul says, of course, in Romans 2 that the Law can be written on the heart/mind of a Gentile non-believer.[25] 7:22 thus means no more than that such a person rejoices in the Law in his or her innermost being. Paul does not identify the "flesh" with the "I." Rather in a limited dualistic way he distinguishes the "I" and its mind and "will" from the "flesh," which is associated with misdeeds. Paul does not argue for a divided "I" or a divided "Law" (as if all the uses of the term nomos here must refer to the Law of God).[26]

Käsemann at this juncture wishes to interpret "law of the mind" (v. 23) as a reference to human conscience,[27] which was certainly referred to earlier in chs. 1 and 2. This may well be correct, but "the law of the mind" seems to be paralleled with "the Law of God" (v. 22), which could be a reference to the Mosaic Law as an external authority. In v. 23 nomos may mean Law, or again it may simply be, as in v. 21, "another rule/principle at work within me...." The person in v. 23 has two principles at work within him at the same juncture. One is of God, and one is not, and a war is going on inside this person. At present this person is losing the battle. He cries out that he is a miserable person and asks who will deliver him. This must be contrasted with 8.2, where Paul speaks of freedom from such death in the Christian. Even Augustine felt he

23. See Cranfield, Romans, 1:364-67.

24. Against Barrett, Romans, p. 141, who takes very much the same line as Cranfield on this point.

25. See pp. 82-90 above.

26. On this sort of bifurcated interpretation of the self and the Law even in the case of Christians see especially Dunn, Romans 1–8, pp. 388-89. But the Mosaic Law does not belong to the epoch of Christ, in Paul's view, anymore than the "I" in bondage to sin belongs to the story of the Christian life.

27. See Käsemann, Romans, pp. 205-6.

needed to downplay the idea of the bondage of the will here, reducing it to the problem of concupiscence,[28] when he decided that this cry for freedom took place within Christian life. Cranfield's, like Luther's, attempt to see the Christian as the one experiencing this anguish of the bondage of the will is forced, and does not comport with the context or the rest of the content of these verses.

There is significant debate as to whether v. 24 should be read as referring to "this body of death" or "the body of this death." *Touto* could modify either antecedent. Cranfield insists that this is a cry of a person who wants to die, who wants to be delivered from the physical body, which drags him down.[29] This is quite possible in light of what follows in ch. 8. But is Paul talking about liberation from the body or rather liberation of the self within the body, a spiritual liberation? If the latter, then *sōma* ("body") is used here metaphorically to refer to the habitus of death and sin which dwells within the body, but not necessarily to death. These things have taken up residence in the fallen person, who is indeed fallen and cannot get up without outside help. It is probably of some relevance here that Paul says in 2 Corinthians 5 that Paul does not desire, as his first preference, to be absent from the body, but rather that the present body be further clothed with the resurrection body. So this may be a cry for resurrection.

The language about the wretched man actually has a very close parallel in Epictetus, which again suggests that Paul is arguing in a way that his audience would find intelligible.

> Since these two elements were commingled in our begetting, on the one hand the body, which we have in common with the animals, and on the other reason and intelligence, which we have in common with the gods, some of us incline toward the former relationship, which is not blessed by fortune and is mortal, and only a few toward that which is divine and blessed. . . . For what am I? "A miserable paltry man" say they, and "Lo, my wretched paltry flesh." Wretched indeed, but you also have something better than your paltry flesh. Why then abandon that and cling to this? (1.3.3-6)

For Paul, there is an anthropological tension in both the non-Christian's life and the Christian's life (see the inner-outer discussion in 2 Corinthians 4–5). They differ in that what once was merely an anthropological tension in a fallen person has become an eschatological tension between Spirit and flesh, as Galatians 5 makes apparent. It is thus incorrect to pit eschatological tensions over against anthropological tensions or to read salvation-historical tensions of

28. See pp. 181-83 above.
29. Cranfield, *Romans*, 1:365-67.

already-and-not-yet too strongly into Paul's anthropological tensions.[30] The tension in the Christian life is not between old person and new person, as if one were both simultaneously, much less as if one were still in bondage to the old and fallen ways. It is rather between the inner person which is now being renewed and the outer self or body which is not, and between flesh or sinful inclination and the leading of the Holy Spirit.

V. 25a is most naturally seen as the anticipation of what Paul is going to say in ch. 8. He anticipates the deliverance he will discuss there and celebrates it here in advance. This is effective rhetoric because he has been dealing with a very heavy and serious matter throughout chs. 6–7 and the audience will need some relief. So Paul here lets them know that relief from the lengthy discussion of the bondage of sin, death, and the Law is coming. This way he keeps his audience from despairing or tuning out.

V. 25b then returns to the theme of 7.14-25, bringing this lengthy argument to closure. Here Paul sums up before turning to the joyful news of ch. 8. As with the other contrasts in chs. 6–7 which need to be taken seriously,[31] Paul ends with one last contrast: "I myself, while with my mind am a slave to God's Law, but with my flesh a slave to the rule of sin." This surely cannot be the same person described in 8.2, unless Paul is guilty of a very schizophrenic view of Christian life.[32] No, Paul has here described those living in the shadow of Adam, knowing something of God's will or Law but unable by willpower or by the guidance of that Law to free themselves from the bondage of sin and death. His largely Gentile audience would recognize this discussion about enthrallment as describing not just what the life of a Jew might be like apart from Christ[33] but what the life of any creature of God, Gentile or Jewish, is like apart from the liberation in Christ. Paul has narrated a crisis in the life of such a person, not the person's ordinary day-to-day experience. This person has reached

30. Against Dunn, *Romans 1–8*, pp. 396-97.

31. On which see the chart on pp. 167-68 above.

32. On the inner self described here see T. K. Heckel, *Der Innere Mensch: Die paulinischen Verarbeitung eines platonischen Motivs* (Tübingen: Mohr, 1993).

33. See P. Achtemeier, *Romans* (Atlanta: John Knox, 1985), p. 122: "it represents non-Christian life under the Law seen from a Christian perspective." His helpful survey of the issues can be found on pp. 118-30. As he says, one of the sure signs of a mistaken interpretation of a text is when Paul is made to say the exact opposite of what he seems to say. For example, Achtemeier (pp. 120-21) points to Calvin's reading of v. 17. Paul says, "It is no longer I that do it but sin that dwells in me." Calvin comments, "Paul here denies that he is wholly possessed by sin; nay he declares himself to be exempt from its bondage." Or again Paul says in v. 16, "I do what I do not want." Luther reads this to mean that Paul "does not do the good as often and to such an extent and as readily as he would like." Something is clearly wrong with these readings of Paul's words, for they flatly deny the prima facie meaning of the text.

the point of despair over human inability to please God and do his will and cries out for help. Paul will describe that help found in Christ in ch. 8.

Finally we may ask once more, could Gentiles have seen themselves in this text? The answer is clearly Yes. Consider, for example, Epictetus: "Since the person who is in error does not wish to err but to be right, it is clear he is not doing what he wishes" (2.26.1). Or even more tellingly Medea's complaint in Ovid's *Metamorphoses* 7.19-21: "Oh, if I could, I would be more like myself! But against my own wishes, some strange influence weighs heavily upon me, and desire sways one way, reason another. . . . I see the better and approve; the worse I follow."[34] Of course we can find such sentiments in Jewish literature as well, for example in 4 Ezra 9.36-37, and this is not a surprise because Paul is trying to speak broadly enough to include both the vast majority of his audience, which was Gentile, and the minority, which was Jewish.

Bridging the Horizons

Paul Achtemeier warns about Romans 7: "Those who seek to preach or teach this passage face the problem of overcoming the weight of the long history of interpretation which has distorted Paul's intention in these verses."[35] On the other hand, in an age of not only biblical illiteracy but also ecclesiological ignorance, not that many people, even in the church, know this history of interpretation. It is not necessary to remove a burden of interpretation that does not exist, but it is important to give a modern audience a sense of caution about over-psychologizing the text and especially about using it as a way to deal with modern psychological dilemmas of moral impotence or schizophrenia or the like. Reading this text through the eyes of Freud is about as unhelpful as reading it through the eyes of Augustine or Luther.

If, however, one can convey the sense of the flow of the text and that it deals with a spiritual crisis in the life of the non-Christian described, then this text could be used in fruitful ways. For example, one could ask: What is the nature of conversion? What happens not only to one's worldview but to one's moral compass and willpower when one is delivered from the bondage to sin? If conversion is not merely a cognitive event, what are its potential benefits vis-à-vis one's emotions, will, and conduct? But if one goes down this road, one must also be prepared to talk frankly about the potential tensions in the

---

34. On these texts and other similar pagan texts see C. Talbert, *Romans* (Macon: Smyth and Helwys, 2002), p. 193. In fact Talbert's whole discussion of the matter, pp. 192-203, will repay close examination.

35. Achtemeier, *Romans*, p. 124.

Christian life, the struggle between inner and outer self, between person and persona, between flesh and Spirit. If one loads too much into one's theology of crisis conversion, one will then have difficulty explaining the struggles of the subsequent Christian life.

Argument Seven — 8.1-17: Life in the Spirit; That Was Then, This Is Now

It is clear enough that we have turned a corner when we reach Romans 8. There is no more diatribe and no more impersonation. Instead Paul sets out to describe the Christian life at some length, as he brings his positive arguments to a close. The *probatio* finishes on a high, indeed exuberant and joyful note with the two arguments in ch. 8. There is some debate whether v. 17 goes with what precedes or belongs with the argument in the second half of ch. 8. On the whole it would appear it is more naturally seen as going with vv. 1-16 since v. 18 begins with *gar* and seems to move on to relating what the Christian can hope for as a result of life in the Spirit here and now.

There were of course rhetorical rules about "arrangement" of one's arguments, and we have already seen how Paul leads from strength by beginning with arguments grounded in human experience, then turns to the Scriptures, and then finally argues on the basis of analogies with customs and other commonplaces. Here, as he concludes the *probatio,* his positive case, he returns again to the argument from experience, in this case, specifically Christian experience.

Quintilian has much to say about arrangement, and his advice bears repeating here. He says that the good rhetor tends to descend in his arguments from the common to the particular, or to put it another way one would move from the genus, to the species, to the ultimate species, becoming more and more particular (*Instit. Or.* 7.1.23-28). He also says one can work in the opposite direction as well. This would help to explain what we find in Paul's arrangement.

Paul begins broadly with the story of humanity outside Christ in 1.18ff., then turns to a particular type of Gentile outside Christ, then a particular type of Jew outside Christ in chs. 2–3, then reprises his thesis statement at the end of

207

ch. 3. Paul then reverses the process, starting with the particular case of Abraham in ch. 4, then those who are "in Abraham," then a more general discussion of Christian experience in 5.1-11. Paul then once again takes a particular example, Adam, and does a rhetorical comparison of Adam with Christ in 5.12-21 and then embarks on a long four-part argument in chs. 6–7 about those who are in Adam, comparing and contrasting that existence with Christian existence. The climax of this process comes in 7.7-25 when Paul contrasts in dramatic fashion the life of Adam and those in Adam with life in the Spirit and in Christ in ch. 8. Quintilian reminds his fellow rhetors that "that which as a rule occurs to us first is just that which ought to come last in our speech" (*Instit. Or.* 7.1.25). Paul began his discussion with the Roman Christians by talking about their mutual life in Christ and how he and they could each impart some spiritual blessing or grace gift to each other. Perhaps he was thinking already of what he says here in ch. 8 as he draws the *probatio* to a close by dwelling on the life in Christ all Christians share.

All along the generative narratives about Adam, Christ, Abraham, and those who fit into one or the other of these stories undergird the argumentation. This is absolutely in keeping with deliberative rhetoric for "there is a preference among those who invent such [deliberative] themes for selecting great personages, such as kings, princes, senators, and peoples, while the theme itself is generally on a grander scale. Consequently since the words are suited to the theme, they acquire additional splendor from the magnificence of the matter" (*Instit. Or.* 3.8.61). Historical examples are said to be of the most value in deliberative rhetoric (3.8.36), and Paul uses them to the full. His focus is on founders of the race or of the faith.

Paul's logic is a narrative logic or a salvation-historical logic as he works through the story of the human race, both lost and found, and the effect of the great founders, Adam, Abraham, and Christ, on the human race. It is of course true that Paul deals with important topics like salvation by grace through faith and sin, death, and the Law, but he deals with them neither in the abstract nor by setting up some sort of *ordo salutis* and then pursuing the topic of justification, followed by sanctification, followed by glorification. He does not treat his material like a late western person trained to think in terms of the history of ideas.

Paul's eloquence rises to a climax in ch. 8 precisely because his theme, life in Christ and its consequences, is the grandest one yet discoursed upon in the letter, the theme which most completely fulfills the promise of the announced theme in the *propositio* in 1.16-17. Now finally he can speak fully of the Good News for all Christians, about the power of God for salvation, about life in the Spirit, about how the righteous shall live by faith because the righteousness of God has been revealed through Christ to those who believe.

So now, in no respect condemnation to those in Christ Jesus, for the rule of the Spirit of life in Christ Jesus freed you¹ from the rule of sin and death. For the inability of the Law, in that because it was weak through the flesh, God sent his own Son in the likeness of sinful flesh, and concerning sin, he condemned sin in the flesh, in order that the righteous decree of the Law might be fulfilled in us, to those behaving not according to the flesh but according to the Spirit. For those being according to the flesh devote themselves to the things of the flesh, but those according to the Spirit to the things of the Spirit. For the mentality/outlook of the flesh is death, but the mentality/outlook of the Spirit is life and peace. For the mentality/outlook of the flesh is enmity toward God, for it does not submit to the Law of God, for it is not able. But those in the flesh are not able to be pleasing to God. But you yourselves are not in the flesh, but in the Spirit, if indeed the Spirit of God dwells in you. But if anyone does not have the Spirit of Christ, that one is not of him. But if Christ is in you, on the one hand the body of death because of sin, on the other hand the Spirit of life because of righteousness. But if the Spirit who raised Jesus from the dead dwells in you, the One who raised Jesus will even give life to your mortal body through the indwelling of his Spirit in you.

So then brothers, we are debtors not to the flesh, to live according to the flesh. For if you live according to the flesh you are destined to die, but if by the Spirit you put to death the deeds of the body, you will live. For whoever is led by the Spirit of God, these are sons of God. For you did not receive a spirit of slavery again unto fear, but you received a Spirit of adoption, in whom we cry Abba, Father. For that same Spirit bears witness with our spirit that we are children of God. But if children, also heirs. Heirs on the one hand of God, but on the other hand fellow heirs of Christ if, that is, we suffer with him in order that we also may be glorified with him.

All scholars are in agreement that the material in ch. 8 has to do with the life of the Christian, and it is also clear that the stress is on the believer's relationship to the Holy Spirit and the effect the Spirit has on the believer. The word *pneuma*, "spirit," occurs only five times in chs. 1–7 and eight times in chs. 9–11, but some twenty times in ch. 8.² The theme of the section in this case is indicated by the frequency of word usage. Paul will discourse here about what is true in the eschatological age which has already dawned. The "now" which in-

---

1. Some manuscripts have "us" at this juncture and still others have "me," as a sort of carryover from the first-person singular references in ch. 7. On the basis of the external evidence "you" seems most likely to be the original reading here, though "me" has strong support as well. See B. M. Metzger, *A Textual Commentary on the Greek New Testament* (3rd ed.; London: United Bible Societies, 1971), p. 456.
2. C. E. B. Cranfield, *A Critical and Exegetical Commentary on the Epistle to the Romans* (ICC; Edinburgh: Clark, 1975-79), 1:370-71.

troduces the discussion from the beginning of v. 1 is the "now" of the eschatological age, and more particularly Paul is speaking of what is true for those who
are in Christ. While straightforward forensic language has not been plentiful in
this discourse thus far, at this juncture Paul does indeed use such language. In
light of what has just been said in ch. 7 about the lost but convicted soul crying
out for deliverance, it is not surprising that Paul begins this discourse with the
pronouncement of "no condemnation" for those in Christ. This is certainly
part of how Paul views what transpires at conversion. A verdict is pronounced,
as a result of the finished work of Christ, about the sinner who turns to Christ
in faith. This objective standing that results from pardon or no condemnation
by God[3] is, however, paired with a subjective transformation which is the burden of the discourse here. Paul's focus will be on what the Spirit has done
within believers.

A Closer Look: In Christ and in the Spirit

What exactly does Paul mean by the phrase "in Christ"? Like the similar phrase "in
the Lord" it is possible for this phrase to mean no more than later generations of believers mean by the term "Christian," a term Paul nowhere uses. Thus for instance,
when Paul says in 1 Corinthians 7 that it is permissible for a widow to marry, but only
"in the Lord," he simply means she should marry a Christian. On the other hand,
there are various contexts where the phrase has a more pregnant sense, such as 1 Corinthians 12, where Paul speaks of being baptized by one Spirit into the one body of
Christ. "In Christ" in such cases is the residue of the discussion about the incorporation of the believer into Christ or into his body. Since Paul also believes in the reverse
sort of incorporation ("Christ in us, the hope of glory"), it would appear that we
must take absolutely seriously this sort of language, as Paul is speaking of what he believes to be spiritual transactions that link believers to Christ and vice versa. For example, "Christ in us" does not merely mean Christ for or with the believer.[4]

There is the further complication that one must ask about the relationship between "in Christ" and "in the Spirit." Are they just two ways of speaking about the
same condition or phenomenon? Paul differentiates the Spirit from Christ in various
ways, although they are often said to have the same effect on believers. So the answer

---

3. One crucial point that is often overlooked in the usual discussions of "justification"
is that the verdict for the sinner is *not* "Not guilty." Rather, the guilt is assumed, and the verdict is "pardoned" or "no condemnation" for what one is known to be guilty of. Paul is not in
any way suggesting that God is pronouncing the sinner not guilty, or that God is pretending
that the believer is righteous based on Christ's righteousness. Paul does not speak of imputed
righteousness here or elsewhere in his letters.

4. See my discussion of these matters in *Paul's Narrative Thought World: The Tapestry
of Tragedy and Triumph* (Louisville: Westminster/John Knox, 1994), pp. 245-306.

to this question is not immediately clear. Paul seems to see the Spirit as the agent or instrument of Christ, sent out to implement Christ's agenda for and in the believer. Christ uses the Spirit to grasp hold of those who respond in faith, and by the Spirit they are incorporated into the body of Christ's people (1 Cor. 12.13). It seems clear that "in Christ" has some sort of incorporative sense in texts like 1 Cor. 6.15ff., and it seems very likely indeed that that is how a largely Gentile audience would have heard such language, especially in light of other eastern cults such as the mystery religions. In 1 Corinthians 6 Paul speaks of the physical body of believers being members of Christ, because of which they must not have sexual relations with prostitutes. This is more than just graphic language or grandiose metaphors. Paul believes in real spiritual union and communion between believers and Christ. I would then take this language to say more than what Käsemann suggests when he says that it means to be in Christ's field of force,[5] though Christ's lordship over the believer is involved as well. Paul believes that through the Spirit Christ has taken possession of believers' lives and connected them with his exalted and glorified self by incorporating them into his earthly body of believers. As later Pauline discussion in Colossians will make apparent, Paul sees the head of the body as Christ in heaven, while the body remains on earth. Paul is thus able to speak of Christ operating above and separate from his earthly body, and not merely through it.

In v. 2 we find a surprising but probably original reference to "you" singular.[6] Surprising since Paul is addressing a group of Christians, but the simplest explanation is that Paul wants to emphasize here what is true for each individual Christian when it comes to the work of the Spirit. Furthermore, the singular "you" has a rhetorical purpose and is indeed a carry-over from ch. 7. Paul's audience were to see themselves as formerly the "I" who speaks there. Now here Paul speaks directly and to the heart of each individual in his audience, saying that they are no longer in that condition, thank God. Each of them has been set free from the bondage the "I" expressed.

The text reads literally "for the law of the Spirit of life in Christ Jesus freed you (singular) from the law of sin and death." Here Paul does indeed speak of two laws, not one law seen from two perspectives, and it is most natural to translate *nomos* in both instances as "rule" or "principle."[7] In neither case is the reference to the Torah.[8] Having been set free from one ruling force in one's life,

---

5. E. Käsemann, *Commentary on Romans* (Grand Rapids: Eerdmans, 1980), pp. 212-17.

6. On the text of this verse see p. 209 n. 1 above.

7. See rightly L. T. Johnson, *Reading Romans: A Literary and Theological Commentary* (Macon: Smyth and Helwys, 2001), p. 127, on Paul's punning or playful use of *nomos*.

8. G. D. Fee, *God's Empowering Presence: The Holy Spirit in the Letters of Paul* (Peabody: Hendrickson, 1994), pp. 522-24, is right to emphasize the rhetorical word-play here

which led only to sin and death, one has come under the authority of another. Thus, Cranfield's whole argument that Paul is talking about the Christian now properly being ruled by the Law of God is both unnecessary and incorrect.[9] It is the presence of the Spirit, not of the Mosaic Law, that rules in the believer's life. The aorist tense of "freed" suggests a one-time event completed in the past, at the point of conversion. This comports with the suggestion that 7.14-25 is a narrative of a crisis leading up to conversion.[10]

V. 3 provides a clear contrast between what the Law was able to accomplish and what Christ accomplished. What was impossible for the Law, in that it was weak and had no power to transform human lives, was nonetheless possible for the Son who was sent. The point that Paul makes in various places about the Mosaic Law applies here — one of the major problems with the Law is that, while it can tell what a person ought to do, it cannot transform a fallen human being or empower him or her to do it. The Law is weak because of the fallen human nature or sinful inclinations ("flesh").

In "God sent his Son" we seem to have an early Christian confessional formula about the sending of the Son which Paul adopts and adapts (cf. John 3.16; Gal. 4:4; Phil. 2.5-11). "Jesus Christ was *sent* by his Father; he was neither a man who discovered the truth about God, nor a heavenly rebel, like Prometheus, but a divine envoy, whose authority resided not in himself but in him who sent him."[11] Dunn protests that Paul is only using "Adam" language here, which would be singularly inappropriate since Adam did not preexist and was

---

with *nomos*. Paul then refers to three laws: (1) there is the Torah, which is a holy and good thing, but it cannot give life, nor can it enable or empower a fallen person to obey it; (2) there is the rule/law of sin and death in the fallen person, in particular in the flesh; and (3) there is the rule/law of the Spirit of life. The Law (Torah) is pitted against the law/rule of sin and death (type 2) in 7.14-25. But here in 8.2 it is pitted against type 3, with two non-Torah types of law being in view. Type 3 is the internalization of the rule of the Law of Christ, mentioned elsewhere, and fulfills the intent and essence of type 1 (Torah). The law/rule of sin and death cannot be simply the Law as used by sin for the very good reason that, as Paul explains, sin also uses one's fallen desires to enslave one, and one's desires are certainly not the same as the Law. So when Paul speaks about the rule of sin and death in the fallen person, he is sometimes also saying that the Law has been used to a bad end, but sometimes he is referring to dominating passions. The matter is complex and cannot be solved by simply assuming that *nomos* in Romans always means the Mosaic Law. Against J. D. G. Dunn, *Romans 1–8*, Word Biblical Commentary (Dallas: Word, 1988), pp. 416-17.

9. Cranfield, *Romans*, 1:374-75.

10. Käsemann, *Romans*, pp. 214-15, makes the common mistake of assuming that Paul does not distinguish between Spirit and water baptism, based on a misreading of ch. 6, and therefore assumes that Paul is speaking here of what happens by baptism. On this important matter see Dunn's classic study, *Baptism in the Holy Spirit* (London: SCM, 1970).

11. C. K. Barrett, *A Commentary on the Epistle to the Romans* (Peabody: Hendrickson, 1991), p. 155f.

not *sent* to earth. In all likelihood "God sent" here and elsewhere in Paul implies a concept of preexistence and so of incarnation.[12] *Heautou* is in the emphatic position — God's *own* Son was sent.

The phrase "in the likeness/image of" has been much debated. Paul is not avoiding saying that Christ took on a real physical body. He is no docetist or Gnostic (see Phil. 2.5-11). Nor is he saying that Christ has some sort of special kind of flesh of a different substance than that of fallen human beings. He uses the language of comparison here because of the adjective "sinful." "The likeness of sinful flesh" means Christ had real flesh, but it was not fallen and sinful flesh.[13] In view of the comparison with Adam in 5.12-21 it is quite believable that Paul is thinking of Christ as the new Adam who comes on the earthly scene like Adam before the Fall.[14] The phrase compares human flesh and Christ's flesh, but also distinguishes them. It does not speak of the deeds of Jesus and our deeds and so does not say that the Son came and did not sin like all other human beings, though Paul believes that is also true (cf. 2 Cor. 5.21).[15]

Cranfield suggests that the phrase means that Christ came in the form or likeness of sinful flesh but did not cease to be the Son by doing so. In other words, he was not changed into a human being without remainder, but rather assumed human flesh while still remaining himself, the Son of God. This presumes the preexistence of the Son in Paul's thought, which in my view is exactly what a text such as Phil. 2.5-11 suggests.[16] Christ took on some of the limitations of human flesh, but only some. Paul seems to think that Christ could not have condemned sin in the flesh unless he had taken on real human flesh, without himself having sinful flesh.

Christ was sent "for sin" *(peri hamartias).* This phrase is frequently used in the LXX to refer to a sin offering (cf. Lev. 5.6-7, 11; Num. 6.16; Ezek. 42.13). It

12. Against Dunn, *Romans 1–8*, pp. 420-21. See my treatment of the christological hymn material in *Paul's Narrative Thought World*, pp. 94-119.

13. The sinlessness of Christ is an idea found in various NT documents; cf. John 7.18; 8.46; 2 Cor. 5.21; Heb. 4.15; 7.26; 1 Pet. 2.22. See N. T. Wright, "Romans," in *The New Interpreter's Bible*, vol. 10 (Nashville: Abingdon, 2002), p. 578.

14. This view makes unnecessary the difficult question of whether Christ died for himself, if he too had a fallen human nature. According to the theology of sacrifice and atonement in the OT, the sacrifice had to be without blemish in order for it to be a legitimate substitute for the sinning human being, and in view of Paul's earlier discussion about sacrifice and propitiation (see pp. 107-10 above) this may have been a consideration in the way Paul phrases things here.

15. Cranfield, *Romans*, 1:378-82.

16. Käsemann, *Romans*, pp. 216-17, seems to take a kenotic approach here, based on his reading of Philippians 2, such that the divine Christ's emptying of himself led to his turning into a human being without remainder.

certainly can mean that here as well, especially in the light of what follows and of what has been said in ch. 5 about atonement.[17]

Paul then adds the thought that God condemns sin in the flesh. "No clearer statement is found in Paul, or indeed anywhere else in all early Christian literature of the early Christian belief that what happened on the cross was the judicial punishment of sin. . . . [I]n Jesus' death the condemnation that sin deserved was meted out fully and finally, so that sinners over whose heads that condemnation had hung might be liberated from this threat once and for all."[18] This "condemnation" refers to the judgment on sinful human flesh that Christ endured for believers on the cross, but also to the judgment God rendered on sinful flesh by sending his Son to the cross.[19] In this way, sin was actually condemned in Christ's flesh and in what happened to Christ's flesh on the cross. The condemnation then was not merely a decree, but involved a demonstration, or an affecting event — Christ's death. The declaration of no condemnation on those in Christ (v. 1) is based on the judgment of condemnation on sinfulness exercised on Christ on the cross (v. 3).

V. 4 begins with a *hina* clause which indicates either purpose ("in order that") or result ("with the result that"). Was Christ "sent in the likeness of sinful flesh" for the purpose of fulfilling the decree of the Law? In view of v. 3a this seems quite likely. The sin offering effects God's condemnation on sin.[20] But if Christ fulfilled the just decree of the Law, are we bound any longer to do so, or for that matter to suffer its punishment? The answer would seem to be No. I agree with Cranfield that *dikaiōma* must mean righteous requirement or righteous decree of the Law.[21]

What follows, however, seems to suggest that this requirement is fulfilled "in us" who walk not according to the flesh but according to the Spirit.[22] This might suggest that Christ came so that believers might be enabled to fulfill the Mosaic Law. But what Paul seems to have in mind is Christians being enabled, not to keep the Law as part of the Mosaic covenant, but to do God's will, which was certainly pointed to in the Mosaic Law. Christ took care of the matter of obedience to the Mosaic Law and the Law covenant for believers in his death. In light of texts like Gal. 6.1-2 it would seem clear that Paul means that what the Law really intended and was meant to accomplish is in fact accomplished in the

17. See K. Grieb, *The Story of Romans: A Narrative Defense of God's Righteousness* (Louisville: Westminster/John Knox, 2002), p. 77; Fee, *God's Empowering Presence*, p. 531.

18. Wright, "Romans," p. 575.

19. See F. M. Gillmann, "Another Look at Romans 8.3: 'In the Likeness of Sinful Flesh,'" *CBQ* 49 (1987): 597-604.

20. Dunn, *Romans 1–8*, p. 422.

21. Cranfield, *Romans*, 1:383-84.

22. See J. A. Zeisler, "The Just Requirement of the Law (Romans 8.4)," *AusBR* 35 (1987): 77-82.

life of the believer by means of the death of Christ and the Holy Spirit's presence, which allows the believer to walk in newness of life and to love God and neighbor wholeheartedly.[23] This is what the new Law of Christ is all about. It is a different law from the Mosaic Law, though it has some of the same stipulations and imperatives.[24] "The Spirit himself fulfills Torah by replacing it, and he does so by enabling God's people to 'fulfill' the 'whole of Torah'. . . . Paul does not say that Torah is now 'obeyed' or 'kept' or 'done' — the ordinary language for Torah observance — but that which the Torah requires is now 'fulfilled' *in us*."[25]

V. 5 elaborates what v. 4b has said. Those living according to the flesh concentrate or devote themselves to the things of the flesh, while those living according to the Spirit do the opposite.

In v. 6 we have an anacoluthon and must insert some sort of verb for both halves of the sentence. It does not seem likely Paul is talking about two conditions in one individual, for he has just been talking about two different sorts of people. Thus *estin* seems to be the right verb to insert, and we translate "for the mentality of the flesh is (i.e., amounts to or leads to) death, while the outlook of the Spirit is (leads to) life and peace." Two minds or mentalities are referred to here, not two outlooks of the same mind. One concentrates on the flesh, the other on the Spirit and spiritual things. The proof that this is the correct interpretation is found in the next verse, where Paul explains why or how this is so: "for the outlook of the flesh is enmity toward God, for it does not submit to the Law of God, nor is it able to do so." Needless to say, Paul does not describe the believer as being at enmity with God. *Dioti* here means "for" or "because" and introduces a reason, just as *hoti* does. Those who are in the flesh are not able to please God. Being in the flesh is not an orientation one can simply trade in or forsake on one's own. As ch. 7 makes clear, such a person is a slave to sin.

V. 9 describes the condition of believers. They are not "in the flesh" but rather in the Spirit. *Eiper* here can be translated "if indeed," but since Paul is talking about a fulfilled condition, the conditional clause does not indicate a bare possibility. Paul is not talking merely about a mindset which Christians ought not to have but about a state of being which is no longer the case for a Christian and should never be returned to.[26] Notice the language of mutual indwelling here. The believer is in the sphere of the Spirit precisely because the Spirit dwells in the believer. This verse makes it clear that for Paul the Spirit of

---

23. See C. Talbert, *Romans* (Macon: Smyth and Helwys, 2002), p. 204, who says that the just requirement of the Law is "God's desire for righteousness (= faithfulness) on the part of the people in covenant with Him."

24. See the careful discussion about fulfillment here in Fee, *God's Empowering Presence*, pp. 536-37.

25. Fee, *God's Empowering Presence*, p. 536.

26. Against Dunn, *Romans 1–8*, pp. 428-29.

Christ is the same as the Spirit of God. If one does not have this Spirit, one is not Christ's. For Paul there is no such thing as a believer without the Spirit dwelling in his or her life.[27]

V. 10 also is elliptical and we must insert a verb to make sense of the sentence. Presumably it could mean something like "but if Christ is in you, then the body of death (is not), but rather the Spirit of life through righteousness." But it is important to read this verse in light of the *men . . . de* contrast, and this favors the view that Paul is describing the inner and outer life of the believer. If this is correct, then the body of death is simply the physical body, which is subject to disease, decay, and death.[28] But if "body of death" (6:6) means the same as "body of sin"[29] then *sōma* here means something like what we mean when we say "I have a foreign body in my eye." This may be right, though the inner versus outer interpretation cannot be ruled out, and in fact seems supported by the next verse.[30] One of the main points here is that the Spirit makes possible the personal righteousness that the Law, weakened by sin, could not.[31]

If the Spirit dwells in the believer, then this same Spirit will give newness of life to the believer's mortal body in the future, just as he raised Christ from the dead in the past (v. 11). Paul is speaking about the believer's bodily resurrection in the future, rather than about spiritual transformation at conversion. This favors the view that Paul is talking about the physical body in the previous verse. Paul then is likely contrasting the mortal body (cf. mortal, *thnēta*, and dead, *nekron*) with the work of the Spirit within the believer and later at the eschaton. This idea of the Spirit as the agent of the resurrection is not what we usually find in the NT, but then this text has already told us that this is the Spirit of God, the agent God uses to accomplish the divine purposes. There is a textual problem here: if "his Spirit that indwells you" is genitive, then it is said that the Spirit who now indwells the believer will later be the agent who raises the believer from the dead. If, however, it is accusative, then the meaning is that the indwelling Spirit will be a reason for God to raise the believer later. It is not impossible that Paul is envisioning that those who live until the parousia, instead of being raised, will be internally transformed when Christ comes (cf. 1 Thessalonians 4; 1 Corinthians 15).

27. See rightly Dunn, *Romans 1–8*, p. 429: "only those who have the Spirit can claim to be Christ's; only those whose lives demonstrate by character and conduct that the Spirit is directing them can claim to be under Christ's lordship."

28. This would perhaps mean that the cry in 7.24-25 is indeed for a resurrection body, not to die per se.

29. Käsemann, *Romans*, pp. 223-24.

30. Consider the translation of P. Achtemeier, *Romans* (Atlanta: John Knox, 1985), p. 135: "When Christ is in your midst, although the body means death because of sin, the Spirit means life because of righteousness."

31. Fee, *God's Empowering Presence*, p. 516.

Ara oun in v. 12 introduces a new paragraph, drawing conclusions on the basis of what has just been said, and it should be translated "so then." Believers, like non-believers, are debtors, but not to the flesh so that they would have to pay that debt by living according to the flesh. Those who live according to the flesh are destined to die. Here we are put in touch with the prophetic conviction that deeds produce destiny. There are always consequences to one's actions, even eternal consequences. The person who lives by the Spirit puts to death the deeds of the body (here as in v. 10 *sōma* is used interchangably with *sarx*). What Paul says in v. 13 assumes that the Christian is capable of putting to death such deeds, but this is not true of the person in 7.14-25, who cannot help himself.

Käsemann insists that the verb *agontai* in v. 14 means "driven" by the Spirit.[32] If so, Paul might be adopting language familiar from the Greco-Roman world which speaks of ecstasy. But the verb could also mean "allow oneself to be led or controlled," as Gal. 5.18 would suggest. That the person who is led or driven by the Spirit is a son of God suggests that sonship comes with or through the Spirit. This makes good sense since Paul believes it is the Spirit that puts life into believers and gives them a basis for spiritual kinship with God. Believers are adopted children, Jesus being the only begotten Son.

Paul does not seem to be using "spirit" of the human spirit in its first occurrence in v. 15, but is rather saying that the Spirit, when he enters the believer's life, brings sonship,[33] not bondage (cf. 1 Cor. 2.12; 2 Tim. 1.7). The Spirit has been received (aorist tense), which undoubtedly means received at conversion. Paul knows of no reception of the Spirit subsequent to conversion. Paul does use *pneuma*, "spirit," in more than one sense in this context, just as he was able to use *nomos* in more than one sense earlier in this passage.

"The spirit of bondage which leads to fear" is an excellent summary of what he has described in 7.14-25. By contrast there is the condition of being adopted and so given the right to call God Father. This too is endowed and enabled by the Spirit. It is in the Spirit that we cry "Abba, Father."[34] This language of adoption would be especially appropopriate in Rome, where legal adoption was a means to a brighter future. This practice was very common, even in the imperial family. The language would, however, be surprising if Paul were speaking in a Jewish manner to a largely Jewish audience, because Jews basically did not practice adoption.[35]

The verb "cry" is a strong one, suggesting something of a shout or an

32. Käsemann, *Romans*, p. 226.

33. The term *huiothesia* is used only by Paul in the NT, but it is common in the inscriptions referring to adoption as sons or sonship. See *NewDocs* 4:173.

34. E. A. Obeng, "Abba Father: The Prayer of the Sons of God," *ET* 99 (1987-88): 363-66.

35. See Barrett, *Romans*, p. 153.

emotion-laden outcry prompted by the Spirit.[36] The content of the cry is the same as that of Jesus (Mark 14.34). Laura Ice and I have argued at some length that it is indeed a form of praying Jesus used and taught his disciples to use and that it is characteristic and perhaps even distinctive of the Jesus movement.[37] Cranfield may be right that what Paul envisions here is not the frenzied cry of the pagan ecstatic but rather the fervent prayer of a devotee, as in the LXX version of the Psalms (Pss. 3.4; 4.3; 18.6; 22.2, 5; 34.6).[38] But Paul clearly believes in the powerful presence of the Spirit in the believer's life strongly prompting one to pray, and in this case to pray in an audible and intelligible voice.[39] Paul himself probably used such prayer language and seems to assume that his audience is familiar with this form of addressing God. I would suggest that "Abba" was used by the earliest Jewish Christians and that the Greek word for "Father" was added to the invocation when Gentiles or non-Aramaic-speaking Jews became part of the Jesus movement. The use of the two words for Father favors the suggestion that Paul is not alluding to recitation of the Lord's Prayer here, but rather a Spirit-prompted outcry. It cannot be accidental that it is in contexts where Paul addresses the issue of the believer's sonship, here and in Gal. 4:6, that he uses "Abba." These two terms, "Abba" and "son," are integrally linked, bearing witness to the intimate relationship with God that is conveyed through the presence of the Holy Spirit.

How one interprets v. 16 affects many other matters. For example, "the Spirit bears witness *to* our spirit" is rather different from "the Spirit bears witness *with* our spirit."[40] In either case, the prior thing is the witness of the Spirit that we are God's children, which in turn prompts the Abba prayer. Having been assured that he or she is God's, the believer can then address God in intimate and personal terms. The "witness" is not to be identified with its result, namely our cry of response ("Abba"). Of course the cry reveals that the inward

36. See Dunn, *Romans 1–8*, p. 453.

37. See B. Witherington and L. Ice, *The Shadow of the Almighty* (Grand Rapids: Eerdmans, 2001). So far as I can see, there is still no evidence for God being prayed to as Abba outside of the Jesus and Christian tradition during or before the relevant period. There are a few places where God is called *ab* (father) in early Jewish literature, but *abba* is never used (cf. Ps. 89.26; Sir. 23.1, 4; 51.10; Wis. 14.3; *3 Maccabees* 6.3, 8; 4Q372, 1.16; 4Q460, 5.6 and Blessing 4 of the *Eighteen Benedictions*). See the discussion in Talbert, *Romans*, p. 206.

38. Cranfield, *Romans*, 1:398-99.

39. See Dunn, "Spirit Speech: Reflections on Romans 8.12-27," in *Romans and the People of God*, ed. S. K. Soderlund and N. T. Wright (Grand Rapids: Eerdmans, 1999), pp. 82-91, here p. 84: "the Spirit is the Spirit of sonship precisely because it is the Spirit of the Son. That is to say, the Spirit for Paul links the believer directly to Jesus; the Spirit defines the person as Christian precisely by establishing this link. And it makes this plain by reproducing the prayer relation of Jesus himself with God in believers; like Jesus, believers cry 'Abba! Father.'"

40. See Wright, "Romans," p. 594.

witness of the Spirit has already transpired. If Deut. 19.15 lies in the background here, this may mean that Paul is speaking of two witnesses: the Holy Spirit bearing witness *with* the believer's spirit. That would be seen as a validation of the truth since there were two witnesses. God gives the believer a witness in the Spirit, but requires one of the believer's spirit also. The translation "with" is favored by a comparison of the use of this verb in Rom. 2.15 and 9.1.

Paul uses *teknon* and *huios* interchangeably here. But as he develops his argument, he wants to maintain that there is something that follows from being a child of God, namely that one is an heir of God and a fellow-heir with Christ. But the believer has not yet fully inherited what he or she has been promised. He lives in hope. There is a proviso to inheriting however. One must follow the path Christ followed to glory, the path of self-sacrifice, of suffering with him and for him in the same cause for which he suffered. *Syn* compounds proliferate throughout this passage. Paul is talking about things we share with Christ and with the Spirit. He is likely speaking about suffering for the faith and for Christ, not just any sort of suffering.

Bridging the Horizons

For Paul, the *sine qua non* of Christian existence is the Holy Spirit. It is the Spirit which sets the captive free and gives life, inspires prayer, prophecy, tongues, and a host of other things. There is no such thing as a Christian without the presence of the Spirit in his or her life. Furthermore, the Spirit is seen and depicted by Paul as a being, not merely a presence or a force or a power. This in turn means that when Paul speaks of the Spirit being in the believer's life, he means the person of the Spirit. One can no more have a little bit of the Spirit in one's life than a woman can be a little bit pregnant. My point is that the personal nature of the Spirit rules out treating the Spirit as mere force or power one could acquire in installments. It is not an accident that Paul will contrast the principle of sin and death which rules the fallen person with the principle of life which comes from the presence of the Spirit. Not only do Christians have the verdict of "no condemnation" when they convert, they are also empowered by the vivifying presence of the Spirit to walk in newness of life. The Spirit does not merely convey the Good News. The Spirit enacts that news in the believer.

Argument Eight — 8.18-39:
Life in Christ in Glory

It is possible to divide this section into two parts, with vv. 31-39 introduced by the now familiar rhetorical question "What then shall we say?" But the thematic continuity of the section does not favor this division, and in any case vv. 31-39 bring the entire *probatio*, begun in 1.18, to a climax. 8.31-39 is the conclusion for all these eight arguments, bringing us back to the thesis statement of 1.16-17 and drawing out its ultimate implications for those in Christ.

8.18-39 is not the climax of all Paul's arguments, only the climax of the *probatio*. Too often chs. 9–11 have been taken as something of an afterthought or appendix, which they most certainly are not. Indeed, they more directly address some of the problems in the Roman Christian community, and one of the purposes of 1.18–8.39 is to provide a theological basis for what Paul will say in chs. 9–11 and urge in chs. 12–15. Failure to recognize this has often led to the teaching of chs. 1–8 as if they were some kind of self-contained miniature theological textbook that tells us everything we always wanted to know about Pauline theology but were afraid to ask. This is a mistake. What follows in chs. 9–11 could be understood as the answer to the question — If what you say in chs. 1–8 is true, then what position do the Jews still have in God's salvific plans?[1] This

---

1. It is interesting that the *dikai–* word group language becomes much less frequently mentioned in this epistle after 8.33 (but see 9.14; 9.31; 10.3; 10.10; 14.17). There are thirty-two examples up to 8.33 and only five in the second half of the letter. I would suggest that this is because, having established how God sets people right with him, and having gotten to the point in the argument where he has discoursed on life in the Spirit and in Christ, Paul intends to go on to talk about how Christians should live, no longer discoursing on the means by which they became Christians in the first place. For a helpful chart and survey of every single instance of this word group in Romans see A. J. M. Wedderburn, *The Reason for Romans* (Edinburgh: Clark, 1988), pp. 109-111.

was, I submit, an important question for Roman Christians in light of their social situation, and doubly important for Paul to address after he has told his audience that God sets right the ungodly, even saves the unrighteous Gentiles and the wicked, and is impartial in his graciousness.

What needs to be appreciated about 8.18-39 is that it reveals one of the most masterful dimensions of Paul's theology. Paul shows here that salvation in Christ completes not only God's plans for creation, but also his plans for calling and forming a people for himself.[2] Thus for Paul salvation has both anthropological and cosmological significance and effects. At the end of this passage, in vv. 31-39, we can see what happens when Paul gets caught up in love, wonder, and praise. His prose style becomes almost hymnic.[3]

For I reckon that the sufferings of the present time are not comparable to the coming glory to be revealed to us. For creation with eager expectation awaits the revelation of the sons of God. For creation was subjected to futility, not willingly but through the One who subjects it in hope, so that the creation itself also will be freed from the slavery of decay unto the freedom of the glory of the children of God. For we know that all creation groans together and is in travail until the present time. But not only so, but also ourselves having the first fruits of the Spirit, and ourselves groan within ourselves, awaiting sonship, the redemption of our bodies. For we were saved in hope, but hope that is seen is not hope. For who hopes for what he already sees? But if we hope for what we do not see, we await it with patience.

Likewise also the Spirit helps our weakness, for we do not know how to pray as we ought, but the same Spirit intercedes with inarticulate groans. But the one searching the heart knows what is the mind of the Spirit, so that according to God he intercedes for the saints. But we know that for those who love God, all things work together[4] for good, for those called according to choice/purpose. For those whom he knew beforehand, he also destined beforehand to share the likeness of the form of his Son, so that he might be the firstborn of many brothers. Those he destined beforehand, he also called, and those he called he also set right, and those he set right he also glorified.

What then shall we say to all this? If God is for us, is anyone against us? For

2. See rightly J. D. G. Dunn, *Romans 1–8*, Word Biblical Commentary (Dallas: Word, 1988), p. 467.

3. On the structure of this entire chapter, and its echoes of earlier material, both Pauline and non-Pauline, see P. Von der Osten-Sacken, *Römer 8 als Beispiel paulinischen Soteriologie* (Göttingen: Vandenhoeck and Ruprecht, 1975).

4. It is possible that the original reading here is "God works all things together . . ." which is supported by some important witnesses including p46, A, B, and others. The shorter reading which omits *ho theos* is even better supported, however, and is probably original. See B. M. Metzger, *A Textual Commentary on the Greek New Testament* (3rd ed.; London: United Bible Societies, 1971), p. 458.

he who did not spare his own Son but delivered him up for us all, how will he not with him give us all things? Who will make an accusation against God's chosen? God is the one who sets it right. Who will condemn? Christ is the one who died, rather was raised, who also is at the right hand of God, who also intercedes for us. For what will separate us from the love of Christ? Will suffering or anguish or persecution or famine or nakedness or danger or the sword? Just as it is written "For the sake of you, we die the whole day, we are regarded as lambs for slaughter." But in all these situations we triumph gloriously through the one who loves us. For I am convinced that neither death nor life, nor angels nor rulers, nor things present nor things to come, nor powers, nor height, nor depth, nor any other part of creation is able to separate us from the love of God which is in Christ Jesus our Lord.

8.18 begins with the same verb as 3.28 and 6.11, expressing a firm conviction. It can be translated "reckon" but it does not mean something like "guess" or "think." Rather it means "I have certainly concluded." In other words, it is a verb of deduction used when someone is bringing an argument to closure and trying to focus on conclusions. A conviction has been reached on the basis of rational thinking. Paul is going to make another comparison, much like the comparison found in 2 Corinthians 4-5, where he speaks of the eternal weight of glory in contrast to our light and momentary afflictions. What Paul wishes to say here is that however severe a believer's sufferings may be in the present era of salvation and messianic afflictions, they are not comparable to the glory which will be revealed to the believer. Here the point at issue is what will happen to our human bodies. Paul has in mind the future resurrection, at which point believers will be well and truly conformed to Christ's image, and then be truly revealed as sons of God, like the Son of God.[5]

The word *axia* in v. 18 means "of equal worth or value" and the phrase *eis hēmas* must surely mean "in us," in our very bodies. It indicates the locus of the revelation of glory. What is being discussed here is not present sanctification but the internal and also external and eternal renovation that resurrection entails.

V. 19 has prompted a major debate about the meaning of *ktisis,* "creation." Basically, there are eight possibilities: all humanity, unbelieving humanity alone, believing humanity alone, angels alone, subhuman nature (both creature and creation), subhuman nature plus angels, unbelievers and nature, and subhuman nature plus humanity in general. V. 23 clearly enough contrasts believ-

---

5. S. Eastman, "Whose Apocalypse? The Identity of the Sons of God in Romans 8.19," *JBL* 121 (2002): 263-77, notes that since full conformity to Christ's image does not come until the return of Christ and the resurrection, and since that is also when "all Israel will be saved" and will regain their sonship, it then becomes the case that the futures of believers, Israel, and all creation are linked in chs. 8–11.

ers with creation, and this seems to rule out inclusion of believers here. V. 20 seems to rule out non-believers as well, or even humanity in general, since at least Adam was not subject to such futility or suffering without a choice. So *ktisis* here probably refers to subhuman creatures and nature. Paul does not appear to think that angels in general or in toto have been subjected to the sort of decay and futility spoken of here.[6] It should not be surprising that he uses the rhetorical device of personification again here. Nature is often personified in the OT, particularly in the Psalms.

The word *apokaradokia* means "eager expectation," and it comes from the idea of straining one's neck forward to see what is coming next. V. 19 indicates that the future fortunes of all creation are bound up with the believers' future. What Paul has in mind is the ultimate eschatological hope, not of disembodied life in heaven, but of new creatures in a new earth, though of course he uses slightly different language than we find in Revelation 21–22.[7] All creation is straining, looking forward eagerly to the day when believers will be in the full sense sons of God, being fully conformed even in the body to the likeness of the resurrected Jesus.[8] The reference to groaning may indicate that the messianic labor pains for all creation and creatures have begun.

In vv. 20-21 Paul probably has the Genesis story of the fall and its effects in view (Gen. 3.17-19). This makes perfectly good sense in view of the contrast between Adam, with those in Adam, and those in Christ (7.5, 6 and 8.1-17). Though the subject in v. 20 is implied, it seems clearly to be God that has subjected creation to futility. Perhaps a better translation than "futility" would be "ineffectiveness," inability to reach its goal and raison d'être. The world will not reveal its full glory, nor be able to do so, until believers' full glory is revealed at the resurrection. This is because, apart from God, human beings, not subhuman nature, are the chief actors in the drama of redemption. Christianity, like Judaism, is a religion grounded in history and its future, not a nature religion in the normal sense of that phrase. Hope for creation is bound up with hope for humanity.

Dioti in v. 21 likely means "because" or "for." Creation was subjected in hope because it will be set free, just as believers will, from disease, decay, and

---

6. See C. Bryan, *A Preface to Romans: Notes on the Epistle and Its Literary and Cultural Setting* (Oxford: Oxford University Press, 2000), p. 150 and n. 83.

7. On which see my *Commentary on John's Revelation* (Cambridge: Cambridge University Press, 2003), *ad loc.*

8. Irenaeus's exegesis of this passage includes the belief that all of creation would be restored to its pristine and original condition (*Adversus Haereses* 5.32.1). See the discussion by D. J. Bingham, "Irenaeus' Reading of Romans 8," in *SBL Seminar Papers 2001*, pp. 131-50, here pp. 145-46. "The creation is essentially and substantially worthy of renovation. Its bondage is linked to the bondage of its master, the human. So too, its restoration is linked to the liberty of humanity. It will receive its incorruption only in the glory of the human."

death.[9] It is possible that the idea of the loss of glory in the fall, which is then seen as regained at the eschaton, is in view here.[10] The focus here is on future freedom.[11] Freedom and glory coincide and are seen as future, so far as the material aspect of creation and the life of the believer is concerned.

In v. 22 Paul makes a statement he assumes all will agree with, that all creation has been groaning in unison until now. V. 23 states an additional truth: not only so, says Paul, but also. . . . What follows this grammatical turn in the argument is extremely emphatic with two uses of *autoi* added merely to punctuate the matter. "We ourselves, who ourselves have the first fruits of the Spirit, nonetheless groan within ourselves awaiting the redemption of the body." This sentence makes it likely that the previous discussion did have to do with the redemption of the body. *Aparchē* here, as in 1 Corinthians 15, refers to "first fruits," which always implies that there will be latter fruits. The first fruits are the foretaste or preview of what is to come. Unlike 1 Corinthians 15, where Paul is discussing Jesus' resurrection as the first fruits of the resurrection of believers, here the reference is to the Holy Spirit, given by God. Similarly, *arrabōn* (2 Cor. 5.5) refers to a deposit made on a purchase. In either case, the idea is something we have in part now but will receive the rest of later. There has been a minority opinion that Paul might be referring to the human spirit here. But the subject is the first fruits *of* the Spirit, so this is unlikely. The initial work of the Spirit in the life of the believer is referred to as first fruits. Paul is not likely referring to getting some of the Spirit itself in the present, and more of it later, as if the Spirit were seen as a substance that could be parceled out a little at a time.[12] The word *huiothesian*, "adoption"

9. J. R. Michaels, "The Redemption of Our Body: The Riddle of Romans 8.19-22," in *Romans and the People of God*, ed. S. K. Soderlund and N. T. Wright (Grand Rapids: Eerdmans, 1999), pp. 92-114, makes the interesting suggestion that *ktisis* does not refer to creation but to the creature in these verses. However, it seems odd for Paul to say "the creature waits in eager expectation for the children of God to be revealed," for that implies some sort of dichotomy between "the creature" and the "children of God" such that they can be distinguished here. Also, what would it mean to say the "creature" was subjected to frustration through no choice of its own? This surely was not the case with Adam. Yet the echo of the creation and fall story seems clear here, and Gen. 3.17-19 does indeed speak of how creation participated in the fall with the creature. See B. Byrne, *Romans*, Sacra Pagina (Collegeville: Liturgical, 1996), pp. 257-58.

10. See pp. 63-72 above on lost glory.

11. E. Käsemann, *Commentary on Romans* (Grand Rapids: Eerdmans, 1980), pp. 232-34.

12. See the discussion in G. D. Fee, *God's Empowering Presence: The Holy Spirit in the Letters of Paul* (Peabody: Hendrickson, 1994), pp. 573-74. He suggests that the phrase is appositional such that "first fruits" = Holy Spirit. This may be correct. The imagery is meant to conjure up the larger concept of the eschatological harvest. The Spirit functions as something of a guarantee that God will complete the task of our redemption. C. K. Barrett, *A Commentary on the Epistle to the Romans* (Peabody: Hendrickson, 1991), pp. 156-57, is right that it is not Paul's view that the Spirit is parceled out a little at a time.

(see above on v. 15) is omitted in a few important witnesses (𝔓46, D, G), but is probably original.

In v. 24 Paul expresses the paradoxical nature of his gospel. It is a matter of "already" (we were saved) and "not yet" (in hope). Salvation begins to happen to the believer in this lifetime, with "were saved" referring to the event of conversion, but the story of salvation is not over until the redemption of the body. Only then is the full extent of grace and transformation experienced. By definition, asks Paul, who hopes for what they already see? Notice the emphasis on seeing. Paul is thinking of the visible transformation, even to human flesh, which will transpire (see 1 Corinthians 15). Thus this life is the time of waiting patiently for what is hoped for but not yet seen (cf. Heb. 11.1, where hoping and not seeing are also paired) — the resurrection of believers into a new form of bodily existence, like that which Christ already is experiencing.

Beginning with v. 26 we have a difficult paragraph about the work of the Spirit in or for the believer or both. The first sentence is clear enough — the Spirit helps the believer in his weakness. The major debate in this section is whether it is a special kind of prayer or prayer in general that constitutes the weakness and difficulty the believer is experiencing.[13] What is it that "we do not know"? The Greek is such that it could be what to pray, what to pray for, or even the thing prayed for. Some have even seen here two unknowns — what to pray for and how to pray it. But this is unlikely. *Katho dei* should be seen as a qualifier referring to what is right according to God's will in regard to what should be prayed. Käsemann argues that prayer in general cannot be the problem, for in fact believers do have a model for prayer in the Lord's Prayer. He argues that what is in view is the believer under fire and needing special help from the Spirit. In our weakness the Holy Spirit intercedes for us in some way. How? Does *stenagmois alalētois* refer to sighs that are wordless, or beyond words, or to the inarticulate groans of the ecstatic prompted by the Spirit, or possibly even to glossolalia uttered in worship (1 Cor. 14.14)?[14]

Käsemann describes the following scenario: there were ecstatics who saw their ability to speak in tongues as a sign that the future was now. Paul counters this by indicating that heavenly speech is actually not a sign that believers have already received their glorious future, but rather that in their weakness the Spirit gives them a small foretaste of that future, which makes them long and cry out for more. Cranfield denies that glossolalia is in view here since it is private prayer and praise language while the problem here seems to be bringing the known needs of believers before God in an adequate manner.[15] One might

13. Käsemann, *Romans*, pp. 239-41.

14. On this see Fee, *God's Empowering Presence*, pp. 575-86; cf. Käsemann, *Romans*, p. 241.

15. C. E. B. Cranfield, *A Critical and Exegetical Commentary on the Epistle to the Romans* (ICC; Edinburgh: Clark, 1975-79), pp. 420-24.

have expected a little more explicitness if glossolalia were in view here.[16] And, most decisively, Paul is talking about *the Spirit* uttering inarticulate groans, not the believer.[17] Thus Cranfield is probably right that what is meant are utterances or groanings that are imperceptible to the believer. The Spirit groans along with the believer, just as the believer groans as part of fallen creation.[18]

V. 27 confirms that what Paul is discussing is the Spirit's activity, not ours, even aided by the Spirit. God, the searcher of hearts, certainly knows what is on the Spirit's mind or, to put it another way, what the Spirit urges and desires. In all of this discussion the Spirit is spoken of in profoundly personal terms. Paul does not see the Spirit as merely some sort of force or power or even just the presence of God. The Spirit prays, which is a profoundly personal act, and we are told here the Spirit intercedes for the saints.[19]

In v. 28 Paul makes another statement that he assumes is common knowledge — "we know," though this could be rhetorical, really meaning "we all ought to know." Here we have a rare instance of Paul speaking about the believer's love for God. It is crucial to the argument here that Paul is talking about Christians. For Christians who are called, all things work together. Paul is not talking about some evolutionary or inevitable process that happens like magic for believers. He is referring to the sovereignty and providence of God over all things and processes. God is the one who works things out, as the alternate textual reading, which inserts *ho theos*, "God," makes even clearer. That God is the subject is made clear by the reference just afterward to "those whom he called."[20] Whatever this verse means, it certainly does not grant exemption from the hardships of life, as Paul will go on to suggest when he lists such things later in this chapter. With *panta* ("all things") Paul probably has particularly in mind the sufferings of the present age. Paul believes that God can use such things, weaving them into his plan for a person's life, using all things to a good

16. See C. Talbert, *Romans* (Macon: Smyth and Helwys, 2002), p. 220: "Paul's language however is 'wordless groans.' This does not sound like *glossolalia*, even the private type, which involves words that someone could hear and interpret."

17. See E. A. Obeng, "The Spirit Intercession Motif in Paul," *ET* 95 (1983-84): 361-64, and his "The Origins of the Spirit Intercession Motif in Romans 8.26," *NTS* 32 (1986): 621-32. Cf. N. T. Wright, "Romans," in *The New Interpreter's Bible*, vol. 10 (Nashville: Abingdon, 2002), p. 599.

18. For a good counter-argument that speaking in tongues is in view here see Fee, *God's Empowering Presence*, pp. 577-86.

19. See the helpful treatment of the Spirit references in this chapter by Dunn, "Spirit Speech: Reflections on Romans 8.12-27," in Soderlund and Wright, eds., *Romans and the People of God*, pp. 82-91.

20. However, as Fee avers, the subject may be God the Spirit, since Paul has been discussing the role of the Spirit immediately prior to this section. See Fee, *God's Empowering Presence*, pp. 587-91.

end (cf. 13.4) — namely to the eventual end of the redemption of believers' bodies. The point is that all things can be made to serve the end of our redemption, not necessarily our earthly comfort or convenience.

The next phrase reads literally "those called according to purpose/ choice." "His" is not in the text. Some commentators have urged that *prothesis* could refer to human beings here, in which case the text would mean "those called according to (their own) choice," or, as we would say, "by choice," the free act of choice by which those called respond to God's call.[21] This is grammatically perfectly possible and is in fact how Origen, Chrysostom, Theodoret, and most other ancient Greek commentators who knew Paul's Greek far better than we do took it.[22] Chrysostom, for example: "For if the calling alone were sufficient, how is it that all were not saved? Hence he says it is not the calling alone, but the purpose of those called too, that works the salvation. For the calling was not forced upon them, nor compulsory. All then were called, but all did not obey the call." Thus the choice or purposing is that of the respondent. In support of the view that God's choice is meant here is probably Rom. 9.11 (cf. Eph. 1.11; 3.11; 2 Tim. 1.9; Philo, *Moses* 3.61),[23] and one may point to the general tenor and drift of the passage, particularly the emphasis on divine action for the believer in v. 29. Since, however, this same verse refers to our love for God, the exegetical decision is not so clear-cut and obvious, contrary to the impression left by most translations. Above all, the word "his" should not be inserted. Instead, the matter should be left open.

Hous, "whom," at the beginning of v. 29 must refer back to "those who love God," that is, Christians, in v. 28. The discussion that follows is about the future of believers. Paul is not discussing some mass of unredeemed humanity out of which God chose some to be among the elect.[24] But what are we to do

21. See *NewDocs* 1:64. The word means plan, purpose, resolve, or choice.

22. See Bryan, *Preface to Romans,* p. 153 and n. 94.

23. See Dunn, *Romans 1–8,* pp. 481-82.

24. In his helpful summary of the evidence from the Church Fathers, G. Bray, ed., *Romans* (Ancient Christian Commentary on Scripture; Downers Grove: InterVarsity, 1998), p. 233, says this: "Apart from Augustine, who embraced it wholeheartedly, most of the Fathers found it somewhat puzzling to accept the apostle's teaching at face value. They did not want to deny that the world was planned and ordered by God, but neither did they want to suggest that there were some people whom God had predestined to damnation. They were convinced that predestination did not remove human free will. God's call to salvation was generally understood to be universal. The fact that not all responded was their fault entirely and the result of a deliberate choice on their part." Bray adds: "Only Augustine, and then only in his later writings, was prepared to accept the full implications of divine predestination" (p. 244). A sampling of what the fathers say shows that Augustine was by no means the only voice in the choir, and in fact it appears he was frequently singing solo. For example, Diodore in the *Pauline Commentary from the Greek Church* says about 8.28-30: "This text does not take away our free will. It uses the word 'foreknew' before 'predestined.' Now it is clear that foreknowledge

with *hoti,* the first word in v. 29? It seems likely that it means *for* or *because* here and is not merely an unimportant connective. If so, then vv. 29 and 30 will explain why all things work together for good for believers. This working together for good happens because all along God has had a plan for believers. Therefore v. 29 says that "those believers whom God knew in advance he also destined beforehand to share the form of the image of his Son."

Is Paul then talking about a pretemporal election plan of God where the outcome is predetermined because of God's sovereign hand in and on every step of the process? This of course is how Augustine and his offspring read this text, but it is not how some of the crucial Greek Fathers that came before Augustine read it, including most importantly Chrysostom. Paul is speaking about God foreknowing and destining in advance Christians to be fully conformed to the image of Christ.[25] It needs to be borne in mind that Paul's audience is composed largely of Gentile Christians, who Paul apparently felt needed some encouragement due to suffering or persecution or other calamities they might be facing.

It is possible that in such a situation Paul wanted to tell believers not how they became Christians in the first place but rather how God always had a plan to get believers to the finish line, working all things together for good, showing them how they will be able to persevere through whatever trials they may face along the way. In Christ they have a glorious destiny, and, Paul will go on to stress, no outside power, circumstance, degree of suffering, or temptation can rip them out of the firm grip that God has on their lives. He is working things

---

does not by itself impose any particular kind of behavior. . . . Whom did he predestine? Those whom he foreknew, who were called according to his plan i.e. who demonstrated that they were worthy to be called by his plan and made conformable to Christ" (cited by Bray, p. 235). Theodoret in his *Interpretation of the Letter to the Romans* puts it this way: "Those whose intention God foreknew, he predestined from the beginning" (Bray, p. 237). Or again Cyril of Alexandria in his *Explanation of the Letter to the Romans* says: "He calls everyone to himself, and no one is lacking the grace of his calling for when he says everyone he excludes nobody." (He is discussing 8.28 in light of Jesus' saying "Come unto me all who labor . . ."). Finally there is the much maligned Pelagius, who says in his *Commentary on Romans,* "Those who God knew in advance would believe, he called. A call gathers together those who are willing to come, not those who are unwilling. . . . Paul says this because of the enemies of the faith, in order that they may not judge God's grace to be arbitrary" (Bray, p. 237 for these last three quotations). A few voices took a line closer to Augustine's, particularly Origen, but it was a minority opinion even in Augustine's day.

25. Dunn, *Romans 1–8,* p. 482, argues that the use of "foreknow" here "has in view the more Hebraic understanding of 'knowing' as involving a relationship experienced and acknowledged." This, however, makes no sense. You cannot have a relationship with someone who does not yet exist, and more particularly you cannot have the experience of a relationship that does not yet exist. You can, however, know something in advance without yet experiencing it, and this is what Paul has in mind here. Cf. Acts 26.5; 2 Pet. 3.17.

together for good in every stage of the salvation process. The end or destiny of believers is to become fully Christ-like, even in their bodily form. Paul has just said that the believer's hope is the redemption of his or her body, and here he explains how God will be working to get the believer to that goal.[26] In Paul's use, "foreknow" and "predestine" "do not refer in the first instance to some limitation on our freedom, nor do they refer to some arbitrary decision by God that some creatures are to be denied all chance at salvation. They simply point to the fact that God knows the end to which he will bring his creation, namely redemption, and that the destiny is firmly set in his purposes. . . . In that sense Paul can speak of 'pre-destination.' It means, just as the word says, that the destiny has already been set; and that destiny is the final redemptive transformation of reality."[27]

In short, and particularly in light of vv. 31-39, this comforting text is about the perseverance of the saints, not about the election of some to be saints out of a mass of unredeemed humanity, the choice being determined purely on the basis of God's fiat. That later notion makes nonsense of the very concept which is said to be determining this whole matter, namely love. Not only God's love for believers, but the believers' love for God. It is those who love God who are called according to purpose and whom God foreknew, and that purpose they must embrace freely and fully in love.[28]

Love for God can be commanded, but it cannot be coerced, compelled, or engineered in advance, or else it loses its character as love. The proof that this line of thinking, and not that of Augustine, Luther, or Calvin, is on the right track is seen clearly in 11.2, where Paul says plainly that God foreknew his Jewish

26. See Wright, "Romans," p. 602: "God's purpose for those who are in Christ is precisely Christ-shaped. They are chosen and called in order to advance God's purpose in and for the world. . . . That which is true of the Messiah is true of his people."

27. P. Achtemeier, *Romans* (Atlanta: John Knox, 1985), p. 144.

28. One point which Dunn, *Romans 1–8*, p. 485, and others seem to have clearly missed is that we continue to have reference to the same *hous:* once in v. 29, and three times in v. 30. The import of this is twofold: (1) Paul is deliberately talking about a group of people — "those who." He does not for instance address individuals, as we saw him doing with the "you" singular in 8.2. Election is seen as a corporate matter by Paul. There is an elect group (see below on v. 33). (2) Even more importantly, since vv. 29-30 must be linked to v. 28, the "those who" in question are those about whom Paul has already said that they "love God" — i.e., Paul makes perfectly clear that he is talking about Christians here. The statement about them loving God *precedes* and determines how we should read both *hous* in these verses and the chain of verbs. God knew something in advance about these persons, namely that they would respond to the call of God in love. For such people, God goes all out to make sure that in the end they are fully conformed to the image of Christ. These verses would have had a very different significance had they read "and those God predetermined would love him, he then justified. . . ." But this is not what Paul says or suggests, not least because it does not comport with his theology of the nature of love.

people, and yet not all of them responded positively to his call. Indeed, only a minority have as he writes this letter. God's foreknowledge, and even God's plan of destiny for Israel, did not in the end predetermine which particular individual Israelite would respond positively to the gospel call and which would not. In 10.8-15 Paul will make clear that the basis of that response is faith and confession. Just so, God's plan for his Elect One, Jesus, does not inexorably predetermine who will end up being "in Christ." What Paul does in ch. 8 is to reassure believers, saying "God has always known you and planned for your future, even from before the foundations of the universe."

Paul distinguishes between what God knows and what God wills or destines in advance. Knowing and willing are not one and the same. The proof of this is of course that God knows very well about human sin but does not will it or destine it to happen. What is implied in this is that God loved believers before they ever responded to the call and loved God. Various early Jewish texts speak of God's foreknowledge (cf. 1QH 1.7-8; CD 2.8; Jer. 1.5). *Symmorphous*, "conformed," probably does not have in view the conforming of the believer to the image of Christ that takes place internally and during the process of sanctification, or at least that is not the sole subject here. If it is referred to at all, it is referred to as part of the process that leads to the final act of conforming believers to Christ — namely the resurrection. Paul goes on to say that Christ becomes the firstborn of many brothers and sisters through this process. In view of 1 Cor. 15.20-24 this surely refers to Christ's resurrection, his so-called birth (rebirth) being at the resurrection — first fruits and firstborn being two ways of speaking about the same thing, both of which imply that there will be more to follow. Käsemann is probably right to see the Adam story, grounded in the comparison in Romans 5, behind all of this.[29] Christ is the first of a new race, the race of the resurrected ones, who for now are being conformed internally but not yet externally to Christ's image.

V. 30 then sums this all up, reassuring the Romans that God is in control of all these matters. Those believers whom God foreknew he also destined in advance, those he destined he also called, those he called he also set right, and those he set right he also glorified. The verb tenses make it clear that Paul is looking at things from the eschatological end of the process, with even glorification already having transpired. *Doxa*, "glory," here refers to the future glory of resurrection, as before. Paul's emphasis here is on God's hand of involvement in every step of this process, and so he does not mention the human response, positive or negative. Nor does he mention sanctification. But he has already spoken of believers loving God in v. 28, and that should be kept in view throughout the reading of vv. 29-30. If these latter two verses stood in isolation apart from a clear connection with v. 28, that would be one thing, but they do

---

29. See Käsemann, *Romans*, pp. 244-45.

not, and they must be interpreted in the light of the broader context of Pauline thinking about grace and faith, foreknowing and human purpose, and the like. If vv. 29-30 stood alone then Paul would indeed sound like the most deterministic of early Jews, such as we sometimes find in some of early Jewish literature at Qumran and elsewhere. But what the Romans needed to be assured of was God's involvement, not their own, in the whole salvation process and plan.[30] This text admirably stresses the hands-on nature of God and his providential plan. This truth, when it comes to looking at the Christian life as an exercise in persevering, will be even further highlighted in vv. 31-39.

V. 31 begins in the first person plural, but Paul will become more direct and personal as the passage goes along. *Tauta,* "these things," points back to what he has just spoken of, and so we are meant to see these verses as bringing to light certain conclusions that follow in view of the truths already shared. It is right to see these verses as the climax of the entire first part of the letter, the *probatio.* Cranfield suggests that the theme here is "if God is for us, who can be against us," and he sees this as a concise summary of 1.16b–8.30.[31] This is correct, and it is no accident that Paul rises to an emotional climax here as well, with vv. 38-39 in the first person singular. This conclusion is in the rhetorical form of the diatribe, where questions are again asked and then answered by Paul himself.

In order to demonstrate the theme of "if God is for us," Paul will list some things that are ranked against believers from time to time. V. 32 sets forth the opposition, but puts them in perspective and in their place by saying that the God who did not spare his own Son will also take care of the things that are trials for Christians, so to make sure of their deliverance.[32] The conditional statement (introduced by *ei*) in v. 31 expresses a real condition, not merely a probability.

Some commentators have seen in v. 32 an echo of the story of Isaac (Gen. 22.12, 16 LXX). The traditions about the binding of Isaac were important in early Judaism, but the dating of some of those traditions, especially the one that suggests that the unconsummated sacrifice of Isaac atoned for Israel's sin, probably post-dates the writing of Romans. If there is such an allusion here, then the

---

30. See K. K. Yeo, "Messianic Predestination in Romans 8 and Classical Confucianism," in *SBL Seminar Papers 2001,* pp. 81-107, here p. 90: "One ought to be careful not to read the language of predestination as a divine prediction and a closed system of static fate; otherwise the metanarrative of Christ could be comprehensive and yet rigid, or could be specific and yet exclusive. . . . And foreknowledge of God should be understood in the eschatological view of history, i.e. God intends *all* humanity to have an affectionate relationship with God as God's sons."

31. Cranfield, *Romans,* 1:434-35.

32. On the allusion to the Isaac story see J. Swetnam, *Jesus and Isaac* (Rome: Biblical Institute Press, 1981). In my estimation it is a mistake to make too much of this echo, because of course Isaac was spared, but Jesus was not.

point is that Christ's sacrifice was greater than Isaac's because it was completed. 3.25 might also allude to such a tradition. Rather than sparing his Son, God delivered him up to death "for us all," which at the very least means for all believers. Possibly Isa. 53.12 (cf. Rom. 4.25 for "delivered") is alluded to here.

If God will give up even his Son to death, how will he not give all things to believers? But what are these "all things"? The context makes clear that Paul is not talking about material wealth and the like. He means all that is necessary for salvation, all that is necessary to protect believers from spiritual danger in all sorts of difficult and dangerous circumstances. Again, this is not a promise of continual good health or that believers will never suffer or die, but rather that no third party or power or force or circumstance or lesser supernatural being will be able to separate the believer from the love of God in Christ. Jesus' death and resurrection form the central paradigm out of which Paul interprets all that happens to the believer in the world and all that is past, present, and future.[33] Not an abstract concept of God, but rather God with flesh on, God in Christ reconciling the world to himself, characterizes Paul's understanding of deity. Paul speaks of God only as the God who reveals himself, not as a hidden God whose will and ways are inscrutable and whose hidden counsels might actually be the opposite of his revealed Word. At the end of v. 32 we have a verbal cognate of *charis* which we should translate "give graciously."

In v. 33 Paul enumerates real and probable situations of difficulty and danger that he has experienced and that his audience might well face. In speaking of accusations against believers Paul is perhaps envisioning a courtroom scene. Paul asks who will accuse, but does not answer. Rather he tells why such accusations are fruitless and pointless. If God justifies those accused, who could possibly condemn them (see 8.1)? The highest judge of all has pronounced no condemnation as the verdict. Possibly Paul is drawing on Isa. 50.7-9 here. There seem to be several probable allusions to Isaiah's Servant Songs here as Paul concludes his positive arguments. It seems likely that Paul would indeed have seen Christ as the Suffering Servant. More specifically, the language about God's Elect comes right from OT language about the people of God as a group (1 Chron. 16.13; Pss. 89.3; 105.6; Isa. 42.1; 43.20; 45.4; 65.9-22; Sir. 46.1; 47.22; Wis. 3.9; 4.15; *Jubilees* 1.29; 1QS 8.6; CD 4.3-4). A careful reading of these texts will show that most do not entail the notion that elect individuals have some sort of advance guarantee of salvation. The concept of "the elect" applies to the group, and individuals within the group can, and indeed often are said to, commit apostasy. This is not because they were not chosen to be Jews, or "true" Jews, in the first place. It is because they became unfaithful and chose to wander away.[34]

---

33. Käsemann, *Romans*, pp. 246-47.

34. For more on Jewish ways of thinking about these matters, see pp. 246-49 below. It is telling that it takes a tour de force, full-length argument in a monograph to suggest that Paul

Even if the accusations against believers are valid, Jesus paid the price —
he died for believers and rose again, and furthermore is seated in the seat of
honor and influence beside God in heaven where he intercedes for the believer.
The thought of Jesus as our intercessor is not uniquely Pauline (see also Heb.
7.25; 1 John 2.1). Here we have two relative clauses, the second dependent on the
first. The first seems to be alluding to Psalm 110.[35] Pelagius says in a striking remark that Christ intercedes for us by constantly showing and offering the Father his perfect human nature. The point would be: "Don't judge them; in view
of my work on earth they are redeemable."

The list of difficulties in vv. 35-36 has often been related to similar pagan
lists, but unlike those lists Paul does not include happier circumstances along
with the more difficult ones, and furthermore Paul's list is related to Christ and
his sufferings, mentioned twice in the previous verses. All such experiences are
to be viewed in the light of Christ's death and resurrection, and his intercession
while he sits on the seat of power (a phrase perhaps creedal in origin). Paul is
not simply listing chance misfortunes but rather woes that can and do come to
those who are witnesses for Christ. In short, the context is probably the idea of
the messianic woes, a special sort of suffering or tribulation.[36] All of the words
in this list refer to external experiences, except perhaps *stenochōria*, and it refers
to anguish caused by *thlipsis*, with which it is paired. The same two words are
paired in 2.9. The next word, "persecution," could relate to the same experience
as *thlipsis*. But the next two, "famine and nakedness," go naturally together, as
do "danger and sword." Possibly "sword" is placed last because Paul is thinking
of execution. For Roman citizens capital punishment took the form of beheading (cf. 13.4).[37] Obviously execution would be the last woe a Christian would
face in this life. None of these things can separate the believer from the love of
God received in Christ.

V. 36 quotes Ps. 44.22 (LXX 43.23) with much the same point as one part
of 1 Corinthans 10: no danger that overcomes Christians is anything new or un-

---

had some other view of apostasy than was the dominant one in early Judaism. But see J. M.
Gundry Volf, *Paul and Perseverance: Staying In and Falling Away* (Louisville: Westminster/
J. Knox, 1990). Methinks she doth protest too much. The warning in 1 Tim. 1.19 to Timothy,
coupled with living examples of those who had shipwrecked their faith, is a real one. It is significant that the author of this lengthy monograph does not even properly deal with this text,
nor with similar texts, such as Heb. 6.4-6, which seem to have come out of the Pauline circle
as well. The point that must be stressed about 1 Tim. 1.19 is this — one cannot make shipwreck of a faith one does not have, and Paul or the later Paulinist would not speak of making
shipwreck of a false faith while urging Timothy to keep that same faith.

35. On the use of Psalm 110 here and elsewhere concerning Christ see D. M. Hay, *Glory
at the Right Hand: Psalm 110 in Early Christianity* (Nashville: Abingdon, 1973).

36. Käsemann, *Romans*, pp. 248-49.

37. See pp. 313-16 below.

expected for the people of God. 2 Maccabees 7 also uses this psalm verse of the martyrdom of a mother and her seven sons. *Hoti* functions here simply as a colon to introduce the quotation.

V. 37 makes evident that Paul expects his listeners to experience many if not all these calamities, and to triumph over and through them. "But in all these circumstances we triumph gloriously through the loving one." *En toutois pasin* may be a Hebraism meaning "in spite of all these things,"[38] but more probably it just means "in all these things."

In v. 38 Paul states a firm conviction that nothing in all creation (*ktisis,* again referring to subhuman creatures and nature) can separate Christians from God's love. The stringing together of Jesus' titles and names, "Christ Jesus our Lord," is also found in 5.1. Believers truly know the love of God only in Christ Jesus and experience it in him. No natural or supernatural malevolent forces, even if they are capable of taking the believer's life, can separate the believer from God's love. Indeed, to take a believer's life is to send him directly into the presence of Jesus. No experience, present or potential, can separate the believer from God's love. Angels and archangels perhaps represent here the cosmic forces ranged against the believer (see Eph. 6.12). It is possible, however, that "powers or rulers" refers to earthly authorities before whom the Roman Christians might be brought. "Height" and "depth" were used traditionally of things above the sky and beneath the earth.

There is one item that Paul does not include in the list of things that cannot separate the believer from God's love, namely the believer himself. Paul's point is that no forces, experiences, or events external to the believer's own heart or mind can get in the way of God's love. Thus the believer has nothing to fear from the world in this respect. The scope of God's love is greater than the scope of the world's powers, whether natural or supernatural. This is a great reassurance indeed and is meant, as is this whole passage, to bolster the idea of the perseverance of the saints and their salvation so long as they rest in the firm grasp of the hand of the Almighty.

Note the hymnic character of this entire passage. Paul has gone into a doxological mode here at the end of his positive arguments.

> The Scholastics dispute whether a righteous person could lose his virtues, since Paul says: "Who shall separate us from the love?" as if he wanted to say: "In what way could we lose our love?" They thought that love should be interpreted of our virtues, that is, the love with which we love God. But this is unsound interpretation and must be rejected. It is certain that saints can fall and lose the Holy Spirit, faith, and love, as the prophet Nathan condemns David on account of adultery.

38. Cranfield, *Romans,* 1:440-41.

Why then does he say that the love of God is everlasting? I answer: As the evangelical promise is perpetual and valid, but in such a way that it requires faith, so Paul is here speaking to believers, as if he said: "As long as you believe, as long as you do not fall from faith, it is most certain that the love of God toward you is in force." The meaning is this: Without doubt the love with which God loves us is always valid, firm, and certain for the believer. . . . Others have twisted this to refer to predestination, but there is no need to turn to that in this passage, for he is speaking of our victory. . . . The meaning will be simple and plain if it is understood of believers.[39]

We might not endorse all that Melanchthon has said here, though he is right that this passage is about those who are already Christians and that Paul believed in the dangers of apostasy. Even within the Reformed, in this case Lutheran, tradition of interpretation, there were varying views on controversial texts like those we find in Romans 7 and 8.

Bridging the Horizons

Picture a father crossing a busy highway with a small child by his side holding his hand quite firmly. The father has good judgment and he is capable of shielding the child from any calamity and protecting him from any outside force harming him as they make their way across the highway. The one eventuality the father cannot prevent is the child being willful and wrenching himself free from his grasp, running off, and being struck by a vehicle. This it seems to me is an adequate parable of what Paul means in the last powerful paragraph of this argument. God has a firm loving grip on the believer, and no outside force can separate the believer from God and God's love. A believer cannot lose his or her salvation as one might lose one's glasses. But by willful rebellion there is the possibility of apostasy, of making shipwreck of one's faith. The Good News, then, is that one cannot lose or misplace one's salvation or simply wander away by accident. Indeed, only by an enormous willful effort could one throw it away. Such is the loving grasp God has on his children.

39. P. Melanchthon, *Commentary on Romans*, trans. F. Kramer (St. Louis: Concordia, 1992), pp. 183-84.

Argument Nine — 9.1–11.36:
God's Justice and Israel's Future

The argument in chs. 9–11 is of a piece, though it has several parts to it.[1] Paul will answer a series of rhetorical questions centered on whether God will keep his word to Israel or has abandoned his first chosen people. The issue of the actual status and standing of Gentiles in the people of God in relationship to Jews is also addressed at some length. This means as well that the subject that Paul has been dealing with since the very beginning of this epistle is indeed God's justice and righteousness insofar as it has a bearing on human fate, either positively or negatively, by way of either commendation or condemnation, salvation or damnation. The discussion is theocentric, and only after that anthropocentric, but part of that theocentrism is Paul's focus on Christ, and part of the anthropocentrism is a focus on Jew and Gentile united in Christ and not just humanity in general.

Paul will once again use the diatribe style and personification to present his case.[2]

> The section is in some ways the most rhetorically striking of the entire letter, and makes extensive use of virtually the entire range of techniques of the podium and the classroom. There will be rhetorical questions (9.14, 21; 10.8, 14-15, 18, 19; 11.1, 7, 11); there will be dramatic intervention by and argument with imaginary opponents (9.14-21), there will be protestations of the author's own passion and sincerity (9.1-4; 10.1; 11.1); there will be direct

---

1. On this entire section, and on Paul's view of Israel in general, see my *Jesus, Paul, and the End of the World: A Comparative Study in New Testament Eschatology* (Downers Grove: InterVarsity, 1992), pp. 99-128. On the analysis of this material through the ages see C. Talbert, *Romans* (Macon: Smyth and Helwys, 2002), pp. 240-45.

2. On these rhetorical devices see pp. 180-84 above.

appeal to the hearers (11.13, 25); there will be antithesis and parallelism (11.15-16); there will be illustrative parable (11.16-21); and there will be extensive citation of authority — naturally in view of the subject, scriptural authority.[3]

It is a very serious error indeed to treat these chapters as an afterthought, unrelated discussion, or mere appendix to chs. 1–8.[4] It is nearer to the mark to call it the climax of the theological portion of the letter.[5] It is an argument for the defense of both God and of Israel and as such is meant to refute certain assumptions Gentiles in Rome seem to be making about God and Israel, and about Israel's future. Paul takes on the role of the witness for the defense, beginning with the oath in 9.1-5 and then proceeding with his testimony. He follows the normal rhetorical convention that suggests that emotion should be displayed at the outset and at the conclusion of a speech or argument, in the first instance to draw on the sympathies of the audience, and so draw them into the discussion, and at the end to reinforce and seal the discussion in the hearts of the audience. So 9.1-5 and 11.33-36 have pathos and involve an appeal to the emotions.[6]

The argument has three basic parts: 9.6-29; 9.30–10.21; and 11.1-32. The first and third parts address the question whether God's Word or plan or character has failed: Is God still faithful to Israel? We have here an essentially theocentric argument, though, as the middle part of the argument shows, the focus can shift to Israel and its failures and future, so that both God and Israel are defended and misconceptions about both and about God's salvation plan are refuted.

From a rhetorical viewpoint this section of the letter is part of a *refutatio*. Paul is refuting certain ideas and arguments apparently held by Gentile believers in Rome, or at least Paul fears that they hold such views of Jews and Jewish Christians. It is hard to tell whether he is forestalling potential problems based on some rumors or reports he has heard or is actually trying to correct an existing problem. In light of chs. 14–15, it would appear that what Paul deals with here is far from hypothetical.

This section of Romans is the most Scripture-saturated in the whole letter. In fact, 31% of the Scripture citations in the undisputed Pauline letters are

3. C. Bryan, *A Preface to Romans: Notes on the Epistle and Its Literary and Cultural Setting* (Oxford: Oxford University Press, 2000), p. 160.

4. See C. H. Dodd, *The Epistle of Paul to the Romans* (London: Collins Fontana, 1959), pp. 161-63.

5. See J. A. Fitzmyer, *Romans* (New York: Doubleday, 1992), p. 541; K. Stendahl, *Paul among Jews and Gentiles* (Philadelphia: Fortress, 1977), p. 4; N. T. Wright, *The Climax of the Covenant* (Edinburgh: Clark, 1992), p. 234.

6. E. Käsemann, *Commentary on Romans* (Grand Rapids: Eerdmans, 1980), pp. 257-60.

in Romans 9–11, some 28 citations or partial citations in all. Paul needs all the support he can muster in his argument against perceptions of Jewish Christians that Gentile Christians would be inclined toward, and so he resorts to inartificial proofs based on the commonly shared authority known as Scripture. He cannot appeal to experience here, except in passing to his own at the outset of his argument. The argument here is in fact dependent on the earlier discussions in chs. 2–3 with the Jewish teacher. Some of the questions raised, for example, in 3.1-9 are fully answered only in 9.6-29.[7]

Paul often refers to himself in the first person in chs. 9–11. While he does so only seven times in 1.18–8.39, and two of these are asides (3.5; 6.19), in chs. 9–11 the first person refers to Paul some twenty-seven times. He is speaking not only personally here, but also as a Jew on behalf of other Jews, making a personal appeal to Gentiles.[8]

In any rhetorical discourse there is a twofold division that can readily be made in the arguments. The *probatio* involves the arguments for a case, and the *refutatio* provides arguments against the opponent's case. It was indeed the normal procedure to save the *refutatio* for later in the discourse (Quintilian, *Instit. Or.* 5.13.1), unless one's argument were forensic, making refutation necessary immediately. But Paul's argument is deliberative, and he has deliberately saved the major bone of contention and division until the end of his theological arguments, well after he has established rapport with the audience and led them through a series of arguments they are likely to consent to, or at least be favorably disposed to on the whole. Furthermore, we are probably dealing here with what Quintilian calls *prolepsis,* an anticipatory rebuttal which forestalls certain arguments Paul might expect to hear when he gets to Rome (see *Instit. Or.* 4.1.49-50).

Quintilian tells us that generally speaking no strong appeal to the emotions of the audience is made in a refutation, though the author may show his own emotions (5.13.2). The principles of argumentation are to be the same as in the preceding *probatio,* using the same ideas, thoughts, figures, and topics. Invention is not at a premium in a refutation; rather rebuttal is. So Paul amplifies here on the already discussed topic of God's justice and righteousness as it has bearing on the people of God, both Jewish and Gentile, and their relationship to God. Paul has an advantage normal defenders did not, namely that he was able to prepare his defense after reflection, whereas normally a *refutatio* must be conjured up on the spot.

One of the parts of a defense that could be used, if absolutely necessary,

7. See, rightly, N. T. Wright, "Romans," in *The New Interpreter's Bible,* vol. 10 (Nashville: Abingdon, 2002), p. 635.

8. See S. K. Stowers, *A Rereading of Romans: Justice, Jews, and Gentiles* (New Haven: Yale University Press, 1994), p. 292.

was pleas for mercy (*Instit. Or.* 5.13.4-5). It is not an accident that the subjects of God, who is the judge in all these matters, and God's mercy come up prominently in this section of Paul's discourse, especially at the end of the argument in ch. 11. The point will be that all stand only on the basis of God's mercy and grace. Thus, while Paul is defending Jews and Jewish Christians to his largely Gentile audience, he is also reminding those Gentiles that the final judge of such matters is not they but God, and all must rely on God's mercy if salvation is to be had by anyone. Notice what Quintilian says: "When pleading before an emperor or any other person who has power either to acquit or condemn, it is incumbent on us to urge that, while our client has committed an offense that deserves the death penalty, it is still the duty of a merciful judge to spare him despite his sins" (5.13.6).

Quintilian stresses that since this is ultimately a matter for the judge and not for the adversary "we shall have to use the deliberative rather than the forensic style" (5.13.6). So we see that a *refutatio* and a deliberative argument do indeed mix, and can be part of a larger deliberative discourse. The goal, Quintilian says, is to get the judge to focus on the glory that will accrue to him for clemency. The final peroration to this argument, especially in 11.31-36, which refers to the mercy, judgments, and glory of God the judge, is exactly what we would expect in the conclusion of a *refutatio*. Paul knows very well what he is doing, and he is following the form of a proper *refutatio* very clearly.

In terms of rhetorical strategy, in a *refutatio* one could dispose of the opponent's arguments en masse, if they were weak, but singly if they had some individual strength (*Instit. Or.* 5.13.11). Paul follows the latter course, which shows that he knows he is dealing with some substantial objections to his views. "The cumulative force of these arguments is damaging. But if you refute them singly, the flame which derived its strength from the mass of fuel will die down as soon as the material which fed it is separated, just as if we divert a great stream into a number of channels we may cross it where we will" (*Instit. Or.* 5.13.13).

The passion of Paul's words in chs. 9-11 reflects the urgency of the matter as he plans to go to Rome. There must be some semblance of concord between Jewish and Gentile believers in Rome before he gets there. He is thus exercised to remove the impediments to such unity here and in the following ethical sections of the discourse. Chs. 1–8 have provided the theological foundation (salvation is by grace through faith for all, for all have sinned and fallen short of God's glory) for the argument here and those that follow in chs. 12–15. But now Paul has arrived at the real matters at issue, and he will deal with them seriatim.

Finally, one needs to not overlook that we are dealing with the diatribe form of debate or discussion here once more. This explains the inordinate number of questions, including rhetorical questions which provide some of the division markers of the discourse (cf. 9.14, 19-22; 10.14-15, 18-19; 11.15), and are usually followed by declarative answers and then scriptural support.[9] Paul seeks to justify the ways of God to his largely Gentile audience, showing how God's current dealings with Jews, including non-Christian Jews, and also with Gentiles are fully consistent with what Scripture says and what Paul preaches.[10]

I speak the truth in Christ, I am not lying, my conscience bears witness with me in the Holy Spirit, that it is a great sorrow to me, and a continual pain in my heart. For I could pray to be "anathema," I myself [separated] from Christ for my brothers and kinsmen according to the flesh. Who are Israelites, whose are the sonship, and the glory, and the covenants,[11] and the legislation of the Law, and the worship, and the promises, whose are the fathers, and from whom came the Christ, according to the flesh, [but] above all who is God, blessed unto all eternity, amen.

But it is not, of course, that the Word of God has failed, for not all of those who are from Israel are Israel. Nor is it that the seed of Abraham are all children, but "In Isaac will be acknowledged [those] who are your seed." That is, it is not the children of the flesh that are the children of God, but the children of promise are reckoned as seed. For the word of promise is thus: "According to this time I will come, and there will be a son for Sarah." But not only so, but also Rebecca from one of our fathers had on a marriage bed Isaac. For not yet bearing children, nor do they do what is good or bad, in order that the plan/purpose of God be preserved/remain according to free choice, not from works but from the calling told to her that "the older will be slave to the younger," just as it is written "Jacob I loved, but Esau I hated."

What then shall we say? Is there not injustice with God? Let it not happen! For to Moses he says "I will have mercy on whom I will have mercy, and I will pity whom I will pity." So then it is not the one who wills, nor the one who runs, but it is of the mercy of God. For the Scripture says to Pharaoh: "Unto this same thing I raised you up, thus to show in you my power, and thus proclaim my name in all the earth." So then whomever he wills, he has mercy on, but whomever he wills he hardens.

---

9. See the detailed analysis of the structure in J. W. Aageson, "Scripture and Structure in the Development of the Argument in Romans 9–11," *CBQ* 48 (1986): 265-89, especially pp. 286-87.

10. See my discussion of this in *Jesus, Paul, and the End of the World*, pp. 111-25.

11. Some good manuscripts (𝔓46, B, D, and others) have the singular, "covenant," but the plural is even better attested (ℵ, C, K, and many others). It is certainly more likely that a plural would be altered to a singular, than vice versa, because the plural might be thought to involve theological difficulties. See B. M. Metzger, *A Textual Commentary on the Greek New Testament* (3rd ed.; London: United Bible Societies, 1971), p. 459. In fact, however, Paul does speak of covenants plural, as Gal. 4.24 shows. He does not believe that God gave only one covenant in several administrations or forms. Indeed, he sees the Mosaic covenant as an interim one between the Abrahamic and new covenants, with the latter being the fulfillment or completion of the Abrahamic covenant.

You will say to me then "Why then is there any blame? For can anyone resist his will?" "O mere human being, who are you to answer back to God?" Does the molded one/creature say to the Molder/Creator "Why have you made me thus?" Does not the potter of the clay have power/authority to make from his lump on the one hand the vessel unto honor, and on the other hand one unto dishonor? But if God wishing to show wrath and make known his power endures with much patience the vessels of wrath who have been preparing themselves for destruction, and in order that he might make known the wealth of his glory upon the vessels of mercy who are prepared beforehand unto glory, even us whom he also called, not only from the Jews, but also from the Gentiles/nations, as it even says in Hosea: "I shall call those not my people 'My people,' and she who is not my beloved 'beloved.' And it will be in the place where it was said 'You are not my people,' there you will be called children of the living God." But Isaiah cries out for Israel: "But even if the number of the sons of Israel be as sand of the sea, those left behind/the remnant will be saved.[12] *For the Lord will make upon the earth the Word of accomplishment and of limitations," and just as Isaiah foretold, "Unless the Lord Sabaoth left to us seed, we would become as Sodom and become like Gomorrah."*

What then shall we say? That Gentiles who did not pursue righteousness attained righteousness, but righteousness that comes from faith? But Israel pursuing a law of righteousness in the Law did not attain it? Why is this? Because [it was pursued] not from faith but as from works? They struck the stone of stumbling just as it is written "Behold, I put a stone of stumbling in Zion and a rock of scandal/offense, and the one believing in him will not be put to shame."

Brothers, the deep desire of my heart, and my petition to God for them is for salvation. For I bear witness about them, that they have a zeal for God, but it is not according to knowledge. For failing to recognize the righteousness of God, and seeking to establish the same, they did not submit to the righteousness of God. For Christ is the end of the Law for righteousness, unto all those believing. For Moses writes about the righteousness from the Law, that "The person doing it shall live in it." But the Righteousness from Faith speaks thus: "Do not say in your heart, 'Which one will ascend into heaven?' (that is, to bring Christ down) or 'Who will descend into the abyss?' (that is, to bring Christ up from the dead)." But what does it say: "The word is near you, in your mouth and in your heart." This is the word of faith which we preach, for if you confess with your mouth the Lord Jesus and believe in your heart that God raised him from the dead, you will be saved. For you believe in your heart unto righteousness, but you confess with your lips unto salvation. For the Scripture says: "All those believing in him shall not be put to shame."

---

12. As R. B. Hays, *Echoes of Scripture in the Letters of Paul* (New Haven: Yale University Press, 1989), p. 68, points out, this citation from Isaiah is meant to be hopeful, and there is no justification for inserting the word "only" before the word "remnant" in the text. No Greek manuscript supports such an insertion.

For there is no distinction of Jews and Gentiles, for the same [is] Lord of all, of riches unto all who call upon him, for "all whoever call upon the name of the Lord, shall be saved."

How then shall they call unto one in whom they have not believed? But how shall they believe in whom they have not heard? And how shall they hear without preaching? But how can they preach unless they have been sent? Just as it is written: "How beautiful the feet of those proclaiming the good." But not all obey the proclamation. For Isaiah says "Lord, who has believed our oral report?" For faith [comes] from hearing, but hearing through the word of Christ. But I say, have they not heard? Certainly they did. "Unto all the earth, the voice of them has gone out, and unto the limits of the inhabited world the word of them." But I say, "Did Israel not understand?" First of all, Moses says: "I myself will make you jealous of those not a people. A people without understanding will excite your anger." But Isaiah shows greater daring and says: "I was found among those who did not seek me, and I became visible to those who did not inquire after me." But to Israel he says: "The whole day I stretched out my hand to a disobedient and resistant people."

God has not pushed away/rejected his people, has he? Let it never happen! For I also am an Israelite, from the seed of Abraham, the tribe of Benjamin. God has not rejected his people whom he foreknew. Or do you not know in Elijah what the Scripture says, how he pleaded to God against Israel: "Lord, they have killed your prophets, they have dug up your altars, and I alone am left remaining, and they seek my life"? And what does the oracle say to him? "I have left behind/remaining for myself seven thousand men who have not bent the knee to Baal." So then in the present time there is a remainder according to the free choice of grace. But if it is from grace, then it is no longer from works since grace is no longer grace [under those circumstances]. What then? Israel sought it, but did not attain it, but the chosen attained it. But the rest were hardened, just as it is written: "God gave them a spirit of torpor, eyes of those not to see, and ears of those not to hear, until the present day." And David says: "May their table turn into a snare and a trap, and into a scandal and a requital to them, May their eyes be darkened so as not to see, and their backs always be bent over."

I say then, have they stumbled so as to fall? Let it never happen! But their false step/trespass was the salvation of the Gentiles, unto the making of them jealous. But if their misstep meant riches for the world, and their failure riches for the Gentiles, how much more will the full number of them mean?

But to you Gentiles I am speaking. I, so far as I myself am apostle of the Gentiles, I am honoring my ministry, so somehow I might make jealous the flesh [kin] of mine and might save some from among them. For if their rejection [means] the reconciliation of the world, what will their acceptance [mean] if not life from the dead? But if the first fruits are holy, then also the mass of them, and if the root is holy, so also the branches.

But if some of the branches were broken off, but you a wild olive branch were *grafted on in them and are fellow sharers in the root, of its sap of the olive tree,*[13] *do not exult over the branches. But if you individually exult, bear in mind that you do not carry the root, but the root carries you. You will say then, "Branches were broken off in order that I might be grafted in." Very well, they were broken off for unbelief, but you remain standing by faith. Do not preoccupy yourself with thoughts of grandeur, but rather be afraid. For if God did not spare the natural branches, is it likely that he will spare you? Behold then both the kindness and the severity of God. Upon the falling on the one hand severity, but upon you on the other hand kindness, if you individually persevere in the kindness, otherwise you individually will also be cut off. And those others, if they do not persevere in unbelief they will be grafted back in. For God is able to graft them back in again. For if you from the against nature wild olive tree were cut out and contrary to nature grafted into the cultivated olive tree, how much more those who are according to nature might be re-engrafted by the same mercy.*

For I do not wish you to be ignorant, brothers, of this mystery, in order that you might not be wise in yourselves, because a hardening in part has happened to Israel until the fullness of the Gentiles comes in, and thus in the same manner all Israel will be saved as it is written: "The Deliverer will come from Zion. He will turn away the ungodliness from Jacob, and this to them shall be my covenant, when I take away their sins." On the one hand they are enemies according to the gospel because of you, but on the other hand according to the election they are beloved because of the fathers. For the grace gift and the call of God are irrevocable. For in the same way once you were disobedient to God, but now you have found mercy because of their disobedience. Thus also those now have disobeyed on account of mercy shown to you in order also that they might receive mercy.[14] *For God shut up all of those unto disobedience in order that he might have mercy on all. Oh the depths of the riches and wisdom and knowledge of God, how inscrutable his judgments and untraceable his ways. For "who has known the mind of the Lord? Or who has been his adviser? Or who gave to him beforehand, so as even to have it repaid to him?" Because from him and through him and unto him are all things. Glory to him unto eternity. Amen.*

---

13. C. K. Barrett, *A Commentary on the Epistle to the Romans* (Peabody: Hendrickson, 1991), p. 196, suggests the translation "in the rich root of the olive tree," which is possible. The phrase is difficult and some mss. have "of the richness of the olive tree" (𝔭46, D, G, old Latin, Irenaeus); others have "of the root and of the richness of the olive tree" (A, Vulgate). These are likely later simplifications.

14. Some manuscripts (ℵ, B, D) add a *nyn* modifying the verb "receive mercy," failing to notice the eschatological nature of Paul's argument here. But the "now" is omitted by 𝔭46, A, some Western manuscripts, and important Church Fathers such as Chrysostom, Origen, Theodoret, and others. On balance the "now" is probably a later addition. See Metzger, *A Textual Commentary,* p. 465.

Though it was not the intended effect of Paul's discourse up to this juncture, most everything that Paul has said up to now in one way or another raises
questions about the status of Israel, especially if righteousness or being set right
is obtained through faith in Christ and if Israel by and large has rejected Christ.
It is understandable how Gentiles might conclude that God has forsaken his
first chosen people for another one, or at the least that Jews no longer have any
privileged status since God is impartial and the people of God are to be defined
as Jew and Gentile united in Christ, and furthermore since all come to God on
the basis of grace and faith.

Paul then writes chs. 9–11 to refute certain wrong deductions about the
status of Jews and God's relationship to them, and also about whether God
might renege on his promises to them, which would mean that the Word of
God had failed or was unreliable. There are profound issues of theodicy, the
character of God, ecclesiology, election, and the truthfulness and trustworthiness of Scripture involved in this discussion. This section is the climax of Paul's
theological discussion, not a mere appendix to that discussion. Indeed, this section builds on what was said in chs. 1–3 about God's impartiality and faithfulness, in ch. 4 about Abraham, and in ch. 8 about predestination and the final
goal and outcome of God's salvation plan. Failure to see the eschatological drift
of this discussion has often led to misunderstanding about the future of Israel
and the nature of election.

Another of the major issues this section of Romans raises is: Who is Paul
discussing in this section? All Jews? All Jews who have rejected Christ? All Jews
who have accepted Christ? That Jews are the focus of the discussion is not really
a matter of scholarly debate. That is accepted almost without question. Once
one begins to think about salvation by grace through faith and the majority of
Jews, who do not believe in Jesus, one has a theological problem.[15] If God has
abandoned his plan for Israel, what sure and certain hope can Gentiles have in
regard to the future? If God's love for Israel has ceased, is it really true that
nothing can separate the believer from the love of God? Some of the pitfalls
that need to be avoided in the interpretation of this section of Romans have
been ably summed up by N. T. Wright:

> The controversial revolution in Pauline studies that produced the so-called
> new perspective of the 1970s shifted attention away from late-medieval
> soul-searchings and anxieties about salvation, and placed it instead on (in
> Sanders's phrase) the comparison of patterns of religion. It was a self-
> consciously post-Holocaust project, aimed not least at reminding Paul's
> readers of his essential Jewishness. But this should not blind us to the fact

15. C. E. B. Cranfield, *A Critical and Exegetical Commentary on the Epistle to the
Romans* (ICC; Edinburgh: Clark, 1975-79), 2:445-50.

that, precisely as a Jewish person, Paul begins this section with grief and sorrow — because he sees his fellow Jews rejecting the Gospel of their own Messiah. Paul is not writing a post-Enlightenment treatise about how all religions are basically the same; nor is he writing an essay on a modified version of the same project — namely how the one God has made two equally valid covenants, one with Jews and the other with Christians. Nor is he writing a postmodern tract about how everyone must tell their own story and find their own way.[16] . . . these chapters remain profoundly Christian — that is, centered on Jesus as Messiah and Lord. Paul does not accommodate himself to our agendas and expectations any more than he did to those of his contemporaries.[17]

Once again in this section we are confronted with the issue of God's righteousness, just as we were at the outset of Paul's discourse in ch. 1, and by righteousness Paul means a variety of things, here especially God's being true to his Word, and so his faithfulness, even in spite of his people's unfaithfulness and rejection of Jesus as Messiah. Vindication is at issue here, God vindicating his own Word, as well as delivering or saving his own people. Their rejection of Jesus has prompted something of a crisis of hope, if not a crisis of faith in someone like Paul, and so he must wrestle through it to an answer about God, about God's salvation plan, and about the future of his own kin according to the flesh, his fellow Jews. But on top of all that, he has to deal with Gentiles in Rome who apparently believe that God is indeed a supersessionist, having by and large replaced his first chosen people with another one. Paul will and must deny what appears to be the case, and he must undercut Gentile hubris and make clear the Gentile Christians' indebtedness to the "root" and their status as grafted-in "wild olive branches."

Paul is not introducing the "Israel" question for the first time in ch. 9–11. He has already had a dialogue with a Jewish teacher in chs. 2–3, and already in 2.28-29 he has raised the question of who is a true Jew. He has already made clear that he operates with a remnant theology. Wright stresses that what actually happens in 9.6–10.21 with its plethora of OT references is a retelling of Is-

---

16. In these last two sentences Wright is critiquing Stendahl, and also J. G. Gager, *The Origins of Anti-Semitism* (New York: Oxford University Press, 1983), and L. Gaston, *Paul and the Torah* (Vancouver: University of British Columbia, 1987). A decisive rebuttal to the view that Paul opts for a two covenant/two ways of salvation theory can be found in H. Räisänen, "Paul, God and Israel: Romans 9–11 in Recent Research," in *The Social World of Formative Christianity and Judaism: Essays in Tribute to Howard Clark Kee,* ed. J. Neusner et al. (Philadelphia: Fortress, 1988), pp. 178-206. Cf. E. E. Johnson, "Romans 9–11: The Faithfulness and Impartiality of God," in *Pauline Theology,* ed. D. M. Hay and E. E. Johnson, vol. 3: *Romans* (Minneapolis: Fortress, 1995), pp. 211-39.

17. Wright, "Romans," p. 621.

rael's story from the time of Abraham until Paul's own day.[18] But it is more than that.

Paul is using the scriptural references and stories to refute a bad theology, held, even if not openly espoused, by the majority of his audience, who are Gentiles. The scriptural references prove two things, that God is faithful to his Word and that God has historical purposes that have always taken into account Israel's faith and unfaithfulness, promises made to Israel, and Israel's apostasy. God was not taken by surprise when most Jews rejected Jesus.

The discussion of election in chs. 9–11 is a discussion of corporate election, in the midst of which there are individual rejection by some and selection for historical purposes of others. In other words, Paul will give equal emphasis to election and apostasy in his discussion. This is especially clear when he starts addreessing a singular "you" in ch. 10. To those Gentile Christians who are already saved he warns sternly that they could be broken off in a heartbeat if they choose to become unfaithful and unbelieving. Neither God's foreknowledge nor corporate election prevents individuals from becoming unfaithful and committing apostasy. If it happened in Israel, it can happen to Gentile believers as well if they do not watch out. In other words, there is nothing in this discussion of election that suggests that the election results are rigged in advance for particular individuals or that Paul was an early advocate of "once saved always saved" if by that one means that apostasy is impossible for those truly chosen by God.

Rather, Paul's views on predestination, election, the remnant, apostasy, and salvation fall within the parameters of such discussions in early Judaism, rather than within the framework of later Augustinian, Lutheran, and Calvinist discussions of the matter. Those early Jewish discussions make full allowance for both corporate election and the meaningful choices of individuals who may commit apostasy and opt out of the people of God.

A Closer Look: Predestination, Election, Salvation, and Apostasy in Early Judaism

Paul's concepts of election, salvation, predestination, and the like are not examples of creatio ex nihilo. He is writing out of and into a rather specific social and historical context. Some of the vocabulary he uses, such as the verb *proorizō*, is not found in previous Greek literature, including the LXX. The related term *proginōskō*, to foreknow, is found, for example, in Philo *De Somnis* 1.2, and the concept and term are also present in Wis. 8.8. OT references to God knowing someone or his people, that is, to

---

18. Wright, "Romans," p. 622.

his inclination toward or love for them, sometimes refer to a concept of election (Amos 3.2; Deut. 9.24; Exod. 33.12, 17; Gen. 18.19; Deut. 34.10), and such passages lie in the background here.

It is, however, a mistake to draw conclusions about Paul's views on these matters just on the basis of word studies of certain key terms in earlier literature, not least because Paul has reenvisioned whatever he believed as a non-Christian Jew about such matters in the light of Christ and his new-found eschatological beliefs, since he believes that the Christ-event has inaugurated the end times. Furthermore, the language about God knowing and determining in the OT does not stand in isolation, but needs to be correlated with references to Israel's apostasy, rebellion, and falling away. Such references can be found especially in the prophetic literature (e.g., Hosea) but also in later Jewish literature such as *Jubilees* 23.14-23, where, as in Paul, apostasy is connected with certain eschatological and apocalyptic ideas.

The very texts that stress God's sovereignty also stress viable human choice in moral matters. For example, Sirach 15.11-17: "Say not it was the Lord's fault that I fell away . . . say not, He led me astray. . . . He made man from the beginning, and left him to his own counsel." *Psalms of Solomon* 9.4: "Our deeds are in the choice and power of our soul, to do righteousness and iniquity in the works of our hands." 4 Esdras 8.55-56: "Ask no more about the multitude of those who perish . . . for they themselves, having freedom given them, spurned the Most High and despised his law and abandoned his ways."

In the rabbinic literature, there is the famous saying of Rabbi Akiba: "Everything is foreseen (by God), and freedom of choice is given (to man), and the world is judged with goodness, and all depends on the preponderance of (good or ill) doing" (Mishnah *Pirke Abot* 3.15). Simeon ben Azzai, a younger contemporary of Akiba, says the same thing *(Mekilta* on Exod. 15.26). The usual rabbinic prooftexts for freedom of moral choice are Prov. 3.34 and Exod. 15.26. R. Hanina says "Everything is in the power of Heaven, except the reverence of Heaven (i.e., of God)" (Babylonian Talmud *Berakoth* 33b). Especially telling is Babylonian Talmud *Niddah* 16b, which says that God in his providence determines beforehand what a person will be and what will befall him but not whether he will be godless or godly, wicked or righteous. G. F. Moore summarizes the evidence from early Judaism: "religion is the one thing that God *requires* of man; He does not *constrain* him to it. It is unnecessary to multiply examples further; there are no dissentient voices."[19] This is perhaps a bit of an overstatement, as an examination of Josephus's account of the various sects of Judaism shows.

Josephus indicates that determinism or fate or predestination was an issue very much in dispute in early Judaism, and the dispute was chiefly between Paul's former sect, the Pharisees, and other dominant opinions. He says that the Essenes exempted nothing from the control of destiny or foreordination, that the Sadducees took the opposite end of the spectrum, denying that there was any such thing as foreordination, and that the Pharisees held the middle ground, namely that some

---

19. G. F. Moore, *Judaism*, vol. 1 (New York: Schocken, 1971), p. 456.

things but not all are the work of divine destining. Some things, such as whether one responds to divine grace or continues in one's faith, are within the control of human beings. Yet Josephus recognizes that there is some tension within Pharisaic thought on this matter. For example, *War* 2.8, 14 says that the Pharisees ascribe everything to destiny and to God, except that to do right or wrong lies mainly in the hands of human beings, though God's hand can be seen as an auxiliary force involved in these choices as well. There is a fuller statement of the matter in *Antiquities* 18.1-3: "While the Pharisees hold that all things are brought about by destiny, they do not deprive the human will of its own impulse to do them, it having pleased God that there should be a cooperation and that to the deliberation (of God) about destiny, humans in the case of the one who wills should assent, with virtue or wickedness."

The relevance of Pharisaism for what Paul says should be clear. He was a Pharisee before his Damascus Road experience, and he affirms both God's foreknowledge, his destining of some things, and human responsibility for sin and the awful possibility of radical rebellion against God by a believer, namely apostasy. It is not an either/or matter for Paul when it comes to viable human moral choices and God's sovereignty, but rather both/and. This means that, while he certainly affirms that all human beings are sinful and have sinned and fall short of God's highest and best for them, he also affirms the possibility by grace and through faith to avoid sin. He stands directly in the line of the early Jewish discussion by affirming that in the most important matter of all — one's salvation and possibility of virtuous behavior, humans must respond to the initiative of grace freely, and continue to do so freely after initially becoming a new creature in Christ. The divine and human wills are both involved in such matters.

There is nothing quite like Luther's later concept of *simul justus et peccator* in Paul, nor would we expect one from early Jewish discussion of such matters. There is however the issue of the "inclination to do evil" which is affirmed in various places in the early Jewish literature, and also in Paul. Paul speaks of it at some length in Galatians 5 and sees the work of the Spirit as more powerful and as pulling a person in the opposite direction. The discussion Paul is furthering there goes back at least to Jesus ben Sira, who stresses that God is absolutely not the author or destiner of human sin: "Do not say, 'From God is my transgression,' for that which God hates, he does not make. Do not say, 'He . . . made me to stumble,' for there is no need to do that to evil men. . . . God created humans from the beginning and placed them in the hand of their own inclinations (*yetzer*)" (Sir. 15.11-14). There is also the notion of the transmission of such an inclination to do evil from Adam to his offspring in 4 Ezra 3.21: "For the first Adam clothed himself with an evil heart and transgressed and was overcome and not only so but also all who were begotten from him." The cure for the evil impulse is said in one source to be repentance.[20]

But there is also an affirmation in some early Jewish literature of an inclination

20. See the discussion by W. D. Davies, *Paul and Rabbinic Judaism* (New York: Harper, 1948), p. 23.

to do good within fallen human beings: "Therefore if the soul takes pleasure in the good impulse, all its actions are in righteousness" (*Testament of Asher* 1.6). Paul does not talk about a natural impulse toward good in humans, but he does talk about the work of the Spirit, which in his view is even more powerful. But there is an eschatological tradition that bears repeating as well: "In the world to come God will bring the evil impulse and slay it in the presence of the righteous and the wicked" (Babylonian Talmud *Sukkoth* 52a). This may be part of what Paul affirms about the new creature in Christ in texts like 2 Cor. 5.17, or at least he believes that in the Christian life, "greater is he who is in you" than the inclination to sin.

In sum, it is important to set Paul in the context of early Jewish, especially early Pharisaic, discussions of such matters, to the extent that we can discern them. When we do so we find that Paul sounds rather like various of his contemporaries who certainly affirm divine providence and election and destining and also human sin and viable human choice, especially about the crucial matters of salvation and moral rectitude. We will have more to say about Paul's concept of election and salvation as we discuss particular texts.

The tour-de-force argument in chs. 9–11 begins abruptly with Paul swearing an oath. The rhetorically astute audience would recognize this as a prelude to a specific kind of argument, namely one having to do with a testimony of witnesses, Paul as witness and Scripture as witness, as well as God himself speaking through the divine Word. Paul must rebut the notions that God has forsaken his first chosen people, that the Word of God has failed, and that Israel has stumbled so as to be permanently lost. Underlying these rebuttals is the refutation of the assumption of Gentile superiority in the Roman church. Here as elsewhere Paul is seeking to level the playing field so as to make clear that all are "in" the people of God by God's mercy and grace and that no one has a right to boast in his or her own accomplishments. He also wants to make clear that the salvation of Israel is still part of God's game-plan, despite how things now appear.

There may be another and even more subtle sort of rebuttal going on as well. Wright argues that

the retelling of Israel's story in 9.6–10.21 is itself designed not only to suggest a new way of reading Israel's own history but also quietly to undermine the pretensions of Rome itself. Rome, too, told stories of its own history, going back to the brothers Romulus and Remus a thousand years earlier, coming through the long story of the republic and finally arriving at the emperor who was now enthroned as lord of the world. Paul, having declared in 9.5 that Jesus, the Messiah, is "God over all, blessed forever" . . . returns to the point in 10.12: Jesus is Lord of all, Jew and Gentile alike. Israel's history, climaxing in Jesus, is designed to upstage Roman history, climaxing in Augustus.[21]

Paul asserts right from the beginning that he is telling the truth, and he seems to be suggesting that the rule of testimony by two witnesses has been met, because both he and his conscience attest that he is telling the truth, but he also affirms that the Holy Spirit is involved, so that what he says are Spirit-inspired words. In 2.15 as well conscience was seen as a co-witness.[22]

Paul explains his continual heartache and sorrow for his Jewish kin, by which here he must mean non-Christian Jews. He even goes so far as to say that he could wish himself accursed *(anathema)* by Christ for the sake of these fellow Jews. By "anathema" Paul seems to mean something like "separated" since he speaks of being anathema *from Christ.*[23] The theme of self-sacrifice for one's own people came up often in the literature of Greece and Rome and was particularly important in Jewish literature. And Paul also echoes Moses' plea for the people of Israel (Exod. 32.32; Num. 11.15).

In v. 3 Paul calls his fellow Jews his brothers as well as his kin according to the flesh. Here "brother" is used not in the spiritual sense of fellow Christian, nor in the literal sense of a member of Paul's own physical or extended family, unless one includes all Jews as his extended family. In v. 4 he describes them as "Israelites," indicating something of their spiritual nature as God's chosen people. He is probably already setting up the argument which is to follow, because he wants to maintain that God has not rejected non-Christian Jews as no longer part of Israel. Indeed, the term Israel is going to be used in 11.26 to refer quite specifically to non-Christian Jews. But Paul will go on to say in v. 6 that not all those who are from Israel are Israel. He does not use the qualifier "true" Israel, and it is probably not appropriate to bring it into the discussion. He is saying that the term "Israel" does not apply to some Jews. He will use the righteous remnant concept in his discussion, as we shall see.

Paul lists the spiritual credits or benefits of Israel, trying to build up the honor rating of the Jews in the eyes of his largely Gentile audience. But it is precisely those benefits that make it all the more puzzling that the majority of Jews have rejected their own Messiah. Here Paul builds on what he said in 3.1-8.[24]

---

21. Wright, "Romans," pp. 623-24.

22. See Barrett, *Romans,* p. 165.

23. This makes it rather clear that Cranfield, *Romans,* 2:451-594, and others cannot be right in suggesting that Paul views non-Christian Jews as already saved persons apart from faith in Christ. Paul would not be wishing himself cut off for their sake if he believed that there was no need for such a heroic gesture since they were not in fact lost or cut off from God's people. What he believes is that they are cut off, but only for a time. His is an eschatological argument, not a purely theological one, for it brings future events into the mix.

24. See P. Achtemeier, *Romans* (Atlanta: John Knox, 1985), p. 156.

Their "sonship" means that they have a family relationship with God, with all the benefits that pertain thereto. "Glory" refers to the divine presence dwelling in the midst of God's people, or less likely to the hope of eschatological glory at the resurrection. But Paul is not talking about hope here but about what the Jews already have. They also have "the covenants," by which he means at least the Abrahamic and Mosaic covenants, and new covenant. That they do is why Paul says "to the Jew first" in his thesis statement in 1.16-17. The promise of eschatological redemption and renewal was for them first. In Paul's pre–A.D. 70 context, *latreia* would likely refer to the worship carried out in the Temple in Jerusalem. So Paul's largely Gentile Roman audience would probably have understood it, since pagans associated worship with temples, not with meetings in synagogues or homes. The Jews also have the rule of law, or, more literally, "the legislation of Law," probably referring in particular to the Mosaic Law.[25] Paul is building up the impression that Israel is a duly and indeed divinely constituted people with many gifts from God.

With "the promises" (such as those to Abraham) Paul goes beyond heritage or history to that which has to do with the future, a benefit which is still outstanding. By "the fathers" Paul means the great patriarchs of the faith — Abraham, Isaac, Jacob, Joseph, and so on. Then finally Paul names what is in his mind the Jews' greatest asset and gift to humankind — the Messiah. *Kata sarka*, according to physical descent, the Messiah came from the Jews. Paul elsewhere indicates that on the basis of other criteria, or in other ways, Christ came from God.[26]

V. 5b is one of the most debated verses in all of Pauline literature. Is Paul actually calling Christ God here? The question hinges on punctuation. There is no question but that it is better Greek to regard the *ho ōn* which follows "the Christ" as referring back to Christ rather than forward to *theos*, "God."[27] Furthermore, whenever we find a doxology elsewhere, including in Paul, it begins with "blessed" or some similar term, not with *ho ōn*. Those who want to find an independent doxology to God here are hard-pressed to explain why the doxology does not follow this normal pattern.

In fact, the one real objection to Christ being called God here is that Paul supposedly does not do so elsewhere. But this is not true. He does do so in

25. Notice that Paul counts the Law, in principle, in the blessing or asset column.

26. As I have said in *Jesus, Paul, and the End of the World*, p. 115, Paul is probably thinking through a logical historical sequence in this list. First he mentions that Israel was made sons and daughters in the Exodus, they saw the glory cloud, and God made a series of covenants with them; then he relates how the Law and divine worship were set up and God obligated himself to the promises in the covenants; this in turn leads to Paul's mentioning the patriarchs who received the promises, and of course finally to the Promised One — the Messiah.

27. See the discussion in Bryan, *A Preface to Romans*, pp. 170-71.

equivalent terms in Phil. 2.5-11, and furthermore when he calls Christ "Lord," he is predicating of Jesus the divine name used for God over and over in the LXX. We find Jesus called divine Lord, indeed confessed as such in Rom. 10.9, and then an OT passage (Joel 3.5 LXX) in which God is called "Lord" is applied to Jesus at 10.13. Paul has christologically redefined how he understands monotheism, and 9.5 is just further evidence of the fact.

There remain, however, two ways to translate v. 5 recognizing that Christ is called God here, "Christ, who is God over all, blessed forever" or "Christ, who is over all, God blessed forever."[28] At any rate, Paul is perfectly capable of talking about the Messiah in both his human and his divine dimensions in the same breath.[29] But this Christ is not through with Israel yet, and precisely because he is also the God of mercy he will return to turn Jacob back to his God, as the end of this entire argument will urge.

The preamble now being over, the argument proper begins at v. 6. Paul immediately gets to the point — the Word of God to Israel has not failed. Rather, one must understand the concept of the remnant. The remnant proves that the Word of God to Jews has not failed. But who is this remnant? Paul apparently is referring to persons like himself, Jews who are followers of Jesus.[30] And furthermore, he will argue that God is not finished with non-Christian Jews either.[31] Indeed, he will say in the third part of his argument that God has

---

28. The detailed arguments of Metzger, *A Textual Commentary,* pp. 459-62, are telling. Note especially that if the clause which begins with *ho ōn* was intended to be an asyndetic doxology to God, then the word *ōn* is totally pointless and superfluous. It is more likely that the text would have read *ho epi pantōn theos* if God was being distinguished from Christ here. Furthermore, Pauline doxologies are never asyndetic (cf. Gal. 1.5; Rom. 1.25; 2 Cor. 11.31; Rom. 11.36; Phil. 4.20).

29. Wright, "Romans," p. 630.

30. While I agree with Wright, "Romans," p. 635, that Paul does argue in Galatians 3–4 that Christ turns out to be the remnant, in the sense of being the seed of Abraham, Paul is not arguing that way in this context. Jesus is not equated in these chapters with Israel; rather, Jesus is said to be Israel's Messiah, which is not the same thing.

31. It is a mistake to argue, as Wright and others do, that Paul has two different definitions of Israel running in chs. 9–11. This is simply not true. Paul's concept of Israel involves the wider notion of the elect and the narrower notion of those Jews selected for special purposes, but the latter is but a subset of the former, and in any case Paul is always talking about ethnic Jews. Unfaithful Israelites are still considered Israelites, though they are temporarily broken off, and faithful Gentiles are still considered Gentiles before or after they are saved. Furthermore, Jewish Christians are still seen as Jews as well as Christians. The olive tree is indeed a symbol used to refer to Jew and Gentile being part of the same people of God. But Israel or Jews are not equated with the church, nor is Israel said to contain Gentile Christians. Paul is using the term "Israel" in this discussion in an ethnic sense, just as he uses the term "Gentile" in this context. That some Israelites are not "Israel" in the select or true sense does not mean that Paul has redefined Israel to mean the church. It is interesting that while D. J. Moo, "The

temporarily hardened some Jews so that the Gentiles could be grafted in to the
people of God, and so in fact the other Jews could be regrafted into the people
of God on the basis of grace and faith in Jesus. Then all will have been saved on
the basis of faith in the promises.

So when Paul is referring to the hardening of some, he is not talking
about eternal damnation. He is talking about a process in history that is temporal and temporary. Therefore, Paul speaks in 9.22-23 not of those saved or
damned from before the foundation of the world, but rather vessels that are
currently positively related to God and vessels that currently are not.[32]

In vv. 7-10 Paul provides some scriptural backing for what he has just asserted. The examples are meant to show that not all Israel turn out to be children of the promise, even though they are all children of Abraham. The most
telling example of course is Esau, who before he had done anything was given a
certain lot in life. He and his brother Jacob were the product of one act of intercourse (which is probably what the euphemistic reference to the marriage bed
is meant to convey).[33] The elder would serve the younger, not because the
younger deserved better or had done better deeds, but because God in his unmerited favor decided to do it that way, showing mercy on Jacob more than
Esau. But Esau's historical role, however determined by God, does not mean
that God cursed Esau and damned him for eternity. As the OT context of the
saying "Jacob I loved and Esau I hated" (Mal. 1.2-3) shows, the subject there is
two nations, not two individuals, and, as we have said, even when individuals
are in the picture, it is not their eternal destiny that is spoken of. The quoted
verse, then, may speak of God's elective purposes, but the concern is with roles
they are to play in history, not their personal eternal destiny.[34] So when Paul
speaks of Israel, his concern is with the history of God's choices and historical

Theology of Romans 9–11," in Hay and Johnson, eds., *Pauline Theology*, vol. 3, pp. 240-58, rejects Wright's theory concerning "two definitions of Israel" (one of which refers to the church,
see p. 252), he still maintains Calvin's "two definitions of election" theory, one corporate, and
one individual (p. 255); but this theory is equally problematic if one wants to urge that individual election is to salvation. At least one of the individuals Paul refers to early in his argument in ch. 9, namely Pharaoh, whom God has elected for a specific historical purpose, is certainly not said to be elected to salvation. So, then, do we have both individual election for
historical purposes and a separate individual election for salvation? This theory has as many
problems as Wright's "two Israels" theory.

32. See Cranfield, *Romans*, 2:480-84.

33. D. Moo, *The Epistle to the Romans* (NICNT; Grand Rapids: Eerdmans, 1996), p. 579,
points out that the phrase "having a marriage bed" can refer to having a marital relationship
or to an act of intercourse or even to a seminal transmission of sperm. It is probably the second in this text.

34. See the helpful discussion by G. B. Caird, "Expository Problems: Predestination —
Romans ix–xi," *ET* 68 (1956-57): 324-27.

purposes, not the history of a race.[35] The story being told here is that of God's dealing with Israel as it illustrates his righteous character and plan. Paul does also want to squelch the notion that physical descent determines the elect, and he does this by carrying his argument through more than one generation of patriarchs. There is nothing here about the replacement of one Israel by another or about a true Israel. The concern is rather with how the one people of God have developed through time.

Paul uses the Scripture to demonstrate that God has always done things a certain way, namely that there has always been selection for special purposes within election and that there has always been a remnant concept operating as well. These two ideas are juxtaposed, but they are not identical. Paul explains that, though the large majority of Jews have currently rejected Christ, this should not be taken as a sign that God has rejected them, not least because there have been various times in Israel's history (e.g., the wilderness wandering period) when the majority of Jews rejected God's plans and purposes for them. In fact, Paul will argue that God knew that they would reject him, and so he planned for and made room for the acceptance of Gentiles in large numbers and the acceptance of all on the basis of grace and faith and his mercy toward all, not on the basis of some obligation. This separation is, therefore, not an illustration of God's inscrutable judgment but ultimately of his mercy over all, though of course God does not cease to be just.[36]

It is too seldom noticed that the concept of the righteous remnant is used to further the discussion of God's historical purposes, and in particular his purposes to produce a Jewish messianic figure to save the world. The concern is not with a saved group of Israelites as opposed to a permanently non-elect group of Israelites, for Paul will go on to say that even those Jews temporarily and temporally broken off from the chosen people can and will be regrafted in. He also describes the remnant process to make clear how God works to create a people for his purposes. Israel was chosen or created not primarily for its own benefit, but to be a light to the nations. Paul is describing that process of election and selection for such purposes. Israel's or anyone else's salvation is not finally completed until the eschaton. Until then, there can be assurance of what is hoped for, but this assurance always stands under the proviso that one must persevere until the end of life, which is possible only by God's grace and through faith, working out one's salvation with fear and trembling, as Paul puts it in Philippians.

Unless we see salvation from the end of the process we will not understand this discussion. It does not happen in full or come to its completion before Christ returns and the dead are raised. This is so not only because salvation

35. See, rightly, Achtemeier, *Romans*, pp. 157-59.
36. Cranfield, *Romans*, 2:493-96.

in its final form applies only to a resurrected person who even in the flesh is conformed to the image of the resurrected Jesus. It is also because Paul believes that even the saved person faces the danger of unfaithfulness and apostasy in this life. One is not eternally secure until one is securely in eternity. Paul also believes that since all have sinned and fallen short of God's glory, God owes salvation to no one, and none can merit it. It is all a matter of mercy and grace. Thus God is free to choose and use whomever he will for the divine purposes, without injustice. One can be chosen for God's purposes, like Cyrus or Pharaoh, and not be saved. Being chosen for historical purposes and being saved are not one and the same thing. Salvation for individuals is by grace and through faith. Election, insofar as the creation of a people is involved, is largely a corporate thing — it is "in Israel" or "in Christ," but the means of getting in is by faith.[37] "[E]lection does not take place . . . arbitrarily or fortuitously; it takes place always and only *in Christ*. They are elect who are in him; they who are elect are in him (cf. Gal. 3:29). It is failure to remember this that causes confusion over Paul's doctrine of election and predestination."[38]

Paul roundly repudiates the suggestion contained in v. 14's rhetorical question — "is there injustice with God?"[39] The quotation in v. 15 from Exod.

---

37. See the helpful and nuanced remarks of Achtemeier, *Romans,* pp. 160-65, especially pp. 164-65:

> The difficulty lies in the fact that those who have understood these verses to be statements of eternal truth about how God deals with each individual, rather than a statement of how God has dealt with Israel in pursuing his plan for the redemption of a rebellious creation, have also tended to understand these verses in terms of a rigid and symmetrical predeterminism. God had determined before each individual was born whether or not that person would be saved or damned. Nothing that individual could do would alter that fact. Those who were damned got what they deserved as rebellious creatures. Those who were saved were saved only by grace. . . . That is simply not what Paul is saying in this passage. He is not writing about the fate of each individual. He is making a statement about how God dealt with Israel, and continues to deal with it, even when it rejects his Son; namely he deals with it in mercy, even when it deserves wrath. That is why one so badly distorts Paul's point if one assumes these verses tell me about my fate, or anyone else's, before God: damned or saved. Rather, what these verses tell me is that the same gracious purpose at work in the election of Israel is now at work in a new chosen people to whom I can now belong, by that same gracious purpose of God. The passage is therefore about the enlargement of God's mercy to include Gentiles, not about the narrow and predetermined fate of each individual.

38. Barrett, *Romans,* p. 171.

39. Actually there are two rhetorical questions here, the first of which is "What then shall we say?" as we also found at 6.1, 15; 7.7 and will find again at 9.30. Paul then regularly introduces segments of his discussion with rhetorical questions, which is yet further proof of the need to see the divisions in this letter's discourse in rhetorical terms, not merely in theological or logical terms.

33.19 says nothing about "I will judge those whom I will judge." Both phrases speak of mercy. "Mercy" could be said to be the theme of this and the following two chapters. The word occurs seven times in some form, but only five times in all the rest of Paul's letters.

God's mercy explains this separation and temporary hardening process (v. 16).[40] So it arises from the character of God, not from the worthiness or unworthiness of this or that vessel. God's elective purposes should never be taken outside the context of his mercy and his revelatory and salvific work in Christ. Election is in Israel in the first instance, and then in Christ. It is not some abstract or inscrutable will of God that lurks behind the revealed will of God, for God's will and heart are truly revealed in Christ. Whatever is not known about God must comport with what God has revealed to the world in Christ. Thus it is not helpful to talk about pretemporal eternal decrees by God, unless one is talking about what God decreed about and for his Son, the chosen and destined One.

V. 17 offers another illustration. Pharaoh was raised up to demonstrate God's saving power on behalf of Israel and thus to show the glory of God throughout the earth.[41] That he was judged or hardened is a byproduct, but God acted to redeem his people. It is a regular feature of God's work that redemption for one person may require or involve judgment on another person. Liberation of the oppressed requires judgment of the oppressor. Nothing is said about Pharaoh's eternal state, but rather only how he was used by God during the exodus. "Raise up" does not refer to resurrection here, but rather to God bringing Pharaoh onto the stage of history and hardening him to reveal his mercy and power to save Israel.[42]

V. 18 speaks of this dual process: God has mercy on whom he wills and hardens whom he wills. This remark must not be isolated from the rest of what Paul is saying here. If Israel is any analogy, then "hardening" does not mean damning. It involves a temporal action of limited duration. The point of this discussion in any case is to deal with the fate and condition of Israel, not Pharaoh. How does one explain the Jews' rejection of their Messiah? What hope do they still have? Thus far Paul has talked about predestination of two groups — Christians in ch. 8 and Israel in ch. 9. Israel was destined to stumble so that Gentiles might rise, but also so that all might rise up by the grace of God. This

40. Wright, "Romans," p. 638, helpfully puts it this way: "the status of being God's promise-bearing people has in the last analysis nothing to do with whether Israel intends to do what God wants . . . or whether Israel expends energy on the task. . . . What matters, what carries the saving plan forward even though all human agents let God down, is God's own mercy."

41. Paul's quotation of Exod. 9.16 differs from the LXX at various points. See Cranfield, *Romans,* 2:485-86.

42. See Wright, "Romans," p. 639.

destining is not to heaven or hell, but for God's historical purposes, as was the case with Pharaoh.[43]

"Reading this part of Romans is like riding a bicycle: if you stand still for more than a moment, forgetting the onward movement both of the story of 9.6–10.21 and of the letter as a whole, you are liable to lose your balance — or, perhaps, to accuse Paul of losing his."[44] Proof-texting, or taking certain verses of this section out of the flow and context and trajectory of this rhetorical argument, has led to all sorts of bad theology. When the effect of an argument is intended to be cumulative, and there are deliberately an ebb and flow, assertions and then qualifications, involved in it, it is a major mistake to focus on one or another verse to get at Paul's "theology" of election and the like. In any case, what we have here is Paul's active theologizing into a specific situation, not Paul's theology as we often speak of it today.[45]

Vv. 22 and 23 belong together and may seem particularly harsh. Paul is in the middle of using Jeremiah's metaphor (Jer. 18.6) about the potter and the clay to discuss the relationship of God to his creatures. That it is a metaphor must be stressed again and again. V. 22 is problematic because it involves a conditional sentence without an apodosis, so we must supply the first part of the sentence to make it work. In view of vv. 14-18 it is clear enough that Paul is dealing with what he believes to be a real condition here, not merely a possible or probable one. The real question about v. 22 is whether it should have a causal or concessive clause beginning with *thelōn*. If causal, then the meaning is "But what if God endured vessels of wrath, prepared for destruction with much long-suffering, *because* he willed to show forth his wrath and to make known his power, and in order to make known the riches of his glory upon vessels of mercy?" If concessive, then the sentence will read: "What if God, *although* he willed to show forth his wrath, . . . nevertheless endured vessels of wrath with much long-suffering in order to make known the riches of his glory upon the vessels of mercy?" Paul could be saying that, though God would show forth his wrath against the vessels of wrath, nonetheless he had patience with them for an extended period of time. It is difficult to imagine Paul saying that God endured the vessels of wrath *because* he wanted to show forth his wrath. It is clear enough that Paul does believe there will be a wrath to come (see 2 Thessalo-

43. See, rightly, Hays, *Echoes of Scripture,* p. 66: "Thus the allusion to Jeremiah 18 in 9.20-21, like other allusions and echoes earlier in the text, anticipates the resolution of Paul's argument in Romans 11. The reader who recognizes the allusion will not slip into the error of reading 9.14-29 as an excursus on the doctrine of the predestination of individuals to salvation or damnation, because the prophetic subtexts keep the concern with which the chapter began — the fate of Israel — sharply in focus."

44. Wright, "Romans," p. 639.

45. I intend to address this matter in the future in my forthcoming volume on NT theology.

nians 2), though in Romans 1 he could also talk about a wrath in the midst of time being exercised by God. Thus it seems clear that the *thelōn* clause in 9.22 is concessive. God's endurance of the vessels of wrath shows his patience and mercy, giving time for amendment of life.

What is often overlooked is that Paul is also drawing on the sapiential reading of the story of Israel found in Wis. 12.3-18. The passage emphasizes God's forbearance toward the wicked, the inappropriateness of the created and fallen person challenging God's right to judge, God's righteousness, which includes his justice and not just his mercy or faithfulness, and God's right to judge mercifully if he so chooses. In Wis. 15.7 we read about the Potter who forms from the same clay "both the vessels that serve clean uses and those for contrary uses, making all alike." Both Paul and the author of Wisdom assert that "God has the right both to remake nations and peoples in a new way and to withhold judgment for a while in order that salvation may spread to the rest of the world."[46] Furthermore, Paul seems to be aware of Sir. 33.12-13, which speaks of God distinguishing among persons.[47]

Paul uses two different verbs when talking about the vessels of mercy and the vessels of wrath. The latter are framed/prepared/fit/put together for wrath, while the former are prepared beforehand for glory.[48] *Katērtismena,* used of the vessels of wrath, is a perfect passive participle. *Proētoimasen,* used of the vessels of mercy, is an aorist active indicative. This change cannot be accidental, and it suggests that Paul means that the vessels of wrath are ripe or fit for destruction.[49] Indeed, one could follow the translation of John Chrysostom here and understand it in the middle voice: "have made themselves fit for" destruction. If so, this verse certainly does not support the notion of double predestination. Rather it refers to the fact that these vessels are worthy of destruction, though God has endured them for a long time.[50]

Furthermore, it is not said that the vessels of mercy are destined for glory beforehand, but that they are prepared for glory beforehand. So the subject is not some pretemporal determination, but rather what ch. 8 has referred to — namely that God did always plan for believers to be conformed to the image of his Son, and during their Christian lives, through the process of being set right and being sanctified, they have been prepared for such a glorious destiny. Thus Paul would be alluding to the process of sanctification here, which has a

---

46. Wright, "Romans," p. 641.

47. See E. E. Johnson, *The Function of Apocalyptic and Wisdom Traditions in Romans 9–11* (Atlanta: Scholars, 1989), p. 132.

48. See the discussion by Bryan, *A Preface to Romans,* pp. 163-64, on the different verbs and deliberately different ways in which these two sets of vessels are described.

49. Bryan, *A Preface to Romans,* p. 163; cf. 2 Cor. 9.5 on the use of this verb by Paul.

50. See rightly Cranfield, *Romans,* 2:496-97.

pretemporal plan behind it. Furthermore, as Eph. 2.3-4 makes quite evident, someone can start out as a vessel of wrath and later become a child of God by grace through faith. The issue is where one is in the story of a particular vessel, not some act of divine predetermination of some to wrath.

In vv. 30-33 Paul sums up some implications of what he has just said. Gentiles who did not pursue righteousness attained it, but it was a form of righteousness that came through faith. On the other hand, Israel pursued the Law of righteousness and did not attain it. The Israelites were pursuing a ruling principle of righteousness in their lives, by means of the Law. The Law then did bear witness to righteousness. It was a law about that. The problem was not that Israel realized that God required obedience. The problem was that they pursued righteousness by works of the Law, not by faith in Christ, and therefore did not attain it. "Because not by faith, but as from works they pursued it, they did not attain it" (v. 32). The fault was not that Israel used the Law in a legalistic way or were glorying in works-righteousness. The problem in part was with the Law itself. It could not empower a person to obey or keep it (cf. Galatians 3–4, Romans 6–7). Nor could the Law create or give the faith or righteousness it spoke of. These came only from Christ and through the Holy Spirit. The Law is not evil. Indeed it is holy, just, and good. But it is impotent, and inadequate to help fallen persons keep it.[51]

Beginning at vv. 32b-33 Paul seems to be drawing on a traditional catena of Scriptures from Isa. 28.16 and 8.14 in the LXX. The Israelites stumbled or struck their foot on the stone of stumbling. It is God who raised up that stone of stumbling, according to the quotation in v. 33a. But v. 33b adds that those believing on him shall not be put to shame (or we might translate "shall not be disappointed"). The shame in view here is the eschatological shame of appearing at final judgment naked — that is, in the wrong condition. Thus, Paul clearly has had a future wrath in mind in this discussion, not merely a present wrath (cf. 5.5). Käsemann says that "Judaism must take offense at Christ to the degree that the requirement of faith enforces a break with its religious past. It cannot see that precisely in this way it is summoned back to the promise it has been given. The continuity of the fleshly conceals the continuity of the divine word maintained in Scripture. It thus conceals the eschatological goal."[52] The problem with this assessment is that it seems to assume that faith was not a requirement before Christ, which is not so.

10.1 begins somewhat as 9.1-2 did, expressing Paul's heartache about his

---

51. Johnson, "Romans 9–11," p. 219, is quite right that Paul enunciates a double problem here. On the one hand the Gentiles have obtained what they did not seek, and on the other hand Jews have not obtained even though they sought righteousness through the Law. It is both Gentile belief and Jewish unbelief that constitute the problem here.

52. Käsemann, *Romans*, p. 279.

fellow Jews, who, it will be noted, are seen as lost and in need of salvation. Paul's heart's desire and what he prays for repeatedly is their salvation. He is thinking, as 11.26 will show, of future salvation on the last day; otherwise he would speak not only of prayer but also of proclaiming. In v. 2 he speaks of the Jews having a zeal for God that is not according to knowledge. Too often people mistake earnestness for truth. One can be zealous for the wrong cause, and it may well be that Paul puts it this way precisely because he was exhibit A of such zeal when he was wrongly persecuting the followers of Jesus as a Pharisee. He believes that non-Christian Jews lack understanding, and in some cases they have been rebellious and rejected God's Word to them.

The matter of righteousness, both God's and human righteousness, comes up again at this juncture. Non-Christian Jews, despite their zeal, are ignorant of the righteousness that comes from God, not least because they have been seeking to "stand" by their own righteousness. Notice the language Paul chooses here. He is not talking about "getting in" but rather "staying in," to use Sanders's terminology. He is saying that Jews seek to stand on the basis of their own righteousness, having already been granted the gracious privilege of being part of God's people. It may be doubted that Paul would call this "covenantal nomism," for he speaks of "their own" righteousness, and not the righteousness of the Law per se. There is an issue of their not submitting to the righteousness of God. Here *diakaiosynē* certainly does not mean "right standing with God," for they already had that. The issue lies elsewhere. As those who were already God's people, they were standing in the wrong place and not submitting to the right righteousness.

V. 4 then reads literally "for end/termination/purpose/goal of the Law [is] Christ for righteousness to all those believing." This is one of the most debated verses in the Pauline corpus. It is of course true that Paul believes that no longer being under the Law does not mean no longer being required to behave in a righteous manner. On the other end of the spectrum, it is not true that Paul is simply talking about badges or marks of righteousness such as Sabbath-keeping and circumcision when he says that Christ is the end or termination of the Law. Something more profound is going on.[53]

Telos, "end," can indeed have several possible meanings.[54] End as completion or termination does not exclude end as goal.[55] But in Paul's writings *telos*

53. See the discussion on pp. 115-25 above.
54. See Bryan, *A Preface to Romans,* pp. 171-72.
55. The translation by Stowers of this portion of ch. 10, *A Rereading of Romans,* p. 311, is worth pondering: "I pray to God that my fellow Jews might be saved from God's anger. They want to do God's will but they are ignorant about God's plan for making things right. They have tried to work out a plan of their own for making things right instead of accepting God's plan. For Christ is the Law's goal with respect to God's plan for making things right, for all who believe [not just Israel]."

seems always to include the notion of termination, whatever other nuances it may have (cf. 1 Cor. 1.8; 10.11; 15.24; 2 Cor. 11.15; Phil. 3.19).[56] "When an object has served its purpose," thus having reached its goal, "it may be discarded."[57] It is a mistake then to translate *telos* as "aim" here, as though Paul meant merely that the Law points to Christ.[58] He will go on to say that righteousness for those who believe is available now through *another* means — not through the Law but through faith. Now if this is the contrast in mind, then righteousness should logically mean the same thing in both cases. Righteousness is not attained nor maintained by means of the Law but by another means.[59] Christ has put an end to the Law as a way of pursuing righteousness.[60]

V. 4 explains what has been said in v. 3. The righteousness that comes from God is very different from "their own righteousness," from the pursuit of right standing before God by keeping the Law. Refusing to submit to God's righteousness is a mistake *because* Christ has put an end to any other means of righteousness. Christ, not the Law, is now the means of righteousness for believers, whether we mean by that right standing, sanctification, moral behavior, or final righteousness. Paul will refer to the law of Christ, not Torah, when he speaks of the code or standard of righteousness for Christians.[61] The argument here is salvation-historical, not merely christological. He is not trying to argue that Christ embodies the Law's righteousness or is the aim of the Law, though he might well agree with those ideas. The sense here is close to 2 Cor. 3.13-14, where the point is the end of the Mosaic covenant, spoken of metaphorically as the end of the glory of Moses' face, which was being annulled.

Paul juxtaposes two different voices in vv. 5-7. Moses says about the righteousness from the Law that the one doing it shall live in it (Lev. 18.5, also quoted in Gal. 3.12). But then the voice of a personified concept speaks: "the Righteousness from Faith says. . . ." But what it says are the words of Moses in Deut. 9.4 and

56. Thus the translation "goal" in itself is not adequate. But see Wright, "Romans," pp. 645-46.

57. Barrett, *Romans*, p. 184.

58. On the interpretation of this verse by the Church Fathers see R. Badenas, *Christ the End of the Law: Romans 10.4 in Pauline Perspective* (Sheffield: JSOT, 1985), pp. 515-20. Many of them (but by no means all of them) do interpret Paul to mean goal or culmination, but this ignores the way Paul uses the term elsewhere.

59. For a strong argument for the goal interpretation see Wright, "Romans," pp. 656-57.

60. This does not mean, of course, that Paul thinks the Law as part of Scripture ceases to have a function for believers or ceases to tell the truth. His regular citation of it in support of his argument proves otherwise. The Law's function, however, is as witness to the truth and promises of God, not as moral code or Mosaic covenant that the believer is under and obliged to keep.

61. See my discussion in *Grace in Galatia* (Grand Rapids: Eerdmans, 1998), pp. 235-37.

30.12-14 (the latter is applied to personified Wisdom in Baruch 3.29-30, but here to Christ), so in a sense Moses is pitted against himself. The point of the quotations in v. 6 is that righteousness is not a matter of human searching and striving. The righteousness from faith makes house-calls! One does not need to be transported in a vision up into heaven to find Christ, or make a subterranean journey, as is sometimes described in apocalyptic literature, to bring him up from the dead.[62] No, the Word, both written and incarnate, is near at hand, as Deut. 30.12-14 shows.[63] Paul is talking about something that can be both embodied and confessed, the word of faith about Jesus and the righteousness from faith that comes from having a relationship with Jesus. He may also be calling Jesus "the Righteousness from Faith," which might explain the personification.[64]

Paul says in v. 8 that it is this righteousness that he has been preaching. He follows the same techniques of commentary that we find at Qumran, citing a verse and then interspersing a comment introduced by "that is" (vv. 6-8; cf., e.g., 1QpHab 2.10-11, quoting Hab. 1.6).[65] But he uses these texts in a way similar to what one finds in earlier Jewish sapiential literature (Sir. 24.5; Bar. 3.29-30), where Wisdom is the assumed subject that is sought for in the abyss and in the heavens, only Christ now replaces "Wisdom" as the one sought after in such out-of-the-way places.[66] Paul appears to have been a trained exegete well before he became a Christian, but then too he seems here and elsewhere to function as something of a sapiential prophet as well.[67]

In vv. 9 and 10 the issue is salvation. A true confession coupled with true believing leads to salvation. The confession here is parallel to the one in 1 Cor. 12.3, which suggests that Paul is using a set formula his audience will recognize.

62. See E. M. Humphrey, "Why Bring the Word Down? The Rhetoric of Demonstration and Disclosure in Romans 9.30–10.21," in *Romans and the People of God*, ed. S. K. Soderlund and N. T. Wright (Grand Rapids: Eerdmans, 1999), pp. 129-48. Among other things, Paul is denying here that there is any need for a visionary experience in order to hear the word of Christ and respond. It is a matter that has already been openly revealed in the gospel.

63. As Barrett, *Romans*, p. 185, suggests, Paul may be saying here that humans could not have precipitated the incarnation. If so, we have a reference to the preexistence of Christ here. On the quotes of Lev. 18.5 and Deut. 30.12-14 in this passage see J. D. G. Dunn, "'Righteousness from Law' and 'Righteousness from Faith': Paul's Interpretation of Scripture in Romans 10.1-10," in *Tradition and Interpretation in the New Testament*, ed. G. F. Hawthorne and O. Betz (Grand Rapids: Eerdmans, 1987), pp. 216-28.

64. On the rhetorical devices of Personification and "Impersonation" see pp. 179-81 above.

65. See Barrett, *Romans*, p. 185.

66. See rightly, Hays, *Echoes of Scripture*, pp. 80-83.

67. See C. A. Evans, "Paul and the Prophets: Prophetic Criticism in the Epistle to the Romans (with Special Reference to Romans 9–11)," in Soderlund and Wright, eds., *Romans and the People of God*, pp. 115-28.

The confession of Jesus as Lord is followed immediately by reference to God raising Jesus from the dead. Both are confessed together precisely because Jesus is the risen Lord. Furthermore the resurrection would clearly distinguish confession of Jesus as Lord from other such confessions in the Greco-Roman world.[68] Jesus, unlike other so-called lords, had died and been raised from the dead and fully assumed the role of Lord only at and by means of the resurrection.

V. 10 is especially crucial for our purposes. Righteousness and salvation are in parallel object clauses: just as salvation has an experiential dimension, Paul likely means that righteousness does as well. Thus Barrett's translation: "faith works in the heart to produce righteousness."[69] After all, believing in the heart is an internal matter, not merely a matter of some objective status or standing. "Righteousness" perhaps refers here not only to being set right by God but also to the beginnings of being made righteous, what is normally called sanctification. What is certainly nowhere on the horizon here is the notion of Christ's alien righteousness being predicated of the believer in lieu of the believer's own personal righteousness.

With the quotation of Isa. 28.16, v. 11 raises the matter of honor. A person who believes in Jesus will not be put to shame (at the eschaton, when all is revealed and all are evaluated). In fact Paul has modified the quotation by adding "all" up front to stress the intended universal scope of God's salvation plan.

In v. 12 Paul reiterates God's impartiality, a theme we heard enunciated much earlier in the letter. There is no distinction between Jews and Gentiles because there is one Lord over all, and this Lord is prepared to bestow blessings on one and all who call upon him.[70] In 3.22 the absence of distinction between Jew and Gentile had to do with all being sinners, but here with all being under the same Lord who wishes to bless all.

Again in v. 13 we have the verb "saved" in the future tense. Joel 2.32 is quoted, and the emphasis is on "all." All who call on this Lord will be saved. Paul here is countering any notions that God has plans to save only a few or desires to bless only a few. On the contrary, anyone who responds to the gospel and calls upon and confesses the name of the Lord will be saved. Paul's stress is on the wideness of God's mercy, not the narrowness of the size of the remnant or elect group.

---

68. Barrett, *Romans*, p. 187.

69. Barrett, *Romans*, p. 188.

70. Paul seems to be drawing on Joel 2.32 (3.5 in the LXX) here. See J. Dupont, "Le Seigneur de tous (Ac 10:36; Rm. 10.12). Arrière-fond scripturaire d'une formule christologique," in Hawthorne and Betz, eds., *Tradition and Interpretation in the New Testament*, pp. 229-36, here p. 230. The interesting thing about that verse is that it also speaks of the deliverance of those called by God happening on Mount Zion and in Jerusalem. In other words, it seems to relate to Paul's Scripture quotation at 11.26a, which in the main has been associated with Isa. 59.20-21 and 27.9.

Beginning at v. 14 we have a chain or sequence of events required for someone to be saved. There is nothing in this chain about God's predetermined decrees of election. Salvation happens because someone has been sent, that person has preached, someone else has heard, the one who has heard has believed, and the one who has believed has called on the Lord and so been saved. The emphasis is on the necessity of preaching and of response to preaching.

But then Paul gets to the heart of the problem: not all respond to the gospel positively, or, as Paul puts it, not all "obey" the preaching. In v. 15's quotation of Isa. 52.7 he is nearer to the Hebrew than the LXX. It may be suggested that he knew both and, like other early Jewish exegetes, used the version that best illustrated his point.

He amplifies the problem in vv. 18-19. He is still concerned with non-Christian Israel, which he refers to again in v. 19. Israel has heard and does know about the gospel. He seems to assume that the gospel has already in the 50s gone out to a large portion of the empire (cf. 15.19, 23; Mark 13.10; 14.9). This is of a piece with his assertion in ch. 15 that he has completed his work in the eastern half of the empire and wishes to move on to Rome and further west.[71]

The quotations of Deut. 32.21 in v. 19 and Isa. 65.1 in v. 20 provide the basis for Paul's analysis in ch. 11 of what is happening with Israel. God is making non-Christian Jews envious by bringing into the people of God Gentiles, who are characterized as "not a nation" and as lacking understanding. God has revealed himself to those who were not seeking him. Paul thus has a rationale for what has happened with Israel and for why so many Gentiles are responding to the gospel when so many Jews are not. It is a story with many twists in it, and it is interesting that Paul relies mainly on Isaiah and the Pentateuch to provide the storyline and the explanations. V. 21 is plaintive, with God presented as a parent stretching out his arms toward a wayward child all day long, but the child is obstinate and wayward.

11.1 brings us to the third major part of Paul's argument and reflects his major concern. He does not want the audience in Rome to think that God has rejected Israel.[72] He emphatically rejects such a notion. The proof he gives immediately is himself: he is an Israelite, from the seed of Abraham and the tribe of Benjamin.[73] God has certainly not rejected his people whom he foreknew. Foreknowledge here is predicated of a whole group of people, ethnic Israel,

---

71. On which see pp. 362-63 below.

72. As T. L. Donaldson, *Paul and the Gentiles: Remapping the Apostle's Convictional World* (Minneapolis: Fortress, 1997), pp. 239-43, says, the issue in Paul's view is "delay" not "displacement," and so Paul's theology in regard to Israel should not be seen as supersessionist.

73. On the structure of Romans 11 see D. G. Johnson, "The Structure and Meaning of Romans 11," *CBQ* 46 (1984): 91-103.

many of whom are not, in Paul's view, currently saved. Foreknowledge does not mean foreordination to salvation, clearly enough, unless one *assumes* that in v. 26 Paul is predicting the salvation of every Jew who ever existed.[74] In v. 2 then we also have a non-restrictive use of "foreknew" applied to God. Here the term clearly does not refer to something like a prior choice on God's part.[75]

Vv. 2-4 paraphrase the story from 1 Kgs. 19.10-14 about Elijah.[76] Paul was not the first to complain and worry about Israel's unfaithfulness. Elijah did so and was told[77] that there were in fact many not worshiping the gods of this world — seven thousand in this case. There was a leftover left. V. 5 speaks of a remnant or remainder "according to the free choice of grace." *Eklogē* could be translated "election," but that would not really convey the essence of what Paul is getting at. This "free choice" probably refers to God's choice of a group — the remainder. Again election or selection is corporate.

V. 6 once again states the fundamental contrast between the free choice based on grace and a choice based on works, in this case works of the Law. The point is that God's free choice was not based on the remnant's works of the Law. This is not a contrast between libertinism and legalism. Paul's critique of the Mosaic Law is based on the assumption that it is obsolete, for Christ is the end of the Law as a way of righteousness. It has no power to enable a fallen person to keep it. This is a salvation-historical argument with the Christ-event being the crucial turning point.

C. H. Talbert seeks to argue that Paul is opposing legalism, by which he means that Paul is opposing "doing works of the Law" as a means of striving to stay in the people of God and then obtain final or eschatological salvation.[78] But this hardly plumbs the radical nature of Paul's argument. Paul is not merely opposing a legalistic way of approaching the Mosaic Law or the Mosaic covenant. And in any case, he is all for his converts keeping the Law of Christ and

74. Nor does foreknowledge mean foreordination in 8.29, where Paul distinguishes the two concepts.

75. 11.2 must be compared with 8.29. It leads to hopeless contradictions to suggest either that (1) "foreknew" is used in a restrictive sense of the final elect in 8.29, but not in 11.2, or (2) that "foreknew" simply means God's predetermined choosing in both places. J. M. Gundry Volf, *Paul and Perseverance: Staying In and Falling Away* (Louisville: Westminster/ J. Knox, 1990), pp. 170-71, recognizes that Paul does use "foreknew" in 11.2 in a nonrestrictive sense, but then she has no adequate explanation of how this comports with her view (see pp. 9-10) that something else is going on in 8.29. The simple way to resolve this dilemma is to recognize that Paul does not mean "predetermined" by "foreknew," as should be clear from 8.29, where two different terms are used to convey what Paul wants to say.

76. As Barrett, *Romans*, p. 193, says, he gives the sense of it, not directly quoting.

77. The term *chrēmatismos* here refers to a divine utterance rather than an oracle specifically; see *NewDocs* 4:176.

78. C. H. Talbert, "Paul, Judaism, and the Revisionists," *CBQ* 63 (2001): 1-22.

tells them that they must avoid the deeds of the flesh and do the Law of Christ if they want to enter the kingdom (Galatians 5–6). In other words, Paul is an advocate of just what Talbert thinks Paul is critiquing. Paul affirms a sort of covenantal nomism, though it is grace-empowered and Spirit-driven. It is just not the Mosaic covenant that he wants Gentiles to keep. It is a mistake to call any demand or requirement to obey a law "legalism" in a context where salvation is by grace and faith. The obedience that necessarily must follow from and depend on living faith is not legalism. Paul's problem is not with obedience or good works, or laws per se. Those are all seen as good things by him. His problem is with anachronism in a fallen world where the Mosaic Law cannot empower fallen persons to keep it and where Christ has brought it to an end as a way of righteousness, especially when Christ and the Spirit *can* empower obedient living.

Paul then contrasts in v. 7 the "remainder" or "elect" within Israel who obtained what all Israel sought. Not all who are from Israel are Israel, as Paul has said earlier in this argument. Election of Israel as God's chosen people was no automatic guarantee of salvation. Paul then applies the "hardening" principle to the rest of Israel and cites two sets of Scriptures to back up the claim — first Deut. 29.4 and Isa. 29.10 and then Pss. 69.22-23 and 35.8. In both sets of texts hardening is described as spiritual darkness, blindness, or imperceptiveness. "The rest" were made impervious to hearing or seeing the Word. Paul in fact has sharpened Deut. 29.4 by placing "not" with "to see" and "to hear" rather than with "gave."[79]

In vv. 11-25 we have the conclusion of Paul's major argument in chs. 9–11 about God, the Jews, and their future. Again, he is not talking about Jews who are followers of Christ in this segment any more than he was in the previous two parts of this argument. He says that he is going to reveal an apocalyptic *mystērion*, a "mystery," something a person knows only because God has revealed it to him or her. It is indeed possible that Paul is describing part of a vision that he has had. He was indeed a visionary (see 2 Cor. 12.2-10).[80]

What Paul has said in 9.6–11.10 could easily lead to the conclusion that the unbelieving Jews were lost altogether, God having rejected them in favor of the Gentiles. So once again Paul begins a segment of his argument with a rhetorical question: Have they stumbled so as to fall (permanently)? Here *hina* could mean "in order to": God made them stumble so that they would fall. But here the focus is not on divine determination but on the outcome for the Jews. Therefore "so as to" is to be preferred as a translation. "Fall" here then would mean fall into ruin, into irrevocable disfavor with God. Paul's response is "ab-

---

79. See Barrett, *Romans*, p. 195.

80. See my discussion on this in *Conflict and Community in Corinth* (Grand Rapids: Eerdmans, 1995), pp. 459-64.

solutely not!" He is surely not dealing here with a purely hypothetical question. It must have occurred to some Gentiles at some juncture.

In fact, as a result of the Jews' stumbling/trespass *(paraptōma),*[81] salvation has come to the Gentiles.[82] Part of the reason it has come to the Gentiles at this juncture is to make non-Christian Jews jealous. 10.19 has already quoted Deut. 32.21 about making Israel jealous. Now Paul hints that he hopes for and indeed sees his mission to the Gentiles as an indirect way to bring some Jews as well into the Christian faith. Furthermore, this is not mere wishful thinking on the part of Paul. Rather he sees it as God's mysterious plan revealed to him.[83]

V. 12 argues from the lesser to the greater: if it is true that the temporary lapse of some Jews from their place in the people of God means riches for the Gentile world,[84] what will their reinclusion mean? *Plērōma,* "fullness" or "full number,"[85] appears here and again later in this argument. Other early Jewish apocalyptic texts speak of the "full number" of the elect being collected, brought in, reunited before the eschaton (see 4 Ezra 6.25; 2 Baruch 81.4).[86] Paul inverts such references, which have the full number of Jews reunited and saved before the Gentiles stream to Zion or become part of God's people. Paul instead has the full number of Gentiles saved before all Israel is saved.

The emphasis in *plērōma* is probably not on a set number of the elect, but rather on a full or large number, a great multitude. Paul's vision of salvation is grand. He does not believe that only a tiny remnant of Jews and Gentiles will be saved. Käsemann suggests that what is in view is the filling up of the remnant, so that eventually "all Israel" is saved.[87] Some have interpreted *plērōma* to mean something like the full restoration or conversion, but this is unlikely. Here Paul is making a quantitative comparison between a small remnant and a fullness of

81. The word has both senses, and Paul may be playing on this fact.

82. Stowers, *A Rereading of Romans,* pp. 312-15, takes the whole passage to be referring to a footrace in which some Jews have temporarily stumbled, but have not fallen out of the race, and will one day complete the race. Paul does use such a metaphor here, but only briefly, and the more important point is that he expects the turnaround of the Jews to transpire when Christ comes, not by continued striving on their part.

83. In both 11.12 and 11.16 we have elliptical sentences where the predicate must be supplied. The careful study of S. R. Llewelyn of ellipses when found in conditional sentences beginning with *ei* leads to the conclusion that in each case the verb must be supplied or inferred from the immediately preceding clause. See *NewDocs* 6:68.

84. *Kosmos* here means not just the inhabited world but the Gentile world, as it is parallel to *ethnē* (Gentile nations) in the next clause.

85. Barrett, *Romans,* p. 198, helpfully suggests the translation "full strength," contrasting the cutting down of the numbers of Israel to the fact that they will later be brought up to full strength once more.

86. Johnson, *The Function of Apocalyptic and Wisdom Traditions in Romans 9–11,* p. 124.

87. Käsemann, *Romans,* pp. 304-6, 312-14.

the saved. The only question is whether he sees this as the adding of the unbelieving majority to the believing minority of Jews, which then amounts to "all Israel." Or is he talking about adding the unbelieving majority of Jews to the whole people of God and so the whole people are brought up to "fullness," both Jew and Gentile united in Christ. But if in v. 25 Paul means by *plērōma* those Gentiles now converted plus those yet to be converted, the parallel would then suggest that "fullness" here and "all Israel" in v. 26 is the adding of the now unbelieving Jews to believing Jews to make a full complement.

In v. 13 Paul emphatically and directly addresses the Gentile majority of his audience. He has a right to single them out and address them, not least because he is the Apostle to the Gentiles (*eph' hoson* means "insofar as"). Paul says he honors his ministry. *Diakonian* has the more specific sense of "ministry," not just any service in general here. Paul honors and glories in this ministry because it is an honor to lead people to Christ, and he hopes it will even have some good effect on his Jewish kin. Paul sees his mission to Gentiles as indirectly a mission to Jews as well. To judge from 2 Cor. 11.24-25 Paul did indeed evangelize in synagogues, as Acts confirms, and he paid a price for it. Even the Apostle to the Gentiles took seriously the gospel priority of "for the Jew first, and also for the Gentile," though his focus was on Gentiles.

V. 14 brings a note of realism. Paul hopes to make his fellow Jews jealous and so save *some* from among them *(tinas ex autōn)*. He does not expect by himself to bring the fullness of Israel into the Christian faith. Käsemann is likely wrong in saying that Paul thought his own mission would result in "all Israel being saved."[88] 1 Cor. 9.22 illuminates what Paul is talking about here, which is that there will be an eschatological miracle at the return of Christ.[89] "Evidently, though Paul can hope for the final salvation of all Israel (vs. 26), he does not hope for it in terms of the actual conversion of all individual Israelites; salvation of them all is a mysterious eschatological event, which is only prefigured in occasional personal conversions."[90] It is the latter Paul refers to when he says "some" here.

V. 15 makes clear that Paul sees these unbelieving Jews as temporarily rejected or pushed away *(apobolē),* which comports with his later metaphor that God has broken them off from the tree of his people temporarily. This verse provides yet another argument from the lesser to the greater. The rejection of the Jews could be either their rejection of Jesus or God's rejection of them, or the latter based on the former and so both. Since the focus here seems to be on

---

88. Käsemann, *Romans,* pp. 306-7.

89. As Cranfield, *Romans,* 2:561, says, Paul expects an eschatological act and result of God's plan, but he neither states nor implies that he sees his own work as the last-ditch effort before the end of the world that will produce this "all Israel."

90. Barrett, *Romans,* p. 199.

God's role, the stress would seem to be on the latter. On the word *katallagē* we should compare 5.10-11. Cranfield urges that "reconciliation" here refers specifically to Christ's death.[91] If so, what might be in view here is that the rejection of Jesus that led to his death and the world's reconciliation was at the same time God's rejection of such Jews. V. 15b must be taken seriously and probably literally. The acceptance by these Jews of Christ, or their re-acceptance by God will mean resurrection of the dead. If, as I think, we should take this as a literal reference to the resurrection at the end of human history, then Paul is admitting that he does not envision a gradual progressive conversion of the Jews, but a large or mass change at the end of history which will usher in the resurrection of the dead and the messianic or millennial age.[92]

In short, Paul has no delusions that he will participate in the end during his lifetime. *Ei mē* in v. 15b must mean "except," though a literal rendering would be "if not." "Life from the dead" is similar to what we see in John 5.24 and indicates that Paul sees the conversion of the Jews in an eschatological light. On the one hand, it will not transpire until God's timing for it (that is, until the full number of Gentiles come in). On the other hand, God, not Paul, will bring about this result at the end of things. What Paul envisions is the unifying of the people of God, Jew and Gentile, in Christ at the end of things.

Vv. 16-17 begin to illustrate by metaphor some of what Paul has in mind. I take the reference to "first fruits" here to mean the first fruits of conversion to Christ among Jews. Paul's point, contrary to what Cranfield suggests,[93] is not that a few Jewish Christians sanctify the mass of non-Christian Jews. Paul is not using the holiness language here in that way. His argument is, rather, that if the first few Jewish converts are set apart to God and are in truth a sort of first fruits and so a harbinger of things to come, then the mass of Jews are still ultimately "set apart" or "holy" unto God and set apart for salvation. God has not finally rejected them.

Many have been misled by dwelling too much on Paul's use of Num. 15.20-21, but I think Paul is simply drawing on OT language and ideas here to make his point. Cranfield rightly notes that though early Jewish teachers did talk about the first fruits sanctifying the rest, neither Paul nor the OT says anything to this effect elsewhere.[94] A closer parallel than later Jewish discussion would be 1 Corinthians 15, where Christ is called "the first fruits from the dead," which implies that more will be coming in similar fashion and condition. That is also the point here.

91. Cranfield, *Romans*, 2:562.
92. Origen and many of the Church Fathers understood this to be a reference to the literal resurrection here. See Bryan, *Preface to Romans*, p. 187.
93. Cranfield, *Romans*, 2:484-88.
94. Cranfield, *Romans*, 2:484-88.

There has also been endless debate about what "root" refers to in v. 16. This second analogy is not about root and tree but about root and branches, probably because it allows Paul to go on and talk about branches broken off. The root, of course, gives nourishment to the tree and so to the branches. In view of v. 28, the root likely represents the patriarchs, though it could refer to Jewish Christians. If the patriarchs are the root, then the mass of Israel, even unbelieving branches, have a special place in God's plan as a result of the faith of the patriarchs, or, better said, as a result of the promises made to them. Root and first fruits need not refer to the same thing here.[95] Rather we have two different illustrations of the same point in principle.

Why does Paul choose the olive tree metaphor for the people of God rather than the more usual vine metaphor in v. 17?[96] Jer. 11.16 and Hos. 14.6 use the olive tree metaphor, and in both texts the focus is on God's judgment, about broken branches, and in Hosea about restoration to a beautiful condition beyond judgment. So it is Israel's broken condition that calls for use of the metaphor of the olive tree.

Some have faulted Paul for being ignorant in what he says here, and others have defended him, saying that the grafting of a wild olive branch into a domesticated olive tree was not unknown in antiquity. But clearly he is not trying to give a lesson in horticulture, as is made clear as he goes on to speak of the regrafting in of natural branches, which was never practiced in antiquity. Strict verisimilitude should not be expected.[97] A figure of thought is being used to talk about the relationship of Jews and Gentiles in the people of God. We do not have a full-blown allegory here as in Galatians 4, but the talk about root, branches, pruning, grafting, and regrafting falls under the heading of such a figure of thought. Quintilian calls it *inversio,* where we present one thing in words, but another in meaning (*Instit. Or.* 8.6.44). He says that such figures are usually interspersed with more literal or plain speech to make the meaning clear (8.6.47). "In this type of allegory the ornamental element is provided by the metaphorical words and the meaning is indicated by those which are used literally" (8.6.48-49). Quintilian has no problem with multiple metaphors or short allegories, but he is opposed to mixing of metaphors.

Paul begins with the assertion that some of the branches were broken off (the passive suggests that God broke them off). Only *some.* Had God totally rejected his people once and for all, we would have expected Paul to say "all," and we would have expected there to be no Jewish Christians like Paul. But this was certainly not God's plan. Paul addresses the Gentiles in his audience directly,

---

95. Cranfield, *Romans,* 2:564-65.

96. See A. G. Baxter and J. Zeisler, "Paul and Arboriculture: Romans 11.17-24," *JSNT* 24 (1985): 25-32.

97. See Barrett, *Romans,* p. 201.

using singular "you," which suggests that he has individual Gentiles in mind. They are all wild olive branches that have been grafted "into them." *En autois* must mean "in among them," not "in place of them." This strongly suggests that for Paul the continuity with the OT people of God is in Jewish Christians, and before them, in Christ, and before him, in the patriarchs. Paul's understanding that the gospel has gone out into the Diaspora also supports the conclusion that the "remnant" in his day is viewed as Jewish Christians, rather than just any pious Jews.[98] He is also not suggesting that these Christian Gentiles were mysteriously and secretly grafted into non-Christian Israel of his own day. The remnant for Paul is not pious Jews in general but rather Jewish Christians like himself, who have the job of mediating the Jewish heritage to Gentiles.[99]

Thus Paul reminds the Gentiles: you were grafted into them and became fellow sharers in the fatness (that is, the sap) of the root of the olive tree. This is presumably a symbol of the blessings of that religious heritage and the promises that go with it. How this works is made abundantly clear in Galatians 3–4. Wild olive trees never produce useful oil. Since Paul clearly identifies the Gentiles with wild olive branches that have been grafted in, he is seeking to put overweening Gentile Christians in their place in two ways: He makes it clear that Jewish Christians, and before them the patriarchs, are the natural part of the tree, thus giving Jews precedence in the people of God, and that as wild olive branches the Gentiles bring nothing into the union. God simply grafts them in by pure grace.[100] They should not exult over the broken-off branches or over Jewish Christians because they do not carry the Jewish heritage. Rather, "the root carries you." On the basis of 1 Enoch 93.5, 8; Philo, *Quis rerum divinarum heres* 279; and *Jubilees* 21.24, "root" probably refers to the patriarchs, perhaps Abraham in particular. This conclusion may be supported by Rom. 4.1-2, where Abraham is called "*our* father according to the flesh."[101]

Paul's understanding of why all this has happened begins to become apparent in v. 19. Here again we have diatribe, and the interlocutor is a Gentile advocate of a different theology, one that says "the branches have been broken off so that I myself may be grafted in." The *hina* clause here surely indicates purpose. Paul actually agrees with this argument so far as it goes (v. 20), but it does not go far enough. This breaking off and grafting in is not some arbitrary process. Those whom God broke off were unbelieving, and those he grafted in he

98. See my discussion in *Jesus, Paul, and the End of the World*, p. 117.

99. This is what Paul is attempting to do for his Gentile audience in chs. 9–11. He wants them to embrace and appropriate this heritage, as well as gain newfound respect for Jews and Jewish Christians.

100. On the use of this analogy or metaphor see J. C. T. Havemann, "Cultivated Olive — Wild Olive: The Olive Tree Metaphor in Romans 11.16-24," *Neotestamentica* 31 (1997): 87-106.

101. See pp. 115-17 above.

grafted in by faith, and they stand only by faith. The datives of *pistis* and *apistia* are causal: the breaking off was "because of unfaith," not arbitrarily decided and done by God, and the standing was "because of faith." The corollary should be clear: if the Gentiles also manifest unfaith, they too may be broken off. They have an arbitrary or irrevocable privileged status no more than unfaithful Jewish individuals do. This being the case, Gentiles should not get high-minded but should fear God and realize that they are not beyond apostasy and unfaith and therefore not immune to the wrath of God should they behave in such fashion.

The logic of v. 21 should be clear. If God did not spare the natural branches from such a breaking off, from such a judgment (which nonetheless was not final), why should he spare the Gentiles from it? Thus there is absolutely no basis for Gentile boasting. V. 22 points out that God has more than one attribute — kindness and severity are mentioned. Thus God must be not only loved but also honored and obeyed. The Jews who fell away received severity, but the Gentiles kindness. It is necessary to persevere in that kindness, otherwise even Gentiles may be cut off. But if any do not remain or persevere in their unbelief, God has the power to graft them (namely unbelieving Jews) in again. V. 24 brings the analogy to a close. If a wild olive branch received mercy and was grafted into the natural olive tree, how much more should God have mercy on the natural branches temporarily broken off.

Paul makes a new beginning at v. 25 and explains that he does not want the Gentiles in the audience to be ignorant of the "mystery" of God's future plan of salvation for both Gentile and Jew and how it will work. Käsemann thinks that the mystery is the future salvation event itself for the Jews.[102] Some have suggested that Mark 13.10 might stand in the background here, and this is possible. That Paul reveals this mystery as something new may well suggest it was a special revelation Paul himself received, and like a prophet or seer he is proclaiming it here. 1 Cor. 13.2 groups mysteries closely with prophecies. Paul is talking about insight into the eschatological reality God will bring about. He seems to see salvation happening in three stages: rejection by Jews, acceptance by the full number of the Gentiles, and then all Israel will be saved. This is certainly different from the notion found in numerous OT and Jewish texts (Ps. 22.27; Isa. 2.2-3; 56.6-8; Mic. 4.2; Zech. 2.11; 14.16; Tobit 13.11; 14.6-7; *Psalms of Solomon* 17.34; *Testament of Zebulun* 9.8; *Testament of Benjamin* 9.2), in which the Gentiles flow into Zion after Israel has first been restored to its intended glory.

Paul's use of the language of hardening is interesting. In 9.18 he used the verb *sklērynō*, which normally has the sense of "harden" or "stiffen." In 11.25, however, we have a noun cognate of *pōroō*, which has the basic sense of "pet-

---

102. Käsemann, *Romans*, pp. 311-12.

rify" and in the passive the metaphorical sense of "become deadened" or "become insensible" (cf. Mark 6.52; 8.17; John 12.40; 2 Cor. 3.14). The OT sources of such ideas include Deut. 29.4 and Isa. 29.10, which have indeed been cited in 11.8. For Paul, when this judgment falls on Israel, it is temporal and not final judgment, as becomes clear in 11.25. This hardening happens "until" *(achris)* a particular point in time.

V. 25 says explicitly that the hardening came *apo merous* on Israel. Should this phrase be taken as adjectival or adverbial? In view of vv. 5, 7, and 17, Paul could affirm that hardening has come on all of Israel. Käsemann rightly points to the contrast with the *plērōma* which is mentioned just afterward.[103] Thus I must disagree with Käsemann's conclusion that what is meant is that all Israel experienced a partial hardening. This is not true of Paul and other Jewish Christians. Rather what must be meant is that a part of Israel, a large part, were hardened, but this condition was of a limited duration. *Achris* here must mean until — until the full number of the Gentiles enter into the kingdom. *Plērōma* must mean here what it meant earlier in this argument. It thus refers either to all the Gentiles who will be saved or to the additional number of Gentiles yet to be saved after Paul wrote. It does not mean the Gentile world as a whole. The implications of this verse must be allowed to have their full force — temporarily some Jews, but not all, are not part of the people of God because they have rejected Jesus' messiahship. Paul nowhere in Romans 9–11 suggests that there are two peoples of God.

In v. 26, one of the most controversial verses of these chapters,[104] the quandary is over whom "all Israel" refers to, (1) Jews and Gentiles in Christ,

---

103. Käsemann, *Romans,* pp. 312-13.

104. It is clear from G. Bray's survey (Bray, ed., *Romans* [Ancient Christian Commentary on Scripture; Downers Grove: InterVarsity, 1998], pp. 297-302) of the evidence from the early Church Fathers that the majority opinion was that after the full number of Gentiles were saved, then "all Israel" would be saved, which was understood to mean many Jews, if not all, and this would transpire when Jesus returned. For example, Theodoret, in *Interpretation of Romans,* says: "After the Gentiles accepted the Gospel, the Jews would believe, when the great Elijah would come to them and bring them the doctrine of faith." On the meaning of the "all" in the "all Israel" phrase, Diodore, in *Pauline Commentary,* says: this "does not mean that every one of them will be but that either those who were understood by Elijah or those scattered all over the world will one day come to faith." Pelagius, in *Commentary on Romans,* says: "Christ will come again to set them free." Cyril of Alexandria, in *Explanation of Romans,* says: "Israel will be saved eventually, a hope which Paul confirms by quoting this text of Scripture. For indeed Israel will be saved in its own time and will be called at the end, after the calling of the Gentiles" (all cited by Bray, pp. 298-99). Finally, we may quote what Ambrosiaster says of the future of Jews in his *Commentary on Paul's Epistles:* "they will be received with joy when they return to the faith, because God's love for them is stirred up by the memory of their ancestors" (Bray, p. 299). It is true that Augustine believed "all Israel" here meant Jews and Gentiles united in one people (*Letters* 149), but as usual his is a minority opinion.

(2) all the elect of Israel, (3) the whole nation of Israel including every individual, or (4) the nation of Israel with certain exceptions.[105] It is extremely problematic to understand "Israel" in v. 26 to mean something different than it means in v. 25, where it surely does not refer to any Gentiles, especially since v. 26 is linked to v. 25 by *kai houtōs*. Furthermore, since Jews and Gentiles are contrasted throughout vv. 11-32, one would expect that to be true in v. 26 as well.

Houtōs in itself normally has the meaning "so" or "in this manner," but combined with *kai* it could refer to a temporal rather than just logical sequence, with the sense "and then" or "and thus." Van der Horst produces various examples where *kai houtōs* has the temporal sense of "thereafter" or "and then."[106] For example, in Theophrastus's *Characters* 18, after checking to ensure that all of the house is locked up, only then *(kai houtōs)* is the owner able to go to sleep. In Plato *Protagoras* 314c Socrates and Hippocrates are said to finish their discussion, and "thereafter" or "only then" go into the house. The temporal sense of *kai houtōs* is especially clear in Epictetus 2.15.8 (see also Plato, *Gorgias* 457d; Xenophon, *Anabasis* 7.1.4; *Cyropedia* 2.1.1; Aristotle, *Poetics* 1455b1). There are also examples from Jewish literature (e.g., *Testament of Abraham* 7.11) and the NT, for example in Acts 7.8, where the sense is surely that "God gave Abraham the covenant of circumcision and thereafter *(kai houtōs)* Abraham begot Isaac." "Luke does not want to inform his readers about the physical condition in which Abraham begot the son that would be the heir of the covenant, but about the fact that this happened only after he had received the sign of this covenant!"[107] Acts 20.11 seems even clearer. In 1 Thess. 4.16-17 a temporal sequence is clearly in view, as is made evident by the use of *epeita* in v. 16: "the dead in Christ will rise first; *thereafter* we who are alive, who are left, will be caught up in the clouds together with them to meet the Lord in the air, *and then* we will be with the Lord forever" (see also 1 Cor. 14.25).[108] "Quite apart from the grammatical and lexical possibilities that the word *houtōs* had, it is also the context of Rom. 11 that makes it very probable that it was the temporal meaning of *houtōs* that the author had in mind here."[109]

Even if, less probably, *houtōs* does mean "in this manner,"[110] then the combination of vv. 25-26 should probably be read: "some Jews have been hardened until the full number of Gentiles are brought in (by grace through faith), and *in the same manner* all Israel will be saved." The discussion then of this

---

105. See the full-length monograph on the subject by F. Refoulé, ". . . *Et ainsi tout Israel sera sauvé*": *Romains 11,25-32* (Paris: Cerf, 1984).

106. P. W. Van der Horst, "Only Then Will All Israel Be Saved: A Short Note on the Meaning of *kai houtōs* in Romans 11.26," *JBL* 119 (2000): 521-25.

107. Van der Horst, "Only Then," pp. 523-24.

108. Van der Horst, "Only Then," p. 524.

109. Van der Horst, "Only Then," p. 524.

110. See the discussion by Wright, "Romans," pp. 690-91.

verse should also not be isolated from what Paul has already said in v. 15 — first the reconciliation of the Gentile world while Jews are temporarily rejected, then these Jews will be accepted, which will be the signal for the resurrection. Dunn recognizes a reference to the parousia in the Scripture quotation which follows, but seems to think that in this verse Paul is talking about the effect of the full number of Gentiles coming in, provoking Israel to jealousy and so to conversion.[111] But Paul could just as well be paralleling the way Israel will finally be brought back in to the way Gentiles were brought in — by mercy, grace, and faith, without linking the two events. The grammatical and lexical evidence produced above in any case favors the temporal sense of *kai houtōs* here, as does the context of Paul's discussion.[112]

Against view (3) above of v. 26, elsewhere in this chapter Paul has made very clear that he believes apostasy happens. Persons do not remain saved unless they remain or stand in and on their faith. We cannot assume that Paul would say anything here to vitiate his previous argument about salvation being by grace and through faith. Thus, it would appear that (2) and (4) above are the only really viable views of this verse. The problem with arguing that all the elect from Israel are meant is that such a view would be self-evident, even absurdly so in light of what Paul has already said. More importantly, he is speaking about something that transpires at the eschaton. Furthermore, in 1 Sam. 7.5; 25.1; 1 Kgs. 12.1; 2 Chron. 12.1; Dan. 9.11; *Jubilees* 50.9; *Testament of Levi* 17.5; and Mishnah *Sanhedrin* 10.1 "all Israel" does not mean literally every single Israelite (cf. also 1 Sam. 18.16; 2 Sam. 2.9; 3.21; Deut 31.11; Judg. 8.27). There are some exceptions. Mishnah *Sanhedrin* 10.1 deserves to be quoted: "All Israel have a share in the world to come . . . except he that says that the Law is not from heaven . . . and he that reads heretical books, or that utters charms over a wound. . . . Also he that pronounces the Name with its proper letters." The idea then is that the great mass of Israelites or a very large number are saved.[113]

We must remember that Paul has been discussing non-Christian Jews. He already knew of many saved Jewish Christians and it is hardly likely he has them in view here. Rather, he says this "all Israel" group will be saved after the full number of Gentiles has come in. Therefore, he is talking about a mass conversion of non-Christian Jews at the end of salvation history. As we have seen, *houtōs* here probably means "then." Some commentators have thought on the

111. J. D. G. Dunn, *Romans 9–16*, Word Biblical Commentary Series (Dallas: Word, 1988), p. 681.

112. See Talbert, *Romans*, p. 264.

113. Volf, *Paul and Perseverance*, p. 185, thinks Paul has in mind the great mass of Jews who have responded either positively or negatively to the gospel in the gospel era. But this makes a mockery of the bold pronunciation that all Israel will be saved, because in fact Paul would be talking about only a small minority of the many generations of Jews.

basis of this word alone, translated "thus," that what Paul has just mentioned is the end of the process: when the fullness of the Gentiles comes in, this itself will be "all Israel" being saved. V. 15 is definitely against such a view.[114] And it was Israel which was hardened in v. 25, not saved, unlike the Gentiles, and in v. 26 this same Israel is then said to be saved. *Testament of Dan* 6.4; *Testament of Judah* 23.5; and 4 Ezra 4.38-43 say that Israel has missed the mark, needs to repent, and will do so before the end, at which time the end will come and salvation will come to the Gentiles. Paul has just inverted the order of this sequence.

Paul quotes Isa. 59.20-21a as a sort of proof-text to show that this truth he is conveying about Israel was already mentioned in the OT. He has altered the text, which speaks of a Deliverer coming *to* Zion (MT) or *on behalf of* Zion (LXX), to "from" Zion. He has in mind the new Jerusalem (see Gal. 4.26). The quotation refers to what will happen to non-Christian Jews when the Deliverer comes, namely at the parousia.[115] There is some evidence from later Jewish discussions that Isa. 59.20-21 was referred to Messiah rather than God, and Paul may be following a tradition of that understanding of the text. Cranfield suggests that we compare 1 Thess. 1.10 at this juncture.[116] Thus, when Christ comes again he will turn back unbelief among his Jewish kin. Then indeed he will come for the lost sheep of Israel, and they will finally hear. But this quotation also clearly implies that only the Deliverer will accomplish this, not some present plan to evangelize Jews.

Vv. 30 and 31 contrast the present status of Jews and Gentiles in two different ways. According to the gospel the Jews are "enemies" (or one might translate this "hated") for the Gentiles' sake. But according to the election they are loved for the sake of the fathers. The free gift and call to Israel are irrevocable, even if individual Jews choose to opt out of God's salvation plan for them. For in the same way that Gentiles were once disobedient to God, but now in the eschatological age have been ushered in and have found mercy through Christ and through the Jews' disobedience, so also the Jews have been disobedient so that they too may find mercy.

V. 32 sums this all up nicely: God shut up all to disobedience in order that he might have mercy on all. This means that all Paul has said about hardening and Israel being vessels of wrath was a *temporary* condition and had the ultimate purpose of God having mercy on all,[117] or, to put it another way, that God did this so all would have to relate to him on the basis of grace and faith, so

---

114. See Barrett, *Romans*, p. 206.

115. Against the special pleading of Wright, "Romans," pp. 692-93. It is interesting that Theodoret was very clear on this matter: "After the Gentiles accepted the Gospel, the Jews would believe, when the great Elijah would come to them and bring them the doctrine of faith." See Bray, ed., *Romans*, p. 298.

116. Cranfield, *Romans*, 2:578-79.

117. See Chrysostom, *Homily on Romans* 19: "None of these things is immutable; neither your good nor their evil." See Bray, ed., *Romans*, p. 295.

none would think they had God in their debt, or that he owed them something. It also means that God did it this way so that all would recognize that he alone sets right sinners, the ungodly, which includes all the human race, even pious humans of all sorts.[118]

This was a very scandalous and unconventional gospel that Paul preached, and it is clear that Paul sees all things in light of his understanding of God's righteousness, which involves both wrath and salvation.

> The whole epistle stands under the sign that no person [not even a Jew] is justified by works and that even the pious do not enter the kingdom of God on the basis of their piety. . . . Paul is bold enough to view both each individual and world history from the standpoint of the doctrine of justification. The end of the old world and the beginning of the new world can be thought of only as justification of the ungodly. Logically then the problem of Israel can only be solved under the same theme.[119]

While Käsemann's forensic way of putting this does not capture the scope of what Paul means by *dikaiosynē*, he is basically correct, and as the doxology which follows will show, all humans are indebted to the riches of God's mercy.

And it is precisely the contemplation of the mercy of God that leads Paul into an outburst of doxological praise in vv. 33-36, which conclude this magisterial argument. Paul first extols the infinite resources of God. The juxtaposition of "depth" and "riches" suggests a bottomless treasury of mercy.[120] God understands all, wishes to have mercy on all, and has the wisdom to work out a plan where even those temporarily left out can be grafted back in, because he is a God of second chances and forgiveness. The means he devised to have mercy on all was not something one could figure out, even from close study of the OT. This doxology, like a good deal of the discussion in chs. 1–11, is rooted in the Jewish wisdom tradition (cf. 2 *Baruch* 14.8, 9; 20.4; 1QH 7.26-33; 10.3-7). It is the longest of Paul's doxologies. God's judgments, his decisions about the world and about human matters, cannot be figured out by human beings.

In v. 34 Paul quotes Isa. 40.13 (LXX). A full forty percent of Paul's OT quotations in this section, and for that matter in Romans, are from Isaiah. God's mind is unknowable unless he reveals it. Hence the need for the revelation of his apocalyptic secret of a salvation plan.

Furthermore, God is in no one's debt. V. 35 quotes Job 41.11 from some source other than the LXX. "With God, man never earns a recompense; he can only be loved and treated with mercy."[121] It is striking that in his concluding

118. See Talbert, *Romans*, pp. 265-67.
119. Käsemann, *Romans*, p. 315.
120. Dunn, *Romans 9–16*, p. 699.
121. Barrett, *Romans*, p. 211.

words of this last of the theological arguments, Paul speaks of God in what seem to be Stoic, but also biblical, terms. Marcus Aurelius, *Meditations* 4.23 says: "From thee are all things, in thee are all things, unto thee are all things" (cf. Seneca, *Epistulae* 65.8). God is the source, the means, and the goal of all things, all historical purposes, and all salvific events. Paul's largely Gentile audience may well have known this familiar saying, and he may have used it here precisely because, rhetorically speaking, it would help him to win over his audience to his remarkable view of Jews and Gentiles in God's plan of salvation. The God Gentiles had known only vaguely through sources like nature (Romans 1) and Stoic thought, Paul is now glorifying because he is the God of all peoples in all ages. God's plan is for Jews and Gentiles to be saved in and by Jesus Christ and to be united in Christ.

It may be that this doxology is theologically rather than christologically focused precisely because Paul is speaking for the Jews that he has just said are yet to be saved, the "all Israel" who can speak this doxology, but not one focused on Jesus. The God of the Bible then, as described in this climactic argument, is the one to whom all praise and glory should be given forever, for this God alone is the one who can judge all and still extend mercy to all. When Paul turns to the parenesis in ch. 12, he will build precisely on the lessons learned in chs. 9–11 about the saving mercy and great righteousness of God which believers appropriate the benefits of, and try to live on the basis of, through faith in Jesus Christ.

Bridging the Horizons

I grew up in a neighborhood in High Point, North Carolina that was substantially Jewish. My closest neighborhood friends with whom I laughed and cried and played and stayed were Jews. I played basketball with them, attended basmitzvoth, and broke my arm in their yard, showing off for Sheryl and Dana, my closest Jewish friends. Even though my family moved to another part of town, Sheryl and I continued to be friends and to go through school together. I now lived closer to the synagogue and would play basketball with Harvey and Larry after Hebrew school, and I enjoyed going to functions there. There came a day when Sheryl approached me at school about going to a dance. You could tell she felt a little awkward about asking me, but we had been friends a long time. She wanted to go to the dance at the Country Club, and her regular date had stopped seeing her. She asked if I would take her. I of course said yes, but there was a cloud over this matter. This was the 1960s, and country clubs with an all, or almost all, W.A.S.P. membership did not permit any Jews to attend functions, much less be members. Undaunted, Sheryl and I decided to go and try to have a good time, which we managed to do. It taught me a lesson in life, namely to try to see the world from the point of view of those who faced far more discrimination than I had every known.

Prejudice in any age is an ugly sin, and Paul deals with just such prejudice in chs. 9–11. His largely Gentile audience seems to follow the normal Roman understanding of Jews, namely that Jews are an inferior race and, more to the point, a religiously inferior race. The great danger after the edict of Claudius in A.D. 49 was that Gentile Christians in Rome would believe that God had quite rightly rejected his first chosen people for people like themselves. So Paul must offer a tour-de-force argument to counter such prejudice, which is combined in a deadly amalgam with bad theology. The truth is that such battles have to be fought and won in every generation of human history because humanity is still a fallen lot.

Argument Ten — 12.1-21:
Living Sacrifices and Loving Service

Romans 12–15 has sometimes been viewed as an ethical miscellany without connections or coherence. But, as Dunn says, "chaps. 12–15 follow naturally from and constitute a necessary corollary to the overall argument of chaps. 1–11; they should not be regarded as a piece of standard parenesis which has not direct material or thematic connection with what has gone before and could have been discarded or wholly reordered without loss."[1] Campbell rightly stresses that Paul is trying to create a community ethos in Rome so that there can be unity in the midst of diversity, a church of Jews and Gentiles, not a third sort of entity which is neither Jewish nor Gentile.[2] The Christian faith and praxis which the Roman Christians share in common should distinguish them from others more than their differences divide them from each other. In regard to these differences, "Gentiles must not regard observance of the Jewish Law as incompatible with Christian faith, and Jews must not regard it as essential to the Christian faith. Justification by faith demands freedom of lifestyle in faith."[3] Stowers puts things a bit differently: Romans "12–15 sketches an ethic of community based on the principle of faithfulness as adaptability to others."[4] These very qualities of adaptability and self-sacrifice for the sake of the community

1. J. D. G. Dunn, *Romans 9–16*, Word Biblical Commentary Series (Dallas: Word, 1988), p. 703.

2. W. S. Campbell, "The Rule of Faith in Romans 12.1–15.13," in *Pauline Theology*, ed. D. M. Hay and E. E. Johnson, vol. 3: *Romans* (Minneapolis: Fortress, 1995), pp. 259-86, here p. 278.

3. Campbell, "The Rule of Faith," p. 283.

4. S. K. Stowers, *A Rereading of Romans: Justice, Jews, and Gentiles* (New Haven: Yale University Press, 1994), p. 318.

are precisely what one would expect a rhetor to speak about when the goal is unity, concord, harmony in a fractured or divided community.

Deliberative rhetoric quite frequently included exhortations, as the rhetor would try to persuade the audience to take action in one way or another (Aristotle, *Rhetoric* I 1354a3-6). We do indeed have coherent arguments in this portion of Romans that center on issues that divided or were likely to divide the church in Rome.[5] Paul is dealing with various matters that detract from the unity or stability of the Roman Christian community, at the center of which is the Jew-Gentile question. He wishes to see the gospel fully realized in Rome, which involves Christian Jews and Gentiles not merely getting along with each other but actually forming a unified people of God.[6] "The unity/disunity theme ties together the whole of 12.1–15.13."[7]

Paul clearly knows of some things that are disturbing and dividing Christians in Rome. The aim of chs. 1–11 has been to produce a situation where the audience understands that Jews and Gentiles are on equal footing in grace and in disgrace, in salvation and in sin. All stand under the mercy of God and have need of it. The *refutatio* in chs. 9–11 was meant to counter anti-Semitic feelings or attitudes of Roman Gentile superiority, which were impeding the coming together of a unified body of Christ, Jewish and Gentile, in Rome. Paul made clear there that God has not given up on Israel, nor have God's promises to Jews failed. But it is one thing to dismantle the intellectual underpinnings of hubris, division, discord, and dissension by establishing that all are saved by grace and through faith and that God has not reneged on his promises to anyone, but another thing to deal with the ethical manifestations of such attitudes and beliefs. In chs. 12–15 Paul will attempt to bring harmony to the praxis of the Roman church, to its members' relationship with the state, and to other matters as well.

Ch. 12 serves as something of a tone-setting exercise or preamble to the more particular exhortations, which begin in ch. 13. Paul will try to establish the ethical basis for all Christian conduct in a two-part argument — 12.1-8 and 9-21. Rhetoricians called the hortatory portion of a letter *parainetikon,* from which our word parenesis comes (*Instit. Or.* 9.2.103). It was a regular part of such ethical arguments to stir the audience up by appealing to the stronger

5. Dunn, *Romans 9–16,* p. 707: "Paul begins with an exhortation which summarizes the claim of his gospel . . . which sets out the basis for all Christian lifestyle and relationships, and which deliberately indicates the balance necessary between personal commitment and divine enabling. . . . the verses pick up previous threads of the discussion in a parenesis which reflects the course of the complete discussion to this point."

6. P. Towner, "Romans 13.1-7 and Paul's Missiological Perspective," in *Romans and the People of God,* ed. S. K. Soderlund and N. T. Wright (Grand Rapids: Eerdmans, 1999), pp. 149-69, here pp. 152-53.

7. Towner, "Romans 13.1-7 and Paul's Missiological Perspective," p. 153.

emotions of love or hate and the like. Paul will do that, especially in vv. 9-21 where he will draw on the teachings of Jesus about love. His theological argument was undergirded throughout with the notions of grace and faith, and his ethical argument will be undergirded with the notion of love in action, and he will indeed try to create pathos in the audience by the time he reaches the *peroratio.* These are, then, emotion-charged ethical arguments and not merely a grab-bag of ethical ideas.

As we will see, after developing the theme of mercy in chs. 9–11 Paul immediately builds on this theme in ch. 12, making God's compassion for his audience the basis for his appeals, and he will return to the same theme near the end of the parenesis, in 15.9. More importantly, while chs. 9–11 have been an intertextual exploration using the OT, one could say that chs. 12–15 are an inter-traditional exploration in which Paul will quote, allude to, paraphrase, and echo the oral teaching of Jesus at various junctures (especially 12.14, 18; 13.7, 8-10; 14.10, 13, 14, 17, 18; 15.1-2).

Dunn sees this *a-b-c-d-c-b-a* pattern in the parenesis: *a* 12.1-2 — the basis for responsible living by implication other than the Mosaic Law, *b* 12.3-8 — the body of Christ as the social expression of God's people, *c* 12.9-21 — love as the fundamental moral imperative in human relationships, *d* 13.1-7 — Christians and the powers that be, *c′* 13.8-10 — love of neighbor as fulfillment of the law in human relationships, *b′* 13.11-14 — Christ as the pattern of Christian living, *a′* 14.1–15.6 — the basis for social interaction by implication other than the Mosaic Law.[8] The large size of the final section, which in fact has various facets and parts, is a problem for this outline. But Dunn has established that there is an order to this material. Paul will visit the same themes more than once to drive home the point. This is a good rhetorical strategy when one is trying to change behavior patterns, and it becomes clear that Paul's call to obedience is fundamentally grounded in the teaching of Jesus, rather than the Mosaic Law, with which it differs in certain key respects. The difficulty of course is that Paul also reaffirms, as did Jesus, some but not all portions of the Mosaic Law as applicable to the life of Jesus' followers. Paul does not see a solution to the ethical dilemmas in Rome in the submission of all to the Mosaic Law.[9] Instead, his moral vision is both wider and other than that of Moses, for it is grounded in Jesus' eschatologi-

---

8. Dunn, *Romans 9–16,* p. 706.

9. While Paul does in effect discourse here on the Law of Christ established for believers, Christ having been the termination of the Mosaic Law as a way of righteousness, he does not label it as such, something he does do in Galatians 6 and 1 Corinthians 9. In Paul's view, the Law of Christ includes: (1) the teaching and example of Christ; (2) portions of the Mosaic Law that Christ reaffirmed; and (3) Christian teaching of various sorts, including the reuse of some Greco-Roman and early Jewish teaching, particularly sapiential and apocalyptic teaching from early Judaism. See my discussion in *Grace in Galatia* (Grand Rapids: Eerdmans, 1998), pp. 418-26.

cal vision of a community ethic,[10] as the eschatological references, for instance in 12.1-2 and 13.11-14, make clear. It is not just a matter of a new law or ethic but of a new and eschatological situation in which the Spirit of God has been fully poured out, enabling God's people to press on to the "obedience of faith."

Brothers, I call upon you because of the compassion of God to offer your bodies as living sacrifices, holy, pleasing to God as your reasonable/logical worship, and not model yourselves on this aeon, but be transformed by the renewal of mind,[11] for the determining of what the will of God is — the good and pleasing and perfect.

For I say through the grace given to me to all those among you not to esteem [yourselves] higher than it is necessary to think, but to think so as to be of sound mind, to each as God has divided according to the measure of faith. For thus in one body we have many members, but all members do not have the same function, thus the many are one body in Christ, individually members of one another. But having grace gifts differing according to the grace given to you, either prophecy according to the proportion of faith, or serving in practical service, or the one teaching in teaching, or the one exhorting in exhortation, or the one giving a share in simplicity, or the one ruling in diligence, the one having mercy in gladness.

Love without hypocrisy, abhorring the evil, clinging to the good. Love one another, be warm in affection, take the lead in honoring one another, be diligent, not inert, fervent in spirit, serving unto the Lord, rejoicing in hope, bearing up in distress, continuing faithfully in prayer, sharing in common the needs of the saints, seeking to practice hospitality. Bless those persecuting [you],[12] bless and do not curse. Rejoice with those rejoicing, mourn with those mourning. Think along the same lines with one another, not thinking too highly, but associating humbly with one another. Not being wise in your own estimation, never rendering evil for evil, having a regard for what is honorable before all human beings; if possible, for your part be at peace with all human beings, not seeking to vindicate yourself, beloved, but leave a place for the wrath [of God], for it is written: "Vindication is mine, I will repay" says the Lord. But if your enemy is hungry, feed him. If thirsty give him drink. For by doing this you will heap coals of fire upon his head. Do not let yourself be conquered by evil, but conquer the evil in the good.

10. See especially R. B. Hays, *The Moral Vision of the New Testament: A Contemporary Introduction to New Testament Ethics* (San Francisco: Harper, 1996), pp. 16-59. N. T. Wright, "Romans," in *The New Interpreter's Bible*, vol. 10 (Nashville: Abingdon, 2002), p. 700, rightly says: "Romans 12–16 is the ultimate answer to those who suggest that Paul's 'ethics' are not really related to his 'theology.'"

11. The word "your" is found in ℵ, D, L, P, and most minuscules, but the text without it has strong support in 𝔭46, A, B, D, F, G and is probably original. See B. M. Metzger, *A Textual Commentary on the Greek New Testament* (3rd ed.; London: United Bible Societies, 1971), p. 466.

12. In my view the "you" is probably original, as Paul is quoting a saying of Jesus — Matt. 5.44/Luke 6.28.

Religion and religious rituals were indeed a major and appropriate theme for deliberative rhetoric. In v. 1 Paul will use the language of sacrificial ritual to talk about the posture of Christian living as an offering up to God of self. The first words out of his mouth are not a command but an appeal because he understands that the way to deal with ethical matters is by means of persuasion. There is a place for imperatives, but they must be used in a context in which the audience has been appealed to to make the right moral choices. The matter lies in their hands, and Paul places the onus on himself to persuade them to take the right course. He calls his audience "brothers," seeking to establish a clear Christian bond with them after all the discussion about Israel in chs. 9–11. The basis for his appeal is the compassion of God. *Oiktirmon*, "compassion," is not the term used in chs. 9–11 for mercy, but the sense is close, and the cognate verb has been used in 9.15. This appeal justifies the dictum that for Paul, if all theology is "grace," all ethics is a matter of "gratitude," the response of the grateful heart to God's merciful gift of salvation.

The audience must offer themselves up to God. In fact, Paul will say that they must offer their very bodies up to God,[13] for their bodies are the vehicles through which they act and behave in various ways. The body, indeed the whole self, must become a living, as opposed to dead, sacrifice, which is holy and acceptable or pleasing to God.[14] "Body," as opposed to "limbs," is appropriate here because sacrifice entailed the offering of the entire animal.[15] But animal sacrifices are no longer necessary in Paul's view. Something more demanding is now required. One must give oneself totally to God, and God will accept no substitutes, not least because the process of substitution was brought to its climax and completion in Christ's death. Paul then says that this *is* their reasonable or logical worship.[16] He thus unites worship with ethics, adoration with behavior. Those who have presented their bodies to God as a sacrifice belong no longer to themselves but to God. The offerer no lon-

---

13. E. Käsemann, *Commentary on Romans* (Grand Rapids: Eerdmans, 1980), p. 327, stresses that "body" refers to our being in relationship to the world, or the outward expression of our being.

14. Chrysostom, *Homily* 20 on Romans: "How is the body to become a sacrifice? Let the eye look on no evil thing, and it has already become a sacrifice. Let the tongue say nothing filthy, and it has become an offering. Let your hand do nothing evil, and it has become a whole burnt offering. But even this is not enough for we must have good works also. The hands must do alms, the mouth must bless those who curse it, and the ears must find time to listen to the reading of Scripture. Sacrifice allows no unclean thing. It is the first fruit of all other actions" (see G. Bray, ed., *Romans* [Ancient Christian Commentary on Scripture; Downers Grove: InterVarsity, 1998], p. 306).

15. Dunn, *Romans 9–16*, p. 709.

16. The term *latreia* is the same as the one used in 9.4 for Israel's worship, and there is no good reason not to translate it as "worship" here.

ger has the final say over his behavior. He or she is now God's property and
must behave according to God's dictates. But God does not want a dead human sacrifice but a living and lively one. He does not want something *from*
us; he wants *us*.

Worship is where the creature recognizes that he or she is a creature and
God is the Creator. It is an act of submission or ordering oneself under the Divine. It is also by implication a denial of one's own divinity, a denial that one is
lord of one's own life. If one does what this verse says, then it follows that one
has committed herself to obeying the commandments and exhortations that
follow. But, more than this, Paul is suggesting that all of life should be
doxological, an offering up to God, an act of worship.

Believers must present themselves in a pleasing manner, and God will indeed be pleased with what we offer. "This is counterintuitive for many Christians, schooled to insist that nothing we can do can commend ourselves to God.
But Paul insists . . . that Christian worship and obedience, holiness and unity do
indeed please God. . . ."[17] "Those in the flesh" cannot please God (8.8), but
those "in the Spirit" can.

This self-offering is our "reasonable" or "logical" worship (cf. 1 Pet. 2.2,
5).[18] Here the Jerusalem Bible is helpful with its paraphrase: "worship worthy
of thinking beings." Worship, that is, reflective of what we know and recognize to be true of God and what God has done. Humans are capable of being
rational and recognizing that God is worthy of worship. Paul here is again
perhaps drawing on a connection with thought that would be familiar to his
Roman audience. Epictetus 1.16.20-21 says: "If I were a nightingale, I should
be singing as a nightingale; if a swan as a swan. But as it is I am a rational
(logikos) being, therefore I must be singing hymns of praise to God." Paul is
also in some respects close here to Philo, who says "The soul . . . ought to
honor God not irrationally nor ignorantly, but with knowledge and reason"
(*Special Laws* 1.209).

But there may be more meaning. As Wright suggests, Paul may mean the
worship to which our logic or arguments have been pointing.[19] Paul's arguments have led to doxology at the end of chs. 8 and 11. Furthermore, *oun*, the
connective "therefore," means that what Paul says in 12.1 is based on what he has
argued previously. It is a conclusion based on the preceding arguments. So he
can be saying "in light of what we have argued in chs. 1–11 about the compassion of God, I appeal to you to present yourselves to God in a form and sort of
worship toward which our logic or arguments have been pointing." This does

17. Wright, "Romans," p. 704.
18. See M. Reasoner, "The Theology of Romans 12.1–15.13," in Hay and Johnson, eds.,
Pauline Theology, vol. 3, pp. 287-99, here pp. 294-95.
19. Wright, "Romans," p. 705.

full justice to the connection, especially between the end of ch. 11, with its theme of mercy, and what we find here.[20]

V. 2 offers a deliberate and stark contrast. One is not to be conformed but rather transformed. Paul will contrast the way "this age" tries to mold a person and the way the eschatological situation now present in the midst of this age seeks to change a person. Paul often uses the phrase "this age" (1 Cor. 1.20; 2.6, 8; 3.18; 2 Cor. 4.4; Eph. 1.21 and cf. Gal. 1.4; 1 Cor. 3.19; 5.10; 7.31). He believes that, while believers live in this world and this age, the form of this world is passing away. It is foolish to conform oneself to what is obsolescent and on the way out. More importantly, conforming to this age involves conforming one's life to something other than the pattern of Christ.[21] Paul is not calling for believers to abandon this age, but to live in it while not being "of" it.

Instead, there is to be a metamorphosis of the believer's mind. The verbs translated "conform" and "transform," while imperative, are in the present continual tense. Paul is talking about a process of de-enculturation and reorientation. There may be some force to the suggestion that, since the term *schēma* is at the heart of the first verb and *morphē* at the heart of the second, the latter refers to the outward expression of what one is within, whereas the "schema" refers primarily to the outward form of the person. Outward conformity, then, as opposed to inward transformation which is outwardly expressed, seems to be in view.[22] Here again, Paul is using a concept familiar in Stoicism, that of moral or inward transformation (see Seneca, *Epistulae* 6.1).

Since it is the mind that is being transformed, Paul is talking about a change in worldview, a Copernican revolution in one's thinking, not just an attitude adjustment. He is speaking about a new or "renewed"[23] and Christlike way of looking at the world. In the light of the previous verse, Paul must surely also mean that to offer proper and rational worship one must have a renewed mind. For one thing, one's concept of God, the one true God, must be renewed

---

20. See K. Grieb, *The Story of Romans: A Narrative Defense of God's Righteousness* (Louisville: Westminster/John Knox, 2002), p. 117: "'I appeal to you, *therefore*, . . . by the mercies of God' represents the most important 'therefore' in the epistle. Paul's request that the Roman Christians order their lives according to the pattern of Christ is based on everything that has gone before."

21. Dunn, *Romans 9–16*, p. 712.

22. C. K. Barrett, *A Commentary on the Epistle to the Romans* (Peabody: Hendrickson, 1991), p. 213, is of course right that there was much more to paganism than mere rote ritual or outward conformity. It also engaged the mind and the heart of many. Yet when one studies how worship was a matter of the perfect performance of a sacrifice and the ritual involved (or else it had to be done all over again), there was a very strong emphasis on the perfect form of worship, through the offering of the perfect sacrifice. It is thus understandable how Paul might emphasize that element in his contrast here.

23. *Anakainōsis* occurs for the first time in Greek literature here.

or transformed. Renewal of mind and presentation of body are two parts of what must happen if one is to offer true worship to God. But Paul also says that the renewal of the mind is the prerequisite to discerning the will of God, and so to behaving as well as believing in a way that worships and glorifies God. "Paul holds forth a different (eschatological) spirituality (not cult-focused) and ethic (not law-determined) for the Roman congregations."[24] Discernment of what is good and pleasing and perfect in God's will and eyes is possible only if the fallen person has had a transformation and renewal of his or her mind. Precisely because the believer is a new eschatological creation, though living in an old and obsolescent world, new modes of behavior are expected, indeed required.[25] As Wright suggests, v. 1 focuses on the body but with the mind involved, and v. 2 focuses on the mind but with implications about what the body does.[26] These two verses then together refer to the whole person dedicated to God in all things and orientations.

Notice that Paul expects not just obedience from believers, but moral discernment.[27] For many, perhaps most, situations in life, there is not a specific biblical rule to tell one precisely what to do. Therefore, one must have a renewed mind, gain a moral vision, and develop a competency in moral discernment to determine what is indeed good and pleasing and perfect in God's sight. One will be able to do this only if one's mind is being renewed and one is also consciously disengaging from the world's orientation and prevailing assumptions. Phillips's translation expresses the latter half of this well: "Don't let the world around you squeeze you into its mould." There are thus both disengagement and new orientation going on at the same time. God's will is the definition of what is good and pleasing and perfect, but discerning what this looks like in specific incidents in the fallen world is often difficult.

With the preamble or presuppositions addressed in vv. 1-2, Paul turns in v. 3 to addressing particular concerns. The connection between what precedes and what we have here is made clear by Wright: "Offer God the true worship; be transformed by having your minds renewed, because you should be thinking as one people in the Messiah."[28] Paul's ethic is not for isolated individual Chris-

24. Dunn, *Romans 9–16*, p. 715.
25. See V. P. Furnish, *Theology and Ethics in Paul* (Nashville: Abingdon, 1968).
26. Wright, "Romans," p. 705.
27. P. Stuhlmacher, *Paul's Letter to the Romans* (Louisville: Westminster/John Knox, 1994), p. 186, rightly points out that Paul is dealing with samples of moral discourse and issues here, not some sort of comprehensive treatment. He expects the audience to take the examples and then extrapolate from them, using moral discernment, to figure out what is good and pleasing in other situations. Stuhlmacher adds that Paul "does not know, and has also never approved of a justification which does not introduce and lead to a life of righteousness."
28. Wright, "Romans," p. 708.

tians, but rather it is a community-forming ethic. "We would rightly expect, therefore, that Paul's description of the community whose minds are renewed to conform to the image of Christ would at the same time largely consist of recommendations for actions and attitudes that lead to living in peace."[29]

We have already seen from chs. 1–2 and 9–11 that the Gentile Christians in Rome, who make up the vast majority of the audience for this letter, have a hubris problem.[30] It is wrong then to see the material here as just generalized exhortations, with Paul hoping that some will strike the mark. He is talking about an appropriate estimate of oneself. No one should overestimate himself or herself, or esteem himself or herself higher than is necessary. This echoes what Paul has already said specifically to Gentiles in 11.25. The Greco-Roman world used much hyperbolic rhetoric about one's status and standing and abilities, as on the honorific columns and in the imperial decrees. A sound or sober mind neither over- nor underestimates itself. It is interesting that sober-mindedness was among the virtues Aristotle stressed (*Nicomachean Ethics* 1117b 13).[31] The essence of the meaning is soundness of mind, discretion, and moderation with regard to things.[32]

Paul makes it clear that it is God who has bestowed varying abilities on persons, and in fact God has also given different measures of faith to different persons. The phrase "measure of faith" in v. 3 must be compared with the similar phrase in v. 6.[33] Paul is saying that believers need to evaluate themselves honestly on the basis of the gifts and measure of faith God has given them. After the verb *merizō*, the phrase is most naturally taken to refer to the apportioning of different measures, in this case of faith. This is the meaning of such a phrase in 1 Cor. 7.17 and 2 Cor. 10.13, which is the closest usage to our text.[34] This comment is a prelude to the discussion of the exercising of spiritual gifts and is meant to be a guiding principle of sorts. "Faith" here does not refer to saving faith but to some particular or special kind of faith, such as faith for healing and the like (see 1 Corinthians 13), faith that gives one a power to do special things. If a person constantly remembers that his spiritual abilities are gifts he has received from God, this is a major hedge against inflated thinking. "The man who is humble before God is unlikely to be arrogant before his fellow-creatures."[35]

Another part of how one is to think about oneself is to see oneself as part of the body of Christ, not as an isolated or individual entity. Thus, v. 4 reminds

29. Grieb, *The Story of Romans,* p. 120.
30. See pp. 73-76 above, and pp. 236-56 above.
31. See B. Byrne, *Romans,* Sacra Pagina (Collegeville: Liturgical, 1996), p. 368.
32. See Barrett, *Romans,* p. 217.
33. See Dunn, *Romans 9–16,* pp. 721-22.
34. See Dunn, *Romans 9–16,* pp. 721-22.
35. See Dunn, *Romans 9–16,* pp. 721-22.

one and all that the body has many members and not all have the same function. This counters divisions in a very similar way to the argument in 1 Corinthians 12. If one understands oneself as but one member among many in the body of Christ, then one will not have an overinflated view of oneself. And, further, if one recognizes that there is no gift or function that should be exalted over others, there need be no competition to do particular tasks, for not all persons have the same function in the body.

According to v. 5, Christians are one body in Christ and not, by implication, in some other body, such as the body politic (cf. Plato, *Republic* 402c-d; Plutarch, *Aratus* 24.5; *Coriolanus* 6.2-4) or the empire, seen as the emperor's body. Livy's discussion of the senate and people being like body parts which cannot do without each other provides something of a parallel (*Historia* 2.32). But it is not just that believers are connected to Christ in a profound and spiritual way. They are also members of each other and therefore must have regard for each other as members of the body of Christ, as persons whom Christ loves and for whom he died.

Each believer has one or more grace gifts, according to the grace given to them by God. It is interesting that the first gift mentioned in v. 6 is that of prophecy, a gift highly valued in Rome because it was the political hub of the empire, where some were always trying to find out which way the divine wind was blowing. One who is prophesying is to do so "according to the proportion of faith."[36] Though the Reformers often thought Paul was talking about some kind of "analogy of faith," that is, prophecy according to the pith and content of the salvation message that runs like a red thread through the Bible, this is highly unlikely. For one thing, the phrase here is too similar to the one in v. 3, which refers not to "the faith" but simply to "the measure of faith."[37] For another thing, Paul has already suggested that some have more faith and some less, and he will go on to say that some have strong faith and some weak (chs. 14–15). The point here is that, if one prophesies beyond the measure of one's faith, the prophecy will be five parts inspiration to perhaps three parts perspiration or mere wishful thinking.[38] This is probably why Paul says in 1 Corinthians 14 that Christian prophecy needs to be critically sifted, weeding out the inspired part from the rest. In this, Christian

36. Dunn, *Romans 9–16*, p. 726: "Paul is not simply echoing 1 Cor. 12–14, which is much more sharply focused on particular problems in Corinth, but is in fact providing a more generalized picture of the earliest Christian congregations. . . . It is a striking fact, worth noting once again, that Paul can so confidently take it for granted that congregations that he has neither founded nor visited would be charismatic. . . . This must imply that the pattern was widespread at least in the diaspora churches."

37. See, rightly, Käsemann, *Romans*, p. 335.

38. See Chrysostom: "Although prophecy is a grace, it does not flow forth freely at random but is given only in proportion to our faith" (*Homily* 21 on Romans; see Bray, ed., *Romans*, p. 312).

prophecy is seen as something rather different from the "thus says Yahweh" sort of pronouncements where prophets are just mouthpieces for God.[39] As Dunn puts it, it is a matter of a prophet speaking forth in proportion to his or her dependence on and hearing of God's message.[40]

Prophecy, as inspired speech, is mentioned only here in Romans, but it is clear that Paul sees it as one of the most important spiritual gifts. He gives it a prominent place in 1 Cor. 14.1, 39 and 1 Thess. 5.19-20. Prophets are ranked just behind apostles in 1 Cor. 12.28 and Eph. 4.11. Perhaps Paul gives it prominence here because of the way he views its function: it builds up the body of Christ (1 Cor. 14.3-5), and Paul's deliberative rhetoric of concord and division healing is to the fore here.

Paul next refers to practical service, then teaching,[41] exhorting, generosity, leading, and having compassion on persons. This is a list of Spirit-inspired or grace-endowed functions rather than a list of church offices and so is like what one finds in 1 Cor. 12.8-10, as opposed to 1 Cor. 12.28.[42] Paul says nothing about elders, deacons, overseers, or apostles in Rome. Nevertheless, Käsemann is right in saying that we have not just a community ethic here but also the fledgling stages of a community order or structure.[43] Paul never mentions Peter or any other leader in this sort of context, unlike, for example, what we find in 1 Corinthians 1 or Galatians 1–2. The impression we get is that, while there are certainly gifted Christians and even Pauline coworkers in Rome (see Romans 16), there are no towering leaders or apostolic figures that Paul feels he must deal with there.[44] Of

39. See my discussion of such matters in *Jesus the Seer: The Progress of Prophecy* (Peabody: Hendrickson, 1999), pp. 293-328.

40. Dunn, *Romans 9–16*, p. 728.

41. As Dunn, *Romans 9–16*, p. 729, points out, that Paul lists teaching as one of the Spirit-inspired gifts (cf. Gal. 6.6) shows that he is not just talking about the passing on of learned traditions when he refers to this gift. In the interpretive role, the teacher must rely on the Holy Spirit.

42. See Barrett, *Romans*, p. 219.

43. Käsemann, *Romans*, p. 332.

44. As M. Y. MacDonald, *The Pauline Churches* (Cambridge: Cambridge University Press, 1988), p. 60, says: "The picture of the organization of the Pauline communities as being purely pneumatic, which represents the starting point for much writing on the development of the church, is deficient because it does not fully take into account the relationship between beliefs, social structures and social setting. The leadership structures of Paul's communities are not shaped in a straightforward manner by his theology; the relationship between the structures and the ideas is dialectical. . . . A purely charismatic ministry and concept of authority based exclusively on Spirit endowment presents an unrealistic picture of the human society of the Apostle." What is fascinating about Romans is that Paul is busily trying to refashion the leadership structure of a church he did not found by all that he says in this letter, especially in chs. 13–16. The strategy seems to entail the elevation of the status and roles of his co-workers and other Jewish Christians in Rome (see pp. 375-80 below), hence the lengthy greetings in ch. 16, and at the same time a combating of bad theology, elitism, and prejudice

course the list of grace gifts here is not intended to be exhaustive, as is shown by a comparison to the lists in 1 Corinthians 12 and elsewhere. This is merely a representative sampling. The reference to "leaders" or "rulers" indicates that the Roman church was not leaderless. There was some sort of hierarchy of leadership, or at least some had the gift of leadership and exercised it in the various house churches. Leaders are to act with zeal, and deeds of mercy are to be done with cheerfulness. Paul then is focusing to some degree on the attitude with which one exercises one's gifts. Dull, listless, grumpy, and overly somber saints need an attitude adjustment in order to exercise their gifts in a Christlike manner.[45]

In v. 9 the focus turns to the manner in which one exercises one's gifts and relates to others in the body of Christ. Dunn has provided a helpful presentation of the second division of ch. 12, vv. 9-13, as though it were ethical words to the wise:

> Genuine love: hating what is evil, devoted to what is good;
> Family affection in brotherly love for one another,
> Showing the way to one another in respect;
> Not negligent in eagerness aglow with the Spirit,
> Serving the Lord;
> Rejoicing in hope, steadfast in affliction,
> Persistent in prayer;
> Sharing in the needs of the saints, aspiring to hospitality.[46]

This is far from random ethical notes. It is unitive rhetoric, meant to help the community establish *koinōnia* and to help them survive in a difficult environment. "Paul evidently was particularly mindful of the fact that the little congregations in Rome were an endangered species, vulnerable to further imperial rulings against Jews and societies. He therefore urges a policy of living quietly, and of nonresponse to provocation. The counsel is chiefly rooted in Jewish traditional wisdom regarding human relationships."[47] Exactly so. Some of that wisdom comes in the form of the use of early Jewish traditions and the OT, and some in the form of the use of the Jesus traditions, in vv. 14-21.[48]

---

of the Gentile believers which produces divisions. There are also the tempering of the use of gifts beyond the measure of one's faith and the exhortation to love and self-sacrificial behavior. Finally, there is the promise of his own visit in which he intends to impart a "gift," which refers to his teaching on various and sundry things.

45. There is no evidence in the text, against J. A. Fitzmyer, *Romans* (New York: Doubleday, 1992), p. 645, that Paul is simply addressing the charismatic element in the congregations at Rome.

46. Dunn, *Romans 9–16*, p. 738.

47. Dunn, *Romans 9–16*, p. 738.

48. It is interesting that at Qumran, which at least by the Dead Sea had no temple, the

This section is made up of clauses containing only participles. Some have suggested that the participle could be used for the imperative, but the case is not compelling. A better suggestion is that of Barrett and others. In early Jewish sources in Hebrew or Aramaic participles are used to express rules and codes.[49] The participles do occur in similar code-like fashion here, and there is a parallel usage in 1 Pet. 2.18; 3.1, 7-8; 4.7-10. This would suggest that this part of Paul's discourse represents a translation of a Semitic source from early Jewish Christianity. "These verses present a very interesting picture of early Christian life. . . ."[50] One might wish to compare the summaries in Acts 2.42-47 and 4.32-35, which describe communal life in Jerusalem among the followers of Jesus.[51] Even more to the point, as Johnson notes, Rom. 12.9-13 expresses imperativally what was in the indicative mode in 5.2-5. Christians are exhorted to work out what God's Spirit and life's experiences have worked into them.[52]

It may not be an accident that the next segment of this discourse, beginning with v. 14, has allusions to the teaching of Jesus combined with some partial OT quotations. This also may go back to the early Jewish Christians in Jerusalem. Paul then would be passing on received traditions from v. 14 on. This makes good sense as part of Paul's larger rhetorical strategy to unify the believers in Rome by offering the rhetoric of concord, in both theological and ethical forms, by creating an ethos that the Jewish Christian minority would find familiar and comfortable and that the Gentile majority could accept as well. Could it, in fact, be that Paul envisions the Jewish Christian minority as marginalized and in need of hospitality, charity, and the like, and that this drives this portion of the letter? Could it be that the reference to the needy among the saints would be understood as referring to Jewish Christians in Rome rather than in Jerusalem?[53] This is certainly a plausible scenario.

In a sense this second half of ch. 12 functions rather as 1 Corinthians 13 does in the midst of the discussion there about gifts, showing the body in Corinth the

---

community was seen as an alternate "spiritual temple" with the observance of the rules as a kind of spiritual sacrifice. See 4QFlor. 1.6; 1QS 8.6-8; 9.3-11.

49. Barrett, *Romans*, pp. 220-21.

50. Barrett, *Romans*, p. 221.

51. See my *Acts of the Apostles: A Socio-Rhetorical Commentary* (Grand Rapids: Eerdmans, 1998), pp. 157-63 and pp. 204-210.

52. L. T. Johnson, *Reading Romans: A Literary and Theological Commentary* (Macon: Smyth and Helwys, 2001), p. 195.

53. We must follow the logic of this letter, and thus far Paul has not mentioned Jerusalem, so the Roman audience would not likely think of Jerusalem Christians when they hear this part of the discourse. What we are suggesting above would also mean that Paul is not just offering up a rehash of general maxims. His words have a specific function and pertinence for the audience he is now addressing. The term "saints" certainly was sometimes a code word for Jewish Christians, as a careful reading of Eph. 1-3 will show.

more excellent way to behave and use one's gifts. Paul speaks of love without hypocrisy (see 2 Cor. 6.6) because there is a kind of loving that can lead to evil, and so Paul adds that one must love in a pure and sincere way, while clinging to the good. By unhypocritical love he probably means love that is genuine, with no playing of a part or pretending (a *hypokritēs* is an actor). We are not to project an image and hide behind a mask that is not in accord with what is in our hearts.[54]

Paul uses very strong language here: loathe what is evil, cling to what is good.[55] In v. 9 he is probably talking about love of God, and in v. 10 about love of the brothers and sisters in the body of Christ. *Philadelphia,* which literally refers to sisterly love, does not seem to have been in use in a metaphorical sense before the time of Paul. Paul urges the Roman Christians to be warm, affectionate, and seeking to honor one another. This entire other-directed attitude is the antidote to a self-seeking attitude. In an honor and shame culture, honoring oneself or establishing one's own and one's family's or tribe's honor was a paramount concern. One honored others, but Paul is talking about a sort of mutual honoring of one another that pays no attention to hierarchical pecking orders or social status. Paul, in fact, is deconstructing or redirecting some of the major values of the culture. A good way of rendering the command here is "go first and lead the way in showing honor to one another."[56]

Paul is not content simply to use the body metaphor; he feels a need to say how the various parts should relate to one another, as well as to others. "Christian use of these typically family words does rather stand out in its consistency, and the combination of both words [*philadelphia, philostorgos*] underscores the point. This too is a part of the redefinition of boundaries in which Paul engages — a sense of family belongingness, which transcended immediate family ties and did not depend on natural or ethnic bonds. The organic imagery of the interrelatedness of the body requires to be supplemented by the emotional bond of family affection."[57]

As v. 11 shows, Paul has little patience with laziness or inactivity when there are important and good things to be done. He is all for fervency of spirit, or perhaps what is meant is fervency created by the Holy Spirit,[58] with the aim of one's activity being serving as to the Lord. The participle *zeontes* means "boiling over" and can be used to refer to a burning passion that simply bubbles up and pours out of a person's life (Plato, *Republic* 4.440C; Philo, *Sacrifices* 15).

54. Dunn, *Romans 9–16,* p. 740.
55. See Wright, "Romans," p. 711.
56. See Wright, "Romans," p. 711.
57. Dunn, *Romans 9–16,* p. 741.
58. We cannot be sure, since the term "holy" is not appended here. Acts 18.25 shows that Paul may be using a stock phrase here, for the same thing is said of Apollos in Acts, and there, too, it is unclear whether the human spirit or the Holy Spirit is meant.

Dunn is right when he suggests that Paul seeks to keep the human emotional/ spiritual dimension correlated to the Spirit (cf. 8.15-16, 26; 1 Cor. 14.14-16; Gal. 5.22-23).[59]

The picture given in v. 12 of the Christian is of one who rejoices in hope or, as the NEB puts it, "let hope keep you joyful." Such a believer is always looking forward hopefully to what God will do next, but also knows how to persevere through trials and distressful situations. One of the keys to that perseverance is constant or persistent prayer.

V. 13 may well look forward to what Paul will say in ch. 15 about the collection for the saints in Jerusalem, but a more plausible suggestion has already been mentioned.[60] If we compare 1.7, where the letter is addressed to "the beloved of God" and "those called to be saints," it is possible to believe that this refers to Gentiles and Jews in Christ respectively. Since Paul is primarily addressing Gentiles, he mentions them first. Again, if the letter is primarily addressed to Gentiles, with Jewish Christians listening in, then this portion of the letter becomes an exhortation for one part of the body of Christ, the larger Gentile part, to do a better job of helping and being understanding of the Jewish Christian minority. It becomes a word on target, which comports with the rest of the unitive rhetoric of the letter.[61] To share or participate in common with the needs of the saints suggests an active concern and giving so that those needs are met. The visual picture is of persons who take other people's needs as if they were their own. Practicing hospitality is a natural next exhortation. *Philoxenia* literally means "love of strangers" but can refer to hospitality to fellow Christians, as 1 Pet. 4.9 shows. Hospitality as Paul has in mind involves more than just providing lodging or food for travelers, particularly traveling Christians unknown to the host. Paul also envisions actual hospitality to strangers as part of the gospel witness to the world. The exhortation to hospitality is common in early Christian literature, and it is interesting that much of such exhortation seems to be directed to the church in Rome (cf. Heb. 13.2; *1 Clement* 1.2; 10.7; 11.1; 12.1; Hermas, *Mandate* 8.10), perhaps because it was particularly fragmented.[62] There appears to be a word-play in vv. 13-14. "Pur-

59. Dunn, *Romans 9–16*, p. 742.

60. A further possibility is offered by R. Jewett in *Christian Tolerance: Paul's Message to the Modern Church* (Philadelphia: Westminster, 1982), pp. 92-114, namely that Paul is concerned that those Jewish Christians who were exiled in 49 and have come back to Rome destitute be taken care of.

61. Interestingly, in some later western manuscripts of v. 13, we have *mneiais* instead of *chreiais*. This is unlikely to be an accidental slip of the pen. More probably, it reflects the early practice of praying for the departed saints. See Käsemann, *Romans*, p. 346.

62. For a very helpful treatment of this tradition of Christian hospitality, see C. D. Pohl, *Making Room: Recovering Hospitality as Christian Tradition* (Grand Rapids: Eerdmans, 1999).

suing *(diōkontes)* hospitality to strangers" is followed by "bless those pursuing *(diōkontas)* you."[63]

In vv. 14-21 Paul turns from how Christians treat each other to how they relate to the world, which may persecute or harm them. His words echo the Jesus tradition, in particular the central section of the Q material, the Sermon on the Mount. Such echoes come again in Rom. 14.10 as well. It appears that Paul knows a section of this famous "sermon" rather well.[64] In particular, he knows about Jesus' teaching of love of neighbor and enemy, and ch. 13 will show that he also knows Jesus' teaching about the "state." There is a connection. Paul is concerned with Christians both doing their civic duty and also avoiding unnecessary confrontation in a potentially volatile situation, especially in the wake of the edict of Claudius. Christians did not need to be further restricted, marginalized, or exiled.

V. 14's reference to blessing one's enemies rather than cursing them seems to be a paraphrase of the Q saying in Matt. 5.44/Luke 6.28. In fact, this text and the Q saying are the only two instances of this contrast between blessing and cursing in the NT. Blessing is a boundary-removing act, just as cursing is a boundary-defining act. Invoking God into one's relationships was a powerful thing to do. Again, what Paul is asking for is counter-intuitive. He believes that such things are possible precisely because the eschatological Spirit, with its character-forming power, dwells within the Christian community. What Paul is asking for is not natural but supernatural. There is little evidence for non-retaliation as a code early Jews lived by, outside the community of Jesus. What few such exhortations there are refer to vengeance not being exercised against fellow Jews.[65] Jesus' exhortation goes further than that. As Dunn says, Paul treats Jesus' words as something familiar and as a living tradition, so there is no need to cite it verbatim or identify the source.[66]

What v. 15 calls for is perhaps less abnormal, but Paul is urging that one truly and actively enter into the joys and sorrows of others. We find such exhortations in Jewish wisdom literature (Sir. 7.34). Paul is not talking about ritualized celebrating or mourning as a cultural duty. Just as loving must be done sincerely, so must these activities. What is inculcated here is at the opposite end of the spectrum from the Stoic notion of impassiveness.

V. 16 returns to the theme of arrogance and overinflated egos, but first it

63. See, rightly, Grieb, *The Story of Romans*, p. 121.

64. See D. C. Allison, "The Pauline Epistles and the Synoptic Gospels: The Pattern of the Parallels," *NTS* 28 (1982): 1-32, here pp. 11-12.

65. See K. Yinger, "Rom. 12.14-21 and Nonretaliation in Second Temple Judaism: Addressing Persecution within the Community," *CBQ* 60 (1998): 74-96. There is, of course, also the record of the more normal response, for instance when the seven brothers call down curses on their tormentors as they go on to martyrdom (2 Maccabees 7).

66. Dunn, *Romans 9–16*, p. 745.

exhorts the audience to "think the same among one another," that is, to be of one mind. We return here to the participles, which again suggests Paul may be drawing on his early Jewish Christian source. If so, it is in order to see that virtually the same thing is said of the Jerusalem community in Acts 4.32. Paul stresses that all believers should think along the same lines with one another. As Käsemann says, this does not mean that all have the same thoughts, but rather "it is a matter of orientation to the single goal of the community united in grace."[67]

The anti-hierarchal theme comes in when Paul says that all should humbly associate with one another, or, better translated, "be carried away to the lowly/ lowly tasks."[68] Paul wants a wholehearted and self-effacing kind of service that embraces the lowly and takes on even menial tasks. Paul is speaking against both Roman patrician notions about menial labor being beneath one's dignity and the stratifying tendencies of the culture. He is particularly speaking to Gentiles for whom humility and treating all the same were not familiar and widespread virtues. Paul does not want these Christians to be so self-absorbed and self-focused that they become "wise in their own eyes," as if their self-appraisal were the most important criterion in evaluating things. Paul wants self-esteem rather than overestimation or over-focus on self to rule the community.

V. 17 is emphatic about not returning evil for evil. It should never happen that way with Christians. Here we have an echo of Matt. 5.38-42/Luke 6.29. Is it an accident that the two allusions to the Jesus tradition found in close quarters here are also found together in Q? Perhaps not, since it seems likely that Paul is drawing on early Christian sources here. He wants to stress that Christians should not engage in shameful behavior. One should strive to do what is considered honorable by all people. The verb here means "take thought of in advance." Paul is calling for Christians to do their best to adhere to the best of the Roman cultural virtues and so provide a point of contact and be a source of honor and witness for the Christian community in Rome.

Christians are called (vv. 18-19) to strive to be at peace, so far as possible,[69] with all persons, not seeking to vindicate themselves. This seems to allude to Matt. 5.9. They are to break the cycle of negative reciprocity in the form of honor challenges and enmity conventions.[70] They are to leave such vindicating, much less vindictiveness, out of their codes of behavior. Instead, they are to leave room for the just judge, God, and God's wrath to deal with situations that

---

67. Käsemann, *Romans*, p. 347.

68. See Dunn, *Romans 9–16*, p. 747.

69. Notice the note of realism here on Paul's part. He knows it will not always be possible to live at peace with a neighbor.

70. On which, see my *Conflict and Community in Corinth* (Grand Rapids: Eerdmans, 1995), pp. 154-61.

require such measures. V. 19 echoes both Lev. 19.18 and Matt. 5.39 in regard to non-retaliation. The reference to wrath recalls Rom. 1.18-32 and prepares for what will be said in 13.4. From the latter one may conclude that Paul believes that authorities do have a limited right to exercise force and do so as agents of God, but he does not believe that private individuals, in particular Christians, should try to take justice into their own hands.

V. 20 also involves quotations, in this case of Prov. 25.21-22 and Matt. 5.44, in regard to providing food and drink for the enemy.[71] Heaping burning coals on the enemy's head probably refers to some sort of shaming convention meant to drive a person to remorse and better behavior.[72] Or could it be a metaphor for what the penitent feels and does? There is some evidence of an ancient Egyptian practice in which penitents would carry a tray of burning coals on their heads.[73]

V. 21 continues the same thought by speaking of not succumbing to evil but overcoming it with good. "This is not merely prudential; it is the way God himself has proceeded against his enemies (cf. v. 8). The mercy of God . . . will triumph over the rebellion and disobedience of men (11:32); the mercy of those on whom God has had mercy may similarly prove victorious."[74]

Bridging the Horizons

In an odd form of overcompensation, those with the least self-esteem are those most likely to make the most hyperbolic claims about themselves and their accomplishments. Their sense of self comes from what they think they have accomplished and the praise they believe they deserve. There is then an elusive quest for more attention, more praise, because nothing can fill the God-shaped

---

71. On the advice about treatment of enemies in early Jewish and Greco-Roman literature, cf. Seneca, *De Ira* 2.34.5, Epictetus, *Encheiridion* 42; *Epistle to Aristeas* 225-27; *Testament of Benjamin* 4.2-3; *Joseph and Aseneth* 23.9; and the discussion of such texts in C. Talbert, *Romans* (Macon: Smyth and Helwys, 2002), pp. 292-93. What these texts show is that a merciful ethic in regard to enemies did exist in early Judaism and paganism, even if Johnson, *Reading Romans*, p. 196, is correct about the majority of the evidence in saying: "The moral code of the ancient world — that of both Judaism and Hellenism — recognized the validity of having enemies and of paying back harm done to oneself or one's loved ones."

72. See Grieb, *The Story of Romans*, p. 122.

73. See W. Klassen, "Coals of Fire: Signs of Repentance or Revenge?" *NTS* 9 (1962-63): 337-50. After saying "overcome evil with good," it is surely unlikely that Paul with this metaphor wants to encourage any form of vengeance. Cf. the comment by Käsemann, *Romans*, p. 349.

74. Barrett, *Romans*, p. 223.

vacuum in such a person except God. Paul here is concerned to help his converts have a proper sense of self, which leads neither to overinflated or under-
developed senses of self-worth and self-esteem. V. 3 suggests that there is a level
of self-esteem necessary to be a healthy functioning person capable of normal
relationships. But this same verse also strongly suggests that a key to a sound
mind is evaluating oneself not according to the measure of one's brain power,
willpower, or emotional capacity, but according to the measure of faith. At the
root of what Paul is saying is that we must evaluate ourselves according to the
way God evaluates us, which entails the measure of faith God has given to the
individual. What matters is our faith capacity, not our "face" value. Paul recognizes in vv. 1-2 that what he is suggesting is counter-intuitive, that it is not how
the world evaluates things, and so Christians must continually strive for the renewal of their minds, deprogramming themselves from the world's code. "The
renewed mind also sees itself not as an isolated individual around which the
world revolves (the star of our own show) but as part of a larger community
with legitimately competing needs and interests that have to be taken into account if the community is to live in peace."[75]

Chrysostom had this to say about love: "Love by itself is not enough;
there must be zeal as well. For zeal also comes out of loving and gives it warmth,
so that the one confirms the other. For there are many who have love in their
mind but do not stretch out their hand. This is why Paul calls on every means
he knows to build up love."[76] Like Paul before him, Chrysostom is keenly aware
that ideological abstractions or rhetoric without accompanying action fails to
create or sustain community. But stretching out one's hand requires great cour-
age since there is always the legitimate risk of rejection, on both micro and
macro levels. Nonetheless, v. 1 calls us to be "living sacrifices" — a wholehearted
and whole identity endeavor. Just as our Exemplar stretched out his arms at
Golgotha, in abandoned defiance of the unprecedented rejection he experienced, we must do likewise. "To claim the comfort of the Crucified while rejecting his way is to advocate not only cheap grace but a deceitful ideology."[77] Yet
how alluring are comfortable but illegitimate means of "following" Christ!
"There are no mere spectators, only subjects and rebels."[78]

Paul's appeal is for the people of the Roman house churches to become
subjects, to follow the way of the King, the way of the cross. The divisions that
characterize the Roman churches trouble Paul, and he realizes that the community's failure to overcome these differences arises from the Christians' failure to

75. Grieb, *The Story of Romans*, p. 120.
76. *Homily on Romans* 21, in Bray, ed., *Romans*, p. 315.
77. Miroslav Volf, *Exclusion and Embrace: A Theological Exploration of Identity, Otherness, and Reconciliation* (Nashville: Abingdon, 1996), p. 24.
78. Wright, "Romans," p. 706.

apprehend fully their "in Christ" identity. Only such radical identification with Christ dispels the fear of the other that falsely enthralls us, stifling all genuine intimacy. Fear compels human beings in one of two directions: either we distance ourselves from others or we cling to them. Both are self-protective strategies that only serve to feed the voracious tyrant fear. The great paradox of Kingdom living is that, as we surrender to the death of our demanding selfishness, life-giving self-discovery emerges.[79]

Despite the ethnic, cultural, and religious differences between the Jewish and Gentile believers, the old world-conforming pattern of exclusion, division, and segregation may, indeed must, be overcome. The ethos of the "in Christ" community is not an afterthought for Paul. V. 1's "therefore" makes it clear that chs. 1-11 are inextricably and logically linked to chs. 12-15. Contemporary western categories that bifurcate belief and action would be inconceivable to Paul, whose Christian worldview is firmly embedded in the inherent coherency of the Jewish *Shema*. He is not changing the subject from faith and mercy; rather, he is appealing to his readers to live as they claim to think.

The transforming, indwelling Spirit of Christ continuously renews believers' minds and thus enables new thought patterns. From this new way of thinking, the praxis of the newly inaugurated Kingdom can be enacted. Athanasius shares St. Anthony's thoughts on the basis of renewed minds: "I want you to know this, that Jesus Christ our Lord is himself the true mind of the Father. By him all the fullness of every rational nature is made in the image of his image. Therefore, we should love one another very much. For he who loves his neighbor loves God, while whoever loves God, loves his own soul."[80] In this quotation also we see the mind change linked to its behavioral results with "therefore."

Paul's appeal is extremely appealing: transformation is possible, the status quo can be disrupted, problematic habits and practices can be overcome, and substantial healing can occur *in this life*. In other words, through moments of crisis and seasons of processive growth, we who have whole-heartedly sacrificed our entire selves to the renewing, reshaping work of our Creator become increasingly holy and whole persons. As our values and our virtues align, faith and ethics or belief and praxis become congruent. We become integrated persons displaying Christlike behavior. But a decision must be made, and Paul urges his original audience and us to opt for transformation. Will we present ourselves as willing, readied, compliant sacrifices, willing to follow the ways of our Exemplar, Jesus the Christ? Will we sacrifice the thought patterns and thereby the behavioral patterns of this world? Will we submit to a paradigmatic

79. Wright, "Romans," p. 706.
80. Athanasius, *Life of Anthony*. Quoted in *Essential Monastic Wisdom: Writings on the Contemplative Life*, ed. Hugh Feiss (San Francisco: HarperSanFrancisco, 1999), p. 183.

shift in worldview? Will we surrender our obsolescent but oh-so-comfortable and instinctual ways of thinking and embrace God-inspired renewed ideas and concepts? And, as the present continual tense of "transform" and "renew" reveals, will we continually choose transformation through the agency of renewed thinking — minute by minute, day by day, year by year, and situation by situation?

Living sacrifices are not pinch-faced legalists, ruled by fear of a misstep. Henri Nouwen, citing psychologist Erwin Goodenough, says fear-based living frequently compels us to seek stultifying routine akin to "a vividly patterned curtain which both shields us from the unknown and shows us how to behave."[81] "When routine behavior begins to dominate our daily lives, and suggestions of change call forth violent resistance, fear has begun to poison the roots of our existence."[82] Such an inclination both blinds us to the delight of ecstatic breakthroughs made possible by renewed thinking and eventually deadens our souls, destroying the spaciousness of the dynamic relationship that we originally entered. Affirming Goodenough's thesis that Jesus was a "supralegalist,"[83] Nouwen calls Jesus one who "bursts through the socially provided curtain, at least on some points, to fresh perceptions and judgments."[84] It is to that alluring, risky, and growing-edge adventure that Christ beckons those willing and eager to follow him.

Another behavioral pattern that emanates from fear-based legalism is rootlessness. "Fear can make us into wanderers who go from one place to another without direction or goal. Our emotions and feelings then become like a wild river that leaves its bed and destroys the land, instead of irrigating it. Lashing out, self-mutilation, erratic talking, running away, aimless wandering — all can be responses to a fear that has become too great for us to face."[85] Both obsession with routine and rootlessness seek to maintain idolatrous personal power over life, circumstances, those who threaten us or who call us to change, and so on. The counter-intuitive way of the living sacrifice is to present the entirety of our existence willingly and obediently, in humble surrender to the only one who possesses absolute power, always exercised with absolute love.

A number of years ago, I was sitting on a pier that extended into the Sea of Galilee. Intent on my reading, I was oblivious to my surroundings until I heard a young child's voice shouting, "Abba, Abba!" As I looked up, a five- or

---

81. Henri J. M. Nouwen, *Lifesigns* (New York: Doubleday, 1990), p. 93.

82. Nouwen, *Lifesigns*, p. 90.

83. Nouwen, *Lifesigns*, p. 93. Goodenough, *The Psychology of Religious Experiences* (New York: Basic Books, 1965), pp. 102-3.

84. Nouwen, *Lifesigns*, p. 93. Cf. Goodenough, *The Psychology of Religious Experiences*, pp. 102-3.

85. Nouwen, *Lifesigns*, p. 93.

six-year-old boy, face alight with a broad smile and eyes fixed upon the sole oc-
cupant of a fishing boat that had pulled alongside the pier, was traversing the
length of the dock at full speed. Then, without pausing, he leapt off the pier, utterly abandoned to the confidence that he would be caught in the arms of his
attentive Abba. That iconic scene typifies the radical and joyful trust that enables the surrender and abandonment displayed by living sacrifices.

When living sacrifices refuse to dwell within the confines of fear, the divine gift of joy is received. Regrettably, "[m]any people hardly believe anymore
in the possibility of a truly joy-filled life. They have more or less accepted life as
a prison and are grateful for every occasion that creates the illusion of the opposite: a cruise, a suspense novel, a sexual experience, or a few hours in a
heightened state of consciousness."[86] While none of these pursuits are sinful or
inappropriate in and of themselves, when they are sought as opiates for fear or
as means of avoiding reality, the pursuers become conformed to the world, reflecting its obsession with fleeting pleasure, rather than seeking lasting, satisfying God-granted joy. Nouwen describes joy as ecstasy, "a divine joy that does
not leave us during times of illness, poverty, oppression, or persecution. It is
present even when the world laughs or tortures, robs or maims, fights or kills. It
is truly ecstatic, always moving us from the house of fear into the house of love,
and always proclaiming that death no longer has the final say."[87] The reason we
are able to celebrate life regardless of circumstances? Christ is sharing his own
ineffable joy with us. We are participants in Emmanuel, God with us, joy.

Living sacrifices are also not self-fascinated narcissists, ruled by pride displayed in one of its two guises: rabid but generally unaware denial of Rom.
3.23's assertion that "all have sinned and fall short of the glory of God," or unhealthy preoccupation with personal shortcomings. Such misguided introspec-
tion only exacerbates the shrieking me-centered inner need and urges a hasty
return to the complacency and false (albeit enticing) security of worldly conformity. The yawning trap of the latter tendency is that it elicits personal attempts at salvation through self-willed disciplines. While such efforts often
masquerade as righteous acts, they mask the ultimate sin of pride — rejection
of the once-and-for-all atonement of Christ in favor of works-righteous
strivings of self-atonement. The futility of such efforts is obvious. The community of the church serves as a vital antidote to the self-absorption of either manifestation of narcissism. In the *Life of Syncletica*, Amma Syncletica, a desert
mother, advises, "When we live in community, let us choose obedience over discipline; for the latter teaches arrogance, while the former calls for humility."[88]

To all who struggle with pride of either stripe (and who does not?), An-

86. Nouwen, *Lifesigns*, p. 97.
87. Nouwen, *Lifesigns*, p. 99.
88. *Life of Syncletica*. Quoted in Feiss, ed., *Essential Monastic Wisdom*, p. 153.

thony, the fourth-century Egyptian desert ascetic, offers insightful wisdom regarding the enticing and illusory nature of conformity to the world by elevation of self: "Truthfully, my children, I tell you that everyone who delights in his own will and is subdued in his own thoughts, and takes up the things sown in his own heart, and rejoices in them, and supposes in his heart that these are some great chosen mystery, and justifies himself in what he does — the soul of such a man is the breath of evil spirits."[89] Naturally, his wisdom applies to women as well as men.

Instead of self-absorption, living sacrifices focus on the Lord who transforms. They are committed to intimate relationship with the triune God, who has wooed them and who now is accomplishing renewal within them. Living sacrifices accept the truism that "what gets our attention gets us." In the freedom and spaciousness of devoted loving attention, living sacrifices are receptive of and responsive to the one who is everything to them. Within the beauty of divine action and human responsiveness, changed behavior occurs from a changed pattern of thinking, a transformation that reaches to our very deepest subconscious levels.

Such holy submission is inviting, liberating, and expansive in a way that can be comprehended only by those who have experienced initial justifying and sanctifying grace. The way of transformation eludes the uninitiated for, to them, it is virtually indiscernible and incomprehensible (1 Cor. 2.7-8). Accordingly, the transformed way of life appears as foolishness to those who think as the world does (1 Cor. 2.14). Rom. 1.21 and 22, however, assert that it is the world's thinking and the behavior that follows from it that is foolish (cf. 1 Cor. 3:19). So in this age of prevailing spiritual blindness, living sacrifices must suffer the ignominy of being "fools for Christ" (1 Cor. 3.18; 4.10).

Living sacrifices accept the reality that increasingly renewed thinking often is birthed in the crucible of dark nights of the soul. In a paradoxical way, illumination frequently comes as darkness, not the darkness of broken relationship with God (for that is always a decision to reject divine action and, therefore, to opt for sin). Nor is this darkness that of clinical depression, a physical condition that impacts emotional well-being. Rather, this perfecting darkness is a season of being shaped by the rigor of naked faith, refined in seemingly barren, desert places with an Always Present One who is choosing to remain silent so that we might become strengthened disciples. Such seasons feed the certitude of the deeply assured and convinced faith depicted in Heb. 11.1.

In such times of soul darkness, Benedictine Abbot Louis de Blois's 1538 work *Mirror for Monks* counsels, "When you are afflicted with sensory distractions, depression, dryness of heart, headache, or any other misery and temptation, beware of saying: 'I am abandoned. The Lord has cast me off. My service

---

89. Anthony, *Letters*. Quoted in Feiss, ed., *Essential Monastic Wisdom*, p. 153.

does not please him.' These are things that the faint-hearted often say. Instead, bear all things patiently and cheerfully for the sake of him who called and chose you. Believe for certain that he is near to those who are troubled in heart." Since the very word "bearing" implies the presence of the burdensome, patient and cheerful bearing cannot mean living in Pollyanna-like denial of the very real pain or difficulty of our circumstances.

Abbot Louis's words lead us to another posture and practice of living sacrifices. Emotions are not to be denied but honestly recognized, acknowledged, and mined for whatever insight they may offer to the growth that is under way. However, they are never the plumblines of reality for living sacrifices, nor are they the indicators of God's love, compassion, and enduring presence. Over time and often through our experiences of being tested, we discover that our feelings have been schooled and our emotional responses correlate more closely to the renewed way of thinking that God has wrought in us. Frequently, that discovery comes as a surprise because our very closeness to the situations of our lives withholds from us the perspective of seeing how we are taking on the shape God intends. Others within the community of faith often provide this essential perspective — if we permit them to do so.

That permission is granted when we are vulnerable before God and others. It seems self-evident that to be a sacrifice is to be vulnerable. But we too often choose to conceal that vulnerability from fellow believers, forgetting that our lives are not our own and that we do not live for our own benefit. Transparency in all of life's events points others and us to the author of the changes that have occurred and are continuing to occur. This vulnerable posture fosters humility, enabling us to acknowledge and recognize that it is not our initiative but rather Christ's that accomplishes all transformation. Humility, while universally affirmed as an essential virtue, remains difficult to describe.

Recently I received a letter from Dan Colborne, a Baptist Union of Western Canada pastor in Victoria, BC, which offers insight regarding this necessarily elusive virtue. Referring to God-given gifts, abilities, and talents, he wrote, "Humility does not consist in thinking these things are not, but in knowing they are not enough. Life humbles us by showing us immensity, and thus that we are small. If to be humble were simply to be small, we would all be humble. Humility lies not in being small but in letting God be big." He continues by affirming the priceless gift that is given when we risk transparent living: "We permit others to see how grace works, we [serve as living] lessons in humility. In this vain and pompous world, such lessons go unnoticed. They are like the mountain flowers trampled by thoughtless hordes of prospectors. They are little valued, but even Solomon, in all his gold and finery, was not adorned like one of these." May we, as living sacrifices, let God be big and risk transparent living so that all can benefit from lessons in humility!

Argument Eleven — 13.1-14:
Taxing Situations and the Debt of Love

Many scholars have seen this material as rather loosely connected with what precedes in 12.14-21, or have argued that 13.8-14 is a natural sequel to 12.9-21. The usual corollary of this reasoning is that 13.1-7 is a preexisting piece inserted here by Paul.[1] But we must recognize not only the connections with what comes before,[2] especially in the latter half of ch. 12, but also between 13.1-7 and 13.8-14.

N. Elliott has put his finger on the rhetorical pulse of the second half of Romans:

> The broad rhetorical movement across chapters 12-15, like that across chapters 8-11, is meant to quell Gentile-Christian arrogance and to evoke sympathy and solidarity with Israel. That context suggests that Rom. 13:1-7 was intended to head off the sort of public unrest that could have further jeopardized the already vulnerable situation of the beleaguered Jewish population of Rome. Paul meant simply to deflect the Roman Christians from the trajectory of anti-Jewish attitudes and ideology along which they were already traveling, a trajectory that would implicate them even more in the scapegoating of the Jews already visible in Roman culture.[3]

1. There are even a few who think that this is a non-Pauline interpolation. See discussion in L. E. Keck, "What Makes Romans Tick?" in *Pauline Theology,* ed. D. M. Hay and E. E. Johnson, vol. 3: *Romans* (Minneapolis: Fortress, 1995), pp. 3-29.

2. See, for example, J. D. G. Dunn, *Romans 9–16,* Word Biblical Commentary Series (Dallas: Word, 1988), p. 758, who notes the numerous echoes of Rom. 2.7-11 with terms such as "good," "the good," "honor," "praise," "the evil," "wrath," and "conscience."

3. N. Elliott, "Romans 13.1-7 in the Context of Imperial Propaganda," in *Paul and Empire,* ed. R. A. Horsley (Harrisburg: Trinity, 1997), pp. 184-204, here p. 196.

There needs then to be careful discussion of the social situation Paul is address-ing if this text is to be understood in its intended sense and context.[4] Dunn and others are right that Gentile Christians, who welcomed Jewish Christians back to Rome after Claudius died in A.D. 54 and his banishment edict lapsed, were perhaps putting themselves and their congregations at some risk of imperial scrutiny.[5] The edict would have only confirmed the prejudices of some Gentiles that Jews, including Jewish Christians like Priscilla and Aquila (Acts 18), were trouble and probably were under the judgment of God. Nero's ascent to the throne brought a new rhetoric of peace, unlike the Augustan one, which re-quires a bit more detailed examination.

A Closer Look: The Accession of Nero and the Rhetoric of Peace

Claudius was eliminated in A.D. 54 by family plotting. More specifically, he was killed by Agrippina, his wife since 49, who wanted to advance her son Nero to the throne. Nero was only sixteen in 54, and so required advisors and those who would serve in a sense as his guardians. His military advisor was A. Burrus, and Seneca, the Stoic philosopher, served as a spiritual and moral advisor. It is due largely to the tutelage and guidance of these two men that the first five years of Nero's reign were not noted for corruption or disruption.

Nero had been coached enough and so was wise enough to allow the Senate more power and to do away with private treason trials of prominent persons, a vice in which Claudius had indulged.[6] He also immediately allowed Jews to return to Rome on his accession, which was three years or a little less before Paul wrote Romans in the spring of 57.[7] Until 59, there was relative peace and calm, especially in Rome, and there was much hope that the emperor would continue along the positive track he was fol-lowing. He had, after all, promised such at his accession. That event was carefully struc-tured, with Seneca giving a series of speeches meant to establish the tone of Nero's reign in distinction from the days of fear, reprisals, and literal backstabbing of Clau-dius's last years. Seneca's famous discourse *De Clementia* urges the emperor to say

---

4. It is very interesting to compare what Paul says here and how he describes Christian community life to what Tertullian (*Apology* 39) says at the end of the second century: "We are an association bound together by our religious profession. . . . We meet together as an assem-bly and society. . . . We pray for the emperors. . . . We gather together to read our sacred writ-ings. . . . After the gathering is over the Christians go out as if they had come from a school of virtue."

5. See Dunn, "Romans 13:1-7 — A Charter for Imperial Quietism?" *Ex Auditu* 2 (1986): 55-68.

6. See M. T. Griffin, *Nero: The End of a Dynasty* (New Haven: Yale University Press, 1985), pp. 50-66.

7. See above, pp. 11-15.

I am the arbiter of life and death for the nations. . . . All those many thousands of swords which my peace restrains will be drawn at my nod; what nations shall be utterly destroyed, which banished, this is mine to decree. With all things thus at my disposal, I have been moved neither by anger nor youthful impulse to unjust punishment. . . . With me the sword is hidden, no, it is sheathed; I am sparing . . . even the meanest blood; no man fails to find favor at my hands though he lack all else but the name of man. (1.2-4)

There was then to be a very different sort of peace during the time of Nero. Not the Pax Romana established by force of arms during the time of Augustus, but rather a true peace, which involved restraint and resistance to using force by governing authorities. Another of Nero's propagandists, Calpurnius Siculus, said that

the unholy War-Goddess [Bellona] shall yield and have her vanquished hands bound behind her back and, stripped of weapons, turn her furious teeth into her own entrails. . . . Fair peace shall come, fair not in appearance alone. . . . Clemency has commanded every vice that wears the disguise of peace to take itself unto some far place: she has broken every maddened sword blade. . . . Peace in her fullness shall come; knowing not the drawn sword blade. . . . (*Ecologue* 1.45-65)

These speeches are of significance for what Paul will say about Roman officials and the wearing of the sword. Seneca was to go on to say in *De Clementia* that Nero could boast of having ruled the state at a time when no blood had been shed (11.3), and the arms he wore were for adornment alone (13.5). Without question, Paul will have heard of the imperial rhetoric. In Romans 13 he is encouraging not merely political quietism but, in fact, a form of nonresistance and pacifism so that no suspicion will be thrown on Christians, either Jewish or Gentile. He could in good faith exhort his audience to pay their taxes and do their civic duties and live at peace with their neighbors because there was great and widespread hope, and not only in Rome, that Nero would keep the peace and govern wisely, fairly, and justly. It is, of course, true that, once Nero committed matricide in 59, lost both Seneca and Burrus, and then persecuted Christians, he dashed all such hopes of a golden era of true clemency. But Paul wrote this letter well before then.[8] It is seldom stressed but should be that Paul is trying to make clear that Roman officials, including Nero, are unwitting servants of the true God. When they practice justice and mercy, they do so as servants of *the* God, whether they know it or not, and so it can be a part of honoring the true God to honor and cooperate with the efforts of the Roman state.[9] If we consider what later Roman historians say about the early years of Nero (Tacitus, *Annales* 13.51; Suetonius, *Nero* 10-18), even though they know about the excesses and evil of the later years, it becomes understandable why Paul, a Roman citizen, might well be hopeful that Rome was capable of operating normally and as it ought to when he wrote this letter.

8. See the helpful discussion by Elliott, "Romans 13.1-7," pp. 200-204.

9. For similar conclusions see C. Bryan, *A Preface to Romans: Notes on the Epistle and Its Literary and Cultural Setting* (Oxford: Oxford University Press, 2000), p. 205.

But it is also possible, and has been strongly advocated by R. Jewett, that there is a subversive dimension to what Paul is saying here.[10] The Roman authorities would not have been pleased to read this passage in Romans, since it suggests that they are serving the God of the Jews, indeed, even the God who expressed himself in Jesus Christ, who was crucified by Roman authorities. This would have been offensive especially to strong advocates of the imperial cult. The emperor was a "god upon the earth," and the notion that he and his officials served the Jewish God would have been doubly offensive to the *auctoritas* and projected self-image of the emperor as inculcated by his cult. But this is forgetting that Paul's audience is Christian, not pagan, and Paul seeks to give them the true picture of things. The situation is not like Daniel speaking to Nebuchadnezzar in Daniel 1–4. Paul is giving the best advice he can in the form of deliberative rhetoric to divided Christians in Rome who need to avoid drawing negative attention to themselves, while still trying to make room for and welcome Jewish Christians, both those who stayed in Rome between 49 and 54 and those who left and then returned at the end of that period.

Rom. 13.1-7 does not justify the sins of the state, as if might makes right and whatever the state is able to do is a reflection of God's will. Paul is not calling for the resignation of Christian conscience, especially not in the face of a pagan state. There is no full-blown theology of church and state here; there is rather, by implication, a limited endorsement of the state in principle until Christ returns — if the state truly operates as servant of God and minister to the people, bringing justice and peace. But the focus is on an exhortation to Christians as to how they should respond to the *legitimate* claims of the state on them for respect, honor, and resources. "Paul speaks not of the state as such but of the political and civic authority as it would actually bear upon his readers."[11] It is what Christians do in reaction to the state that Paul is concerned about here. Christians are not to become zealots like Saul of Tarsus, taking the Law into their own hands.[12] They are not to curse, they are not to resist, they are not to take justice into their own hands, and they are not to abstain from paying taxes and tolls.

That Paul could say very different and negative things about the state when the state was malfunctioning at the end of Claudius's reign seems clear enough from 1 and 2 Thessalonians, particularly in 2 Thessalonians 2. But Paul's anti-imperial rhetoric there and elsewhere in his letters is set in the context of the not yet, which is to say the return of Christ, at whose coming every knee will bow and every tongue confess him to be Lord. When Jesus is finally and fully Lord over all on earth, no one else will be lord at all.

But Rom. 13.1-7 is an "in the meantime" passage, written at a moment of some peace in the realm, and is guiding Roman Christians as to how to respond if the state is operating in a just and fair manner. The legitimate claims of the state should not be resisted or rejected. But Roman officials are severely demoted in this passage, for they

10. See R. Jewett, "Response: Exegetical Support from Romans and Other Letters," in *Paul and Politics*, ed. R. A. Horsley (Harrisburg: Trinity, 2002), pp. 58-71.

11. Dunn, *Romans 9–16*, p. 759.

12. See M. Borg, "A New Context for Romans XIII," *NTS* 19 (1972-73): 205-18.

stand under the authority of the one true God and have power and authority only insofar as he has given it to them.

> Romans 13 constitutes a severe demotion of arrogant and self-divinizing rulers. It is an undermining of totalitarianism, not a reinforcement of it. . . . The main thing [Paul] wants to get across to Roman Christians is that, even though they are servants of the Messiah Jesus, the world's rightful Lord, this does not give them carte blanche to ignore the temporary subordinates whose appointed task, whether they know it or not, is to bring at least a measure of God's order and justice to the world. Government and magistrates may be more or less good or bad; but — and this is Paul's basic point — government qua government is intended by God and should in principle command submission from Christian and non-Christian alike.[13]

Finally, it perhaps needs to be added that this passage does not speak to the issue of international conflict and so neither raises nor answers questions about a just war. Tax police are not soldiers, and what is expected of Christians in this passage is respect and resources. Nothing is said or implied about war or joining the military. This is not surprising since Roman legions had patron deities, and Christians would not have been able to participate in honoring them, as was required. Nor is anything said to suggest that the state has no right to use force to enforce its legitimate policies. Indeed, the opposite is said. Paul's ethic of pacifism and/or nonresistance in Romans 12–13 is an ethic for Christians and the Christian community. It is not an ethic he seeks or believes should be imposed on the non-Christian state.

Let all human beings submit to superior authorities,[14] *for there is no authority except from God, but those existing are appointed by God, so that those opposing the authority are resisting the order that is of God, but those resisting receive judgment on themselves. For rulers are not a fearful thing to good works but to evil ones. But do you wish not to fear the authorities? Do the good works, and you will have praise from them. For they are servants of God for your good. But if you do evil, then fear, for not in vain does he wear the sword. For he is a servant of God, an avenger for wrath against the evil of the wrongdoer. Therefore, it is necessary to submit, not only because of wrath, but also because of conscience. Because of this,*

13. N. T. Wright, "Romans," in *The New Interpreter's Bible*, vol. 10 (Nashville: Abingdon, 2002), p. 719.

14. Some western witnesses (𝔭46, D*, G, and others) simply have "to all higher authorities you (should) submit." B. M. Metzger, *A Textual Commentary on the Greek New Testament* (3rd ed.; London: United Bible Societies, 1971), p. 467, suggests that this is an attempt to avoid the Hebrew idiom "all souls," which begins the verse. This may be so, or it may be that, in fact, later church situations required an exhortation to submit to *all* superior authorities, even the ones persecuting them.

also pay tribute, for the ministers of God are occupying themselves with the same thing. Pay to all what is due, to the customs official, the customs, to the toll collector, the toll, to the fear-inspiring, the respect, and to the honorable, the honor.

Owe no one anything except love to one another. For the one loving has fulfilled the other Law.[15] For the [commandments] "do not commit adultery, do not murder, do not steal, do not covet"[16] and any other commandment is brought to a head/summed up in this word: "Love your neighbor as yourself." For the love of neighbor works no evil. The fullness of the Law is love. And do this knowing the time, for the hour has already come for you to rise up from sleep, for the hour of our salvation is nearer than when we [initially] believed. The night is far advanced, the day is near. So then we put away the works of darkness, but we put on the armor/weapons of light. Let us walk in the day without shame, not [involved in] orgies, drunkenness, and acts of intercourse, and debaucheries, nor rivalry and zeal. But clothe yourselves with the Lord Jesus Christ and take forethought not to do the desires of the flesh.

Though 13.1 begins by making a point about what ought to be true for all, there can be little doubt that Paul has in view the Christians in Rome, the seat of the empire's government. Some have seen in this material an adaptation of Diaspora synagogue rhetoric, which is not impossible. More clearly it relates to early Jewish reflections on such matters (Wis. 6.3-10; Sir. 10.4; 17.17; *Epistle of Aristeas* 224; 1 *Enoch* 46.5; 2 *Baruch* 82.9; John 19.11; Mishnah *'Abot* 3.2; cf. *Martyrdom of Polycarp* 10.2). Josephus is rather emphatic that the "cosmos" is subject to the Romans by God's intent and act (*Wars* 5.366-68; cf. 2.390). Some of the vocabulary has been illuminated by recent sociological studies of the situation of the Roman government during this era. What probably prompts this portion of the discourse is the involvement of some Christians in Rome in the expulsion under Claudius in A.D. 49, and pressure on some to conform to or, on the other hand, rebel against the Roman authorities. Käsemann thinks Paul is reacting here and elsewhere to "enthusiasts" in Rome who had little or no respect for civil authorities.[17] There may be some truth to this, but more impor-

15. This could be translated "for the one loving the other has fulfilled the Law." But the order of the words is such that it is more natural to take the word "other" with "Law." It reads literally "For the one loving the other law has fulfilled." I take this to be a rather clear indication that Paul is referring to the Law of Christ in which the pith of the Mosaic Law is summed up and fulfilled but to which is added the teaching of Jesus and other early Christian teaching. See pp. 337-40 below.

16. Some witnesses (notably ℵ, P, and others) insert "do not bear false witness" under the influence of Exod. 20.15-17; Deut. 5.19-21. This reflects the later tendency to fill in perceived gaps or omissions in the text, for Paul has cited four of the commandments in the second table of the Ten Commandments. See Metzger, *A Textual Commentary*, p. 467.

17. E. Käsemann, *Commentary on Romans* (Grand Rapids: Eerdmans, 1980), pp. 350-59.

tantly Paul wants the Christian community both to be unified and not to draw negative attention to itself, especially after the expulsion. Now was a time for quietly living at peace with one's neighbors, including government officials. We know from Roman historians that in A.D. 57-58 there were considerable unrest and complaining about the extortionate practices of tax collectors in Rome and elsewhere (Tacitus, *Annales* 13.50-51; Suetonius, *Nero* 10.1).

In regard to the technical vocabulary here, the following can be noted: *exousiai*[18] and *tetagmenai* are terms for prominent Roman officials; *leitourgos* refers to an authorized representative of an administrative body such as the Senate, the proverbial "public servant"; *archē* refers to a municipal or city official; the phrase *tou theou diatagē* was used to characterize the state's power, which was given divine authority to establish order; *kalos* and *agathos* characterize politically good conduct; and wearing the sword was characteristic of the emperor but also of various deputies beneath him in the power structure. In view of all this, Paul's exhortation to pay customs and tolls fits in well as a proper Christian response to the state when it operates properly. Other expressions of allegiance such as emperor worship could not be assented to, so Christians had to be doubly diligent to perform fully the civic duties they could carry out. "All that is asked of the readers is that they 'do good,' 'pay taxes,' and 'honor and respect those in power.' All that is legitimately ascribed to the authorities is punishing the evil and rewarding the good. This limited homage is far from an enthusiastic endorsement of the empire."[19]

Traditionally, there have been three major interpretive approaches to this text. O. Cullmann and others have seen *exousiai* as a reference to supernatural or angelic powers who were believed to be behind or in cooperation with the civic authorities.[20] On the basis of 1 Cor. 2.8, this argument has a certain plausibility, and, furthermore, every other occurrence of plural *exousiai* clearly refers to invisible angelic powers. But such texts do not mention civic authorities, and here we certainly have that. More importantly, when Paul talks about *exousiai*, he is referring to hostile powers; here Paul is talking about civic authorities being God-ordained or at least divinely empowered and ordered. There is nothing in the context to suggest that Paul is talking about hostile or supernatural powers, and, of course, he would not exhort Christians to be subject to such powers.[21] Clearly, with the reference to the sword and taxes, the main focus in this

18. Notice, for example, how this term is used in Josephus, *Wars* 2.350; Wis. 6.3; and Luke 12.11 of human magistrates. There are in addition plenty of inscriptions where *exousia* refers to governmental authorities. See *NewDocs* 2:83-84.

19. C. Talbert, *Romans* (Macon: Smyth and Helwys, 2002), p. 296.

20. O. Cullmann, *The State in the New Testament* (London: SCM, 1957).

21. But see W. Wink, *Naming the Powers: The Language of Power in the New Testament* (Philadelphia: Fortress, 1984). Contrast C. K. Barrett, *A Commentary on the Epistle to the Romans* (Peabody: Hendrickson, 1991), p. 225.

text could not be on such powers, and, in fact, there is no positive evidence Paul has supernatural powers in view at all here. He is, rather, talking about human officials who can serve as servants of God.

A second major line of approach to this text maintains that God merely orders the governing officials and does not ordain them.[22] But what Paul says is that the higher authorities are to be submitted to by everyone because all authority comes from God. This is surely a statement about earthly authorities, indicating the source of their authority or power. Furthermore, it seems unlikely that Paul would call these authorities "servants of God" if he did not believe in the divine source of these offices or civic functions. Here it is likely that, again as in various other places in this letter, Paul is drawing on Jewish sapiential traditions such as we find in Wis. 6.1-2, which says that the source of a ruler's dominion is from God (cf. Prov. 8.15-16). There are, of course, numerous OT texts about God setting up and bringing down governments and nations, and this involves not merely setting up or toppling individuals but whole civic institutions (cf. 2 Sam. 12.8; Jer. 27.5-6; Dan. 2.21, 37-38). All such texts indicate that no one rules unless God puts them in power.

A third and more promising line of approach is offered by V. P. Furnish, who argues that Paul is advocating the paying of both direct and indirect taxes, and the one wearing the sword is the tax police.[23] One strength of this argument is that *phoros* and *telos* are indeed terms for direct and indirect taxes.[24] The latter was collected by Roman "knights" and was more subject to abuse. It consisted of harbor fees, duties on exports, and the like. The direct taxes were collected by proper government officials. Furnish concludes that this text is mainly about Christians paying their taxes of various sorts and that nothing is said here about capital punishment or even the penal use of the sword to terminate a life during a rebellion, only about the use of force, if needed, to collect taxes. Paul is simply presenting the fact that, in principle, this is what governments are supposed to do. But in response to Furnish one must say that vv. 1-2 in particular, but also vv. 3-5, refer to higher officials in general, not just tax officials, though tax officials seem to be the illustration of the general principle Paul chooses to focus on.[25]

---

22. The most famous of such treatments in recent years is J. H. Yoder, *The Politics of Jesus*, 2nd ed. (Grand Rapids: Eerdmans, 1994).

23. V. P. Furnish, *The Moral Teaching of Paul* (Nashville: Abingdon, 1979), pp. 115-41.

24. See now the discussion of B. Winter, "Roman Law and Society in Romans 12–15," in *Rome in the Bible and the Early Christian Church*, ed. P. Oakes (Grand Rapids: Baker, 2002), pp. 67-102, here pp. 83-85.

25. The dangerous tendency in later Christian history to take this passage as some sort of blanket endorsement for Christian submission to any and all forms of government, or any and all actions of a particular government, is easy to chronicle but should not be laid at Paul's doorstep. Usually the Church Fathers would qualify such endorsements of government with

The text uses the verb *hypotassō* in v. 1 and then again in v. 5. This verb means not "obey" but "submit." Paul does not counsel blind obedience.[26] Three Greek verbs could be translated "obey," and Paul uses none of them here. *Hypotassō* refers to a proper ordering of oneself under the order God has established. Since the verb is in the middle voice here, the focus is on the voluntary or self-impelled nature of the submission. It is a matter of accepting the relationship God has placed one in, and on this point one should compare Paul's advice in 1 Corinthians 7 to remain in the state, condition, or social status one found oneself in when converted.

Paul wrote this during the good years of Nero's reign, before Christians were persecuted. The proviso is that one should submit to the government as and when it is doing what God set the government up to do. Paul is saying that Christians should not resist the *legitimate* demands of the government. Non-resistance is not the same as passive resistance or civil disobedience, though Paul would have agreed that one should not compromise one's faith when the law demands something ungodly. Thus, one could be civilly disobedient to a given law and submit to the authority's right to punish such disobedience, thereby showing that one is not in rebellion against the state. Paul, then, is opposing rebellion, disruption, or resistance against the legitimate functions of the state. This view gives credence to what Käsemann suggests, namely that Paul is opposing certain notions that one need not pay taxes. Cranfield is also likely right in saying that Paul is drawing on the Jesus tradition about rendering unto Caesar.[27] More certainly, when Paul says that God ordains all authorities that exist, he is repeating what other early Jews said (cf. Josephus, *Wars* 2.140: no ruler obtains his office except by God's will; Wis. 6.3; Prov. 8.15-16; and especially Dan. 4.25).

Exousiai hyperechousai could be translated "superior authorities," and so some have seen here a reference to the emperor, with his dagger in v. 4, in this case Nero (cf. 1 Pet. 2.13), who not incidentally was about to institute tax reform right when Paul was writing this letter. But in view of the verb that follows it is unlikely that the emperor himself is in view. Rather, it is simply the governing officials who are over the people (cf. Wis. 6.5; 2 Macc. 3.11) and under whom the

provisos like "if anyone thinks he ought to submit to the point where he accepts that someone who is his superior in temporal affairs should have authority even over his faith, he falls into an even greater error" (Augustine, *Commentary on Romans* 72); or cf. Basil, *The Morals* 79.1: "It is right to submit to higher authority whenever a command of God is not violated thereby." See the samples of opinions from the fathers in Bray, ed., *Romans* (Ancient Christian Commentary on Scripture; Downers Grove: InterVarsity, 1998), pp. 324-29.

26. On the difference, see, helpfully, D. Moo, *The Epistle to the Romans* (NICNT; Grand Rapids: Eerdmans, 1996), pp. 807-10.

27. Käsemann, *Romans,* pp. 353-55; C. E. B. Cranfield, *A Critical and Exegetical Commentary on the Epistle to the Romans* (ICC; Edinburgh: Clark, 1975-79), pp. 669-70.

Christians are to arrange themselves — submitting to their authority. This means submitting to a pagan and non-democratic government. Paul's advice comes to Christians in a non-democratic situation in which there was little that could be called free elections or elected officials as we know them today. Since Christians could not change the government by voting, they were limited to praying, respecting, submitting, and paying taxes. What they were not to do was rebel or resist legitimate requests or demands from officials.

In v. 1b Paul says that no authorities "exist" except by being appointed by God. He does not say none function except by God. The issue here is their existence. This favors translation of *tetagmenai* as "ordained" or "appointed" not merely "ordered." The person who opposes the powers God has set up is, in fact, opposing the order God set up, and so is opposing God. Paul assures the audience that they will receive condemnation for such resistance. *Krima* must mean the sentence of condemnation for such resistance; thus, a legal judgment. These officials do not cause the good to fear, only those who resist, and so do evil. Paul's advice is simple: if you do not want to live in fear, do not buck the system. When the government is functioning properly, which is what Paul seems to assume here, one who does good receives praise from the government. In an honor and shame culture, public praise was crucial to improving one's status and honor rating. This is, indeed, a serious concern of Paul's in order to move the Christian community in Rome out from the shadows of suspicion and doubt. The perfect participle "those who rebel" in v. 2 indicates a determined and persistent approach: "those who are determined to resist."[28] Paul apparently has some sort of zealot in mind.[29] "The words are directed against anarchy rather than single-issue protest."[30]

B. Winter has argued that vv. 3-4 are about benefaction, and Christians who are able are exhorted to practice benefaction and so improve the honor rating of the Christian community.[31] This is perhaps part of what Paul intends, but I agree with P. Towner that the exhortation seems to be somewhat broader, aimed at all the community not just at the few Christians in Rome who could practice benefaction in the conventional sense. More likely, Paul is using this language to refer more broadly to Christian service to the community of whatever

28. Dunn, *Romans 9–16*, p. 762.
29. It is intriguing that Rom 13.3, about rulers holding no terror for those who do right, is found in a mosaic in a Byzantine monastic building, perhaps referring to obeying the religious rulers who were over the monks, though a reference to secular rulers cannot be ruled out. See *NewDocs* 1:101.
30. *NewDocs* 1:101.
31. B. Winter, *Seek the Welfare of the City: Christians as Benefactors and Citizens* (Grand Rapids: Eerdmans, 1994), pp. 26-38. Key here is the exhortation to "do the good work" in v. 3, which is a sort of coded language for "offer benefactions." See further Winter, "Roman Law and Society in Romans 12–15," pp. 67-102, here pp. 81-85.

sort, including honoring those in authority and paying taxes or tolls.[32] Christians are to take the lead in doing good to all, even to the secular authorities.

V. 4 is often controverted, but surely the text means "they are God's servant to you for the good." The Christian is to look at the governing officials as God's instrument and as an instrument of the good. In fact, even if the Christian is harmed or killed, this may rebound to God's glory because of the peaceful witness borne against the injustice. But the one who does evil should fear the authorities and their swords. Thus far, Paul has been talking about authorities in general terms. He adds that such an official is the servant of God precisely when he exercises wrath on the evildoer, as the executor of justice. Barrett notes that the magistrate, by executing justice or a preliminary manifestation of God's wrath, restrains evil and so postpones the final manifestation of God's wrath (2 Thess. 2.6-7).[33] If this view of Paul's presentation of the state is correct, then the state turns out not to be in cooperation with the demonic powers if it is operating properly. On the contrary, it is a restrainer of such powers and an example of God's long-suffering. The restraint of evil by judicial authorities gives space for the proclamation and acceptance of the gospel and so postpones the need of final judgment.[34]

But does "the sword" refer to the general functions of government, or is Paul already thinking more particularly about the tax police? I believe that the reference to taxes in vv. 6-7 is just a pertinent illustration of the general principle that officials do have the right to use force. But it is unlikely that Paul has capital punishment in view, for which the weapon mentioned was not used. Romans practiced crucifixion, or beheading by a much more lethal weapon. The "right of the sword," the *ius gladii,* was the authority of provincial governors to impose capital punishment, but here Paul is speaking about officials in Rome.[35] Later in this passage he will speak about the enforcement of tax law against resistance. But if v. 4 is speaking in general, and the tax issue will be only an illustration of what he says here, then there is nothing here that absolutely rules out that Paul might have agreed that the government had the right to use lethal force in extremis. Whatever degree of force is in view, Paul is saying that the state is charged with doing what Christians have just been prohibited from doing.[36] Paul does not appear to envision Christians assuming such public responsibilities.

32. See P. Towner, "Romans 13.1-7 and Paul's Missiological Perspective," in *Romans and the People of God,* ed. S. K. Soderlund and N. T. Wright (Grand Rapids: Eerdmans, 1999), pp. 149-69, here p. 168.

33. Barrett, *Romans,* p. 227.

34. Barrett, *Romans,* p. 229.

35. Cranfield, *Romans,* 2:667; see A. N. Sherwin-White, *Roman Society and Roman Law in the New Testament* (Oxford: Clarendon, 1963), pp. 8-11.

36. F. F. Bruce, "Paul and the Powers That Be," *BJRL* 66 (1983-84): 78-96.

In v. 5 Paul concludes that since authorities are servants of God and since they bear and have the right to bear the sword, it is necessary to submit to them, not only to avoid the wrath of the governmental official, but also for the sake of conscience. This means not "because if you don't, you will feel guilty," but that critical moral reflection of a positive sort will reveal that it is the right thing to do. The official has a role to play in the divine plan, and so taxes should be paid. This "minister of God" occupies himself with doing the task of God and should be respected. V. 6 is perhaps best called the climax of this argument, rather than just an illustration of it.[37]

V. 7 seems to have some connection with Mark 12.17, which also refers to the necessity of paying tribute.[38] The obligation to pay what is due goes beyond just money to respect and honor as well. Nero had promised to abolish indirect taxes because of the abuses, but his advisors did not let him do so, which led to some general consternation. There were even open protests in Rome about such taxes when Paul wrote this letter.[39] So Paul seeks to temper such sentiments among the converts in Rome, lest they draw negative attention to themselves.

V. 8 may be seen as a transitional verse leading to the next section of this chapter. Indeed, it can be seen as the negative form of v. 7. Paul returns to the love theme of the preceding chapter. *Ei mē* has its normal meaning of "except" here. The debt of love we always owe, for it is an unlimited debt. It is not certain whether "one another" here means just fellow Christians or fellow human beings. In view of the more general reference to "neighbor" which follows in vv. 9-10, it is probably the latter.

The one who loves has fulfilled "the other law," which might mean the divine Law as opposed to human law. Against this, however, Paul's previous exhortations on paying tribute are based on Jesus' teaching to "render to Caesar," just as his exhortation on nonresistance and love is based on the teaching of Jesus, and Paul would have seen such teachings as divine law as well. Therefore, it is more likely he means by "the other law" law other than the Mosaic Law. Less likely is the suggestion that Paul means "the one loving the other person has fulfilled the Law" because, in fact, Paul says quite the contrary in Galatians where he insists that if his converts get themselves circumcised they are then obligated to keep the whole Mosaic Law, not just its heart or summation. Least likely is that *heteron nomon* means "the rest of the law." Paul speaks of fulfilling, not obeying, in any case.

If one fulfills the other law, the Law of Christ, which has as its centerpiece love, then one has in fact carried out the Mosaic Law's core demands. Paul believes that the Ten Commandments are summed up in the love commandment

---

37. See Dunn, *Romans 9–16*, p. 766.
38. Dunn, *Romans 9–16*, p. 768.
39. See the discussion in Tacitus, *Annales* 13.50-51.

and obedience to it. This other law, the Law of Christ, contains the sum and substance or heart of the Mosaic Law. When one fulfills Christ's Law, one has accomplished the intent or aim of the previous law. One, therefore, need not go on to keep the Mosaic Law as well, especially since Christ was the end of that Law as a way of righteousness (10.4).[40]

It is right to detect echoes of Jesus' own teaching here (cf. Matt. 22.37-39 and Jas. 2.8). Like Jesus (cf. Mark 12.31 and par.), Paul sees Lev. 19.18 as the heart of the human-oriented part of the Law. One may compare what Rabbi Akiba says about Lev. 19.18 (*Sifra* on Lev. 19.18)[41] being the greatest general principle of Torah. But Paul is also following a longer Jewish tradition that suggested that the pith or heart of the Law could be summed up in one phrase (*Testament of Issachar* 6; Babylonian Talmud *Shabbat* 31a). "Neighbor" in this text was seen as restricted to fellow Jews, and this tradition seems to have continued at Qumran, where, in fact, it seems to be even further narrowed to fellow Qumranites.[42] But Hebrew *gêr*, which refers to the stranger in the land, is translated by "neighbor" in the LXX, and the Greek term *plēsion* does have a wider significance in some early Jewish texts (cf. Sir. 13.15; *1 Enoch* 99.15; Josephus, *Wars* 7.260). There is then something of a precedent for what we find in the teaching of Jesus and Paul on this matter.

It is four of the Ten Commandments[43] and "whatever other commandment there is" that is summed up in the love commandment. 1 Corinthians 13 says much the same, only more eloquently. The specific commandments show what the quality of this love is meant to be. It has a concrete shape: it does no harm to the neighbor in any of the ways mentioned.[44] Love in the NT is not mainly or merely a warm, mushy feeling or sentiment but a decision of the will to do what God commands in regard to the neighbor. It involves commitment and action, not just feelings or intentions or attitude. If the second table of the Law is summed up as love for neighbor, we may assume that Paul saw the first five commandments as summed up and fulfilled in love for God.

Paul is not saying that love completes the Law, like icing on a cake or a *donum superadditum*. He is saying rather that "another Law" has replaced and fulfills the heart of the old Mosaic Law.[45] The new Law represents the quintes-

---

40. See pp. 260-61 above.

41. See Dunn, *Romans 9–16*, p. 778.

42. See Dunn, *Romans 9–16*, p. 778.

43. Notice that Paul nowhere in his letters reaffirms the sabbath commandment. Indeed, he warns against those who insist on keeping it and who judge others if they do not; see Col. 2.16.

44. Wright, "Romans," p. 725, helpfully cites the famous line from Samuel Johnson that doing no harm is the praise of a stone not a human being. But Paul's point is that this avoidance of harm is necessarily implied by the command to love.

45. Barrett, *Romans*, p. 231.

sence of the old one, plus more and other commandments. He is saying that this is the heart of what God requires in regard to the neighbor.[46] To love is, of course, to carry out the commandments that Paul lists. Love is not a substitute for the Law but the perfect expression and fulfillment of what the Law aims at and desires of God's people. Indeed, love is, in a sense, a Law unto itself, for it goes well beyond the avoidance of doing harm, or even respecting and helping the neighbor.

Vv. 11-14 present what can be called an eschatological sanction, and Furnish is right to point out this whole section is bracketed by such language (cf. 12.2).[47] V. 11 argues that one should do just what Paul has been insisting on in vv. 1-10, especially considering the time on the eschatological clock. It is already time to wake up. There is little reason to dispute that Paul entertained the possibility that the end might come in his lifetime, but he does not insist on some particular timing for it or that he would live to see it (cf. 4 Ezra 4.26). Paul did not foresee two thousand years of church history, but when the timing of the second coming is allowed to be uncertain while the event is believed to be certain, one can treat it like company coming from afar. One needs to be prepared always, because one does not know just when it will show up. "Salvation" here probably should not be equated with the second coming, though that is not impossible. It is, as usually in Paul, seen as future (cf. 1 Thess. 5.8-9), not brought to completion until Christ comes and "all Israel is saved."

In saying that "the night is far spent and the day near at hand" (v. 12), Paul perhaps has in view the "age to come," which is dawning on the horizon and shedding light backward on the present age.[48] In view of the eschatological situation, Paul exhorts the Romans to put off the deeds of darkness and put on the weapons or armor of light. This language of baptismal disrobing and re-robing is used here not to indicate what happens at baptism, but to exhort the audience to continue to shed the old ways of this world and clothe and equip themselves in ways to fend those ways off, and to live in newness of life. Christians are to walk properly as in the day. Thus, in some sense, the eschatological day or its light is already at hand, for Christians can walk in it. *Hōs* here means "as is actually the case."[49] Believers are already standing under the sign of a new day. Thus Paul uses this eschatological language in an "already and not yet" fashion.

46. That this would have come as a surprising exhortation to many Romans is stressed by Winter, "Roman Law and Society," p. 88: "Binding obligations, often financial, towards committed relationships, including family, masters and patrons, formed the fabric of Roman society. The obligation to love, let alone love an immediate neighbor or those within proximity, must have struck a highly unfamiliar note in the mind of any inhabitant of Rome who heard it for the first time."

47. V. P. Furnish, *The Moral Teaching of Paul* (Nashville: Abingdon, 1979), pp. 115-20.

48. See Cranfield, *Romans*, 2:683.

49. Käsemann, *Romans*, pp. 362-63.

Walking in the day is explained negatively as not doing the sorts of things that often happen in nighttime revelry: drunken orgies, spite, pride, rivalry, and fighting. In short, believers are to clothe themselves with Christ, and not give any forethought to the desires of the flesh, by which Paul means sinful inclinations. On putting on Christ, one should compare Gal. 3.28-29. There is an interesting parallel in Dionysius of Halicarnassus 11.5 where to "put on Tarquin" means to play the role of Tarquin. Perhaps this is part of what Paul has in mind here: imitation of Christ.[50]

> To put on the Lord Jesus Christ means here to embrace again and again, in faith and confidence, in grateful loyalty and obedience, Him to whom we already belong, and (in Chrysostom's words) "never to be forsaken of Him,"[51] and His always being seen in us through our holiness, through our gentleness. It means to follow Him in the way of discipleship and to strive to let our lives be moulded according to the pattern of the humility of His earthly life.[52]

Bridging the Horizons

In his challenging study of Romans R. Jewett draws the following conclusions:

> There is a global sweep to Paul's view of the gospel mission; it reaches, particularly in Romans, to the end of the earth, to Spain (Rom. 15:24, 28). The exclusive claims of both Jews and Gentiles are countered and transformed by this gospel. It is Paul in particular who wishes the new community to be marked by persuasion rather than coercion. He stresses that its Lord is the crucified one, not the emperor; he exults that its citizens are mostly the rank and file of men, women, and children, both slave and free; its sustenance is the love-feast rather than the imperial dole granted to privileged citizens; its liturgy centers on the crucifixion and resurrection of Jesus rather than on the triumph over enemies in the civic cult and the theater; its honor comes through the imputation of righteousness rather than through the advantages of birth and achievement; it is more committed to *agapē* than to order; and its reach includes Barbarians, as well as Greeks and Romans, Gentiles as well as Jews.[53]

---

50. See Dunn, *Romans 9–16*, p. 790.
51. I.e., never to forsake him.
52. Cranfield, *Romans*, 2:68-89.
53. Jewett, "Response," in Horsley, ed., *Paul and Politics*, p. 71.

Paul was in the business of trying to create a Christian countercultural option in the empire. Christians were to be respectful and kind to all and to submit to governing authorities, but there can be no doubt that their ultimate allegiance was to be elsewhere, to the God from whom all power and authority ultimately flow. When there was a clash of worldviews between what Christ and Caesar said, there could be no doubt where a Christian needed to take his or her stand. This meant that when there was too great a gap or worse too great a clash of values between the macro-culture and the micro-culture, between the state and the Christian community, Christians would inevitably be called on to be prepared to suffer injustice as Christ suffered. What they were not called to is violent reaction to injustice. This much is clear from Romans 13. The rise and spread of the emperor cult during the first century exacerbated the problems Christians faced in maintaining both their faith and their witness.

This text raises questions for modern believers: Where do we see the tendencies of government to misuse the authority God has granted it? Where do we sense a call for absolute allegiance to the state at the expense of one's allegiance to God and the Christian faith? What should the Christian response be when there is injustice, even wickedness, in high places? What would it mean in a pluralistic culture to take seriously the "under God" part of "one nation under God"? And, if it is true that Paul "demobilizes Christians from the worship of Roman gods . . . and enlists them in the spiritual worship of the God who raised Jesus from the dead,"[54] what sacred cows do we need to be skewering? What idols in our culture do we need to stop genuflecting before? Where in our culture do we see the dangers of worshiping ourselves and our standard of living? One thing is certain: Rom. 13.1-7 should never be taken as a call for blanket or blind obedience to the state. A Christian's primary allegiances lie elsewhere.[55]

As I write this, Operation Iraqi Freedom is under way. Nationally and internationally, Christians are sharply divided regarding this particular initiative. Shortly after commencement of the war, a local church televised an advertisement claiming "every battle the USA has ever won was through prayer to Jesus, the commander in chief in the sky. So, don't just pray for the safety of the troops, pray for the victory of God's people — Americans. Jesus is the instigator of this action in Iraq." The Lexington *Herald-Leader*'s Faith and Values section advised that forty-eight percent of persons polled in a 2002 Pew Research Center for the People and Press poll "said they think the United States has had special protection from God for most of its history." Further, it asserted that seventy-one percent of white evangelical Protestants "think the United States has special divine protection. Among white non-evangelical Protestants and Catholics, four in 10

54. N. Elliott, "Paul and the Politics of Empire," in Horsley, ed., *Paul and Politics*, p. 39.
55. See K. Grieb, *The Story of Romans: A Narrative Defense of God's Righteousness* (Louisville: Westminster/John Knox, 2002), pp. 122-26.

took that position."[56] Anti-war protests abound, but are countered by gatherings declaring that voicing such sentiments in the midst of war is unpatriotic and reflects a disregard for the morale of the "Coalition of the Willing" troops. In the midst of such confusion, where and how does a Christian make her or his stand? What is our primary allegiance and how is that allegiance enacted?

Reflecting on violence and peace, Miroslav Volf diagnoses a strong disposition among Christians:

> The crucified Messiah is good for the inner world of our souls tormented by guilt and abandonment. He is the Savior who dies in our place to take away our sins and liberate our conscience; he is the fellow sufferer who holds our hands as we walk through the valley of tears. But for the outer world of our embodied selves, where interests clash with interests and power crosses sword with power, we feel we need a different kind of Messiah — "the King of Kings and the Lord of Lords," who will make our wills unbending, our arms strong, our swords sharp. Superimposed on the image of the helpless Messiah hanging on the cross is the image of the victorious Rider on the white horse, his eyes "like the flame of fire" and his "robe dipped in blood," coming "to tread the wine press of the fury of the wrath of God the Almighty" (Revelation 19:11-17). We will believe in the Crucified, but we want to march with the Rider.[57]

Identity confusion lies at the heart of the matter. Volf believes it is essential that we consider what kind of social agents Christians are to *be* before we begin to posit preferred social arrangements. Only in that way can we, as such social agents, "fashion healthy social arrangements instead of simply being molded by them."[58] Considering Paul's counsel to avoid being conformed to the patterns of the world, he most certainly would have voiced a hearty Amen to Volf's assertion.

Like amniotic fluid, our culture forms the substance in which, from our conception, we are protected and nurtured until we are birthed as new creations through the quickening of the Spirit of God at work within us. Within our cultural milieu, we quickly learn what attitudes, mores, and behaviors are acceptable and what is disdained or wholly contemptible. The environment is so familiar that we often behave by instinct, from a posture of thoughtless complacency. Deviations from the norm are instantly recognizable and various degrees of ostracism ensue, seeking to conform and re-conform us to the prevailing cultural norm.

No culture is inherently superior or inferior to another. But the urge to

---

56. Lexington *Herald-Leader,* April 5, 2003 edition.
57. M. Volf, *Exclusion and Embrace* (Nashville: Abingdon, 1996), p. 276.
58. Volf, *Exclusion and Embrace,* p. 22.

conform and be acceptable is so strong that without thoughtful, intentional embrace of our Kingdom identity, we think and behave ethnocentrically — oh so quick to recognize and then reject the "other" in our midst, a phenomenon Volf terms "distancing." In addition, ethnocentrism creates blind spots, and we become unaware of the shortcomings of our own cultures. This ethnocentric combination of shortsightedness and blindness puts us at odds with the God of all cultures, whose Kingdom vision is intent on the creation of a peculiar people comprised from all tribes, tongues, and nations.

Without espousing a pie-in-the-sky in the sweet by-and-by ethos, in Phil. 3:20 Paul confirms that the Christian's "citizenship is in heaven." This theme of wholly new identity pervades the New Testament. For example, the one who is "in Christ . . . is a new creation; old things have passed away; behold, all things have become new" (2 Cor. 5.17). In Galatians, Paul affirms that we are all children of God (3.26), "Abraham's seed, and heirs according to the promise" (v. 29), "heirs of God through Christ" (4.7). Galatians also contains the paradigmatic verse of God's cultural milieu: "There is neither Jew nor Greek, there is neither slave nor free, there is no male and female; for you are all one in Christ Jesus" (3.28; cf. Col. 3.11). Eph. 2.19 continues the good news: "Therefore you are no longer strangers and foreigners, but fellow citizens with the saints and members of the household of God." Col. 1.13 establishes a contrast: "He [the Father] has delivered us from the power of darkness and conveyed us into the kingdom of the Son of his love" (cf. 1 Thess. 2.12). Furthermore, we have "put on the new person who is renewed in knowledge according to the image of him" (Col. 3.10) and are "the elect of God, holy and beloved" (v. 12). In 1 Pet. 2.9-10 descriptions abound: "chosen generation . . . royal priesthood, a holy nation, his own special people . . . now the people of God." V. 11 sums up our condition: in this world we are "sojourners and pilgrims."

Clearly, Scripture identifies us with the Kingdom inaugurated at the ascension and enthronement of the resurrected Jesus. But the reign of God "is not a place, it is a process — a process of turning and deliverance — a process of peace, justice. . . . Jesus anounces that the reign of God is already beginning, and he also promises a future grand fulfillment. The key is to know when . . . the key is to be ready, which means to be doing,"[59] and I would add being, as Jesus commands. As such, believers are resident aliens, called to embrace the mores and values of the Kingdom rather than acquiescing to the cultural patterns that shaped our unregenerate selves. It seems evident that "Paul wrote to the communities of faith under his jurisdiction in order to nurture in them a distinctive identity as the people of God."[60] Despite this new identity, the not yet fully real-

59. Glen H. Stassen, *Just Peacemaking: Transforming Initiatives for Justice and Peace* (Louisville: Westminster, 1992), p. 41.

60. C. B. Cousar, *The Letters of Paul* (Nashville: Abingdon, 1996), p. 142.

ized eschatological reality compels believers to live in submission to the legitimate leadership of the state. Anarchy and violence must never characterize the responses of those who would claim to follow the crucified Lord. Yet, simultaneously, "believers are to manifest the reality of the new age, even in the face of the continuing presence of the old."[61]

Exegeting Matt. 6:33, Henri Nouwen says that, rather than declaring all issues related to worldly affairs as "unimportant, valueless or useless," Jesus "asks us to shift the point of gravity, to relocate the center of our attention, to change our priorities. . . . Jesus does not speak about a change of activities, a change in contacts, or even a change of pace. He speaks about a change of heart."[62] In fact, "the whole purpose of Jesus' ministry is to bring us to the house of his Father. . . . He came to lift us up into loving community with the Father."[63] From that relationship, we can obediently fulfill the commission to go into the world as Christ did when he was sent to the world by his Father (John 17.18). "What is new is that we are set free from the compulsions of our world and have set our hearts on the only necessary thing. What is new is that we no longer experience the many things, people, and events as endless causes for worry, but begin to experience them as the rich variety of ways in which God makes his presence known to us."[64]

Mutual compatibility no longer forms the foundation of relationships in this new community, the household of God. Astutely, Nouwen reminds us: "Similiarities in educational background, psychological make-up, or social status can bring us together, but they can never be the basis for community. Community is grounded in God, who calls us together, and not in the attractiveness of people to each other."[65] While

> many groups . . . have been formed to protect their own interests, to defend their own status, or to promote their own causes, . . . none of these is a Christian community. Instead of breaking through the walls of fear and creating new space for God, they close themselves to real or imaginary intruders. The mystery of community is precisely that it embraces *all* people, whatever their individual differences may be, and allows them to live together as brothers and sisters of Christ and sons and daughters of his heavenly Father.[66]

---

61. Cousar, *Letters*, p. 145.
62. Henri J. M. Nouwen, *Making All Things New: An Invitation to the Spiritual Life* (New York: HarperCollins, 1981), p. 42.
63. Nouwen, *Making All Things New*, pp. 50-51.
64. Nouwen, *Making All Things New*, p. 57.
65. Nouwen, *Making All Things New*, p. 83.
66. Nouwen, *Making All Things New*, p. 83.

Christians must never merge or collapse the community of Christ's one body into mere facsimiles of our birth cultures, for that is always a movement toward idolatry. Although too often used to support blind, unquestioning worldly conformity, Romans 13 was not intended by its author for such an ill-conceived purpose.

Volf ponders how Christians are to live "under the rule of Caesar" while they await full realization of the reign of justice and truth that only our Lord's return will accomplish. He concludes "that the crucified Messiah (the theology of the cross) and the Rider on the white horse (the theology of judgment) do not underwrite violence but offer important resources for living peacefully in a violent world."[67] First, the cross breaks the cycle of violence by absorbing it through nonresistance, for "the crucified Messiah is not a concealed legitimation of the system of terror, but its radical critique. Far from enthroning violence, the sacralization of him as victim subverts violence."[68] Second, the cross exposes the mechanism of scapegoating by unmasking it through suffering, for Jesus was hated without cause, albeit "his truthfulness and his justice was reason enough for hatred" and he posed a threat as "threatening innocence."[69]

As vital as both absorbing and unmasking are, Volf stresses that "nonviolence must be part of a larger strategy of combating the system of terror."[70] Accordingly, in addition to the passive responses to violence, thirdly, the cross is "part of Jesus' *struggle* for God's truth and justice . . . [for] active opposition to the kingdom of Satan . . . is . . . inseparable from the proclamation of the kingdom of God."[71] As believers, we must enter the spaces occupied by the enemy in the struggle against deception and oppression. When we do so, nonviolence, itself solely a negativity, becomes "a creative possibility . . . a foundation of a new world."[72] Finally, "the cross is a *divine embrace of the deceitful and the unjust.*"[73] Because God embraced sinners through atonement, we are called to embrace them in forgiveness.

But how do we connect the rider on the white horse with the crucified Messiah? The wrath of God displayed in judgment must be reconciled with the love of God displayed in self-sacrificial forgiveness, or God is incongruous, perhaps even the ultimate perpetrator of violence and oppression. On this point, Volf's counsel is insightful. He begins with the reminder that the cross is also God's way of overcoming the world's injustice and deception. Therefore, "those

67. Volf, *Exclusion and Embrace*, p. 278.
68. Volf, *Exclusion and Embrace*, p. 292.
69. Volf, *Exclusion and Embrace*, p. 292.
70. Volf, *Exclusion and Embrace*, p. 293.
71. Volf, *Exclusion and Embrace*, p. 293.
72. Volf, *Exclusion and Embrace*, p. 293.
73. Volf, *Exclusion and Embrace*, pp. 294-95.

who take divine suffering (the cross) as a display of divine weakness that condones violence — instead of divine grace that restores the violator — draw upon themselves divine anger (the sword) that makes an end to their violence. The violence of the Rider . . . is the *symbolic portrayal of the final exclusion of everything that refuses to be redeemed by God's suffering love.*"[74]

Whatever the nature of the limited "permission" granted by God to the state's use of the sword, 1 Pet. 2.21, 23 and Rom. 12.18-21 indicate that "Christians are not to take up their swords and gather under the banner of the Rider on the white horse, but to take up their crosses and follow the crucified Messiah."[75] God and God alone is the judge, and when we presume to be God we engage in the "be like God" sin as old as Eden, the sin that marred the embrace of the garden, setting us into the world of violence in which we find ourselves. Judgment must occur for violence to be overcome, but it must be judgment that transcends the doomed pattern of human overcomers. And the outcome of the final divine judgment is "the Lamb at the center of the throne, [where] the distance between the 'throne' and the 'subjects' has collapsed in the embrace of the triune God."[76] Come, Lord Jesus.

74. Volf, *Exclusion and Embrace*, pp. 298-99.
75. Volf, *Exclusion and Embrace*, p. 302.
76. Volf, *Exclusion and Embrace*, p. 301.

Argument Twelve — 14.1–15.13: The Weak and the Strong and What Goes Wrong

Just as Paul saved the most contentious theological matter until the end of the theological section of his discourse (chs. 9–11), here Paul has saved the most controversial ethical matter until the end of his ethical arguments. This is an effective rhetorical technique and allows the rhetor to gain assent on lesser matters from the audience and build up momentum for the more difficult issues. There is some debate as to where this section of the letter ends, but since we have seen the rhetorical pattern in which Paul concludes a section with a doxology (at the end of chs. 8 and 11), it seems feasible to see 15.9-13 as the end of this rhetorical unit. There are in fact clear parallels between 15.9-13 and 11.32-36. Both end sections with doxologies addressed mainly to God, and both bring up the theme of mercy. Therefore, it is reasonable to see 15.9-13 in the same light as the end of ch. 11.

One of the first and most important topics in deliberative rhetoric is the discussion of religious rituals and practices (see *Rhetoric to Alexander* 1423a). Deliberative speeches on this subject usually support the status quo rather than arguing for a change in rituals. Paul's unity-driven rhetoric here wants each to continue to practice as one sees fit in food and sabbath matters, and the appeal to conscience, being self-persuaded, and not acting when one has doubts is standard, as is the urging to avoid disputes and meddling when it comes to other people's convictions on non-essential matters.

The deliberative orator "aims at establishing the expediency or harmfulness of a proposed course of action: if he urges its acceptance he does so on the ground that it will do good; if he urges its rejection he does so on the ground that it will do harm" (Aristotle, *Rhetoric* 1.3.21-25). Paul argues both ways, urging that a welcoming posture by all is expedient and arguing against destroying the weak in faith by insisting on one's rights. He will also urge that the weak not judge the strong. What works to build community and what does harm are at the forefront of Paul's discussion.

The argument that Paul is not merely offering up generic ethical remarks in chs. 12–15 receives strong support from 14.1–15.13.[1] There are echoes here of earlier Pauline discussions in 1 Corinthians and elsewhere, but that does not prove that Paul is simply recycling generic material without addressing specific concerns in Rome.[2] It simply means that Paul is consistent when he teaches on the same subject. Furthermore, he is approaching matters carefully since the Roman house churches were not started by him and so he cannot take the same rhetorical approach as he did in letters written to his own converts.[3] The key thematic differences between the discussion here and in 1 Corinthians 8–10 are as notable as the similarities. For example, the issues there are idol meat and knowledge, but here the discussion is more Jewish, involving clean and unclean and sabbath observance.[4] Paul seems to be genuinely aware of some issues that need to be dealt with, issues between the Jewish Christian minority and the Gentile Christian majority, as we shall see.[5]

What Paul offers is also not simply a treatment of "things indifferent," adiaphora.[6] Unity of the fellowship could hardly be described as an indif-

1. See J. D. G. Dunn, *Romans 9–16*, Word Biblical Commentary Series (Dallas: Word, 1988), p. 795.

2. But see the argument of R. J. Karris, "Romans 14.1–15.13 and the Occasion of Romans," in *The Romans Debate,* ed. K. P. Donfried (2nd ed., Peabody: Hendrickson, 1991), pp. 65-84, and the responses by K. P. Donfried and W. Wuellner, pp. 102-46.

3. See the discussion on pp. 7-20 above.

4. See my discussion at length on 1 Corinthians 8–10 in *Conflict and Community in Corinth* (Grand Rapids: Eerdmans, 1995), pp. 186-230.

5. The merit of the treatment of A. J. M. Wedderburn, *The Reason for Romans* (Edinburgh: Clark, 1988), is that he does think there are concrete situations undergirding and underlying all of Paul's argument in Romans. However, he fails to realize that there is no evidence of Judaizing in Roman churches, or for that matter of pure libertinism. He is caught in the old mode of thinking that Paul has Judaizing opponents in Rome that he is arguing against indirectly. But there is absolutely nothing in Romans that suggests that anyone was arguing about circumcision, which was the sign of the Mosaic covenant. The Gentiles in Rome were in danger of anti-Semitism, not Judaizing! The argument in Galatians differs markedly from that in Romans in this respect, and in others. Romans needs to be read on its own terms, and not through the filter of Galatians and the problems that existed in Galatia.

6. C. Talbert, *Romans* (Macon: Smyth and Helwys, 2002), p. 312, is careful to qualify that while eating or not-eating may be an indifferent thing, how and in what context one does so is not, as others may be caused to stumble. Though what Paul is talking about does not involve ethical absolutes (it is not absolutely wrong to eat meat, for example), it does involve an absolutely essential and not optional ethical principle, namely loving one's fellow believers and not causing them to violate their conscience. Nevertheless, Epictetus's remark (*Dissertationes* 2.19.13) should be quoted: "Now the virtues and everything which shares in them are good, . . . while vices are evil. But what falls between these . . . are indifferent matters (adiaphora)."

ferent matter. But how does one achieve unity without insisting on uniformity?[7]

There are several sections to the argument in 14.1–15.13, but the argument
needs to be treated as a whole to show how the discussion about the weak and
strong develops. As in 1 Corinthians, Paul identifies with the strong to a certain
degree in terms of the freedom issue, but he also wishes to defend the weak. He
does not want the weak to despise the strong or the strong to look down on the
weak. But there is another aspect of this section very reminiscent of 1 Corinthians: Paul is using deliberative rhetoric about peace and upbuilding and being of
one mind in order to unify the Christians in Rome.

The rhetoric of concord is found throughout this argument in a very
clear way. This means that Paul was quite convinced that there were significant
divisions in Rome that needed to be overcome, and, to judge from chs. 9–11,
they largely fell along the lines of the ethnic division in the church there. Furthermore, the divisions especially involved the marginalizing of the Jewish
Christians. So Paul must offer a strong exhortation to the dominant Gentile
Christians to welcome, receive, be hospitable to, and not offend the weaker Jewish Christians, who have more scruples about food and observance of days.
"Paul is engaging here the issue of multiculturalism. How can people share a
certain unifying community identity without having to lose completely their
particular cultural heritage? Which differences divide and disable the community and which ones should be celebrated as enriching it? How much diversity
can a specific community tolerate before it disintegrates?"[8] In 11.13-24 and 12.3,
16-17 Paul has already warned Gentile Christians against hubris and, in particular, against thinking too highly of themselves in relationship to Jews and Jewish
Christians. 14.1–15.13 will draw out the practical implications of those previous
remarks.[9]

In chs. 9–11 Paul dealt with particular theological issues of dispute and
concern among the Romans. Here Paul will build on that discussion with his
longest ethical discussion on any subject to hammer home certain practical and
ethical conclusions about all being equal in grace and equally under the mercy
of God. A stylistic feature of this argument will be Paul's oscillation between
the second person singular (14.4, 10, 15, 20-22; 15.2) and plural (14.1, 7-8, 13, 16,
19; 15.1-2, 4-6).[10] More often than not, he speaks to the group. But the direct ad-

7. See E. Käsemann, *Commentary on Romans* (Grand Rapids: Eerdmans, 1980), p. 370:
"Christian life suffers distortion when uniformity is enforced and there is uncritical subjec-
tion to conventions."

8. L. T. Johnson, *Reading Romans: A Literary and Theological Commentary* (Macon:
Smyth and Helwys, 2001), p. 212.

9. C. K. Barrett, *A Commentary on the Epistle to the Romans* (Peabody: Hendrickson,
1991), p. 235.

10. See Dunn, *Romans 9–16*, p. 795.

dress to individuals shows that Paul is concerned about individual behavior
and will be bold enough to pinpoint a specific problem that needs correcting.

Though Romans is not a problem-solving letter to the degree 1 Corinthians is, it is still meant as a word on target for the Roman Christians. The character of the discourse, in both its theological and ethical dimensions and parts, is
intended to persuade the Roman Christians to take a particular course of action
— to unite and build up the body of Christ in Rome, which is composed of
both Jews and Gentiles, and to see themselves as part of God's eschatological
plan to unite all peoples in Christ throughout the world by grace through faith,
never forgetting that the Good News about the Jewish Messiah Jesus is for the
Jew first, and also for the Gentile.[11]

*Welcome those who are weak in faith, without disputes for deciding [the issue].
Someone on the one hand trusts to eat everything, but the weak on the other hand
eat vegetables. The one eating should not despise the one not eating, but the one
not eating should not judge the one eating, for God welcomed him. Who are you to
judge another's servant? He stands or falls unto his own master. But he will be
made to stand, for the Lord has the power to hold him up. Someone on the one
hand judges one day in comparison to another, someone else on the other hand
judges all days [the same]. Let each be absolutely convinced in his own mind. The
one observing the day observes it to the Lord.[12] And the one eating eats to the Lord,
for he gives thanks to God. But one not eating abstains unto the Lord and gives
thanks to God. For none of us lives to himself [alone], and none of us will die to
himself. For if we live, we live to the Lord, and if we die, we die to the Lord. For if
we live or we die, we are of the Lord. For because of this Christ died and he lived,[13]
in order that he might be Lord of the dead and the living. But you, why do you
judge your brother? Or you also, why do you despise your brother? For all will
stand before the judgment seat of God, for it is written: "As I live, says the Lord,
that every knee will bow to me, and every tongue will publicly confess to God." So
then each of us will give an account concerning himself.*

So let us no longer judge one another, but rather decide to do this — not to

11. On rhetorical considerations in this part of the letter see further J. L. Jaquette, "Life
and Death, *Adiaphora*, and Paul's Rhetorical Strategies," *NovT* 38 (1996): 30-54.

12. At this juncture the Textus Receptus and other later witnesses (L, P, and others) add
a clause that is the opposite of the one just given, to balance the text, since we then have
clauses about both those eating and those not eating. This is typical of Byzantine witnesses
seeking to fill in the gaps. See B. M. Metzger, *A Textual Commentary on the Greek New Testament* (3rd ed.; London: United Bible Societies, 1971), p. 468.

13. Various witnesses either replace the verb "lived again" with some form of the verb
"raise" (perhaps on the basis of 1 Thess. 4.14), or they add the more common term "raise."
The witnesses for the simple reading "lived again" are strong and include ℵ*, A, B, C, and
others, and this reading best explains the others. See Metzger, *A Textual Commentary*, p. 468.

put an obstacle or temptation in the way of a brother. For you know I am also con-
vinced that nothing is common/unclean in itself, unless someone considers it to be
unclean, to that one it is unclean. For if your brother is caused grief because of
food, you are not walking according to love. By your food, do not destroy that one
for whom Christ died. Do not let what is good for you be blasphemed, for the Do-
minion of God is not food and drink but righteousness and peace and joy in the
Holy Spirit. On this principle, he who serves Christ is pleasing to God and ap-
proved by human beings. So then we pursue[14] the ways of peace and the building
up of one another. Do not for the sake of food destroy the work of God. Everything
is clean, but it is evil for the person eating with offense. But good for the one not
eating meat or drinking wine nor by whom your brother does not stumble. Your
faith which you have, have to yourself before God. Happy is the one who does not
condemn himself by what he approves. But the one beginning to doubt will stand
judged if he eats because it is not from faith. But everything which is not from faith
is sin.[15]

But we the strong ought to bear the weakness of those without strength/
power, and not to please ourselves. Let each of us please his neighbor unto the good,
for upbuilding, for even Christ did not please himself. But, just as it is written,
"The reproaches of those who have reproached you have fallen upon me." For

14. Many manuscripts have the subjunctive verb form here, but everywhere else in Romans the indicative form of the verb always follows *ara oun* (cf. 5.18; 7.3, 25; 8.12; 9.16, 18). See Meztger, *A Textual Commentary,* p. 469.

15. It can be said that the doxology that NT translations have at 16.25-27 was a doxology looking for a home. Some manuscripts (A, P, 5, 33, 104, Armenian) have this doxology *both* here after v. 23 and at 16.25-27. Some manuscripts have the doxology only here (L, and various Byzantine witnesses). Some omit the doxology altogether and end the manuscript at 16.24 (G, 629). Ḍ46, an important early witness, has the doxology at 15.33 and goes on to include 16.1-23, ending at 16.23. Finally, some Vulgate and Old Latin witnesses conclude the manuscript with 14.23, followed only by 16.24 and the doxology. What do we make of all this? The whole discussion in Metzger, *A Textual Commentary,* pp. 470-73, should be consulted. It appears that there was a shorter version of Romans in circulation, perhaps from the hand of Marcion, perhaps not including chs. 15–16. There is, however, no good early evidence for the omission of chs. 15–16 apart from the possible Marcionite text. The doxology found at 16.25-27, however, is another story. There is evidence of its omission in several texts such as G, and its chronic displacement or multiple placement has suggested to many that it was not original. This may well be so. At the same time the witnesses for the traditional text, including 16.25-27 at the end, are diverse and strong, including ℵ, B, C, D, and others. Thus, the nod must go to that doxology being an original part of the text, though in view of its vocabulary it may have been adopted and adapted by Paul from a source. H. Gamble's discussion of these matters in *A Textual History of the Letter to the Romans* (Grand Rapids: Eerdmans, 1977) should be consulted in full, and leads to the conclusion that even ch. 16 does indeed belong to the original text of Romans, perhaps including 16.25-27. See pp. 5-7 in the Introduction above.

whatever was written beforehand was written for our instruction, in order that through patience and through the counsel/comfort of the Scriptures we may have hope. May the God of patience and counsel/comfort give to you the same mind among one another according to Christ Jesus, in order that with one mind in one voice/mouth you may glorify the God and Father of our Lord Jesus Christ.

Therefore, welcome one another as Christ also welcomed you, unto the glory of God. For I say Christ became the servant of the circumcised, for the sake of the truth of God, that he might confirm the promises of the fathers, but the Gentiles glorify God for mercy, just as it is written: "Because of this I will confess you publicly among the nations/Gentiles and sing praise to your name." And again he says "Rejoice, Gentiles, with his people." And again "praise the Lord, all the nations, and let all the peoples praise him." And again Isaiah says "There shall be the root of Jesse, and the One arising to rule the nations. In him the nations will hope." May the God of hope fill you with all joy and peace in believing, unto your abounding/ overflowing in hope in the power of the Holy Spirit.

14.1 begins abruptly with an exhortation to welcome the weak without disputing with them about matters.[16] This definitely suggests that there was such disputing. Paul assumes his Roman audience knows exactly whom he is referring to, and so it is in order for us, who do not have the advantages of Paul or his audience, to consider more closely who these people might be, through an analysis of two different views of the matter, that of W. S. Campbell and the more controversial views of M. Nanos.

A Closer Look: The Weak in Rome — Jews, Christians, or Jewish Christians?

There has always been some debate over whether there was some close connection between the synagogues in Rome and the house churches. On a surface reading of Romans, one would not guess that there was; indeed, in view of the apologetic in chs. 9–11 for Jews and Jewishness, one would guess the opposite. M. Nanos gives us an opportunity to reexamine the text in light of a broader range of possibilities.

The theses of Nanos can be enumerated as follows: (1) Paul is a good Jew, an observant Jew who has not broken with the essential truths and praxis of his people. (2) The Christians in Rome have not separated from the synagogue. Even the Gentiles are still meeting in the synagogues, though they have additional meetings as well, though under supervision from the synagogue. Paul is addressing the Gentile question of how Gentiles should behave in the Jewish communities in Rome. (3) Paul is still committed to the missionary pattern of sharing the gospel with the Jew first, even

16. The verb *proslambanō* means to receive into one's home or group. See 2 Macc. 10.15; Acts 28.2.

at enormous cost to himself. (4) Paul believes in the restoration of Israel. (5) "The weak" referred to in chs. 14–15 are Jews, not Jewish Christians. (6) The problem Paul seeks to address is "Gentilizing" not "Judaizing." (7) 13.1-7 is about Christian (Gentile in particular) obedience to synagogue authorities, particularly in relationship to the paying of taxes, in particular the Temple tax.[17]

There is some merit in various of these arguments. We have already seen in chs. 9–11 that Paul is worried about Gentiles writing off Jews and Jewish Christians. The issue in Rome does in part seem to be rising anti-Semitism and "Gentilizing." Nanos is right both in his assertion that God intends to restore Israel and also in the likelihood that Paul did indeed go to synagogues wherever he went to make sure the gospel priority of "the Jew first" was met, even though Paul's focus would be on Gentiles. Nanos is right to take seriously both Luke's presentation of this matter and the clear hints in texts like 2 Corinthians 11 that Paul was indeed beaten for his attempts to evangelize in synagogues.

But there are problems with Nanos's views. First, Nanos does not have an adequate explanation for why Paul speaks in chs. 9–11 about the current lostness of Jews broken off from the people of God, especially since for Paul the people of God are now Jews and Gentiles united in Christ. Paul does not see allegiance to Christ as optional if one is to be part of the people of God. To the contrary, in Paul's view it is Jewish Christians who now carry forward the Jewish heritage in the new era, not the synagogue or non-Christian Jews. Jewish Christians like Paul are both the proof that God has not abandoned his first chosen people and the "root" and "tree" into which Gentiles have been grafted.

Second, in view of the similarities between ch. 13 and both other early Jewish discussion of pagan officials[18] and discussions such as we find in 1 Pet. 2.13-17, it is highly unlikely that Paul is speaking about synagogue officials in ch. 13. He does not use any synagogue-specific terms such as *archisynagōgos*. This, in turn, means that Paul is also not referring to the Temple tax.

Third, the discussion of the weak and the strong is couched in specifically Christian terms. The weak abstain "unto the Lord" and there is no evidence that Paul means something different in 14.5-8 by "Lord" than in v. 9 — namely Jesus. Paul is not trying to quell dissensions in the synagogue caused by a "Gentile" question. He is trying to unite a divided Christian group who are disunited over a "Jewish" question, among other things. 14.15 is an insurmountable objection to Nanos's reading of this material. He has clearly misread the historical situation in the late 50s in Rome, insofar as the connections between church and synagogue are concerned. The split between the two communities came well before Paul wrote Romans, and Acts 28 does not suggest anything to the contrary. In fact, it suggests that the synagogue officials in Rome know little about what is going on with Christians, including those in their own city.[19]

17. M. Nanos, *The Mystery of Romans* (Minneapolis: Fortress, 1996).
18. See pp. 304-15 above.
19. See the critique of Nanos by A. J. Levine, "Nanos: The Mystery of Romans," in *JQR* 89 (1998): 222-24, which is along the same lines as the one offered above.

Fourth, Nanos's attempt to suggest that Christians in Rome, in particular Gentile Christians, were being urged to keep the apostolic decree of Acts 15, which was a form of the Noahic commandments, is not well supported. It is doubtful that the apostolic decree is based on the Noahic commandments. It has to do with avoiding the sort of things that go on in pagan temples, including participating in idol feasts. It is not an attempt to impose general food laws on Gentiles per se, and, in any case, Paul's position is that all foods are clean, as Rom. 14.20 states.[20]

Far nearer the mark is the treatment of W. S. Campbell.[21] Campbell reviews the argument that the terms "weak" and "strong" primarily have social rather than theological significance. On this showing, the strong would be the Gentile who was a Roman citizen or who had a proclivity for things Roman. Campbell also reviews the contention that the language about "judging" and "despising" has power connotations, so that Paul is trying to convince the powerful not to oppress the weak.[22] There is some truth in this, but Paul is very explicit that he is speaking about the weak "in faith," which certainly means that the category he is most interested in is theological and ethical rather than primarily social.[23] There is also no indication in our text that the strong are Roman citizens, though the hints we have certainly suggest they were likely to be Gentiles.

That the weak are referred to in 14.1, 2 and 15.1 shows that one should not separate chs. 14 and 15. They are parts of the same discussion. But Paul is not just interested in defending the weak and exhorting the strong. He is trying to bind the two groups together, if we can speak of distinct groups (and I think we can).[24] "Paul's intention is to promote harmony *within* diversity rather than to remove the diversity — otherwise what would be the significance of saying 'Let everyone be fully convinced in his own mind' or 'whatever is not of faith is sin'?"[25] Campbell rightly concludes that there were in Rome Christian groups who followed some aspects of the Jewish lifestyle and other Christian groups, probably the Gentile majority, who despised or

20. See pp. 340-41 above.

21. Campbell, "The Rule of Faith in Romans 12.1–15.13," in *Pauline Theology,* ed. D. M. Hay and E. E. Johnson, vol. 3: *Romans* (Minneapolis: Fortress, 1995), pp. 259-86, here pp. 268-69.

22. He is here repeating the suggestions of C. Osiek, "The Oral World of the First-Century Christians," a paper delivered at the SBL meeting in 1993.

23. See Barrett, *Romans,* p. 236: "The weak are weak in faith; they are weak but they have faith; they have faith but they do not draw from it all the inferences that they should draw."

24. Campbell, "The Rule of Faith," pp. 270-72, carefully reviews the argument as to whether groups are in view, or if types are being discussed without thinking of clearly demarcated groups. He asks whether there is really enough in calling someone weak, and a vegetarian, and perhaps also a sabbath observer, to distinguish a group. My answer to this would be yes. This is why Paul is able to identify with one group (the strong) while defending the other (the weak). In fact, Campbell goes on to conclude rightly that "Paul is dealing here with conflicting groups rather than with differing types of individual Christians" (p. 273).

25. Campbell, "The Rule of Faith," p. 272.

were arrogant toward those Christians who followed some aspects of the Jewish life-style and who saw little reason to welcome or fellowship with them.[26]

Campbell astutely observes that Paul's ethical stance did not include a requirement that all Christians in Rome follow the same lifestyle. Paul does not see diversity of lifestyle as the major problem, rather attitudes about those diverse lifestyles were.[27] "Paul has no quarrel with those who continue to observe the law so long as they do not seek to compel others to live like them! Gentiles must not regard observance of the Jewish law as incompatible with Christian faith, and Jews must not regard it as essential to Christian faith."[28] Campbell is also right that Paul is combating pride, arrogance, boasting, and presumptuousness, and I would add anti-Semitism, among the largely Gentile audience he addresses. The Roman persona, which included elements of assumed superiority in culture, race, and matters religious, is what Paul must deal with if he is to build bridges between Jewish and Gentile Christians in Rome. Faith and love are to determine one's attitude and approach to fellow Christians, not these other more natural or human considerations. In my judgment, Campbell is too reticent to identify more clearly "the weak" as probably Jewish Christians, as was the case in Corinth as well.

Horace in *Satires* 1.9.68-72 describes an interesting conversation that transpired in Rome and is of relevance to our discussion of Romans 14. One person refuses to talk to another and adds, "Today is the thirtieth sabbath. Would you affront the circumcised Jews?" The other replies, "I have no scruples." The first rejoins, "But I have. I am a somewhat weaker brother, one of the many. I will talk another day." This discussion clearly links Jewishness or sympathy with Jewishness with being a weaker brother, in the context of Rome. There is, furthermore, the discussion in Cicero's *Tusculan Disputations* 4.26 where he speaks of the morally weak person as one who has an intense belief that something ought to be avoided, even though in actuality it need not be avoided. He calls it "an act of judging that one has knowledge where one has none."[29]

Even more to the point, the term *koinon* in Rom. 14.14 is used in contexts where Jewish dietary rules involving clean and unclean food are in view. This means that Paul is indeed dealing with a situation in Rome that involves the *kashrut* laws.[30] In short, Paul is dealing with a Jewish Christian versus Gentile

26. Campbell, "The Rule of Faith," p. 275.

27. Campbell, "The Rule of Faith," pp. 282-83.

28. Campbell, "The Rule of Faith," p. 283.

29. Thanks to Charles Talbert for pointing out this reference to me (see his *Romans*, p. 315).

30. See the discussion in M. Reasoner, "The Theology of Romans 12.1–15.13," in Hay and Johnson, eds., *Pauline Theology*, vol. 3, pp. 287-99, here p. 290.

Christian issue here, even if there were a few Gentile food laws in Rome, perhaps among former God-fearers who also had interest in keeping Jewish food
laws, and even if there were a few of Paul's Jewish Christian protégés in Rome,
such as Aquila and Priscilla,[31] who already agreed with Paul's views on these
matters. Paul recognizes that these are disputable matters at the outset and does
not want such differences to lead to the judging of persons. We are, in Paul's
view, in the realm where differences of opinion about lifestyle are fine but
should not be allowed to create disunity in the body of Christ.

The second half of v. 1 probably means that the weak are to be welcomed.
One should not use that welcome as an opportunity to lecture them or argue
with them about the things they have doubts about. The basic sense of "weak in
faith" seems to involve a failure to trust in God without qualification in one or
more aspects of one's life.[32] The issue here is not just actions. As Grieb says,
"Paul argues that Christians are just as accountable to God for their *attitudes*
towards their brothers and sisters with whom they disagree as they are accountable for the *decisions* they have made that divide them from one another."[33]
Judging or despising others has as much to do with attitude as action, and Paul
is correcting both. Paul's ethics then goes beyond the regulation of behavior, as
did Jesus' (cf. Matt. 5.28).

V. 2 refers to those who believe it is permissible to eat everything, and the
"weak" who eat only vegetables. Why only vegetables?[34] (1) The OT Law allowed some meats. But meat sold in public meat markets would not all have
been slaughtered according to Jewish rules (for example, it would likely have
blood in it),[35] and most of it would have come to market from pagan temples.
So for a Jew who did not want to risk eating ritually impure meat, the only option was abstinence from meat. Josephus tells of Jewish priests imprisoned in
Rome subsisting on nuts and figs for fear of eating meat that was contaminated
with blood or tainted by association with idolatry (*Life* 14; cf. 2 Macc. 5.27).
(2) After the debacle among Jews, apparently caused by disputes over Jesus, and
the expulsion of the Jews in A.D. 49, "the officials who controlled the meat market would have withdrawn the provision of 'suitable food.' There may have

31. See below pp. 381-82.

32. Dunn, *Romans 9–16*, p. 798.

33. K. Grieb, *The Story of Romans: A Narrative Defense of God's Righteousness* (Louisville: Westminster/John Knox, 2002), p. 128.

34. See the argument of Dunn, *Romans 9–16*, pp. 800-801, dismantling the assumption
that the reference to vegetarianism means that the discussion is not about Jews. On Jewish or
Jewish Christian vegetarianism see Dan. 1.8; Judith 12.2; *Testament of Reuben* 1.10; *Testament
of Judah* 15.4; *Joseph and Aseneth* 8.5; Philo, *De Vita Contemplativa* 37 on the Therapeutae, and
Eusebius, *Historia Ecclesiae* 2.23.5 on James the brother of Jesus; and on the Ebionites see
Origen, *Matth.* 11.12; Epiphanius, *Haereses* 30.15.3.

35. On which see Lev. 3.17; 7.26-27; 17.10-14; Deut. 12.16, 23-24; 15.23.

been some in Rome who were no longer eating meat because kosher meat was not available in the markets. Given the official control of the market it would have required the action of a senior official, with the emperor himself giving his approval, for the reopening of the segment of the market for the Jews."[36] (3) Then, after the Jews' return under Nero, the few Jewish butchers in Rome might have been unwilling to service Jewish Christians, and Jewish Christians might have avoided synagogues, which might have cut them off from sources of acceptable meat. (4) Furthermore, the poor or marginalized could seldom if ever afford to buy meat, and the opportunities they would have to eat meat would be at public festivals connected with pagan celebrations and temples, or perhaps if a Gentile Christian invited them to dine at his home (see 1 Corinthians 8–10).[37]

For one or more of these reasons, Jewish Christians may have chosen to be vegetarians. But the primary message that that would send to many Gentiles, since the ability to purchase and regularly eat meat was a privilege of the socially better off, was that these Jewish Christians were of poor or lower social status. They thus might be doubly looked down on, both for their foreignness and their supposed poverty.

In fact, the latter, according to v. 3, is precisely what Paul seems to assume. The meat-eaters are looking down on the abstainers. The reverse side of the coin is that the abstainers condemn the meat-eaters, presumably for defiling themselves, and for offending Jews in the bargain. Paul reminds both that God has accepted the person in question, and so should they — despising and condemning are not Christian attitudes.

Paul must come up with a rhetorically effective leveling device to strengthen his exhortation; he chooses the metaphor of slaves and masters. V. 4 thus suggests that one's fellow Christian has one hierarchical relationship to be concerned about, and that is with his or her master — Christ. Now, if Christ is the only person in the socially superior position, then all Christians are at the same social level — they are all simply slaves or servants. The weak have no business judging someone else's household slave, nor do the strong. Neither has a superior position over another in Christ; they are in the very same position with regard to the Master. Neither should assume that they alone occupy the moral high ground. Furthermore, Paul makes clear that the Master makes his servants stand. He does not set them up for a fall, nor does he allow them to fall. The implication is that the believer has no business in trying to judge or trip up or put down another believer because of what they will or will not eat.

---

36. B. W. Winter, "Roman Law and Society in Romans 12–15," in *Rome in the Bible and the Early Church*, ed. P. Oakes (Grand Rapids: Baker, 2002), p. 90.

37. See my discussion of these matters in *Conflict and Community in Corinth*, pp. 186-230.

Paul chooses another illustration of the principle of not judging in v. 5. He says that some regard particular days above others, while others consider every day alike. Paul does not specifically mention sabbaths here, but presumably this is because he wants to include the notion of any and all special days, including festival days and the Day of Atonement as well as sabbaths (cf. Gal. 4.10; Col. 2.16). Paul, in this case, does not take either side; he simply says that each should be convinced in his or her own mind about what he or she is doing, and do it unto the Lord. This is an important point.[38]

Paul recognizes that there will be differences of opinion and belief within the body of Christ, and in non-essential matters he is content for it to be so. He believes that people should be allowed to make up and be convicted in their own minds about such issues. In other words, he expects some of these differences to reflect deeply held convictions, and that too is okay. And yet he still seeks to build a firm unity in the group of Christians he is addressing.[39] The attitude expressed here is much like that expressed much later by John Wesley and others: in essentials unity, in non-essentials one thinks and lets think, in all things charity or love. While Paul believes in persuasion and in imperatives, he also believes in allowing people the freedom to make up their minds on a host of things, so long as it is within the realm of what could reasonably be said to be in accord with the will of God and the Law of Christ.

The expansion of the argument in vv. 6-8 makes clear the underlying principle. Christians are not to live to themselves, by which Paul means that they are not to think they live just for themselves and their own benefit and pleasure.[40] To the contrary, Christians belong to Christ and are to live as though they are constantly under his watchful eye and have the task of trying to please him. They are to live in a context where they realize that they have been bought with a price; their lives are not their own to do with as they please. All they do should be done in the context of realizing that their lives are a gift from God, and their actions, whether eating, abstaining, worshiping, or whatever, should be suitable for offering up to God in thanks. Their actions should be doxological, bringing praise to God and edifying others. The reference to "giving thanks" is probably a telltale sign that Paul is thinking of these actions transpiring at the table, when food is shared within the Christian community.[41] In v. 7 Paul says that not only do believers not live to themselves alone, they are also

38. F. Watson, "The Two Roman Congregations: Romans 14.1–15.13," in Donfried, ed., *The Romans Debate*, pp. 203-15. While Watson may overplay the separation of Jewish and Gentile Christians in Rome, especially since this letter assumes the two groups will even eat together, nonetheless he is right to see significant divisions falling largely along ethnic lines.

39. See Dunn, *Romans 9–16*, p. 806.

40. See N. T. Wright, "Romans," in *The New Interpreter's Bible*, vol. 10 (Nashville: Abingdon, 2002), p. 737.

41. See Käsemann, *Romans*, p. 371.

not free to take or leave their lives as they will. They belong to another, the Lord. Thus, not only their religious actions, but their entire lives fall under the rubric of attempting to please and honor God. There are no secular moments in a Christian life.

V. 9 provides the theological basis of the previous exhortation. First, Paul asserts that Christ is Lord of all persons, dead or living, precisely because he lived and died for others.[42] Lordship commenced once *Christ* rose again from the dead. It is probably because he has been discussing the living and the dead that Paul uses the unexpected verb *ezēsen* here rather than the usual term "rose." There seems to be here no idea of Christ as exemplar. Rather, the focus is on Christ's unique role in relationship to all persons: he is Lord.

The eschatological train of thought continues in v. 10. The diatribe format is found here once more, and this verse makes it quite clear that Paul knows of and is addressing distinguishable groups of Christians in Rome.[43] The rhetorical question about why someone judges a brother and sister presumes the fact that Christ the risen and alive Lord is to be the judge, and therefore believers are not. 2 Cor. 5.10 mentions Christ's judgment seat, but here the reference is to God's judgment seat. For Paul, these ideas are interchangeable since Paul believes Christ is not only capable of fulfilling divine functions and taking on divine roles, Jesus is indeed the divine Lord.

In v. 11 Paul backs up his exhortation with a quotation mainly from Isa. 45.23 ("to me every knee shall bow . . .") though the initial oath is probably based on Isa. 49.18. Paul does not draw out the christological implications of his use of Isa. 45.23 as he does in Phil. 2.10, but what he is driving at is clear enough. The sense of the verb *exomologeō* is probably "acknowledge" rather than "praise." And this is probably acknowledgment in connection with obeisance rather than the eschatological confession of sins.[44] All will have to acknowledge on judgment day that God is God, even if they have not confessed him or believed in him till then. Christians will be judged for their judging and despising of one another. That they are saved by faith does not mean they will not be held accountable for their actions.[45] Furthermore, by judging one another, they have usurped the role that Christ will, and is solely sufficient to, play when he returns.

Wright is correct in saying that Paul believes that God is already setting up an outpost of the Kingdom of Heaven right under the noses of the Roman

---

42. Cf. Plutarch, *Vita Cleomachi* 31.

43. See Dunn, *Romans 9–16*, p. 808.

44. Käsemann, *Romans*, p. 372.

45. Dunn, *Romans 9–16*, p. 810: "It is clearly important for Paul that faith does not exempt any, far less every, believer from the final reckoning of God's judgement" (see especially 2.6-16; 1 Cor. 3.12-15; 2 Cor. 5.10).

authorities. Everyone in Rome knew well who claimed to be the master of the known world and who had a houseful of slaves. Everyone knew that Caesar was the court of last resort in the empire. But Paul says here that there is another Lord who will judge in a different court and to whom every knee will eventually bow. So Paul is indeed offering a sort of anti-imperial rhetoric and worldview here. If Jesus is and will be truly Lord of both the living and the dead, then Caesar's claims to be such are bogus. Rather, Caesar, like his own officials, are unwitting servants of the true God and his Son, who is the true Lord. Paul recognizes that such Roman officials have a legitimate role to play as public servants and servants of God (ch. 13), but he denies and rebuts the emperors' grandiose claims to lordship and divinity, and he also denies the rhetoric that the Roman Empire is the greatest domain of all. That claim, he says, belongs to God's Kingdom.[46]

V. 12 then tells believers not only that there will be a review of their actions and that God already knows all they have done, but also that each one will have to render an account, an explanation, for their behavior. To do so before the all-knowing Lord of all is a daunting prospect, especially when Jesus is the one person a believer would especially not want to disappoint or be shamed before. Thus, there is a powerful eschatological sanction being applied here to enforce the exhortations, which is an effective rhetorical move.

V. 13 provides something of a transition to the next subsection of this argument. Paul sums up what has been said before by saying his audience should resolve to stop judging one another, but this does not mean he wants them to give up judging altogether. In fact, he wants them to exercise good judgment so as not to set up any obstacles for a brother or sister. Probably he is drawing on the Jesus tradition we find in Mark 9.42 and par.[47] It is probably important that his argument be grounded in this way, especially for the Jewish Christians in the audience, who would need some convincing, for instance about the cleanness of all food.[48]

Paul then will say in both vv. 14 and 20 that he is quite convinced that no food is unclean in itself. The strong emphasis here is noteworthy. This means that Paul did not want food laws to be used as boundary markers or determiners for the church, even in the church he did not found in Rome.[49] According to

---

46. See Wright, "Romans," pp. 738-39.

47. See Dunn, *Romans 9–16*, p. 818.

48. Käsemann, *Romans*, p. 374, puts the matter strongly: "Jewish-Christians, who still felt obligated to keep the law of holiness, must have experienced a constant personal threat in dealing with Gentile-Christians, and must have seen in their free-thinking colleagues something like defectors."

49. One may suspect that Paul is so adamant here, almost swearing an oath, because he had often been challenged on this view, for it meant a sharp break with one of the crucial and distinctive aspects of early Judaism, and in this case he is doing the rhetorically apt thing by

Mark 7.18-19, and in particular according to Mark's comment on the parabolic saying of Jesus, this was also Jesus' view. It would appear that Paul, perhaps through his contact with Mark on the first missionary journey, had learned that this was the implication of the teaching of Jesus. Needless to say, this is a radical posture for a Jew to take, and, whether or not this teaching does go back to Jesus, it is certainly Paul's view. This, in turn, means that Paul does not see the Mosaic requirements about such things as obligatory for Christians, even Jewish Christians, and it also means he agrees with "the strong" or Gentiles on this point, rather than with "the weak" or Jewish Christians. But the second half of v. 14 is distinctive and shows some ethical nuancing on Paul's part. If a person regards something as unclean or "common" (that is, profane, as the word actually means), then it is unclean for him or her.

And furthermore, if one's perfectly legitimate choice of food and drink causes another to stumble, and one insists on doing it one's own way and scandalizing a fellow Christian, v. 15 indicates that such a person, even though he has not violated his own conscience, has violated the law of love for the brother or sister. Indeed, one could even "destroy"[50] the faith of fragile or young or weak Christians by brazenly violating what they deem to be proper Christian scruples. The parallel in Mishnah *Sanhedrin* 4.5 is worth citing: "If any one has caused a single soul to perish, Scripture imputes it to him as though he had caused a whole world to perish."

It appears likely that the social setting Paul has in mind is the Christian fellowship meal, for Paul envisions the weak seeing the strong eat the offensive meat, and he envisions the strong noticing the ones eating only vegetables and drinking no wine. He also envisions a setting in which the weak might be tempted by the strong's behavior to violate their own conscience.[51] All of this points to the meals early Christians were sharing with each other as a community. It is, therefore, in order to notice that Paul assumes there will be such joint meals in Rome involving Jewish and Gentile Christians. The community may be divided on some issues, but they are not entirely split into completely separate or rival factions.

Paul is concerned throughout this passage to inculcate behavior that unites rather than divides the weak and the strong in Rome. It is a bad witness to allow something that is not evil in itself to be spoken of as evil in public by those who are scandalized by a person's conduct. It is a matter of love, unity,

---

forestalling any challenge to this view by any of the "weak" in the audience. Paul got this idea from Jesus, either through revelation or through tradition or both, and for Paul this is a nonnegotiable point. See Käsemann, *Romans*, p. 375.

50. The verb refers here to final eschatological ruin and judgment, as opposed to acquittal by God or Christ. See Dunn, *Romans 9–16*, p. 821.

51. See Barrett, *Romans*, p. 242.

and witness, and it is also a matter of priorities. By "your good" in v. 16, Paul likely means one's knowledge that all foods are clean.[52] As Paul will say in v. 17, drawing on themes already enunciated in 5.1-5,[53] the Dominion of God[54] does not consist in food and drink and insisting on one's own way about such things, but rather in far more important things: righteousness, peace, and joy in the Holy Spirit. This cuts both ways, against both the strong and weak, against both making too little of others' scruples about food and making too much of abstaining or eating only certain foods due to religious scruples. The implication is that Paul is talking about qualities within the Christian life here, including righteousness, as well as peace and joy.[55] One who serves Christ on the basis of these factors will be pleasing to God. One who serves Christ on the basis of exercising one's own freedom and selfishly indulging one's own preferences and predilections, that person will not please God at all. In fact, says Paul in v. 18, behavior on the basis of what is right and peace-making and joyful will receive not only the praise of God but also the praise of one's fellow human beings.

Wright calls vv. 19-21 a second coat of paint on the same argument,[56] and he is correct that Paul is reiterating some things here. Every effort must be made to behave in a way that makes for peace and leads to the upbuilding[57] of one's fellow Christians. If that means one has to resist the temptation to eat and drink in public in a way that offends other believers, so be it. According to v. 21, it is better to abstain from all behavior that offends, so as to avoid causing a fellow believer to stumble or lose faith. Whereas Paul has said previously that food is unclean to the weak who deem it so, here he says food becomes evil if one eats it in a context where it causes someone else to stumble. I stress the word "context" here, because Paul is not referring to any and all occasions when a person eats. This is clear enough from his discussion in 1 Corinthians 8–10. The verbs

52. See R. A. J. Gagnon, "The Meaning of *hymōn to agathon* in Romans 14.16," *JBL* 117 (1998): 675-89.

53. See, rightly, Wright, "Romans," p. 741.

54. Though this term does not occur often in Paul, and especially not frequently in references to something in the present, we can mention 1 Cor. 4.20; 6.9-10; 15.50; Col. 4.11; 1 Thess. 2.12; 2 Thess. 1.5. See my discussion of these texts in *Jesus, Paul, and the End of the World: A Comparative Study in New Testament Eschatology* (Downers Grove: InterVarsity, 1992), pp. 51-58. Paul is talking about God's saving reign in the Christian's life, which, by the Spirit, produces such qualities in the believer.

55. Again, the term *dikaiosynē* refers to an attribute of a believer; the focus is not on a relationship here. See Barrett, *Romans*, p. 243.

56. Wright, "Romans," p. 741.

57. On this term cf. Jer. 12.16; 31.4, 28; 33.7; 42.10; 45.4. The metaphor of upbuilding was part of the regular arsenal of terms used to argue both in and out of rhetorical contexts for concord and unity; cf. Epictetus 2.15.8.

here refer to particular acts of consumption: "The infinitives 'to eat' and 'to drink' are aorists, and the meaning seems to be that, if on any particular occasion it seems likely that to eat flesh or to drink wine will cause a brother to stumble, it is right on that occasion to abstain. . . . Eating and drinking are not wrong in themselves, and on other occasions the danger may not arise."[58]

Clearly, this exhortation is primarily for the "strong." Paul tells them in v. 22 that they should keep their beliefs about what they are free to eat and drink to themselves. V. 22b has the only beatitude in the Pauline corpus.[59] There is a danger of condemning oneself by approving eating and drinking things one can legitimately consume without violation of conscience, but which, if one does so in public, will alienate the eater from the "weak" and provide a witness that can only harm their fragile faith.

In v. 23, Paul turns around and speaks to the "weak," indicating that they should not eat or drink anything they cannot do in good faith, because, though such eating or drinking may not be a sin in itself, it will be a sin for the weak because they thus violate their consciences and so are unable to offer the act up as an act of thanksgiving to God. Indeed, they will see themselves as condemned by God for doing it. There is perhaps an echo here of what is said in 4.20-21 about Abraham, the model of faith, who did not waver in doubt but grew "strong in faith."[60] But Paul may also be reflecting here knowledge of a principle enunciated in Roman discussions about what is appropriate. Cicero (*De Officiis* 1.30) says: "It is an excellent rule that they give who urge us not to do a thing, when there is doubt whether it is right or wrong; for righteousness shines with a brilliance of its own, but doubt is a sign that we are thinking of a possible wrong."

15.1 begins the final two subsections of the final argument in Romans, and Paul chooses in these two sections to say the same thing in two different ways. In vv. 1-6 the message will be "do not selfishly focus on your own preferences, for Christ did not please himself." In vv. 7-13, Paul will turn around and say the same thing in a positive manner: "welcome one another because and as you were welcomed by Christ."[61]

Vv. 1-2 show that Paul clearly identifies with the strong and says three principles should be maintained: bear with the weaknesses of the weak, and do not judge them; do not make pleasing yourselves the basis of your actions; and rather, seek to please the neighbor in ways that build up his or her weak faith. V. 3 presents Christ as an example of one who did not please himself; indeed, he even took the reproaches meant for others on himself, as the quotation of Ps.

---

58. Barrett, *Romans*, p. 245.
59. Wright, "Romans," p. 742.
60. Wright, "Romans," p. 742.
61. Wright, "Romans," p. 744.

69.9 makes clear.[62] Christ was other-directed rather than self-centered. The portrait of the righteous Jew who unjustly but self-sacrificially suffers for others is very appropriately applied to Jesus.[63] With the title "the Christ" with the definite article Paul is deliberately calling Jesus the Jewish Messiah.[64] We may compare 2 Cor. 8.9 and Phil. 2.5-8 on Christ's humbling of himself.

V. 4 makes a statement about the virtue and value of Scripture for the Christian life. It is suitable for teaching and helps believers to endure and be encouraged so that they may look forward to the future in hope. This should be compared to what is said in the later Pauline text 2 Tim. 3.16.[65] We must distinguish between Scripture as a source of instruction and encouragement on the one hand and the keeping of particular covenants contained within the OT on the other hand, in this case the Mosaic covenant with its Law code. Paul believes Christians are not under the Mosaic Law, but this does not mean that he thinks there is nothing to be learned from the OT as a book of prophecy, promises, and instruction. Quite the contrary. He believes the OT is still the inspired word of God and is profitable for teaching and encouragement. Christians are under a different covenant and obliged to its commandments. They still should learn from previous revelation and covenants, not least because God operates in a consistent way throughout salvation history, and what he requires under the new covenant, which involves both grace and obedience, is not radically different from some of what he required under the Law, which also involved grace and obedience. There is overlap, and so there are things to be learned from the old covenants and from the OT as Scripture.

Vv. 5-6 constitute a benediction of sorts in which Paul invokes the aid of God in creating a unified group of Christians in Rome. Those Christians need to be of one mind in regard to how they respect and treat one another. *Homothymadon* occurs regularly in the early part of Acts when Luke describes the like-mindedness of the earliest Jerusalem fellowship (Acts 1.14; 2.46; 4.24; 5.12; 7.57). One reason for Christians to be unified is so that they may collectively and with one heart and voice glorify God. "If praise in worship no longer bears witness in this way to daily fellowship, the community cannot ex-

---

62. For those trying to find this verse in either the MT or the LXX, one must keep in mind that the numbering system differs in the English text from either one of these sources. The verse in question is 69.10 in the MT and 68.10 in the LXX. On this verse see J. Zeisler, *Paul's Letter to the Romans* (London: SCM, 1989), pp. 337-38, who rightly sees Paul's use of the psalm as christological, with the focus on Christ's death as a form of self-giving that believers can emulate.

63. Barrett, *Romans*, p. 247: "The use of Scripture at this point is significant. It means that the example of Christ is more than an example; it belongs to the pattern of revelation."

64. See Dunn, *Romans 9–16*, p. 838.

65. I am in agreement with L. T. Johnson that 2 Timothy probably does go back to Paul, even though he may not have been the actual composer of the document.

ist."[66] Paul is consciously concluding his final argument with echoes of where he began his discourse. He began with prayer in 1.9-12 and ends there as well.[67]

V. 7 makes the connection between ethics and worship even clearer. By accepting one another as the Christ has accepted them,[68] the Christians thereby praise God. Unifying conduct is doxological by its very nature, and it reflects the character of God, who is patient and merciful.

It becomes apparent in vv. 8-9 that Paul is thinking back to and building on the discussion in chs. 9–11. There are especially echoes of 9.4-5. One could argue that 15.8 and 9 sum up much of the argument and rhetorical aims of the whole deliberative argument. W. Meeks points out the strangeness of the indirect claim being made here. Christ has welcomed Gentile Christians by being a servant to Jews, in order to fulfill promises made to Jewish patriarchs about Gentiles! "This extraordinarily compact statement constitutes a reprise of themes Paul has developed in chaps 9-11 and, more than that, in the whole letter, leading up to Paul's restatement of the goal of his own mission, which follows in the remainder of this chapter."[69] These verses indicate that Paul believes that the destiny of Jews and Gentiles is intertwined, and God always intended it that way, for the Good News is for all persons of whatever ethnic background.

Christ is called here "the servant of the circumcision" for two very good reasons. Paul is mainly exhorting the Gentile Christians to be the servants of their circumcised fellow Christians, and he is also countering anti-Semitism by reminding them that God has not given up on his first chosen people. In fact, there are still promises made to the patriarchs that are yet to be fulfilled for Jews. God's truth would be put in doubt if Christ had not become a servant of Jews so that the promises given to the patriarchs might be confirmed.[70] These

66. Käsemann, *Romans*, p. 383.
67. Wright, "Romans," p. 746.
68. Again we have the titular use here with the definite article as in v. 3. This is surely deliberate, since Paul goes on in the same passage to use Christ as a virtual name, omitting the definite article. This rhetorical ploy is probably meant to remind the Gentile majority that Jesus is the Jewish messiah.
69. W. Meeks, "Judgment and the Brother: Romans 14.1–15.13," in *Tradition and Interpretation in the New Testament,* ed. G. F. Hawthorne and O. Betz (Grand Rapids: Eerdmans, 1987), pp. 290-300.
70. Here Wright, "Romans," p. 746, in his pursuit of his thesis that Israel is summed up in Christ and all the promises are fulfilled in him, goes awry. Paul does not say here that the promises to the patriarchs are fulfilled in Christ. He says that they are confirmed by Christ, which is a different matter. Paul believes that they still remain to be fulfilled in Israel when Christ returns. Israel's history has not come to an end in Jesus Christ, though he will be the one who brings it to its intended goal at the eschaton. Dunn, *Romans 9–16*, p. 847, is right that the parallel usages of the verb and its cognates in 4.16 and 11.29 point to the translation "confirm" or "guarantee," as does the usage in the papyri as well. In light of Paul's argument in ch. 11, he is surely speaking about the confirmation of the promises to the Jews who are currently

promises will be fulfilled through the work of Christ at both his first and second comings, but they will be fulfilled for the Jewish people of God as well as those Gentiles who join them in the one people of God.[71] This is simply another way of saying that the gospel is for the Jew first, and Paul's largely Gentile audience must never forget that. V. 10 probably also echoes Mark 10.43-45, where Jesus presents himself as the servant who came to give his life as a ransom for the many.

The end result of recognizing how God is still working with and for Jews and Jewish Christians should be that Gentiles praise God for his mercy on both Jews and themselves. Johnson insightfully calls vv. 9-12 a counter-catena of quotations to what we find in 3.11-18, where texts that speak of humans turning away from God are used. Here we hear of Gentiles turning to and praising God.[72] V. 9 has a composite citation from 2 Sam. 22.50 and Ps. 18.49, and v. 10 cites Deut. 32.43 to the effect that the one true God's praise should resound forth from the midst of the Gentile nations, not just from Jews.[73] V. 11 simply adds the imperative to the indicative, urging Gentiles to praise God (quoting Ps. 117.1). V. 12 involves a quotation of Isa. 11.10 and is an ideal conclusion to this catena of quotations. It reminds Paul's Gentile audience that they have salvation only through the root of Jesse,[74] through the Jew Jesus, and, in fact, he rules over the Gentile nations, and they will place their hope in him. Here we have an echo of the initial remarks on Christ found in 1.3-4. We have come full circle.[75] The Jewish Messiah is Good News for the Jew first, and also for the Gentile, and the aim of his mission was to produce one people of God, Jew and Gentile, united in him. One purpose of these Scripture citations is to make clear that including Gentiles in the people of God was not just a happy afterthought of God. Rather it was always part of the divine plan.[76]

V. 12 may also be an implied critique of Roman attitudes about the subjugated Jews and about the Roman emperor as ruler over all nations. Not so, says Paul, for in the end all glory, honor, and praise will accrue to Jesus, not Caesar.

V. 13 provides a further benediction, which focuses on the theme of hope.

"broken off," which Jesus will bring when he comes again. He is not speaking here of the fulfillment of the promises to Abraham in the conversion of the Gentiles, though that is a theme he addresses elsewhere (see Gal. 3.14, 22).

71. See J. R. Wagner, "The Christ, Servant of the Jew and Gentile: A Fresh Approach to Romans 15.8-9," *JBL* 116 (1997): 473-85 on these verses.

72. See Johnson, *Reading Romans*, p. 219.

73. Here Paul follows the LXX, which speaks of the nations praising God, whereas the MT exhorts the nations to praise God's people.

74. This was clearly a messianic title. See Isa. 11.1-5; Sir. 47.22; Rev. 5.5; 22.16; 4QPat 3-4; 4QFlor. 1.11.

75. See Wright, "Romans," p. 748.

76. Barrett, *Romans*, p. 249.

God is a God of hope, and so the audience should overflow with such hope, which means in turn being forward-looking and hopeful about the future of both Jews and Gentiles in Christ. But it is only by the power of the Spirit that one can abound in hope or be filled with joy and peace. When one is filled with those attributes, which are called "fruit of the Spirit" in Galatians 5, then one is enabled to trust God in all circumstances. L. Keck sums things up well:

> Romans 15.7-13, then, expands this unity [of the strong and the weak in Rome, united with each other in the univocal praise of God] by showing that it is not simply a mutual, intra-mural accommodation to be reached in Rome, but a local instance of God's saving purpose in Christ — the eschatological unity of all people, concretely Jew and Gentile. By coming back to this theme, Paul draws a thread through the entire letter and shows that in Scripture God has indeed promised in advance the gospel for all humanity (1.2). Second, the theme of the universal praise of God is, in Paul's view, much more than a rhetorical flourish. It is the actual material soteriological alternative to the root problem of humanity: not giving praise to God or honoring God [cf. 1.21; 2.23].[77]

Bridging the Horizons

Origen offers a telling comment on this section of Paul's discourse: "Eating meat and drinking wine are matters of indifference in themselves. Even wicked people may abstain from these things, and some idol worshipers, in fact, do so, for reasons which are actually evil. Likewise quite a few heretics enjoin similar practices. The only reason abstinence of this kind is good is that it may help to avoid offending a brother."[78] This brings to light a fundamental principle of a truly Christian ethic — it is other-regarding. A Christian does not demand his or her own rights and privileges, especially when the issue is not a matter of ethical principle but rather just of personal preference.

The quotation from Origen also brings up another point. There is no inherent spiritual merit in certain disciplines like fasting or abstention from certain foods and drinks. One can praise God as well by eating as by abstaining. There may be and often are health benefits to abstention. But abstention in itself does not make one a good person or draw one closer to God. The same can be said in regard to abstention from sexual activity. Such abstention is not a

---

77. L. Keck, "Christology, Soteriology, and the Praise of God (Romans 15.7-13)," in *The Conversation Continues: Studies in Paul and John*, ed. R. T. Fortna and B. R. Gaventa (Nashville: Abingdon, 1990), pp. 85-97, here pp. 93-94.

78. See G. Bray, *Romans* (Downers Grove: InterVarsity, 1998), p. 350.

good in itself any more than sexual expression is inherently evil. There is a context in which all such activities can be done to the glory of God. Abstaining is not inherently a more holy activity. Holiness has to do with doing all things to the glory of God. Some things cannot be done to God's glory such as hating one's neighbor or being selfish and self-centered. But, more importantly, holiness has to do with real *agapē* love expressed wholeheartedly to God and to others. When holiness becomes primarily defined by what one abstains from, one has missed the heart of the holiness ethic in the Bible, which Paul is enunciating in part in Romans 14–15.

Paul's concern with dietary issues and the underlying attitude of acceptance of difference that must prevail in the Christian community stems from the compelling need to maintain table fellowship in the neophyte Roman house-churches. Since shared meals prefigure, reveal, and reflect the Kingdom, they provide "the context for instruction on equal recognition and respect . . . to portray a clear message — that of equality, transformed relations, and a common life."[79] Eating was and still often remains a bounded activity and, so, when we intentionally include the other in such times, social, economic, and cultural boundaries are transcended through the relationship forged at the common table. Such is the subversive aspect of hospitality.

15.7 contains the basis for, means for, and result of genuinely *Christian* hospitality: "Welcome one another, therefore, just as Christ has welcomed you, for the glory of God." Since Christ is our exemplar and we are the church called to embody the living Word in this world, the mandate to practice hospitality toward and receive hospitality[80] from *all* others cannot be ignored or rejected. Welcoming, that is, hospitality, "is a way of life fundamental to Christian identity."[81] Since Christ is *the* host, we are all guests by divine grace. That received grace must flow through us or its ongoing reception becomes blocked. Hoarded grace quickly becomes rotting manna. In a very real sense, hospitality requires us to trust in the breadth of divine love and the inexhaustible nature of our Creator's resources, convinced that such divine love and provision are sufficient for the day.

Paul knew that a major portion of what we term "sin" consists of obsession with "otherness," xenophobia (literally "fear of strangers"). With the Fall, the richness of creation's diversity within a framework of relatedness was de-

---

79. C. Pohl, *Making Room: Recovering Hospitality as a Christian Tradition* (Grand Rapids: Eerdmans, 1999), p. 32.

80. St. John Chrysostom in his *Homily* 41 on Genesis 18 reminds us that "the person exemplifying . . . [hospitality] with enthusiasm receives something rather than gives it" (*Homilies on Genesis 18–45*, trans. Robert C. Hill, Fathers of the Church series [Washington: Catholic University of America Press, 1986-92], 3:409).

81. Pohl, *Making Room*, p. x.

formed into a differences-as-divisions understanding. Relationship gave way to suspicion and its inevitable fruit of alienation[82] — the ultimate refugee experience. Strangers are essentially "people without a place"[83] and thus vulnerable. Yet, within the Christian hospitality tradition, only strangers depending on God are capable of truly welcoming other strangers. The Babel account depicts the inevitable segregation that ensues when the good gift of shared culture and language is employed in the quest of "mak[ing] a name for ourselves."[84]

Graciously, God's commitment to risk-taking, costly love transcended the essential otherness between Creator and created as he set about restoring the relational nature of creation itself. God called Abram, Sarai, and their family to "leave your country, people, and parent's household and go to the land I will show you."[85] Inherent in that experience of divine invitation and human surrender was a promise: distinctive blessing granted so that "all peoples on earth will be blessed through you."[86] From the divine viewpoint, particularity always serves universality, for God is essentially hospitable, welcoming all who are willing to come. Whenever God's people lose touch with the essential unity of our chosen and alien aspects of identity, the framework of the Kingdom is fractured.

With establishment of the post-exodus covenant, God repeatedly reminded the Israelites that, as inhabitants of the land of promise, they were tenants of the divine owner[87] and had to remember they too were once, and in some sense still were, aliens and sojourners.[88] That identification and memory were to shape an ethos of relationship and care for the alien/sojourner, enacted through intentional, Torah-mandated hospitality. Remembering would protect the Israelites from subsequent hubris and alienation from God and others. But the lesson proved difficult and the people called to be God's agents in the world grew forgetful and presumed upon the purported irrevocability of the divine-Israel relationship. That arrogance and disobedience occasioned the exile — a second period of refugee status intended to restore meaningful relationship with God from which essential moral hospitality could flow to others.

With the return to the land of promise, fear of being dispossessed again prevailed, diluting and eventually overcoming the God-prescribed risky way of living, the way of hospitality. So the Law, intended to provide shelter and rela-

---

82. From humanity's perspective, the alienation is total and irrevocable. The relationships between God and humanity, human being to human being, humanity and nature to lesser creatures and creation have experienced brokenness. Cf. Gen. 3:14-19.

83. Pohl, *Making Room*, p. 87.

84. Gen. 11:4.

85. Gen. 12:1-3.

86. Gen. 12:3.

87. Lev. 25:23 and Deut. 26:1-15. Cf. Gen. 15:5-18.

88. Exod. 23:9; Lev. 19:33-34; Deut. 10:18-19; 24:14-22.

tionship for all humanity through the creation of a distinctive people capable
of embracing others, was perverted into self-protective thinking and behavior,
the framework of exclusion, wholly opposite to divine hospitality. Clean-
unclean, insider-outsider, Jewish-Gentile paradigms prevailed, paradigms antithetical to hospitality's recognition of commonality expressed in "shared living" (cf. Rom. 12.9-16).

Philip Hallie's *Lest Innocent Blood Be Shed* recounts a story of the transforming, subversive power of shared living — what the author terms a "kitchen
struggle":[89] Nineteen hundred years after Paul wrote Romans, André Trocmé, a
Huguenot pastor in the village of Le Chambon in the Haute-Loire region of
France, underscored the recognition of commonality. Refusing to ostracize the
Jews of France despite their religious "otherness," he affirmed, "We do not
know what a Jew is. We know only men."[90] Pohl asserts, "When, by acknowl-
edging difference, we only endanger, then we must only acknowledge our common human identity."[91] Trocmé's commitment and that of his village to such a
way of living made Le Chambon the safest place in Europe for Jews during
WWII. Through the subversive practice of Christian hospitality, a kitchen con-
spiracy of goodness, this small, impoverished village of three thousand in occupied France saved an estimated five thousand Jewish refugees from the Nazi ex-
termination camps. Like the Israelites before them, the Huguenots of Le
Chambon recalled their own history of persecution and realized that Christian
faith demanded a refusal to participate in oppression and violence, always the
first fruits of focusing on differences.

Alongside the fear of provoking God's wrath by failing to "protect" the
Torah (as if God requires human protection), the Roman occupation of Palestine exacerbated the sense of threat. The Law became known as "the yoke of Torah" and now burdened rather than heartening the people, who then sought to
preserve their identity by strict separation from others. Thankfully, God did not
abandon his engagement with humanity, but chose to display mercy and grace
to draw all people into the household of the Lord. Rather than maintaining the
only legitimate wholly other identity, the Son descended from heaven and accepted the inherent vulnerability of the human condition (a reality shared by
all persons) to show us the way to truly becoming human,[92] the way of kenotic
selflessness.

The penultimate refugee experience is constituted in God willingly surrendering relationship within the trinity and divine privileges to enter first-

89. Philip Hallie, *Lest Innocent Blood Be Shed* (New York: HarperPerennial, 1994), p. 9.
90. Hallie, *Lest Innocent Blood Be Shed*, p. 170.
91. Pohl, *Making Room*, p. 83.
92. This way of considering salvation as the process of becoming fully human is described in Jean Vanier's *Becoming Human* (New York: Paulist Press, 1999).

century Palestine as part of a subjugated ethnic group that practiced an unpopular and widely misunderstood faith. Then God encased in frail human infancy, accompanied by his earthly family, became a refugee, fleeing the persecution of Herod and seeking and receiving shelter in Egypt, a land of former enslavement. It is no wonder that Jesus' ministry exemplified hospitality, with radical leveling of guest and host status/roles. Accordingly, the paradigmatic text for the hospitality tradition of the Christian church is Matt 25.31-46, with its assertion that what we do or do not do for others is reckoned as done or left undone for Christ. It is not surprising that St. Benedict insisted that all guests "be received as Christ himself."[93] Indeed, John Wesley also warned that our very reception in eternity is influenced by whether we practice hospitality.[94]

Christians are called to be "strangers in the world,"[95] aware of our own essential "otherness" so that fear of strangers gives way to divinely enabled *philoxenia* ("love of strangers").[96] Therefore, distinctions of "weak" and "strong" disappear in the face of love-based hospitality. The locus of Christian citizenship is the household of God,[97] and when we live out that identity the Lord is glorified. Indeed, the early church asserted that hospitality was "one of the pillars of morality on which the universe rests" and considered it the primary witness of the gospel. May we who are God's guests enter into the risky but faithful proposition of loving one another through the power of the Holy Spirit, who truly is God with(in) us.

93. *Rule of St. Benedict,* quoted in Owen Chadwick's *Western Asceticism* (Philadelphia: Westminster, 1979), p. 324.

94. J. Wesley, Sermon XCVIII, "On Visiting the Sick."

95. 1 Pet. 1.1-2, 17-19.

96. Rom. 12.13. Cf. Hebrews 13 and 1 Peter 4.

97. 1 Pet. 2.9-12.

Peroratio I — 15.14-21:
The Knowledge and Apostle of the Gentiles

The *peroratio* is found in 15.14-21, with v. 22 being a transitional verse to get one to the epistolary section known as travel plans. In fact, Paul intersperses the travel plans in the midst of this *peroratio,* so that its emotional conclusion, full of pathos, is found in vv. 30-33.[1] One could argue that 16.17-19 also sounds like a *peroratio.* I will argue that it is the conclusion for the "weak" minority or Jewish Christians (and some God-fearers), whereas 15.14-21 is the conclusion for the "strong" majority, who are by and large Gentile Christians. This comports very nicely with Paul's rhetorical strategy in ch. 2 where he addressed first an arrogant Gentile followed by a Jewish teacher too full of himself, using the diatribe format. It bears asking why Paul used that format so frequently in this letter from ch. 2 on, far more than in his other letters. The answer is that he really is dealing with a divided house in Rome, and so he must address one group and then the other repeatedly, both in the theological section of the letter and also in the ethical section, and now in two *peroratios* as well.

I also maintain that the people listed in 16.3-16 are those that the Gentile majority are urged to greet and treat hospitably, after having been told to assist Phoebe. They are Jewish Christians and God-fearers in Rome, who in the main have returned from Corinth and elsewhere in the east after Nero came to power

---

1. On which see W. Wuellner, "Paul's Rhetoric," in *The Romans Debate,* ed. K. P. Donfried (2nd ed.; Peabody: Hendrickson, 1991), pp. 128-46. Paul is juggling both rhetorical and epistolary elements in the end of ch. 15 and in ch. 16, trying to bring both to closure. Since he has offered his discourse in the context of a letter this is not a surprise, and so Romans is in some respects like ancient diplomatic letters which used deliberative rhetoric, or like the *logos protreptikos;* see D. E. Aune, "Romans as a *Logos Protreptikos,*" in Donfried, ed., *The Romans Debate,* pp. 278-96.

in A.D. 54, or have come to Rome at that juncture for the first time. They now need to be integrated or reintegrated into the church in Rome, which is largely Gentile. Their eastern origins or time spent in the east is why Paul knows so many of them and is related to some of them. Some hold the opinions of the "weak" and so need the encouraging word found in the second *peroratio* in 16.17-19. The final greetings from Corinth in 16.21-24 are directed to these Jewish Christians whom Paul and his host and coworkers know.[2]

There were various possible functions of a *peroratio*, and while Quintilian tends to urge one to pick one or another form of conclusion (*Instit. Or.* 6.1.1-2), in the Greek tradition it was considered fine to combine the functions (see Aristotle, *Rhetoric* 3.19.1; cf. *Rhetorica Ad Herennium* 2.30). These functions included a final emotional appeal, appealing to the stronger emotions; summation of the major themes or thesis of the discourse; recapitulation and amplification of some earlier important material; and a final remark to stimulate empathy for the speaker and his discourse — in this case for Paul and his ministerial tasks as apostle to the Gentiles. This last was sometimes called the *conquestio.*

What then would Paul hope to accomplish in his *peroratio* to the Gentiles? Since he was planning to visit them, hopefully soon, and since he wanted to solicit their support for his journeys to Jerusalem and Spain, he had to awaken empathy and support. He knew full well that in deliberative oratory an appeal to the deeper emotions is crucial since you want the hearer to take action in the near future on behalf of the causes and exhortations you have urged (see *Instit. Or.* 3.8.12). Paul seeks almost immediately to achieve this aim by urging support of his upcoming journey and then his further work in the west, not least in the form of prayer with Paul about such matters (vv. 30-33), and by pushing the Gentiles to reach out to the Jewish Christians in Rome by offering a long "greeting card" and urging the Gentiles to come together with these named persons. If I am right in my hypothesis, we can stop trying to figure out how Paul could know so many people in Rome. In a sense, all the arguments in Romans lead up to ch. 16, to this very practical conclusion, for the gospel was for all persons, the Jew first and also the Gentile.

But how would Paul get to the point of trying to effect this rapprochement between the Gentile majority and Jewish minority in the church in Rome? He must first reawaken empathy for himself and his mission, and must

---

2. If I am right in this analysis, it demonstrates how divided the Roman Gentile and Jewish Christians actually were, for they can be addressed separately, though in the same letter. It also shows that ch. 16 is part of Paul's rhetorical strategy to get the Christians in Rome unified. Paul reinforces what he has argued for in chs. 12–15 by his concluding double *peroratio* and by his exhortation to be hospitable and loving toward one another. The Gentiles are especially urged to reach out to these named Jewish and God-fearing Christians.

one final time try to establish rapport with the Gentiles. He does this by the technique of recapitulation. First, he revisits the themes of both the prescript and the *exordium*/thanksgiving prayer that led to the *probatio* and the initial theological section of the discourse (cf. 15.14 and 1.8; 15.15-21 and 1.13b; 15.22 and 1.13a; 15.23-24, 28-29 and 1.11-12; 15.25-27 and 1.14; 15.30-32 and 1.9-10; 15:33 and 1.8).[3] Then he revisits the initial ethical argument as well (cf. 15.16 and 12.1-2). Paul's work and his exhortation to the Gentiles are seen to correspond. Paul amplifies on his mission to the Gentiles — his job was to preach to the Gentiles so that they would obey God, preaching where Christ was not known. 15.17-20 is an amplification of vv. 15b-16. Then finally, in the quotation of Isa. 52.15 in 15.21, we have the *conquestio*, where Paul cites an unimpeachable source, the OT, as justification for his continued missionary approach to the Gentiles. If this were not enough, Paul returns briefly to make a final emotional appeal in vv. 30-33, after digressing about his travel plans.

What we do *not* find in this *peroratio* (15.14-21, 30-33) is a rehearsal or summation of the thesis statement in 1.16-17. Nor in the second *peroratio* is there one either. Paul says only that he has written to his audience boldly with a series of arguments, "by way of reminder," thus appealing to them as people who already know or should know these things. The "summation" was not required in deliberative oratory, unlike forensic rhetoric, where it was almost de rigueur.

We also do not find in the first *peroratio* any appeal to the deeper negative emotions such as anger, hate, grief, and the like. The Roman Gentile Christians, with a few possible exceptions, are not Paul's converts, so he cannot afford to alienate them, and in any case he does not want to arouse anything that could further divide the Christians in Rome. To the contrary, he must win them over to his side and establish rapport before he arrives in Rome, especially if he wants their support for his further missionary ventures. This he does admirably, to judge from his reception when he finally reached Rome (see Acts 28).

But I myself have been fully persuaded, my brothers, concerning you, that you yourselves are full of goodness, filled with all knowledge, being able also to admonish/instruct one another. But rather boldly I wrote to you in part, so as to remind you, because of the grace given to me by God, so that I might be a public servant of Jesus Christ unto the Gentiles, serving in the capacity of priest of the gospel of God, in order that the sacrificial offering of the Gentiles might be acceptable, consecrated in the Holy Spirit. I have then a matter for boasting in Christ Jesus, the [work I do] for God. For I will not dare to speak of anything which Christ did not accomplish through me unto the obedience of Gentiles, in word and deed, in pow-

---

3. J. D. G. Dunn, *Romans 9–16*, Word Biblical Commentary Series (Dallas: Word, 1988), p. 857.

erful signs and wonders, in the power of the Spirit of God,[4] *with the result that from Jerusalem making a circle to Illyricum, I have completed the gospel of Christ, but thus seeking the honor to preach where Christ has not been named, in order to avoid building on someone else's foundation. But just as it is written: "To those to whom nothing was announced about him, they will see, and those not hearing will understand."*

At the beginning of this epic letter, Paul discoursed about four things: himself and his apostleship to the Gentiles (1.1, 5), his gospel about Jesus (1.2-4), the world-renowned faith and spiritual gifts of the Roman Christians (1.8, 11-12), and Paul's eagerness, deep desire, and plans, until now frustrated, to go to Rome and share the faith (1.10, 11, 13, 15), not least because it was the hub, the center, the mecca for Gentiles in a largely Gentile world. It is these themes which are recapitulated in the *peroratio* in 15.14-21, and in the travel plans section in 15.22-33.

V. 14 begins with a compliment (or *captatio benevolentiae*), not unlike the compliment already paid the Roman Christians in 1.8, 12. Paul had all along wanted to ask for the assistance of the Roman church, but much was needed before such a request, including a presentation of some of his gospel. Now he will fully alert the audience he is coming, having waited until now to knock on the door. The long discourse was necessary in part because "Paul carefully guards against falling into the house as soon as the door opens."[5] While we have echoes of the *proem* in this passage (see 1.8, 12), here the focus is on the Romans being full of goodness and knowledge. Paul is courting or wooing his audience. "He has written strong words, and does not wish by tactlessness to ruin his relations with the church in Rome before setting foot in the city. Of course this does not mean he is insincere in what he says."[6] What it does mean is that Paul knows from a rhetorical standpoint that he must end on a positive or affirming note with this Gentile majority if he is to be received in Rome when he gets there. He wants to be received on the basis of who he is in Christ and on the basis of his gospel and mission to Gentiles, not on the basis of some social status he may have, for example as a Roman citizen.

What does v. 14 actually assume about the Roman Gentile Christians? They are, at their best, people of genuine goodness, faith, and considerable

4. It is not clear whether the original text read "Spirit of God" or "Holy Spirit" here. Since our earliest manuscript, p46, has the former reading, and it is followed by other good manuscripts, this reading has a slight edge. See B. M. Metzger, *A Textual Commentary on the Greek New Testament* (3rd ed.; London: United Bible Societies, 1971), p. 473.

5. E. Käsemann, *Commentary on Romans* (Grand Rapids: Eerdmans, 1980), p. 390.

6. C. K. Barrett, *A Commentary on the Epistle to the Romans* (Peabody: Hendrickson, 1991), p. 252.

knowledge, quite unlike the Gentiles described in 1.29ff. Paul, though he has instructed them at great length, will call this instruction a "reminder" (v. 15) and thus reiterates that he is reinforcing what they already know, at least for the most part.[7] He trusts their goodwill and that they now know all they need to know so that, among other things, they can instruct or admonish one another. Paul does not address leaders here, perhaps because there are not that many or the leadership structure is not that developed, but in any case he expects the Roman Gentile Christians in general to participate in instructing or exhorting. Nothing we find in Romans suggests that the Christian community there has an apostolic foundation, much less a Petrine apostolic foundation.

This leads to another point. While Paul makes much out of the fact that he does not want to build on another's foundation, yet he has instructed the Roman Christians at great length in this letter, and he longs to go to Rome to do even further sharing of the gospel and Christian instruction. He seems to think he has a right, as apostle to the Gentiles, to do so. He seems to assume, though he says he knows the Roman Gentile Christians have knowledge, that they have not had a proper apostolic undergirding. The foundation of the church in Rome seems to have happened not only without the help of Paul, but also without any intentional or planned missionary strategy involving a mission to Gentiles, which Paul is in charge of for the early church. So he has written this letter in part to ensure that the Roman church has the right theological and ethical foundation, since what they have received in the past is uncertain or unclear, at least to Paul.

In v. 15 Paul admits that he has exhorted them boldly, but he says it was "in part" by way of reminder.[8] What does "in part" modify? Is Paul saying that part of his letter was bold or blunt, or is he saying that what he has written is partially a reminder? It could be either. Dunn suggests that Paul means that in a particular part of the letter, namely 12.1–15.13, he has been so bold as to directly exhort an audience he did not convert,[9] though Dunn admits this may well refer to the whole letter. Barrett thinks Paul is saying that he wrote partially to remind the audience.[10] I think this is likely to be correct. Paul surely knew, especially in his argument in chs. 9–11, that he was breaking some fresh ground for his audience, not least because he characterizes what he is doing as the revelation of what previously had been a mystery or secret. So Romans is only in part a "reminder."

Paul explains that what enabled and permitted him to write in this way to

---

7. But as Käsemann, *Romans*, p. 392, notes, to say that one is reminding someone of what he already knows is a standard rhetorical device, used to ingratiate oneself with the audience.

8. See B. Byrne, "Rather Boldly (Rom. 15.15): Paul's Prophetic Bid to Win the Allegiance of the Christians in Rome," *Biblica* 74 (1993): 83-96.

9. Dunn, *Romans 9–16*, p. 858.

10. Barrett, *Romans*, p. 252.

such an audience was the grace given him by God to be a minister to the
Gentiles. One should not put it down to Paul simply being an imposing and as-
sertive person. The grace given him was not merely, indeed not primarily, for his
own benefit (v. 16). It was given "in order that" he might be a religious public
servant, a minister, to Gentiles. The term *leitourgos* here surely has its cultic sense
as in Neh. 10.39; Isa. 61.6; Sir. 7.30; and Heb. 8.2. Paul presents himself as a
priest,[11] serving the Good News of God, offering up the Gentiles to God as a
consecrated sacrifice, trusting that it will be acceptable to God. "In keeping with
the rest of the NT, Paul assumes an eschatological transformation of the OT
cultic ministry, in which animal sacrifices are replaced by obedient Christians
(cf. 12.1) and the praise they offer God (Heb. 13.15). . . ."[12] The echo here of Rom.
12.1-2 is clear, only in this case it is Paul rather than the Gentile audience doing
the offering. The term *hierourgeō* refers to performing the work of a priest.[13]
This is the only place in the Pauline corpus that Paul so clearly presents himself
as a priest doing priestly service. Notice the very natural trinitarian progression
here — Paul is a minister of Christ, serving the gospel of God, offering the
Gentiles who have been consecrated by the Spirit. Paul clearly sees the divine
functions and existence parceled out in three persons and ways. Only ritually
clean or pure sacrifices were acceptable, which is why we have the language
about consecrated and acceptable juxtaposed. But Paul may also be thinking of
the actual effect of the Spirit on believers and may not be limiting the term
hagiazein to the meaning "to be set apart" for God.[14] One should compare Acts
26.17-18 to this verse and to v. 31 (see also 16.20). This verse is but one more confirmation, if we needed one, that Paul is addressing a largely Gentile audience,
and certainly in this *peroratio* that is whom he is talking about and speaking to.

Boasting was a regular part of an honor and shame culture, especially
when there was a sort of competition involved between two or more persons or
groups. It is noteworthy then that v. 17 wants to talk about appropriate sorts of
boasting, in this case, in what Christ has accomplished through Paul, and specifically in spiritual matters. In Paul's view, inoffensive self-praise must take one
of two forms: it must either be a sort of mock boasting about self (as in 2 Cor.
11.16-33),[15] or it must be a boasting in what God in Christ has done through

11. Not a Levite; see H. Schlier, "Die 'Liturgie' der apostolischen Evangeliums (Römer
15, 14-21)," in *Das Ende der Zeit. Exegetische Aufsätze und Vorträge* (Freiburg: Herder, 1971), pp.
171-76.

12. D. Moo, *The Epistle to the Romans* (NICNT; Grand Rapids: Eerdmans, 1996), pp.
890-91.

13. See Josephus, *Antiquities* 5.263; 6.102; 7.333; 9.43; cf. Philo *Legum Allegoriae* 3.130; *De
Plantatione* 164.

14. See C. Talbert, *Romans* (Macon: Smyth and Helwys, 2002), p. 329.

15. See my *Conflict and Community in Corinth* (Grand Rapids: Eerdmans, 1995), pp.
432-41.

Paul, as in this text. Paul will not boast about what anyone else has done, or what God has done through anyone else. He must speak from his own experience and not make presumptions about others' experiences. We have already seen this sort of boasting by Paul in 5.11.[16] The aim of Paul's work, as v. 18 makes clear, is the obedience of the Gentiles. It is not just faith or obedience he is after, but the obedience that flows forth from faith.[17]

How did Christ accomplish this work through Paul and in the Gentiles? Paul says it involved word and deed, the power of signs and wonders, and the power of the Holy Spirit.[18] There were then various components that made this ministry effective. "Signs and wonders" echoes similar phrases in the OT and early Jewish literature (cf. Exod. 7.3, 9; 11.9-10; Wis. 8.8; 10.16; Bar. 2.11). We may compare the use of the phrase in 2 Cor. 12.12 (cf. Gal. 3.5). What this verse makes clear is that Paul did perform miracles, or, better said, miracles were performed through Paul. There are of course various accounts of this in places like Acts 13–14, but Paul is notably reticent to talk about such things, probably precisely because it would lead people to focus too much on himself rather than on his Lord. The same sort of considerations may be in play with this matter as in regard to Paul's reticence to talk about his social status as a Roman citizen. Paul wants the gospel and the gospel work to speak for itself without the usual honor and status conventions coming into play. What Paul adds in v. 19b is that his preaching has "completed" or fulfilled the gospel of Christ. "As the world is permeated by the Gospel, the Gospel itself comes to fulfillment. It is of the essence of the Gospel that it is not just proclaimed but that it fashions an earthly sphere of validity for the lordship of Christ."[19]

Paul amazingly then goes on to say that he has completed the gospel work in the arc from Jerusalem to Illyricum. The Roman province of Illyricum was founded in 35-33 B.C. Presumably Paul is speaking in general terms in three ways: he means that his work has been in the top half of the Mediterranean crescent as far west as Illyricum, which corresponded roughly with the territory we call Albania plus what was once known as Yugoslavia; he probably does not mean he specifically evangelized in Jerusalem and Illyricum (we have no record elsewhere in Paul's letters of his doing so in either place)[20] but in the arc that covers that general part of the empire;[21] and he means he has completed the

---

16. See Dunn, *Romans 9–16*, p. 862.

17. See pp. 34-36 above.

18. See K. Grieb, *The Story of Romans: A Narrative Defense of God's Righteousness* (Louisville: Westminster/John Knox, 2002), p. 138.

19. Käsemann, *Romans*, p. 394.

20. But see Acts 9.28-29; and 2 Tim. 4.10 says that Titus went to Dalmatia, which is another name for the same territory.

21. L. T. Johnson, *Reading Romans: A Literary and Theological Commentary* (Macon: Smyth and Helwys, 2001), p. 227, is right, however, that the mention of Jerusalem here shows

work in the region God wanted *him* to do, which was an exercise in representative church planting, especially involving an urban strategy focusing on Roman colony cities and other crucial cities like Ephesus. As Paul says, he views his work as a matter of laying the foundations. He does not see it as his task to assemble all the superstructure.[22] As v. 20 says, Paul must go where Christ has not been named, a ministry which he believes there is a scriptural call to fulfill, based in Isa. 52.15. The verb *philotimeomai* means "love or seek honor," and this whole passage is a kind of honor discourse. The sort of honor Paul seeks is the privilege of reaching those who have never heard of Christ with the Good News about him.[23] Paul is equally concerned not to build on another person's apostolic foundation. But this may explain why he was prepared to write to and visit the Romans — their church had no such foundation. It is also perhaps relevant to note that a letter like Colossians or Philemon shows Paul exercising some authority in churches he did not directly found, it would appear.

The importance of the quotation in v. 21 needs to be stressed. It is a verbatim rendering of the LXX of Isa. 52.15. This text comes near the beginning of the crucial fourth Servant Song (Isa. 52.13–53.12) and brings to light an interesting part of Paul's self understanding. This song speaks of the servant's impact on the Gentile nations. Did Paul see himself as that Servant? The answer seems to be, in and through Christ, yes he did. It must be remembered that early Jews did not read those texts in an exclusively messianic way. Paul the servant of Christ sees his ministry as an extension of Jesus' ministry, and, as v. 19 says, he sees his mission as a completing of the gospel of Christ. "We should beware of the assumption that the Christological interpretation of such passages prevented all other reference for them, or that Paul would think it blasphemous to see his own mission as 'completing the Gospel of Christ.'"[24] What does applying such a text to himself suggest about Paul's self-understanding? "Only an apocalyptic self-understanding can find the criterion of one's own action prefigured in Scripture in such a way that its prophecy is directed personally to the apostle and makes him the executor and therefore the predestined instrument of salvation history."[25]

---

that Paul found the Jerusalem church to be of great significance, perhaps even a commissioning church for his Gentile mission (see Galatians 2). The collection also supports the conclusion that Paul saw the Jerusalem church as crucial.

22. See rightly, Dunn, *Romans 9–16*, p. 864.

23. The suggestion in *NewDocs* 1:88 that it means here merely "strive eagerly" misses the context where honorable behavior of some sort seems to be being inculcated.

24. Dunn, *Romans 9–16*, p. 866.

25. Käsemann, *Romans*, p. 396.

Bridging the Horizons

This passage, as much as any in the Pauline corpus, conveys the missionary zeal of Paul. He is, in so many ways, the paradigm for all later Christian pioneers and evangelistic trailblazers. He is a church planter, but the evidence of his extended stay in Corinth also suggests that he was a church nurturer. He boldly goes where no missionary has gone before, believing that that is a part of his calling.

But such a calling is not for every Christian, as Paul knows all too well. He does not ask all those in Rome to emulate him in his church planter/trailblazer role. He does ask for their support in various ways. Romans 12 teaches that different Christians have differing gifts and so differing callings, so one should not measure the degree of one's commitment or faithfulness to one's calling by whether one has done what Paul did, which is to say, get involved in overseas missions. Were that the criterion by which Christians should really be judged effective witnesses and believers, then James, the brother of Jesus, who was the head of the Jerusalem church but seems to have never wandered from his home base there, would have come up very short by such a test. They also serve who stay at home and work. It all depends on what one is gifted and called to do, but, of course, God's call on a person's life can change over time, and so one must always be open to new leadings and challenges.

Yet there is something especially inspiring about stories like that of Jim Elliot, the missionary who lost his life working with the fierce Auca Indians in South America, giving the last full measure of his devotion by pouring out his life. Shortly before Elliot died, when he was asked about why he kept risking his life with such an inhospitable and seemingly ungrateful and unpromising audience, he said, "He is no fool who gives up what he cannot keep, to gain what he cannot lose." Recently, one of the Auca tribesmen spoke at an evangelistic event in Florida. After Elliot died, this man was converted to the Christian faith, in part due to the enduring impact of Elliot's witness. Now there is a significant group of Christians among the Aucas. There is then still truth to Tertullian's older claim that "the blood of the martyrs is seed for the church."

That quotation speaks to the reality of pre-Constantinian evangelism — Paul's proclamation was counter-cultural, subversive, imaginative, and prophetic and sought to advance the formation of a new community of transformed persons with renewed ways of thinking (and, therefore, behaving). Similarly, Jim and Elisabeth Elliot discovered the costliness of initial penetration of a culture wherein the Christian message was utterly new and, thus, utterly threatening.

Contrast that transforming evangelism with contemporary revivalism that, like Constantinian "faith," presumes an unholy alliance of church and state wherein the thought patterns and ethos of the two cultures become so enmeshed as to be virtually indistinguishable. Revivalism presumes an awareness of Christianity or at least the intermingled quasi-Christianity and then seeks to awaken response, generally in an individualistic, inward, Gnostic fashion. Accordingly, author Rodney Clapp asserts, "Today's evangelism is marketing, and today's pastor is expected to be a marketer . . . [who] appeals to desires that already exist among the unevangelized . . . in the form of 'felt needs.'"[26] Such a domesticated God is incongruent with the God of Abraham, Sarah, Isaac, Rebekah, Jacob, and Rachel and would be inconceivable to the apostle Paul.

The God of Israel and the New Testament is keenly interested in human history, not in escapist theology of eternal life in the sweet by-and-by. "The goal or proper end of human life . . . is . . . the enjoyment of wholeness in communion with God and God's people, amid a healed and no longer strife-driven creation."[27] Although that eventuality is not yet fully realized, Pauline (and post-Constantinian) evangelism is not an information dump into "empty" minds; it is a transformational dialogue of invitation to enter a worldwide "in Christ" community and subsequent initiation into the ways of that peculiar people.

The foundation of that community is its relational nature, congruent with its triune God. Private faith is antithetical to legitimate Christianity, and the tyranny of individualism must and will be supplanted whenever and wherever the gospel is proclaimed as a way of life, the following of an enthroned suffering Messiah, not as an isolated acceptance of a concept. Clapp underscores that "vital involvement in the life of Christ demands public confession and practice of . . . faith."[28]

Likewise, evangelism emanates from a communal posture and is itself a corporate activity, since the embodied/enacted nature of the gospel is winsome and essentially hospitable; again, the Body is like its God. "Faithful and effective Christian evangelism can occur only as part and parcel of Christian culture."[29] As Paul did, twenty-first-century evangelists must persuade people to enter the kingdom, rather than imposing, coercing, or manipulating "belief" (the way of Constantinian evangelism). Clapp describes this persuasion as "proposing" a new way of understanding and a new way of being. In the task of persuasion, listening and relating supersede speaking as tools of proclamation. Also, "[g]enuinely proposing means that evangelism is honest persuasion, a matter of fully informing others and allowing them to choose as they will."[30]

26. Rodney Clapp, *A Peculiar People: The Church as Culture in a Post-Christian Society* (Downers Grove: InterVarsity, 1996), p. 164.
27. Clapp, *A Peculiar People*, p. 165.
28. Clapp, *A Peculiar People*, p. 167.
29. Clapp, *A Peculiar People*, p. 170.
30. Clapp, *A Peculiar People*, p. 171.

In our post-Christian context, the early church affords guidance. The epistle to the Romans presents a model for contemporary evangelism when we, its readers, understand that the theology of welcome delineated in chs. 12-16 is inextricably correlated to the theology set out in chs. 1-11. From that perspective of unity, Paul's concern for hospitality and surrendering of false categories of thinking that lead to exclusion becomes transparent. The apostle to the Gentiles was not momentarily distracted from important theological ideas in favor of details of entertainment. Rather, he understood that, without communities of invitation that embrace others and model alternative ways of perceiving "felt needs," the organic spread of the gospel of transformation is sabotaged.

Yet, in looking to the early church, we do not seek

> general, technical, once-for-all answers to challenges set in the way of Christian endeavor . . . [for] Christianity is not about compartmentalization or withdrawal: it is radically and relentlessly life-encompassing . . . a living tradition, a continuing argument, a still-unfolding history. It is about being engaged by a God who is not through wooing, harassing, changing and redeeming an estranged creation.[31]

Nor do we overlook the kingdom outposts that already exist, for we indeed are en route to this new way of being and poised for a new way of seeing. In this Christianity as distinctive culture paradigm, the evangelist is "part of and . . . able to point to a community worthy of attention and respect"[32] where curiosity, questioning, and seeking are validated and welcomed.

31. Clapp, *A Peculiar People*, p. 188.
32. Clapp, *A Peculiar People*, p. 171.

Good News Heading West — 15.22-33: Travel Plans, Apostolic Parousia, *Peroratio*

As with various other documents in the NT, for instance Revelation, the beginning and the end of the document have epistolary elements intermingled with other elements of a non-epistolary character. In this case, Paul is mixing epistolary elements and rhetorical elements to bring his discourse to a closure. The so-called apostolic parousia (promise of a visit of an apostle) and travel plans are non-rhetorical elements, and we find the conclusion of the first *peroratio* in vv. 30-33, which in fact go with 15.14-21. Indeed, one could leave out 15.22-29 and it would not be missed. What vv. 30-33 provide is the pathos or emotional appeal portion of the *peroratio*.[1] The echoes of ch. 1 in the travel plans section of ch. 15 are noteworthy and show that Paul has been thinking through to this conclusion of his discourse from the outset.

For this reason I have been hindered many times from coming to you, but now, having no longer a place/opportunity in this region, but having a longing to come to you for many years, when I go to Spain, for I hope while passing through to see you and you send me on my way there, when I have been satisfied/enjoyed you first for a while, but now I go to Jerusalem caring for/rendering service to the saints, for Macedonia and Achaia decided to make a certain contribution/sharing in common with the poor among the saints in Jerusalem. For they decided to do so, and indeed they are debtors of them, for if the Gentiles share in common in their spiritual resources, they even owe material resources to them as a public service. Having accomplished this, and having sealed to them this fruit, I will come by way of you and on to Spain. But I know in coming to you I will come in the fullness of the blessing of Christ.

But I urge you, through our Lord Jesus Christ and through the love of the

---

1. On the various rhetorical functions of a *peroratio* see pp. 350-51 above.

Spirit, to strive in company with me in prayer for me to God, in order that I might be delivered from the disobedient in Judea, and my service which I offer in Jerusalem will be well received by the saints, in order that coming to you in joy through the will of God, I might be refreshed together with you. The God of peace be with all of you. Amen.

The importance of the Jerusalem church to Paul was made clear in v. 19, where Paul indicated that his mission went out from, and indeed was authorized by, James and the church in Jerusalem. Now he must speak of bringing a collection to the Jerusalem church for the poor among them. V. 22 is a further statement indicating Paul's desire to come to visit the Roman Christians. If he has been hindered many times from coming, it means that he has repeatedly desired to do so. There are in fact two ways to read the remarks in v. 23. On the one hand Paul might mean that he has completed his work in the east, or he may mean that so much opposition has built up against him in the east, including in particular in Jerusalem (see his prayer to be delivered from the "disobedient" below), that he needs to head west.[2]

It is interesting how much euphemistic language Paul will use in this section of the letter. For example, he will speak of money and material resources in indirect ways as "fruit," or as being "sent on the way," which refers to traveling money. He will speak of the church in Jerusalem as "the holy ones," that is, "the saints." It is my suggestion that this is the term Paul regularly used for Jewish Christians, especially those in the founding church in Jerusalem. We have little or no evidence that there were any Christians in the Jerusalem church other than native and Diaspora Jewish Christians. I would suggest that Rom. 1.7 reflects this — he writes to the "beloved of God" (i.e., the Gentile majority) and to "the called saints" (i.e., the Jewish Christian minority). Here in ch. 15 the discussion is about the poor among the saints in Jerusalem, but Paul clearly contrasts the spiritual contribution of the Jewish Christians in Jerusalem to the Gentiles and in turn the Gentile material contributions to them. The contrast does not work so well if "the saints" includes Gentiles.

Quite surprisingly, Paul in v. 24 announces his intention to go to Spain. He might have chosen the northern coast of Africa or Gaul or Egypt or Mesopotamia, but instead he says that he will go to Spain. Perhaps Wright is correct in saying that Paul was thinking of fulfilling the prophecies about the far-away lands and islands hearing of the one true God (cf. Isa. 11.11; 41.1; 42.4, 10; 49.1; 51.5; 60.9).[3] R. D. Aus has suggested in fact that Paul viewed Spain in light of Isa.

---

2. See L. T. Johnson, *Reading Romans: A Literary and Theological Commentary* (Macon: Smyth and Helwys, 2001), p. 229.

3. N. T. Wright, "Romans," in *The New Interpreter's Bible*, vol. 10 (Nashville: Abingdon, 2002), p. 755.

66.19 as the Tarshish of biblical reference. To go there would mean that he had indeed reached the limit of the west.[4] This might explain why Paul was interested in Spain, but to suggest that Paul wanted to go there before finishing the collection so that all the regions of Gentiles might contribute is unlikely. Paul may have believed that all the Gentile regions must be reached before the "full number of Gentiles" would be saved, but he does not connect this matter to the relief funds for the saints in Jerusalem.

Did Paul ever reach Spain? If he did, it would have to be after his house arrest in Rome ended in A.D. 62. We have the evidence of Clement of Rome (1 Clement 5.7), writing at the end of the first century, that Paul reached "the limit of the west," but we cannot be certain this refers to Spain. It is possible that Paul envisioned finishing church planting in the northern half of the Mediterranean crescent before turning to the southern half, which would include Roman Africa and of course Egypt. But this is mere speculation. What we can be more sure of is that v. 24 makes evident that Paul did not intend to stay in Rome long, much less to become apostle in residence there and take over whatever leadership structure they already had. Rather Paul keeps stressing that he will only be passing through and that he will enlist the Romans' aid so that he can go further afield in his missionary work. "The diplomatic caution evident in the proem still controls the statement here. Paul must avoid the suspicion that he wants to make the world capital his own domain, and he does not want to say brusquely that he regards it merely as a bridgehead. Nevertheless, he states that Spain is the true goal of his journey. . . ."[5]

Paul has spoken similarly in 1 Cor. 16.6b, where he says he hopes that the Corinthian Christians will be able to "help me on my journey," a round-about way of asking them to provide traveling funds and resources to enable him to make it to the next destination. To judge from texts like 1 Macc. 12.4 and 4 Esd. 4.47, this could entail anything such as food, funds, letters of introduction, and transportation, and it became a regular practice in the early church (cf. Acts 15.3; 20.38; 21.5; 2 Cor. 1.16; Titus 3.13; 3 John 6).[6]

This is a short-term and very different matter than placing oneself in either a relationship of "giving and receiving" such as Paul speaks of having with his partners in ministry the Philippians (Phil. 4.15), or placing oneself in the debt of a patron. Paul consistently refused patronage from new converts, had only a parity reciprocity relationship with the Philippians, and otherwise accepted only either hospitality or traveling funds from churches like that in Corinth, or in this

---

4. See R. D. Aus, "Paul's Travel Plans to Spain, and the 'Full Number of the Gentiles' of Romans 11.25," *NovT* 21 (1979): 232-62.

5. E. Käsemann, *Commentary on Romans* (Grand Rapids: Eerdmans, 1980), p. 397.

6. See J. D. G. Dunn, *Romans 9–16*, Word Biblical Commentary Series (Dallas: Word, 1988), p. 872.

case in Rome.[7] It would have been especially unlikely that Paul would accept patronage or even parity from the Roman church for it was not one he had founded, and he was only just now establishing some kind of personal contact and influence over the Christians in Rome. The request for traveling funds was in fact a way for Paul to show his faith and belief in the good character of the Roman church. It was also an overture to establish a somewhat more intimate relationship with them. Basically Paul avoided accepting missionary support while staying with a new congregation to avoid the appearance of offering the gospel for money, but he would allow them to help him in another arena, such as the Philippians did, or at least allow them to provide traveling funds.

In another context I have discussed the collection at length.[8] Here it needs to be noted that the reference to the "poor" in ch. 15 confirms the suggestion that Paul was indeed talking about the collection in Gal. 2.10, and it is germane to note that it is said there to be for the poor in Jerusalem. This simply provides further confirmation for the conclusion that the private meeting Paul refers to in Galatians 2 is not the same as that mentioned in Acts 15, for the latter is not about the collection at all. Rather Galatians 2 corresponds with the visit Luke mentions in passing at Acts 11.29-30, where Paul and Barnabas carry famine relief money to the poor in Jerusalem. Gal. 2.10, then, is a plea to continue to remember the poor in Jerusalem.[9] Paul, some eight years later, is finally ready to deliver on his promise to do so by making a journey to Jerusalem, though he knows that it will be fraught with peril, and so he requests prayer of the largely Gentile Roman audience. Further confirmation we are on the right track comes from Paul's sometime companion, Luke, who records in Acts 24.17 that the collection was intended as alms and an offering for "my nation," that is, Jews, not Gentiles. The saints in Jerusalem are the Jews of the Jerusalem church, with special focus on the poor among them.

Paul is not thinking here of the collection as a way to make non-Christian Jews jealous and so precipitate the big event of the conversion of Israel.[10] Here

---

7. See my discussion of this matter in *Friendship and Finances in Philippi* (Valley Forge: Trinity, 1994), pp. 123-24.

8. See my discussion in *Conflict and Community in Corinth* (Grand Rapids: Eerdmans, 1995), pp. 423-26. On the chronological implications of the mention of the collection in various Pauline letters for dating these letters, particularly Galatians, see A. J. M. Wedderburn, "Paul's Collection: Chronology and History," *NTS* 48 (2002): 95-110. There are now two other full-length studies of the collection: B. Beckheuer, *Paulus und Jerusalem. Kollekte und Mission im theologischen Denken des Heidenapostels* (Frankfurt: Lang, 1997), and S. Joubert, *Paul as Benefactor: Reciprocity, Strategy, and Theological Reflection in Paul's Collection* (Tübingen: Mohr, 2000).

9. See my *Grace in Galatia* (Grand Rapids: Eerdmans, 1998), pp. 144-46.

10. T. L. Donaldson, *Paul and the Gentiles: Remapping the Apostle's Convictional World* (Minneapolis: Fortress, 1997), pp. 256-58.

he only asks for prayer to be delivered from them when he comes to town. He does not believe all Israel will be saved that way. It will happen when the Redeemer (i.e., Christ) returns to Zion. Rather, the intended and hoped-for secondary function of the collection is to help cement the Jewish and Gentile parts of the church together. "For Gentiles to give money and for Jewish Christians to accept it would be a sign that they in turn accepted the Gentiles as part of their family. The collection then was intended to accomplish, *mutatis mutandis,* the same thing that Paul had been urging in 14.1–15.13."[11] To put it in rhetorical terms, all along in this letter Paul's deliberative rhetoric has been intended to produce unity, harmony, concord between the Gentile majority and the Jewish minority in the church in Rome, and here he seeks to show them that they are but a part of his larger effort to produce such concord between his largely Gentile churches and the Jewish church in Jerusalem.

V. 25 refers quite specifically to the "service to the saints." "Saints" is used very frequently in the OT and early Jewish literature to refer to Jews, in particular devout Jews, and the LXX uses the same Greek term as Paul uses here — *hagioi* (Pss. 16.3; 34.9; 74.3; 83.3; Isa. 4.3; Dan. 7.18-27; 8.24; Tob. 8.15; Wis. 18.9; *Testament of Levi* 18.11, 14; *Testament of Issachar* 5.4; *Testament of Dan* 5.12). Paul himself regularly refers to a specific subset of Jews as "saints," namely the Jewish Christians in Jerusalem (cf. 1 Cor. 16.1; 2 Cor. 8.4; 9.1, 12). It "is certainly quite possible that Paul's usage reflects an early self-designation of the earliest Christian church, parallel to its quite common use elsewhere in Judaism at the time."[12] The important conclusion to be drawn is that Paul continued to use this term to refer to Jews, specifically Jewish Christians, and even more specifically on some occasions Jewish Christians in the mother church in Jerusalem.[13] The way Paul puts things in v. 26, he makes clear that neither the poor among the saints in Jerusalem nor even all the Jerusalem Jewish Christians are all of the saints. What we probably do not find in Romans is "saints" being used of Gentiles.[14]

Here we are helped by the treatment of G. W. Peterman of v. 26, where he establishes that this verse is referring to an act which establishes *koinōnia* or a true sharing in common between Paul's largely Gentile churches and the Jewish church in Jerusalem.[15] Paul then points out in fact that it was the Jewish Christians who set the reciprocity cycle in motion, for they had shared their spiritual resources and heritage and had thus put the largely Gentile churches in their

11. Wright, "Romans," p. 756.

12. Dunn, *Romans 9–16,* p. 873.

13. Notice that here the saints in general in Jerusalem are only "among the saints." They are the saints "there," in that location. In other words, Paul does not simply use this term to refer just to the Jerusalem church.

14. There is one possible exception. See pp. 350-51 above.

15. G. W. Peterman, "Romans 15.26: Make a Contribution or Establish Fellowship?" *NTS* 40 (1994): 457-63.

debt. The collection is a material response meant to fund this unfunded liabil-
ity, in a sense. As v. 27 puts it, the Gentile Christians will be providing a liturgy,
that is, a public service, to the Jerusalem church.[16] This will close the circle so
that *koinōnia* actually happens, as both parties share in common with one another. Paul does not mention all his churches, only those in Achaia and Macedonia, perhaps because he is in Corinth when he writes this. In light of 1 Cor.
16.1 it seems likely more of Paul's churches were involved. In fact, as we shall see
when we deal with the end of Romans 16, Paul may even be mentioning some of
the delegates from his various Gentile churches who are going to Jerusalem
with him and the collection.

V. 28 has what seems to be a peculiar phrase. Paul speaks of "sealing to
them the fruit." The "fruit" is the collection, which is seen as a sort of harvest or
fruit of the evangelizing of the Gentiles, proof that they are part of the Christian family and care about the Jerusalem church. But why speak of sealing?
Cranfield suggests that, because sealing is the last act before one hands something over, Paul envisions the handing over of the collection as completing the
matter.[17] There is probably some truth in this, but perhaps Paul sees this act of
handing over the collection as the finishing touch on his ministry in the east,
that which seals or cements the bond between his largely Gentile churches and
the Jerusalem church. He believes that if he can pull off the delivery of the collection and then go on to Rome, he will be coming to the Roman Christians in
the fullness of the blessing of Jesus. V. 29 then may suggest that his success in Jerusalem will reflect that Jesus has blessed his ministry in the east so that he can
come to Rome with that sense of endorsement and approval from his Master
for his work with the Gentiles.

Vv. 30-33 are the emotive conclusion to all of Paul's arguments presented
to the largely Gentile audience in Rome. Here Paul meets the requirement that
the *peroratio* manifest pathos, strong emotion of some sort. There is a sort of
natural trinitarianism to v. 30, where Paul speaks of praying to God, but be-
seeches the Roman Christians through Jesus and through the love which the
Spirit engenders in them.[18] He makes a plea for his audience to join with him in
prayer for himself and his upcoming dangerous trip to Jerusalem. The language
of "striving" together in prayer[19] is "agonistic" language, using the athletic met-

16. In both Rom. 15.27 and 2 Cor. 9.12 the reference is not to a service to God or to a religious service in the narrow sense of a worship service, but to a religious public service rendered to the Jerusalem church. Paul uses *leitourgos* only in the sense of some sort of religious
service. See *NewDocs* 7:105.

17. C. E. B. Cranfield, *A Critical and Exegetical Commentary on the Epistle to the
Romans* (ICC; Edinburgh: Clark, 1975-79), 2:774-75.

18. See C. K. Barrett, *A Commentary on the Epistle to the Romans* (Peabody: Hendrickson, 1991), p. 256, who calls it an unintended trinitarian formula.

19. *Synagōnizomai* is found in inscriptions from before the NT era with the meaning

aphor of the straining of an athlete toward a particular goal (cf. Phil. 1.27; 4.3; Col. 4.12). The Christian is viewed as a spiritual athlete wrestling or striving diligently and earnestly in prayer.[20] Paul does not seem to mean simply that the Romans should strive with him, rather than strive in prayer.[21]

The prayer is to be specifically for Paul's deliverance from the disobedient in Judea, but there is also the positive prayer that his collection will be found acceptable by the Jerusalem church. There are then two causes for anxiety and prayer here. "Disobedient" is how Paul characterizes non-Christian Jews, in particular those who have rejected the gospel (cf. 10.21; 11.30-31). He envisions running the gauntlet in Jerusalem and then heading off to Rome where he can come with joy and enjoy the refreshment of good fellowship for a while before heading on to Spain. Paul is willing to risk his neck for the sake of delivering the collection, for he believes it has an important role in cementing together the more Jewish and the more Gentile parts of the church. But in v. 32 he qualifies this with "through" or "according to God's will," as if he knows very well that it might not turn out the way he hopes. In fact, of course, Acts 21–28 recount how badly it did turn out. Paul was taken captive after a near riot in the Temple precincts, was subjected to house arrest for two years without release or a verdict, and then was shipped to Rome courtesy of the hospitality of the Roman army.

V. 33 is a normal Pauline benedictory phrase without a main verb, indicating the end of the main discourse (cf. Rom. 16.20; Phil. 4.9; 2 Cor. 13.11; 1 Thess. 5.23; 2 Thess. 3.16), though he also uses such phrases to end particular arguments as well. This is his way of entrusting his audience into the hands of God and wishing God's blessing of shalom, wholeness, and well-being on them.[22] But it is important to remind ourselves that Paul expected the performance of this letter to be part of an act of worship. Benedictions in letters are then no surprise when the letter is to be part of a doxological act.

A Closer Look: The Legacy of Paul and Romans — the Early Returns

We spoke briefly at the beginning of this commentary on this subject,[23] and throughout the commentary we have interacted a bit with patristic (i.e., from the third century on into the Middle Ages) use of Paul. But here as we bring the commentary to a

---

"strive together with," referring to a sort of tug of war with ambassadors from other countries. See *NewDocs* 3:84.

20. See Barrett, *Romans*, p. 256.

21. Against Dunn, *Romans 9–16*, p. 878.

22. We will discuss the issues of the placement and authenticity of 16.25-27, which is interestingly enough placed here after 15.33 in 𝔭46, when we get to the end of ch. 16.

23. See pp. 11-13 above.

close will be a good juncture to elaborate on the subject from the earliest period of church history up to the first great commentary written on Romans that we know of — Origen's masterful work.

The place to begin is with the use of the Pauline corpus, and in particular Romans, by the so-called Apostolic Fathers, who wrote from the end of the first century until the middle of the second century. The corpus of writings involved is incredibly varied and includes the *Didache,* the *Letter of Barnabas,* the *Shepherd* of Hermas, and the writings of Clement of Rome, Ignatius of Antioch, and Polycarp of Smyrna. Only the last three mention Paul by name and cite his letters, and in fact only *1 Clement* shows any direct contact with Paul.[24] It is interesting that the only Christians of the NT era mentioned in the Apostolic Fathers are Paul, and to a lesser degree Peter and Mary. Not even James, Jesus' brother, is mentioned in these works. More to the point, no NT source is used more by these writers than the letters of Paul. The profound impact of his writings even in the earliest part of church history is quite clear. Already in the second century Paul's letters were in the hands of churches to which he did not write and were used as authoritative even though there was by no means yet a canon of the NT.

The first reference to Paul from within these three works is found in *1 Clement* 5.5-7, probably written at the end of the first century. Here we notice that it is Paul's life as well as his letters that have made a strong impression. Clement says that Paul preached in both the east and the west and "taught righteousness to the whole world." To this is then immediately added that Paul reached "the farthest bounds of the west." Though Clement is largely indebted to 1 Corinthians, not surprisingly since he is addressing Corinthian Christians, nevertheless these remarks are telling and probably indicate that Clement has read or heard Paul's Romans in Rome. The mention of Paul preaching righteousness to the world seems especially fitting in light of what we find in Romans.

In fact there is considerably more evidence that Clement knew Romans. In chs. 30–34 he discusses righteousness or justification, and his indebtedness to Paul's Romans there seems particularly clear. *1 Clement* 32.4 reads: "We, having been called through his will in Jesus Christ, are not set right through our own efforts or through our wisdom or understanding or piety or works which we wrought in holiness of heart, but through faith, through which the almighty God sets right all persons that have been since the beginning." It is furthermore fascinating that Clement here uses the style of the diatribe to present this material as we find Paul so often doing in Romans. Even the rhetorical style of Paul in Romans has affected Clement.[25] Equally like Paul, Clement indicates that it is incumbent on Christians to be righteous and do righteous works (33.8: "let us work the work of righteousness"). His is not a theology of imputed righteousness but of righteous behavior that flows from being granted right standing with God through faith in Christ. In addition Clement dwells on the

---

24. I am indebted to A. Lindemann's helpful survey "Paul in the Writings of the Apostolic Fathers," in *Paul and the Legacy of Paul,* ed. W. S. Babcock (Dallas: SMU Press, 1990), pp. 25-45, for some of what follows.

25. See Lindemann, "Paul in the Writings of the Apostolic Fathers," p. 33.

theme of "weak" and "strong," and it is clear that he is indebted not merely to 1 Corinthians for this. For example, there is a clear echo of Rom. 12.4 in *1 Clement* 38.4. Finally, there is the prayer in *1 Clement* 61, which includes in vv. 1-2 a prayer for "our rulers and governors on the earth." Clement reflects here the same view of the state that Paul does in Romans 13.[26] But it is not just Paul's ethical teaching in Romans that Clement draws on. In *1 Clement* 12.1 Clement says that through the blood of the Lord there shall be redemption *(lytrōsis)*, which seems to reflect Rom. 3.25.

When we turn to Ignatius there is much less to say, except that Ignatius seems to know several of Paul's letters, particularly 1 Corinthians, Romans, and Ephesians. In his own *Ephesians* 18.2 Ignatius offers a christological formula about the incarnation that seems to be indebted to Rom. 1.3-4: "For our God, Jesus the Christ, was carried in the womb by Mary according to God's plan — and of the seed of David and of the Holy Spirit — who was born and baptized. . . ." Since there is no stress elsewhere in Paul on Jesus being the seed of David, the connection seems clear between these two texts. In *Ephesians* 19.1 there may also be an echo of Rom. 16.25-26: "hidden were the mysteries, then made manifest to the ages," though 1 Cor. 2.6-9 could be echoed here as well. There may be an indication of the knowledge of the material in Romans 14 in *Magnesians* 9.1, which mentions sabbaths and that there is no requirement to observe them if one is under grace.

In Polycarp's letter to the Philippians the theme of "righteousness" surfaces again. Though Polycarp says near the outset (3.1) that he is not writing the audience about *diakaiosynē*, in fact he does do so a bit. In fact chs. 1–12 of this document could be seen as his response to the Philippians' queries about righteousness.[27] In 8.1 Christ is called the down payment *(arrabōn)* of our righteousness, where the condition of righteousness is seen as the believer's eschatological goal. This comports well with some of what Paul says about righteousness in Romans.[28] Equally clearly, in 3.3 Polycarp speaks of how, if a believer is occupied with faith, hope, and love, he has "fulfilled the commandment of righteousness." He seems to be echoing the discussion in Rom. 13.8-10, where all commandments are said to be summed up in the love command.[29]

In some ways, it is not a surprise that only the more formidable of the somewhat later Fathers really begin to take the measure of Paul's writings, including Romans. I am referring particularly to Origen and to a lesser degree Clement, both in the major Christian center of Alexandria, Chrysostom in Antioch, and of course Augustine.[30]

---

26. Lindemann, "Paul in the Writings of the Apostolic Fathers," p. 35. It is interesting how Lindemann also recognizes the echo of 1 Tim. 2.1-3 and concludes that that letter must have been written in and available to the Roman church. If so, it must have been written prior to the writing by Clement of this letter to Corinth.

27. Lindemann, "Paul in the Writings of the Apostolic Fathers," p. 43.

28. See pp. 64-65 above.

29. Lindemann, "Paul in the Writings of the Apostolic Fathers," p. 44.

30. R. Clement, "(Re)Constructing Paul: Origen's Reading of Romans in *Peri Archōn*," in *SBL Seminar Papers 2001*, pp. 151-74, deals with Origen's hermeneutic and his anti-Semitic tendencies, which affected his use of the literal versus spiritual ways of reading Paul.

Origen's commentary on Romans, written in about 247, was to our knowledge the first full-scale attempt to plumb the depths of Romans.[31] Origen, like Clement, interpreted Paul through the lens of Platonism, which had been liberally imbibed in Alexandria, as with Philo before them. Origen was certainly a creative thinker, but he was no systematician, nor was he afraid to speculate and change his mind from what he had written earlier so far as it involved his understanding of Pauline thought. Particularly crucial for Origen were Rom. 8.18-39 and 9.6-24 as he chose to grasp the nettle of Paul's doctrine of election and salvation. In fact Romans and 1 Corinthians are the Pauline letters most used by Origen throughout all his works, but this also seems to have been the case with many other Fathers, including the earlier Apostolic Fathers.[32]

Origen's discussion of Romans 8–9 must be set in the context of the wider discussion in Greek philosophy about determinism and free will. The difference is, as R. Wilken makes clear, that what was largely a moral problem for Greek philosophers (since determinism seems to be a result of impersonal forces controlling human destinies) became in the Christian discussion a theological as well as an ethical problem.[33] For Origen the nub of the problem comes to light in Romans 8–9. "There are in the Scriptures ten thousand passages that prove the existence of free choice with utmost clarity . . . [but] . . . certain sayings in the Old and New Testaments incline us to the opposite conclusion" (De Principiis 3.1.6-7). Origen then cites Exodus 4 on the hardening of Pharaoh's heart, Ezek. 11.19-20 on God giving a new heart that replaces the stony one, and Romans 8 and 9, where he places the emphasis. The theological dilemma is put this way by Origen: "Since the teaching of the church includes the doctrine of the righteous judgement of God . . ." the discussion of "free choice" becomes imperative (De principiis 3.1.1). Origen is quite frank about the impact of the legacy of Paul's discussion in Romans 9. He calls it the "famous problem concerning Jacob and Esau" (Commentary on John 2.191) and says that it will and does "disturb the many with the belief that human beings do not possess free will, but that God saves and destroys whomever he wills" (De principiis 3.1.7).

Origen noticed that Paul had been using the diatribal format for a good portion of his discussion in Romans and came to the conclusion this was so in Romans 9–11 as well. Thus he assigns to a fictive opponent or dialogue partner statements like "it depends not on human will or exertion but upon God's mercy" (9.16). Origen also discusses the fact that Paul talks about two different kinds of justice or righteousness, that which justifies before God and the relative justice or righteousness by which one person can be adjudged to be just or fair or righteous in comparison to the deeds of other human beings (Commentary on Romans 5.2 and 6.1). Origen is clearly wrestling

31. See R. Morgan, Romans (New Testament Guides; Sheffield: Sheffield Academic, 1995), p. 134.

32. On Origen's use of Paul's writings see P. Gorday, "Paulus Origenianus: The Economic Interpretation of Paul," in Babcock, ed., Paul and the Legacy of Paul, pp. 141-63, and in the same volume R. Wilken, "Free Choice and the Divine Will in Greek Christian Commentaries on Paul," pp. 123-40.

33. See Wilken, "Free Choice," pp. 125-27.

with the ideas that Paul is presenting and trying to come to grips with their implications.

The exegetes whom Origen mentions who interpreted Paul's Romans before him are mostly Gnostics: Marcion, Valentinus, Basilides, and others.[34] Often deemed heretics even in their own day in the second century, they apparently were some of the first to comment on Romans. Origen sees it as something of a duty to refute them at various points and so reclaim Romans for the orthodox tradition. His commentary is in part an anti-Gnostic polemic. The essential thesis that he will support against the Gnostics is that while the latter maintain a strong doctrine of election and determinism, he will stress that the biblical view is that human beings are free to respond to God's acts and offer of salvation. This he states clearly in the preface to his commentary.

It is no accident, then, that the first text from Romans Origen chose to deal with at length was 9.16 — "it does not depend on him who wills or him who runs, but on God who has mercy." In fact, in his exegesis Origen will return again and again to this passage, since it suited so well the view that the Gnostics were advocating.[35] Origen had actually been formulating his views on these matters for some time as he already addressed this passage in his earlier work *On First Principles*. Origen insists that in all things God is providentially good. Even in the case of the hardening of Pharaoh's heart, it was ultimately for his salvation (*De Principiis* 3.1). Such hardening is part of the process of purification that God puts people through. God supplies the power and knowledge on the basis of which humans can choose to do either good or evil. God determined to create life and then to absorb its flaws as part of working all things together for good in the larger scheme of restoration and redemption.[36] God's electing and selecting process is based on his prior knowledge of how differing persons will respond (*De Principiis* 3.1.17). But not only so, Origen then adds a further theological notion to tidy up all loose ends. Why is it that some are born into unhappy and indeed even miserable lots in life, and others are not? Origen propounds the notion of the preexistence of human souls and suggests that one's earthly lot in life in part is a result of how one behaved and faired before taking on a mortal frame. All souls sin and fall in heaven (except Jesus) and so inherit a degree of misery or bliss in earthly life relative to their behavior in heaven. This explains the story of Jacob and Esau as Paul tells it (3.1.22). It looks as if the Gnostics made strong points based on Romans 8–9 to buttress their theology, and Origen sought to deconstruct that theology over and over again, even at the price of sounding rather like them in the notion that one's earthly lot in life is affected by a premundane set of affairs. For Origen, as for Plato, this world is but a pale copy of the world of heaven, and life in this world involves a process of suffering and purification. "The groaning of the universe in Rom. 8.22f. is, for Origen, a positive experience of the renewal taking place in this penal and therapeutic state of corporeality."[37]

34. See Gorday, "Paulus Origenianus," p. 143.
35. See Gorday, "Paulus Origenianus," p. 146.
36. Gorday, "Paulus Origenianus," p. 147.
37. Gorday, "Paulus Origenianus," p. 149.

For Origen, Romans 8 is all about the love of God, which is indefatigable and shows that his will for all his creation is for good and not for harm, for restoration and redemption and not for judgment, for God desires that all be saved and that all humans be conformed to the image of the Son. This desire of God, however, can be frustrated for particular individuals by willful sin and rejection, by the power of contrary choice, which God has bestowed on humans. In some ways Origen sounds very like Paul, though filtered through Platonic and anti-Gnostic sieves, but in other ways he sounds more Gnostic than Pauline. He in turn would help spur a great chain of reflection and meditation on Paul by other great minds such as Gregory of Nyssa, Theodore, Theodoret, Diodore of Tarsus, Chrysostom, Cyril of Alexandria, Ambrosiaster, Anselm, Augustine, Aquinas, and others. In due course Romans would be in the regular rotation of church liturgy and expository preaching, where it would continue to influence the entire church and not just its scholars. Interestingly enough, it would often prove to be Paul's ethical teaching in Romans that would be the most influential, particularly what he says in 13.1-7.[38]

If it is a measure of the importance and power of a discourse that it calls forth many profound and perplexing reactions, then we can see that already in Clement, Ignatius, Polycarp, and Origen, the impact of Paul was enormous, shaping the very way even profound thinkers viewed God, human beings, salvation, and the human dilemma. He still challenges us today in similar fashion.

Bridging the Horizons

It is interesting that the only sustained discussion of giving in the entire Pauline corpus has to do with the special collection Paul was raising for the saints in Jerusalem. So often when stewardship Sunday rolls around, 1 Cor. 16.1-2 is trotted out as if it were about the weekly offering for the local church. In fact, it is about giving to a special overseas venture, and Paul says there that each should give according to one's income. There is no browbeating here about tithing. Indeed, there is no mention of tithing in any of Paul's letters. What Paul urges is sacrificial giving, following the example of Christ. Sacrificial giving can involve giving a good deal more than a tithe, or it can, in the case of the indigent and poor, involve giving less than a tithe. It is probably not germane to bring up Gospel texts on tithing, where Jesus' audience is Pharisees or other early Jews and the discussion is clearly an intramural Jewish discussion based on the Mosaic Law, a Law that Paul says Christians are no lon-

---

38. Morgan, *Romans*, pp. 134-35, says: "Rom. 13.1-7 is arguably the most historically influential paragraph Paul ever wrote." He cites the way Chrysostom, Thomas Aquinas, and even the Council of Constance in 1415 use this text to argue for honoring and respecting governing officials and opposing tyrannicide.

ger "under." Even Jesus, however, seems to have enunciated a principle of sacrificial giving as the norm for his followers (see Mark 12.41-44). So where does this leave us in the church today? I would urge that bad hermeneutics do not lead to good preaching. If, indeed, Christians are no longer under the Mosaic covenant, then texts from that covenantal agreement should not be used to indicate that Christians are obligated to tithe. If there is an obligation to tithe, it must be found in NT teaching clearly directed to Christians. In my view there is no such text.

What instead Christians are certainly called to is sacrificial giving, and no particular percentage value can be easily attached. Such giving requires faith and prayer and seeking God's will to determine what would be a sacrificial amount to give. Several principles should rule such considerations:

> Christians are not owners of anything they have but only stewards of God's property. They did not bring it with them into the world, and they cannot take it with them when they die, and so what they do with it while living should follow the dictates of what accords with God's will.
>
> As John Wesley stressed, another person's necessity should normally come before one indulges in one's own luxuries. This then requires a process of discerning what is a necessity where and when one lives and what amounts to a luxury.
>
> The examples from Acts 2 and 4 about sharing of property need to be given careful consideration. The principle operating there seems to be that no one claimed any exclusive right to property. Wherever there was a need the Christian community took care of it. Would that the church would still take seriously this responsibility today.
>
> Paul does enunciate some principles about giving. He says that we should do good to all, but especially to the household of faith (Gal. 6.10). There is a responsibility to model for the world what a welcoming and hospitable community looks like, one in which each person treats each other as a family-member. There *is* then a responsibility for Christians to try and help non-Christians in whatever way is needed.
>
> As the collection shows, the church should always and everywhere be concerned about alleviating poverty in whatever way possible. This should be a priority.
>
> The various teachings in the NT, especially from Jesus and James, about not hoarding resources or giving lip service to the needs of others without actually trying to take action must be heeded as well. As John Wesley once said, if you save all you can without giving all you can, you may be a living person but you are a dead Christian. There can be no Silas Marners in the church.

It is time for western churches, especially those in North America, to re-think their edifice complex. Can it really be justified to spend millions and millions of dollars on elaborate buildings, which mainly serve only ourselves, and then struggle to raise money for missions budgets? The church is largely no longer a missionary movement. It is a self-nurturing entity which has a missions committee and budget but spends most of its money on itself. There is a difference between this and what one reads about in Paul's letters.

A Letter of Recommendation and Reconciliation — 16.1-27

Apart from vv. 25-27 and v. 24 (cf. v. 20), there is little or no dispute about the Pauline character of the material in Romans 16. The dispute has to do with whether ch. 16 was originally part of the letter to the Romans or is from a separate document intended for an audience elsewhere or in Rome. The earliest NT papyrus, ℘46, has 16.25-27 at the end of ch. 15, but is not a basis for concluding that 16.1-23 was not an original part of this letter since ℘46 goes on to include 16.1-23 immediately after 16.25-27. Even ℘46 does not know Romans in its supposed shortened form, ending after ch. 15.[1]

It is quite true that 16.1-2 reads like a letter of recommendation,[2] and in 16.3ff.[3] Paul does not himself greet persons but rather exhorts some audience to do so. This is different from the vast majority of closing greetings we find in the undisputed Pauline letters, but it is not uncommon in the papyrus letters we

---

1. See E. Käsemann, *Commentary on Romans* (Grand Rapids: Eerdmans, 1980), p. 408.

2. In fact it appears to be almost a textbook case of such a letter. Pseudo-Demetrius presents the form of such a letter (in *Epistolary Types* 2) as: "So and so, who is conveying this letter to you, has been tested by us and is loved on account of his trustworthiness. You will do well if you deem him worthy of a welcome both for my sake, and his, and indeed for your own. For you will not be sorry if you entrust to him, in any matter you wish, either words or deeds of a confidential nature. Indeed, you too will praise him to others when you see how useful he can be in everything." See the discussion by C. Bryan, *A Preface to Romans: Notes on the Epistle and Its Literary and Cultural Setting* (Oxford: Oxford University Press, 2000), pp. 33-34.

3. A. Schlatter, *Romans: The Righteousness of God* (Peabody: Hendrickson, 1995), pp. 272-73, makes the helpful point that had Paul been writing this material to somewhere like Ephesus he could surely have spoken more briefly and would not have needed an extended commendation of Phoebe or of the Jewish Christians whom he urges his listeners to receive.

know of from the period (e.g., BGU 2349 or P. Koln I.56).[4] Both of these factors may suggest that ch. 16 was originally a separate letter from chs. 1–15, even if it was written to the same audience. We may dismiss the argument which suggests that Paul would not have known and so would not have named so many persons in Rome. Many early Christians were very mobile, and in fact we know that at least some of these Christians had had contact with Paul in the east, for example Priscilla and Aquila, Andronicus and Junia, Rufus' mother, and probably the ones Paul mentions as his relatives. But more can be said.[5]

If we take seriously the edict of Claudius and the fact that for a time many Roman Christians were exiled from Rome and likely headed east, Paul could in fact have met all of these persons in Corinth and elsewhere in his missionary travels in the east. For example, Epaenetus is said to be the first convert in Asia (v. 5). So I suggest that these named persons are the Jewish Christians Paul knows in Rome,[6] most of whom he met in the east between 49 and the writing of this letter, and some of whom he knew because they were his relatives. This letter, whether a part of Romans or simply carried with Romans, is addressed primarily to the Gentile majority in Rome, and is urging *them* to welcome, be hospitable to, build fellowship with these Jewish Christians in Rome, many of whom are in a tenuous position. In other words, ch. 16 is part of Paul's strategy to effect unity and reconciliation among the divided Roman Christians. Apparently not nearly enough had been accomplished on this front since Claudius died on October 13, 54, and Jews, including Jewish Christians, began to return to Rome.

Thus, whether ch. 16 is originally part of the same physical document as chs. 1–15 is unimportant. It is addressed to the same audience and gives names to the Jewish Christians in Rome. This chapter asks the Gentile Christians to do so as well — to receive and honor and have fellowship with these Jewish Christians. As ch. 16 was read before this mixed audience of Gentiles and Jews, perhaps those who are named in vv. 3-16 were turned to and briefly addressed directly as Jewish Christians in the *peroratio* designated specifically for them in vv. 17-19. They are to look out for Gentile Christians ruled by their appetites who might cause them to stumble and so cause further division in the Roman church by insisting on their own customs and eating practices. This latter brief passage is a further development of what Paul was exhorting in chs. 14–15, only now his primary focus is on addressing the weak.

The primary text-critical issues in ch. 16 are the location of the doxology found in most English translations in vv. 25-27 and the originality of the brief

---

4. See the citation and discussion of the latter in *NewDocs* 1:54-55.

5. See pp. 5-7 above.

6. Perhaps also with a few God-fearers and others who were currently associating with or fellowshiping with the Jewish Christians in Rome. Nonetheless, I think the majority of those named are very likely to be Jews.

grace word found in v. 24 in some manuscripts and elsewhere in others. In other words, the textual problems need not affect our assessment of vv. 1-23. Vv. 25-27 occur after v. 23 or v. 24 in some of our oldest and best authorities — namely ℵ, B, D, the Vulgate, and Origen. 𝔭61 also places vv. 25-27 after v. 23, but that fragment includes only those four verses. A few manuscripts known to Origen (though he does not accept their reading), the Harclean margin, and Ω have vv. 25-27 after 14.23. A, P, and 33 have 16.25-27 after both 14.23 and 16.23 or 24. Only 𝔭46 has vv. 25-27 after ch. 15. Arguments from silence are always dicey, but it is worth noting that neither Tertullian, Cyprian, nor Irenaeus ever quotes chs. 15–16 while they do use other portions of Romans, and especially the first two of these Fathers could have readily used some of the material in chs. 15–16 in their arguments.[7] A truncated form of Romans seems to have circulated in their day, perhaps created by Marcion.

What may we conclude about the text of the end of Romans 16? The benediction, in its short form, belonged at v. 20 (without the word "Christ"), not after v. 23 or v. 27, and was an original part of the document at v. 20. This means that v. 24 should be omitted as a duplication or later emendation.[8] It is possible that vv. 25-27 were a post-Pauline doxology added at various places in the manuscript. Yet the traditional location is well supported, and the omission of these verses altogether is not really supported in the manuscript tradition, only their displacement. Accordingly, we will tentatively take these verses to be a Pauline doxology.[9] I agree with Wright that it is unlikely that Paul would end this document without some sort of doxology or benediction, and 16.25-27 is arguably Pauline in character.[10]

I introduce/commend to you Phoebe our sister, who is the deaconess of the church in Cenchreae, in order that you might welcome her in the Lord [in a manner] worthy of the saints and that you might stand by her in whatever matter she may need assistance with, also because she herself has been a patroness/benefactor of many, including me myself.

Greet with every show of affection Prisca[11] and Aquila, my coworkers in

7. See C. K. Barrett, *A Commentary on the Epistle to the Romans* (Peabody: Hendrickson, 1991), pp. 10-13, on all of this matter.

8. See B. M. Metzger, *A Textual Commentary on the Greek New Testament* (3rd ed.; London: United Bible Societies, 1971), p. 476.

9. See Metzger, *A Textual Commentary,* pp. 470-73.

10. N. T. Wright, "Romans," in *The New Interpreter's Bible,* vol. 10 (Nashville: Abingdon, 2002), p. 758.

11. The Textus Receptus reads "Priscilla" here, the diminutive form of the name, following various manuscripts, including 81 and 255. The shorter form of the name is well supported by 𝔭46, A, B, C, D, F, G, and others and deserves to be read here. See Metzger, *A Textual Commentary,* p. 475.

Christ Jesus, who for the sake of my life risked their own necks, for whom not I alone give thanks but also all the churches of the Gentiles, and [greet warmly] the assembly in their house. Greet with every show of affection my beloved Epaenetus, who is the first fruits of Asia in Christ. Greet with every show of affection Maria,¹² who has labored much for you. Greet with every show of affection Andronicus and Junia,¹³ who are my relations and fellow prisoners, who are notable among the apostles, and who were in Christ before me. Greet with every show of affection Ampliatus my beloved in the Lord. Greet with every show of affection Urbanus our coworker in Christ and Stachys my beloved. Greet with every show of affection Apelles, the one proved in Christ. Greet with every show of affection those who are from [the house] of Aristobolus. Greet with every show of affection Herodion my relative. Greet with every show of affection from [the house] of Narcissus, those who are in the Lord. Greet with every show of affection Tryphaena and Tryphosa the laborers in the Lord. Greet with every show of affection Persis the beloved, who has labored much in the Lord. Greet with every show of affection Rufus the chosen in the Lord, and his mother and mine. Greet with every show of affection Asyncritus, Phlegon, Hermes, Patrobas, Hermas, and the brothers with them. Greet with every show of affection Philologus and Julia, Nereus and his sister, and Olympas and all the saints with them. Greet with every show of affection one another with a holy kiss. All the assemblies of Christ greet you with every show of affection.

12. I have chosen to transliterate this name properly rather than with the usual rendering "Mary." In fact, all the women named Mary in the NT who have a Hebrew or Aramaic name are Miriams, and this includes Jesus' mother and the disciple from Magdala. They are all named after the famous OT prophetess. With this "Maria" we cannot be sure. She may have been a Diaspora Jew before she became a Christian and so had the name Maria only in Greek. We have a similar problem with the name of James, which is really Jacob. At least in the case of this woman's name we have the excuse that the Greek rendering of Miriam is Maria, and so we have the modern name Mary. In the case of James, the Greek is Jacobus, which is nowhere close to James and does a much better job of reflecting the form of the original Hebrew name than the English rendering. See my discussion of this in the book I have co-authored with H. Shanks entitled *The Brother of Jesus* (San Francisco: Harper, 2003).

13. The feminine name Junia is attested more than 250 times in Greek and Latin inscriptions, whereas the masculine counterpart Junias is nowhere attested. When the Greek manuscripts began to be accented, the word in question was indeed accented as a feminine noun. See J. A. Fitzmyer, *Romans* (New York: Doubleday, 1992), pp. 737-38, and R. S. Cervin, "A Note Regarding the Name Junia[s] in Romans 16.7," *NTS* 40 (1994): 464-70. See also E. E. Epp, "Text-Critical, Exegetical, and Socio-Cultural Factors Affecting the Junia/Junias Variation in Rom. 16.7," in *New Testament Textual Criticism and Exegesis: Festschrift J. Delobel*, ed. A. Denaux (Leuven: Leuven University Press, 2002), pp. 227-91. It is thus highly unlikely that Paul is referring to two men here, rather than, as is more likely, a man and a woman, probably husband and wife, who are "notable among the apostles." On the meaning of that last phrase see pp. 380-81 below and see the discussion in Metzger, *A Textual Commentary*, pp. 475-76.

But I beseech you, brothers, watch out for those creating the dissensions and the stumbling blocks, bypassing the teaching which you yourself learned, and hold aloof from them. For such people are not doing service to our Lord Christ but their own bellies, and through fair speech and fine words beguile the hearts of the simple. For your obedience has reached to all. I rejoice then over you but I wish for you to be wise about the good, innocent about the evil. But the God of peace will quickly crush Satan under your feet. The grace of our Lord Jesus be with you.

Timothy my coworker greets you with every show of affection, and Lucius and Jason and Sosipater my relatives. I, Tertius, the writer of this letter, greet you with every affection in the Lord. Gaius my guest/host greets you with every show of affection and the whole of the assembly. Erastus greets you with every show of affection, the treasurer of the city, and Quartus the brother.[14]

To the one who is able to make you stand according to my gospel and the preaching of Jesus Christ, according to the revelation of the mystery having been kept secret from eternity, but now revealed through the writings of the prophets according to the command of the eternal God for the obedience of faith made known to all the nations, to the only wise God through Jesus Christ, to whom the glory forever.[15] Amen.[16]

I have dealt with this passage elsewhere,[17] but here the text demands a fuller treatment. On any showing there are many unique features to ch. 16. First, Paul does not directly greet his friends and coworkers and relatives in Rome. He has the dominantly Gentile audience do it for him as part of his rhetorical strategy to help effect some sort of reconciliation or unity among the Christians in Rome before he arrives there. In particular, he wants the marginalized Jewish Christians, many of them newly back in Rome from exile, to be embraced. It is not at all an accident that Paul again and again in this passage uses the verb

14. V. 24 is a repetition of v. 20, and it belongs at the earlier location, not here.

15. These verses are impressively supported by p61, ℵ, B, C, D, 81 and a host of other manuscripts and likely deserve to be seen as part of the original text of Romans. See Metzger, *A Textual Commentary*, pp. 476-77.

16. There are some very interesting subscriptions to this letter, some of which simply affirm that it was written to the Romans, some that it was written to the Romans from Corinth, and still others of which interestingly say that the letter was written *dia Phoibēs* from Corinth (35 and 201), some with "the deaconess" added to "through Phoebe" (42, 90, 216, 339, 462, 466*, 642). See Metzger, *A Textual Commentary*, p. 477. These are of course clarifications, and while *dia* with the genitive could amount to suggesting that Phoebe was the scribe of the letter ("through the hand of Phoebe"), there is one manuscript, 337, which clarifies that what was meant is that while Tertius wrote the letter, it was sent to the Romans with the deaconess Phoebe. This simply confirms what 16.1-2 suggests and as such is a likely deduction.

17. See my *Women in the Earliest Churches* (Cambridge: Cambridge University Press, 1988), pp. 113-17.

aspazomai. This verb does not merely mean "greet" in some perfunctory way. It literally means to wrap one's arms around and embrace someone, and when coupled with the command to offer the holy kiss as well (v. 16), it amounts to a command to treat those named as family, to welcome them into one's own home and circle. Paul is going all out to create a new social situation in Rome, overcoming the obstacles to unity and concord dealt with in chs. 14–15. His arguments have intended to deconstruct the social stratification in the Roman church, creating a leveling effect by making all debtors to the grace and mercy of God, so that the Gentile majority will treat the Jewish Christian minority as equals and with respect. The righteousness of God is to be mirrored in the righteous and fair conduct of believers.

Second, Paul names and knows some twenty-six persons in Rome. He stresses his close personal relationship with several of these people: Andronicus, Junia, and Herodion are said to be Paul's relatives. At a minimum this means they are Jews, and more specifically Jewish Christians, but it may also mean that they are some sort of close kin of Paul's. Prisca, Aquila, and Urbanus are all called Paul's coworkers, not in Rome since he has not been there yet, nor as an advance guard that he has sent to Rome. That is Phoebe's role, as we shall see. Paul calls Phoebe and those with Philologus "saints," which is probably a code word for Jewish Christians. Paul calls some of those named "beloved" by him: Epaenetus, who was also Paul's first convert in Asia, Ampliatus, Stachys, and Persis.

Paul also refers to various people who have worked hard for the Roman Christians he is addressing: Maria, Tryphaena and Tryphosa, and Persis. Three of these four are women. Paul uses various honorific descriptions of several other of these persons to make clear their worth and importance: Andronicus and Junia are outstanding, Apelles is tested and approved, Rufus is elect in the Lord, and his mother is also Paul's mother (in some sense).[18] Only those mentioned as connected to a household (those of Aristobolus and Narcissus) or a household assembly (probably those listed in vv. 14-15) are not described in some special way.

In other words, at least sixteen of the twenty-six named persons are singled out in some special way. This is no ordinary greeting card. It is more like an honor roll. The suggestion of Lampe that "it is possible that many of the 26 persons had been expelled from Rome under Claudius and had returned after Claudius' death — just like Aquila and Prisca (Acts 18.2; Rom. 16.3)"[19] is more than just a possibility. It is a likelihood, and this likely means that they were all

18. If Paul means this literally, of course this would mean that Rufus is another relative of Paul's.

19. P. Lampe, "The Roman Christians of Romans 16," in *The Romans Debate*, ed. K. P. Donfried, 2nd ed. (Peabody: Hendrickson, 1991), p. 219.

Jews, albeit Jewish Christians. In fact Lampe is prepared to go further. He says that leaving aside the ten persons briefly mentioned in vv. 14-15 who are quite intentionally at the end of the list, we must assume that at least twelve of these persons named had seen Paul in person in the east somewhere — "the comments added to their names leave hardly any room for another interpretation."[20] Indeed, not only had various of these people been Paul's coworkers in the east, Andronicus and Junia had even been in jail somewhere with Paul, and Prisca and Aquila had put their lives on the line for Paul.[21]

It appears that we have various husband and wife ministry teams mentioned in this chapter, including Prisca and Aquila and Andronicus and Junia. Since this practice seems to have arisen out of Jewish Christian circles, to judge from these two couples, it is then germane to compare not only 1 Cor. 9.5, which speaks to the matter, but also to think of the practical consideration that there were places and settings where only men or women could go in the Greco-Roman world, and so by having a couple who minister the outreach for the gospel would be broadened. Käsemann, following J. Jeremias, thinks there may be something to the notion that the Jewish idea of the testimony of two witnesses may be behind not only Jesus sending disciples out to witness in pairs, but also the early Jewish Christian community doing so as well.[22]

The rhetorical effect of this list is severalfold: (1) These are not persons the Gentile majority in Rome can afford to ignore, dismiss, minimize, or treat in a condescending fashion. They are important Christians in Rome and are to be fully welcomed, supported, and bonded with in fellowship and mission. (2) This list establishes that Paul himself already has quite a social network established in Rome among these people. Thus Paul himself and his special emissary Phoebe must be received. Paul's authority and teaching cannot be ignored or dismissed. (3) The rhetorical function of many of the special descriptions appended to the names of some sixteen of these persons is to make clear that these are devout hardworking Christians, in whose debt the Roman Christians are, whether they know it or not. (4) It is no accident that only here in Romans do we have the global greeting from "all the assemblies of Christ" in the east (v. 16). Paul is finished with his work there, and the effect of this remark is that the eyes and thoughts of these churches are now all turning toward Rome as Paul plans to go there. The Roman church is part of a much larger entity, and its members have certain responsibilities toward the churches in the east. This is why Paul enlists the Roman Christians to pray as he goes to Jerusalem with the collection. This chapter comports with the larger rhetorical agendas of this letter and brings

20. Lampe, "The Roman Christians of Romans 16," p. 220.
21. Schlatter, *Romans*, p. 274, makes the interesting suggestion that this imprisonment may have transpired in Antioch.
22. See Käsemann, *Romans*, p. 413.

them to a remarkable and practical conclusion. Armed with these preliminary remarks we are prepared to examine this important chapter in more detail.

In vv. 1-2 Paul commends Phoebe to the Gentile-dominated church in Rome. The name Phoebe comes from Greek mythology, which may suggest that she was a Gentile, but Jews in the Diaspora often had non-Jewish names. He will go on not merely to mention but to praise seven women who are active in the Roman church, which is more than the number of men he praises, and he will mention by name seventeen men and only nine women. Letters of recommendation were well known in antiquity (cf. 1 Macc. 12.43; 2 Macc. 9.25; 2 Cor. 3.1), and it was customary to commend or recommend the courier of the letter, especially if he or she was unknown to the audience.[23]

It was also customary, as we can see in the Christian papyri and here, to call the bearer a brother or sister, making clear that the person should be received as a fellow believer.[24] Here we have the feminine Greek form *adelphē*, which was regularly used in early Christianity in a spiritual sense (cf. 1 Cor. 7.15; 9.5; Phlm. 2; Jas. 2.15). "Our" implies a universal brotherhood and sisterhood of all Christians.[25] Phoebe is not only a Christian sister, she is also a deacon of the church in Cenchreae, one of the ports of Corinth. The form *ousan diakonon* suggests that she had an ongoing ministry. She seems to be the first mentioned deacon in Christian history.[26] She should not be called a deaconess because the masculine form of the word is used here and because the specific order of women church workers called deaconesses did not exist for another three hundred years.[27] A sixth-century inscription found on the Mount of Olives speaks of a deaconess named Sophia who is called "the second Phoebe."[28] The use of "deacon" here should be compared to Phil. 1.1 and 1 Tim. 3.8 and 12.[29]

For the first time in Romans, here we find the word *ekklēsia*, assembly, applied to a group of Christians, though not those in Rome. The absence of the

23. See E. R. Richards, *The Secretary in the Letters of Paul* (Tübingen: Mohr, 1991), pp. 70-73.

24. See P. Oxy. LVI 3857 in *NewDocs* 8:171.

25. J. D. G. Dunn, *Romans 9–16*, Word Biblical Commentary Series (Dallas: Word, 1988), p. 886.

26. Dunn, *Romans 9–16*, pp. 886-87.

27. See rightly Wright, "Romans," p. 762. It is interesting, however, that Origen takes this passage to indicate that women were ordained in the church's ministry by apostolic authority. Pelagius in his commentary on Romans indicates that in his day women were allowed to baptize other women and preach the word to them. See G. Bray, ed., *Romans* (Ancient Christian Commentary on Scripture; Downers Grove: InterVarsity, 1998), p. 369. Cf. K. Romaniuk, "Was Phoebe in Romans 16,1 a Deaconess?" *ZNW* 81 (1990): 132-34.

28. See *NewDocs* 4:239-41; cf. 2:193-94.

29. See C. E. B. Cranfield, *A Critical and Exegetical Commentary on the Epistle to the Romans* (ICC; Edinburgh: Clark, 1975-79), 2:781.

word otherwise perhaps reflects Paul's knowledge that the Christians in Rome were not united and not regularly meeting together as a group, but rather taking the safer route of meeting in small numbers in various homes in Rome. The term itself originally referred to the political assembly in Greece, a place where policy would be discussed and debated and acts of persuasion would be undertaken. It is possible that Paul carries some of this notion forward into his conception of the Christian assembly, for he certainly sees such meetings as places where rhetoric, the art of persuasion, should be used.[30]

V. 2 urges that Phoebe be welcomed or received "in a manner worthy of the saints." The verb "welcome" here is the normal one indicating the providing of hospitality to someone, perhaps particularly someone who has been traveling. The sentence is awkward: "Welcome her in the Lord, worthy of the saints." This way of putting it suggests that Paul is saying receive her in a Christian manner, treat her as one of the saints. This would suggest she is a Jewish Christian and is to be treated with the same respect Paul has been inculcating for such persons throughout chs. 9–15. The audience is then exhorted to assist her in whatever practical way she may need assistance. This is a telling remark. It suggests that she is coming to Rome to work among the Roman Christians. She is the vanguard, preparing the way for Paul's visit. Among other things she would likely be the one who delivers Paul's letter and who begins to make arrangements for Paul's accommodations, and perhaps also collects resources for his further missionary work.[31]

Paul then calls her a *prostatis*. If one examines the cognate term in 12.8, this suggests that we are talking about a person in charge of some sort of practical charitable work, which also comports with calling her a deacon. The notions of care and of some sort of structured leadership role in adminstering that care, benevolence, or patronage are not mutually exclusive. R. Oster has shown how in the inscriptional use of this language in Ephesus the two concepts go hand-in-hand.[32] Normally such work would not be assigned to a person who needed such assistance but rather one who could provide it. If the term is taken at face value it means something like helper or protector or perhaps even *patroness*.[33]

---

30. See my discussion in *Conflict and Community in Corinth* (Grand Rapids: Eerdmans, 1995), pp. 90-93.

31. Though I think R. Jewett makes too much of Paul's mission to Spain insofar as it affects the content and nature of Romans, he has much that is helpful about Phoebe and Paul's plans in "Paul, Phoebe, and the Spanish Mission," in *The Social World of Formative Christianity and Judaism*, ed. J. Neusner et al. (Philadelphia: Fortress, 1988), pp. 142-61.

32. See *NewDocs* 4:74-82, here p. 82. In other words, modern concerns to try to deny that women had leadership roles in the church by distinguishing the meaning "care" from the sense "lead" or "rule" or "direct" are artificial and should not be imposed on the NT text.

33. The term *prostatis* is used of a woman who is a patroness at least as early as 142 B.C. See the discussion in Bryan, *A Preface to Romans*, pp. 38-39.

In both Philo and Josephus its masculine equivalent has this specific sense (cf. Philo, *De Virtutibus* 155 to Josephus, *Antiquities* 14.157, 144). This is also what the term means in two Jewish inscriptions found in Rome (CIJ 100, 365), and we now have fresh evidence that the feminine form *prostatis* had this sense.[34] In fact we have an inscription from Corinth, from this very period, which speaks of a woman named Junia Theodora who is said to be a patroness noted for providing hospitality to those traveling to Corinth.[35] B. Brooten has shown that there is evidence of Jewish women fulfilling the role of patroness and benefactor of a synagogue.[36] Phoebe apparently fulfilled a similar role in the church, in this case for Paul and others.[37] "Given the fact that Paul has consistently designated his collection as a *diakonia* . . . and that *prostatis* can bear the meaning financial patron . . . we are justified in our evaluation of Phoebe as something like Paul's 'financial agent' in his negotiations with the Roman church."[38]

Now this is striking not least because Paul has rejected patronage in Corinth from the church itself, choosing rather to continue his tentmaking trade. But he accepts it from Phoebe. This suggests that Paul has very great respect for and trust in Phoebe and does not fear that she will treat him merely as a client who has obligations to her and who must keep the reciprocity cycle going. It may also be that she provided Paul with some protection, perhaps a place in Cenchreae to hide from trouble in Corinth (cf. Acts 18.18).[39] Clarke rightly points out that though it seems clear that Phoebe is a person of considerable social status and perhaps wealth as well, since she has been the "patroness of many," that she provides practical service as a deacon on an ongoing basis shows very clearly Paul is not commending her primarily for her social status.

34. See *NewDocs* 4:242-44.

35. See R. A. Kearsley, "Women in the World of the New Testament," *Ancient Society* 15 (1985): 124-77, which has since been revised and updated in "Women in Public Life in the Roman East: Iunia Theodora, Claudia Metrodora, and Phoebe Benefactress of Paul," *TynBul* 50 (1999): 189-211. See also the helpful discussion by A. D. Clarke, "Jew and Greek, Slave and Free, Male and Female: Paul's Theology of Ethnic, Social, and Gender Inclusiveness in Romans 16," in *Rome in the Bible and the Early Church*, ed. P. Oakes (Grand Rapids: Baker, 2002), pp. 103-25, here pp. 115-18. Käsemann, *Romans*, p. 411, is quite wrong that women could not take on legal functions or be patronesses at this juncture in Roman history. He is correct, however, that the participle in v. 1 indicates that she has an ongoing ministry as a deacon.

36. See B. Brooten, *Women Leaders in the Ancient Synagogues* (Chico: Scholars, 1982).

37. Perhaps in view of Paul's general policy in regard to receiving patronage from converts (see pp. 363-65 above), what Paul received from Phoebe was housing and hospitality rather than full patronage. Or perhaps Phoebe is the exception in Corinth and was his patron there in his later days. We cannot be sure.

38. L. T. Johnson, *Reading Romans: A Literary and Theological Commentary* (Macon: Smyth and Helwys, 2001), p. 233.

39. See Pausanias, *Descriptions of Greece* 2.2.3.

40. Clarke, "Jew and Greek," p. 117.

Indeed he is depicting her as one who steps down the social ladder and uses her social advantages in the service of others, in this case especially the church, even taking on menial tasks.[40]

The first people Paul asks to be warmly received are Prisca and Aquila. Paul stresses not only that they have risked life and limb for him but also the impact of their work for the Gentile churches in general. To judge from this text, 1 Cor. 16.19, and Acts 18 they must have been some of Paul's closest coworkers. They seem to have been involved in a variety of churches, including those in Ephesus, Corinth, and Rome.[41] Four of the six times this couple is mentioned in the NT, Priscilla's name comes first. This is very unusual in a patriarchal culture. It is possible that she is from Rome (only her husband is said to be a Jew from Pontus in Acts 18.2). That she is mentioned first has also been explained on the basis of her being of higher social status than her husband or more prominent in the church.

What seems a secure conclusion is that Paul was not responsible for converting them, unlike Epaenetus. "That a Jewish couple expelled because of the conflict with Christians in Rome deliberately gave a Christian missionary work and shelter is far more improbable than that Paul found lodgings [in Corinth] with Christians who had fled from Rome."[42] Acts 18 informs us that among other things Priscilla and Aquila were teachers. They instructed even a church leader as prominent as Apollos. John Chrysostom was one of the Greek Fathers who commented on Priscilla as a teacher and saw it as noteworthy *(Homily on Acts 18)*.

Paul's most used designation for those who aided him in his ministry is *synergos*, "coworker," not brother, apostle, servant, or any other spiritualized term. All but one of the thirteen uses of this term in the NT occur in Paul (the exception being 3 John 8). It is not a term Paul uses in general of Christians (cf. 1 Cor. 3.9; 1 Thess. 3.2; Rom. 16.3, 9, 21; Phil. 2.25; Phlm. 24; 2 Cor. 8.23; 1.24). 1 Cor. 16.16-18 makes evident that the term indicates a leadership position, for in that text the congregation is urged to be subject to Paul's coworkers.[43] Thus we may rightly conclude that Priscilla and Aquila were an important husband and wife ministry team, and that if either was better known for Christian work it was Priscilla. It is possible that she was a freedwoman of Roman extraction named after a member of the Priscillian gens, but we cannot be certain of this. What we do know is that the name was exceedingly common in Rome, as the Greek inscriptions from Rome mention the name some two hundred times.[44]

41. See my discussion of them in *Women in the Earliest Churches*, pp. 153-54.

42. E. Haenchen, *The Acts of the Apostles* (Philadelphia: Westminster Press, 1971), p. 533 n. 4.

43. See my discussion in *Women in the Earliest Churches*, pp. 111-13.

44. See Lampe, "The Roman Christians of Romans 16," p. 226.

We do not know which occasion Paul is referring to when he says this couple risked their lives for his sake, but presumably it had something to do with their time together in Corinth or perhaps Ephesus.[45]

"All the churches of the Gentiles" indicates that there were a goodly number of such churches and that Priscilla and Aquila had put them in their debt in various ways. That these churches were predominantly or overwhelmingly Gentile in character made them like the church in Rome. This is as opposed to the church of the "saints" in Jerusalem, by which is meant Jewish Christians. We may also compare the phrase in v. 16 "all the churches of Christ," which would presumably include both predominantly Jewish and predominantly Gentiles churches. Paul may say "all the churches of the Gentiles" to help establish, or reestablish after some years of absence, the authority of Priscilla and Aquila in the Roman church. They are Jews, but their mission work has been among Gentiles, and so it is appropriate for them to be recognized and supported by the predominantly Gentile church in Rome.

We are furthermore told in v. 5 that there is an assembly of Christians who meet in the house of Priscilla and Aquila. Paul does not speak of *the* assembly of God in Rome, but of household assemblies (plural) in Rome. This is probably a telltale sign of the lack of unity among Roman Christians, something Paul is trying to change in this letter. He will mention the household of Aristobolus, apparently not a Christian, but here an assembly that meets in a Christian household. It seems logical to conclude that while many Christians, especially slaves, were a part of a religiously mixed household, Christian meetings were held in homes where the household owner or owners were Christians.

V. 5 also asks for a warm greeting and reception for Epaenetus, the first convert (presumably of Paul's, but possibly of Prisca and Aquila's) in Asia.[46] Paul uses the term "first fruit" to indicate that Epaenetus is but a harbinger of the harvest of Gentiles in Asia (see similarly of Stephanus, 1 Cor. 16.15). He was by no means the only convert. The reference to Asia could mean that he was from Ephesus, but at present he is in Rome and is called Paul's beloved. Paul is making clear he has many close contacts in Rome, and many persons he cares deeply about. This of course indirectly confirms what we know from Acts, namely that Paul did do missionary work in Asia. If we are to judge from Acts, Paul began his missionary work in the synagogue in a city, and the first converts were normally Jews, or in some cases God-fearers. It is probable then Epaenetus is one or the other of these sorts of persons.

In v. 6 Maria is mentioned as someone who has worked very hard in

---

45. Notice the use of the term *psychē* in v. 4 to refer to Paul's physical life, not his "soul."

46. Perhaps, as Käsemann, *Romans,* p. 413, suggests, he went to Rome from Ephesus with Prisca and Aquila.

Rome. For whatever reason, Paul uses the verb *kopiaō,* which means to work hard, only of women in this passage. Possibly this reflects the fact that women in general had more time to devote to Christian service in Rome than some men did. Whatever the reason for this emphasis, it reminds us that women were prominent in the Christian movement both in Rome and elsewhere in the first century.[47] Chrysostom, commenting on this verse, says: "The women of those days were more spirited than lions, sharing with the Apostles their labors for the Gospel's sake. In this way they went traveling with them and also performed all other ministries."[48] Maria is not given a title. Like Priscilla, the name Maria comes up a great deal in Greek inscriptions from Rome — over 100 times. Of the names in this chapter, only Maria, Julia, and Rufus appear in Jewish inscriptions from Rome. Maria's work must have been some sort of Christian work, though we cannot be sure of what kind. Her name is consistent with the conclusion that she is Jewish, and in fact 𝔭46, ℵ, and other texts render the name as *Mariam,* which makes clearer the Jewish character of the name.

In v. 7 we hear of Andronicus and Junia, likely another ministry couple, and we may be quite certain they are Jewish since Paul claims them as relatives.[49] Chrysostom calls this verse an "encomium" to this couple and indeed remarks on all the encomia Paul gives to various persons, many of them women, in this passage. The term *syngeneis* never occurs in Paul's other letters, but Paul uses it here of this couple and in v. 11 of Herodion.[50] Part of Paul's reason for mentioning that these three are his relatives is to remind the predominantly Gentile church that God has not given up on Israel.[51] But this does not mean that the others he lists are not Jews. Had Paul wanted to call these three fellow Jews or Israelites, he could have done so. He speaks very specifically in 9.3-4 when he wants to talk about Israelites in general being his kin. But his emphasis here is on his own relatives within the larger group who were Jews.[52]

Paul also calls Andronicus and Junia his fellow prisoners. We do not know when this imprisonment happened, and it is even conceivable that Paul merely

47. See the excursus below, pp. 388-89.

48. In this very same passage he explains that 1 Tim. 2.12 does not mean that Paul is forbidding women from teaching; he is only hindering them from coming forward in public assemblies. Chrysostom then sees the issue as a matter of public vs. private instruction, though he allows that when her husband is unable to do the job, a woman could do it.

49. The first commentator to suggest that these might be two men seems to be the medieval exegete Giles of Rome (1247-1316). See Fitzmyer, *Romans,* p. 738. Thereafter this view became prominent, if not the dominant opinion, right through the nineteenth century.

50. This is a name that never occurs in the Greek inscriptions in Rome.

51. Lampe, "The Roman Christians of Romans 16," p. 224.

52. Against Barrett, *Romans,* p. 259. The proof that Barrett is wrong that others listed must be Gentiles is of course Priscilla and Aquila, whom Paul does not call his kin, but who are clearly Jews.

means that they were imprisoned for the faith as he was, rather than that they were all in jail together. 2 Cor. 11.23 tells us that Paul was imprisoned on various occasions, and to judge from Acts 18 and 2 Cor. 11:24 it was frequently connected with his witness in the synagogue. The "thirty-nine lashes" of the latter verse was a punishment for false teaching in the synagogue. It may be that Andronicus and Junia were involved on such an occasion and were also imprisoned.

A Closer Look: Was Junia also Joanna?

One of the most helpful, intriguing, and complete recent treatments of Junia is that of R. Bauckham.[53] It is Bauckham's thesis that Junia is in fact Joanna mentioned in Luke 8.3 and elsewhere in that Gospel.[54]

Early Jews who had regular contact with the Greco-Roman world in one way or another often took Latin names, favoring those which sounded like their Jewish names if possible, and Junia is close in sound to the Jewish name Yohannah. To the objection that Palestinian Jews would avoid Latin names and instead choose Greek ones so as not to raise the ire of fellow Jews, Bauckham is able to point out that those Jews who had close association with Romans, such as the entourage of Herod Antipas, might well choose Latin names.[55]

Bauckham takes pains to deal at length with the arguments of M. H. Burer and D. B. Wallace (on which see below), who argue that "prominent among the apostles" does not identify Andronicus and Junia as apostles. Indeed the evidence from the parallels makes it perfectly possible that the phrase can have an inclusive meaning in 16.7.[56] "Writers such as Origen and John Chrysostom were educated native speakers of Greek. They had no reason for Andronicus and Junia to be apostles other than supposing this to be the meaning of Paul's Greek. If Burer and Wallace's conclusion is right, then it is inexplicable that these Greek patristic interpreters should have read the Greek of Romans in the way they did."[57]

---

53. R. Bauckham, *Gospel Women: Studies in the Named Women of the Gospels* (Grand Rapids: Eerdmans, 2002), pp. 109-202.

54. Bauckham conjures with the possibility that her husband Chuza may also have had the Latin name Andronicus, but he also recognizes that Andronicus could have been her second husband after Chuza died or possibly divorced her (perhaps for being a follower of Jesus?).

55. Bauckham, *Gospel Women,* p. 182: "Thus it is not surprising that the majority of those [Palestinian Jews] who are known to have had Latin names are found within the sphere of the Herods and the Herodians."

56. See Bauckham, *Gospel Women,* pp. 172-80. Bauckham in fact shows that Burer and Wallace have engaged in a tendentious presentation of the evidence in order to favor their case that Junia was not an apostle.

57. Bauckham, *Gospel Women,* p. 179.

It has been suggested that Paul means by "apostle" here nothing more than what he means in 2 Cor. 8.23 and Phil. 2.25, where the word refers to official messengers or emissaries of a local church. But Bauckham answers that "such people are clearly designated 'apostles of churches' (2 Cor. 8.23) and 'your . . . apostle' (Phil. 2.25). It is hard to see how they could form a known body of people among whom Andronicus and Junia could be said to be outstanding."[58] Since "apostles" is used without further qualification in Rom. 16.7 it is very likely it means what Paul normally means by the term — namely one who has seen the Lord and has been commissioned as an apostle of Christ. Furthermore, Bauckham notes, Andronicus and Junia could not have been apostles of Christ in Paul's eyes unless they had become apostles before Paul did, since Paul calls himself last of the apostles, the last to see the risen Lord, in 1 Corinthians 15.

Bauckham then goes on rightly, in my judgment, to point out that since Paul adds that Andronicus and Junia were in Christ before Paul this surely strongly suggests they must be Palestinian Jews who became followers of Jesus. It is not impossible that after Pentecost they were among those Jews who went to Rome and carried the message of the gospel to that city. In any case, in the 50s Paul expects even the Gentile majority in Rome to acknowledge them as outstanding among the apostles, which is to say he expects the Gentile Christians to recognize their authority in Rome. Presumably they have returned to Rome with others after the edict of Claudius lapsed. "No one else Paul mentions in Romans 16 has comparable standing."[59]

Bauckham additionally suggests that Paul has mentioned first three of his co-workers in the Aegean mission and then three who pioneered and led the Christian missionary efforts in Rome. This is certainly plausible and it supports my thesis that these are all Jewish Christians Paul is referring to at this juncture.

Bauckham's thesis that Junia may be Joanna would perhaps help explain not only the reference to her and her husband being both in Christ before Paul and apostles before Paul, but also their prior apostolic work, which seems to have left them incarcerated at one juncture, perhaps with Paul. Though we cannot be sure Bauckham is correct in connecting Junia and Joanna, it is certainly possible, and in any case the rest of his strong case for Junia being a Jewish Christian apostle with connections with Palestine and Paul does not depend on identifying her as Joanna.

Paul makes two important remarks about this couple. First, they were "in Christ" before Paul was. That is, they were converted before the late 30s and before the beginning of the Gentile mission. So very probably they not only were Jews but were from the mother church, or less probably, from one of the two other major cities where Christianity first took root — Damascus and Antioch.[60]

58. Bauckham, *Gospel Women*, p. 180.
59. Bauckham, *Gospel Women*, p. 181.
60. See Johnson, *Reading Romans*, p. 234.

Paul also says that they were well known or prominent or outstanding "among the apostles." Only in the NT is *episēmoi* used in a somewhat metaphorical sense. Literally the term means something like "stamped" or "marked," hence "notable," "noteworthy," or even "noted." Paul is making clear their honor rating in the apostolic circle. But does "in the apostles" mean "in the eyes of the apostles" or "among the apostles"? The patristic witnesses take the phrase to mean the latter rather than the former, and the examples cited in the Greek lexicon (BAGD) where "in" means "in the eyes of" include these specific words or some like them.[61] M. H. Burer and D. B. Wallace have tried to argue for an elative force for "in the apostles," saying that Paul would have used a genitive form of "apostles" if he meant "among the apostles."[62] But, as Moo points out, it would surely have been more natural for Paul to use *hypo* or a simple dative form if that were what he wanted to say.[63] Furthermore, there would have to be a good reason that the Fathers, who knew this Greek far better than we do, overwhelmingly assumed that Paul meant "noted among the apostles."[64] It is then appropriate to conclude that Paul means that these two persons were not only apostles but were noteworthy within the apostolic circle.

Paul twice uses "apostle" of someone who is simply an agent or emissary of a particular church sent on a particular mission (Phil. 2.25; 2 Cor. 8.23), but by far the most common way he uses the term is to refer to apostles of Jesus Christ, those who have seen the risen Lord and have been commissioned by the Lord to share the Good News. This is surely how Paul uses the word here. Andronicus and Junia may be among those mentioned in 1 Cor. 15.7 as apostles to whom Jesus appeared. They are not merely celebrated or appreciated or commissioned by some local church.

The conclusion then follows that Paul has no problem with women as teachers (Priscilla) or leaders, proclaimers, or missionaries of the Good News. Indeed, it is hardly likely that a woman would be incarcerated in Paul's world without having made some significant public remark or action. Junia said or did something that led to a judicial action. Chrysostom recognizes that Paul is referring to a woman apostle and says of her that she had a keen interest in *philosophia;* indeed "the supposition that Paul was addressing a female apostle Junia dominated among the patristic exegetes and the early Translations (Old Latin, Vulgate, Sahidic, and Boharic)."[65]

61. See my discussion in *Women in the Earliest Churches*, pp. 115-16 and the notes.

62. Burer and Wallace, "Was Junia Really an Apostle?" *NTS* 47 (2001): 76-91.

63. D. Moo, *The Epistle to the Romans* (NICNT; Grand Rapids: Eerdmans, 1996), p. 923.

64. Burer and Wallace, "Was Junia Really an Apostle?" p. 90, are in the end forced to admit that there are other cases where *en* plus the dative of a personal object is used in an inclusive sense, as seems surely to be the case here.

65. Clarke, "Jew and Greek," p. 119.

A Closer Look: Women and Their Roles in Rome

In his landmark study, J. P. V. D. Balsdon says clearly that women in Rome in the first century A.D. did not live in the sort of seclusion that was common for oriental women.[66] Much depended on the social class of a woman. For example, a Roman matron seems to have been freer, better educated, more influential, and more respected than women in Greece (Macedonia was an exception) and in the eastern part of the empire. Jewish women in a Roman setting, such as Prisca, Junia, and probably Mary, may have had a narrower range of permitted activities, not least because Jews in Rome were under scrutiny, especially after the edict of Claudius in A.D. 49.

Marriage laws and other laws had become less severe in their restriction of women during the empire, though Augustus did try to provide incentives for patrician women to marry,[67] have a certain number of children, and assume traditional roles within the family.[68] In fact, Augustus's laws show that many women were seeking other avenues of self-expression as businesswomen, in religious cults, and in various other ways. Furthermore, even among poorer families, including some financially strapped patrician families, daughters did go to school, even though tutors were available only for those who could afford them. Romans saw education of women not as an extravagance but rather as a way to enhance a woman and her worth.[69]

Within the home, Roman women, and matrons in particular, had considerable status and power. They were generally speaking not housewives in the normal sense of the term. Though they bore a major responsibility for the home, they would normally assign menial tasks to servants. They regularly would go to markets, festivals, games, and the like. They would also often supervise their children's education. They might well be the de facto head of all things that went on in the home, especially if their husbands were traveling merchants, soldiers, or ambassadors.

Obviously, women played prominent roles in Roman religion, with the Vestal Virgins the most obvious example. Though they were dedicated to virginity and tending the sacred flame for thirty years, they were not under the power of any man, not bound by any oath other than their sacred one, and could testify in a court. They were also wealthy women as they were given a good-sized dowry in recognition of their service to Rome, a dowry twice that of a rich matron. Outside their eight-hour duty period they were free to go to dinner parties, visit matrons, and go to certain religious festivals. They even had the power to remit the sentence of a prisoner if they passed one on the street and were implored to do so. They were emissaries of peace for the emperor and the state, and when some misfortune hit Rome, they would do propitia-

---

66. J. P. V. D. Balsdon, *Roman Women: Their History and Habits* (London: Bodley Head, 1962), p. 45.

67. Suetonius, *Augustus* 73; CIL 112.

68. See my discussion in *Women in the Earliest Churches*, pp. 16-23.

69. See Plutarch, *Parallel Lives: Pompey* 55; cf. F. E. Adcock, "Women in Roman Life and Letters," *Greece and Rome* 14 (1945): 1-22.

tory acts. Obviously while these women were in a distinct minority among Roman women, nonetheless they show what was possible.[70]

Eastern religious cults had been entering Rome and attracting women since at least the third century B.C., when the cult of the Idean mother was introduced into the city. So popular did some of these cults become, including especially that of Isis, that Petronius in the first century A.D. groans that Roman women neglect the traditional cults almost entirely for the eastern imports (*Satyricon* 44). The cult of Isis was important because it was "non-political" in the sense that it was participated in not for the benefit of the state, but rather for the benefit of individuals, a trait it shared in common with another sect which came to Rome somewhat later — Christianity. The rituals of Isis were flexible, and one might well see rites for prostitutes followed by other women spending the night in the temple to dedicate themselves to chastity. The only Roman traditional cults which gave women prominent roles were those of Vesta and Ceres, whereas women could readily become priestesses in the cult of Isis, the goddess with sympathy for the pain and suffering of women, who promised healing, blessing, and understanding. Most strikingly, in the cult of Isis women of lower class held the same status or standing as women of the upper classes.[71] The inscriptions testify to at least six women priestesses in this cult, including one of a family of senatorial rank and one an Italian freedwoman (CIL 2244-2248). The attempts by Augustus and Tiberius to abolish this cult failed miserably, and it is certainly no coincidence that the rise of women to more freedom in Roman society during the empire parallels the rise of the prominence and popularity of this cult.

We have insufficient knowledge of status and roles of freedwomen and female slaves in Rome, but we can say a few things. There is evidence that they played a wide range of roles, from shopkeeper to artisan to domestic to physician to commercial entrepreneur to brickmaker even to owning shipyards or brick factories.[72] It seems clear that many women of whatever status had more disposable income in Rome than in the eastern parts of the empire. Since both slaves and freedpersons had ways of prospering and accumulating wealth during the empire, one could have relatively high social status economically even if one was not part of or connected to a patrician family. In other words, there were different forms of social status and influence in Rome during this era, and we find women playing a wide variety of roles, religious and otherwise.

It is then not a surprise at all to find women like the eight that Paul mentions in Romans 16 playing a variety of roles in the Roman church, and indeed probably a wider variety than they could have played in the synagogue. This is probably one reason women were attracted to the Christian movement as it spread west across the empire.

Paul certainly shows no qualms about having women as coworkers in a wide va-

70. Cf. Livy 1.20.3; 1.70.1; Tacitus, *Annales* 4.16.6; Pliny, *Letters* 7.19.
71. See Balsdon, *Roman Women*, p. 246.
72. See H. J. Loane, *Industry and Commerce of the City of Rome (50 BC–AD 200)* (Baltimore: Johns Hopkins University Press, 1938).

riety of roles. He did not set out to change secular society's patriarchal structure, but he did try to help create a Christian subculture where men and women could all be one in Christ and where what determined roles in the church was one's gifting and calling, not one's gender or social status. Even in his discussions of family in 1 Corinthians 7, Colossians 3–4, and Ephesians 5–6 we see him starting where he found the social structures but seeking to reform the patriarchal family structure in various ways so that women, children, and slaves would be treated as Christian persons worthy of respect, honor, and love in the context of mutual service and submission.[73] It is the husband/father/slaveowner that would be surprised by the new duties and obligations to other members of the household that Paul imposes on *them,* by "submit to one another out of love for Christ" (Eph. 5.21), "the body of the husband belongs to the wife" (1 Cor. 7.4), and "no longer as a slave but as a brother" (Phlm. 16). Reform within the community as the leaven of the gospel was kneaded into the lump was Paul's way of trying to implement the social implications of his gospel. We see those implications in practice in Romans 16 when it comes to the religious roles of women.[74]

Vv. 8 and 9 refer to three men whom Paul calls either "beloved" or "coworker," so they are all men he knew from the east. Ampliatus and Urbanus are fairly common names in the Roman inscriptions (occurring eighty and ninety-five times respectively), while Stachys is rarer (eleven occurrences).[75] The name Urbanus does not suggest a person who was a slave or a freedman. We cannot tell if these men are Jews or Gentiles, but nothing rules out the suggestion that they are either Jews or God-fearers, or at the very least those who regularly fellowship in the Jewish Christian household of Prisca and Aquila or another Jewish Christian household. The same applies to Apelles "the tested" (v. 10).

The second half of v. 10 mentions "those of the household of Aristobolus," probably indicating that Aristobolus himself was not a Christian. Those Paul mentions were slaves or freedmen and freedwomen. The name Aristobolus occurs only twice in all the many Roman inscriptions, which suggests that this Aristobolus was from the east. It has been conjectured he was a member of the Herodian family.[76] We know of an Aristobolus who was the grandson of Herod the Great and brother of Herod Agrippa I.[77] According to

73. See the discussions at length in *Women in the Earliest Churches,* pp. 16-23 and in our forthcoming commentary on Ephesians, Colossians, and Philemon.

74. On the interesting inscriptional evidence for women assuming leadership positions in the church into the fourth century as teachers, deaconesses, and the like, see *NewDocs* 1:121.

75. See Lampe, "The Roman Christians of Romans 16," p. 226.

76. See pp. 387-88 above.

77. See Josephus, *War* 2.221.

Josephus, Aristobolus went to Rome with Agrippa I in the forties when Agrippa
was taken hostage, and then Aristobolus maintained a low profile in Rome,
never holding public office (*Antiquities* 18.273-76; *Wars* 2.221). If this is the
Aristobolus mentioned here (and the name is quite rare), he brought his slaves
with him from the east, and probably he and his household were Jewish or affil-
iated with the synagogue before some of them became Christians.[78] The juxtaposition of Aristobolus with Herodion (v. 11), who is said to be a kinsman of
Paul, has set this train of thinking in motion. Herodion was certainly a Jew,
probably a freedman of the Herodian family, for freedmen took their owners'
names in some form. Narcissus may be another famous name. Again, the
householder is not a Christian, but there are Christians in his home. A freedman named Narcissus came to prominence as a close aide of Claudius and had
a household in Rome in the early fifties (Juvenal, *Satirae* 14.329-31). His household likely became absorbed into Nero's once Claudius fell in A.D. 54, and he
himself was a victim of Agrippina's wrath (Tacitus, *Annales* 13.1). We do not
know if the members of that household here greeted were Jews or Gentiles.

In v. 12 Paul refers to two women with slave names meaning "dainty" and
"delicate" — Tryphaena and Tryphosa. It is germane for our purposes to say
that the inscriptions do mention a Jewish woman with the former name.[79] Next
mentioned is Persis, whose name was a popular slave name. All three were
probably freedwomen, since they had the time to work hard for the church.[80]
Persis is called "beloved," but not "my beloved," unlike the men in vv. 5, 8, and 9,
perhaps because Paul did not want to give the wrong impression about his relationship with her. Nevertheless, the term of endearment here reminds the audience that she was widely loved and respected.

Rufus (v. 13) is a Latin name. Since the Gospel of Mark was likely written
to Roman Christians,[81] the Rufus mentioned in Mark 15.21 may be the same
man, especially since the Christian community in Rome was apparently not all
that large. Mark's Rufus is the son of Simon of Cyrene, who carried Jesus' cross.
It is not clear why Paul calls him "the elect" or "the chosen," but of course it indicates that he is a Christian.[82] It is also very likely that he is a diaspora Jew,
since Simon of Cyrene was apparently in Jerusalem for the Passover.

78. It must be remembered that his brother Agrippa I had lived in Rome even as late as
the 40s, and so there would have been a Herodian household connection in Rome for
Aristobolus to be involved in or assume the headship of after Agrippa's death. See Moo,
Romans, p. 925.

79. See Lampe, "The Roman Christians of Romans 16," p. 150.

80. Dunn, *Romans 9–16*, p. 897.

81. See my *The Gospel of Mark* (Grand Rapids: Eerdmans, 2000), p. 394.

82. Notice that the Greek phrase is "elect in the Lord," not "elect in himself." Even in
this passing reference, Paul makes clear that election takes place "in the Lord" or "in Christ,"
for Christ is *the* Elect One of God.

But what does it mean that Rufus's mother is also a mother to Paul?[83] Possibly she provided for or helped Paul when he lived in Jerusalem before his conversion, but we cannot be sure. Whatever made her Paul's "mother" happened somewhere outside Rome, but presumably Rufus and his mother went to Rome once the edict of Claudius expired. It is unlikely that Paul means that this woman was his literal mother, who was a resident of Tarsus.[84]

Vv. 14-15 name two groups of five people, and those "with them," "the brothers with them" and then "all the saints with them." It is possible that Philologus and Julia were slaves in the Emperor's household, since Julia was a common name in that setting, but we can not be sure.[85] Paul does not pause to say much about all these people other than that they are to be warmly greeted. Lampe is probably correct that we should see two house-churches here, with their most prominent members named.[86] I would suggest once again that "saints" indicates Jewish Christians, which may suggest that the named persons are also Jewish Christians, or at least are part of one of the house-churches where Jewish Christians meet. Perhaps some of them were God-fearers before they became Christians. Paul uses "brother" more generically of either Gentile or Jewish Christians.

But it needs to be asked again: Why has Paul exhorted his largely Gentile audience to embrace these named persons and those associated with them? Why has he distinguished the main audience addressed in the letter from these named persons, whom the audience is to treat in a Christian manner? In my view the answer is that these named persons are the Jewish Christians in Rome and those who closely associated with them, some of whom are likely former God-fearers, and some perhaps Gentiles just sympathetic to Judaism. In my view these people, or at least a significant number of them, are "the weak" Paul has referred to in chs. 14–15. If I am right about this, it helps to explain not only the *peroratio* which follows but also the greetings from Corinth, as we shall see.

V. 16 refers to the holy kiss, which was a regular part of Paul's communities (1 Cor. 16.20; 2 Cor. 13.12; 1 Thess. 5.26; also 1 Pet. 5.14; Justin, *Apology I* 65). That it is a holy or chaste kiss may suggest that it is a matter of ritual,[87] but,

83. There is plenty of papyrological evidence for the use of the term "mother" or "father" in a metaphorical sense. See P. Oxy. X 1296; P. Oxy. XLVIII 3396, and P. Oxy. LVI 3859. See *NewDocs* 6:158, n. 178.

84. As Barrett, *Romans,* p. 260, says, the mention of Rufus probably confirms that all these greetings are directed to people in Rome.

85. See Dunn, *Romans 9–16*, p. 898.

86. Lampe, "The Roman Christians of Romans 16," p. 230.

87. See Clement of Alexandria, *The Instructor* 3.11: "But there are those who do nothing but make the church resound with a kiss, not having love in themselves. For this very thing, the shameless use of a kiss, which ought to be mystic, occasions foul suspicion and evil reports. The apostle, however, calls the kiss holy."

more importantly for our purposes, Paul is sealing or concluding this section of exhortations to greet with an exhortation to kiss, which means he wants these people treated as family and welcomed wholeheartedly into the fellowship of the majority.[88] It is striking that he can then turn and conclude v. 16 by saying to the Gentile-dominated audience "all the churches of Christ warmly embrace you." In short, Paul is saying "do unto your own fellow Christians in Rome what has been and is being done to you." But this is also a way of making clear that all these other churches are watching what they will do. Christian eyes in the east have turned westward to the capital, and Paul, the representative apostle of many of those churches, is coming their way. It is time for them to get their houses and house-churches in order.

We have sought to make a case that those named in Romans 16 thus far are Jewish Christians or their affiliates in their household groups. Some are Paul's relatives, some are his coworkers, and some are simply Jewish Christians who have returned to Rome and need to be recognized and reconciled with the "strong," the dominantly Gentile Christian community in Rome.

Paul has a word of advice for these named Jewish Christians and their confreres which he offers in a second *peroratio* in vv. 17-20.[89] "[T]he apostle speaks here with an authority which he does sometimes. . . in relation to the Romans but which for the most part he carefully avoids. He does it with a kind of fury which does not appear elsewhere in the epistle. . . ."[90] The explanation for this is part rhetorical (this is natural in a *peroratio,* where one is supposed to stir up the deeper emotions) and part based on the fact that Paul is addressing Jewish Christians, indeed Jewish Christians whom he already knows, has worked with, is related to, or has converted. He has an authority over them that he does not have over the Gentiles in Rome. Hence his candor and strong words, which also mirror his belief that there is a serious problem in Rome for these Christians.

V. 17 begins very much as 12.1 began. The *de* here connects this exhortation to the immediately preceding greetings, and strongly suggests that Paul has primarily in mind that named group of people as the audience for this final exhortation.[91] Here Paul will exhort the "weak" and those who associate with

88. On this practice see my discussion in *Conflict and Community in Corinth,* pp. 322-23, and see S. Benko, "The Kiss," in his *Pagan Rome and the Early Christians* (Bloomington: Indiana University Press, 1984), pp. 79-102.

89. Barrett, *Romans,* p. 261, assumes that Paul is advising the Gentile "strong" to stay away from the over-scrupulous, who are ruled by food laws. This would be quite the opposite of what Paul was saying in chs. 14–15, where it is the strong who are doing the tempting and who do not need shielding. Far more probable is the view that Paul is addressing the Jewish Christians, especially the "weak" among them, here.

90. Käsemann, *Romans,* p. 419.

91. J. Zeisler, *Paul's Letter to the Romans* (London: SCM, 1989), pp. 348-49, even consid-

them and provide a warning for them, in the same way that he identified primarily with the "strong" in various ways in chs. 12–15 and exhorted them.[92] Here Paul exhorts these Christians, whom he calls "brothers," to look out for, or critically examine the motives and behavior of, those who cause divisions. This is very different from the exhortation to the Gentile strong in chs. 14–15 to stop causing divisions and stop causing "the weak" to stumble. Here we have the other side of this advice, directed to the other part of Paul's audience in Rome.

Paul advises them to stay away from the division-causers. The rents in the fabric of the Roman church garment do not need to get any bigger. Paul also says that the teaching they have learned is against such behavior which causes divisions and leads people into temptation and so to stumble. If Paul is indeed addressing Aquila and Priscilla here, and others who have been in the east, then it is germane to note that 1 Corinthians is a letter focusing quite specifically on unitive, deliberative rhetoric and seeking to overcome divisions and factions. In other words, we have specific evidence of the sort of teaching Paul has in mind simply by examining his rhetoric in 1 Corinthians. It would be in Corinth and elsewhere in the east that these Christians will have heard this advice before. For the "weak" who cannot handle the freedom with which the "strong" eat all sorts of things and seem to be lax in their religious rituals, the advice is to stay away from those who do not heed Paul's earlier exhortation in chs. 14–15 but rather persist in flaunting their freedom and tempting the weak. As Grieb says, polemical parting shots are not anything surprising in Paul's letters (cf. Gal. 6.11-17).[93]

Paul makes clear in v. 18 that he is not just talking about people who simply live like Gentiles, but those who advocate that all Christians should behave as they do. Paul's reference to their rhetoric — involving smooth talk and fine-sounding speech — makes clear that his complaint is in regard to those who are attempting to persuade the weak to violate their consciences. It is these persons, presumably only a few of the Gentile strong, that Paul advises the Jewish Christians and those who fellowship with them to avoid. He does not want the weak

---

ers that this passage must be directed to another church, because he has failed to pick up the rhetorical and grammatical signals here of the connection with those just mentioned.

92. Dunn, *Romans 9–16*, p. 904, is right to note the difference in tone from what we have in 14.1–15.6. This is because: (1) Paul is offering an emotional *peroratio* here, and (2) he is focusing on a different audience here by and large, and is concerned that the weak may succumb to temptation, hence the sternness of the warning. Those who do not recognize the rhetorical signals and clues linking this with the previously named persons and the weak among the Jewish Christians have little explanation for what Paul is doing here. On the connection with chs. 14–15 see, however, K. P. Donfried, "A Short Note on Romans 16," in Donfried, ed., *The Romans Debate*, pp. 44-52.

93. K. Grieb, *The Story of Romans: A Narrative Defense of God's Righteousness* (Louisville: Westminster/J. Knox, 2002), p. 146.

to stumble or be scandalized. He is especially concerned about the deception of the hearts of the "simple," those who are weak in faith and have too many scruples about food and other religious matters.

In v. 19 Paul commends these Christians for their obedience, which they have gained a reputation for. But obedience to clear teaching is one thing, discernment in situations which seem ambiguous and in which a person weak in faith can be led astray is another. Thus Paul urges them to be wise about the good, and innocent of the evil. He seems to be echoing here the teaching of Jesus about being wise yet innocent (Matt. 10.16).[94] For a person weak in faith, it is never wise to step on the slippery slope of an ambiguous situation for "whatever is not of faith is sin" at least for the person who violates his or her own conscience.

This *peroratio* can be said to be at the same time reiteration, amplification with specific application for the weak, and also an appeal to the stronger emotions,[95] especially fear of doing evil. Thus Paul closes it with a strong statement about God stamping out evil and reassuring the weak and offers a benediction to conclude this segment of the discourse. God will take action to deal with Satan. Paul does not exhort Christians to do so. Perhaps he is thinking of the Hebrew text of Gen. 3.15 here. *En tachei* can be translated either "quickly," indicating how God will deal with Satan and so modifying the verb, or "soon," telling when God will crush Satan.

There is a definite article before "Satan," as usual in the NT, which may reflect the fact that this is a description or title rather than a name: the Satan, that is, the adversary (cf. 1 Cor. 5.5; 7.5; 2 Cor. 2.11; 11.14; 12.7; 1 Thess. 2.18; 2 Thess. 2.9). Paul does not speak much about Satan, and even less about demons per se, though he does mention "powers and principalities." The hope of Satan being crushed under foot is common in apocalyptic Jewish and Christian contexts (*Jubilees* 5.6; 10.7-11; 23.29; *1 Enoch* 10.4, 11-12; 13.1-2; 1QM 17.5-6; 18.1; Rev. 20.10).[96] It has a special relevance in the Roman context in light of the image in Roman triumphs and on coins of the victor standing on the neck of the defeated with an inscription like "under the yoke of Rome."[97]

Paul calls God "the God of peace" because Satan is ultimately the one who tempts and instills divisions among God's people and because the God who wants concord and harmony among his people must therefore deal decisively with Satan. This verse thus indicates that God will deal with the problem that is troubling the weak in Rome, and will do so with dispatch. It is thus un-

---

94. See P. Stuhlmacher, *Romans* (Louisville: Westminster/J. Knox, 1989), p. 253; Moo, *Romans*, p. 932.

95. On the function and types of the *peroratio* see pp. 350-55 above.

96. See Dunn, *Romans 9–16*, p. 905.

97. See Käsemann, *Romans*, p. 418.

likely that Paul is referring here to the second coming of Jesus, though in light of 2 Thessalonians 2 this is possible. The benediction asks that the grace of Jesus be with those Paul is addressing and is direct and clear. Equally clear is the fact that Paul is concerned about these marginalized Christians, who are in a minority in Rome and are being tested and tempted to violate their consciences.

The greetings in vv. 21-23 are from those who are in Corinth with Paul. Those they would have known in Rome were those who had been in Corinth before, such as Prisca and Aquila. It is thus likely that these final greetings are at least mainly directed to those named in vv. 3-16 — Jewish Christians who have returned to Rome from the east, and those with them. B. Beckheuer suggests that those who send greetings in vv. 21-23 are in fact delegates from various Pauline churches who have gathered in Corinth before going to Jerusalem with Paul.[98] There is a certain overlap with the list in Acts 20.4: Timothy is mentioned in both texts, and Sopater may be Sosipater. Both lists contain a Gaius, but that was a very common name. This conjecture is worth pondering, but would those delegated have really traveled west to Corinth with money only to head back east to Jerusalem with Paul?[99]

Timothy is called Paul's coworker,[100] and Lucius, Jason, and Sosipater are relatives of Paul. Lucius is possibly, but probably not, Luke (cf. Phlm. 24; Col. 4.14; 2 Tim. 4.11). It is more possible that Jason and Sosipater are those mentioned in Acts 17.5-9 and 20.4 respectively. Paul's relatives in Corinth are greeting his relatives in Rome, among others, if we are right that these greetings are directed to those just named in this chapter. Romans 16 is the only place in the Pauline letters Paul refers to his own relatives. He mentions them because he is trying not only to establish stronger social networks in Rome before his arrival but also to connect with the Jewish Christians in Rome. His relatives' greetings to Jewish Christians they know in Rome helps achieve this aim.

In v. 22 Tertius inserts his own greeting.[101] He states that he is the writer who took Paul's dictation in this letter. Paul regularly used scribes (cf. 1 Cor. 16.21; Gal. 6.11; Col. 4.18; 2 Thess. 3.17). "In the Lord" comes at the end of the sentence rather than after "greet warmly," which may suggest that Tertius is saying that he has been doing his scribal work "in the Lord."[102]

---

98. B. Beckheuer, *Paulus und Jerusalem: Kollekte und Mission im theologischen Denken des Heidenapostels* (Frankfurt: Lang, 1997), pp. 168, 202.

99. See A. J. M. Wedderburn, "Paul's Collection: Chronology and History," *NTS* 48 (2002): 106-7.

100. According to Acts 16, Timothy is Jewish and Paul has him circumcised, making him all the more useful in witnessing to Jews. Clearly Timothy and those listed as Paul's relatives are Jews. Erastus, on the other hand, is clearly not a Jew.

101. Often scribes were well-trained slaves (see *NewDocs* 1:70), but there is no indication here that Tertius was a slave.

102. On Paul's use of scribes see my discussion in *The Paul Quest: The Search for the*

Gaius in v. 23 is said to be either Paul's guest or host. *Xenos* typically means "stranger" and so "guest," but it can also mean "host," which is more probable here. He may be mentioned in 1 Cor. 1.14. Erastus is in all likelihood the Erastus called an aedile in a paving inscription in front of the theater in Corinth. He, like Gaius, is a high-status Christian that was probably converted by Paul through contact in the marketplace when Paul was making tents and had to pay fees to Erastus.[103]

Though various scholars have doubted that the doxology in vv. 25-27 is either Pauline or an original part of this letter,[104] a good case can be made that it is both Paul's and an original part of Romans.[105] One must take into account that Paul is using liturgical language here, not ordinary speech. Doxologies often concluded religious texts (cf. *4 Maccabees* 18.24; *1 Clement* 64.2; *2 Clement* 20.5; *1 Enoch* 39.10; *Didache* 8.2; 9.2-4). D. Moo has shown how some key phrases and ideas in this doxology have parallels earlier in Romans:

v. 25	who is able (power)	1.4, 16
	establish you	1.11
	my gospel	1.1, 9, 16; 2.16
	revelation	1.17
v. 26	prophetic writings	1.2; cf. 3.21
	all nations (Gentiles)	1.5
	believe and obey	1.5
27	only God	3.29-30
	wise God	11.33-36[106]

Most of these echoes are from the beginning of the letter. Paul has come full circle, and what he asserted earlier in the letter he will reiterate here, only now he will thank God for these truths and promises.

It is God, not Paul, nor even the Roman Christians themselves, who can enable them to stand. Furthermore, Paul distinguishes between "my gospel" and the preaching of Jesus Christ, though the latter may be a subset of the former, and certainly there is overlap between the two. What we have in Romans is

---

Jew of Tarsus (Downers Grove: InterVarsity, 1998), pp. 99-109; and cf. R. E. Richards, *The Secretary in the Letters of Paul* (Tübingen: Mohr, 1991).

103. See my discussion in *Conflict and Community in Corinth*, pp. 32-35.

104. See J. K. Elliott, "The Language and Style of the Concluding Doxology to the Epistle to the Romans," *ZNW* 72 (1981): 124-30.

105. For this view see especially Cranfield, *Romans*, 2:808-9. For the view that it is Pauline, see I. H. Marshall, "Romans 16.25-27 — An Apt Conclusion," in *Romans and the People of God*, ed. S. K. Soderlund and N. T. Wright (Grand Rapids: Eerdmans, 1999), pp. 170-84; cf. Wright, "Romans," p. 768; Moo, *Romans*, pp. 936-37.

106. D. Moo, *Encountering the Book of Romans* (Grand Rapids: Baker, 2002), p. 209.

the gospel message for those who are already "in Christ," not, by and large, Paul's evangelistic preaching, as in his other letters. His letters are all addressed to Christians, though of course they contain echoes and sometimes brief summaries of the gospel preaching. The kerygma is not the same as the acts of persuasion that take place in Romans. It is therefore interesting that today we preach on the basis of Paul's persuasion and teaching, rather than on the basis of his kerygma, but then again we do normally preach to the converted.

Romans is by no means "the preaching about Jesus Christ" if by that one means that it is a long exercise in christological preaching retelling the story of Jesus' life, death, and resurrection. As is often noted, Romans is more theocentric than christocentric, though the latter is a subset of the former. Rather, such preaching or kerygma is presumed and built on in this letter and Paul's other letters.[107] Sometimes there is a christological focus (e.g., ch. 5), but only sometimes. Sometimes the underlying stories of the kerygma and the Bible (e.g., ch. 4) bubble to the surface, but only sometimes. Romans cannot be called, in short, "the preaching about Jesus Christ." Believers stand according to the gospel, but they have come to stand in the first place through the preached word about Jesus (see 10.8-15).

Both the kerygma and the gospel involve "the revelation of a mystery." We may compare here 1 Cor. 2.6-10 in regard to the revelation of the salvific mystery. Paul may be specifically alluding to God's salvation plan to include both Jew and Gentile in Christ on the basis of grace, faith, and the pure mercy of God, which he makes especially clear in Romans 9–11. This "mystery" was sealed from eternity but is now revealed in time through the writings of the prophets. Since Paul is recapitulating here he may well have ch. 1 in view, in particular the *propositio*, which quotes Habakkuk about these matters. There is then this relationship between the prophetic Scriptures and evangelistic preaching about Jesus which together make known God's salvation plan, which was to produce the obedience of faith in Gentiles, but also in Jews. The eternal God commanded that these things be made known.[108] Paul is a man under orders and constraints and he must obey the orders. The orders involve bringing all Gentile nations under the discipline of the obedience of faith by making known the only wise God and his plan of salvation.

Paul ends his letter at v. 27 by dedicating it all to the only wise God who acted through Jesus Christ. Glory might be given here to Christ, who is the nearest antecedent, or to God, or perhaps Paul would say it is to both. We still

---

107. See, rightly, Käsemann, *Romans*, p. 417: "the gospel is more than the kerygma. It is the norm of this."

108. *NewDocs* 2:86 provides us with an example from an inscription to a deity in which we have the phrase *kat' epitagēn* meaning "according to the ordinance/command" of the god. See the use in 1 Tim. 1.1 and Titus 1.3 of this phrase as well as here.

have miles to go, before we have truly taken the measure of and plumbed the
depths of all Paul tells us in these sixteen remarkable chapters.

Bridging the Horizons

Paul's specific commendation of seven of the nine women named in this chapter
and his reference to Phoebe's role as a deacon are extremely significant. While
contemporary believers divide over ordination of women, women teaching men,
and the like, this chapter suggests that such objections, in general, would have
puzzled Paul. Despite his Jewish tradition's understanding of the value and role of
women, Paul was able to affirm and accept the radical leveling of first-century
Christianity. "There is neither Jew nor Greek, there is neither slave nor free, there
is no male and female; for you are all one in Christ Jesus" (Gal. 3:28). Sadly, that
God-ordained equal status between the genders was quickly subsumed.

"[E]arly in church history women were shunned as evil — 'the devil's
gateway,' in the words of one church father (Tertullian) — and during the Middle Ages belief in this innate female evil led to an exaggerated fear of witchcraft
among women."[109] Augustine believed Scripture required women to cover their
heads in order to cover their brains, which were "filled with thoughts of 'lower
things.'" Augustine also held that "Eve fell into deception because she lacked
the image of God," because, that is, she was a woman.[110] It is only "in compara-
tively recent times" that "the church changed its stance . . . [to] saying women
are inferior *positionally* instead of *in essence*."[111]

In contrast, Mary Stewart Van Leeuwen underscores the surprising gender equality within early Christendom:

> Pentecost has sometimes been called "women's emancipation day," because
> of women's inclusion with men in the outpouring of the Spirit. Before, it
> had been the Jewish custom to recognize only males as full members of the
> community through the sign of circumcision. After Pentecost, the church
> baptized men and women alike. Before, it was considered at best unneces-
> sary and at worst scandalous for women to study the Scriptures beside men
> in the synagogue. Now they broke bread and participated in worship ser-
> vices with the men. Before, women's freedom of movement was rigidly re-
> stricted because of the rabbinic assertion that public contact between non-

109. Rebecca Merrill Groothuis, *The Feminist Bogeywoman* (Grand Rapids: Baker,
1995), p. 5.
110. Sarah Sumner, *Men and Women in the Church: Building Consensus on Christian
Leadership* (Downers Grove: InterVarsity, 2003), pp. 61-62.
111. Patricia Gundry, *Heirs Together* (Grand Rapids: Zondervan, 1980), p. 117.

married women and men was bound to produce lust. Now women assumed positions of leadership even in mixed gatherings and were acknowledged and praised by Paul at various points in his letters.[112]

She then asserts that, whenever the church is in a time of revival and rapid expansion, women's gifts are recognized, affirmed, and utilized. But Van Leeuwen cautions, "At other times (let's admit it) men and women alike seem to regress to a pre-Pentecost anxiety about gender roles and become preoccupied with details concerning headship and submission."[113]

Her words seemed chillingly relevant as I read a column in *Christianity Today* stating that seventeen Southern Baptist missionaries have been fired due to their refusal to sign the denomination's 2000 Baptist Faith and Message statement. "The more controversial sections of the BFM have to do with disallowing women pastors and asking wives to 'graciously submit' to their husbands."[114] A further twenty missionaries resigned and ten took early retirement. To date, seventy-seven have "declined work in harmony with the 2000 BFM," but, ominously to me, "nearly ninety-nine percent of the denomination's 5,500 overseas missionaries have affirmed it."[115] None of this takes into consideration the Southern Baptist churches, academics, and clergy who chose to leave the convention rather than affirm such blatantly sexist statements.

A second example of misguided "zeal" was recounted in a 1999 issue of *Christianity Today*.[116] Anne Graham Lotz, the daughter of evangelist Billy Graham, was invited to speak at a conference of pastors. Many of the pastors registered for the event, paid the applicable fees, traveled to the event and, when she rose to preach, collectively turned their backs to the podium and this fellow believer. She demonstrated great aplomb (and Christian commitment to love) by preaching to their backs. Even if these men believed her teaching was sinful (only because the instruction came from the lips of a woman), surely such unloving "correction" and remaining in the presence of "unbiblical disobedience" could never be considered Christ-like.

Perhaps the most alarming aspect of the current polarization within evangelical Christian communities is the lack of genuine dialogue, which then diminishes a united effort to speak on behalf of authentically biblical Christianity. Further, as previously asserted, the Pentecost energy of Christianity is diffused as we sink to lobbying for hierarchical positions, rights, and roles — even though Jesus firmly denounced such seeking of privilege.

112. Mary Stewart Van Leeuwen, *Gender and Grace* (Downers Grove: InterVarsity, 1990), p. 35.

113. Van Leeuwen, *Gender and Grace*, p. 35.

114. *Christianity Today* 47, no. 7 (2003): 24.

115. Ibid.

116. Wendy Murray Zoba, "Angel in the Pulpit," *Christianity Today*, April 5, 1999, p. 58.

The vitality of the evangelical church in the late nineteenth and early twentieth centuries, with its strong inclusion of women preachers, belies two arguments that are frequently employed against women's leadership and ordination. The first asserts that biblical Christians have always renounced women leaders and pastor/preachers, while its corollary states that Christian feminism "is simply a misguided mimicry of the secular feminism flowing from the 1960s."[117] An unbiased exploration of women's participation in evangelicalism in the late nineteenth and early twentieth centuries reveals an alarming recidivism from that time that Paul and his coworkers in the first century would find deplorable and thoroughly incongruent with the in-Christ identity of believers, regardless of race, gender, or economic status.

In her short booklet entitled *The Feminist Bogeywoman*, egalitarian Rebecca Merrill Groothuis points out that what she terms "evangelical feminism" is thoroughly biblical and has a long history. In no way is such evangelical feminism an outgrowth of secular feminism, for the former is based on the authority and instruction of Scripture while the latter is based on women's experience as its final authority. "Evangelical feminism has a different beginning and a different end. It arises from a different theology and a different history, and it aspires to a different purpose. Theologically, evangelical feminism is based on the biblical principle of the equality of all people before God."[118] Furthermore, "the roots of evangelical feminism can be found in the goals and values of the nineteenth-century women's movement, which arose from an interaction of the political ideals of classical liberalism (equality under the law for all) with the religious zeal of the Second Great Awakening and, later, the Third Awakening (or Holiness Movement)."[119] Also, the purpose of evangelical feminism is to serve rather than to pursue power — the "ultimate goal is the good of the church and society rather than simply the empowerment of the individual woman."[120]

Although theologian Sarah Sumner is quick to discount any personal connection with feminism (even of the evangelical variety), her belief regarding the value of women remains clear-cut.

> Feminism is not something that must be added to Christianity in order for the church to honor women. The gospel itself is pro-women. It is quintessentially Christian to be pro-people. Hence it is just as unnecessary for a Christian to be a feminist as it is for a Christian to be a humanist. There's no need to blend a humanist worldview into a Christian worldview, because Christians already have the highest view of humanity in the world. Our Lord Jesus is himself the all-time greatest Advocate for men and

117. Van Leeuwen, *Gender and Grace*, p. 243.
118. Groothuis, *The Feminist Bogeywoman*, p. 9.
119. Groothuis, *The Feminist Bogeywoman*, p. 9.
120. Groothuis, *The Feminist Bogeywoman*, p. 10.

women and children. Anyone who thinks that treating women fairly is a feminist thing to do, not a Christian thing to do, doesn't understand Christianity.[121]

Accordingly, Sumner makes a sharp distinction between historical Christian thinking (in her opinion, strongly misogynistic) and genuinely biblical thinking about women (as evident in Romans 16). Even John Piper and Wayne Grudem — both avid "complementarians" — concur that they are "uncomfortable with the term 'traditionalist' because it implies an unwillingness to let Scripture challenge traditional patterns of behavior."[122]

In fact, Sumner believes that polarization regarding the issue of women in vocational ministry extends far deeper. She says that female ordained leadership is a "presenting" issue and is "convinced that the current debate on men and women in the church effectively unearths people's buried thoughts about their sexuality, their concept of marriage, their view of the authority of Scripture, their theology of God and their philosophy of natural order."[123] Coupled with that is the human tendency to inhabit a paradigm (i.e., men lead, women follow) without being aware of how it shapes our understanding of Scripture and, thus, our behavior.

Yet the belief that equality endangers the family, destroys marriages, or threatens to weaken the very foundations of society is erroneous. Rhetoric that makes such claims must be countered with biblical instruction and baring of the fear or lust for power that lies behind such statements. Groothuis rightly underscores that the

> focus is the gospel of Jesus Christ. Biblical equality is seen as an effect or implication of the gospel; the heart of the gospel is repentance and forgiveness of sin through the grace of God in Christ. . . . The main point of the gospel is not the destruction of patriarchy, but the destruction of the stronghold of sin in the human heart, which impels not only patriarchy but a host of other evil deviations from God's intended order.[124]

Early in Romans, Paul states there is "no partiality" with God (2.11). He closes with this listing of men and women working alongside one another to establish churches throughout the Roman Empire. May we in the twenty-first century learn to do likewise and not be preoccupied with dissensions and stumbling blocks, which Paul has urged us to avoid.

121. Sumner, *Men and Women in the Church*, p. 28.
122. John Piper and Wayne Grudem, eds., *Recovering Biblical Manhood and Womanhood* (Wheaton: Crossway, 1991), p. xiv.
123. Sumner, *Men and Women in the Church*, p. 283.
124. Groothuis, *The Feminist Bogeywoman*, p. 10.

Index of Modern Authors

Index of Biblical References

Index of Other Ancient Writings